CONCISE ENGLISH-SCOTS DICTIONARY

Edited by
Iseabail Macleod
and
Pauline Cairns
Drawing upon materials supplied
by William Graham

POLYGON
AT EDINBURGH

Dedication
For William Graham
whose generous gift of manuscript material
made this dictionary possible.

Polygon at Edinburgh

An imprint of Edinburgh University Press Ltd
22 George Square, Edinburgh

First published 1993 by Chambers Harrap Publishers Ltd
This edition published 1999 by Polygon at Edinburgh

Printed and bound in Finland by WSOY

A CIP Record for this book is available from the British
Library

ISBN 1 902930 04 5 (paperback)

Contents

Introduction

The aim of this dictionary is to give as much help as possible within a comparatively short book to all who want to use the Scots language, from writers to schoolchildren, for creative work or just for pleasure. Scots has in recent years gained considerably in prestige and acceptance in the community. School pupils were formerly criticized or even punished for the use of their native language, but today's educational policies are to encourage its use and also to arouse an interest in its long literary tradition. This is being added to more and more by modern writers of high calibre, often in poetry but also in prose, and in particular in drama. Many people simply want to familiarize themselves with words and phrases which are embedded deep in their backgrounds but often refuse to come to the surface. It is hoped that this book will be of help to all of these.

The emphasis is mainly on the language of the twentieth century, but a few words from earlier times have been included where they might be likely to be used in writing about a particular period (see p viii below).

The main sources of the dictionary are the Scottish National Dictionary Association's Scots–English dictionaries (see list on p xvii), its growing data base of new research, and manuscript material generously donated to the Association by William Graham. Being acutely aware of the need for an English-Scots reference work, he collected this material over several decades, and although, in this concise dictionary, we were not able to include all of it, we are deeply grateful to him for allowing us to use the fruits of his long and patient labours.

How are the entries organized?

See the entry for **care** on p 32. The main headword section, divided where appropriate into part-of-speech sections and further into meaning sections, is followed by: derivatives, eg **careful**; compounds, eg **caretaker**; phrases, eg **take care of**.

Grammar

A word's part of speech is given only where there are two or more (eg both noun and verb) in an entry or where this information is helpful in clarifying a meaning. The following descriptions are used:

adjective	past tense	preposition
adverb	past participle	interjection
noun	present participle	conjunction
verb		

Past tenses and part participles are inserted, where necessary, in their own alphabetical place, with a cross-reference at the main verb, eg

stung *past tense of* **sting** stang.
sting *verb, see also* **stung;** stang; . . .

How many Scots words?

In cases where there is a very large number of Scots words for a concept (see **hit**, **blow**, for example), a selection of the most widely used is included. To help the user in the search for other words, many near-synonyms are cross-referred one to the other. This arrangement gives the user a wider choice by indicating other entries where a suitable Scots word might be found (see also p vi). These can if necessary be checked further in one of the Scots–English dictionaries, such as the *Pocket Scots Dictionary* (see list on p xvii).

Order of Scots words

The aim is to give the most likely equivalent(s) for the commonest meaning of the English word first, ie the one(s) closest to this in meaning and most widely used throughout Scotland, where appropriate indicating the areas where the words are used (see pp viii, ix). The less common meanings then follow in order of importance. Often a cognate form is commonest, eg **part** pairt; ..., and these often cover more than one meaning of the word. In some cases, however, other Scots words are more widely used and the cognate comes later in the list, eg **child** bairn, wean, chile, . . .

Explanatory words

Different meanings of a word are distinguished in various ways, often by the use of 'indicating words' of various kinds:
subject labels, eg (*law*).

synonyms of the headword, eg
about . . . (*concerning*) anent, on, o; (*approximately*) lik(e).
thoughtful . . . (*considerate*) considerin.

collocations, eg
bail . . . (*a boat*) owse . . .
blow out (*a candle*) whiff.
termination (*of a lease, term of office etc*) ish; (*of a contract etc*) expiry.
thin (*of persons*: *see also* **skinny**) slink, nairra-boukit, . . .

other brief notes to help to distinguish meanings, eg **thread** threid; (*broken or frayed*) raivel; (*shoemaker's*) lingel, en(d), souter-en(d), . . .

illustrative phrases are included occasionally to show how the word is used,

eg **wits** judgement: *'oot o yer judgement'*, . . .
to . . . (*in telling the time*) o(f): *'a quarter o fower'*.

Cross-references

In many cases, shades of meaning of the Scots and English words are very difficult to distinguish from one another. For this reason, many synonyms or near-synonyms are cross-referred to each other, and this allows the user to check further for other words which might fit the context better, eg

tale *see also* **story;** sonnet NE, . . .

bright (*of personality: see also* **lively**) gleg, trig, . . .

Where no exact equivalent has been found in Scots, sometimes a cross-reference is given to a word of more or less similar meaning for which Scots equivalents exist, eg

buffoon *see* **fool, idiot.**

sarcasm *see* **mockery.**

canter *see* **gallop, trot.** (No precise equivalent for 'canter' has been found, but 'gallop' and 'trot' give other words for the movements of a horse.)

Spelling

The lack of standardization in spelling has long been a problem to writers in Scots. The *Scottish National Dictionary*, and to a lesser extent the *Concise Scots Dictionary*, give lists of variants, thus displaying the variety of Scots spelling – historical, regional, accidental, idiosyncratic.

In the *Concise English–Scots Dictionary*, however, space does not permit such liberal treatment and usually only one spelling is given, or in some cases two or more, especially where there are regional variants, eg **abuse** abuise, abeese N: . . . Sometimes additional variants are given at the word's main appearance in the dictionary, eg **hand** haun(d), han, . . . Elsewhere the information is given in a more compressed form, eg -han(d).

It is often very difficult to decide which spellings to include, since those which are historically preferable do not always help the user towards a modern Scots pronunciation. In selecting spellings, the following criteria have been applied:

The first headword from the *Scottish National Dictionary* (and therefore usually also from the *Concise Scots Dictionary* – see p xvii) is used unless:

a) it could mislead as to the common modern pronunciation. Therefore *hoose* rather than *house*; *cowp* rather than *coup*; *deef* rather than *deaf*.

b) there is a more distinctively Scots spelling which also conforms to a) above. Therefore *cannie* rather than *canny*.

English spellings are given where the word is used mainly in formal (eg legal) contexts or where it is in most frequent usage, eg

Sunday Sawbath, Sabbath.

Apostrophes are avoided where they represent a 'missing' English letter, as in *wi, himsel, o.*

Where it is possible to do so succinctly, alternative spellings are given, covering dialect and other common variations, eg

-a(w) as in *ba*(w), *ca*(w) and -a(u)- as in *spra(u)chle, tra(u)chle*, to cover regional variation in this vowel (see Pronunciation, p x); in some North-Eastern words however, -aa- is used, as in *aager.*

-n(d) as in *grun(d)*

-l(d) as in *aul(d), chiel(d)*

-lik(e), -rif(e) when used as suffixes, as in *wicelik(e), caul(d)rif(e).*

Some preferred spellings:

-ae, -ai-, -a- are used for the vowel in Scottish Standard English 'maid', according to modern usage, as in *brae, sair, hame*

-ei-, -ie-, -ee- for the vowel in Scottish Standard English 'bleed', as in *heid, eediot, deef, stieve*

-ie rather than -y at the end of a word, as in *bonnie, cannie*

-i-, -y-, -ei- or -ey- for the diphthong in Scottish Standard English 'wife', as in *ile, dyke, eydent, aye* (= always)

-i- or -y- for the diphthong in English 'buy', as in *rive, ay* (= yes)

-oo- is normally used for the vowel in Scottish Standard English 'good' or 'groove', as in *aboot, doon, droon, hoose, oot, coo, flooer*

-ow- is normally used for the vowel in Scottish Standard English 'down', as in *cowp, lowp, smowt, howk, lowse*; -owe at the end of a word, as in *growe, thowe, lowe.*

But for the two preceding, -ou- is used:

a) where both pronunciations are used (even if varying regionally), as in *roup* meaning to cry, shout, roar [pronounced roop or rowp] and

b) where one spelling is established in modern usage, eg *souch* [always pronounced sooch]; *roup* meaning auction [usually pronounced rowp]

-ul for the vowel in English 'dull', as in *ful, pul*

-ch- rather than -gh-, as in *loch, dreich, sprauchle*

-tch- rather than -ch- for the consonant combination in English 'beech', as in *fleetch, pootch*; at the beginning of a word, ch- is used, as in *chap.*

Verb endings:

-in for present participle and verbal noun ending, as in *girnin*, *raxin*.

for past tense, past participle:

-it after -b, -d, -g, -k, -p, -t, as in *biggit*, *howkit*

-t after -il, -en, -er, -ch, -tch, -sh, -ss, -f, as in *laucht*, *fasht*, *fleetcht*

-(e)d, as in *kaimed*, *hained*, *breenged*, *chowed*

-elt for verbs ending in -le, as in *sprauchelt*, *trauchelt*.

Punctuation

A comma separates synonyms; where there is an additional different meaning, a semicolon is normally used, almost always preceding an indicating word. Occasionally, where the distinction in meaning is only slight, a comma suffices: **atmosphere** . . . (*thick, stuffy*) smuchter NE, (*in a crowded place*) stech N; . . . **bowl** . . . (*esp wooden*) bicker . . . , (*with handles*) luggie; . . .

A colon is used:

(a) where a word or label refers to the whole entry, eg **gleam** see also **glimmer, shine**: *verb* . . .

(b) in some cases where two pieces of information are given in parentheses, eg **flash** *noun* (*of light*: *see also* **gleam**) . . .

(c) before an example phrase, eg **failed** (*in a profession*) stickit: '*stickit minister*'.

Time and place

The conventional dagger † precedes words which, as far as our evidence goes, are no longer in current use. It is also used for words which are still used but only in historical contexts, eg **smuggling** †free trade; **spelling book** †spell(-book); **cap** . . . (old woman's) †mutch; . . . ; **cattle-raider** †reiver.

Where a word, meaning or phrase is restricted to a particular locality, this is indicated in broad terms using the wider dialect areas, eg N(orth), S(outh-) W(est) etc, and only occasionally the old county names, eg Fife, Ayrshire, as in the *Concise Scots Dictionary*.

The dialect areas are listed below, and the maps on pp xii and xiii show the areas referred to. The modern map on pp xiv, xv shows the post-1975 regions and districts, and their relationship to the old counties can thus be seen approximately.

SHETLAND
ORKNEY
N (North)   includes Caithness

NE (North-East)	includes Aberdeen (the city)
E COAST (East Coast)	mainly fishing terms, found along the eastern seaboard
CENTRAL	covers E Central, W and SW
E CENTRAL (East Central)	includes Angus, Perthshire, Fife, Lothian, Edinburgh
W (West Central)	includes Glasgow, Argyll, Ayrshire
SW (South-West)	
S (South)	
SE (South-East)	covers South E Central, south of the Firth of Forth, as well as South
ULSTER	

Scots is spoken much less in the Gaelic-speaking (or recently Gaelic-speaking) parts of Scotland but a few words from these areas, mostly of Gaelic origin, have been included, labelled HIGHLAND.

How to use the words

As well as some indication of the geographical spread of a word or meaning, information is given, where appropriate, as to how and in what circumstances it is used. These labels, listed below, are usually placed after the word to which they refer, eg **if** . . . gif *mainly literary*. Occasionally, however, they are given before the word to avoid repetition, eg **rabbit** . . . (*pet name*) mappie, map-map, . . .

informal

slang

literary = in literary usage only, at least at the present time

(in) poetry

archaic = still in use but having an old-fashioned ring to it,
    eg **ratify** . . . homologate *archaic*; . . .

child's word, often a word used to, as well as by children,
    eg **bed** . . . beddie-ba(s) *child's word*, . . .

pet name

humorous

contemptuous

law = not strictly a legal term, but a word used mainly in legal contexts,
    eg **across** . . . atour *law*; **in good time** timeous *law*; for legal terms (*law*) comes
    before the word, eg **security** (*law*) caution; . . .

gipsy eg **go away** . . . abree *gipsy*

taboo = for terms used, especially by fishermen, as substitutes for names and expressions avoided because of taboo: **pig** . . . Sandie (Campbell) *taboo*, harkie *taboo*, SHETLAND; . . .

Other indications of register are occasionally given, eg **little finger** . . . peerie-winkie *in nursery rhymes*; **mother** . . . minnie *affectionate name*.

How to pronounce Scots words

The following notes may be helpful in using the Dictionary for speaking Scots. Efforts have been made throughout to select those spellings which most closely mirror modern Scots pronunciation for the modern Scots user, but note the following:

(1) **ng** in Scots, eg in *ingle, ingan, hunger*, is pronounced as in English 'sing', not as in English 'single'.

(2) In Scots, **ch** occurring in the middle or at the end of a word is most often sounded as in *loch* or *dreich* or in the place-names *Buchan* or *Brechin*.

(3) At the beginning of a word, **ch** has its usual English sound as in 'cheese'. Where the pronunciation occurs later in a word, it is usually spelt -tch- in this dictionary, eg *fleetch*.

(4) **gh**, which normally occurs only in the middle or at the end of a word, has the same sound as **ch** in (2) above.

(5) **th** in Scots has the same two pronunciations as in English, one as in 'the, that, breathe', the other as in 'thank, thin, three, teeth'.

(6) **wh** is pronounced *hw-*, not *w-* as in southern English, eg *wheech* [pronounced hweech].

(7) In some dialects north of the Tay, the **k** in initial **kn-** in eg *knife* is or was pronounced either as *k-* or, near the Tay, as *t-*, so that *knife* in these dialects is pronounced either k(e)nife or t(e)nife; similarly with the **g** in **gn-** as in *gnash* in some of the same dialects; elsewhere **kn-** and **gn-** are pronounced simply as n- as in English.

(8) **ui** varies with the dialect:

in some conservative dialects (eg Shetland, Orkney, Angus, South Scots), the pronunciation is similar to the vowel of French 'peu' or German 'schön'

in North and East Fife, the pronunciation is like *a* in Scottish Standard English 'late' or 'blade' or *ai* in 'pair' or *ay* in 'day'

in many other dialects, the pronunciation in some words is like *i* in English 'bit', so that *buit* is pronounced like 'bit'

in the Northern mainland dialects this sound does not occur; -ee- is used instead.

(9) **oo** as in Scottish Standard English 'groove' or 'moon'.

(10) **ey** as in *gey* (very) is the same as the vowel in the Scots (and Scottish Standard English) pronunciation of 'mine' or 'tile'.

(11) *Stress*. In Scots, in words of more than one syllable, stress most often falls on the same syllable as it would in English, eg words such as *hoolet* have stress on the first syllable, but prefixes such as *dis-* in *disjaskit* or *un-* in *unbraw* are usually unstressed.

Further information on Scots pronunciation can be found in the Scots-English dictionaries (see list on p xvii).

Abbreviations

These have been kept to a minimum, most words being spelt out in full, with the following exceptions:

eg	for example
esp	especially
etc	et cetera
ie	that is
specif	specifically
usu	usually

See also the list of dialect areas on pp viii, ix.

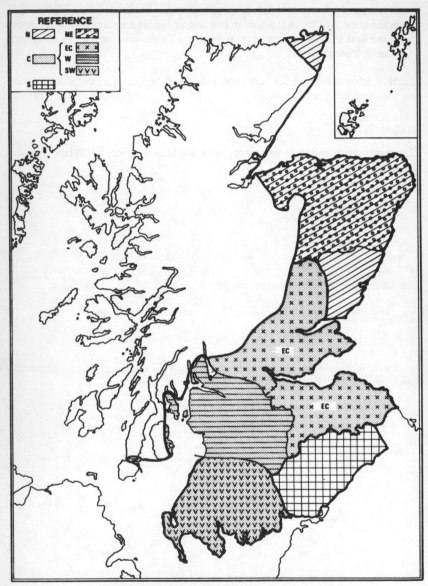

Map 1 Scotland: the main dialect divisions of Scots

Map 2 Scotland: pre-1975 counties

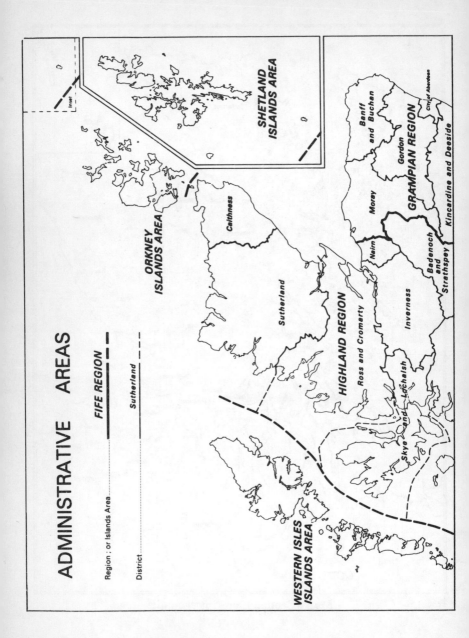

ADMINISTRATIVE AREAS

Region ; or Islands Area .... **FIFE REGION**

District .... Sutherland

SHETLAND ISLANDS AREA

ORKNEY ISLANDS AREA

WESTERN ISLES ISLANDS AREA

HIGHLAND REGION

Caithness

Sutherland

Ross and Cromarty

Skye and Lochalsh

Inverness

Nairn

Moray

Badenoch and Strathspey

GRAMPIAN REGION

Banff and Buchen

Gordon

City of Aberdeen

Kincardine and Deeside

Inset

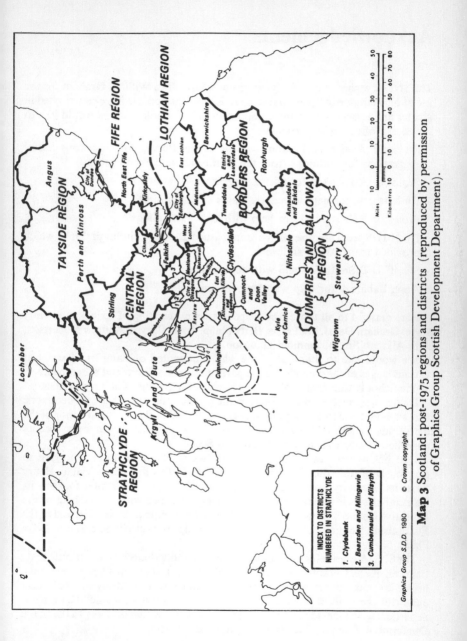

Map 3 Scotland: post-1975 regions and districts (reproduced by permission of Graphics Group Scottish Development Department).

INDEX TO DISTRICTS
NUMBERED IN STRATHCLYDE

1. Clydebank
2. Bearsden and Milngavie
3. Cumbernauld and Kilsyth

Graphics Group S.D.D. 1980   © Crown copyright

Acknowledgements

The SNDA wishes to express its gratitude above all to William Graham for the use of his manuscript material (see p iv). Many other people have contributed in greater and lesser ways in the compilation of this book, and we would like to thank the following in particular:

Professor Alexander Fenton and Dr David Purves for numerous useful suggestions for additions from the North-East and South areas.

Professor A J Aitken for useful suggestions.

Ruth Martin for help with early stages of this project.

Professor Robert Black for help with legal terminology.

Dr H-H Speitel for use of his unpublished thesis (Edinburgh 1969) which provided many useful additions.

Sheriff D B Smith for help with curling terms.

Anna Babarczy for help with keyboarding.

We are grateful to all those who helped with the checking of scripts at an early stage: Graham Davis, Ian Petrie, Betty Philip, Jessie Purves, Andrew Robertson, Ann Aikman Smith, Jennifer Thomson.

We would like to thank all those who commented on samples of script at various stages of the compilation, in particular Lorna Smith and other members of the Schools Committee of the Association for Scottish Literary Studies.

Dictionaries such as this are built on the firm foundation of their predecessors, and we would like to thank especially David Murison, the principal editor of the ten-volume *Scottish National Dictionary*, whose untiring labour over decades underlies so much in the lexicography of Scots.

Last but by no means least, we would like to thank all those who give so generously of their time in helping to keep the SNDA financially viable. Henry Pirie, its Secretary and Treasurer, gives unstintingly of his time to keep its financial affairs in order. There would be little finance without the help of the Executive Council, above all of its Chairman, Sir Kenneth Alexander, and of the Fundraising Committee, under the chairmanship of Ann Aikman Smith: Betty Philip, Sheila Davies, Jessie Purves.

The SNDA is grateful to all those bodies and individuals who contribute to its finances. Recent grants from the Scottish Office Education Department have helped to make the Association financially more secure. Many Scottish local authorities have given generously in stringent times, and we would like to thank in particular Strathclyde and Highland Regions. We would also like to thank the Dunfermline Building Society for a generous donation.

Scottish National Dictionary Association Limited

As indicated above, this book is based largely on the SNDA's other dictionaries:

The Scottish National Dictionary, in ten volumes, 1931-76

The Concise Scots Dictionary 1986

The Pocket Scots Dictionary 1988

The Scots Thesaurus 1990.

All these dictionaries contain, in greater or lesser detail, information about the Scots language and its history.

The SNDA has recently embarked on a new research scheme to monitor the language and its developments. If you would like to help, or would like more information, please write to:

The Scottish National Dictionary Association,
27 George Square,
Edinburgh EH8 9LD.

A

aback: taken aback mesmerised, taen tae the fair, dumfoonert.

abandon pass, gie ower, forleet; (*a task*) fa(w) throu, (*a nest*) forvoo, forhoo(ie).

abandonment (*law: of something owned*) dereliction.

abashed hingin-luggit, hingin-heidit.

abate (*of pain*) liss; (*of wind etc*) quall.

abattoir *see also* **slaughterhouse**; butch-hoose.

abdomen *see* **belly.**

abhorrent scunnersome, ugsome, laithlie.

abhorrence scunner, ug NE, grue.

abide (*tolerate*) bide, thole, dree.

ability abeelitie, can N, feerich NE, clivveralitie, ingine.

abject *see* **obsequious.**

ablaze ableeze, alowe.

able *see also* **cannot, could;** yable S, yibble S, (*competent*) ticht, feckfu, lik(e)ly.

able-bodied hail, yauld.

be able to get: '*ye'll get swimmin the morn*'.

be able to do easily hae easy deein SHETLAND, NE, nae hae ill deein NE.

abnormal no richt, orra, by-or(di)nar.

abolish *law, see* **annul.**

abort (*miscarry*) pairt wi bairn; (*of an animal*) pick, slip.

aborted animal pick, slink.

abortion slip.

abound *see* **swarm.**

abounding hoatchin, hotchin.

about aboot; (*concerning*) anent, on, o; (*approximately*) lik(e).

above abuin, abeen N, bune SW.

above-mentioned foresaid.

get above yourself misken yersel NE.

abreast abreist, fit for fit, han(d) for nieve.

keep abreast (of) keep till (wi) NE, keep tee till NE.

two abreast twa in a raw.

abridgement (*law*) abbreviate.

abroad (*over a wide area*) abreed.

abrupt (*in manner*) snottie, cuttit, snappit, snappie.

abscess *see also* **whitlow;** income, bealin; (*on backs of cattle etc*) warble.

absent: absentee *see* **truant.**

absent-minded forgettle, nae in.

absent-mindedness forget.

absence: note explaining absence from school line.

absolute fair, evendoon; (*in bad sense*) black: '*black lees*'.

absolutely fair, evendoon, rump an stump, stoup an roup.

absorbed oot ower the lugs.

abstain from gae fae.

abstemious cannie.

abstract *noun* abstrack; (*law*) abbreviate.

abstracted *see also* **absent-minded;** (*of the eyes*) far ben.

absurd *see* **ridiculous.**

abundance rowth, fouth, feck.

abundant rowth(ie), ruch.

abuse *verb* abuise, abeese N: **1** *see* **illtreat. 2** (*verbally*) misca(w), tongue, ill-gab, ill-tongue N, wallipend NE.

noun abuise, abeese N; (*abusive language*) snash, ill-tongue, tongue, ill-jaw, ill-win(d) NE, back-jaw.

abusive ill-mou'd, ill-tonguit; (*of the tongue*) ill-scrapit.

abusive verbal contest (between poets) flytin(g).

1

heap abuse on someone ca(w) someone for a(w)thing.

term of abuse *see* **contemptuous term**.

accelerate (*a curling stone, by sweeping in front of it*) gie (a stane) feet.

accent *noun, see also* **affected**; tune, tin, teen NE, souch.

accept accep.

access ingate, ingang, wey in, wye in NE.

accessory pertinent.

accident amshach NE, stramash, skavie NE.

accidental casual.

accommodation up-pittin; (*for farmworkers*) bothy, hyne hoose NE, chaumer, berrick.

accompany convoy, set, follow, get: '*We'll get ye doon the stair*'; (*as a friend*) chum; (*part of the way*) see by the hen's mait, see the lenth o . . .: '*We'll see ye the lenth o the bus stop*'.

accompanying of a person convoy; (*part of the way*) Scotch convoy.

accomplish *see* **achieve**.

accomplished far seen.

accord *verb, see also* **agree**; cord.

in accordance with conform tae.

according to him (by) his wey o't.

accordion box HIGHLAND.

account *noun* accoont: **1** (*long description*) scrift. **2** (*in a shop*) line: '*pit it on the line*'.

of no account nochtless.

on account of o.

on your own account on yersel.

accumulate hudge NE.

accumulation (*of things*) rake, hirst NE, harl, gedderie.

accurate *see* **right**.

accurately pintitlie.

accuse wyte, faut.

accused *noun* (*law*) panel.

accustom brither NE.

accustomed (to) yaised (wi), eest (wi) N; (*of animals to a new pasture*) heftit.

ace ess, yiss SE.

ace of spades furl o birse NE.

ache *noun, see also* **pain** 1; stoun(d), gowp.

verb stoun(d), nip, stang, yerk, yawk, rug, soo; (*violently*) gowp.

achieve get roon(d), pit ower.

achievement dirdum (*mainly sarcastic*).

acid *adjective* (*of taste*) *see also* **bitter** 1; wersh.

acid drop soor drap.

acknowledge lat licht NE, tak wi; (*as a relation*) awn.

acknowledge the truth of haud wi.

acorn (*large, ripe, on its stalk*) pipe SE.

acorn cup and stalk 'smoked' by children puggie pipe.

acquaint acquant, acquent.

acquaintance acquantance, acquentance; (*knowledge*) kennin.

acquainted acquant, acquent.

acquire *see* **get**.

acquisition (*lucky*) caption NE, pirkas CAITHNESS.

acquit free SHETLAND, NE; (*law*) assoilzie.

acre *see table on p 302.*

acrid *see also* **bitter** 1; reekit, snell.

acrimony nip-lug.

acrimonious tuithie, snell.

acrobatic feat henner EDINBURGH.

across *preposition* athort, throu, thorter, atour *law*.

adverb athort, thorter; (*at a place understood in the conversation*) owerby.

act *noun, verb* ack.

action (*at law*) law plea, †ploy; (*stopping the execution of a writ*) suspension.

raise an action (*at law*) pursue.

active acteeve; (*of persons*) feerie, fersell, trig, swack, forcie SHETLAND, NE, kibble NE, throu-gaun, yaul(d), leish SW, S; (*of children*) steerin, steerie NE, stourie; (*of animals*) swack.

activity throu-pit, feenish NE, traffeck SHETLAND, NE.

actually ackwallie.

acute 1 (*mentally*) *see also* **shrewd**; gleg, snack(ie). **2** (*of pain etc*) fell.

Adam's apple knot o yer craig *or* thrapple NE.

adamant *see also* **stubborn**; positive.

adaptable (*of an animal*) handie NE.

add (*to something*) eik.

  addition addeetion; (*something added*) eik.

  additional tither; (*eg before numeral*) ither: '*the ither fower*'.

  in addition tae the buit.

  in addition (to) *see also* **besides**; forby, an a(w).

adder ether, edder, nether, veeper.

address *noun* (*on a letter*) backin.

  verb (*a letter*) back.

  familiar, friendly term of address (*to a man*) Jimmie, guid man: '*Hoo are ye the day, guid man?*'; (*to a woman*) hen; (*to a small man or boy*) wee man; (*to a big man*) big man.

adept *adjective* fell, kittle.

  noun, see **expert**.

adequate eneuch, anew.

adhere clap.

  adhesive *adjective, see* **sticky** (*under* **stick**^{2}).

adjoin mairch wi.

adjourn (*a legal case*) continue.

adjust (*an implement*) tune; (*a garment etc*) turse; (*put right*) sort.

administer admeenister.

  administration admeenistration.

  administrator *see* **manager**.

admire respeck.

  admirable braw.

admit *see also* **acknowledge**; awn.

  I admit that I winna say but (whit).

  admission admeeshion.

admonish speak a word tae.

  admonition tellin, lesson.

ado *see also* **commotion, fuss**; adae, adee NE.

adolescence, adolescent *see* **youth** 2.

adopted child foster.

adorn *see also* **decorate**; munt, busk, dink, mense.

adroit *see also* **skilful**; cannie, knackie, gleg.

adult *noun* man-bodie, wumman-bodie.

  adjective muckle, man-big, man-grown, man-lenth, man-muckle, wumman-grown, wumman-lenth, wumman-muckle.

advance *verb* (*further*) forder, win forrit.

  advancement forder.

  in advance (of) (*in place*) afore.

  paid in advance fordel N.

advantage better; (*esp in bargaining*) nip NE; (*unfair*) grab NE, backspang; (*unexpected*) kinch.

  advantageous *see* **favourable**.

  having an eye to your own advantage lang-nebbit.

  to little advantage tae little maitter.

advent *see* **arrival**.

adverse thrawart SHETLAND, ORKNEY, conter, ill.

advertise adverteese.

  advertisement adverteesement.

advice: lead *or* **guide by advice** wice.

advise speak a word tae.

adze eetch, hack; (*ship's carpenter's long-handled*) fit-eitch SHETLAND, ORKNEY, N.

aerated water *see* **lemonade**.

aeroplane airieplane.

affable *see also* **pleasant**; couthie, crackie; (*excessively*) aw hinnie an jo.

affair *see* **matter**.

  this state of affairs this o't.

affect affeck; (*physically*) tak on; **affect with** smit wi.

  affected (*in manner*) mim, pitten-on, prick-ma-dentie, primsie, stringie; (*esp in dress*) primpit, fussy; (*in speech*) tattie-peelin, mim-mou'd.

  affected way of speaking pan loaf, Kelvinside, Morningside, high English, dichtie watter English.

  speak affectedly hae a bool in yer mou(th), mump, yap, knap, get roon(d) the mou(th) wi an English dishcloot, talk gless haunles, speak lik(e) a prent buik.

  be affected pit it on.

affection hert-likin, fraca, fainness.
  affection for notion O.
  affectionate *see also* **fond of**; lithesome, innerlie, naitral-hertit, fain; (*deeply*) hert-warm.
  bound by affection sib.
affinity sibness.
affirm threap, uphaud.
  affirmation threap.
afflict *see* **harass**.
  afflicted afflickit.
  be afflicted with thole.
  affliction pine.
affluent *see* **well-off**.
afford affuird; **can't afford** canna fa SHETLAND, ORKNEY, NE.
affront *verb* heelie.
  noun heelie, dunt, tash.
afoot afit, agait.
aforementioned foresaid.
afraid feart (at, for, o), afeart, frichtit (for); (*of the supernatural*) eerie.
  be afraid (that) misdoot (that).
afresh in the new.
aft eft.
after efter, aifter, ahin(t).
  afterbirth (*of an animal, esp a cow*) cleanin.
  aftermath eftercome, eftercast.
  afternoon efternuin, efterneen N.
  aftertaste guff.
  afterwards efterwa(i)rds, efterhin, syne.
  a little after, not long after (at) the back O: '*the back o six*'.
  have a child named after you get the name.
again agane.
against agin, conter, gin.
  go against (*oppose*) conter.
age *verb* (*of a person*) get up in years, turn ower in years.
  aged (*old*) eildit.
  old age *see also* **old**; eild.
  under age within eild.
  be the same age as be ages wi, be eildin(s) wi.
  of the same age heidiepeer.

  fail to live to a ripe old age no claw an auld man's heid.
agent (*who manages property*) factor.
  through the agency of inthrow NE.
aggregate (*total*) tot.
aggressive *see also* **belligerent**; randie.
aggrieved *see also* **annoyed**; sair made.
aghast dumfoonert.
agile lichtsome, soople, swack, swank, swankie, kneef, kibble NE, swipper(t) NE, wannle S.
  agilely soople, swipper(t) NE.
agitate 1 (*make nervous*) fluffer, flocht NE, kittle (up) NE. **2** (*shake*) jummle, rees(h)le, shoogle, pirl SHETLAND, NE.
  agitated wowf, skeer(ie), yivverin NE.
  become agitated roose.
  agitation (*mental*) carfuffle, jabble, feem NE, firr NE.
  in a state of agitation up tae high doh.
agnail ragnail.
ago syne, sinsyne.
  a moment ago eenoo.
  some time ago a while back, a filie back NE, no lang syne.
agony *see* **pain**.
agree gree, say thegither; (*be in harmony (with)*) draw (wi), say ae wey (wi), gae in (wi), see thegither (wi), quader (wi) NE; (*come to an agreement (with)*) say wi, gree; (*fit in (with)*) complouter (wi).
  agreeable 1 *see also* **pleasant**; couthie. **2** (*in agreement*) greeable.
  agreeably condinglie N.
  agreement 1 (*harmony*) greement, greeance. **2** (*esp conspiratorial*) paction, pack.
  agree to meet tryst.
ahead *see also* **forward**; aheid.
aid *see also* **help**: *verb* (*financially*) turn someone's han(d).
  noun forder.
ail: ailing *see also* **ill**; badly, no weel, traikie, dowie, dwinin(-lik(e)), pyauvin N, hard up SE.

ailment *see also* **illness**; tribble; (*slight*) waff, towt.

aim *verb* **1** (*a blow etc*) ettle, mint NE, draw; **aim blows** lat breenge, loonder. **2** *see also* **take aim** *below*; (*a weapon etc*) ettle, wice, pap. **3** (*curling, bowls: a shot to land near the tee*) draw. **4 aim at** *or* **to** ettle at *or* tae, mint at *or* tae, haud for, airt for.

noun **1** (*act of aiming*) gley, airch N, vizzy SHETLAND. **2** (*intention*) mint.

aimless knotless, paidlin.

aimless person knotless threid.

work aimlessly plowter, scutter, picher NE, poach S.

take aim mark, airch, gley NE, vizzy SHETLAND.

air *noun* **1** *see* **atmosphere**. **2** *see* **tune**. **3** (*conceited*) **airs** tantrums, mollops S.

verb (*clothes, in the open*) haizer.

air-bladder (*of a fish*) soom.

aircraft *see* **aeroplane**.

stream of air pew.

aisle trance, pass.

ajar ajee.

akin sib, freen(d)s (wi) NE, neibours (wi).

alarm *verb, see also* **scare**; alairm, skeer, flichter, fleg.

noun, see also **fright**; alairm, terrification, fleg.

alas wae's me, wow (me), waesuck(s), dool, ochone *literary, esp* HIGHLAND, †waly, †walawa, †alake.

alcoholic *adjective* (*of a person*) drouthie.

alcove bole, neuk; (*to sit out a dance etc*) sit-ooterie *humorous*.

alder aller, arn.

wood of the alder Scotch mahogany.

ale yill; (*strong*) nappie *literary*; (*newly-brewed, weak*) swats; (*thin, weak*) penny-wabble NE; (*weak or sour*) jute ORKNEY; (*foaming*) scuds.

alehouse *see* **inn**.

alert *see also* **quick-witted**; gleg, smairt, smert, in, kneef, thorow S.

on the alert on the keevee.

algae (*type of*) slake; (*river or marine*) wrack.

alien *adjective* fremmit, ootlin.

noun ootrel.

alight[1] *see* **dismount**.

alight[2] (*on fire*) in (a) lowe, alowe.

set alight *see also* **kindle**; spark.

align raw.

in exact alignment (*of a door etc*) parpen NE.

alike equal-aqual, sic an sae, sib; (*all alike*) eeksie-peeksie, a(w) ae oo.

alive tae the fore, abuin the muild SHETLAND, ORKNEY, NE, in life, on fit.

be alive leuk up.

all a(w).

All Fools' Day *see* **April Fool's Day**.

All Saints' Day Hallowday.

eve of All Saints' Day Halloween.

all alike *see* **alike**.

all kinds of orra.

all and sundry ilk ane.

all the . . . the hail . . .

all told at a slump.

allay *see* **relieve** 3.

allege threap.

allegiance *see* **loyalty**.

alleviate lichten, souder.

alley close, pend, entry, trance, througaun, througate, wynd, vennel.

allocate (*work etc*) stent.

allot stent.

allotted task stent.

allotment paffle.

allow alloo, lat, leave.

be allowed get: '*Can we get tae the park the noo?*'

allow to go demit.

allude: allude to mint.

allure *verb, see* **entice**.

alluvium sleetch.

ally *noun* (*supporter*) stoop.

almanac prognostic NE.

almighty a(l)michtie.

the Almighty the Michtie.

almost amaist, amest, near(aboot(s)), maistlie, maistlins, fecklie NE, halflins NE, (gey) near.

alms awmous.
  almshouse †bede-house.
aloft alaft.
alone alane, aleen NE, (by) his *etc* lane, im *etc* leen NE, lanerlie, misslie; (*completely*) burd-alane, hert-alane.
  leave alone lat abee.
along alang, yont, awa: '*come awa tae yer bed*'.
  alongside *preposition* anent.
  adverb sidelins.
  right along endlang.
aloof *see also* **shy, disdainful**; freff, abeich.
aloud alood.
already a'ready, areddies.
also *see also* **too**; an a(w), forby.
alter *see* **change**.
alternately time aboot, tour aboot; (*in a game etc*) shots each.
altitude heicht, hicht.
altogether a(w)thegither.
always aye, ayeweys, still an on.
am *emphatic* ur W: '*Ah'm ur*'.
  am not amna, amnae, urnae W.
amalgamate *see* **mix**.
amaze *see also* **astonish**; dumfooner.
amber lammer.
ambition ambeetion, ettle, ettlin.
  ambitious ambeetious, high-bendit.
amble *see* **stroll**.
amenable (*of an animal*) handie NE.
amends mends.
amiable *see also* **pleasant**; douce, couthie.
amiss: take amiss tak ill.
  taken amiss ill-taen, mistaen.
ammunition ammuneetion.
among amang.
amorous fain.
amount *noun* amoont, thing: '*Will ye hae a wee thing soup?*'
  fair amount kit, sort S.
  large amount *see* **lot, many**; lump, feck, wecht, mask, hudge ORKNEY, N; (*of money, possessions*) sowd.
  small amount lick, pickle, inklin, smell, smatterin, scent, drap, drop: '*a*

wee drop cheese'; (*very small*) tait, snuff; (*of liquid*) jirble, spark.
ample (*in quantity*) lucky, fouthie, lairge NE.
amuse *see also* **entertain**; haud oot o langour ORKNEY, N.
  amusement divert, ploy.
  amusing shortsome, pawkie.
  amusing person *or* **thing** divert.
  amuse yourself play yersel.
ancestors forebeir(er)s, forefolk.
  ancestral stock kin.
ancient *see also* **old**; auncient.
and an.
anecdote *see* **story**.
anemone *see* **sea anemone**.
anger *noun, see also* **temper, wrath**; corruption, birse: '*His birse is up*'; **fit of anger** *see* **rage**.
  verb fash, pet.
angry wraith; (*of looks*) atterie; (*furiously*) wuid, dancin mad, bealin, reid mad.
  become angry roose, crab, set up yer humph; **become angry at** lowp up at.
  show anger reek.
  tremble with anger pirr.
angle: at the wrong angle squeegee, (a)sklent.
angler-fish wide-gab, oof NE, keth(r)ie.
anglicized *see also* **affected**; Englified.
anguish *see* **pain**.
animal 1 baist, beas; **animals** cattle, beas. **2** (*weakling*) jabart; (*not thriving*) piner, scrunt; (*lean, scraggy*) rag, scrog, scaddin NE; (*large, worthless*) rammock NE; (*small, bad-tempered*) spitten NE.
animate: animated skeich, on the keevee, heich, sprack, birkie.
  animation *see* **spirit**.
animosity ill-will, unfreen(d)ship.
ankle cuit, queet NE.
announce annoonce, lat ken.
  announcement (*from the pulpit*) intimation.
annoy fash, taiver, teen, wink, pest,

chaw; (*esp with talk or noise*) deave; (*tease*) kittle, towt.

annoyance fash(erie), botherer, bucker NE, deavance.

annoyed mad, thin.

be annoyed that someone has appeared see someone far eneuch.

annoying *see also* **troublesome**; fashious, weary, uggin, sorrafu.

exclamation of annoyance hoot!, howt! SE.

annual ilka year, ilkie ear N.

annul (*law*) elide, reduce.

anoint *see* **smear**.

another anither, anidder.

answer (*in argument or rudely*) speak back.

ant eemock, emerteen NE, pismire.

antagonistic: be antagonistic towards hae yer horn in someone's hip.

anticipate *see also* **expect**; ettle.

in anticipation of gin NE.

anticlockwise withershins, widdershins.

antics cantrips.

antipathy *see* **disgust**.

antique auld-warl(d).

antiquity eild.

antirrhynum *see* **snapdragon**.

anus (erse)hole *slang*.

anvil stiddie.

anxiety anxeeitie, thocht, cark, hert's care, wanrest.

anxious thochtie; (*restlessly*) lik(e) a hen on a het girdle, on eggs, on hecklepins.

any onie.

anybody *see also* **anyone**; oniebodie, emdy W.

anyhow, anyway oniewey(s), onie road.

anyone onie ane, onie yin, oniebodie.

anything oniething, ocht, owt, ochtlins.

anywhere oniegate, oniewey(s).

anywhere else onie ither wey NE.

in any way onie: '*he canna fish onie*', oniewey(s), ochtlins.

apart apairt, oot ower.

apart from leave aside.

apartment *see* **flat**.

apathetic caul(d)rif(e), caul(d)-watter.

apex peen.

apiece the piece.

apologise apologeese.

apothecary droggist, poticary SW.

appal *see also* **frighten**; gliff.

apparatus graith.

apparent *see* **obvious**.

apparently appearinlie NE.

apparition *see also* **ghost**; (*foretelling death*) foregang SHETLAND, N.

appealing *see* **attractive**.

appear kythe; (*in a court etc*) compear.

appearance 1 (*act of appearing*) ootcome. **2** (*look*) cast, hue; (*showing family resemblance*) swap.

having a good appearance *see also* **good-looking**; weel tae be seen.

put in an appearance pit in a face.

appease (*thirst, wishes, desires of*) slock.

appetite appeteet, cut, heck.

appetizing gustie, guid kitchen.

having an appetite for able for, yibble for S.

having a good appetite hertie, maithail.

have a healthy appetite be a man o yer mait.

whet the appetite taste the gab, gust the gab.

applaud (*by stamping the feet*) ruff.

apple *see also* **crab apple**; aipple, yap *child's word*, EDINBURGH.

apple core stump, runt, casket.

the apple of someone's eye someone's ae ee.

apply yourself hing in, claa aff NE.

appoint appint; (*a minister, esp a first charge*) place.

appointment appintment; (*to meet at a certain time and place*) tryst.

fail to keep an appointment mistryst.

make an appointment (with) tryst (wi).

apportion

apportion (*work*) stent.

appraise *see* **value**.

 appraising look swatch, cannie squint.

appreciate apprise, prize.

apprehension 1 (*understanding*) kennin. **2** (*suspicious*) ill dreid.

apprehensive eerie.

 be very apprehensive be sittin on preens, be on nettles.

apprentice *noun* prentice, boy; (*cobbler's*) snab.
 verb prentice, pit tae.

approach *verb* (*slowly; also a specific time*) weir intil.
 noun oncome.

approaching (*a time*) risin: '*it's risin fower*'.

appropriate *verb* (*to your own needs*) skech.
 adjective lik(e).

approve appruve; (*ratify*) homologate.

 express approval *see* **applaud**.

approximately lik(e).

April Aprile.

 April fool gowk, April gowk, huntiegowk.

 April Fool's Day gowk's day, magowk's day, huntiegowk.

 April fool's errand gowk's errand, huntiegowk, gowk.

 make an April fool of magowk, gowk.

 go on an April fool's errand hunt the gowk, gang on a gowk's eerin NE.

 2 April (*when children fix paper tails to backs of unsuspecting victims*) Tailie Day.

apron awpron N, peenie, daidle, brot NE; (*esp coarse, workman's*) brat; (*for rough work*) scodgie brat; (*household overall*) wrapper.

apt lik(e), fettle sw; habile *law*.

arable land pleuch lan(d), ploo grun(d).

arbitrator arbiter, thirdsman; (*chief, to settle a deadlock*) owersman.

arch *noun* erch, airch, pen(d), bow, boo NE.
 arched coomed.

archery: ground for archery practice butts.

argue *see also* **dispute, quarrel, wrangle**; argie, argifee, argufy, argiebargie, threap, tulyie SHETLAND, ORKNEY, NE, dibber-dabber NE.

argument airgument NE, threap, thraw, tulyie SHETLAND, ORKNEY, NE, dibber-dabber, twa words.

aristocratic *see* **lordly**.

arithmetic coonts.

 arithmetical problem quirk SHETLAND, NE.

 do arithmetic coont.

arm *see also* **sea**; airm, erm.

armchair bow-cheer NE; (*large*) muckle chair; (*winged*) lug-chair.

armful oxterfu.

armhole (*of a garment*) oxter; (*tailoring*) sey.

armpit, underpart of the upper arm oxter.

 walk arm-in-arm, link arms cleek, link.

 with your arms folded wi yer airms in yer oxters.

 hold *or* **carry under the arm** oxter.

 lend an arm to (*someone walking*) gie an oxter tae NE.

 take, support *etc* **by the arm** oxter.

army airmie.

aroma *see also* **smell**; (y)oam SHETLAND, ORKNEY, NE.

around aroon(d).

arouse 1 *see also* **waken**; rowst; (*from sleep*) raise. **2** (*sexually*) kittle.

 sexually aroused radg(i)e, yeukie.

arrange (*put in order*) redd (up), sort; (*manage*) cast aboot.

arrangement (*display*) ootset.

array *see* **dress**.

arrears 1 by-rins NE. **2** (*of work*) lie-by NE.

 be in arrears rin ahin(t), be ahin(t) han(d), rest.

arrest *verb, see also* **seize**; (*stop*) reest; (*of police etc*) lift, tak in; (*goods*) reest S.

arrive at win at, win till.

 arrival (*act of arriving*) income.

arrogant heelie(fu), pridefu, heich, heich-heidit, stinkin, croose NE.
  behave arrogantly sneist.
arrow arrae, arra W, airra NE, prog SHETLAND, ORKNEY, CAITHNESS.
arse *see also* **buttocks**; erse.
arson (*law*) fire-raising.
art *see also* **skill**; airt.
  artful *see* **crafty**.
arthritic joint shot joint.
article airticle, objeck.
articulate *verb* (*express*) mou-ban(d).
artificial artifeeshul; (*of speech etc*) *see* **affected**.
  artificial flowers gumflowers.
as is; in: '*in a gift*'.
  as if as, (the) same as.
  as much, far *etc* **as** whit: '*she cried whit she could*'.
  as well an a(w).
  as it were lik(e).
ascend *see also* **climb**; rise SW.
ash[1] (*tree, wood: see also* **mountain ash**) esh.
ash[2] (*from burning*) ass, ess SHETLAND, NE, aise.
  (piece of) coal burnt to ashes ghaist.
  ashen (*very pale*) gash *literary*.
  ash-bucket (ass) backet, baikie.
  ashpit midden, ass-midden.
ashamed: be ashamed hae a rid face.
  be (very) ashamed think (black burnin) shame.
ashlar aislar.
aside *adverb* sidelins.
  set aside (*for future use*) pit past, pit by, lay past.
ask ax, speir; (*a person*) ask at, speir at *or* o; (*law: from a court*) crave.
  ask after ask for, see aboot.
  ask for seek; (*persistently*) craik, thrain.
  ask to go, come *etc* seek tae, intae *etc*: '*he's seekin intae the hoose again*'.
askance (a)sklent.
  look askance sklent, gledge.
askew *adverb, see also* **awry**; squint, asklent, skyow NE, skew.

adjective squeegee, skave.
asleep awa(y): '*Is he awa yet?*'
  fall asleep fa(w) ower, dwam ower, dover ower.
aspect (*appearance*) cast.
  every aspect (the) reet an (the) rise NE.
aspen esp, tremmlin tree, quakin aish, quakin trei S.
aspersion: cast aspersions on *see* **slander**.
aspire to seek tae, ettle efter N.
  aspiring *see* **ambitious**.
aspirin asp(i)reen.
ass *see* **donkey**.
assail *see* **attack**.
assault *see* **attack**.
assemble forgaither, semmle; (*of a school etc*) gae in.
  assembled in: '*the scuil's in*'.
  assembly forgaitherin, gaitherin.
assent *see* **agreement**.
assert *see also* **harp on**; threap.
  assertion (*vehement*) threap.
assess *see* **estimate**.
assiduous eydent.
  assiduity thrift.
assignation tryst; (*law: of property*) disposition.
  make an assignation tryst.
assist pit tae yer han(d).
  assistance (*helping hand*) cast, heeze NE; (*support*) supply.
  assistant (*minister's or teacher's*) helpender NE.
associate *verb* **associate with 1** troke wi, neibour wi, middle wi, frequent wi, forgaither wi; (*for bad purposes*) colleague NE. **2** (*connect with*) liken wi.
  admit being associated with own.
  association 1 (*dealings*) troke. **2** (*of tradesmen in a burgh*) incorporation.
assorted sindry.
  assortment *see* **collection**.
assure asseer NE.
  assured croose.
  assuredly atweel, tweel.
  I assure you there's ma han(d), I sure ye NE, weel I wat.

astern astarn.

asthma the wheezles; (*among miners*) stifle.

   asthmatic pechie; (*and fat*) purfelt.

   asthmatic wheeze pech.

   cough asthmatically peuchle SHETLAND, NE.

astir asteer, on steer.

astonish *see also* **astound, surprise;** dumfooner, ca(w) the feet fae, pall SHETLAND, ORKNEY, NE, daumer NE, denumb, whummle.

   astonished bumbazed, fraized, dumfoonert.

   astonishment maze.

   exclamation of astonishment jings!, help ma boab!, crivvens!, losh (me)!, michtie (me)!, govie (dick)!

astound *see also* **astonish;** stoun(d), mesmerise.

astray wull ORKNEY, NE, agley; (*morally*) aff yer fit.

   go astray (*esp morally*) gae gleyed.

   lead astray mislippen.

astride stridelegs, stridlins.

   sit astride striddle.

astute *see also* **shrewd;** cannie, pawkie, fell, soople.

asunder sinnerie, sindert, abreed.

at it.

   at all at a(w), ava NE, ochtlins.

ate *past tense of* **eat** ett.

athletic *see also* **active, supple;** swankin, swack, leish SW, S.

athwart athort, thort, thorter.

atmosphere (*warm, stuffy*) (y)oam SHETLAND, NE, moch(ie); (*hot, damp*) muithness; (*thick, stuffy*) smuchter NE, (*in a crowded place*) stech N; (*thick, suffocating*) smore, stife, scomfish.

atom: not an atom no a haet, no a rissom.

atone *see* **compensate.**

atrocious *see* **awful.**

attach (*fasten*) steek.

   attach yourself to hing tae.

attack *verb* **1** (*physically*) invade, yoke on, licht on, set tae, raise on; (*vigorously*) get tore in(tae). **2** (*verbally*) lowse oot on, roose on, wauken on.

   noun **1** onding. **2** (*of illness*) drowe, toit; (*slight*) towt.

attain win.

attempt *see also* **try:** *verb* ettle, mint, offer.

   noun ettle, mint, offer, skelp.

attend *see also* **heed: attend to** see efter, tend, tent.

attendance onwaitin.

attendant *see also* **servant;** (*of sportsmen in Highlands*) gillie, (*who carries golf clubs*) caddie.

attention tent; (*to what a person says*) audiscence NE.

   pay attention to tent, tak tent o.

   pay great attention preen yer lugs back.

   person needing a lot of attention onwait.

   spring to attention lowp.

attentive tentie, eydent, thochtie, gleg, in.

   attentively graithlie.

attestation clause (*law: authenticating a deed*) testing clause.

attic ceiling coomceil, camceil.

attire *see* **clothes, clothing.**

attitude shape, set, souch.

attorney *see* **lawyer.**

   power of attorney factory.

attract *see* **entice.**

   (much) attracted by (fair) taen on wi, taen up wi, browdent on.

   be attracted by kythe tae.

attractive bonnie, no bad; (*mainly of people*) sonsie, settin, wicelik(e); (*superficially*) fair-farran(t); (*good-natured*) smirkie.

   attractive woman stoater.

attribute *verb* (*something to someone*) even.

auction *noun, verb* roup, unction; (*of animals*) action mart NE.

   auctioneer's clerk clerk o the roup N, roupin clerk.

   arbiter in disputes at auction judge o the roup N.

building for livestock auction mart.
bid at an auction simply to raise price wheel NE; person who does this white-bannet.
record of goods at auction roup(in) roll.
starting price at an auction upset price.
sell by auction roup.
audacious *see* bold, courageous.
audience owdience SHETLAND, NE.
auger aeger, aager N, wummle; (*used red-hot*) hirsel; (*cooper's*) scillop.
  auger-hole wummle-bore.
augment eik.
augur *see* omen.
august lairdlie NE.
aunt auntie.
  Aunt Sally (*at a fair*) molly-dolly.
aurora borealis merry dancers N, streamers.
auspicious cannie, happy.
austere stere, dour, stench NE, snell.
authentic sevendle, rael, jonick, richt.
  authenticate qualifee; (*officially*) dinnagill NE.
author owthor.
authority 1 heid room, poustie, owerance. 2 (*source of information*) author, talesman.
  those in authority (high) heid yins.
  at the height of your authority in yer potestator SHETLAND, NE.
  authorization 1 (*law: of one person to act for another*) procuratory. 2 (*piece of written*) line.
autocrat maister an mair.
autumn hairst; (*late*) back-en(d).
  autumn holidays (*from school*) tattie holidays.
auxiliary *noun* helpender NE.
available (*to do something*) open tae.
avalanche *noun* whummle.
  verb shuit.
avarice grippiness.
  avaricious *see also* greedy, mean[1], miserly, stingy; grippie, grisk, hungry,

nippie, near-begaun, grabbie.
  avaricious person gled, scrub, grab, sneck.
avenue (*leading to a house*) inlat, entry.
average: on the average owerheid.
  average person *or* thing (common) five aicht(s), a scone o the day's bakin.
averse ill-willed.
  aversion scunner, staw, ill-will (at).
  cause *or* get a feeling of aversion scunner.
avid hyte, yeukie.
  avid for mad for, wuid for.
avoid evite, miss, get by, haud wide o; (*bad weather etc*) scug.
  avoid doing (*something*) scoff NE.
await wait on, wait, bide (for).
awake *adjective* waukened.
  verb, see waken.
  easily awakened waukrif(e).
  awakening waukenin.
  be awake wauk.
  stay awake wauk, keep up.
award awaird.
aware awaur; aware of ware o.
  become aware wit.
awash: be awash sail: '*the flair's sailin*'.
away awa, wa, aback; (*distant*) hyne; (*further away*) yont.
  away from aff o, back oot ower NE, furth o(f) *literary, law*, NE.
  send *or* turn someone away pit someone by the door.
awe dare.
  awful awfu, awfie, aafu NE, yafu NE.
awkward *see also* clumsy; ackwart; (*of a person*) han(d)less, stammerel, gawkit, ill-shakken-up SHETLAND, ORKNEY, NE, tuckie NE; (*of things*) uncannie.
awl elsh; (*fine*) meenie N.
awn baird.
awry *see also* askew; agley, gley(e)d, athraw, ajee.
axe aix, bullax N.
axle aix-tree, assle-tree.

B

baa mae, maa, meh.

babble *see also* **chatter:** *verb* blether, haiver, blabber, yatter, yammer, maunner, gibble-gabble, slabber, glaiber.
noun blethers, haivers, yatter, clack, gibble-gabble.

babbler blether, haiver(el), blether(um)skite, clatterer NE.

baby babbie, bairn, wean CENTRAL, get, geet NE, littlin.

babyish (older) child sook-the-pappie.

baby's binder †barrie.

baby boy laddie bairn, laddie wean, loon(ie) N, FIFE.

baby girl lassie bairn, lassie wean, quin(i)e (bairn) NE.

toast the baby's health weet the bairn's heid.

bachelor bacheleer, wanter, young man, lad; (*still living with parents, at any age*) boy.

back *noun* 1 (*rear*) hin(t), hin(t)side; (*back part*) hinneren(d), hinderen(d). 2 (*of a person or animal*) rig, riggin.
adjective hin(t).

having backache through stooping hippit, hip-grippit.

backbiting nip-lug.

backbone rig, riggin, rig-bane, riggin bane, (*bottom of backbone, where it joins sacrum*) couplin.

backdraught (*in chimney*) blawdoon, flan SHETLAND, ORKNEY, N.

back garden kail yaird.

backside *see* **buttocks.**

backstairs backstair, back.

backward 1 backart, back, (a)hint-the-han(d); (*in progress*) far back N; (*of crops*) blate. 2 (*of a person: see also*

stupid) glaikit, preen-heidit, willyart, bauch.

backwards backarts, hintside foremaist, backlins.

backwards and forwards *see also* **to and fro;** back an fore.

backyard back coort, back green.

back to front backside foremaist, hintside foremaist.

back up uphaud.

back water (*in rowing*) shue SHETLAND, ORKNEY, CAITHNESS.

having a long weak back lingel-backit SW, S.

never look back nivver leuk ower yer shouder.

get your own back on get yer penny(s)worths (oot) O.

put someone's back up set up someone's humph, get up someone's birse.

bacon ham, Sandy *humorous.*

side of bacon flake SE.

bad *adjective, see also* **nasty, useless, malevolent;** baud; (*evil*) ill, ill-deedie, ill-hertit, ill-kindit, wickit, coorse, shan *originally gipsy.*

badly bad, baud, ill, sair.

badly-behaved ill-contrivit SHETLAND, N, ill-gaitit, coorse, ill-trickit.

badly-nourished ill-thriven.

badly off ill-aff, sair aff.

badness ill.

bad child blastie.

(come to) a bad end (*gang*) a gray gate.

bad habit ill-gate.

bad manners ill laits.

bad temper *see* **rage.**

bad-tempered *see also* **sulky, peevish, surly;** crabbit, wickit, girnie,

12

cankerit, glumsh, nippit, natterie, ram-gunshoch, ill-natured, ill-faured; (*esp of a child*) pe(r)neurious NE.

bad-tempered person catter-wurr NE; (*esp a woman*) randie.

go to the bad gae an ill gate.

in a bad mood in (a) bad cut.

one's as bad as the other there's no ane o them tae mend anither.

you're as bad as I am gin I be pottie ye're pannie NE.

badger brock.

baffle (*puzzle*) pall SHETLAND, ORKNEY, N, bleck NE, fickle.

bag *see also* **sack**[1]; poke, pyoke NE; (*esp leather*) walgan NE; (*polythene*) poly poke.

bagpipe *see also* **grace note**: bagpipes pipes; **set of bagpipes** pair of bagpipes SHETLAND, ANGUS, (*complete set*) stand.

bagpipe band pipe band.

bass pipe of the bagpipe drone; **socket of this** stock.

melody pipe of the bagpipe, separate pipe for practice chanter; **bell-end of this** sole.

classical music of the bagpipe pibroch; **theme of this** urlar.

play on the bagpipes pipe, doodle; (*shrilly*) skirl.

bail[1] *noun* (*law*) caution.

bail[2] *verb* (*a boat*) owse SHETLAND, ORKNEY; (*bail a boat*) lave.

bailer spootcher.

bait *see* **worm**.

bake byaak NE, (*referring to heating process*) fire: '*fire them in a het oven*'.

baked *past tense* beuk NE.

past participle baken.

baker batchie, †baxter.

baking board bake-board, bake-brod.

baking plate (*used over fire or other heat*) girdle.

balance: equally balanced equal-aqual.

in the balance on the hing.

lose your balance fa(w) aff yer feet.

balcony (*esp at top of outside stair*) plettie DUNDEE.

bald bell, beld NE, bauldie(-heidit).

bale[1] *noun* (*of straw etc*) turse.

verb turse.

bale[2] *see* **bail**[2].

balk *noun* (*beam*) bauk.

ball ba(w), pallet, bool; (*used in shinty*) nag.

ball-game *see* **football, handball**.

keeping a ball in the air keepie-up.

ballad ballant; (*street-ballad*) strowd NE.

balmy (*of weather*) leesome NE, saft.

balustrade ravel.

bamboozle *see also* **perplex**; bumbaze, taigle.

banana banannie.

band[1] (*which binds*) baun(d), ban.

band[2] (*group*) baun(d), ban, curn; (*of reapers etc*) boon.

bandmaster (*of a pipe-band*) pipe major, pipie *informal*.

bandage *noun* cloot; (*dipped in beeswax etc*) trate.

verb rowe.

bandit *see* **robber**.

bandy *verb* **bandy words** giff-gaff.

bandy-legged bowlie(-leggit) w, bowdie(-leggit), bow-hoched, shammie-leggit.

bang *noun, see also* **blow**[2]; (*sound*) blaff, (*of a gun etc*) tooch SE.

verb, see also **knock, strike**; dunner, rattle, dird N, dang, knell; (*a door*) dad.

with a bang dird N.

banish bainish.

bank[1] baunk; (*of river etc: steep sloping*) brae; (*overhanging*) broo, hag SW, S, (*where fish lurk*) haud; (*of land: steep*) scaur, skerr S; (*esp of peat*) bink; (*for shellfish in the sea*) scaup; (*of earth etc at roadside*) bunker.

bank up (*a fire*) rake, (*for the night*) rest, reest.

bank[2] (*financial*) baunk; (*in a game*) puggie; (*child's*) lucky box.

banknote paper note; (*for £1*) note, single (note).

bankrupt *adjective* broken, runkit.
noun †dyvour, †Abbey laird *jocular*.
verb runk, tak doon ORKNEY, N.
bankruptcy brak.
bring to bankruptcy bring tae the roup.
go bankrupt gae throu it, cowp, set doon (yer barra).
proclaim as a bankrupt †put to the horn.
banns cries: '*pit in the cries*'.
have the banns proclaimed be cried.
banquet *see* **feast**.
bantam bantim, buntin.
banter *verb* jamph, chairge SW, S.
noun jamph, heyze NE: '*haad a heyze*', mows NE.
baptize bapteese, kirs(t)en.
baptism bapteesim, kirs(t)enin.
offer (*a child*) **for baptism** present.
bar *noun, see also* **crossbar, window bar**; baur; (*wooden*) spaik; (*long, wooden*) stang; (*for specific purposes*): **1** (*eg for a door, window*) slot; **2** (*in window-grating*) staincher, stainchel; **3** (*over a fire to hold potchain*) rantle-tree; (*movable*) swey, swee; **4** (*in a grate*) rib; **5** (*wooden, on which fish are hung to dry*) tenter.
barb *noun* prog SHETLAND, ORKNEY, CAITHNESS, porr CAITHNESS; (*of a fishhook etc*) witter SHETLAND, ORKNEY, N, otter S.
barbed (*having barbs*) pikie, wittert SHETLAND, N.
barbed wire pikit weer NE.
barbarous *see* **boorish, rough**.
barber baurber.
bare *adjective, see also* **naked**; (*of land*) scabbit.
completely bare as bare as birkie.
barely *see* **scarcely**.
barefoot(ed) barfit(tit).
bare feet baries.
bare patch (*in a field*) blain.
bare skin scuddie.
bargain *noun* **1** (*agreement*) block, paction, troke, tack, niffer; (*esp unfair*) rug NE; (*esp dishonest*) grab NE; (*easily broken*) bairn's bargain. **2** (*something cheap*) wanworth.
verb troke, niffer, cowp, prig, dacker.
bargainer troker; (*hard*) scrub.
hard-bargaining *adjective* snappie ANGUS.
drive a hard bargain prig.
into the bargain tae the buit, an a(w).
make a bad bargain sell yer hen(s) on a rainy day, ca yer hogs till a huilie market NE.
strike a bargain with chap.
withdraw from a bargain duff, rue.
barge *noun* bairge, scowe, gabbart; (*type of one-masted sailing*) wherry.
verb breenge.
bark (*of a dog etc: see also* **yelp**) *verb* bouch, wow, yowf, yaff, youch; (*esp of a large dog*) bowf; (*in a suppressed way*) wowff; (*in a sharp, suppressed way*) whink; (*rapidly*) yabble.
noun bouch, yamph, wow, yowf, bowf; (*low-pitched*) wowff; (*sharp, suppressed*) whink.
barley 1 (*type of hardy four- or six-row*) bere, big(g). **2** (*barley with husks removed*) pot barley.
grain of barley barley pickle.
barn granzie *gipsy*.
barnacle claik SHETLAND, ORKNEY, NE, scaw CAITHNESS.
barometer mercury NE.
barrel bowie; (*set on end*) stan(d).
barrel hoop gird.
barrel stave scowe.
stack of barrels stowe.
barren 1 (*of animals*) yeld, eil(d). **2** (*of land*) lea, dour, scabbit; (*of soil*) deef, hi(r)stie.
barren cow *etc* yeld.
barren piece of land hirst.
barricade (*defensive palisade*) †peel.
barrister advocate.
barrow (*wheelbarrow*) barra(e), borra; (*handcart*) hurlie, hurl-barra; (*without sides*) paddy barra.

barrow-handle, **barrow-shaft** (barra-)tram, (barra-)stiel.

barter *verb* troke, niffer, hooie, giffgaff, cowp, cose, wissel.
noun troke, niffer.

base[1] *noun* **1** (*foundation*) foond(s), larach, steeth SHETLAND, ORKNEY, CAITHNESS. **2** (*in games*) den, dale, steesh ANGUS.

basement laich, dunnie.

base[2] *adjective, see* **contemptible, worthless.**

bash *see* **beat.**

bashful *see also* **shy**; baushfae, blate, laithfu, strange, timmer, unco, shan.

bashfully laithfu.

basic (*of wages*) upstannin.

basin *see also* **bowl** 1; bowl(ie), leem N, bowie; (*wooden*) cap; (*for mixing meal etc*) bossie NE; (*broad, shallow, for skimming milk*) bine, boyne.

basis grun(d).

bask beek.

basking shark bridgie SHETLAND, ORKNEY, N, muldoan.

basket (*esp for meal, potatoes*) skep; (*esp for bread*) maun; (*shallow, scoopshaped, eg for fish*) scull; (*round, for fish-bait etc*) murlin NE; (*round, for fish, eggs*) rip; (*deep, eg for peat, fish*) creel; (*for seed*) happer; (*straw, for seed, meal*) ruskie; (*of strips of wood*) spail basket; (*deep, carried on back*) creel.

bastard *noun* luve-bairn, come-o-will NE; (*also term of abuse*) bastart, bastardin, get, geet NE.
adjective, see **illegitimate.**

baste (*sewing*) baiss.

bat (*animal*) bawkie (bird).

batch: batch loaf plain loaf.

bath: take a bath dook.

bathe *verb, noun* dook.

snack eaten after bathing *see* **snack.**

baton *see* **stick**[1].

batter *verb, see also* **beat**; lewder, nevel, massacker, cloor, mell.

battered (*worn*) dashelt.

battle *noun, see also* **fight, struggle**; stour.

battle-axe (*type of*) Lochaber axe.

battle-cry slogan.

bauble whigmaleerie, flumgummerie NE.

bawdy ruch, coorse.

bawl *see also* **yell, howl**: *verb* goller, gullie, gollach, yowl, buller NE.
noun goller, buller NE.

bay[1] (*inlet*) *see* **creek, inlet.**

bay[2] *see also* **bark**: *verb* bowf, wow SHETLAND, NE.
noun bowf, wow.

bay[3]: **keep at bay** weir aff.

bay[4] (*tree*) *see* **laurel.**

be *see* **am, are, is, was, were.**

beach *see also* **foreshore**; brae, stron ORKNEY.

beacon fire bleeze.

bead: beading rin(d); (*narrow, between floor and wall*) moose mouldin.

string of beads pair o beads.

beak neb, gob, gab, gebbie.

beaker bicker.

beam *noun* **1** (*of wood: see also* **crossbeam**) bauk, simmer, sile, tree, pall, caber; (*supporting*) sole. **2** (*of light: see also* **gleam**) blink, leam.

bean pod *see* **pod.**

bear[1] *verb* **1** *see also* **carry**; beir. **2** (*endure*) thole, bide, dree.

bearable tholeable.

bearing (*demeanour*) cast.

hard to bear sair, dreich, ill tae thole.

bear[2]: **bearberry** gnashick NE.

beard baird.

bearded bairdie.

bearded woman Katie beardie.

the rubbing of another's face with a stubbly beard (chinnie) bairdie, dry shave.

beast *see also* **animal**; baist, beas.

beat *verb* **1** (*strike, thrash: see also* **strike, slap, spank, thump, batter**) bate, ding, dunt, bash, (*specif a person*) pey, skelp, belt, yerk, kill, dump, lamp, mell, melt, pran NE, tabour, baitchel S, claw someone's hide, gie someone a sarkfu o sair banes; (*severely, heavily*) dunt, loonder, rummle. **2** (*cloth, flax: see also* **full²**) knock; (*clothes etc*) bittle, beetle. **3** (*a drum*) ruff, †touk. **4** (*of rain etc*) blatter, bla(u)d. **5** (*of the heart: violently*) *see* **palpitate**. **6** (*overcome: see also* **surpass**) lamp, bang, cowe, ding, ootding NE, win NE. **7** (*eggs*) switch.

past tense bate, bet.

noun **1** (*of a drum*) †ruff, †touk. **2** (*of the heart: violent*) wallop, dunt.

beaten *past participle* bate, bet, baitten.

beating 1 clearin, loonderin, skelpin, lick(in)s, paikin, thuddin, rummle, come-again NE, reemis(h) NE, payment NE, peggin; (*thorough*) sairin, rummle, laldie: '*gie him laldie*'. **2** (*with 'the tawse'*) palmies, scuds, sculte, pandies, luiffies, wheechs, tag N.

beat down (*by treading*) patter, stramp; (*crops, by wind*) buff NE; (*in price*) prig.

beat time (*to a dance tune*) treeple NE.

beat up *see verb* 1.

that beats all that cowes a(w), that dings a green thing NE, that palls a SHETLAND, ORKNEY, NE.

beauty brawness.

beautiful *see also* **handsome**; bonnie, braw, wallie, loosome *literary*, lillie *literary*.

beautifully bonnie, bonnilie, braw(lie).

beautiful things braws.

because cause, kis, cas, acause.

because of ower the heid(s) o, for.

beckon wag.

become turn, get: '*she's awfie cheeky gettin*'.

becoming settin, wicelik(e).

become of come o.

bed *noun* lair, lie, scratcher *slang*, beddie-ba(s) *child's word*, baw-baw(s) *child's word*; (*built into wall*) box-bed, close bed, bun(-in) bed NE; (*truckle-bed*) hurlie-bed, whirlie(-bed), wheelie-bed; (*divan bed*) sattle-bed.

bedcover (*esp thick woollen*) (bed-)mat; (*tartan*) (bed-)plaid.

bedfellow neibour.

bedridden bedfast.

bedridden person bedal NE.

be bedridden lie.

bedroom chaumer.

out of bed oot ower.

get(ting) up out of bed rise.

get out of bed in a bad temper rise aff yer wrang side.

tucked up in bed skeppit.

bedaub *see* **besmear**.

bedeck *see also* **deck**; bedink.

bedevil (*torment*) murther.

bedraggle (be)draigle, tra(u)chle.

bee (*honey-bee*) skep-bee; (*wild bee: see also* **bumblebee**) bumbee, bummer; (*moss (carder) bee*) foggie (bee), foggie toddler; (*bee with red markings behind*) reid-arsie NE; (*black and yellow striped*) gairie-bee; (*miner bee*) yirdie (bee).

beehive skep, byke, bink; (*straw*) ruskie.

hole in beehive for bees port.

bee in your bonnet maggot, pliskie NE.

put (*a swarm*) **into a beehive** skep.

beef: cut of beef (*from shoulder to loin*) sey, (*from shoulder*) foresey, (*from loin*) backsey, (*from upper foreleg*) shouder lire, (*from the hindquarters: compare* Eng *topside and silverside*) round steak, rump; (*from the hip: compare* Eng *rump*) pope's eye, heukbane.

shin of beef skink.

beer *see also* **ale**; (*newly-brewed, weak*) swats; (*with a head*) scuds; (*strong*) pundie SE.

measure of beer given to brewery workers pundie SE.

beetle¹ *see also* **cockroach**; clock; (*large*) clocker; (*carnivorous ground*) golach; (*death-watch*) chackie mill NE, deid-watch, elf-mill N; (*dung*) dirt bee NE, dirt flee NE; (*humming*) bumclock;

(*night-flying*) nicht-clock; (*red*) sook-the-bluid.

beetle[2] *see* **pestle**.

befall (*of a misfortune etc*) befa(w), come ower, fa(w).

before *preposition* afore, or, gin; (*prior to*) in front o.
conjunction afore, or, gin, till, ere.

befoul *see also* **foul, soil, dirty**; nestie, fyle.

befuddled *see* **fuddled**.

beg 1 (*go about begging: see also* **scrounge**) cadge, tap, thig; (*importunately*) †thig and sorn. **2** *see* **beseech**.

beggar *see also* **tramp, vagrant**; thigger, sorner, gaberlunzie (man); (*licensed*) †bluegown.

beggar's bag †scran bag, †mealie poke.

began *past tense of* **begin** begood.

begin stert, stairt, fa(w) tae, tak on; (*vigorously*) yoke (tae).

beginning stert, stairt, fore-end, affgo; (*of a season, event etc*) mou.

begrimed reekit.

beguile *see also* **deceive, bewitch**; wile, begunk, begowk.

behave guide yersel.

badly-behaved ill-daein, coorse, ill-trickit SHETLAND, N.

behaviour fashions: '*fair fashions*', laits: '*ill laits*', ongauns.

bad behaviour ill-daein; (*rowdy*) ongang NE.

behead †heid.

beheld *past participle of* **behold** behauden, behadden, behudden.

behind *preposition* behin(t), ahin(t), hin(t), aback o, the back o.
adverb behin(t), ahin(t), aback.

behindhand back, hint-hand, ahin(t)-han(d).

behind you *etc* at yer *etc* back.

behold *see also* **beheld**; beha(u)d, leuk till.

beholden behauden, behadden, bunsucken NE.

being (*living*) *see* **person**.

belch *noun, verb* rift, boak, byock NE, yesk, guff, rowt.

bring liquid into mouth by belching brash.

belief: it's my belief it's ma thocht.

believe trew; (*think*) hae.

bell *noun* (*handbell*) skellet (bell); (*passing bell*) deid bell.

bell-heather *see* **heather**.

bell-rope bell-towe.

belladonna *see* **deadly nightshade**.

bellicose *see* **warlike** (*under* **war**).

belligerent randie: '*randie beggar*'.

bellow *see also* **roar**: *verb* bellie NE, bullie, belloch, buller, gullie NE.
noun buller.

bellows bellies, bellises.

belly *see also* **intestines**; wame, wyme N, painch, kyte, cag.

bellyful wamefu.

large-bellied *see also* **corpulent, pot-bellied**; wamie, baggit, kytie.

bellyflop gutser.

belly-band (*on harness*) neir-leather.

belong belang.

belongings (*personal*) guids an gear, graith.

belong to (*a place*) belang: '*he belangs Glesca*'.

to whom does this belong? wha's aucht this?, whase awe this?

beloved †lief *in ballads etc*.

below *see also* **beneath**: *preposition* (in) ablow, (in) alow.
adverb ablow, alow.

belt (*of trees*) beltin, beltie NE, strip, plantin; (*teacher's, for punishing*) tawse, tag NE.

bemuse *see* **confuse, daze, perplex**.

bench bink, binch, furm, firm; (*of turf*) sunk; (*settle*) sattle; (*small*) sunkie; (*long wooden, with chest below*) lang-settle.

bend *verb, see also* **bent, sag**; boo; (*into a knee-shaped angle*) knee; ((*part of*) *the body*) loot; (*eg the limbs*) crom NE; (*of the limbs, under you*) faul(d).
noun (*curve*) boo NE; (*fold*) boucht NE; (*in a river: see also* **meander**) jouk.

beneath *see also* **below**; aneath, (in) anaith.

benediction *see* **blessing.**

beneficial cannie.

benefit *see also* **advantage.**
  get the benefit of get *or* ken the guid o.

benevolent *see* **generous, friendly.**

benighted benichtit.

benign *see* **favourable, kindly.**

bent *adjective* (*crooked*) camshachelt, bowsie, bowlie, bowlt, wrang, aff the strecht; (*with age*) twa-faul(d), cruppen doon; (*over a task etc*) oot ower; (*forward*) forrit ower.

bequest bequeyst NE.

berate *see* **scold.**

beret tammie, Tam o Shanter.

berry *see* **blackcurrant, cloudberry, cowberry, cranberry, crowberry, gooseberry, raspberry, redcurrant, white currant.**
  berry-picking the berries.

beseech beseik, prig, fleetch; (*ingratiatingly*) peuther.

beside aside, forby, inby.
  besides forby, an a(w), mair at(t)our, asides.
  be beside yourself be by yersel, be forby yersel.

beslobber slabber, slubber, slaik, slaiger.

besmear cla(i)rt, clort, clary, clag NE, slaik, slaister, slaiger, slair(ie), slitter, skaik NE.

besotted *see* **infatuated.**

bespatter *see* **beslobber.**

bespectacled speckie.

besprinkle *see* **sprinkle.**

best: best clothes Sunday('s) claes, kirk claes.
  best man young man ORKNEY, NE.
  best room room, ben, but NE; (*in a but-an-ben*) horn-en(d) NE.
  best of a bad lot ill-best.
  the best of the bunch the stang o the trump NE.
  one of the best the hert o (the) corn.
  make the best of it tak on.

bestir yourself steer yer fit, turn yer thoum, shak yer feathers, lift a leg.

bestride striddle.

bet *verb* bate, beat N, haud, wad.
  noun bate, beat, wad.
  betting slip line.
  I'll bet I'se warran, I'se swag.

betide *see* **befall.**

betray *see* **deceive, cheat.**

betroth tryst; (*as trial marriage*) †handfast.

betrothal han(d)fastin.

better: better-class bettermais(t).
  better-looking better-faured, better-lik(e), nae sae ill-faart NE.
  I had better I'm better tae, I better, I'll better, I'll need tae.
  get better (*from illness*) mend (o), haud forrit, mak better, cower NE.
  get the better of *see also* **surpass;** gae ower, win in ahin NE, get yer penny(s)worths o, waur, ding; (*in bargaining*) nip SW.
  go from better to worse gae fae the hauch tae the hedder.

between atween, tween, atweesh, (a)tweesh(t), atwix, betweesh NE.
  between-maid go-between.
  between times *see also* **meantime;** atween whiles.

bevel *verb* wash doon.
  noun suit stock N.
  bevelled edge wash.

beverage *see* **drink.**

bewail *see also* **mourn;** mak (a) murn for.

beware bewaur.
  beware of tak tent o.

bewilder *see also* **confuse, daze;** stoun(d), stammygaster, conflummix NE; (*with talk*) taiver.
  bewildered bumbazed, dumfoonert, dumfouttert NE, raivelt, wull NE, willyart.
  bewilderment jabble.

bewitch blink, †glamour.
  bewitched forespoken, taen(-lik(e)).

beyond beyont, ayont, yont, atour, oot ower.

beyond belief past a(w).

beyond the confines or limits of outwith, furth of *law, literary*, NE.

bib 1 daidle, brat. **2** (*fish*) siller-fish NE, bressie, jackie downie.

Bible the (Guid) Buik.

large family Bible †ha-Bible.

bicker *see* **squabble.**

bicycle *see* **penny-farthing.**

bid *verb* **1** (*invite*) seek. **2** (*at an auction, to raise the price*) wheel NE.

past tense bad.

noun (*esp at auction*) bod(e).

bidden socht.

person who bids at an auction to raise the price white-bonnet.

bide: bide your time hing on.

bier buird NE.

big muckle, mickle, meikle, wappin; (*substantial*) sonsie; (*physically*) muckle-boukit; (*and strong*) maisterfu; (*and stout*) great, sture SHETLAND; (*and fat*) bowsie; (*bulky*) bouksome NE.

bigoted begottit, kirk-reekit, nairra-nebbit.

bilberry blaeberry, blivert NE, blairdie NE, *child's word*.

bile ga(w).

bill[1] (*in a pub, restaurant etc*) lawin.

bill[2] (*of a bird*) neb, gob, gab.

bill and coo (*of lovers*) rookettie-coo.

billow *noun, see* **wave** 1.

verb spue.

bin *see* **dustbin.**

bind bin: *verb* **1** (*tightly*) yerk, yark SHETLAND, ORKNEY, N; (*esp by splicing etc*) wup, wap. **2** (*legally*) astrict; (*by ties of affection etc*) thirl.

bind round sweel, wup roon(d).

birch birk; (*for whipping*) cowe NE.

small wood mainly of birch birks.

bird *see also* **fowl**; burd; (*young*) *see* **nestling.**

bird's call *see also* **call, cry, twitter, croak, coo, chatter, chirp**; chirm.

bird-cherry *see* **cherry.**

be birds of a feather be sic mannie sic horsie NE, be buckelt wi ae hesp.

birth hamecomin(g), howdiein.

birthmark rasp.

birthplace cauf kintra, cauf-grun(d), native, original NE.

give birth shout; (*of an animal*) cleck, (*esp prematurely*) cast.

give birth to bring hame.

good birth gentry, gentrice.

biscuit (*usually thick or soft*) bake; (*hard, with pinhole surface*) heckle(d) biscuit; (*hard, butter*) hardie NE; (*butter*) butterie; (*with uneven edge*) raggie biscuit; (*oatmeal, ginger*) parkin, perkin; (*rectangular, ginger*) parlie; (*fancy, originally costing a penny*) penny thing.

bisect half, hauf.

bit[1] *see also* **piece, amount, fragment**; (*small*) bittie, bittock.

bit by bit gnipper for gnapper NE.

bits and pieces orrals.

bit[2] *past tense of* **bite** bait.

bitch bick.

bite *verb, see also* **bit**[2]; chat NE, gnap NE, chack; (*esp of a dog*) snack.

noun **1** *see also* **morsel, mouthful**; gnap NE, rive. **2** (*esp of a dog*) snack. **3** (*on a fishing line*) rug.

biting 1 (*of wind*) snell, haarie, nitherin. **2** (*of speech*) *see* **bitter.**

bitter *adjective* **1** (*to taste*) wersh, shilpit, sharrow, soor as roddens. **2** (*of beer*) heavy. **3** (*of weather*) snell, gurlie, thin, thrawn NE, atterie. **4** (*of persons*) snell, soor as roddens; (*of speech*) nebbie, tuithie; (*of the tongue*) ill-scrapit.

noun (*beer*) heavy: '*a pint o heavy*'.

bittern bog-bluiter, bluiter, bull-o-the-bog, mire-drum.

bitumen pick.

bizarre *see also* **strange**; no wicelik(e).

blab *see* **tell tales, telltale.**

black *adjective, see also* **dark**; bleck, mirk, glog *literary*; (*very*) as black as the pot, pot black, black as the Earl o Hell's waistcoat.

verb (*boots etc*) bleck NE.

blacken blecken; (*dirty*) coom, barken; (*esp the face with soot etc*) bleck(en).

blacking (*for boots etc*) bleck(nin): '*broon bleck*'.

blackberry brammle, bramble, ladies' gartens S.

blackbird blackie, merl(e) *literary*; (*that nests on the ground*) grun blackie.

blackcurrant blackberry.

black eye (blue) keeker.

blackguard *see also* **rogue, villain**; blackguaird, bleck, kithan CAITHNESS.

blackhead shilcorn.

black lead wad.

black person bleck.

black pudding bluidie puddin, bleedie puddin NE.

black sheep (of the family) ooterlin.

blacksmith bruntie, brookie NE, burn-the-win(d), gowe *literary*; (*farrier*) ferrier.

blackthorn *see* **sloe**.

bladder bledder, blether.

blade 1 (*of a spade etc*) mou(th). **2** (*of grass*) pile, girse NE.

blame *noun* wyte, dirdum, barm NE.
verb wyte, faut.

blame someone for something blame something on someone, wyte someone for *or* o *or* wi something, gie someone the wyte o something.

blameless saikless.

bear no blame for hae nae sin o.

bland wersh.

blandishments *see* **flattery**.

blanket *noun* hap; (*hard, unbrushed*) Scots blanket; (*with thick nap*) English blanket; (*tartan*) (*bed*) plaid.

one large blanket doubled pair o blankets.

blaspheme *see also* **curse**; spell.

blast *noun* (*explosion*) pluff; (*of wind: see also* **gust**) skelp, howder NE, bleester, blooter NE, brattle NE, bla(u)d, tud SHETLAND, ORKNEY.

blasted (*expressing exasperation*) given: '*We'd tae wait twa given oors*'.

blatant *see* **obvious**.

blaze *noun* bleeze, lowe.
verb bleeze, lowe, lunt.

blazing (*of a fire*) reevin NE, rovin NE.

go to blazes! kiss yer luckie!, gae tae Hexham!, gae tae Freuchie (an fry mice)!, gang tae Buckie (an bottle skate)! NE.

bleach *verb* (*clothes* (*in the open air*)) haizer.

bleak dreich, dour, (*esp of weather*) oorlich N, starrach CAITHNESS.

bleat *verb* blait, blare, blea S, mae, meh.
noun mae.

bleed bluid, blood.

blemish *see also* **stain**: *noun* smit, smad SHETLAND, ORKNEY, N, blain NE, gaw, smitch.
verb mank, smad SHETLAND, ORKNEY, N.

blench *see also* **flinch**; resile.

blend *see also* **mix**; bland, mell.
noun, see **mixture**.

bless bliss, sain.

blessed seilie, weel-lookit-tae NE.

blessing blissin, (*act*) sain.

blight *noun* blicht *literary*.
verb blicht *literary*; (*plants*) scowder.

become infected by blight canker.

blind *adjective* blin; (*completely*) stane blin(d); (*in one eye*) gley(e)d.
verb blin.

blind man's buff jockie blindie, belly-blin(d), glim-glam.

blink *verb* blent; (*of the eyes*) pink, glimmer NE.

blinkers blinners, goggles NE.

bliss seil.

blissful seilfu.

blister *noun, verb* blush SE.

raise a blister blush SE.

blithe *see also* **cheerful, merry**; blide SHETLAND, cadgie.

blizzard stour, nizzer NE, yowdendrift *literary*.

bloated fozie; (*with too much food*) brosie, hoven.

blob (*of moisture: see also* **drop**) blab

NE, bleib NE, glob, drib; (*large, of something messy*) slag.

block *noun* (*of wood*) (hack) stock NE; (*small, of wood or stone*) blunk NE.

block up stap, clag.

blockhead *see also* **idiot**: stot, puddin, stammeral, stookie, nowt, sumph, gype, neep(heid).

blood bluid, blid CENTRAL, bleed N.

bloody bluidie.

bloody nose jeelie nose, jeelie neb.

not a blood relation no a drap's bluid, nae freen(d), no sib.

bloodshed *see* **slaughter**.

bloodshot bluid-shed, blood-run NE.

it makes my blood run cold it gars me grue.

bloom *see also* **blossom**: *noun, verb* blume, bleem N.

blossom *see also* **bloom**: *noun* (*esp on hawthorn*) flourish, fleerish NE.

verb flourish, fleerish NE, blaw NE.

blot *noun* 1 spleiter NE. 2 (*on character*) tash.

verb (*stain with ink*) blotch.

blotting pad blad.

blotting paper blot-sheet.

blot out blotch out.

blotch *noun* tash.

blotchy measelt N, mizzelt N, skaikit NE.

blouse *see* **overall**.

blow[1] *verb* 1 (*of wind etc: see also* **puff**) bla(w), byauve NE COAST, waff; (*very hard*) tear, rive, bla(u)d; (*in gusts*) dad, flan, flaff, hushle; (*with a shrill noise*) skirl; (*gently*) fuff. 2 (*the nose*) snite.

blown about jachelt.

blown up (*of cattle etc, with fodder*) hoven.

blow out (*a candle*) whiff.

blow[2] *noun* (*hit: see also* **knock, slap, thump, punch, prod, beating**): 1 bla(w), chap, straik, cloot, cloor, dunch, belt, ding, dab N, scoor NE, cob, da(u)d, yark SHETLAND, ORKNEY, N, crunt. 2 (*heavy*) loonder, clap, dunt, doose, yerk, dird NE, leather, rees(h)le, pergad-

dus, swinge; (*eg with a stick*) lewder, yether SW, S; (*esp with the hand or foot*) fung; (*esp with a whip*) whang; (*esp on the head*) souse. 3 (*light: with something flat*) flaff; (*with the hand etc*) punce. 4 (*sharp*) jag, knap, knoit, snap SHETLAND, N, knack, leerup N, ramiegeister NE; (*swift*) pap; (*smart*) clyte; (*smart, recoiling*) stot; (*glancing*) skite, glent SW. 5 (*stunning*) stoun(d), fell; (*resounding*) dirl, rummle, whinner SHETLAND, ORKNEY, feuch NE; (*esp on the ear*) ring(er); (*whizzing*) souch, sing, wheech.

aim a blow lat breenge, let fung, let flist N.

with a sharp blow skite.

blubber (*weep*) bubble, bibble NE, snotter, sneeter.

blubbering bubblie, bibblie NE, snotterie.

blubbering person bubblie: '*Stoap greetin, bubblie!*'

bludgeon *noun, verb* rung.

blue *see also* **pale**: bew; (*dark, greyish*) blae.

bluish blae, bluachie NE.

bluebell (*Scottish*) harebell, blawort, blaver, gowk's thimmles NE; (*English*) wood hyacinth, gowk's hose, crawtae(s).

bluebottle bummer, muck flee, mauk(ie) flee.

bluetit blue bonnet, ox ee.

bluff[1] *adjective, see* **blunt** 2.

noun, see **headland**.

bluff[2] *verb, see* **deceive**.

blunder *verb* **blunder about** bummle, stammle; (*headlong*) ramstam, reemis(h) NE.

blundering *see* **awkward**.

blunder on stavel.

blunt *adjective* 1 (*of an edge*) bauch. 2 (*of speech etc*) raucle, tongue-betrusht NE, ruch-spun.

verb (*esp tools*) fluise SW.

bluntly richt oot, fair oot, stra(u)cht oot.

blurt out blooter oot.

blush *noun* (*blushing face*) rid face, beamer, ridder, riddie.

bluster *verb* **1** *see also* **boast**: blouster, gowst, gowster, bloust N. **2** (*of wind*) thud, whidder.

noun blouster; (*boasting*) swash.

blustery gurlie, scoorie, grumlie NE, gowsterie.

boar gaut, chattie NE, brawn SW, S.

board *noun* brod, buird, boord; (*plank*) clift; (*for laying out a corpse*) streekin buird NE, stra(u)chtin brod, deid-deal; (*of a book*) brod; (*of a large book*) lid.

verb buird, boord.

boast *verb* bla(w), craw croose, gange, bum, puff, blaw yer ain horn, gandie NE, sprose, creest SW, S; (*about possessions*) craw on yer ain midden.

noun bla(w), ruise.

boastful *see also* **conceited**: great, massie(lik(e)), vauntie *literary*.

boastful person, boaster *see also* **braggart**: bum, bla(w).

boat *noun, see also* **barge, fishing boat**: bait N; (*small cargo steamboat on W Coast*) †puffer; (*toy, of folded paper*) cock-a-bendie boat NE.

boat-hook bottick SHETLAND, N.

boat-pole sting.

bob boab.

bob up and down hobble, hotch.

bobbin pirn, spule.

bodice jump(ie); (*underbodice*) slip-body.

body (*of a person: see also* **corpse**) buddie, bouk, (*living*) corpus.

bodyguard (*of a Highland chief*) †luchtach.

body-snatcher corp-lifter NE.

full of body (*of food*) stieve.

bog *see also* **marsh**: moss, sowp; (*quaking*) quakin-bog, bobbin-quaw.

boggy *see also* **marshy**: mossie.

boggy ground (*flow*) moss; (*esp with surface water*) flush.

become bogged lair.

bog oak moss aik.

bog(e)y 1 bogle, bockie, boodie NE,

doolie, (wirri)cow. **2** (*in the nose*) black man.

bog(e)yman black man, bowzie-man, murmichan.

boil[1] *verb* bile, plot; (*slowly: see also* **simmer**) sotter; (*steadily*) hotter.

boiled sweet boilin, bilin.

boil up bummle, hotter.

up to the boil throu the boil, aboil.

noise of a boiling liquid hotter.

boil[2] *noun* (*on the skin*) bile, bealin, income, brook, blushin SW, ULSTER; (*which does not come to a head*) blin lump.

core of a boil dottle.

boisterous bowsterous, rummlin, teirin, randie, ramstam; (*unruly*) royet, roit NE, tousie; (*merry*) rantin.

behave boisterously gae yer dinger.

bold *see also* **courageous, impudent**: baul(d); (*and impudent*) forrit(some), gallus, facie; (*rash*) frush, raucle.

bollard (*mooring post*) pall.

bolster *noun* bowster.

bolt *noun* bowt, slot; (*small*) snib; (*wooden, for door*) spar.

verb bowt, slot; (*with small bolt*) snib.

like a bolt from the blue lik(e) a slung-stane NE.

bond *noun* †band.

bondstone ban(d)stane SHETLAND, parpen, throu-ban(d).

bone bane.

rounded part of bone at joint knockle.

(pieces of) bones used as castanets clatter banes.

bonfire bleeze; (*at Halloween, Midsummer etc*) tannel; (*at Halloween*) shannack, sownack.

bonnet *see also* **cap, cloth cap, sun bonnet**: bannet, bunnet; (*traditional Scottish, flat woollen*) Kilmarnock bonnet, Tam o Shanter, scone bonnet; (*with tassel*) toorie bunnet; (*woman's, with large side-flaps*) †mutch.

bonus (*extra pay*) bountith; (*for drink*) drink siller.

book buik, b(y)euk; (*small*) buikie.
  book-boards brods, batters.
  book-learning buik-lair.
  bookshelf (*in a pew*) buik buird.
boom (*loud echoing sound*) knell NE.
  make a booming sound bung.
boor *see also* **lout, yokel**; tike, pilsh NE, cowt.
  boorish *see also* **loutish, rough**; menseless, coorse, rum, hull-run, orra.
boost *verb, see* **further.**
boot *noun, see also* **hobnailed**; buit, beet N.
  bootee (*baby's*) fottie S.
  bootlace whang, steeker, pint.
  bootnail tacket.
booth buith.
booty *see* **plunder.**
booze *see* **drink.**
border *noun* (*of land: see also* **boundary**) mairch; (*of cloth*) ruind; (*of a garment etc*) walt.
  have a common border with mairch wi.
  ride out on a Border raid †ride.
  Border raider †reiver.
bore[1] *verb* (*hole*) thirl; (*with drill*) kirn.
  boring tool boral.
bore[2] *verb* (*weary*) sta(w); (*esp with talk*) deave.
  noun sta(w).
  bored *see also* **fed-up**; scunnert, seecksair(t) ORKNEY, NE, seeck-stawed, langsome.
  become bored weary, sta(w).
  boredom langour.
  boring *see* **tedious, dreary.**
born: be born come hame.
borough burgh.
borrow borrae, get a len (o).
bosom bosie.
boss *noun* maister; (*often sarcastic*) heid bummer, heid pilliedacus; (*male*) himsel(f); (*female*) hersel(f); **bosses** high heid yins.
  verb drum-major.
botch *verb, see also* **bungle, spoil**; bootch, broggle, moger, stick, fa throu

NE, mauchle SW, S, bla(u)d, connach.
  noun, see also **bungle, mess, muddle**; bootch NE, tooter NE, scutter, plaister, moger, connach.
both baith.
  both of them, us, you baith the twa o them, us, ye.
bother *verb, see also* **annoy, fuss**; bather, budder SHETLAND, N, fash, middle; (*someone about something*) be at.
  noun, see also **trouble, difficulty, fuss**; bather, budder SHETLAND, N, fash(erie), sussie, neef NE.
  don't bother dinna fash yersel, dinna fash yer thoum, nivver heed, nivver leet.
  not bother (your head) no jee yer ginger.
bottle (*large, for wine or spirits: see also* **decanter**) gardevine; (*two-quart*) magnum bonum.
  bottle-stand (*in a bar*) gantry.
  open a new bottle, crack a bottle brak a bottle.
bottom *noun* boddom, boddam N: **1** *see* **buttocks. 2** (*lowest part: see also* **foot**) grun(d).
  bottom drawer hope kist, providin.
bough *see also* **branch** 1; †beuch.
bought *past tense, past participle of* **buy** bocht, boucht, coft *literary*.
boulder boolder, knab(lick) NE, whun, muckle yuck.
bounce *verb, see also* **bound**[1]; bunce, stot, stoit; (*jolt*) dird NE.
  noun stot; (*jolt*) hotch, dird NE, sowt SW.
  bouncing *adjective* stottin; (*vigorous*) bensin NE.
  with a bounce stoit.
  without bounce (*of a ball etc*) diffie.
bound[1] *noun* **1** *see also* **limit**; boon. **2** (*leap*) lowp, spang, stend, spend.
  verb, see also **bounce**; spang, stend, stunt; (*suddenly*) spoot; (*of an animal*) stot.
  go beyond all bounds ding doon Tantallon.
bound[2] *past tense of* **bind** ban(d).
  past participle bun(d); (*with ties of affection etc*) thirlt.

bound

bound³ *adjective* (*ready to set out*) boun, bun.

boundary *see also* **border**; mairch; (*esp of burgh land*) lanimer, meiths.
  boundary marker meith, prap.
  boundary stone mairch stane.
  boundary wall mairch dyke, fail dyke, hill dyke.
  ride round boundaries *see* **ride**.
  mark the boundary of mairch.

bounty boontie.
  bountiful *see* **plentiful**.

bouquet flooer, bob.

bourgeois *noun* half-knab(bie).

bout (*contest, eg of some leisure activity*) yokin; (*of something*) match: '*greetin match*'.

bow¹ (*of ribbon etc*) doss N.
  bow-legged *see* **bandy-legged**.
  bow-tie made tie.

bow² (*of a ship*) beuch NE.
  bowsprit bowsplit.

bow³ *verb* (*respectfully*) boo, beck, jouk, loot.
noun (*respectful*) boo, beck, jouk.
bowed *see* **bent**.

bowel *see also* **intestines, internal organs, enteritis**; thairm; **bowels** painches, intimmers *humorous*.

bower †bour.

bowl 1 *see also* **basin**; bowlie; (*esp wooden*) bicker, cap, cog(gie), (*with handles*) luggie; (*drinking*) nap(pie). **2** (*in the game*) bool.
  bowls bools.
  bowl along hurl, trinnle; (*swiftly*) scrieve.
  bowl over (*physically*) whummle, tirl, ca(w) ower.

box¹ *noun, see also* **chest 1**; boax, buist; (*tin, with a lid*) mull(ie) NE; (*small, of wood-strips*) spail-box.

box² (*on the ear*) scoor NE, sclaff.

boy *see also* **lad, youth 2, baby**; lad(die), boay, loon(ie) N, cowlie EDINBURGH; (*male child*) man-bairn, †lad-bairn; (*small*) laddie, loonie N, boy-ackie N, mann(ik)ie, chappie, cockie-bendie; (*adolescent*) hauflin; (*bright but small*) sprug; (*small, mischievous*) knip N; (*mischievous*) *see* **rascal**; (*wild, rough*) ruchie N.

boyfriend lad(die), click, cleek.
  get a boyfriend click, cleek.

brace *verb* **1** (*prop up*) rance. **2** (*the limbs against strain*) stell, spar NE.
noun **braces** (*for trousers*) galluses.
  braces button gallus button.

bracing (*of air*) caller; (*too much*) snell, shairp.

bracken brachan, breckan, fern, rannoch.

bracket *noun* brecket; (*for a roof-gutter*) crampet NE.

brackish sautie.

bradawl brog, stob N.

brad(nail) sprag.

brag *see* **boast, exaggerate**.
  braggart bla(w), blicker, blouster, cracker, flist, blether(um)skite.

braid (*gold or silver*) †passments.

brain(s) ha(i)rns.
  brainless boss, harnless.
  brainy heidie.
  brainstorm wuiddrim *literary*.

brake *see* **thicket**.

bramble *see also* **blackberry**; brammle.

bran pron N, sheelin seeds.

branch *noun, see also* **brushwood**: **1** (*of a tree*) brainch, cowe, rice, grain, †beuch. **2** (*of a river*) grain *now in place-names*.

brand *verb* (*cattle etc*) buist.
noun (*ownership mark: see also* **sheep-mark**) kenmark.
  brand-new brent-new, split-new, spleet-new, splent new, spang-new, fire-new.

brandish wag, swirl, wadge, mint NE, swap SHETLAND.

brash *see also* **bold, impudent**; frush, forrit(some).

brass bress.
  brass neck hard neck.

brat *see also* **rascal**; get.

24

brave *see also* **courageous, bold;** campie, wicht *in poetry.*

brawl *noun, see also* **disturbance, free-for-all;** rammie, tulyie, brulyie, hurry, wap.

verb tulyie.

bray *see* roar.

brazen(-faced) braisant, hard-neckit.

breach *noun* 1 *see* gap. 2 (*in relations*) slip.

breach of trust (*law*) malversation.

bread breid, haben *gipsy;* (*of wheat as opposed to oats etc*) laif(-breid), (*baked in batch loaves*) plain breid; (*baked in separate tins*) pan breid; (*bread kept more than a day*) owerday's breid.

piece of bread (*spread with butter, jam etc*) piece: 'jeelie piece'; 'piece an jeelie'; 'cheese piece'; (*with butter spread with the thumb*) thoum-piece; (*soaked in soup etc*) dooker.

pieces of bread soaked in (hot) milk (milk) saps, breid-berry.

bread roll *see* roll 3.

breadth breid(th), brenth.

in breadth abreed.

break *verb* 1 *see also* **crack, smash, snap;** brak, brek; (*snap*) knack; (*stones for building*) knap. 2 (*of frost*) lowp N.

noun 1 (*in continuity*) slap. 2 (*from work*) speel; (*in school day*) leave, meenit NE. 3 (*in clouds*) (blue) bore NE; (*in coal stratum*) cowp.

breaker jaup, jaw NE.

breakfast brak(e)fast, brakwast, pottitch NE.

at breakneck speed ramstam.

breakwater fleet dyke.

break down (*in the middle of a job*) stick; (*collapse: of a person*) foon(d)er.

breakdown (*in health*) foon(d)er.

break even (*of an enterprise*) wash its face.

break in (*a young animal or new shoes etc*) track NE.

break in two gae in twa NE.

break out (*violently*) brainyell.

break up (*of a meeting etc*) skail; (*of cloud*) rive.

break wind *see also* **belch;** lat aff, rift, pump, rowt.

without a break oot o (the) face.

bream braze.

breast *noun* breist, brisket; **breasts** bubbies.

breast-feed sook.

breast-milk pap-milk.

breast-pocket oxter-pootch, gushet.

breath 1 *see also* **gasp;** braith, win(d), aynd SHETLAND, pew SHETLAND; (*deep*) souch, wa(u)cht. 2 (*of fresh air*) gliff; (*of wind etc*) pew SW.

crush the breath out of *see* suffocate, choke 1.

breathless, out of breath pechin, pech(l)t, burs(t)en, fobbin NE; (*from being overweight*) gowstie NE.

under your breath intae yersel, laich doon.

breathe (*hard: see also* **pant**) pech, fob NE, blast NE, hech; (*on something before polishing*) hauch, haw, hooch; (*heavily: see also* **wheeze**) wheezle, souch, snocher, snotter, groozle, thock S; (*and with difficulty*) fesh.

breathing (*heavy*) souch; (*convulsive*) draucht; (*hard, before polishing*) hauch, haw.

breathe your last souch awa.

breeches breeks.

breed *verb* (*of small animals etc*) cleck.

noun (*often contemptuous*) etion NE.

breeding (*good*) gentrice *literary*, gentry.

breeding season ridin season, ridin time.

breeze tirl NE; (*gentle*) gray, saur; (*sudden*) pirr SHETLAND, NE.

breezy blowsterie.

brew *verb* (*ale etc*) mask; (*of tea*) mask.

brewing browst, brewst; (*of tea*) maskin.

brewer brewster, browser NE.

briar breer.

briar pipe gun.

bribe *verb* buy, sweeten, creesh (someone's) luif, line (someone's) luif.
bridesmaid best maid.
bridge brig.
  bridge parapet ravel.
  bridge a gap kep a catch.
bridle *noun* branks.
brief *noun* (*law: to one's counsel*) instructions.
briefly short an lang.
brigand brigan(n)er, †brigane; (*Highland*) †cateran.
bright 1 bricht, licht, skire, skyrie, skyrin ORKNEY, NE, glancie NE; (*of colours*) vieve, (*showily*) roarie; (*of weather*) leesome NE; (*esp deceptively*) gowanie, gowan-gabbit. **2** (*of personality: see also* **lively**) gleg, trig, mirkie NE, kneef, lifie.
  brighten lichten.
brill bonnet fleuk.
brilliant *see* **bright**.
  brilliance glister.
brim *noun* (*of a hat*) flype SHETLAND.
  brimful as fou as a partan, lip-fou.
  brimming over jaupin fou, sweelin ower, lipperin, lip-fou.
brindled riach SHETLAND, ORKNEY, N, brandit.
brine brime NE, brack, saut bree SHETLAND, NE.
bring *see* **brought**.
  bring about rise.
  bring in inbring.
  bring up (*rear*) fess up NE; (*badly or cruelly*) misguide.
brink (*of a stream etc*) lip.
brisk (*in personality: see also* **alert**) gleg, sproosh, trig, lifie, keen, birkie.
  briskly gleglie.
bristle *noun* birse, birsle; **bristles** birse. *verb* birsle; (*of hair etc*) stert.
  bristly jaggie, jabbie, stobbie NE.
brittle brickle, bruckle, (*of wood etc*) frush, freuch NE; (*of ice etc*) crumpie, crumshie NE; (*of pastry etc*) free, frush.
broach (*a subject*) mint.
broad braid.

broadsword (*types of*) †Andrew Ferrary; (*Highlander's basket-hilted*) claymore.
broil *verb* brile, birsle, brander.
broken bracken, brucken.
  broken-down (*in health*) awa wi't, fair duin, crazed; (*in spirit*) *see* **depressed**.
  broken in (*of a horse*) dra(u)chtit NE.
broker cowper, troker.
brome-grass guse-grass.
bronchitis broonchadis, broonkaities, the wheezles.
brood *noun* brod, breed NE, (*of animals, contemptuously of people*) cleckin; (*of chickens etc*) lachter, clatchin. *verb* (*of birds*) clock.
  broody (*of a fowl*) clockin, sittin.
  broody hen clocker, clockin hen.
  smallest and weakest of a brood *see also* **weakling, litter**; weirdie, shargar.
brook *noun* burn, rin, stripe SHETLAND, ORKNEY, N, keechan N, stran(d) SW.
  brooklime watter purpie, wallink.
broom 1 (*plant*) brume, breem NE. **2** (*brush*) besom; (*of heather twigs*) heathercowe; (*of broom*) breem cowe NE.
broth *see also* **soup**; NB 'broth' in Sc means a thick vegetable soup, usually made with mutton or other meat; (*esp made with kail or cabbage*) kail; (*on second day of use*) yaval broth NE; (*without meat*) watter kail, barfit broth NE, (*thin, without meat*) muslin kail; (*with a small amount of barley*) scadlips.
brothel bordel hoose NE, †bordel.
brother brither, billie.
  brother-in-law guid-brither.
brought *past tense of* **bring** brocht, brang. *past participle* brocht, broucht, brung.
  badly brought up ill-guidit.
brow *see also* **eyebrow, forehead**; (*of a hill*) broo, brae.
  browbeat threap at SW.
brown broon; (*pale, yellowish*) faughie N.

brownie (*benevolent spirit*) billy blin, whuppitie-stourie; **brownies** the guid fowk.

brown paper gray paper SHETLAND, ORKNEY, N.

browse *see* **graze**^{2}.

bruise *verb* brizz, birse, broozle, knuse, massacker, dinge, pran NE, cloor.
noun brizz, birse; (*by nipping etc*) chack, check.

brush *noun, see also* **broom**; s(w)ooper; (*of feathers, straws etc*) wisker NE.
verb, see **sweep**.
brushwood scrogs, rice, hag NE.
brush against skiff.
brush off skiff, scuff.

brusque *see also* **curt**; nebbie, snotterie, nippie.

brute bruit, breet NE.

bubble *noun* bibble NE, blob, bell.
verb bibble NE, bummel, fro; (*esp in cooking*) hotter, prinkle, plapper NE, sotter.
bubbling *noun* (*of boiling liquid*) hotter.
bubble over ream.
come bubbling out sotter.
bubble up papple, buller NE.

buck (*of a horse*) yunk.

bucket *see also* **tub, pail** (*which, in Sc, is commoner than bucket*); bowie, cog; (*narrow-mouthed, for carrying water*) stowp, watter-kit.
bucket handle bool.

budge jee, mudge, fitch SHETLAND, ORKNEY, CAITHNESS.
refuse to budge (for) stan(d) the kicker (o) NE, no jee: '*he winna jee*'.

buffet *verb* buff; (*of a storm*) *see* **beat**; (*of wind*) daidle.
buffeted (*by wind*) jachelt.

buffoon *see* **fool, idiot**.

bug *noun* bog.

bugbear *see* **bog(e)yman**.

bugle (*plant*) deidman('s bellows).

build *verb* big, beeld; (*roughly and hurriedly*) rickle; (*a drystone wall*) rickle; (*carelessly*) sclatch.
noun (*of a person*) set.

builder (*of drystone walls*) *see* **drystone wall**.

building biggin; (*carelessly built or ruinous*) raible; (*imposing*) †wark; (*large, divided into flats*) tenement.
building site steadin.
projecting wing or addition to a building jamb NE.

built *past tense* biggit, bug.
past participle biggit.
built on biggit.
built up upbiggit NE.
badly built ricklie.
loosely built (*of a person*) ill-shakken-thegither NE.

bulge *noun, see also* **bump** 2; bumfle.
verb (*of a wall, and collapse*) shuit.
bulging baggit, bumflie.

bulk *noun, verb* bouk.
bulky boukit, bouksome NE, scowthie NE, great.
the bulk of the feck o, maist o.

bull bul, bill, jock SW.
bullock *see also* **ox**; nowt NE; (*young*) stot, stirk; (*castrated when fully-grown*) bull-seg(g) NE.
bull's eye (*sweet*) black man.
bullfinch bullie FIFE.

bully *noun* bangster.
verb ool, hatter.
bullying behaviour bangstrie.

bum *see* **buttocks**.

bumble *see* **babble, mumble**.

bumblebee bumbee, bummer, bummie, droner; (*which deposits light dust*) dusty miller; (*yellow, stingless*) cannie nannie.

bump *verb, see also* **thud, thump**; dunt, dird NE; **bump against** rap on, junner SW; **bump about** hotter, dad; **bump up and down** howd.
noun 1 *see also* **thud, thump, blow**^{2}; dunt, dunch, dird NE, deesht NE. 2 (*swelling*) knap, knoit.
bumper (*of liquor*) cauker.
bumpy knappie.
with a bump stoit, dird NE.

bumpkin *see* **yokel**.

bumptious

bumptious gumptious, pitten-on, massie, muckle, pauchtie.
small bumptious man cockie-bendie, yaff SE.
bun *see also* **cake;** NB in Sc now usually less sweet than in Eng; (*plain, round, glazed, of yeast dough*) cookie: '*cream cookie*'; (*glazed, with currants, orange peel, sugar*) Lon(d)on bun; (*wedge-shaped, glazed*) heater NE; (*sweet, sugar-topped, sponge-like*) Pa(i)ris bun; (*treacle sponge in pastry case*) puggie bun; (*large, round, flattish*) Porter biscuit; (*currant*) loafie NE; (*baked with sweets or raisins*) sweetie scone.
bunch *noun, see also* **bundle;** toosht(ie) NE; (*of things tied with string*) strap; (*of flowers*) flooer: '*here a wee flooer tae ye*'.
verb **bunch together** rally.
tie in a bunch strap.
bundle *noun, see also* **bunch;** bunnle, banyel, knitch, pauchle, turse; (*small*) tulshoch NE; (*heavy*) fang N; (*untidy*) toosht(ie) NE, fussoch NE, farkage ORKNEY; (*small, untidy*) dilgit NE, dulshet NE; (*large, untidy*) dunshach NE; (*of hay, straw*) wap, bottle; (*of straw*) stook, windlin SHETLAND, ORKNEY, N; (*of straw etc for thatching*) stapple, wase; (*small, of hay, corn*) tait.
verb bunnle, bottle, knitch; (*truss*) turse.
bung (*of a cask: see also* **stopper, spigot**) spile, dook NE.
bungle *see also* **botch, muddle:** *verb* blooter, broggle, durk, bootch, scutter, moger, pauchle, bucker NE, misguggle.
noun bummle, sclatch, scutter, tooter NE, bootch, bucker NE, moger NE.
bungler fouter, tooter NE, scutter, bummler, puddle, fauchle, plowster.
bungling *adjective, see also* **clumsy, careless, unskilful;** fouterie, fouterin.
noun fummle, bucker NE, mafflin.
bunion werrock, knoit.
bunting *see* **reed-bunting, snow-bunting.**
buoy bowe NE.

buoyant *see also* **cheerful;** sonsie, gawsie, cantie, croose.
burden *see also* **load:** *noun* (back) birn, lift, cairry, fraucht; (*heavy*) fang; (*handicap*) haud-doon; (*person*) cess.
verb (*with work etc*) tra(u)chle.
be heavily burdened (*eg needlessly*) hulster.
burdensome *see* **heavy.**
burial *see also* **bury, funeral;** burial, beerial NE, hame-gaun.
burial ground (*latterly private*) howf.
burial plot lair, grun(d).
burly buirdlie, muckle-boukit, thick, sture SHETLAND.
burn *see also* **singe, scorch, scald, smoulder:** *verb* birn, brenn, scowder, sneyster; (*blaze*) lunt; (*with bright flame*) lowe.
noun birn, brenn, scam, scowder.
smell of burning yowder.
burnt brunt; (*in cooking*) setten-on.
burr (*in speech*) rattle, whurr.
speak with a burr rattle, whurr.
burrow *noun* (*animal's*) bourie, clap.
verb burrae, howk.
burst *verb* brust, birst, rive; (*out of a container*) lowp; (*of a pudding*) spue; (*of the heart*) leap oot o the huil; (*a garment at a seam*) skail.
past tense burstit.
past participle burs(t)en.
noun, see also **cloudburst;** brust, birst.
burst open leap.
burst out (*with a spluttering noise*) spleuter NE.
filled to bursting burs(t)en, fair stappit.
bury *see also* **burial;** beerie, eard, yird, grave, pit awa, lay doon NE, lair.
buried yirdit.
bus: bus station *or* **terminus** (bus-)stance.
bush *noun* buss; (*stunted*) scrog.
bushy bussie, bouzie.
business (*piece of business: see also* **transaction**) ploy, handlin; (*small*) troke; (*transacted away from home*)

oot-aboot NE; (*line of business*) wey; (*work, occupation*) thrift.

businesslike *see* **efficient.**

bustle *noun, see also* **fuss, bother, commotion, confusion, fluster;** fizz, foorich, feerich NE, dirl, behss NE, farrach, thrangitie, kauch SW, steer(ie).

verb, see also **fuss;** bizz, fizz, stichle, bummle, feerich NE.

bustling (*of a person*) breengin, steerie; (*of a place*) thrang.

bustle about stot aboot.

a state of perpetual bustle ratton's nest.

in a state of bustle lik(e) a cried fair.

busy *adjective* thrang; (*occupied*) fest NE; (*diligent*) eydent.

busybody (*talkative*) clishmaclaver NE.

busy time thrang.

busy with in hand wi, in the heid o.

but bit.

butcher *noun* flesher.

verb, see also **slaughter;** butch.

butchering (trade) fleshin.

butcher's meat butcher meat, beef, flesh.

butt[1] (*of an animal*) *verb* buck, dunch, dush ORKNEY, NE, putt, box N.

noun dunch, doose, putt.

butt[2] (*target*) bob.

butt[3] *see* **cask.**

butter *noun* freet CAITHNESS; (*crumbly from being churned too hot*) short butter.

verb (*a slice of bread etc*) spread (a piece).

butter biscuit butterie.

butterbur tushilago, wild rhubarb, puddock pipes.

buttercup yella gowan, sit-fast, sit-sicker; (*meadow or creeping*) craw-tae(s); (*creeping*) hen-taes.

butterfly butterie NE.

buttermilk soor-dook, soor milk, bledoch, whig, kirn (milk), pell S: '*soor as pell*'.

butter-pats han(d)s, Scotch han(d)s, (butter) clappers, butter-brods.

butter up *see* **flatter.**

pat of butter with decorative motif prent.

free butter from impurities with a knife hair the butter.

buttocks *see also* **bottom;** dowp, hurdies, hint-en(d), hinderen(d), hinders, nether en(d), dock, droddum NE, fud; (*often to a child*) behoochie, bahookie.

button *noun* (*esp trouser*) gornal CAITHNESS; (*metal used in game of 'buttony'*) bossie NE.

buxom sonsie, pretty NE, bowsome, fodgel NE.

buy *see also* **bought;** coff; (*trade, esp horses*) cowp.

buyer (*customer*) merchant NE.

buzz *see also* **whizz:** *verb* bizz NE, bum, shoom NE.

noun bum, dirr, shoom NE, birr.

buzzard gled N, puttock S.

by be; (*of paternity*) tae; (*before*) gin: '*gin this time*'; come: '*come Sunday*'.

bygone bygane.

byway bygate.

by and by *see* **soon.**

by and large near aboot(s).

by the time . . . comes come . . .: '*come Sunday*'.

C

cab (*light, two-wheeled*) †noddy.

cabbage cabbitch, kail, cabbage kail NE, bow-kail; (*with developed head*) bow-stock NE.

   cabbage leaf kail blade.

   cabbage stalk castock, cabbage stock, runt.

   cabbage and potatoes mixed kail kenny, cabbelow.

cabin caibin.

cabinet *see* cupboard.

   cabinet-maker caibe, (square-) wricht.

cable *see* rope.

cache *noun* plank, posie NE.

   verb plank, pose N.

cackle caikle, keckle; (*with laughter*) keckle, guff.

cadaver *see* corpse.

cadet †caddie.

cadge *see* beg.

cage (*in a mine*) towe.

cajole *see also* flatter, coax; fleetch, smool, treesh wi.

   cajolery whillywha NE.

cake *noun, see also* wedding cake, bun; kyaak NE; (*sponge, with paper band*) sair heidie; (*small iced sponge*) French cake; (*fancy, originally costing a penny*) penny thing; (*type of round cake*) tod(die) S; (*rich fruit, with almonds on top*) Dundee cake; (*very rich fruit, in pastry case*) black bun, bun, Scotch bun, curran(t) bun; (*types baked on Michaelmas Eve in the Hebrides*) St Michael's cake, struan.

   cakes snysters, snashters *often contemptuous*; (*fancy*) gulshichs NE, sweetbreid SHETLAND, ORKNEY.

   verb (*of soil etc*) lapper NE.

caked clottert.

calamity *see* reverse, misfortune.

calceolaria mappie('s)-mou(s).

calculate coont.

   calculated calculat, coontit (up).

   calculation wirkin oot; (*rough*) *see* estimate.

calf 1 (*animal*) cauf, ca NE; *plural* caur; (*reared or killed for food*) vale ORKNEY; (*aborted or newly-born*) slink. 2 (*of leg*) cauf, bran.

   not in calf (*of a cow*) farra.

call *verb* 1 ca(w), cry; (*of birds*) clatter; (*of birds, animals: loudly*) rair, roup, yammer; (*shrilly*) wheep. 2 (*give a name to*) cry CENTRAL; be called get: '*He aye gets Jockie fae her*'. 3 (*pay a short visit*) cry in.

   noun 1 ca(w), cry. 2 (*short visit*) cry, roar. 3 (*to animals*) (1) (*to horse etc, to move*) how, tchick, wha-hup; (*to approach*) cop cop; (*to turn right*) hup, haud aff ye, weesh; (*to turn left*) hi here, hey up, come ather NE, vane, yain, heck, wynd; (*to stop*) stan(d), haud up, wo-back. (2) (*to a cow*) proochie, pree-leddy, troo; (*to a calf or a lamb, to food*) sook (sook), sick sick NE. (3) (*to a pig*) chat NE, gussie. (4) (*to a dog: to attack*) hish, hisk. (5) (*to a cat*) piss, cheet(ie-pussy). (6) (*to chickens, to food*) tick(ie), tuck, teek teek teek NE. (7) (*to ducks*) wheetie. (8) (*to a rabbit*) mappie, map map map. (9) (*to drive or frighten off animals*) hish, hisk, hoo NE; (*birds*) hush.

   call in (*make a short visit*) cry in (by), rin in(tae), roar.

   call on (*a person for help*) cry on.

   call to mind mind.

   call (someone) names misca(w), cry

(someone) names, no leave (someone) in the likeness o a dug, ca(w) (someone) oot o his name.

callipers (*one leg with short bend, the other with point*) jennies.

callous 1 (*of people: see also* **indifferent**) upsittin, dowf. **2** (*of skin*) waukit.

callus hauch SE.

calm *adjective* **1** (*of weather: see also* **mild**) lown, quate; (*of a place*) lithe; (*of the sea etc*) sma. **2** (*of a person*) at yersel. *noun* lown; (*at sea*) sma.
verb **1** (*of the wind etc*) *see* **die down. 2** (*a person*) soother.

calm yourself sattle.

calmly lown, quatelik(e).

calm down come tae.

keep calm keep a calm souch, keep the heid.

calumny *see* **slander.**

calve ca SW: '*new ca'd*'.

cambric camrick.

came *past tense of* **come** cam, come.

camisole slip-body.

camomile camovine NE.

camp-follower †ligger-lady.

campion: bladder campion coo-cracker.

can[1] *see* **able, could, cannot.**

can[2] (*for liquids*) tinnie.

canal canaul W, nollie W.

cancel *law, see* **annul.**

candid(ly) *see also* **frank;** fair oot, furth the gate NE, stra(u)cht oot, strecht oot.

candidate: list of candidates leet: '*short leet*'; '*long leet*'.

put on a list of candidates leet.

candle *see also* **wick;** cannle, caunle; (*fir wood used as substitute*) candle fir NE, fir candle NE.

candle-end cannle-dowp.

Candlemas Canlemas.

candlestick (*tall*) carle SW.

candy gundie; (*in blocks or sticks*) candy rock.

cane (*for punishing*) spaingie (wan) NE.

caning *see also* **beating;** hazel oil.

canister mull(ie) NE.

cannonball bool.

cannot canna, cannae.

cant[1] (*insincere talk*) phrase NE.

cant[2] (*slope*) sklent.

cantankerous *see also* **ill-natured, bad-tempered;** pernicketie, contermacious NE, neukit NE, canker(i)t.

canter *see* **gallop, trot.**

canvas cannas NE; (*wax-coated for floor and table covering*) waxcloth.

canvass (*votes by flattery*) peuther.

cap *noun, see also* **cloth cap, bonnet, nightcap;** kep, caip; (*close-fitting woollen*) cool; (*woman's*) curch; (*old woman's*) †mutch; (*round woollen, worn by curlers*) rinker; (*boat-shaped, pointed front and back*) Glengarry, cockit bonnet.

capable cawpable, feckfu, purpose-lik(e), lik(e)ly; (*and energetic*) fell.

capable of up wi.

capacity 1 (*for work*) throu-pit. **2** (*esp for drink*) bind.

capacious *see also* **roomy;** sonsie NE.

full capacity fou.

have capacity for thole.

cape *see* **cloak.**

caper *verb* flisk, fling, link NE, daff. *noun* flisk, pant, kick; **capers** jeegs NE.

capital letters muckle letters, dooble letters.

caprice *see* **whim.**

capricious flauntie, flichtie, aff an on aboot, kittle, licht-heidit, maggotie.

capsize cowp, whummle.

captain *see also* **skipper;** (*of a curling rink*) skip.

capture *verb, see also* **catch;** fang; (*lands, goods*) grip; (*a person*) lay violent hands on.
noun, see also **plunder;** tak.

car caur, machine.

carafe cruet NE.

caraway carvie.

carcass carcage, (*of a slaughtered animal*) bouk; (*of a fowl*) closhach NE.

scraps from a carcass emmledeugs.

card

card[1] *noun* caird, (*esp playing*) cairt;
cards cairds, cairts, deil's picter buiks NE.
card-playing cairtin NE.
pack of cards pair o cairts, stock.
trick at cards *noun* lift.
card[2] *verb* (*wool etc*) caird; (*mechanically*) scribble.
noun caird N.
care *noun* 1 *see also* **anxiety, worry**;
thocht, kauch SW. **2** (*attention*) tent.
verb **1** (*trouble oneself*) fash. **2** (*pay attention*) tent.
badly cared for ill-towdent NE.
carefree lichtsome.
careful carefu, carefae, cannie, eydent,
tentie NE; (*scrupulously*) perjink; **careful!** huilie!
carefully cannie (lik(e)), graithlie.
go carefully ca(w) cannie.
careless *see also* **reckless, heedless,
untidy**; hashie, tentless, haiveless N,
owerlie NE, owerheid SHETLAND,
ORKNEY, hither an yon(t).
carelessly owerlie.
work carelessly slowth, slim; (*and
hastily*) skiff by SHETLAND, N.
work done carelessly hash.
caretaker (*esp of a school*) janitor, jannie *informal*.
careworn *see* **anxious, exhausted**.
care for *see also* **look after, pamper**;
keep, notice SHETLAND, ORKNEY, NE,
see till; (*esp children, animals*) guide.
not care no sussie SHETLAND.
not care a fig no care a docken, no
care a tinker's curse, nae care a rodden
NE, no care a buckie.
take care of *see also* **care for**; tak tent
o, leuk ower, keep, tak aboot SHETLAND, ORKNEY, NE.
career *verb, see* **headlong**.
at the height of your career in yer
potestator SHETLAND, NE.
caress *verb* daut, smoorich, slaik.
cargo cargae SE.
carnage *see* **slaughter**.
carouse *verb* gilravage, splore, bend the
bicker.

carp *verb* threap, yatter, yirp, rane.
carpenter *see also* **joiner, cabinet-maker**; wricht, †squareman.
carpet *see also* **rug**; cairpet.
carriage *see also* **cab**; cairriage, charrit.
carrion ket SE.
carrion crow huidie (craw), huidit
craw, corbie.
carry *verb* cairry; (*goods*) convoy; (*loads,
parcels*) cadge; (*grain etc from the field*)
lead; (*something very heavy*) hump(h),
haigle S; (*under the arm*) oxter.
carrying cairryin; (*of a child on the
shoulders*) shooderie: '*gie me a
shooderie*'.
carry on (*continue*) wag awa, haud on,
ca(w) the girr; (*with difficulty*) chaave
NE, haggle S.
carry-on oncairry, set.
cart *noun* cairt; (*tipping, also closed for
carting manure etc*) cowp-cairt; (*long,
two-wheeled, for grain*) lang cairt; (*flat,
without sides*) float; (*small, low, used in
mining*) hill-cairt; (*refuse collector's*)
scaffie('s)-cairt; (*child's home-made*)
cairtie, hurlie (cairt), piler, guider
E CENTRAL, bogie W.
verb cairt, lead, whurl, draw; (*in small
loads*) clood NE.
carter cairter, whiplicker, whipman.
carthorse aiver.
cart-load cairt-draucht, cairtle NE.
cart road (*on a croft*) ca CAITHNESS.
cart-shaft tram, stang.
horse and cart (*in harness*) yoke.
**detachable board for the side of a
cart** shelvin, wing.
**framework to allow greater load on
a cart** heck NE, taps.
front part of a cart breist N.
cartilage girsle.
carve *see also* **whittle, scrape**; kerve S.
cascade *verb, see also* **pour, splash**;
plash.
noun, see also **waterfall**; spoot, jaw,
plowt.
case: in any case *see* **anyhow**.
in that case syne.

cash *noun, see also* **money**; clink, penny, brindle NE; (*in silver*) white siller.
hard cash dry siller.
ready cash lyin money, lyin siller.
cask *see also* **barrel, keg**; bowie; (*large*) hogget; (*set on end*) stan(d).
cast *verb* kest, kist, kiest NE, thraw, skail; (*fishing lines or nets*) shot NE; (*fishing line*) wap.
past tense kist, kiest NE.
past participle casten, cassen, cuisten.
noun **1** (*in the eye*) *see* **squint-eyed**. **2** (*of features*) swap.
cast iron yetlin SHETLAND.
cast on (*knitting*) warp on.
casting on (*knitting: of first row of stitches*) oncast.
castanets crackers; (*of pieces of bone*) clatter banes.
castrate (*livestock*) lib, sort SHETLAND, NE.
castrating knife libbin knife.
casual happenin; (*of a job*) orra.
casually owerlie.
cat cheet(ie-pussy); (*affectionate name*) (pussy-)baudrons; (*esp castrated*) gib(bie), gib-cat.
catgut thairm.
call to a cat *see* **call** *noun* 3 (5).
let the cat out of the bag lat the cat oot o the poke.
catapult *noun* guttie, cattie; (*forked stick for making*) shangie.
cataract 1 *see* **waterfall, cascade**. **2** (*on the eye*) pearl.
catarrh defluction.
speak through catarrh slorach.
catastrophe *see* **disaster**.
catch *verb, see also* **caught: 1** *see also* **capture, seize**; nick, nip, grip; (*as with a hook*) cleek; (*as by a loop*) hank; (*falling or thrown object*) kep; (*a person, in order to punish*) get yer hands on. **2** (*fish: by the gills*) ginnle w, (*by groping under banks of streams*) guddle, gump SE. **3** *see also* **tangle**[1]; (*eg fingers in a door*) check, chack.
noun **1** (*act of catching*) kep. **2** (*of fish*)

drave, tak. **3** (*eg marriage partner*) rug ORKNEY. **4** (*of a window etc: see also* **latch**) snib, sneck. **5** (*drawback*) thraw *or* whaup i the raip.
catch up on 1 (*overtake*) mak up on, tak in NE. **2** (*a piece of work*) owertak.
good catch (*of fish*) goshens.
object which is easy to catch, person who is good at catching kepper.
catechism catechis, carritch(es).
catechize catecheese, speir questions.
category *see* **kind**[1].
cater (*provide food*) mait.
caterpillar caterpeelar, kailworm; (*hairy*) hairy oobit, hairy worm, grannie; (*large hairy*) hairy grannie; (*of the cabbage butterfly*) green kailworm.
caterwaul *verb* waw ORKNEY, NE, loll S.
caterwauling caterwailin NE.
Catholic *noun* (*contemptuous*) left-fitter CENTRAL, pape CENTRAL, Dan(nie boy) CENTRAL, Tim CENTRAL, green grape *slang*.
be a Catholic kick wi the left fit.
cattle *see also* **livestock**; kye, baists, beasts, beas; (*kept for fattening over winter*) winterers; (*ill because of fairy action*) †elfshot cattle.
cattle-dung sha(i)rn.
cattle-food (*of turnips and straw*) dry keep N.
cattleman herd, (cow) bailie, byreman.
cattle-raid †spreach.
cattle-raider †reiver.
cattle-raiding †reivin, †liftin.
cattle-shed byre.
cattle-stall boose, sta(w).
cattle-track loanin.
lease of cattle on land bowin.
caught *past tense, past participle of* catch caucht, catchit, cotch, claucht.
become caught in a net (*of fish*) strik(e).
caul (*on a newborn baby*) seelie hoo, hallie hoo.
cauldron caudron, muckle pot.

cauliflower cauliflooer.

cause *noun, see* **reason.**

verb (*someone to do something*) gar.

caustic *noun* cowstick.

adjective (*of speech*) *see* **impudent.**

cauterize sneyster.

caution *noun, see* **attention.**

cautious cowshus, cannie, sicker, tentie NE.

cautiously cannie, cannilie, sickerlie NE.

proceed cautiously ca(w) cannie.

cave cove, clift; (*sea-cave*) gloup SHETLAND, ORKNEY, CAITHNESS; (*into which tide flows*) hellyer SHETLAND.

cavern *see* **cave.**

cavil *see* **wrangle.**

cavity *see also* **hollow;** howe.

cavort *see* **prance.**

caw *verb, see also* **call;** caa NE, croup, craw NE.

cease *see also* **stop;** lat (a-)be, stint NE, lin SHETLAND, ORKNEY.

cede *see* **give up.**

ceiling ruif; (*sloping in an attic*) coom, camceil CENTRAL.

with a sloping ceiling coomceiled, camsiled CENTRAL.

celebrate (*something new*) han(d)sel; (*with a drink*) slocken; (*a special event*) pit a hack i the cruik *or* post.

be celebrated (*of a special occasion*) haud.

celebrated *see* **famous.**

celebration (*of a special occasion*) foy.

cellar laich room, laich hoose; (*in a shop*) laich shop.

cement *noun, see* **mortar.**

verb (*a bargain etc*) souder NE, sowther NE.

cemetery *see also* **churchyard;** ceemetery; (*esp private*) howf.

censorious *see also* **critical;** sair.

censure *see* **scold(ing).**

centipede Meg(gie) moniefeet, Jenniehunner-legs, Jennie-hunner-feet, Jennie-monie-feet, jeck wi the monie feet.

centre mids.

cerebral haemorrhage shock.

ceremony: stand on ceremony mak ceremony.

certain 1 *see also* **sure;** certaint, sicker. **2 a certain** . . . ae . . ., yae . . . W, S.

certainly *see also* **assuredly, indeed;** certie, atweel, fy ay NE, fairly (at) NE.

certainly not hoot na, fy na NE, nivver at NE, na-say: '*Are ye gaun tae the picters?*' '*Na-say!*'

make certain mak siccar.

certificate *noun* (*legal*) brief; (*of church membership*) lines.

marriage certificate mairriage lines.

certify certifee.

cessation *see* **stop.**

cesspool *see* **sewer.**

chafe *verb* chaff, freet.

chafed chattit NE.

chaff *noun* **1** (*of corn etc*) caff, sheelocks NE, sheelins. **2** (*banter*) jamph, heeze NE. *verb* tak on, chairge SW, S.

chaffinch chaffie, briskie, brichtie SW, shilfa, shilfie, chye NE, spink S.

chagrin *noun* anger, teen. *verb* chaw.

chain *noun* cheen, chine NE, rackle; (*attaching draught-horse to plough*) soam; (*tying animal to stall: esp round neck*) sell NE, (*linking the post to the 'sell'*) thrammel NE.

verb cheen, chine NE.

chair *noun* cheer, chyre.

verb (*a Presbyterian church court*) moderate.

chairperson *see also* **president;** preses; (*esp of a committee etc*) convener; (*of the general assembly: see* **church court**) moderator.

draw in your chair (*to a table etc*) sit in.

chalk *noun* cauk, kalk.

chalk up, mark with chalk cauk, kalk, caak (up) NE.

challenge *verb* (*to fight*) scart someone's buttons.

noun brag; (*to a feat of daring*) hen, henner EDINBURGH, coosie ANGUS.

blow as a challenge to fight cootch-er, coorgie, cooardie lick; (*by a school-boy*) fugie.

chamber chaumer.

chamberpot chantie, Michael, mick-ey, pish-pot, charlie, dirler.

champ *verb, see* **munch.**

champion *noun* kemp *literary.*

chance *noun* **1** (*opportunity*) kep w, s, kyle, cast; (*to improve*) scowth, dunt SHETLAND. **2** (*probability*) lik(e)ly. *adjective* antrin.

chancy mischancie.

chancel queir.

chandelier (*gas*) gasolierie.

change *verb* cheenge, chynge; (*clothes, job etc*) shift. *noun* cheenge, chynge; (*of abode or employment, or of clothing*) shift.

changeable 1 (*of a person: see also* **capricious, moody**) aff an on. **2** (*of weather: see also* **unsettled**) flichtersome NE, flichterie, tooterie NE.

changeling taen-awa.

change your clothes change yersel, shift.

change your mind tak the rue.

change places (with) shift (wi).

change your shoes change yer feet, shift yer feet.

channel *noun* (*water: see also* **drain**) trink; (*small*) rin; (*drainage*) gaw, dreep; (*in a byre*) gruip, greep NE; (*to a mill*) lade; (*narrow, between rocks in sea*) trink, gullet SW; (*esp rough*) troch.

chant chaunt.

chaos *see also* **muddle;** reel-rall, soss, sotter, heeliegoleerie, ruther NE.

chaotic *see also* **disordered;** throuither, throwder NE, tapsalteerie, mixter-maxter, in a richt soss NE.

in a chaotic state in a pauchle.

chap[1] *noun* (*in the skin*) hack, gaig, pick ORKNEY, NE. *verb* (*of the skin*) hack, gaig.

chap[2] *see also* **fellow;** stock NE, knap NE, knipe NE.

chapel chaipel.

character *see also* **disposition;** (*reputation*) word; (*strength of character*) fushion NE, smeddum.

characteristic *noun* (*personal*) par-ticularity, set.

of respectable character famous.

charge *verb* **1** *see also* **load;** chairge, cherge; (*someone with something*) even. **2** (*recklessly*) breenge, ramp. *noun* (*mining: explosion*) plug; (*fuse*) strum.

give up a criminal charge desert the diet.

charity chairity, cherity, chirity NE.

charity begins at home keep yer ain fish guts for yer ain sea maws NE.

charlatan swick.

charlock skelloch(s) NE, shelloch(s) NE, wild kail SW.

charm *noun* chairm, cherm; (*magic*) cantrip. *verb, see also* **bewitch;** chairm, cherm.

charmed taen up (wi), browdent (on).

chart ca(i)rd.

charwoman: work as a char-woman gang oot amang fowk.

chase *see* **tig.**

chasing game leave-o, jinks, jinkie, hunt the staigie NE.

chasm cleugh.

chaste (*of a woman*) †leal *literary.*

breach of chastity mistak; (*resulting in birth of a child*) misfortune.

chastise *see also* **beat, scold;** chastify, gie someone his coffee, pike, norter NE.

chat *see also* **chatter:** *verb* crack, blether, tove, news. *noun, see also* **chitchat;** crack, blether, gab, tove, news.

chatty bletherin, gabbie, newsie.

chatter *verb* **1** shatter, yitter, yabble; (*of teeth*) chitter, chack NE, yatter. **2** *see also* **chat;** blether, clack, gab, gibble-gabble, tittle, clishmaclaver NE, claik; (*endlessly*) paiter, yatter, crack lik(e) a pen-gun, gang on lik(e) a tuim mill; (*irritatingly*) natter, nyatter NE; (*esp *of birds, animals*) yammer.

noun, see also **chitchat**; blethers, clack, clatters, gab, yatter, gibble-gabble, clavers; (*aimless*) natter, nyatter NE, jibber.

chatterbox *see also* **gossip**; blether(er), clatterer, yap, yatter, haiver, newser, natter, nyatter NE, jaunner SW, S, yabber, yaff, shammy-leather *slang*.

cheap chape.

cheapen *see* **beat down**.

cheat *verb, see also* **deceive**, **swindle**; chate NE, chet, begowk, begunk, blink, swick, sconce, nick, jouk, quirk NE, pauchle; (*esp by wheedling*) whillie.

noun chate NE, chet: **1** (*act of cheating*) swick. **2** (*person who cheats*) swick, intak, rap FIFE.

cheated (*in a bargain*) burnt.

cheating chaterie, swickerie NE.

check[1] *verb* chack; (*oppose*) conter; (*turn back*) kep again.

noun, see also **reverse**; chack.

check[2] (*pattern*) chack.

checked *see also* **chequered**; checkit, chackit.

black-and-white check shepherd's tartan.

cheek 1 (*side of face*) haffet *literary*; **cheeks** chowks, ginnles, chafts. **2** *see* **impudence**.

cheeky *see also* **impudent**; facie, sneistie, forrit.

cheekbone chaft-blade.

cheek by jowl cheek for chow(l).

cheep *verb* peek, wheetle, queak NE.

noun peek.

not a cheep nae a chowp NE.

cheer *verb* lift.

cheered liftit.

cheerful cheerisome, hertie, blythesome, cantie, croose, joco, lichtsome, shortsome.

cheering hertsome, lichtsome.

cheerless *see also* **dreary**; unheartsome; hertless; (*of a building*) gowstie SE.

cheers! slainte (mhath)!

cheery *see* **cheerful**.

cheese (*whole, esp home-made*)

kebbock; (*soft*) crowdie; (*soft, from milk of newly-calved cow*) new cheese NE, caufie's cheese; (*cream*) ream cheese NE; (*from skimmed milk*) sweet-milk cheese N; (*small, hung in cloth*) hingie NE.

cheese-paring nippit, pea-splittin.

cheese-press chessart, cheswell.

the big cheese the heid pilliedacus.

end of a cheese heel.

chemise †sark.

chequered (*pattern*) chackert NE, dambrod.

cherish mak o, culyie.

cherry chirrie; (*wild*) gean; (*bird-cherry*) hagberry.

cherrystone (*dried, as counter in children's game*) paip.

chessboard diceboard.

chest 1 (*box*) kist, chist, buist; (*esp one used as a seat*) bunker; (*for meal etc*) ark, girnel. **2** (*of the body*) kist, chist, scroban N, W.

get something off your chest clear yer crap NE, hoast something up.

corner of a chest for valuables kistneuk.

hollow in the chest slot o the breist.

put in a chest kist.

chestnut chessie.

chevron (*of non-commissioned officer*) strip.

chew *verb* chaw, chow, chat NE, hash; (*partially*) hum(mle); (*awkwardly*) nattle; (*something hard, crisp*) scrump; (*vigorously*) ramsh.

noun chow.

chewing gum chuddie, chuggie.

chicanery *see* **cheating**.

chick chuck(ie) NE, E CENTRAL, chookie CENTRAL.

chicken chuck(ie) NE, E CENTRAL, chookie CENTRAL, chucken, poullie ULSTER, tuckie (hen) *child's word*, tickie *child's word*, NE; (*as food, often*) hen; (*large* (*young*), *for the pot*) howtowdie.

chicken-hearted *see also* **frightened**; hen-hertit.

chickenpox watery pox.

chicken run *see also* **hen-coop**; ree, reeve.

chicken soup hen broth, hen bree; (*with leek*) cock-a-leekie.

chickweed chickenweed, chickenwort.

chide *see* **scold**.

chief *adjective* heidmaist, (*person*) maist. *noun, see also* **boss**; (*of a clan*) chieftain; (*male*) himsel(f).

chilblain mool.

affected with chilblains moolie.

child *see also* **boy, girl**; bairn, wean CENTRAL, chiel(d), chile NE, chillie NE, sproot, get *often contemptuous*, bilch *contemptuous*; (*small: see also* **toddler**) bairnie, wee thing, littlin N, E CENTRAL, smowt, tottie, totum, smool, eeshan N, getlin *often contemptuous*; (*affectionate term*) cuttie, bird, doo, poutie, lambie, trootie, taid NE, posie; (*mischievous: see also* **rascal**) tike, smatche(r)t, sorra, wick, dirt *contemptuous*; (*precocious*) nacket; (*restless*) stourie; (*petted*) sookie, mither's bairn, minnie's bairn, mammie-keekie; (*wheedling*) flairdie SW; (*bad-tempered*) girnie-gib, blastie.

children childer; (*group: contemptuous,* NE) geets, smytrie; (*young*) wee yins.

childhood bairnheid.

childish bairn(l)ie, weanish CENTRAL, weanlie CENTRAL.

childishness bairnliness.

childlike bairnlie, bairn-lik(e).

childbed *see also* **confinement**; jizzen *in poetry*.

childbirth *see also* **labour**; shoutin.

moment of childbirth cannie moment.

pains of childbirth showers.

chill *verb* daver NE. *noun* (*coldness, illness*) jeel.

be *or* **feel chilled** sterve (wi caul(d)).

chilly *see also* **cold**; shill, chilpie NE, airish, greeshach N; (*specif of weather*) oorie, caal kin NE.

chimney lum, chim(b)ley; (*in rock*) lum NE.

chimney-cowl win(d)skew; (*rotating*) aul(d) wife, grannie, whirlie(gig).

chimney corner ingle-neuk, chim(b)ley neuk.

chimney pot lum can, (chim(b)ley) can.

chimney-stack lum, vent, stalk, shank W.

chimney top lum-heid, chim(b)ley-heid.

chimney on fire lummie.

chin: double chin chollers, chirles ORKNEY, flyte-pock.

having a long jutting chin gash-gabbit, shan-gabbit, sham-gabbit.

china cheenie, wallie CENTRAL, S, lame SHETLAND, ORKNEY, N.

china dogs wallie dugs, cheenie dugs.

broken pieces of china wallies, lamies N.

chink jink, bore, gaig.

chip *noun* (*of wood*) spail; **chips** (*of stone*) shivers. *verb* (*a blade etc*) lip.

chirp *see also* **cheep**; *verb* cheetle, chirl, chirm, chilp NE, twit, weeack NE, wheetle(-wheetle), whitter. *noun* cheetle, chirl, chirm, chilp NE.

chisel *noun* (*stonemason's*) cloorer, (*broad-faced*) drove CAITHNESS, NE, (*serrated*) tuithtuil. *verb* (*stone*) cloor.

chitchat *see also* **chat**; clack, claik, clash, claver, clishmaclaver, gab, whitter.

chivalrous *see* **courteous**.

chives sithes, syes NE.

chock *see* **wedge**.

choice *noun* chice, wale, wile. *adjective* han(d)-waled.

no (other) choice but nae (ither) ho but NE.

choir 1 (*mainly church*) ban(d), kire NE. **2** (*part of church*) queir.

choke chock, chowk SW, S; **1** (*a person: see also* **suffocate**) tak (someone's) breath, smuir, smore SHETLAND, NE, whirken S. **2** (*of a person*) scomfish, smuir, smore SHETLAND, NE, whirken s; (*convulsively or with laughter*) kink; (*on food*) worry. **3 choke up** (*a channel etc*) gurge up.

choked 1 (*with weeds etc*) grown-up; (*of a pipe etc*) tippit NE. **2** (*with the cold*) smorin.

choose chaise, chuse, chyse NE, E CENTRAL, cheese NE, wale, (*esp sides in a game*) chap, chaps.

choose between wale amon SHETLAND, NE.

chop *verb* chap, champ, hack, hash, (*esp wood*) hag.

chopped up (*of meat, vegetables*) shorn.

chopping block hack(in) stock, hag block SW, S, hackstock NE.

choppy (*of the sea*) ralliach ARGYLL.

become choppy jabble.

choppy sea lipper.

choppiness chap SHETLAND, ORKNEY, N.

chop off sned, sneg.

chops *see* **jaws**.

chore *see* **job**.

chortle keckle.

chorus 1 *see* **choir**. **2** (*refrain*) owercome, owerword.

chough reid-leggit craw.

christen kirsten, gie (a bairn) a name.

christening kirstenin.

Christendom Christendie *literary*.

Christian name given name.

Christmas Chrissenmas N, Yule, Yeel N; (*Old Style*) Auld Yule, Aal Eel SHETLAND, NE.

Christmas Day Yule Day, Yeel Day N.

Christmas Eve Yule Een, Yeel Een N; (*Old Style*) sowans nicht NE.

Christmas present Christmas: '*Whit wad ye like for yer Christmas?*'

Christmas and New Year period the Daft Days.

chronic (*of a cold etc*) sitten-doon.

chrysalis tammie-nid-nod.

chub skellie S.

chubby chibbie, fluffie, pluffie, chuffie; (*of the face*) buffie NE, guffie S; (*of a child*) sonsie.

chubby-cheeked (*esp of a child*) chuffie-cheekit.

chuckle *noun* keckle.

chum *see* **friend**.

chunk *see also* **lump**; junk, knoit, knot NE, fang NE, whang, knoll.

church kirk; (*main in a town*) high kirk.

churchy kirkie, kirk-greedy, gospel-greedy.

church court *see also* **chairperson**; (*lowest, managing a congregation*) kirk session; (*of an area*) presbytery; (*of a group of presbyteries*) synod; (*highest*) general assembly, (*in some of the smaller churches*) synod.

churchgoer hearer; **churchgoers** kirk-fowk.

church-membership certificate lines.

church organ kist o whustles.

church service diet o worship.

dispersal after church service kirk-skail(in).

churchyard kirkyaird.

ceremonial attendance at church kirkin: '*kirkin o the Cooncil*'.

move to another church lift yer lines, shift yer lines.

churl *see* **boor, lout**.

churlish nabal NE.

churn *noun* kirn; (*upright*) stannin kirn, plowt kirn ORKNEY, plump kirn NE, plumper NE. *verb* kirn, jummle; (*of the stomach*) wammle.

churnful kirn.

churning motion kirn.

form in the churn (*of butter*) gaither.

cigarette end dowp, dowt, tabbie, dottle.

cinder cinner, shunner, shinner NE; (*esp in a furnace etc*) dander.

Cinderella Rashiecoat.

cinema picter hoose.

cinnamon ceenamon, †cannel.

cipher (*nonentity*) ceepher.

circle *see also* **ring**[1]; (*round tee in curling*) hoose, broch NE, cock NE.
circular roon(d).
circular motion birl, sweel.
circumspect *see also* **cautious**; cannie, mows NE.
circumstance: in straitened circumstances taen-doon ORKNEY, N, sair aff, nae weel aff NE.
not under any circumstances at nae rate.
cirrus (cloud) gait's hair.
cistern cistren.
cite (*before a court*) *see* **summon**.
citizen ceetizen.
city-dweller *see* **slum-dweller**.
civic ceevic.
civic head (*of a town*) provost; (*of a city*) Lord Provost.
civil *see also* **polite**; ceevil.
civil court *see* **court**.
claim (*lay claim to*) awn, own.
I claim chaps me, chucks mei S.
clamber clammer NE, sclammer, spra(u)chle; (*hastily*) scrauchle.
clamber up speel.
clammy clam.
clamour *noun, see also* **uproar**; sclammer NE, stramash, narration, jargle; (*of voices*) yabble, yammer.
verb sclammer NE, yammer, craik.
clamp[1] *noun* clams NE, glaums, glaun.
clamp[2] (*of potatoes*) tattie pit, tattie bing.
clandestine hidlins.
clandestinely (in) hidlins.
clang (*of a bell*) *see* **toll**[2].
clank *noun* (*eg of a chain*) rackle N.
clannish hing-thegither.
clap: clapper (*of a mill*) (mill) clap, clack.
clapboard knappel.
claptrap *see also* **nonsense**; palaver.
clarify 1 *see* **clear up**. **2** (*fat*) rind, mouten NE.
clash *noun* (*dash*) swinge, slash.
clasp *noun* clesp; (*hasp*) hesp.
verb clesp, hesp; (*in your arms*) lock.

clasp-knife jockteleg.
clasp hands (*eg to seal a bargain*) chap hands.
class cless.
classify kind.
clatter *see also* **rattle**: *verb* brattle, reemis(h) NE; (*of crockery etc*) rees(h)le.
noun brattle, reemis(h) NE, swack, whinner SHETLAND, ORKNEY; (*clattering noise*) clitter-clatter, rees(h)le.
with a clatter rees(h)le.
claw *see also* **scratch**: *noun* clowe, cleuk, claut; **claws** (*of tongs*) palm.
verb cleuk NE, claut, scrat.
clay cley; (*bluish-grey, hardened*) blaes; (*iron-bearing*) ure SHETLAND.
clayey (*of land*) caul(d).
clean *adjective* claen SW, S.
verb (*thoroughly*) thorow.
noun, see **cleaning**.
cleaning *see also* **wipe**; (*thorough*) thorow; (*hasty*) slaik, dichtin.
clean out *see also* **clear out** 1; redd, claw, dicht; (*with a shovel*) shuil; (*esp a stable etc, of dung*) muck (oot).
clean up *see* **clear up** 1.
clear *adjective* clair; (*of light etc*) skire; (*direct*) plat SHETLAND; (*cleared*) redd.
verb **1** (*eg a space, a passage*) redd; (*a pipe of ash*) ripe, rummle; (*a fireplace of ash*) ripe: '*ripe the ribs*'. **2** (*the throat, nose etc: see also* **throat**) redd N. **3** (*of sky: see also* **clear up**) cast up.
clearance redd, redd-han(d).
cleared redd.
clearing (up) (*act*) redd(in).
clear-sighted gleg (o sicht).
clear away set by; (*to get more space*) redd.
clear out 1 (*ditch etc*) redd, feg; (*bowels etc*) scoor. **2** (*go away*) skice NE.
clear the throat *see* **throat**.
clear up 1 redd (up). **2** (*of weather*) fair, harden (up), rack up, cast up.
clear your way for action *etc* redd yer fix.
keep clear of haud wide o.

cleave rive, rent.

cleavers sticky-Willie, Robbie-rin-the-hedge, guse-grass.

cleft clift, clivvie NE, rift; (*in tree branches*) cloff.

cleft palate wummle-bore.

clench: clenched fist steekit nieve.

clergyman kirk man SHETLAND, ORKNEY, black coat *taboo,* E COAST; upstander *taboo,* SHETLAND; (*esp of a Presbyterian church*) minister.

clerk clark.

chief clerk (*in a bank*) accountant.

clever clivver, heidie, gleg (o the uptak), wice, snack(ie), auld-farran(t), lang-heidit; (*skilful*) crafty; (*shrewd*) fell, pawkie.

cleverness clivveralitie, glegness, ingine.

exceptionally clever person eel-drooner: '*He's nae eel-drooner*'.

be clever hae a hair on yer heid; (*exceptionally*) hae mair than whit the spuin pits in (the heid).

click *verb* (*make a clicking sound*) knick, knack, chack NE.

noun (*clicking sound*) knick, knack.

cliff clift, clint SW, S, craig, sker S; (*esp above sea or a river*) heuch.

climb *verb* **1** *see also* **clamber;** clim, sclim, speel, rink NE, ramp, rise SW; (*with difficulty*) spra(u)chle. **2** (*of plants*) ramp.

noun speel.

climbed *past tense* clam, climmed.

clinch 1 (*a nail*) ruive, plat SHETLAND. **2** (*a bargain etc*) nail.

cling clap.

clinging (*of a child*) glaikit.

clinkers danders.

clip (*esp hair*) cowe, coll; (*very short*) rump, dock.

clipped (*of speech or hair*) dockit.

clippers (*sheep-shearing*) shears.

cloak *noun* clock NE, hap, rauchan, bavarie.

clock *see also* **wall-clock, mechanism;** cloak, knock, time o day.

wall-clock (*with unencased pendulum*) waggitie-wa.

clod *see also* **sod**[1]; claut.

clodhopper *see also* **yokel;** plowt, puddock NE.

clog *verb* clag, cleg; (*with mud*) clatch up.

clogs clampers.

close[1] *adjective* **1** nar SW, ULSTER. **2** (*of a friend*) hameower, curmud S. **3** (*of atmosphere: see also* **muggy, sultry**) lunk(ie), smuchtie NE, smochie; (*and damp*) mochie, muithie.

closely-related near, sib, near freen(d)s.

closer nar.

close-fisted *see* **stingy.**

close-fitting strait, jimp.

close by nar, nearby, nearhan(d), near aboot(s), in aboot, at yer lug.

close to nar, nearby, nearhan(d), aside, inby.

close together (*of persons*) cheek for chow(l); (*of props in a mine*) skin-for-skin.

be close friends (with) be great guns (wi), be chief (wi), be far ben (wi).

sit close cuddle.

sitting close together curcuddoch.

close[2] *verb, see also* **shut;** steek; (*the mouth*) dit NE; (*of a school for a holiday*) gang doon.

noun (*end*) hin(d)maist.

closure (*of business*) shew-up.

close of the day dowp o day.

close with (*in a fight*) come tae grips wi.

clot *noun* **1** *see also* **lump;** clat; (*of blood, milk*) lapper. **2** *see* **idiot.**

verb (*of blood, milk*) lapper.

clotted clottert, lappert.

cloth 1 claith; (*coarse, homespun, woollen*) raploch; (*greyish, homespun, woollen*) hodden (gray); (*coarse linen*) harn, harden; (*wool and linen*) wincey; (*poor, thin*) garb NE. **2** (*piece of cloth: see also* **rag**) cloot; (*coarse, for domestic purposes*) dud NE; (*dirty, thick*) pilsh NE.

cloth cap skippit bunnet, cadie, hooker-doon CENTRAL, doolichter, stem(med) bunnet, snootit bonnet NE.

clothe *see also* **dress**; cleed, cleethe, hap, pit aboot.

clothed cled, cleed, cleedit, clethit.

clothes claes, cloots *contemptuous*, doublets NE, graith; (*best*) (Sunday) braws, regimentals; (*Sunday*) kirk claes; (*everyday, working*) ilkaday('s) claes, scodgie claes; (*second-best, esp after work*) weirin claes, scuddlin claes SHETLAND, ORKNEY, N, shiftin claes.

clothing cleedin, claith.

clothes-beater claes-beetle, posser SW, S.

clothes-brush cloth-brush, claes brush.

clothes-horse claes-screen, winter-dykes.

clothes line (claes) raip.

clothes-moth *see* **moth**.

clothes-prop claes pole, streetcher, stenter, heyser NE, greenie pole.

clothes-rail (*indoor or (formerly) from a window*) perk.

take clothes off tirr.

cloud *noun* **1** clud; (*cirrus*) gait('s) hair; (*cirrus or cirrostratus*) cat's hair NE; (*hump-shaped, indicating rain and wind*) packman; (*large, snowy, indicating bad weather*) Banff bailie NE; (*boat-shaped, indicating high wind*) purse-mou; (*basket-shaped, indicating wind direction*) scullgab NE. **2** (*dense, of smoke, snow etc*) smuir.

cloudy drumlie.

cloudberry knot(berry), noop, nubberry S, averin NE.

cloudburst (thunner-)plump.

cloud formation upcastin.

clouds in motion cairries.

rise in a cloud (*of dust etc*) stour.

clove (*spice*) clowe.

cloven clo'en NE, clowen NE.

cloven hoof cloot.

clover claver, sookie, curl-doddie ORKNEY; (*flower*) sookie-soo; (*of white or red*) plyven; (*flower-head*) sookie-mammie.

be in clover live at heck an manger.

clown *noun, see also* **idiot**; hallion.
verb noise NE.

cloy (*with food*) staw.

cloying (*food*) fousome.

club *noun, see also* **stick**[1], **cudgel, golf club**; mell.

club-foot reel-fit, bowtfit.

club-footed reel-fittit.

club-moss (*stagshorn or fir*) fox-fit S; (*stagshorn*) tod('s) tail(s) N.

cluck *noun* (*of a broody hen*) clock.
verb clock.

clump *noun* (*of trees, or of some low-growing plant*) buss; (*of trees*) beltin, beltie; (*as a shelter for sheep*) stell; (*of rushes*) rash-buss; (*of furze*) whins, fun buss NE; (*of grass*) boss, (*luxuriant*) bob.

clumsy *see also* **awkward, slovenly**; tackie NE, ill-setten; (*incompetent*) han(d)less; (*careless*) bummlin; (*at doing something*) ill (at); (*in walking*) ill-gaein, hochlin; (*and stupid*) gawkit; (*and brutish*) miraculous N; (*and corpulent, often of women*) mardle; (*awkwardly-built*) ill-hung-thegither; (*of things*) untowtherlie NE.

work clumsily blooter.

clumsy person ba(u)chle, gawk(ie); (*large coarse man*) caber NE, howffin NE.

clung *past tense of* **cling** clang.

cluster *noun, see also* **swarm**; boorach.

clutch[1] *verb, see also* **catch, seize, snatch, grasp**; cleek, cla(u)cht.

clutch at play pook at SW.

in the clutches of i the cleuks O N, i the grips O.

clutch[2] (*of eggs*) lachter.

clutter *verb, see also* **muddle, mess**; muck SHETLAND, NE, clamper SW.

coach (*light, two-wheeled*) †noddy.

coagulate *see* **clot, curdle**.

coal 1 coll, quile NE; (*that burns easily*) free coal; (*high-grade, shiny*) jewel-coal; (*volatile, clear-burning*) parrot coal;

(*splintering, hot-burning*) splint (coal); (*shallow-seam*) wee coal; (*small*) chirls; (*very small*) pearls, peas; (*small, smokeless, used by smiths*) smiddy coal; (*inferior*) scraw coal; (*slaty*) sclit; (*burning with sulphurous smell*) stinkin coal; (*unscreened*) tripin; (*supplied to workers at mine*) fire coal. **2** (*piece of coal: see also* **ember**) (*live*) gleed; (*shaly, burnt white*) ghaist S; (*to keep a fire going for a long period*) gaitherin coal, rakin coal, raker, setter; **live coals** (*for starting fire*) kennlin.

coal-box, coal-container (*in or outside house*) (coal) bunker; (*for carrying coal from the face*) hutch.

coal-bucket baikie, backet.

coal-cellar coal-neuk.

coal dust dross, (coal) coom, gum.

coal-face inside: '*gae tae the inside*'; (*length assigned to each miner*) place.

coalfish saithe, rock halibut NE, baddock, bagget NE, gray lord S, coam NE; stenlock; (*young*) cuddie, podlie NE, E CENTRAL, queeth NE, cuithe ORKNEY, prinkle NE, peuchtie, blockan SW; (*in first year*) gerrock NE; (*in second year*) piltock SHETLAND, ORKNEY, get; (*in second or third year*) gray fish SHETLAND, glashan W.

coalman (coal) wheecher.

coalmine, coalpit *see* **mine**².

coal-seam (*first from a mine*) lift.

coarse *see also* **rough**; coorse; (*of persons, manners etc*) teuch, groff, raucle, haskie, ill-faured, ruch-spun; (*of language*) randie; (*of texture*) groff, ramsh, great; (*of flax, fibre*) haskie.

coast *see* **seaside, shore**.

coaster (*for wine-bottle*) wine-slide.

coat cot, quite NE; (*much worn*) loorach NE; (*animal pelt*) sloch.

coating (*surface, of paint*) skaik NE; (*thin, of snow etc*) skirvin S, skimmin(ie) SHETLAND, NE.

coat-hanger shouders.

coax *see also* **wheedle, flatter, cajole**; fleetch, tryst wi N, cook NE, cuittle SW,

s, whillywha, wice, culyie.

coaxing *adjective* fraikie ORKNEY.

cobble *verb* souter.

cobbler *see also* **shoemaker**; souter; (*esp apprentice*) snab.

cobbling *noun* snabbin.

cobblestone causey stane.

cobweb moose wab.

coccyx rumple-bane.

cock *noun* (*bird*) cockieleerie (law), cockmaleerie.
verb (*hat*) scrug.

cocky croose, massie, poochle NE.

cock of the walk wha but he.

cockade hackle, heckle.

cockroach clocker.

cocksure poochle NE.

cod, codfish block NE; (*large*) keelin; (*small*) snappie N, blockie CAITHNESS; (*young*) cabelew; (*young, inshore*) redware cod(lin), warry codlin SHETLAND, NE; (*in poor condition*) sweltin NE, soosler CAITHNESS; (*living among rocks*) rock cod(fish); (*salted wet in hold of a boat*) mudfish SHETLAND, ORKNEY, NE; (*fish of cod family, usually dried for use*) tusk (fish) SHETLAND, ORKNEY, CAITHNESS.

coddle *see* **pamper**.

codicil eik.

coerce *see* **force**.

coffer kist.

coffin kist, deid-kist, deid-box, wuiden jaicket, wuiden overcoat w.

laying of a corpse in a coffin kistin.

cohabitee bidie-in *originally* NE.

co-heir (*female, inheriting an equal portion with others*) †heir portioner.

coil *verb, see also* **wind**²; pirl, wammle, whip; (*specif a rope*) faik, hank.
noun, see also **hank**; lap, pirl, swirl, fank; (*in a ball of wool*) cuffock NE.

coin cunyie, quinie; **coins** *see also* **cash, halfpenny**; clinkers.

coin of low value (*now used only in expressions of worthlessness*) bodle: '*no worth a bodle*', plack.

coincide complouter.

cold caul(d), cald, cowld SHETLAND, ORKNEY, N, ARGYLL, ULSTER: *adjective, see also* **chilly**; *(causing or susceptible to cold)* cauldrif(e); *(feeling very cold)* stervin (wi caul(d)), perished wi caul(d); *(looking cold and miserable)* oorie, nithert S; *(in manner)* cauldrif(e), cauld-wamed, ootward S, freff; *(of weather: bitterly)* snell, thin; *(and raw)* oorie; *(and bleak)* starrach CAITHNESS; *(and showery)* bleeterie NE.

noun **1** *(extreme)* jeel, stervation. **2** *(illness)* dose o the caul(d); *(severe)* snifters, sneevils, snochers, snochles; *(thick, choking)* smuchter NE; *(slight)* glisk o caul(d).

cold spell *(at beginning of spring)* cauld calendars NE, cauld kalends NE; *(in May)* (coo's) quake; *(after July shearing)* yowe('s) trummle.

cold as ice jeel-caul(d) NE, jeelit NE.

run cold *(of blood etc)* grue.

suffering from a cold cauldit: 'ye're still cauldit'.

colewort curly kail, curly greens.

colic *see also* **stomachache**; *(esp in horses)* teenge.

collaborate complouter.

collapse *verb* come in; *(of a wall)* shuit ORKNEY; *(of a person: from exhaustion etc)* foon(d)er, fairrie NE; *(from exhaustion etc or astonishment)* drap aff the spaik S.

noun, see **failure**.

collar *(of a coat or shirt)* neck; *(wooden, for a draught ox)* oussenbow.

collarbone hausebane.

collect 1 *see also* **gather**; lift; *(goods or persons)* uplift; *(money etc)* ingaither; *(eg subscriptions)* gaither; *(eg at a meeting)* tak up; *(taxes, wages etc)* uplift. **2** *(in crowds)* hatter.

collection 1 *see also* **crowd, heap**; mengie N, mardle NE, smytrie NE, gadderie SHETLAND; *(confused, of things)* mixter-maxter, hatter. **2** *(of money)* lift; *(in church as congregation leaves)* retiring collection.

collection box *(with long handle)* (kirk) ladle.

collection plate brod.

collide *(violently)* bairge.

collier *see* **miner**.

collusion paction.

in collusion in pack.

be in collusion collogue, colleague NE.

colour *verb (dye)* lit.

be brightly coloured skire ORKNEY, NE.

colourless *(pale)* fauchie N; *(of personality)* peelie-wersh S.

streak of colour spraing.

colt cowt, clip NE; *(suckling)* cowt foal SW, S; *(one to three years old)* staig; *(male, one to three years old)* frog NE.

coltsfoot tushilago, shilagie, tussilagie NE, doo-docken CAITHNESS.

columbine grannie's mutch(es).

coma *see* **faint**.

comb *noun* kaim; *(for hair)* reddin kaim; *(for holding hair in place)* keppin kaim; *(for textiles)* caird, *(flax comb)* heckle; *(of bird)* tap.

verb kaim, redd.

combat *see also* **fight, struggle**: *verb* kemp.

combine gae thegither.

come *verb, see also* **came**; win.

past participle came, cum(m)ed, comin.

come along! come yer weys!

come away *see* **leave**.

come back soon! haste ye back!

come in come in by.

come on! come awa(y)!, c'way!, quay!; *(in encouragement etc)* gaun yersel!

come together gae thegither.

comely *see also* **attractive**; sonsie, weel-faured, gate farrin NE.

comfort easement, easedom; **home comforts** thack an raip.

comfortable 1 *see also* **cosy, snug**; bien, fine, cannie, codgie NE, cantie, croose NE; *(of a garment)* mawsie NE. **2** *see also* **well-off**; richt eneuch, puist, nae ill aff.

comfortably bienlie.

comic

comic *noun* (*amusing person*) tear, divert.
command *noun* biddin; (*to animals*) *see* call.
Ten Commandments Comman(d)s.
person in command heid bummer, (heid) pilliedacus.
commence *see* begin.
commend ruise, reese NE.
commendation ruise, reese NE.
comment *noun* observe, speak.
commerce traffeck, mercat.
committee comatee, brod SHETLAND, NE, FIFE.
commodious scowthie NE; (*of a building*) gutsie.
commodities *see* goods.
common *adjective* cowmon NE; (*of a person*) raploch; (*jointly owned*) mean. *noun* (*land*) commonty, muir.
commoner carle.
commonly for common.
common sense *noun* smeddum, mense, wit, rumgumption, rummlegumption.
common humanity a(w) Jock Tamson's bairns.
commotion *see also* uproar, fuss, confusion, disturbance; stushie, stashie, splore, steerie, fizz, stour: '*raise a stour*', kippage, tirr-wirr, bizz, hurry, clamihewit, brulziement, whillilu.
communal staircase (*into a block of flats*) common stair; (*along with entrance*) close.
communication traffeck; (*by signs*) blin(d) parables NE.
Communion (*in the Presbyterian Churches*) sacrament, the table(s), occasion.
period around the Communion service (*usu Thursday to Monday*) the sacraments HIGHLAND.
service held before Communion preparatory service.
compact *adjective* 1 *see also* neat; snod, nacketie. 2 (*hard-packed*) saddit. *noun, see* agreement.
companion compaingen N, marrow,

billie NE, fere *literary*; (*female*) cummer.
company (*of people*) *see also* crowd; gaitherin; (*esp convivial*) core, quorum NE.
company of two, three *etc* twasome, threesome *etc*.
keep company with frequent wi, forgaither wi.
compare even (wi).
comparison compare.
in comparison with by, by's, beis, tae, to, in confeerance tae NE, forby.
who can compare with me? fair fa masel N.
compartment (*eg in a trunk, for keeping valuables*) shottle, kist-locker, draarie NE.
compass *noun* (*in a fishing boat*) diacle.
point of the compass airt.
compassion (*deep*) hert-peety.
compassionate innerlie.
feel compassion for rue on, be *or* feel hert-sair for.
compel *see also* necessitate; gar, dwang.
compelled necessitate NE.
compensate †assyth (of).
compensation mends, upmak, †assythment; (*damages*) skaith; (*for breaking a bargain etc*) rue-bargain.
compete (*esp in work*) kemp.
competition competeetion.
competent ticht, lik(e)ly, nae bad (at).
complacent kirr SW.
complain *see also* grumble; compleen, murn, craik, grudge, molligrant, tarrow; (*at length*) rant; (*peevishly*) girn, mump, peefer; (*whine*) yowl, yammer, peenge, pewl, peek NE, yirm S.
be always complaining wurn, narr.
person who is always complaining greetin Teenie.
complaint *see also* grumble; mane, pewl, pleen.
complete *adjective* (*whole*) hail; (*absolute*) fair: '*ye're a fair disgrace*', polisht. *verb, see* finish.

completely fair, black, heids an heels, rump an stump, crap an reet, haillie, evendoon.

complex (*intricate*) quirkie; (*tricky*) pernicketie, kittle.

complexion: of dark complexion din, black-avised, dark-avised.

of fair complexion fair-avised.

compliant bowsome.

complicated *see also* **complex**; misred.

complication wimple.

complicity (*law*) accession.

compliment *see* **flatter(y)**.

comply come tae, complouter; **comply with** (*law*) obtemper.

compose (*write*) clark NE; (*verses*) †clink; (*compose rapidly*) screed (awa).

composed (*of a person: see also* **calm**) cannie.

composer upmakker SHETLAND, NE.

composition composeetion, (*story etc*) upmak SHETLAND, NE, scrift NE.

regain composure come tae.

compost heap midden, yirdie tam NE.

comprehend *see also* **understand**; tak up.

comprehension ken, uptak: '*slow i the uptak*'.

compress *verb, see also* **crush, squeeze**; pran NE, pram SHETLAND, NE, poss S, ULSTER, groze.

compressed panged.

compromise mids NE.

this is a compromise there's aye a mids i the sea NE.

comrade *see* **companion**.

concave howe.

conceal *see also* **hide**[1]; dern; (*by covering*) hap.

conceit consait.

conceited *see also* **proud, haughty**; conceitie, big: '*He's awfie big on it*', bigsie ORKNEY, NE, croose NE, full, pitten-on, set-up, cairried, saucy, up i the buckle, as big as bull beef NE.

be conceited think yersel nae sma drink, think yersel nae sheep shank.

conceive (*a plan etc*) cleck.

concentrate on (*intently*) gang hailheidit for N.

concern *noun* (*care*) fittininment NE.

concerned *see also* **anxious**; thochtit.

concerning *see also* **about**; anent.

concerning this hereanent *law*.

as far as concerns for that pairt o.

have other concerns hae ither towe tae tease.

concert (*of Scottish, esp Highland music*) ceilidh.

concession inlat.

conciliate *see* **reconcile**.

conclude 1 (*end*) *see* **end, finish. 2** *see* **settle**.

conclusion (*of a speech etc*) pirlicue.

come to the wrong conclusion hae the wrang soo by the lug.

draw conclusions draw straes ORKNEY, N.

concoction *see* **mixture**.

concord *see* **harmony**.

concubine *see* **mistress**.

concur *see* **agree**.

condemn *see also* **blame**; (*pronounce sentence*) doom.

condensation (*vapour*) (y)oam SHETLAND, ORKNEY, NE; (*eg on glass*) gum N.

condescend: condescending heich(-heidit).

be very condescending be very high i the bend.

condescend to argue with even yer wits tae.

condiments kitchen, kitchie.

condition *see also* **state**; condeetion, tift; (*of a fishing river*) ply: '*in guid ply*'.

fulfil a condition (*law*) purify a condition.

in good condition bien; (*of animals*) gawsie.

on condition that perconnon that NE, gin.

out of condition (fat an) fozie.

condolence: letter of condolence murnin letter.

condone *see* **excuse, forgive.**

conduct *verb* conduck: **1** (*escort*) convoy, convey NE. **2 conduct yourself** *see* **behave.**

noun, see also **behaviour;** gate NE.

conduit *see also* **channel;** cundie, pend SW, S; (*esp to a millwheel*) trows.

cone *see* **fircone.**

confectionery *see* **sweets.**

confectioner (*male*) sweetie-man; (*female*) sweetie-wife.

confectioner's (*shop*) sweetie-shop.

conference collogue.

confess awn (up till).

confide: have confidence in lippen till.

confident croose.

confidently heid-heich.

confidential parteec(u)lar.

confine *verb* tether ORKNEY, NE, restrick, humfish NE; (*imprison*) †ward; (*animals in a pen*) parrock, criv NE.

noun, see **boundary.**

confined hamperit, crivved in NE.

confinement 1 (*imprisonment*) †ward. **2** (*birth*) inlyin, cryin NE, howdyin, doon-lyin.

beyond the confines of outwith, furth o.

confirm (*esp law*) homologate *archaic*; (*a friendship etc*) souder NE.

confiscate sequestrate.

conflict *verb, noun, see* **fight, struggle.**

conformity (*to customs etc*) rander.

confound *see also* **confuse;** confoon NE.

confront *see* **stand up to.**

confuse 1 (*muddle: see also* **jumble**) taigle, taisle, warple. **2** (*a person*) confeese, raivel, ramfeezle, habble S, mineer NE, conflummix NE, denumb NE, daumer NE.

confused 1 (*in a muddle: see also* **higgledy-piggledy**) throuither, throwder NE, mixter-maxter, reel-rall, misred, rim-ram NE. **2** (*of a person: see also* **dazed**) bumbazit, waun(n)ert, mixit, peerie-heidit, moidert, in a creel, taivert; (*esp because of age*) donnert.

confused story *etc* ham-a-haddie.

confusedly *see* **higgledy-piggledy.**

confusion 1 *see also* **muddle;** hurryburry, swither, steer, jabble, kirn, picher NE, soss, raivelt hesp, heeliegoleerie, gilravage. **2** (*of a person: see also* **perplexity**) throuitherness.

in confusion *see* **higgledy-piggledy.**

confutation (*law*) improbation.

congeal jeel.

congenial couthie, kindly.

conger-eel haivel.

congestion (*respiratory*) closin.

congregate forgaither.

congregation kirk-fowk, church-folk.

withdraw from a particular congregation lift yer lines, shift yer lines.

conjecture *verb, see* **guess.**

conjunction: act in conjunction kep kinches SW.

connect conneck.

connive conneeve.

conquer *see also* **defeat;** vinkish.

conscience: conscientious eydent.

be conscience-stricken tak guilt tae yersel, be vext.

conscious war(e) SHETLAND, ORKNEY.

be conscious of fin(d).

consecrate sain.

consecutive efter ither.

consent *verb, see* **agree.**

noun, see **agreement.**

consequence eftercast; **consequences** efterins, bree.

in consequence of ower the heid(s) o.

take the consequences (of something) dree yer weird, dree the dirdum(s), tak on SHETLAND.

conserve hain, haud in.

consider conseeder, consither N.

considerable gey, bonnie, queer; (*of sums of money etc*) braw; (*of time*) dainty.

considerable number hantle, guid puckle, gey wheen.

considerably gey.

considerate considerin, cowshus NE.

for further consideration (*law*) ad avisandum.

considering confeerin NE.

console mane.

consort *noun* (*spouse*) marrow *literary*.

consort with neibour wi, intromit wi, mell wi, moup wi SW, gang aboot wi.

conspicuous conspeecuous, kenspeckle.

conspire collogue, colleague NE.

conspiracy *see also* **scheme**; pack.

constable *see* **policeman**.

constant 1 (*of work etc*) close. **2** (*faithful*) leal.

constantly daily day, ivverlie, aye: '*he's aye at me for sweeties*', even on.

consternation *see* **perplexity**.

constipation (*in cattle*) dry darn NE.

constrain dwang.

constrained hamperit.

constrict (*of clothes*) nip.

construct *see* **build**.

construe rede.

consult inquire at, see at, speir at.

consume *see also* **eat**; pit ower; (*gradually*) moot SHETLAND; (*frugally*) scrimp; (*waste*) weir throu.

consumption (*amount consumed*) consumpt.

consume a great deal of (*food, drink*) be heavy on, be a heavy neibour on.

consummate *adjective, see* **perfect**.

contact: come into contact with awn, own.

contagion smit: '*gie someone the smit*'.

contagious smittle, smitsome.

infect by contagion smit.

contain *see also* **hold**; conteen; (*restrain*) haud, kep.

container *see* **jug, bucket, pail, tub, jar**[1].

contaminate smit.

contemplate lay the brains asteep.

contemporary (*of the same age*) eil(d)ins (wi), yealins (wi), ages wi.

contempt sneist.

contemptible *see also* **worthless, useless**; dirten, wandocht *literary*.

contemptuous sneistie.

contemptuous term for a person *see also* **good-for-nothing, rogue, rascal, scoundrel**; nyaff, skite, slink, baigle, waff(ie), toalie, wunner N.

exclamation of contempt yer grannie!: '*hopeful yer grannie*'.

contend 1 *see also* **struggle**; kemp. **2** *see also* **dispute**; tulyie.

contention *see* **argument, dispute**.

content *verb, see also* **satisfy**; pleesure. *adjective, see* **contented**.

contented codgie NE, cantie, fine.

contest *noun, see also* **struggle**; tousle, sprattle; (*eg for first place*) kemp.

continue *see also* **carry on**; conteena, haud, dree.

continually *see also* **constantly**; ivver an on, aye.

continuous eend on S; (*esp of rain*) eydent.

continuously even on, eend on S, steady, still an on, nivver upplin N.

contort *see also* **distort**; thraw.

contortion (*esp of the face*) thraw, murgeon.

contract *noun* contrack; (*law: submitting a dispute to arbitration*) submission. *verb* contrack; (*see also* **shrink** 1) gae in.

contractor (*small*) cork.

person bound by a contract (*law*) obligant.

fulfilment of a contract (*law*) implement.

time for renewal of workers' contracts speakin time.

contradict conterdick, conter, contrair, na-say, ca(w) again.

contradiction na-say.

contradictory ill-contrivit SHETLAND, N.

contraption (*fantastic*) whigmaleerie, whirlie, ferlie NE.

contrary *adjective* 1 (*opposite*) contrair, conter. 2 *see also* **perverse, wilful** (*under* **will**[2]); contrair, thrawn, contermacious, maggotive NE, maggotie, thrawart SHETLAND, ORKNEY.
noun contrair, conter NE.
in a contrary direction (*to the sun*) withershins, widdershins.
go contrary to contrair.

contravene *see* **thwart**.

contribute contreebute.
contribution (*of money for some purpose*) inpit.

contrite: be contrite *see* **repent**.

contrive ettle, mak it up, fish, shape.
contrivance *see* **contraption**.

control *verb* guide, maun.
noun poustie, hank, owerance.
have complete control hae (the) heft an (the) blade in yer han(d).
control events guide the gully.
beyond control neither tae haud nor tae bind.
out of control oot o (the) theat(s) NE.
under control sicker.
have (*someone*) **under control** lead (someone) by the neb.
keep under control keep *or* haad in his *etc* ain neuk SHETLAND, NE.

controversy threap, collieshangie NE.
engage in controversy threap.

conundrum *see* **riddle**[1].

convene (*meet*) forgaither, tryst.

convenient hantie.

converse *verb, see also* **chat, talk**; crack, confabble, news, ca(w) the crack.
conversation crack, gab, news, speak, cantation; (*intimate*) corrieneuchin NE; (*whispered*) collogue, toot-moot; (*between two people*) twa-handit crack.
get into conversation (with) get on the crack (wi), hae a news (wi).

convert *see* **change**.

convey *see also* **send, carry**; (*in a wheeled vehicle*) hurl.

convict *verb* convick.

convince insense (intae).

convivial conveevial, hertie, joco.

convolution wimple.

convolvulus bin(d)wood, creepin eevie NE.

convulsion thraw; (*in coughing*) kink.
convulsive cough a richt kinker o a hoast.
cough *or* **choke convulsively** kink.

coo *verb* (*of an infant*) goo; ((*as*) *of a pigeon*) rookettie-coo, croodle, curdoo, buckartie-boo NE; (*of the male*) curroo.

cook *verb* cuik, ready; (*too hastily*) haister S; (*badly*) mismak.
noun cuik.
cooked meal made diet SHETLAND, NE.
fully cooked weel.
cooking pot (*large*) kettle, muckle pot.

cool *adjective* cuil, queel NE; (*of air, water etc*) caller; (*of weather*) airish.
verb cuil, queel NE.

coop *see* **hen-coop**.

cooperate complouter; (*with neighbours*) neibour (wi).
cooperative society (shop) coperative, store, co, copie, sosh ANGUS, FIFE.
cooperative undertaking pairtisay.

coopering *see* **barrel, hoop**.

cope *verb, see* **manage**.

coping caip NE, tablin, skew, peen NE.
coping stone caipstane, peat (stane), putt stone.

copious *see also* **abundant, ample**; lairge NE, rowthie; (*of a drink*) heavy.

copse *see* **wood**.

copulate (*of males*) mow; (*of rams*) tuip, teep NE; (*of cows*) be bulled.

copy *verb, see* **imitate**.
noun, see also **duplicate**; neibour, marrow; (*official, of a court judgement etc*) extract; (*rough*) scroll ORKNEY, NE.
copybook *see also* **exercise book**; copy.
make an official copy of (*law*) extract.

coquettish pawkie.

coracle †currach.

cord *see also* **rope**; towe; (*piece, for tying*) tial SHETLAND, ORKNEY; (*for attaching hook to floating lines*) tome SHETLAND, ORKNEY, N; (*trailing, with hooked lines*) dorro NE; (*to fasten drift net to a rope*) daffin ORKNEY, N; (*for the mechanism of a clock*) therm.

cordial *adjective, see also* **friendly**; hertie, sonsie, guidwillie.

coriander corrydander.

cork *see* **stopper**.

cormorant scarf, scart, Mochrum elder SW.

corn[1] (*on the foot*) werrock.

corn[2] (*grain*) stuff, vittal.

  corn container (corn) ark, corn-kist.

  corncrake craik, weet-ma-fit.

  corn-dolly *see* **last sheaf of corn** *below*.

  cornflower blawort, blaver, blue bonnets.

  corn marigold guil.

  last load of corn winter NE.

  last sheaf of corn at harvest, corn-dolly *see also* **sheaf**; maiden, cailleach, clyack (sheaf) NE, carline NE, kirn (dolly).

  corn-spurrey yarr.

  cornstack *see* **stack**.

corner *noun* **1** cunyie; (*of or in a building*) gushet; (*of the mouth or eye*) wick. **2** (*remote place*) neuk.

  cornerstone scuncheon.

  having corners neukit.

coroner (*law*) the investigative role is carried out by a procurator fiscal, judicial aspects by a sheriff.

corporal: corporal punishment *see also* **beating**; licks, paikin, buttock mail NE.

corporation (*of master craftsmen in a burgh*) trade.

corpse corp, bouk, lyke SHETLAND; (*for dissection, esp stolen*) †shusy.

  corpse candle cannle NE.

corpulent *see also* **fat, stout, buxom**; gurthie, guttie; (*esp of a woman*) mardle.

correct *adjective, see also* **right**; cor-

reck; (*more or less correct*) near the bit.
verb correck, sort.

correspond (*fit*) gree.

  corresponding confeerin NE.

corridor (*in a building*) passage, trance, througang, pass ULSTER.

corroborate (*law*) homologate *archaic*.

corrode *see* **rust**.

corrugated *see* **wrinkled**.

corrupt *adjective* **1** (*of a person or action*) *see* **wicked**. **2** (*of a text*) mankit.

corset steys.

cosset *see* **pamper**.

cost *verb* (*someone something*) stan(d).
noun, see also **expenses**; chairge.

  costliness darth NE.

  legal costs expenses.

costume *see* **dress**.

cosy *see also* **comfortable**; bien, cosh, tosie, snod, feel S.

cot beddie (ba).

cottage cot(tar) hoose; (*two-roomed*) but-an-ben.

  cottages biggins.

  group of farm cottages cot-to(o)n.

  people living in farm cottages cot(tar)-fowk.

  row of farm cottages hinds' raw SE.

cotton: cotton-grass bog-cotton; (*esp harestail*) mosscrop, (pull) ling, canna(ch).

  cotton wool wad, cotton oo.

couch *see also* **bed**; cootch, (*of layers of turf*) sunk.

  couch-grass wrack, quicken(s).

cough *verb* coaf, coch CAITHNESS, hoast, bouch, croichle NE; (*loudly*) bowf (an hoast); (*violently*) husk; (*persistently*) keuch; (*with difficulty*) boich NE; (*huskily, with a wheeze*) craighle; (*esp to clear the throat*) hauch; (*asthmatically, esp to clear the throat*) pyocher SHETLAND, NE; (*in a subdued asthmatic way*) pech; (*with a gurgling noise*) blocher; (*sharply, with a tickle*) kicher.
noun, see also **whooping cough**; hoast, croichle NE; (*loud*) bowf; (*persis-*

tent, tickling) keuch; (*wheezing*) pech; (*rough, wheezing*) cloch; (*persistent, choking*) pyocher NE; (*short, tickling*) kighle, kicher; (*slight*) crickle: '*a crickle i the thrapple*'; (*loose, catarrhal*) blocher; (*so bad as to cause anxiety*) kirkyaird hoast, kirkyairder, graveyaird hoast.

fit of coughing kink.

have a fit of coughing kink.

cough up hoast up, hask.

could *past tense of* **can** cud, cuid.

could not cudna, cudnae.

coulter cooter.

council *see also* **committee**: cooncil.

counsel *see also* **advise**: coonsel.

count *noun, verb, see also* **figure**: coont.

countless undeemous SHETLAND, N, nae mows NE: '*It wis jist a crood nae mows*'.

count on *see* **depend on**.

count out (*money*) tell doon SHETLAND.

countenance *see* **face**.

counter *noun* coonter.

counteract conter.

counterfeit (*of coins*) ill, fause.

counterpart neibour, marrow.

counterweight wither-wecht.

country *noun* countra, kintra, quintra N. *adjective* land(w)art.

countrified *see also* **rustic**; countrifeed NE, E CENTRAL, hedder-an-dub NE.

country girl jennie.

countryman *see also* **yokel**; jock(ie): '*jockie an jennie*', heather-lowper NE.

country person teuchter.

towards the country land(w)art.

county coontie.

couple *see also* **pair**: *noun, verb* cupple, kipple.

courage saul; (*spirit*) smeddum.

courageous *see also* **bold**; croose NE, stalwart, wicht *in poetry*; (*of men*) pretty; (*ready to fight*) fechtie, nae fleggit NE.

course coorse.

in due course in coorse, syne.

of course in coorse.

court *noun, see also* **church court** (*un-der* **church**); coort; (*supreme civil in Scotland*) Court of Session; (*supreme criminal in Scotland*) High Court of Justiciary, *informally* High Court; (*presided over by a sheriff, criminal and civil*) Sheriff Court; (*lowest criminal*) district court.

verb gae thegither, winch; (*someone*) coort (wi), gae wi, be thrang wi, come aifter NE, haud up tae, rush, splunt SW, S.

courting winchin, spluntin SW, S; (*fully clothed in bed*) bundling SHETLAND, HEBRIDES.

court order (*esp by Court of Session before a final judgement*) interlocutor; (*prohibiting something until the right is tried in court*) interdict.

courtyard close EDINBURGH.

courteous *see also* **polite**: hamelie, mensefu; gentie.

courtesy mense.

cousin kizzen; (*child of a parent's sister*) sister-bairn SHETLAND, CAITHNESS.

second cousin hauf-cousin.

cove *see* **inlet**.

covenant *noun* (*agreement*) tryst, paction.

cover *verb* kivver, coor, hap; (*thickly with snow etc*) smore, smuir; (*eg a window with a curtain*) tyld.

noun kivver, hap; **covers** (*of a book*) batters.

covered over happit, owercled SHETLAND.

covering (*esp for protection against cold etc*) hap; (*esp outer*) huil; (*thin, of soil, snow etc*) skirvin S, skimmin.

cover it over a bit gie't a hap(pie).

covet *see also* **long**; hae yer ee in.

covetous *see* **greedy**.

cow[1] *noun* coo, baist, beast; (*young: see also* **heifer**) cuddoch SW, S; (*one-year-old*) eean NE; (*two-year-old in calf*) etterlin; (*fattened for slaughter*) mart SHETLAND, N; (*horned*) hornie; (*with crooked horns, esp pet name*) crummie; (*with white face*) hawkie; (*speckled*) fleckie.

cowberries brawlins.

cow-dung sha(i)rn.

cowhand (cow-)bailie.

cow-lick cauf's lick.

cow parsnip *see* hogweed.

cowpat coo-plat.

cowshed byre.

cowslip lady's fingers.

cow[2] *see* intimidate, humiliate.

cowed oolt NE, (k)noolt SW, S.

be cowed coordie.

coward cooard, cooart, feartie, cootcher, fugie, coof.

cowardice cooardiness.

cowardly cooard(l)ie, hen-hertit, hennie, fugie.

cower coor(ie), slootch, jouk, crulge NE, croodle.

cower down coorie doon.

cowl *see also* chimney-cowl; cool.

cowrie (shell) John o Gro(a)t's buckie, groatie buckie SHETLAND, ORKNEY, N.

coy *see also* timid, shy; skeich.

crab (*esp large edible*) partan, poo SE, cruban; (*small edible*) pulloch N, pallawa; (*with no shell, or about to cast shell*) pillan, piller N, E CENTRAL, peeler NE; (*with no shell*) saftie, sclushach NE.

crab claw partan('s) tae.

crab louse cart NE, cartie SHETLAND; (*disease caused by it*) cart NE.

crab soup partan bree.

crab-apple craw('s) aipple, scrab, scrag SE.

crabbed *see also* irritable, bad-tempered; crabbit.

crack *verb* creck, rive; (*make a cracking sound*) knack, knick ORKNEY, N, nicker SHETLAND; (*a whip*) cleesh S.

noun creck: 1 (*split: see also* split, cleft, scratch) scaum, gaig, jink, rive SHETLAND; (*small, in pottery glaze*) kill-crack; (*on the skin*) *see* chap. 2 (*cracking sound*) knick SHETLAND, ORKNEY, NE, knack ORKNEY, NE; (*of a whip*) cleesh SW, S.

cracked (*of unseasoned wood*) gelled; (*of a wooden container*) gizzen; (*of the skin*) hackit, chappit.

crackle *verb* graisle, crunkle, (*eg of ice*

when trodden on*) crump NE; (*eg when frying*) sotter, skirl.

noun (*of fat etc in a pan*) skirl, sotter.

crackly (*eg of snow or ice*) crumpie, crumshie NE.

cradle beddie (ba).

craft: crafty *see also* smart; sleekit, sleek(ie), sneck-drawin, deep-drauchtit, gleg, pawkie(-wittit), soople, loopie, auld-mou'd NE.

crafty person sneck-drawer.

craftiness sneck-drawin.

craftsman tradesman, wricht.

be crafty hae a link on yer tail SW, S.

crag *see also* cliff; heuch, scaur, skerr S, gairy SW.

cram stap, pang; (*esp with food, see also* gorge) stowe, stech, puist S.

crammed full jam(min) fou; (*of food and drink*) ram-fou, pang-fou.

cramp *noun* (*of legs, in horses*) cleeks NE.

cramped hamper(i)t.

become cramped (*of the limbs*) stock.

crampon (*on boot for climbing trees*) speeler.

cranberry crawberry, crawcrooks, crane S.

crane *noun* (*hoist or bird*) cran; (*of fire engine*) swey N.

verb (*the neck*) rax.

cranefly *see* daddy-long-legs.

cranium *see* skull.

cranny bore, jink.

crash *noun* rattle, stramash, whinner SHETLAND, ORKNEY, reemis(h) NE, doist NE, swack, rennish SW, blaff.

verb (*noisily*) rattle, reird; (*crash about*) reemis(h) NE.

cravat gravat, owerlay.

crave (for), have a craving for *see also* long for; (*of a pregnant woman for certain foods*) hae a greenin for, green for.

craving greenin.

craven *see* coward(ly).

crawl *verb* crowl, wurble; (*laboriously, clumsily, eg through something*) spra(u)chle.

crayon (*coloured*) keel.

craze: crazed *see also* **dazed, confused;** aff (at) the knot NE, wowf.

crazy *see also* **mad, insane;** daft (aboot), gyte, doitit, wuid, hallach NE.

creak *verb* craik, cheep N, chirk, jirg, skirl, jeeg, jarg.

noun jirg; (*light creaking sound*) wheesk.

make a creaking sound graisle.

cream *noun* ream, (*specif from milk*) tap o the milk.

creamy reamie.

cream dish (*esp one for skimming*) reamer, ream pig.

cream jug (ream) poorie.

clotted cream knottit ream NE.

whipped cream with oatmeal froh (milk) NE, foorach NE, crannachan, cream crowdie.

leave (*milk*) **standing for cream to rise** set.

crease *see also* **crinkle, fold**[1]: *verb* cress, lirk, runkle, ruckle, gruggle NE.

noun cress, lirk, kink, runkle, ruckle, gruggle NE.

creased runklie.

creature craitur, baist, beast.

credit *noun* (*honour*) mense.

verb hae: '*Whit hae ye o't!*' = Would you credit it!

be a credit to mense.

book recording goods bought on credit tammie-book.

buy on credit tak on.

spend on credit forenail NE.

demand by a creditor (*law*) requisition.

place (*a person*) **in his due place in a list of creditors** (*law*) rank.

put (*a person*) **further down a list of creditors** postpone.

credulous person bluff NE.

creek *see also* **inlet;** gote, slock, geo SHETLAND, ORKNEY, CAITHNESS.

creep *see also* **crawl;** (*of the flesh*) grue.

crept *past tense* creepit, crap NE.

past participle creepit, cruppen.

cress *see* **watercress.**

crest (*of a bird*) tap, tappin; (*of a hill*) rig, kaim.

crested (*of a bird*) tappi(n)t.

crested hen tappit hen.

crestfallen hingin-luggit.

be crestfallen hing yer lugs.

why are you so crestfallen? wha(e) stole yer scone?

crevice *see also* **cleft;** bore, lirk.

crib *see* **cot.**

cricket (*insect*) charker.

criminal creeminal.

criminal court *see* **court.**

crimson (cloth) cramasie *literary*.

cringe creenge, coorie, sneevil, snuil, beenge.

cringing coorie.

cringing person snuil.

crinkle crunkle, grunkle NE.

crippled *see* **lame.**

crippled person lameter.

crisis: pass a crisis in an illness tak the turn.

crisp *adjective* crumpie, crumshie NE; (*of food*) knappie; (*baked hard*) scrumpit NE; (*of ice, in curling*) keen.

fried until crisp weel-birselt.

make crisp (*food by heat*) harn.

criss-crossed lozent NE.

critic creetic.

critical (*criticizing*) tuithie, ticht.

take a critical look at (*appraisingly*) tak (a) swatch o, (*scrutinize*) scance.

criticize *see also* **blame;** criticeese, puist, quarrel, yaff, challenge, scance (at), pook at; (*severely*) hae yer horn in someone's hip.

never finished criticizing never aff someone's tap.

criticism (*sharp*) heckle.

croak *verb* **1** roup; (*of a bird*) craik, (*esp a crow*) croup; (*of a person coughing*) craighle. **2** (*slang: die*) crock.

noun craik.

croaking (*hoarse*) croupit.

crochet-hook cleek.

crupper

crock: old crock *see* old man.

crockery *see also* earthenware; piggerie NE; (*broken piece, esp used as a toy*) lame N, lamie N, wallie CENTRAL.

croft *noun* craft NE, paffle, placie.

crook *noun* 1 (*shepherd's*) nibbie, crummock. 2 *see* criminal.

crooked *see also* bent; thrawn, gley(e)d, neukit.

crop *noun* 1 crap. 2 (*bird's*) gebbie, caibie N, scroban N, PERTHSHIRE, ARGYLL, BUTE.

verb (*very short*) rump.

come a cropper kiss the causey.

cross *noun* corse.

verb corse: 1 (*with a stride or bound*) spang. 2 (*eg the legs*) plet. 3 (*thwart*) thorter. 4 cross yourself sain yersel.

adjective, see also bad-tempered; crabbit, canker(i)t, tiggie.

crossbar knewel; (*for a door*) steyband, spar, rance; (*on a chair*) rance, sword; (*eg on a cart*) slot, sheth.

crossbeam (*in a roof*) bauk, bougar, owertree.

crossbred (*of a sheep, from Border Leicester ram and Cheviot ewe*) half-bred.

cross-examine cross-speir, backspeir, catechis NE.

cross-examination throu-pittin.

cross-eyed *see* squint-eyed.

cross-question *see* cross-examine.

crossroads sheddins.

cross your mind come up yer back, come up yer humph.

crotch forkin, clift, gowl N, cleavins NE.

crouch *see also* squat; crootch, coorie (doon), clap (doon), clock, crulge NE, croonge NE, hunker (doon), hurkle (doon); (*esp over a fire*) hoker.

crow[1] *noun* (*bird: see also* carrion crow, hooded crow) craw.

crowbar *see also* lever; gavelock, pinch(er), wa-iron NE, guddle, till airn, swey.

crowberry crawberry, crowpert NE, knowpert NE.

crow's feet craw-taes.

crowfoot *see* buttercup.

crowsteps crawsteps, corbie stanes.

gathering of crows craws' waddin.

crow[2] *verb* 1 (*of a cock etc*) craw. 2 (*boast*) blaw.

noun (*of a cock etc*) craw, cockieleerie (law).

crowd *noun* crood, menyie, mardle NE, thrang, clamjamfrie *contemptuous*, vermin *contemptuous*; (*bustling*) thrangitie; (*confused*) cluther, brangle, squatter, currieboram NE, curriebuction NE, gilravage SW; (*noisy*) helm NE; (*esp of children*) smarrach NE, smachrie NE, waller S.

verb, see also swarm; clamjamfrie, clamper SW; (*together*) hotter, rally; (*from cold*) hugger NE; (*in(to)*) cram (in(tae)).

crowded thrang.

crowded out stowed oot.

crown *noun* croon; (*of the head*) powe, cantle NE.

verb croon.

crude (*esp of character: see also* coarse) coorse, raploch, ruch(-spun), ruchsome, raucle.

cruel ill, ill-kindit, ill-set, fell, coorse NE.

cruelly sair.

treat cruelly mischieve SHETLAND, NE.

crumb mealock, millin, pronack, minschie NE, crottle SW, nirl, murlin, murlick NE.

crumble crummle, murl; (*of clay etc*) fa(w); (*away*) moot, moosh CAITHNESS.

crumbly *see also* friable; bruckle, frush, crotlie SW; (*of pastry*) *see* short 2.

crumpet crimpet; NB in Sc usually refers to a large thin dropped scone.

crumple *see also* crinkle, crease; runkle, frumple.

crumpled runklie.

crunch *verb, see also* munch; crinch, crump, cramsh NE, ramsh, scrump NE, scranch.

crunchy crinchie.

if it comes to the crunch if hard comes tae hard.

crupper curple, crupple SW, S, curpin NE.

53

crush *verb* grush, brizz, smush, champ, runkle, pran NE, broozle, groze; (*by striking*) dunt; (*flat, with a slap*) scone.

crust (*surface layer*) scruif; (*thin*) scruiffin; (*of a loaf: flat bottom*) sole, plain Geordie; (*rounded top*) curly Kate.

crusty *see* bad-tempered.

crustacean *see also* shellfish, crab, lobster; (*small, on which herring feed*) croy.

crutch powl, stilt, oxter staff NE.

go on crutches stilt.

cry *verb* 1 *see also* shout, scream, screech; roup, yowt; (*shrilly*) scronach NE. 2 *see also* weep, sob, snivel, whine, whimper; greet, walloch NE; (*loudly*) roar an greet. 3 (*of a bird or animal: see also* call, howl) yowt; (*of a bird, insect*) yirm; (*of a bird*) pew; (*shrilly*) skraich, pleep; claik NE; (*feebly*) peek; (*harshly*) craik.

noun 1 *see also* shout, scream, screech; yowt; (*shrill*) scronach NE, claik NE; (*sharp*) wheep; (*wailing*) pewl. 2 *see also* sob, whine, whimper; greet: 'hae a guid greet'. 3 (*of a bird: see also* call) (*shrill*) skraich, peek; (*esp of curlew*) wheeple.

cry-baby greetin Teenie.

about to cry great-hertit.

apt to cry greetie.

bout of crying greetin match.

crystal kirstal.

as clear as crystal as plain as parritch.

cuckoo gowk, gowkoo.

cuckoo-flower spink.

cuckoo-spit gowk-spit(tle), cuckoo's spittens, puddock spit(tle).

cud cood, cweed NE, quid NE.

cuddle *verb* knuse, oxter (at); (*amorously*) smoorich, soss NE.

noun smoorich, Scotch gravat, bosie.

cuddle in coorie in.

cudgel *noun, see also* stick[1]; rung.

verb, see also beat; loonder, rung, timmer.

cudgelling *see also* beating; kibblin.

cuff[1] (*of a shirt*) han(d)-ban(d).

cuff[2] *see also* slap: *noun* fung, cluff S, ringer.

verb fung NE, ring, souse, cloor.

cultivate (*land*) *see* till.

cultivated (*of land*) biggit.

culvert cundie.

cumbersome *see* heavy.

cunning *adjective, see also* crafty, sly; sleekit, sleek(ie), soople, quirkie.

noun sneck-drawin, slicht.

cup *noun* tass(ie) *literary*; (*esp of wood*) bicker, cap; (*shallow, two-handled, often used as a trophy*) quaich.

cupboard aumrie; (*esp in wall*) press, bole.

cupboard love cat kindness.

cur tike, messan CENTRAL.

curb *verb, see also* restrain, hamper; crub, tak in aboot SHETLAND, NE, pit the haims on, stent, brank, pit the branks on.

noun crub.

curd: curds cruds, yirned milk; (*made from buttermilk*) kirn milk; (*crushed for cheese-making*) gurth.

curdle lapper, yirn; (*of milk*) rin SHETLAND, ORKNEY.

curdled cruddie; (*of milk in churn*) broken.

cure *verb* 1 *see also* heal; cuir, keer NE, mend. 2 (*meat, butter etc*) poother; (*fish, ham etc, by drying or smoking*) reest; (*fish etc, by drying*) rizzer.

noun cuir, keer NE.

shed for curing salmon corfhouse.

curio ferlie.

curious 1 *see also* inquisitive; kwerious NE. 2 *see* odd, strange.

curiosity 1 keeriositie NE. 2 (*marvel*) ferlie.

curl *noun* (*eg of hair*) pirl S, link SHETLAND, swirl.

verb (*eg of hair*) pirl, runkle, wimple.

curler (*first player on each side*) lead.

team of curlers core; (*forming a side of four*) rink.

curly (*esp of hair*) swirlie, pirlie S.

curling (*the game*) the roarin gemm.

curling game (*one of a series in a*

match) rink; (*played by individual as opposed to team*) point game; (*part of, from one end of rink to the other*) en(d).

curling match bonspiel, spiel.

curling rink rack.

curling stone channel stane, ice-stane; (*stone nearest tee*) shot; **undersurface of a curling stone** sole.

curling team *see* **team of curlers** *above*.

play at curling curl, quoit SW, cute W, channel.

curlew whaup, whitterick.

cry of the curlew wheeple.

currant *see also* **blackcurrant, red-currant, white currant, flowering currant**; curran, curn S.

with currants curnie S: '*curnie dumplin*'.

current *see also* **eddy**; (*strong, in sea*) rug; (*of air*) guff.

currency siller: '*Whit kinna siller dae they yaise in France?*'

curry favour sook in, sook up, haud in, smool, sleek.

curse *verb* ban, jeedge NE, voo ORKNEY, NE.

noun butchach: '*she put a butchach on him*'.

a curse upon . . . wae worth . . .

cursory: cursory glance (*quick*) swatch.

curt nippit, snottie, cuttit NE.

curtail jimp, snib.

curtains hingers.

curtsy *verb* beck, jouk.

noun beck, jouk.

show respect by a curtsy mak (yer) obedience.

curve *see also* **bend**: *verb* boo.

noun boo; (*of a street etc*) bow(e): '*Netherbow*'.

curvature of the spine humph.

cushion *noun* cushin, cod.

custard: custard powder custard pooder.

custody: take into custody lift, tak in.

custom 1 *see also* **habit**; haunt, cant NE; (*old*) has-been. **2** (*patronage*) cheenge NE.

customer merchant NE.

the last of an old custom the en(d) o an auld sang.

cut *verb, see also* **slice, chop, slash, reap, wound**[2]; coll; (*whittle with a knife*) white, fite NE; (*cut with a knife or hook*) scutch; (*cut short or off*) snib; (*very short*) rump; (*roughly*) hagger NE, risp; (*unevenly*) haggle; (*hair etc*) cowe, coll; (*peats*) cast, (*from above the bank*) tusk N; (*cloth to a pattern*) shape; (*a groove in stone etc or into the coal-face*) raggle; (*a mussel or limpet from its shell*) sheel.

past tense, past participle cuttit.

noun **1** sned, whack; (*slight*) sneck; (*uneven*) haggle; (*deep, jagged*) hagger NE. **2** (*act of cutting*) sneck, scutch SW. **3** (*of meat: see also* **beef**) tailyie; (*for roasting*) roast; (*from below the breast*) nine holes. **4** (*share of profit*) rug NE.

cutting *noun* (*from a plant, with piece of root attached*) Irishman's cuttin.

cutting remark sneck, stang.

a cut above the ordinary a hack(ie) abeen the common SHETLAND, NE.

cut down (*trees*) hag.

cut the hair of poll.

cut into sneck.

cut off nick, sneg, sneck, sned, snib.

cut off tops of (*turnips etc*) sned, shaw.

cut short *adjective* snibbit NE.

cut up *see* **chop**.

cuttlefish ink-fish, hose-fish, hosack NE.

cylinder ceelinder.

D

dab[1] (*fish*) sand-dab, sautie.

dab[2] *noun* (*light touch*) daub, pap.
verb (*touch lightly*) daub, pap.

dabble 1 (*in liquid*) plowter, plyter NE, skiddle, plype NE; (*in something messy*) slaister, slitter, slatch. **2** (*see also* **potter, waste time**) dauble NE, pingle SE.

dad *see also* **father**; dadie, dey, paw CENTRAL.

daddy-long-legs jennie-lang-legs, jennie spinner, spinner, spinnin jennie, spin(nin) maggie, speeder jennie.

daddy-long-legs grub torie NE, story SHETLAND, ORKNEY, CAITHNESS.

daffodil (yella) lily, glen AYRSHIRE, (*pheasant's eye*) white lily, fite lily NE.

daft *see* **foolish, silly**.

dagger beetyach, bittock; (*short, worn as part of Highland dress: in belt*) dirk, durk; (*in stocking*) sgian dubh.

dainty dentie, conceitie; (*of persons*) jimp, gentie; (*esp of women*) dink.

dainties *see also* **titbits**; daintess, fine pieces, fancy breid.

dairy milk-hoose.

dairymaid dey N.

dairyman *see* **cattleman**.

daisy gowan.

ox-eye daisy horse gowan, (*large*) white gowan.

covered with daisies gowanie.

dale *see* **valley**.

dally with *see also* **flirt**; tig wi, mird wi, haad a heyze wi NE.

dam[1] *noun* (*weir*) caul(d); (*dam of stones in a river*) stem.
verb dem NE.

dam[2] (*animal mother*) †minnie.

damage *verb, see also* **injure, spoil**; da(i)mish, skaith, disabuse, ratch, connach.
noun skaith, disabuse; (*to clothes etc*) tash.

damaged fruit chippit fruit.

damages (*compensation*) skaith, mends.

dame *see also* **lady**; deem NE.

damn *verb* (*in oaths*) dang, daver, confooter NE, weary fa(w).
noun dang.

damned dazent NE.

damn-all deil a haet, fient a haet.

not give a damn no gie a whustle, no care a docken.

damp *adjective, see also* **clammy, close**[1] 3; dunk(ie), clam; (*of weather*) saft, drowie, roukie, weetie SHETLAND, NE; (*and raw*) oorlich N; (*of corn sheaves*) raw; (*of meal*) thane.
noun (*mouldy*) dunk.

damp down (*a fire*) smoor, reest.

damsel damishell NE.

damson ploom damas.

dance *verb* birl, shak a fit, fit the flair, shak yer hochs; (*in a lively way*) lowp, heyze NE; (*lightly*) link NE; (*with a jigging movement*) diddle.
noun bob; (*Scottish country dance: lively*) reel, (*slower*) strathspey; (*first dance at a wedding*) shamit reel; (*dance by men only*) bull-reel NE; (*esp a Scottish dance*) fling.

dancing (*eg at a dance-hall*) jiggin: '*We're gaun tae the jiggin*'.

dancing master dancie.

dance tune spring, sprig.

take (*a lady*) **up to dance** lift.

dandelion dainty-lion, pee-the-bed, pish-the-bed, horse gowan, what o'clock is it?

daze

dandle (*a child*) diddle, daidle, doodle, showd NE.

dandruff scruif, luce SHETLAND.

danger: dangerous uncannie, unchancie, nae mows NE; (*insecure*) crankie.

involving danger sair.

free from danger sicker.

dangle wallop, wammle, wingle SHETLAND.

dapper *see also* **neat**; trig, feat.

small dapper person bodsie NE.

dappled *see* **brindled**.

dare *verb* daur; (*mainly negative*) dow: '*I downa dae it*'; (*past used as present*) durst: '*he durstna*'; (*challenge to do something*) hen.

noun hen.

daring *noun* daur.

adjective, see also **bold**; derf, gallus.

don't you dare . . .! daur (ye). . .!

dark *adjective, see also* **black**; daurk, derk; (*very*) pick; (*sombre*) mirkie; (*gloomy*) mirksome, douth S; (*black*) glog *literary*; (*having dark skin*) din, black-avised; (*having dark hair and eyes*) dark-avised.

dark(ness) mirk(ness).

grow dark gloam, mirken SHETLAND.

make dark dit.

sit in the dark sit lik craws i the mist.

darling *noun* dautie, hinnie, doo, poutie, posie.

darn *verb* dern, ranter.

darning needle stockin needle.

dart *noun* dert, dairt; (*in game*) arra(e); (*weapon*) prog SHETLAND, ORKNEY, CAITHNESS, stug.

verb dert, dairt, skite, glent, skoosh; (*esp of persons*) spoot, jouk, skilt S; (*esp from side to side*) jink; (*in and out of sight*) cook.

darts (*game*) arra(e)s.

dash *verb* 1 (*of liquid: see also* **splash**) jaw, jaup, skelp, swash SHETLAND, ORKNEY, spairge. 2 (*with violence*) ding, dad, wap, swash, toosht. 3 (*hurtle*) hurl.

noun 1 (*of liquid*) sloosh, jaw, jaup, swash, slash, plype NE, jirble. 2 (*with violence*) swinge.

dashing *see* **bold**.

dash about skelp, fleg SW.

date *noun* (*meeting*) tryst.

daub *noun, see also* **smear, smudge**; sclatch, slaik, skaik NE, smyagger CAITHNESS.

verb, see **smear, smudge**.

daughter dochter, lass(ie), lass(ie) bairn, lass(ie) wean, quine NE; (*eldest of a landowner or farmer*) maiden NE.

daughter-in-law guid-dochter.

daunt *see* **frighten**.

dawdle *verb, see also* **potter, waste time, loiter, delay**; daidle, diddle, diddle-daddle NE, dachle NE, scutter NE, set aff, taigle.

dawdler jotter.

dawn *noun* (day-)daw, gray (o the mornin), gray (day)licht, skreich o day, streek o day, (the) morn i e mornin SW.

verb daw, gray, daaken CAITHNESS.

dawn on you come tae yer thoum NE.

day (*sunny in midst of bad weather*) pet (day); (*bitterly cold or depressing*) blue day.

daybreak *see* **dawn**.

daydream dwam, sloom.

daydreaming *adjective* nae in, in a dwam.

day labourer darger.

day labourer's wage day tale.

daylight daylicht, sky; **broad daylight** fair daylicht; **first glimmer of daylight** mornin blink SHETLAND.

day's work (day's) darg.

on alternate days day an day aboot.

during the day throu the day.

in those days than-a-days NE, aan NE: '*fit did e dee aan?*'

daze *verb, see also* **confuse, stupefy, dumbfound**; donner, stoun(d), daiver.

noun, see **daydream**.

dazed dammisht, bumbazit, dozent, doitrified, doilt, modderit.

dazed-looking wull-lik(e) NE.

dazzle *verb* daizzle; (*with wonder etc*) glamour.

dazzling *see* **showy**.

dead *adjective, see also* **lifeless**; deid, gane awa, won awa, pottit heid *humorous*.

deadly deidlie.

deadly nightshade Jacob's ladder.

dead man (*one doomed to die*) gone corbie.

dead of night, dead of winter howe-dumb-deid *literary*.

deaf deef, dull (o hearin), corn beef *humorous*.

deafen deefen; (*esp with noise*) deave, domineer.

deaf person deefie.

deal[1] (*wood*) dale.

deal[2] *noun* dale, troke.

verb **1** *see also* **trade, have dealings with** *below*; dale, traffeck. **2** (*a blow etc*) *see* **deliver**.

dealer dailer, cowper, troker.

dealings traffeck, uptak; (*sometimes undesirable*) troke.

have dealings with mird wi NE, mell wi, parry wi, (*often undesirable*) troke wi; **deal with** pit throu han(d)s, tak an order o.

a great deal *see also* **many**; a gey wheen.

dear *adjective* **1** (*beloved*) †lief *in poetry*. **2** (*expensive*) saut.

noun, see also **darling**: **my dear** my jo *in poetry*; (*to a child*) matsill NE.

dear me! lovanentie!, sakes me!

dearth scant.

death daith, deid, affgaun, hame-gaun, hinneren(d); (*natural*) fair strae death; (*miserable*) ill en(d).

death agony *see* **death throe(s)**.

death rattle hurl, (deid-)ruckle.

death throe(s) deid thraw(s), patient(s) o deid, thratch.

death-watch beetle chackie mill.

cause of (someone's) death deid.

your death of cold mort caul(d), morth o caul(d).

be at the point of death be at ane mae wi't S.

removed by death wede awa *literary*.

sign foretelling death (*will-o'-the-wisp*) daith cannle, lichtie NE; (*shape on candle*) spail; (*sensation of deafness*) deid bell; (*drip on the floor*) deid-drap; (*strange light*) deid-licht(s) NE; (*unexplained knocking*) deid-rap; (*image of a person*) foregang SHETLAND, N.

debate *verb* (*in a court of law*) plead.

noun (*argumentative*) flyte.

debauch *verb* debosh, fyle.

noun guzzle.

debauched-looking blearit.

debilitate *see* **weaken**.

debonair *see* **good-looking, well-mannered**.

debris redd.

debt (*law: owed by the estate of a deceased person, taking precedence over other debts*) privileged debt.

debtor †Abbey laird.

fall into debt rin ahin(t).

in debt to wi.

debut *see* **beginning**.

decamp *see* **run away**.

decant *see also* **pour**; skink.

decanter cruet NE; (*of standard measure, with lid like a hen's tuft*) tappit hen.

decapitate *see* **behead**.

decay *verb, see also* **wither, moulder** (*under* **mould**[2]), mouldy (*under* **mould**[1]); moze SHETLAND, ORKNEY, CAITHNESS; (*slowly*) moot.

decayed *see also* **mouldy** (*under* **mould**[1]); mozie.

decease *noun, see* **death**.

verb, see **die**.

deceased *adjective* umquhile *law or literary*.

the deceased the corp.

deceit *see also* **trickery, deception**; deceiverie, cheatrie, joukeriepawk(e)rie, swickerie NE.

deceitful sleekit, sleek(ie), slidderie, fair-faced, twa-faul(d) NE.

deceitful person *see also* **cheat,**

swindler; sneck-drawer.

act deceitfully gae the back gate, play Jock needle Jock preen NE.

deceive swick, jouk, mislippen, blear (someone's) ee, begeck, begunk, blaf(l)um, blink.

deceiver *see* **cheat, swindler.**

decent *see also* **respectable, decorous**; dacent, weel-faured, honest-lik(e), wicelik(e).

decency honesty.

deception *see also* **deceit, trickery**; intak, swick, sook NE.

decision deceesion; (*of a court of law in a bankruptcy case; of a church court in a committee report etc*) deliverance.

deck *verb, see also* **adorn, decorate**; busk, (be)dink, daiker.

declaim scrift (aff).

declare (*on oath*) depone.

decline *verb* **1** (*in health: see also* **waste away**) dwine, fa(w) awa, traik, torfle S; (*of things*) tyne. **2** *see* **refuse**[1].
noun (*in health*) dwine; (*esp from TB*) decay.

declivity *see also* **slope, hollow**; doon-fa(w), sidelins.

decompose (*of food*) *see* **go off** (*under* **go**).

decorate *see also* **deck, adorn, trim**; decore, daiker; (*esp flags at common ridings*) busk.

decoration *see also* **ornament**; decorement; (*trimmings*) muntin.

decorous *see also* **respectable, decent**; douce, mensefu, richt.

decorum mense, honesty.

decrease: stitches decreased (*knitting*) intaks.

decree *noun* (*law*) *see* **court order**.
verb (*law*) decern, †decreet.

decrepit decrippit NE.

decry *see* **blame, call** (**someone**) **names** (*under* **call**).

dedicate *see also* **inaugurate: dedicate yourself to** stick in wi.

deduce jalouse.

deduction (*of wages*) afftak.

deed *see* **act**.

deep (*innermost, also of sound*) howe.

deep (in) ower the hurdies (in): '*ower the hurdies in debt*'.

deep-set howe.

deep-rooted yirdfast.

deer *see* **roe**[1].

deergrass deer('s) hair, ling.

deface *see also* **damage, spoil**; hash, bla(u)d, mank, tash.

defame *see also* **slander**; bla(u)d, sclave NE, bleck, placad.

defeat *verb, see also* **beat, overcome**; defait, lamp, warsle, win N, whang, pit doon, baist NE.

defeated defait, defeat, bate.

admit defeat spit an gie (it) ower.

defecate drite, drate N, shite, keech, kich NE, loit, cack(ie), fyle, dirt (on) NE, skit SHETLAND; (*of animals*) purl.

defect *noun, see also* **flaw, fault**; defeck, defection, gaw SHETLAND; (*esp weaving*) felter FIFE; (*eg in a fishing line or net*) want.

mentally defective wantin, daft, fuil, feel NE.

be mentally defective want tippence o the shillin, hae a want, be a feel NE.

defence 1 fend. **2** (*law*) exception.

defend *see also* **protect**; fend, weir; **defend yourself** haud aff (o) yersel NE; (*esp in a fight*) keep aff o yersel.

defendant (*law, in a civil case*) defender; (*in a criminal case*) accused, panel.

defer pit ower, refer, supersede *law*.

deferential *see* **submissive, flattering**.

defiance: defiant *see also* **bold, impudent**; forritsome, facie.

in defiance of someone in spite o someone's teeth *or* neck.

act in defiance of maugre NE.

deficient scrimp(it), skybal(d) NE.

deficiency shortcome, ingang; (*esp in wits*) scrimpness, want, wint NE.

be deficient want.

deficit daifeecit.

defile

defile[1] *noun, see also* **ravine, pass;** hause.

defile[2] *verb, see also* **soil, dirty;** fyle, befyle.

definition defineetion.

deflated little-boukit NE.

deflect weir (aff).

deform: deformed *see also* **stunted, distorted;** palie, wrang NE, camsha(u)chelt, misgrown SHETLAND; (*esp of a limb*) tuckie NE.

deformed person knurl, shaird, wirl.

defraud *see also* **cheat, deceive;** snipe NE, slope.

deft *see also* **skilful;** knackie, gleg, weelhandit, slee.

defy thraw (wi).

degrade *see* **humiliate.**

degradation *see* **humiliation.**

dejected *see also* **downcast;** disjeckit, disjaskit, hingin-luggit, hingin-mou'd NE, dowie, hertless, oorit, drum, humdrum.

delay *verb, see also* **dawdle;** dring, taigle, hing, set aff, latch NE, hick; (*a person*) hing on NE.

noun aff-pit, hing-on; (*law: in pressing a claim*) mora.

cause of delay hinder, affset.

causing delay taiglesome.

without delay in a couple o hurries.

delectable *see* **delightful.**

deliberate *adjective* deleebrit, cannie.

verb take to avizandum.

delicate 1 (*in health: see also* **sickly**) dowie, peelie-wallie CENTRAL, peelie-wersh, palie, shilpit, tender, brashie, dortie NE, dorbie NE, nesh. **2** (*difficult, awkward*) kittle, tickly NE.

delicacies *see also* **titbits;** sunkets, fineries SHETLAND.

delicious deleecious.

delight *verb, noun* delicht.

delighted suitit, hert-gled; (*with yourself*) knichtit NE.

delightful loosome, lichtsome.

delinquent *see* **evildoer.**

delirious *see also* **wandering;** deleerit, raivelt, cairried, ree.

be delirious *see* **rave.**

delirium raverie.

deliver (*a blow etc*) len, reak, betak NE, win S.

delivery (*law*) tradition *rare.*

dell *see* **valley, hollow.**

delude *see* **deceive.**

deluded *see* **mistaken.**

deluge *noun, see* **downpour.**

verb, see **pour.**

delusion phrase NE.

demand *verb* (*as a right*) protest.

noun (*persistent*) rane.

make demands on pit at.

demean demain, even; **demean yourself** below yersel.

demeanour cast.

demented *see* **mad, crazy.**

demolish wrack, disannul, ca(w) doon.

demolition demoleetion.

demon wirricow; (*living in water*) kelpie, water horse.

demonstrate *see also* **expound;** kythe.

demoralize bemean.

demure mim (as a Mey puddock), primsie SHETLAND, ORKNEY.

den (*of animal*) *see* **lair.**

denial *see* **deny.**

denote (*mean*) bear.

denounce misca(w), wyte; (*publicly and violently*) sherrack w.

dense 1 (*closely-packed*) thrang; (*of growth*) ruch; (*of mist etc*) blin(d) NE. **2** *see* **stupid.**

dent *noun* dunt NE, dinge, dunkle; (*esp in metal*) cloor.

verb cloor, dunt NE, dinge, dunkle.

dentures seam o teeth.

denude tirl, tirr.

deny na-say.

I won't deny that I winna say but whit.

denial na-say.

depart *see also* **leave**[2]; depairt, tak the gate, ha(u)d awa, steer, leg aff, munt, flit.

departing *adjective* (*esp of a tenant farmer*) wa-gaun, wa-gangin.

departure wa-gaun, wa-gang NE, oot-settin, ootgang.

depend: depend on lippen.

dependable *see also* **reliable**; sicker, stench NE, stieve.

deportment *see* **demeanour**.

deposit *verb* pose N.

noun (*at the bottom of a boat*) growthe.

depraved ill.

deprecate lichtlie.

depredation spulyie, †reif, †herriment, †herschip.

depress: depressed disjaskit, doon o mou(th), wersh, dreich, alagrugous, mump, douth, looch.

depressing *see* **dismal, dreary**.

depression 1 (*see also* **hollow**) howe. **2** (*state of*) glooms, stoun(d) ORKNEY, N, howes: '*be i the howes*'.

deprive (*a person of something*) twin(e); (*of everything*) roop.

be deprived of tyne NE.

depth 1 (*of a furrow*) yird: '*gie the ploo mair yird*'. **2** (*of winter etc: see also* **midwinter**) howe-dumb-deid *literary*.

deputy depute *often after its noun*: '*principal depute*'.

deranged *see also* **insane, mad, crazy**; gyte, wrang NE, superannuate.

deride *see* **mock**.

descend gang doon.

descent (*by birth*) original NE, strin(d), etion *contemptuous*, NE; (*in maternal line*) mither side.

desecrate fyle.

desert *verb, see also* **abandon, leave**[2]; gie ower, forleet.

deserter fugie.

deserts: get your just deserts get yer fairins, get yer whacks.

deserve fa(w) SHETLAND; (*punishment etc*) wirk for.

well-deserved weel-wared.

be just what someone deserves be the price o someone.

design *verb, see* **plan**.

designing *see* **crafty**.

desire *verb, see also* **long (for)**; hae an ee till, wiss, seek (tae), bode NE; (*very much*) ettle efter.

noun ettle, will, crave NE; (*slight*) inklin SHETLAND, ORKNEY, N.

desirous yivverie; (*extremely*) mad (for).

mad with desire gyte.

desk dask.

desolate (*of a place: see also* **dreary**) gowstie, wull NE, wilsome N.

despair *noun* wanhowp.

despatch *see* **send**.

despicable *see* **contemptible, worthless**.

despise *see* **disparage**.

not to be despised nae din-bonnets NE.

despite *see* **in spite of** (*under* **spite**).

despoil *see* **plunder**.

despondent *see* **dejected**.

despot *see* **tyrant**.

dessert (*of whipped cream, sugar, nuts etc*) Edinburgh fog; (*of whipped cream, toasted oatmeal, soft fruit etc*) crannachan, cream crowdie; (*of whipped cream, marmalade, brandy etc*) Caledonian cream; (*of thickened milk and sugar*) Corstorphine cream; (*kind of steamed custard*) Scotch flummery.

destine ordeen, weird.

destiny weird: '*dree yer weird*'.

destitute boss, as peer's the links o the cruik NE.

destitution *see* **poverty**.

destroy *see also* **wreck**; hash, malafooster, mak mice feet o; (*esp a person*) perish.

destroyed *see* **ruined**.

destruction *see also* **wreck, smithereens**; ruinage SHETLAND, NE.

destructive sair: '*she's sair on her claes*'.

detach lowse, twine SHETLAND.

detail *noun* particularity SHETLAND, NE; **details** eeriorums NE, knittins NE. *verb* condescend (up)on.

obsessed by details pernicketie.

detain deteen; (*needlessly*) scutter NE.

detect airt oot SE.
 detective snoot.
detention: pupil in detention after school keepie-in.
deter *see* hinder.
deteriorate gae back; (*in health, fortune*) gae doon the brae, fail.
determined *see also* stubborn; dour, conterm(i)t, positive.
detest *see also* hate; laith, ug.
 detestation scunner, ug NE.
 detestable *see also* repulsive, horrible; laithsome, scunnersome, ugsome, pooshionous SHETLAND, N.
detriment *see* harm.
 detrimental *see* harmful.
devastate *see* plunder.
develop *see* grow.
 development oncome SHETLAND, NE.
deviate twine SHETLAND.
 deviate from the truth slide NE.
device *see* contraption.
devil *see also* fiend; deil, divvil, deevil, the bad man, Auld Nick, Auld Cloots, Auld Hornie, Auld Suitie, Sawtan, the enemy; (*small*) deevilock NE.
 devilish deevilish, divvilish.
 devilry deviltrie.
 devil-may-care *see also* heedless; ramstam, throu-the-muir NE.
 devil take you deil mane ye, sorra fa(w) ye.
 gone to the devil gane tae potterlowe NE.
devious *see also* crafty; scruple.
devise think on NE.
devoid of *see* empty.
devote *see* affectionate.
 devoted to (*a person*) built up on, browdent on.
devour devoor, gaup, gilravage, oof, worry NE; (*use wastefully*) connach NE, rive intil.
devout gracie; (*very*) far ben.
dew deow NE, weet.
dexterous *see* deft, skilful.
diabolical *see* devilish.

dialect: intonation of a particular dialect tune.
dialogue twa-handit crack.
diarrhoea skitter, skit, backdoor trot(s), the thin NE, bloit SW; (*esp in birds or animals*) scoot; (*in cattle*) soft darn.
 have diarrhoea skite, skitter, rin thin.
dibble *verb, noun* dimple NE.
dictate to come the peter ower.
dictionary dictionar.
did not didna, didnae.
die *verb* dee, weir awa, gae hame, cowp the creels, gae awa, get awa, souch awa, crock *slang*; (*peacefully*) slip awa; (*esp after great suffering*) win awa.
 die down (*of wind etc*) lowden, lown, quall NE, lough NE.
 die in harness dee i the harrows NE.
 die of dee wi.
 fated to die fey.
 be dying be a(w) by wi't, be deen wi't N.
diet mait.
differ *see* disagree.
 difference in odds on, odds in.
 different unalik(e).
difficult defeeckwalt, crank; (*tricky*) fickle, kittle, tickly NE; (*troublesome*) ill; (*of tasks*) nae handie, fykie, dreich NE; (*of a road*) stieve SHETLAND.
 difficulty *see also* problem, predicament, obstacle; diffeecultie, defeeckwaltie, hechle SE; difficulties adaes.
 in difficulties raivelt, ill-hauden, in a haud, in the bowfarts NE.
 run into difficulties fin frost N.
 having difficulty (in) ill: '*ill at gyaun*'.
 involving difficulty sair, ill.
 do something with difficulty jauchle throu, wa(u)chle throu.
 difficult to please ill tae dae till *or* wi.
diffident blate.
diffuse *verb, see* spread, scatter.
dig *see also* dug; *verb* howk, hole, sheuch, dell SHETLAND, ORKNEY, N;

(*carelessly*) powk NE; (*a ditch*) cast; (*peats*) *see* **cut**.

noun (*act of digging*) howk.

digger (*person who digs*) howker.

dig up (*eg potatoes*) howk, lift, hole NE.

digest *verb* digeest, disgeest.

digestion digeestion, digeester.

let food digest swage ORKNEY, N.

dignify (*elevate*) heeze.

dignified (*in bearing*) pretty; (*and haughty*) high-bendit.

dignity mense S.

with dignity heid-heich.

dike *see* **dyke**.

dilapidated disjaskit; (*very*) at the ower-faain NE.

dilapidated structure rickle.

dilatory aff-pittin, hint-han(d), dreich, slow as a wee lassie.

be dilatory *see* **delay, dawdle**.

dilemma *see* **predicament, indecision**.

put in a dilemma lant SHETLAND.

diligent eydent.

dilly-dally *see also* **dawdle, delay, shilly-shally**; niffnaff, gamfle.

dilute (*esp spirits*) mak doon, tak doon.

dim *adjective, see* **stupid**.

verb dit.

diminish *see* **shrink** 1.

din *see also* **noise, uproar**; reemis(h) NE, bellum, wap.

dine denner.

dingy (*of colour*) din, pooshiont.

dinner denner, dine, kail.

dinner-bell kail-bell.

dinner-time dine, kail time.

dip *verb* dook.

noun **1** (*in water*) dook. **2** (*in the ground*: *see also* **hollow**) sneck.

dipper (*bird*) essock NE, burnbecker SW, water craw, water meggie, water pyot, water blackbird.

dire *see* **awful**.

direct *adjective* direck: **1 most direct** soonest, seenest NE. **2** (*in manner*: *see also* **frank**) plat (an plain).

verb direck, (*guide*) airt, wice, witter; (*eg a blow*) ettle.

adverb, see **directly**.

direction (*way*) airt, road, han(d), gate, side: '*he's fae Ayrside*'.

in the direction of the wey O, -wan: '*east-wan*'.

in that general direction there awa.

in a contrary direction (*to the sun*) withershins, widdershins.

in various directions athort, aa wye NE.

directly direck, therecklie SW, S: **1** (*straight*) fair, plat. **2** (*at once*) tite.

directly after *adverb* syne.

director *see* **manager, boss**.

dirge †dirgie, coronach; (*mournful noise*) mane.

dirt *see also* **filth, excrement, mud**; cla(i)rt, keech, goor SHETLAND, ORKNEY, N; (*wet, dirty state*) slaister.

dirtied *see* **soiled**.

dirty *adjective, see also* **filthy, soiled, muddy, messy, slovenly, slimy**; cla(i)rtie, mirkie; (*unwashed*) foul; (*grimy*) brookie NE; (*dirty and wet*) slaisterie, cloiterie; (*greasy*) creeshie; (*slimy*) slochie; (*of persons*) haskie, rachlie; (*see also* **slovenly**) trooshlach NE, oozlie SW, ropach HIGHLAND.

verb (*make dirty: see also* **soil, muddy**) cla(i)rt, mairtyr; (*esp clothes*) drabble, slaister, slaiger; (*clothes*) scuddle; (*blacken*) bleck, coom, brook NE.

disable *see also* **injure**.

disabled (*of a limb*) tuckie NE.

disabling (*of pain*) commandin.

disadvantage *see* **hindrance**.

disagree (*quarrel*) cast oot, differ, skew NE.

disagreeable *see also* **unpleasant, nasty, dirty, horrible**; coorse NE, clattie; (*of persons*) menseless, ill-farran(t), pooshionable, (*of weather*) thrawn NE.

disagreement disagreeance; (*see also* **quarrel**) ploy, ootcast, pilget NE, plea.

disappear mizzle; (*gradually*) ely S; (*suddenly*) cook; (*esp mysteriously*) saunt; (*very quickly*) disappear lik snaw aff a dyke.

disappoint disappint, begeck, gunk ULSTER, gie (someone) the gunk; (*greatly*) stammygaster.

disappointed *see also* **dejected**; disappintit.

disappointment disappintment, dunt, drap, begeck N, chaw, set NE, gunk: '*dae a gunk on someone*'; (*great*) sair hert; (*sudden, great*) stammygaster; (*bitter*) het hert; (*source of disappointment*) hert-scaud.

disarrange *see also* **disorder, rumple**; malagrooze NE, fuffle.

disarranged camsha(u)chelt, oot o (the) reel NE, guddelt.

disarray *see* **disorder**.

in disarray throuither, throwder NE.

disaster *see also* **misfortune**; mishanter, stramash.

disastrous: (follow) a disastrous course (gang) a gray gate.

disband *see* **disperse**.

disbelieve misbelieve, misdoot.

discard jeck w, S, sha(u)chle aff.

discern tartle.

discerning *see* **shrewd**.

discharge *verb, see also* **unload**; dischairge; (*a gun*) tuim; (*smoke etc with a small explosion*) pluff.

noun dischairge; (*of a debt*) quittance.

discipline *noun* discipleen; (*very strict*) norter NE.

verb discipleen, keep in aboot, tak in aboot SHETLAND, NE, get the branks on; (*very strictly*) targe, norter NE.

discolour *see also* **stain**; thraw, tash, smad SHETLAND, NE.

discoloured ill-colourit.

disconcert pit aboot.

disconcerted taen(-lik(e)).

disconsolate *see also* **sorrowful**; dowie, sairie, waesome, disjaskit.

discontented worm-eaten, drum; (*noisily*) clamersome NE.

discord *see also* **strife**; plea NE.

discourage ding, daunton.

discouraged hertless.

discouraging hertless.

discourse *noun* discoorse; (*piece of writing*) screed, scrieve, libel.

discourteous *see* **ill-mannered**.

discover *see* **find**.

discredit *verb* hoot, tash, cry doon.

noun tash.

discreet mensefu, cannie.

discretion mense.

discuss (*at length, in great detail*) summer an winter.

discussion (*debate: see also* **argument**) communin NE, twa words; (*talk*) collogue.

disdain *verb, see* **disparage, supercilious**.

disdainful sanshach NE, heelie(fu), heich, stinkin, pauchtie; (*esp of women*) skeich.

disdainfully heich.

act disdainfully sneist.

disease 1 *see also* **illness**; tribble. **2** (*of animals: see also* **sheep disease**; *feverish*) weed; (*of legs and feet*) cruban; (*of cattle, similar to glanders*) clyres; (*of horses: of gums and palate*) skules N.

disembowel (*deer*) gralloch.

disentangle redd, unfankle, unleeze.

disfavour *noun, see also* **dislike**; ill-will.

in disfavour ill-leukit-upon.

with disfavour ill.

disgrace *noun* (*slur*) tash.

disgraced shent.

disgraceful michtie, awfu.

disguise *verb, see also* **hide**[1]; guise.

disgust *verb* scunner, scomfish, ug, set NE, granich NE, skeichen NE; (*intensely*) gar (someone) grue; (*with too much food*) staw.

noun scunner, set NE, alagust NE, hertscaud, forlaithie NE, grue; (*for something edible*) skeichen NE.

disgusted scunnert, uggit NE.

be disgusted at tak a scunner at, tak an ug at NE, tak the grue at.

look disgusted leuk lik(e) Wattie tae the worm.

disgusting *see also* **loathsome, filthy**; scunnersome, scunnerfu, ugsome, uggin, laithfu, fousome, feechie.

disgusting person *or* **thing** scunner, ug NE.

disgustingly laithfu.

cause disgust in someone gie someone the (dry) boak.

exclamation of disgust ech!, gad!, feech!, peuch!; (*esp as a warning to a child*) keech!

object of disgust scunneration.

dish *noun* (*container: see also* **bowl** 1, **plate, crockery**) (*wooden, deep*) cap: '*brose cap*'; (*wooden, esp for milk*) cood; (*wooden, with handles*) luggie; (*oval serving*) ashet.

dishcloth dish-cloot, daily dud NE.

dish-rack *see* **plate-rack**.

dishearten disherten.

disheartened hertless.

dishevelled towtherie, untowtherlie NE, ill-shakken-up SHETLAND, ORKNEY, NE; (*esp of hair*) hudderie, tous(l)ie.

dishevelled person ticket.

dishonest unhonest, unricht, lowse.

be guilty of (minor) dishonesty pauchle.

dishonour *noun* tash.

verb tash.

dishonourable *see* **dishonest**.

dishonourable behaviour hunker-slidin.

disinclined *see also* **disobliging**; sweir(t).

disinclination *noun* sweirtie.

disintegrate *see also* **crumble**; gae (a(w)) tae staps, murl.

disintegrated oot o ither.

disjoint *see also* **dislocate**; lith.

dislike: take a dislike to tak (an) ill-will at, hae a pick at, tak an ug at NE; (*strong*) tak a scunner at, tak a scomfish at.

dislocate *see also* **sprain**; ca(w) oot, shammle, rack, lith, jeck, yerk; (*the neck*) set.

dislocation (*of a joint etc*) rack; (*in a stratum in a mine*) throw, step AYRSHIRE.

disloyal *see also* **deceitful, untrustworthy**; slidderie.

dismal *see also* **dreary**; dowie, dreich, black, unhertsome, hertless, wearifu, oorie NE, weirdlie.

dismay *see* **dishearten**.

look dismayed lat doon the lip.

dismiss 1 (*from a job*) *see* **sack**[1] 2. **2** (*a meeting etc*) skail.

dismissal (*from a job*) leave.

dismount (*from a horse*) lowp aff.

disobedient *see* **naughty**.

disobey misanswer.

disobliging ill-set, ill-willie, stickin.

disorder *noun, see also* **confusion, muddle**; carfuffle, tapsalteerie, towther, sotter, hatter, moger, rummle.

verb, see also **muddle**; carfuffle, raivel, taisle, towther, ball.

disordered, in disorder *see also* **confused, untidy, topsy-turvy, muddled**; throuither, throwder NE, tousie, burbelt SW, sotterie, guddelt.

disorderly throuither, throwder NE, huggerie(-muggerie); (*rough*) ramstougar.

disorganized *see also* **disordered**; in a pauchle.

disparage lichtlie, misca(w), bemean, nochtifie.

disparagement doon-tak, rebaghle.

disparity (between) odds (on *or* of).

dispatch *see* **send**.

dispel *see* **drive away**.

dispense with get by SHETLAND, NE.

disperse (*of a crowd*) skail; (*scatter*) sperfle *literary*; (*of cloud*) rive.

dispersal scatterment; (*of a crowd etc*) skail, upbrak SHETLAND.

dispirited *see also* **depressed, sad**; dowie, douth S, unhertie SHETLAND.

dispiriting *see also* **dismal**; wearie NE.

displace jee.

display *verb, see* **show**.

noun, see also **show**; ootset, set-oot; (*showy*) flumgummerie NE.

displease *see also* offend; miscomfit NE, misfit NE.

displeased *see* touchy.

displeasure displeesure.

dispose of pit by SW, ULSTER, get redd o; (*money, goods etc*) ware.

disposed *see also* well-disposed (*under* well²); set: '*weel set*'; '*ill-set*'.

disposed of by-han(d).

disposition *see also* mood; taik SHETLAND, NE.

of a certain disposition -farran(t): '*auld-farrant*'.

dispossess herrie oot.

disproof (*of a legal deed*) improbation.

dispute *see also* quarrel, wrangle: *verb* argie-bargie, cangle, cabal, thraw, threap, differ, strive SHETLAND, NE, tulyie, haggle-bargain; (*violently*) cattie-worrie NE.

noun argie-bargie, tift(er), tulyie, threap, cabal NE, twa words, haud; (*violent*) collieshangie, currie-wurrie, cattie-worrie NE, cabal NE.

be in dispute with be at heid an aix wi.

disquiet *see* anxiety.

disquieting oorie.

disrepute ill-name.

disreputable *see also* good-for-nothing, contemptible; thief(t)ie, coorse, waff(ie), orra, hingum-tringum NE, scoorie.

disrespect disrespeck.

disrupt (*a group*) skail.

dissatisfaction *see* displeasure.

dissatisfied miscontentit, no (awfie) taen (wi).

be always dissatisfied nae hae a please NE.

dissect disseck.

dissemble *see* cheat, deceive.

dissent *noun* differ.

verb differ.

dissension *see* dispute.

dissipate (*resources etc*) perish, misguide, ware.

dissipated *see* dissolute.

dissolute *see also* disreputable; ill-daein, lowse, randie, torn-doon; (*living in a dissolute way*) ruch-livin.

dissolve mouten NE.

distance (*length of way etc*) lenth: '*this lenth*', gate; (*short*) bittie, bittock, piece, catlowp; (*very short*) tae('s) lenth.

distant 1 *see also* at a distance *below*; far awa, yonder; most distant yonder-maist. 2 (*in manner*) *see* aloof. 3 (*in family relationship*) far oot, far aff, far awa.

distant relative Scotch cousin.

at a distance oot by, oot ower; at a great distance hyne awa, hyndies (awa) *child's word*, NE; at a very great distance at the back o the muin.

distaste scunner, (*specif for food*) skeichen NE.

distasteful *see* disgusting.

distend *see* swell.

distinct sindry.

as distinct from by('s).

distinguish: distinguished markit, guid.

distinguishing mark *see also* sheep-mark; kenspeckle.

distort *see also* make a face (*under* face); showl, bauchle, gashle NE, (*the face*) girn; (*esp a meaning etc*) thraw.

distorted thrawn, camsha(u)chelt, bogshaivelt, bauchelt.

become distorted showl, shile SW.

distortion thraw.

distract distrack.

distracted distrackit.

distraction fry.

distrain upon (*law*) poind, reest S.

distraught in a (dreedfu) wey, aff at the knot, dabbelt NE, hattert S.

distress *noun* 1 *see also* anxiety, sorrow; harm(s) SHETLAND. 2 (*law*) diligence.

verb pit aboot.

distressed made (wi) NE.

be distressed tak it ill oot, tak ill (wi).

distressing sad, sair.

in a state of distress in a (bad) wey, in a go.

distribute distreebute.

distributed distribute.

district destrick, kintra, boons NE, pairt, airt, -side: '*He's fae Ayrside*'.

distrust misdoot, mislippen.

disturb (*annoy*) fash, steer, sturt SHETLAND; (*startle*) start; **disturb yourself** mismak yersel.

disturbed (*of the mind*) ajee.

disturbance *see also* **uproar, commotion, trouble, fight**; rammie, stushie, stashie, strushie, stramash, hubble, hurry, gilravage, collieshangie, wap, ca(w)-throu, mineer NE, carrant NE.

create a disturbance stramash.

ditch *noun, see also* **trench, drain, gutter**; dutch NE, sheuch, gote, trink, rin, dreep CENTRAL, slunk; (*esp field, for drainage*) gruip; (*esp stone-lined*) syver; (*esp natural stream straightened for drainage*) stank; (*surface*) watter-rin.

make ditches, make a ditch in sheuch.

dither *verb, noun, see also* **hesitate, vacillate**; swither, fouter, daiker, ditter.

ditherer swither.

dithering whether-or-no, fouterie.

ditty sonnet.

divan bed sattle-bed.

dive *verb* dook.

diver (*bird: great northern*) Allanhawk, (*great northern or red-throated*) loom NE; (*red-throated*) rain-goose SHETLAND, ORKNEY, CAITHNESS.

diving board dale w.

diverge twin(e), sinder, sinner.

diverse sindry.

diversion (*entertainment*) divert.

divert *see* **amuse, entertain**.

diverting shortsome.

divide *see also* **separate**; twin(e), sinder, sinner; (*into parts*) pairt; (*into two or more parts*) half; (*divide equally*) halve(r).

badly divided ill-pairtit.

dividend deeviden(d); (*from a cooperative*) divvie.

divine *see* **heavenly**.

divination *see* **fortune-telling**.

division 1 (*part, not necessarily one of two equal*) half. **2** (*of land, under old crop-rotation system*) brak.

division sums gizinties.

divulge lat ken, lat licht NE, moot, leet SHETLAND, ORKNEY, N: '*nivver leet*'.

dizzy deezie, shakie-tremlie, licht, waumish.

dizziness deeziness, mirligoes.

do *see also* **did not, done**; dae, dee NE, (*usually emphatic or before a vowel*) div: '*div ye?*'

does dis; **does not** disna, disnae.

do not dinna, dinnae, divna.

do for (*slang*) *see* **kill**.

it won't do (*of a plan etc*) it winna pottie.

to do adae, adee NE: '*I'll hae naethin adae wi ye*'.

docile ill-less SHETLAND, NE, quate.

dock[1] (*plant*) docken; (*broad-leaved*) redshank.

dock[2] (*in court*) †panel.

doctor doacter.

doctrine lair.

document (*formal*) libel; (*legal*) writ, brief, law-paper; (*original*) principal; (*carrying its own evidence of validity*) probative document.

documentary proof evident.

addition to a document eik.

produce a document when challenged to do so in court satisfy production.

dodder *see also* **totter, hobble 1, stagger**; dotter, hochle.

dodge *verb, see also* **avoid**; jink, jouk, (*doing something*) scoff; (*school*) *see* **play truant** (*under* **truant**).

noun, see also **trick**; prottick NE, ginkum NE, fuppertie jig NE.

dodge in and out jouk.

doe †dae.

dog *noun* dug, dowg N, hund, bowf(er) NE, tike *contemptuous*, messan *contemptuous*, deugle *gipsy*; (*small, pet*) messan.

dogged *adjective, see also* **determined**; pludisome NE.

dogfight collieshangie NE, gurrie.

dogfish blin ee, sea dog.

dog-tired tike-tired, fair duin.

call to a dog *see* **call**.

go to the dogs gae tae pigs an whustles, gang tae potterlowe NE, gang tae potterneetion NE, gang tae crockaneetion NE.

doggerel crambo-clink, crambo-jingle.

dogma *see* **doctrine**.

dole: on the dole on the b(u)roo, on the box.

dole money b(u)roo money.

doleful *see also* **sad**; doolsome, dowie, dreich, weest NE, heavysome SW.

doll (*toy or girl*) dall(ie) NE.

dollop *see also* **lump**; slap, da(u)d.

dolphin dunter ORKNEY.

dolt *see also* **fool, idiot**; dult, gype.

doltish *see* **stupid, foolish**.

domestic hamelie, hameart, hamel.

domicile *see* **house**.

become domiciled heft S.

dominate maugre NE, owergang, maun SHETLAND; (*of a wife*) weir the breeks.

domineering ringin, magerfu NE.

domineering boss master *or* mistress an mair.

domineering woman scourge, drum major.

act in a domineering way towards come the peter ower *or* wi.

dominion *see* **control**.

dominoes: tap the table in a game of dominoes to indicate you cannot play chap: '*I'm chappin*'.

game of dominoes with penny forfeits penny chap.

donation *see* **gift**.

done *past participle of* **do** duin, deen N.

done for awa wi't, by wi't, puggelt, deen for NE.

be done for be a gone corbie.

done with past, by (wi('t)).

have done with pit ower, get (something) by wi.

donkey cuddie (ass), lang lugs *humorous*.

doom weird.

doomed (to die) fey.

doomsday deem's day NE.

door door-cheek; (*to a single dwelling, as opposed to a block of flats*) main door.

door-catch sneck, snib.

door-handle hannle.

door-key check.

door-knocker chapper; (*serrated metal, with ring which rattled*) †(tirlin) pin, †risp.

door-latch *see* **door-catch**.

doormat bass (mat).

door-post door-cheek, standart.

door-screen (*in an old cottage*) †hallan(d).

doorstep doorstane.

doorway door-cheek; **front doorway** entry.

front door foredoor.

dormer (window) storm windae.

dose (*of the cold*) *see* **cold**.

dot: on the dot on the minuteheid.

dote: dote on daut.

doting fond, daft (on, aboot *or* for), saft on.

in one's dotage *see also* **senile**; veeand S, dottelt.

be in your dotage dottle N.

dotard dotterel.

double *see also* **two-fold**; dooble.

double chin flytepock.

double-dealing *see* **deceit**.

bent double (*esp with age*) twafaul(d).

doubt *verb* doot, (*disbelieve, distrust*) misdoot, misbelieve, mislippen; (*be in doubt*) swither.

noun doot, misdoot; **state of doubt** swither.

doubtful *see also* **dubious**; dootsome.

without doubt nae mistak but.

dough daich.

doughy daichie.

doughty *see also* **courageous, bold**; douchtie.

douse slock.

dove *see also* **pigeon**; doo.

dovecot doocot.
Dover sole *see* **sole**^{2}.
dowdy *see* **scruffy** (*under* **scruff**^{2}).
dowerless *see* **dowry**.
down^1 (*soft plumage*) doon.
down^2 doon, adoon; *comparative* dooner; *superlative* doonmaist, nethmaist.

downcast *see also* **depressed, doleful**; disjaskit, doon o mou(th), oolt NE, dowf, hingin-luggit, demuired; **looking downcast** wi yer heid under yer oxter; **look downcast** hing yer lugs.
downfall whummle.
downhill doonwith NE.
downpipe rone-pipe.
downpour poor, onding, blash, clash, plump, plash, hail watter, plowt, pishoot, plype NE, peel rushich NE.
downright *see also* **completely**; ring-in, fair furth the gate, plat an plain, evendoon.
downstairs doon the stair.
downtrodden sair hauden doon (by the bubbly jock).
downwards doonwith NE.
down-and-out *see also* **vagrant, tramp** 1: *noun* truaghan N.
adjective on the street(s).
down-at-heel 1 (*of shoes*) ba(u)chelt, sha(u)chlin. **2** (*of a person*) *see* **shabby**.
down the road doon-by.
down there doon-by.
down-to-earth fair oot.
dowry †tocher, †drurie.
dowerless †tocherless.
doze *see also* **snooze**: *verb* dover, snotter, dove NE, gloss NE.
noun dover, gloss, slug W, SW.
doze off dover ower.
dozing (nid) nid noddin.
dozen dizzen.
drab *see also* **dull**; dreich; (*esp of the colour of wool cloth*) riach SHETLAND, ORKNEY, N.
draft *see also* **draught**; (*rough draft*) scroll.
drag *verb, see also* **haul, pull: 1** rug, haal NE, hale *often nautical*; (*violently or roughly*) harl; (*through mud etc; something heavy*) tra(u)chle; (*yourself laboriously*) harl, haik. **2** (*a river etc, for a corpse*) grapple.
noun (*act of dragging*) harl.
dragon draigon.
dragonet gowdie.
dragonfly deil's darnin needle, heather bill, fleein ether, stingin ether.
drain *verb* **1** (*a glass*) tuim, teem N, toot, tak oot, wa(u)cht (oot); **drain a glass** drink cap oot. **2** (*pour liquid from, esp potatoes*) dreep, poor: '*poor the tatties*', teem, sype, sye.
noun, see also **ditch, trench, channel, gutter**; (*drainage channel*) sheuch, gote, dreep, watter-fur, gaw; (*in pasture land*) sheep drain; (*covered*) cundie, syver, pend SW, S; (*formed of stones*) laid drain; (*primitive, eg hole in wall for slops*) †jaw-hole.
drained (*of a glass etc*) oot.
drainpipe (*from a roof-gutter*) rone-pipe.
down the drain doon the jaw-hole: '*Aw the siller went doon the jaw-hole*'.
dram *see* **drink** 3.
drank *past tense of* **drink** drunk.
drape *verb* hap.
draught draucht: **1** (*of air*) waff, souch. **2** (*of liquid*) glut; (*esp of liquor*) wa(u)cht, slock, jaw, howp NE; (*esp large*) sweel NE, blash NE, sowp, swack, swag SHETLAND, ORKNEY.
have a strong draught (*of a chimney*) *see* **draw**.
draughts the dams, the dambrod NE; (*game in which the first to get all men off the board wins*) shuil-the-board; (*draughts-like game*) tod an lambs.
a move in draughts shift.
draw *verb, see also* **pull, haul, drag, tighten**; rug; (*of a chimney*) vent, pou.
drawer (*small, in a chest etc*) shottle.
drawback *see* **snag**.
draw the hand lightly over scuff.
draw in (*of days*) *see* **grow shorter** (*under* **grow**).

drawl

draw off (*liquid*) *see* **drain**.

draw out (*stretch out*) stent.

drawl *verb, noun* draunt.

dread *see also* **fear**: *verb, noun* dreid.

dreadful *see also* **awful**; dreidfae.

dream *noun, see also* **daydream**; drame; (*wild*) wuiddrim.

verb drame; (*muse*) oor SHETLAND, ORKNEY.

dreamy dwamie, dwamish; (*of the eyes*) far ben.

dreamy state *see* **daydream**.

be so lost in dreams that you come to grief leuk at the muin till ye fa(w) i the midden.

dreary *see also* **dismal**; dreich, drearifu; (*of feelings, activities etc*) wersh; (*of places*) gowstie, wilsome, douth s.

drearily eerilie.

dredge *verb, noun* (*esp for shellfish*) dreg.

dregs *see also* **last drops** (*under* **drop**); poorins, quinkins, jute, dreepins.

full of dregs grumlie.

drench(ed) *see* **soak(ed)**.

dress *verb* 1 *see also* **dress up, wrap up**; hap; (*in a slovenly way*) hushle; (*a person in armour*) †graith. 2 (*hooks for fly-fishing*) busk, buss; (*building stone*) cloor.

noun, see also **clothes, garment**; ootrig, habuliment, onpit, graithin; (*esp a trousseau*) muntin.

dressed *see also* **well-dressed, fashionable**; set-on; (*finely*) weel-pit(ten)-on.

dressed-up *see also* **dress up**; primpit, brammed up W; (*esp of women*) dink.

oddly-dressed woman Teenie fae Troon, Teenie fae the neeps E.

ridiculously-dressed person munsie NE.

dresser (*kitchen*) bink.

dressing-down *see also* **scolding**; waukenin, thuddin, reddin-up, dreel N, throu-the-muir, sederunt NE.

dressing-gown wrapper NE.

dressy fussy.

dress up tosh up, tip up NE, doss up NE, pink up, dink up.

dressmaker mantie-maker.

dribble *verb* 1 dreeble, driddle; (*messily*) slitter, slabber. 2 (*in football*) pirl NE.

noun dreeble.

dribbler *see also* **messy person** (*under* **mess**); slitter.

dried *see* **dry**.

drift *noun* (*of snow*) wreath.

verb, see also **wander**; pander.

driftwood wrack, spreath NE.

drill dreel: *verb* (*bore*) thirl.

noun, see **furrow** 1.

drink *see also* **drank, drunk**: *verb* 1 (*deeply*) wa(u)cht (oot *etc*); (*carelessly*) baible; (*heartily*) lay yer lug intae; (*greedily*) slorp; (*quench thirst*) weet yer thrapple; (*drink alcohol*) cock the wee finger, cruik yer elbow, cowp the cog NE; (*in small amounts*) taste; (*continuously in small amounts*) sirple; (*heavily*) blybe NE, blab, bend the bicker, toot.

noun 1 gear. 2 (*a drink: see also* **draught** 2) slock, sowp; (*small*) spairge; (*wishy-washy*) skink, blash, plash, spootrach; (*esp weak tea*) weeshie-washie, skiddle, jute; (*thirst-quenching*) slockener. 3 (*alcohol, esp whisky: see also* **whisky**) wheich; (*a drink*) dram (NB *any size*), sup, drappie, roostie nail, Scotch muffler, refreshment, swallae, toot; (*large quantity of drink*) bucket: '*He can tak a guid bucket*', sowp, blash NE; (*small*) skite NE, snatchack; (*very small*) taste, smell; (*drink on leaving*) deoch-an-dorus; (*to a departing friend*) bonailie. 4 (*types of drink: see also* **liquorice, treacle**) (*hot, esp mulled wine*) plottie; (*to encourage sweating*) coo's drink; (*of spiced ale etc*) het pint; (*of whisky, oatmeal, honey etc*) Athole brose; (*of oatmeal, milk etc*) blenshaw; (*of water, ale, oatmeal*) meal an thrammel NE; (*at harvest celebration*) meal an ale NE; (*of water and oatmeal*) mealie drink ORKNEY, NE.

drinker *see also* **tippler, drunkard**; (*heavy*) drouth, toot.

be a heavy drinker tak a guid bucket;

(*very*) be waur tae watter than corn.

drinking bout splore; (*long*) screed.

on a drinking bout on the bash, on the batter.

give up drinking pit in the pin.

additional drink eik.

drink to the bottom drink cap oot NE.

drink down toot.

drink the proceeds of fuddle.

order drinks without paying for them shuit a craw.

pay your share of the drinks be yer dram.

drink from the same cup in friendship kiss caps.

bring drink secretly from a pub rin the cutter.

drip *verb, see also* **leak, ooze**; dreep, dreeple, dripple, seep, sype; (*of small drops*) pink ORKNEY, NE.

noun **1** dreep, sype. **2** (*person*) Sammy Dreep.

dripping *adjective, see also* **wet, soaking**; seepin, sypin, sappie.

noun **1** (*of liquid*) seep(age). **2** (*fat*) rander, dreepin.

drip-dry *verb* sype.

drive *verb* **1** (*cause to move*) (1) (*a vehicle, animals, a plough, a load*) ca(w); (*animals to market*) lift; (*people or animals in some direction*) hurl. (2) (*specif in a wheeled vehicle*) hurl. **2** (*be conveyed, in any vehicle*) sail SW, S. **3** (*push forward: violently*) ding, whang S; (*esp with blows*) skelp; (*hustle*) dreel NE; (*hard*) haik. **4** (*of wind, rain*) dad.

noun **1** (*in a wheeled vehicle*) hurl. **2** (*energy*) smeddum, virr, throu-ca(w), ca-throu NE, feerich NE, redd SHETLAND, ORKNEY.

driven drien.

driving (*of wind*) rackin.

driving shower onding.

drive away (*by frightening*) fley (awa), boost, gliff S; (*in terror*) ramscooter; (*illness etc*) fleg.

drive in (*nails*) ca(w).

drive off *see* **drive away**.

without drive fushionless, saikless S.

drivel *noun, see also* **nonsense**; haivers, styte, gyter NE.

verb, see also **talk nonsense** (*under* **nonsense**); haiver, slaver, rhyme, gyter NE.

driveller gyter NE.

drizzle *verb* dreezle, smirr, dribble, drabble NE, driffle SW, S, spitter, deow NE, drowe, smizzle SW, S; (*persistently*) smuchter NE.

noun dreezle, weet, smirr, dribble, drowe, rag SHETLAND, ORKNEY, NE; (*soaking*) Liddisdale drowe S; (*often with mist*) skiff, mug NE.

drizzly roukie, muggie, drabbl(ich)ie NE, drappie NE, daggie NE, dawkie.

droll auld-farran(t), pawkie.

drone *verb* **1** (*make a droning sound*) bum, souch. **2 drone on** rhyme, rame, draunt.

noun **1** (*droning sound*) hum. **2** (*of a bagpipe*) burden.

drool *see* **slobber**.

droop (*of plants*) stint; (*of persons*) peenge NE.

drooping (*of plants*) wallan(t) NE; (*of persons*) paewae SHETLAND, NE, FIFE.

drop drap: *verb* **1** *see also* **drip**; rap. **2** (*a stitch in knitting*) lat doon; (*something into a liquid*) plunk; (*suddenly*) plype NE. **3** (*eg from a wall*) dreep.

noun, see also **raindrop**; blob, dribble, drib NE, spark; (*small amount poured out*) poorin, jirble; (*esp of alcohol*) nebfu, skite NE, skirp NE; **drops** (*of wind-driven rain or snow*) spitters; (*of spilt food*) drabbles.

droppings (*of animals*) doldies; (*of cows or sheep*) puslicks NE; (*of sheep, rabbits etc*) purls; (*esp of sheep*) trottles.

fall in drops *see* **drip**.

last drops from a container sypins.

drought drouth, drocht N, drucht NE.

drove *past tense of* **drive** drave, dreeve NE.

noun drave; (*of sheep*) bat SE.

head drover †tapsman.

drown

drown droon.
  drowned droondit.
drowse *see* **doze**.
  drowsy droosie.
drub(bing) *see* **beat(ing)**.
drudge *verb* tra(u)chle, scodge.
  noun scodge.
  drudgery tra(u)chle, pingle, chaave NE.
drug drog NE.
  druggist droggie, droggist.
drum *see also* **beat**.
  drumbeat †touk, †ruff.
  drum roll (*before a proclamation*) †ruff.
  drumming with feet as applause ruff NE.
drunk *adjective, see also* **tipsy, fuddled**; fou, smeekit, roarie, the worse o drink; (*very*) blin fou, bleezin (fou), roarin fou, fou as a puggie, fou as a wulk, miraculous, pie-eyed, mortal (fou), steamin (wi drink), steamboats, mingin; (*hilariously*) fleein; (*at the tearful stage*) greetin fou; (*reeling*) stottin (fou); (*helplessly*) soople; (*disgustingly*) spuin fou; (*habitually*) drouthie, sappie.
  drunkard drouth, drunkart, troch, slaik, toot, tootlie NE, jeet NE, sandbed.
  drunkenness drouthiness.
  be very drunk no be able tae bite yer thoum, glower, hae a rinnin lade S.
  make drunk fill fou.
dry *adjective* (*of weather*) drouthie; (*withering*) bask; (*of wind*) druchtie NE, hard NE; (*parched, shrivelled*) gizzen; (*dry and brittle*) freuch NE; (*of wood etc*) funseless CAITHNESS; (*of touch, taste*) hask; (*stale*) haskie; (*of soil*) hirstie; (*thoroughly, of clothes etc*) hert-dry NE, horn-dry, threiddry, (*sun-dried*) rizzered.
  verb (*by wiping or rubbing*) dicht; (*clothes (partially) in open air*) haizer; (*fish, ham etc*) reest; (*peats, hay etc, in open air or sun*) win, (*by turning*) turn; (*fish, hay etc, to shrink in open air*) pine SHETLAND.

dried (*sun-dried, of fish or clothes*) rizzered.
  dried fish hard fish; (*and split*) speldin SHETLAND, N, speldrin.
  dryish (*of weather*) dryachtie (kin) NE.
  drystone wall dry (stane) dyke, rickle.
  builder of drystone walls dry (stane) dyker, cowan.
  dry weather drouth.
  dry out (*wood etc*) win; (*esp peats*) scrocken SHETLAND, NE.
  dry up (*wither*) spire SE; (*shrivel*) gizzen; (*of ploughed ground*) hair NE.
  keep dry (*of weather*) hing up.
dual *see* **two-fold**.
dubious (*of persons*) jubish.
duck[1] *verb* (*eg to avoid a blow*) jouk, loot; (*in water*) dook.
  ducking dookin.
duck[2] (*bird*) deuk, quackie, deukie quack NE; (*mallard*), mire-duck; (*long-tailed*) coal-an-candlelight; (*golden eye*) gowdie(-duck).
  call to ducks *see* **call**.
  duck pond deuk's dub.
  ducks and drakes (*game*) skifflers, skifters.
  play at ducks and drakes sk(l)iff stanes, scud.
  flat stone used in ducks and drakes skiffer, skiffler.
due (*of direction*) plat SHETLAND.
  due to whit wi, fit wi NE, efter.
dug *past tense, past participle of* **dig** howkit.
dull *see also* **dreary**; dreich, dowie; (*of persons*) dowf, taibetless, timmer; (*stupid*) donsie S, fozie, blate; (*of actions, writings etc*) fushionless, wersh; (*of a blade*) bauch; (*of the sky*) loorie; (*of weather, and chilly*) oorie; (*of sound*) diffie, dowf.
dulse dilse N.
dumb (*struck dumb*) tongue-tackit.
  dumbfound *see also* **confuse, perplex**; dumfooner, dumfoutter NE, mesmerise, kittle.
  dumb person dummie.

dump *verb* **1** (*put down heavily*) plank, plowt. **2** *see* **abandon**.
noun (*for rubbish, or dismal place*) cowp.
in the dumps *see* **depressed**.
dumpling *see also* **pudding**; (*of oatmeal, fat etc*) hodgel S.
dumpy *see* **fat, stocky**.
short dumpy person drochle.
dun *verb* (*for payment*) crave.
dunce dobbie, fits, fittie, dult.
dun(-coloured) fauchie N.
dunderhead *see* **idiot**.
dunes (*area of dunes on E Coast*) links.
dung *see also* **manure**; muck: '*hen's muck*', fulyie; (*esp of cattle*) sha(i)rn; (*of fowls*) hen-pen.
 dung-fly muck flee, sha(i)rnie flee, midden flee.
 dunghill midden, muck midden, sha(i)rn midden NE.
 dunghill foundation (*hollowed out*) midden-hole.
 dunghill site midden-steid.
 dung rake claut, harl.
 (small) balls of dung purls, puslicks N, doldies NE; (*of sheep*) trottles, trintlets.
 large piece of dung doll NE.
 clear dung from muck (oot).
 liquid oozing from dung midden bree, green brees NE, sha(i)rn bree NE, strang.
 scatter (dung) spart.
 smeared with dung sha(i)rnie.
 spread with dung *verb* muck.
dungeon †massymore, †cave.
dunlin pickeril, sea lark, pliver's page.
dupe *see* **cheat, deceive**.
duplicate *noun* (*of a document: see also* **copy**) dooble.
duplicity *see* **deceit**.

durable stark.
 durability docher, lest.
 lacking durability fushionless.
duress (*law*) force and fear.
during in, throu: '*throu the week*', upon.
dusk *see* **twilight**.
dust *noun* dist NE; (*esp in the air*) stour, stew SHETLAND, N; (*esp of coal or peat*) coom; (*of flax*) yowther; (*kicked up by sudden flight or hurry*) sma stanes an stew NE.
 dusting (*cursory*) skift.
 dusty stourie, stewie NE.
 dustbin (ass) bucket, (ass) backet, midgie(-bin), midden *Central*.
 dustbin lorry *see* **refuse collector**.
 dustbin man scaffie, midgie man W.
 cover with dust stour.
 flecked with dust mot(t)ie SHETLAND, NE.
 like a whirl of dust lik(e) stour.
duty 1 (*chore*) turn. **2** *see* **tax**.
 be duty-bound to fa(w) tae, maun.
dwarf *noun* droich, knurl, wirl, crowl SW, crile; (*shrivelled*) blastie.
 dwarfed sutten-on.
 dwarfish drochlin NE, nirlie.
 dwarfish person knurl.
dwell *see also* **stay**[1] 1; bide, dwall.
 dwelt *past tense* bade, bode, dwalt.
 past participle bade, bidden, dwalt.
 dwelling *see* **house**.
dwindle *see* **waste away**.
dye *noun, verb* lit.
 dyer dyester.
 dye-producing lichen crottle.
dyke *see* **wall, ditch**.
dynamic (*of character*) forcie, feckfu.
dysentery: suffer from dysentery (*esp of sheep or cattle*) rush.

E

each ilka, ilkie N, ilk *now literary*; (*apiece*) the piece.
    each one ilk ane, ilkie een N.
    each other ilk ither, ither.
eager aiger SE, awid, yare, willin, gyte, aiver; (*foolishly*) fond; (*excitedly*) yeukie, fidgin fain; (*esp for food or sex*) shairp-set.
    eagerly snell.
    eager for mad for, keen o, on for, illaboot NE, rife for SHETLAND, ORKNEY, wuid for.
    be eager for ettle efter.
    eager to keen o, wuid tae.
    be extremely eager m(y)ang NE.
eagle aigle.
    golden eagle earn.
    sea eagle earn SHETLAND, ORKNEY.
ear 1 lug. **2** (*of corn etc*) aicher, icker SW; (*highest*) tap pickle.
    earmark *noun, verb* (*esp (on) a sheep*: *see also* **sheepmark**) lug-mark.
    earring wup.
    earwig eariwig, forkie(-tail(ie)), forker SE, golach, hornie golach, gavelock, clipshear, scodgebell SE, switchbell.
    long-eared lang-luggit.
    with your ears cocked gleg-eared.
    come into ear (*of grain*) shuit.
earl yerl S.
early *adjective* airlie, air, timeous *now law*; (*early out of bed*) vertie NE.
    adverb air: '*late an air*', ere.
    early closing day shut day.
    very early hours of the morning (wee) sma oors.
    early part (*of a period of time*) foreen(d).
earn (*wages etc*) yearn, yirn, win; (*punishment etc*) work for.

earnings penny fee *mainly in poetry*.
    earn your livelihood mak saut tae yer kail.
    well-earned weel-wared.
earnest: earnest money arles.
    deadly earnest nettle earnest.
    in dead earnest in ettle earnest.
    begin in earnest set on.
earth *noun, see also* **soil**; erd, yird; (*mould, soil*) muild, mool(s).
    earthenware lame SHETLAND, ORKNEY, N, pig.
    earthenware container crock, pig.
    earthenware dealer pigger, mugger.
    earthenware hot-water bottle pig.
    earthy yirdie.
    earthfast yirdfast.
    earthnut *see* **pignut**.
    earth up (*plants*) set up, furr up, heuch.
    face of the earth scruiffin, fit stuil.
ease *see* **comfort**.
    easy-going jack-easy, eedle-doddle N; (*and lazy*) easy-osie.
    easily eithlie.
    do something easily skoosh (it).
    moving easily (*of a bolt etc*) glaid.
    take it easy soss, ca(w) cannie.
east aist.
    eastern easter, easten.
    eastward eastart, eas(t)lins NE.
    eastwards eastle, easel, east the road.
    east wind easter NE.
    east to west sungates, sunweys.
    further east easter.
    furthest east eastma(i)st.
Easter Pace, Pask.
    Easter egg pace egg.
    Easter Monday pace egg day, Pace Day SHETLAND, ORKNEY.

eight

Easter Sunday Pace Day SHETLAND, ORKNEY, NE.

eat *see also* **ate, sup, devour, munch, crunch, nibble: 1** aet, corn. **2** (*quickly*) snap (up); (*heartily*) lay yer lugs intae, tak awa SHETLAND, ORKNEY; (*greedily*) lay intae, guts, rive, haam NE: '*jist haamin intil im*', hunch, gulch NE, pootch NE, worry NE, scaff SHETLAND, heck, gorb(le); (*of animals, down to the roots*) rump. **3** (*without appetite*) pewl amang yer food, chawl, smurl; (*with the mouth nearly closed*) mimp; (*furtively*) smacher; (*of people or animals*) smurl. **4** (*messily*) slaiger, slitter, slaister; (*messily and noisily*) slubber, slabber, slorp, sloch, slorach; (*noisily*) slork.

eaten etten.

eater *see also* **glutton**; (*messy*) slaister, slitter; (*poor, fussy*) pickie, fyke.

eating intak; (*messy, noisy*) slorach NE; slubber; (*excessive*) gulshich NE.

begin to eat lay till, lay yer heid till.

eat a meal mait SHETLAND, NE.

eat up *see also* **devour**; cowe.

eaves easin(s), aesins.

eavesdrop hearken (tae), cran NE, dern, eariwig.

eavesdropper hearkener.

ebb: ebbing (*of the tide*) ootgaun.

ebb-tide (*at lowest point*) grun(d)-ebb SHETLAND, ORKNEY, N.

ebullient skeich, heich.

eccentric unco, orra, Fifish.

eccentricity unconess.

eccentric person jeeger.

ecclesiastic *noun, see* **clergyman**.

ecclesiastical court *see* **church court**.

economy (*saving*) hainin.

economical cannie.

economize scrimp, hain in.

falsely economized ill-hauden NE.

ecstasy: be in ecstasy be (clean) awa wi't.

eddy *see also* **swirl**: *noun* swirl, pirl, weel.
verb pirl.

edge *noun* (*of a stream, pool etc*) lip; (*eg of a hill, a shoe*) laggin S; (*of a piece of land, of a peat-bank*) rind; (*sloping, of a sharpened tool*) cannel.

edging *noun, see* **trimming**.

set (*the teeth*) **on edge** seg; **set** (*someone's*) **teeth on edge** mak (someone) grue.

Edinburgh Edinburrae, Embro, Embra, Auld Reekie.

educate eddicate; (*at university*) college.

education eddication; (buik-)lair.

eel (*young*) needlach N.

eel trap eel ark.

eerie *see also* **uncanny**: oorie, weirdlie, gowstie.

effect *noun* **1** effeck, ootcome, eftercome. **2 effects** *see* **possessions**.

effective feckfu; (*of a blow*) sicker.

effectual effeckwal.

effeminate sapsie.

effeminate man (big) Jessie, Jennie Wullock, kiss-ma-luif, sook-the-pappie; (*garrulous, gossipy*) (auld) sweetie-wife.

effeminate boy lass(ie) boy.

effervesce *see* **foam**.

effervescent fuzzie NE.

efficient feckfu, purpose-lik(e), eydent.

efficiency purpose.

effigy (*in stucco*) stookie.

effluent (*from a dunghill*) midden bree NE.

effort (*attempt*) ettle, fend, ma(u)cht: '*mak a maucht*'; (*struggle*) wa(u)chle, haggle S, tazie, pingle; (*extra*) brash.

make an effort turn yer thoum; (*great effort*) warsle.

not make any effort no cruik a finger.

effrontery *see also* **impudence**; hard neck, bress neck.

effusive *see also* **chatty**; phrasie.

egg goggie *child's word*, W; (*shell-less*) win egg; (*small, yolkless*) cock's egg.

egotistical *see* **selfish**.

eight aucht, echt, aicht.

eighth aucht, echt, aicht.

eighteen auchteen, echteen.

eighteenth auchteent, echteent.

eighty echtie, auchtie.

either aither, ether, edder SHETLAND, NE, onie o the twa SHETLAND, NE; (*with negatives*) etherin(s), edderin(s) SHETLAND, NE: '*We dinna lik it etherins*'.

eject gie (someone) the door (in his face), turn tae the door SHETLAND, N, set oot, oot(pit).

elaborate *adjective* (*over-elaborate*) primpit, fantoosh.

elapse owergae.

elastic elaskit, eleskit S.

elated made up, cairried, upliftit, upmade S, up i the buckle, croose, vauntie *literary*, vaudie, vogie.

elbow *noun* elba(e), elbuck.

verb oxter.

point of the elbow knap SHETLAND.

elder[1]: **elderly** *see also* **old**; up in years, eldren.

elders of a church kirk session.

elder[2] (*tree*) eller S, bourtree, bountree, bull-tree *gipsy*.

elect eleck.

elegant pretty, gentie.

elegy (*esp bagpipe*) lament.

elevate *see also* **exalt**; heeze, heyze NE, upheeze, hyste.

elevation *see* **height**.

eleven eleevin, aleevin.

eleventh eleevint, aleevint.

elf *see* **fairy**.

eliminate elide.

elongate *see also* **stretch**; rax.

elope skirt.

eloquent glib, glib-gabbit.

else ense.

or else or an.

elsewhere itherwhere(s), ithergates, itherroads.

elude *see also* **evade**; jouk, jink.

emaciated *see also* **thin**; shilpit, shirpit, nakit, pikit(-lik(e)), slunken, clinkit, shargart NE.

become emaciated pine.

emaciated person rickle o banes, gaishon SW, S, shargar NE.

embankment watter dyke, mote; (*to prevent erosion*) touk, hutch S.

embarrass gie (someone) a rid face, gie (someone) a richt facer, gie (someone) a riddie.

embarrassed taen(-lik(e)).

become embarrassed get a rid face, get a beamer, get a riddie; (*greatly*) gae throu the flair.

embedded *see* **stuck**.

embellish (*a story*) pit legs an airms tae.

ember aizle, gleed.

embers (*esp of a peat-fire*) greeshoch, drieshach NE.

embezzle pauchle.

embolden *see* **hearten**.

embrace *see also* **cuddle**: *verb* neck, oxter, lock SHETLAND, N.

noun Scotch gravat, bosie.

embroider flourish ORKNEY, NE; (*with designs of flowers etc*) flooer.

embroidery flourishin; (*fine, esp early 19th-century Ayrshire*) flooerin.

embroil: be embroiled in be rowed intae.

emerge: emergence ootcome.

emergency sair fit *or* leg: '*lay somethin aside fur a sair fit*'.

emetic †vomiter.

emigrate lowp the country NE.

eminent *see also* **well-known**; markit.

eminence (*hill*) heich.

emit *see* **send out**.

emotion: emotional strain hert-rug.

filled with emotion great-hertit.

emphatic evendoon.

employ 1 (*use*) wirk wi. **2** (*a servant: see also* **engage**) fee.

employees fowk.

employer (*small*) cork.

employment (*occupation*) thrift; (*new*) stert: '*We'll gie ye a stert on Monday*'.

employment exchange b(u)roo.

empty *adjective* empie, tuim, teem N, tim CENTRAL, S, boss, howe; (*of speech*) pyot.

verb **1** empie, tuim, teem N, tim CENTRAL, S; (*a container by pouring*) poor;

(*by tilting*) cowp, whummle; (*a bag etc*) tusk. **2** (*become empty*) tuim, teem.

emptied (*of a glass etc*) oot: '*yer gless is oot*'.

empty-handed tuim-handit.

empty-headed *see also* **silly, foolish**; tuim-heidit, shaul(d); (*featherbrained*) sodie-heidit.

enamoured *see also* **infatuated**; browden (on) NE.

enchant *see* **bewitch**.

enchantment glamour(ie), gramarie.

enclose (*animals*) faul(d); (*land: with a wall, ditch*) park; (*with a hedge, fence*) hain; (*with an embankment*) lay.

enclosure (*for animals: see also* **pig-sty, sheepfold**) crue, cruive, faul(d), pund, ree, lair; (*usually square*) pumphal NE; (*small*) parrock; (*covered*) coort; (*open, on hillside, for sheltering sheep*) stell; (*for calves*) cauf's ward NE.

encounter *verb* kep NE, meet in wi.

encourage *see also* **hearten**; gie a lift tae, upsteer, kittle.

encouraging hertsome.

encouragement lift, hertenin; (*opportunity*) inlat.

encrust barken, scruif (ower).

encrustation *see* **incrustation**.

encrusted barkenit; (*esp with dirt*) bar-kit.

piece of encrusted skin, hair *etc* scruif.

encumber tra(u)chle, birn.

encumbrance tra(u)chle.

end *noun* en, eyn NE: **1** (*of a period of time*) hint, hin(d)maist, tail; (*of the working day*) lowsin time; (*of a season, tenancy*) ootgang; (*esp of life*) hinneren(d); (*of everything*) mortal en(d). **2** (*lower part*) fit; (*of a loaf*) heel, sole shaif; (*eg of a used candle*) dowp.

verb en, eyn NE.

end product ootcome.

bring to an end mak throu wi.

put an end to (*fighting*) redd NE.

on end oweren(d).

stand on end en, oweren(d); (*peats to dry*) fit.

endearment: term of endearment hinnie, jo, sweetie, wran, ratton, cushie, (croodlin-)doo, cushie-doo; (*to a girl*) dosh SHETLAND, N, galat; (*to a child*) ma wee scone, karriewhitchit NE, burd; (*to a child or lover*) pout(ie), taid NE, posy.

endeavour *see also* **try**: *noun, verb* en-daivour, endeevour NE.

endorse *see* **confirm**.

endow endoo ORKNEY, NE.

endure 1 (*tolerate*) thole, bide, sit wi, dree. **2** *see* **last**^{2}.

endurance thole.

enemy unfreend, fae *literary*.

energy *see also* **drive**; smeddum, birr, virr, ca(w)-throu, fushion NE, throu-pit.

energetic *see also* **vigorous**; speeri-tie, throu-gaun, vertie NE, furthie NE, fendfu, kempie, fersell; (*and capable*) fell.

energetically fell, stark.

energetic movement dirl SHETLAND, NE.

do something fast and energetically leather, skelp on, gae yer dinger, gie it laldie, gie it (big) licks.

work energetically (at) stick in (tae), pelt (at), skelp (at).

set to work energetically lay in.

with all your energy wi a(w) yer pith ORKNEY, N.

give all your energy to gang hail-hei-dit for *or* intil N, wallop at, gang hail teer at NE.

without energy thowless, fushionless.

enervated forfochen.

enfeebled fordwaibelt; (*in mind*) *see* **senile**.

enfold *see also* **wrap**; wimple NE.

enforceable prestable.

engage (*as a servant*) fee, thirl; (*for another term on a farm*) speak tae; (*yourself as a servant*) fee, hire.

engaged 1 (*to be married*) trystit. **2** *see* **busy**.

engine

become engaged (*to be married*) mak (yer) mercat.

person engaged to be married bun(d) shafe NE.

engaging *see* attractive.

engine ingine; (*winding, in a mine*) gig.

engineer ingineer.

English *see also* affected; Sassenach, Southron, †Suddron, the Auld Enemy.

English person Sassenach, †southron, †Suddron.

(well-fed) Englishman pock-puddin *humorous or contemptuous*.

English language †Southron, †Suddron.

enjoyable *see* entertaining.

enlarge eik.

enlighten enlichten, insense intae SW, ULSTER.

enlightenment licht.

enlist (*in the army*) list.

enliven kittle.

enlivening lichtsome.

enmesh mask, mast, fankle.

enmity *see also* hatred; plea NE, un-freen(d)ship SHETLAND, laith ORKNEY.

at enmity striven NE.

enormous *see also* immense; wappin.

enough eneuch, aneuch, anew, enew NE.

enrage *see also* anger; raise.

enraged *see also* angry, furious; hyte.

enrol in (*a class*) or for (*a subject*) tak(e) oot: '*He's takkin oot Maths, Latin an Logic*'.

ensnare (*a man into marriage*) cleek.

ensuing incomin.

ensure mak siccar.

entail †tailyie.

entangle *see also* tangle; fankle, taigle, hank(le), warple, insnorl N, snorl up, wimple NE.

entanglement mink NE, snorl.

enter intil.

entering ingaun: '*ingaun tenant*'.

enteritis (*in children*) bowel-hive(s).

enterprise (*undertaking*) ploy, han(d)lin, ontakkin SHETLAND, NE.

enterprising *see* go-ahead (*under* go).

go into a new enterprise peel yer wan(d)s S.

entertain enterteen.

entertaining shortsome; (*person*) knackie.

entertaining person divert.

entertainment divert, han(d)lin.

enthral *see* bewitch.

enthusiasm birr, t(h)rift.

enthusiastic *see* eager.

do something enthusiastically gae yer dinger, gie it laldie, gie it (big) licks.

first wave of enthusiasm fire edge.

entice enteece, tice, wice, culyie, tryst, treesh (wi) NE.

enticement enteecement.

entire *see also* whole; hail-heidit N.

entirely *see also* completely; as clean as a mackerel.

almost entirely gey near, maist han(d) SHETLAND, NE.

entitle enteetle.

entourage (*of a Highland chief*) †tail.

entrails *see also* bowels, intestines; (*of an animal*) painches, trollie-bags, harigals, ush, draucht; (*specif as food*) puddins; emmlins NE, fa SHETLAND, ORKNEY, inmait S; (*of a deer*) gralloch.

entrance[1] *noun* (*way in*) ingaun, ingang SHETLAND, NE, ingate SHETLAND; (*to a house etc*) entry; (*to a stairway of a block of flats*) close (mou); (*to a tract of country etc*) mou: '*the mou o the glen*'; (*eg to a town*) inlat.

entrance[2] *see* bewitch.

entreat *see also* beseech; fleetch, prig; (*flatteringly*) treesh wi NE.

entrust lippen.

entry *see* entrance[1].

entwine *see* weave.

envelop *see* wrap.

envious *see* jealous.

environment (*of an individual*) heft.

enwrap *see* wrap, enfold.

Episcopal(ian) Episcopaulian, English; (*of the Scottish Episcopal Church*) piskie *informal*.

Episcopalian church English kirk, whustle kirk *now literary*.

the Episcopalian denomination the gentle persuasion NE.

equable: he has an equable temperament he aye keeps a calm souch.

equal *adjective* aqual; (*in every way*) hackum-plackum S; (*in ability etc*) aboot abat, (*in a competition etc*) skleff S; (*in age or height: see also* **contemporary**) heidipeer; **equal to** up wi.

noun aqual; (*of a person or thing: see also* **match**²) marrow, maik.

verb (*match*) peel, come, marrow.

equally aqual, equals-aquals.

equally balanced eeksie-peeksie, equal-aqual; (*on an equal footing*) even han(d)s, a(w) ae oo.

without equal marrowless.

equanimity calm souch: '*keep a calm souch*'.

equip busk, reik, ootrig.

equipment graith, orders, haudin S; (*esp military*) habuliment.

piece of equipment tuil.

equitable *see also* **just**; richt-lik(e) NE.

equivocate parry.

era: end of an era end o an auld sang.

erect *adjective* standin, staunin, upstannin.

verb cantle.

ermine stoat-weasel.

err (*morally*) step aside.

erratic ragglish NE.

erring *see* **misguided**.

erroneous *see also* **wrong**; mislearit.

error skellie SW; (*error in Latin translation*) maxie.

in error in a mistak.

errand eerant, erran, yirran(t), troke.

errand-boy message-boy, message laddie, eeran loon NE.

go an errand gae a message.

(as) a special errand aince erran(d), yince eerant S.

erudite far i the buik, far seen.

erudition buik-lair.

eruption (*on the skin: see also* **rash**¹)

ootstrikin, humour, eemir NE; (*esp of scarlet fever*) rush.

escape *verb* win oot, win awa, win aff, win free; (*something or someone*) miss, evite, win frae, jouk; (*eg a disease*) get throu: '*she got throu the measles*'.

noun ootcome.

escapade ploy, pliskie, splore ORKNEY, NE, prattick NE.

escape the notice of miss.

way of escape ootgate.

escort *verb* convoy, convey NE, set; (*halfway home*) see by the hen's mait.

noun (*escorting*) convoy; (*halfway home*) Scotch convoy.

Eskimo Yack(ie) SHETLAND, ORKNEY, N.

especially maistlie, parteec(u)lar.

essence sense NE.

essential *see* **necessary**.

essential point (*of something*) heid ORKNEY, NE.

establish estaiblish.

become established sit doon.

establishment estaiblishment.

estate *see also* **property**; place, room; (*esp of a small freeholder*) lairdship.

estate agent *see* **agent**.

esteem *verb, noun* respeck.

estimable honest.

estimate *noun* (*building: rough*) slump.

verb (*grain quality, by random sampling*) pruif, pruive NE.

estranged *see also* **loggerheads**; hither-an-yon(t).

estuary firth.

et cetera an (th)at, an siclik(e), an a(w), an things S.

eternity: an eternity a month o muins.

eternally till the morn-come-never, for aye.

etiquette honesty, mense.

evacuate *see* **empty, defecate**.

evade *see also* **avoid, dodge**; evite, jouk, jink, jick, skirt; (*payment, work etc*) slope; (*bad weather etc*) scug.

evasion joukerie; **evasions** weeshie-washies N.

evasive hunker-slidin, slidderie, wheetie NE, hielan NE, joukie.

evaluate comprise.

even e'en, ein SW, aiven; (*level*) evenlie, plat SHETLAND; **even with** (*quits*) eens wi, upsides wi, amen(d)s O NE, skleff wi S.

evenly cut snod.

even as eens.

even if suppose: '*He widna tell ye suppose he kent*'.

get even with see day aboot wi.

evening eenin, een; (*esp winter, as a time of relaxation*) forenicht.

in the evening at een.

event: after the event ahint the han(d), behind the han(d): '*wice behind the hand*'.

at all events whatever, in the hinneren(d).

eventually at *or* i the hinneren(d).

ever ivver, aye.

for ever for aye, till the morn-come-never.

every ivverie, ilka, ilk, ilkie N.

everybody a(w)bodie, ilk ane, ilkie een N.

everyday *see* **plain**.

every day day an daily.

every kind (of) a(w) kin-kind (o).

everything *see also* **the whole lot** (*under* **whole**); a(w)thing(s).

and everything else an a(w).

(in) every way a(w) weys.

everywhere a'where, a(w) wey, a(w)gate, a(w) roads.

evict herrie oot.

evidence (*law: piece of*) evident; (*preliminary*) precognition.

evidence given voluntarily ultroneous evidence.

supply evidence of instruct.

evident weel seen.

evil *adjective, noun, see also* **wicked, malicious;** ill.

evildoer ill-daer.

evil eye ill-ee.

evil-looking ill-faured.

evil-intentioned *see also* **malicious;** ill-hertit, ill-mintit SHETLAND, ORKNEY.

wish evil to ill-will NE.

ewe yowe; (*pet name*) Maillie SW; (*one-year-old*) gimmer; (*thrice-shorn*) twinter, quinter SW, S; (*pregnant*) great yowe; (*that has lost her lamb*) keb(-yowe) S; (*infertile*) tup-yeld yowe; (*past breeding*) slack yowe; (*old*) crock NE.

exact exack, nate; (*of a person*) pointit.

exacting (*of a person*) pointit, perskeet SHETLAND.

exactly exack, nate; (*strictly*) stench NE, tae a shavin.

exaggerate blaw, gange, ca a nail tae the heid NE, win(d) NE, slide NE, rift NE, bleeze awa NE, sprose, spell.

exaggerated account rift NE.

exaggeration whid.

exalt heeze, heyze NE, upheeze, hoise.

in an exalted position up by cairts NE.

in a state of exaltation oot o't NE, fair awa wi't.

examine *see also* **scrutinize;** exaemin, exem, leuk, see, sicht, vizzy SHETLAND; (*esp for stolen property*) ripe.

examination exemination NE, exa(e)min, sicht; (*of conduct: see also* **cross-examination**) throu-gaun; (*searching*) throu the mill; (*of a probationer minister before being licensed to preach*) trials.

exasperate *see also* **annoy;** ug SHETLAND, NE.

exasperated hert-roastit.

exasperating chawin, tantersome NE.

excavate *see* **dig.**

exceed *see also* **excel;** lowp ower, slap, owergang, ootding NE, pall SHETLAND, ORKNEY, NE.

exceedingly *see also* **very;** unco, main, mortal(ly), feerious NE, byous NE, notorious.

excel *see also* **exceed, beat;** bang, bear the gree *literary*, be a(w) their daddies, mak by, bleck.

excellent *see also* **fine**; braw, gran(d), rerr, tap, feerious NE, principal SHETLAND, wallie ORKNEY, barrie *used by schoolchildren,* LOTHIAN, gallus *used by schoolchildren,* W, peesie *slang or child's word.*

something excellent (*of its kind*) stoater, beezer.

except excep, exceppin(s), ceptna NE, by('s), forby, unless, abies, binna.

exceptional(ly) by-or(di)nar, by-common, by-usual, parteec(u)lar, byous.

excerpt swatch.

excessive odious SHETLAND, surfeit.

excessively *see also* **extremely, exceedingly**; ower.

exchange *verb, see also* **bargain, barter**; change, niffer, troke, hooie, blin hooie, cowp, cose SHETLAND, ORKNEY; (*law: land*) excamb.

noun, see also **bargain, barter**; niffer, blin hooie; (*law: of land*) excambion.

exciseman gauger.

excite fluffer, kittle (up), flocht NE.

excitable *see also* **nervous**; reevin.

excited up NE, in a case NE; (*excessively*) up tae high doh, raised, dementit; (*violently or sexually*) radg(i)e; (*of a cow*) rinnin; **easily excited** kittle.

become excited rouse, flichter, fidder; (*ardently*) lowe.

excitement *see also* **commotion**; go: '*in a go*', feerich NE, firr NE, flocht SHETLAND, NE, kip, gloan NE, flichter NE; (*great*) tirrivee, pavie, pelter SHETLAND, NE, yagiment NE, ree; (*panic*) panshit NE; (*pleasurable*) kittle.

exclamation exclaim; *see also under* **annoyance, astonishment, disgust, impatience** *etc.*

exclamation of sorrow, weariness, surprise, contempt hech (sirs)!, hech me!, eh man!

exclude *see* **keep out.**

exclusive (*law: of the jurisdiction of a court*) privative.

exclusively (*law*) allenarly.

excrement *see also* **dung**; keech, shite, drite, drate N, fulyie; (*specif human*) cack(ie), geing; (*lump of*) toalie, doldie NE.

void excrement *see* **defecate.**

excursion (*eg a walk: see also* **outing**) straik.

excuse *verb* excaise, exkeese NE.

noun excaise, exkeese NE; (*hypocritical*) scug SHETLAND, N.

(make) frivolous excuses whittie-whattie.

executioner †hangie, †lockman, †burrio, †staffman.

exempt *verb* exemp.

exercise *noun, verb* exerceese.

exercise book jotter, write-book ORKNEY.

exert: exert yourself fash (yersel), fyke, warsle, chaave NE, kyauve SHETLAND, NE, stent; (*esp physically*) hechle.

not exert yourself no cruik a finger.

exertion (*great*) putt an row NE; (*violent*) fuffle S.

with great exertion sair NE.

exhaust *verb, see also* **exhausted**; exowst, kned ANGUS, trash SW, S; (*land by over-use*) povereese.

exhausted *see also* **tired, harassed, worn out**; wabbit, puggelt, disjaskit, taskit, foonert, (sair) forfoch(t)en, killed, jaupit, socht NE, dirt deen NE, pouskert, traikit, jaffelt SW, stane-tired S, maukit S.

exhausting tra(u)chlesome NE, trashie S.

exhibit *noun* (*law: in court*) production.

exhibition exhibeetion.

make an exhibition of yourself mak a puppie-show o yersel.

exhilaration: shout of exhilaration (*eg when dancing*) hooch!, heech!

exhort threap at, threap wi.

existence: scrape an existence fend.

exit *noun* ootgang, ootgate SHETLAND; (*law: right of exit*) ish.

exonerate *see* **acquit.**

exorbitant oot o a rizzon SHETLAND, N.

exorbitant price *or* rent ransom.

exotic ootlan(d), fremmit, fremd, fantoosh.

expand *see also* **swell**; hove, come, rax SHETLAND, NE.

expatiate expawtiate.

expect expeck; (*rather think*) doot; (*anticipate*) ettle; (*hope for*) bode NE; (*confidently*) lippen.

expectation *see also* **hope**; lippenin, ettlin, wan SHETLAND, ORKNEY, CAITHNESS; (*patient*) onwaitin.

be expected to be supposed tae.

expectorate *see* spit².

expedition expedeetion, carrant.

expel (*from home etc*) herrie oot.

expend ware.

expenditure ootlay.

expense (*cost*) chairge, ootgang; expenses (*mining: additional*) oncost.

experience *noun* expairience; (*unpleasant*) throucome SHETLAND, NE, unction NE.

verb (*have experience of*) hae skeel o, pree.

experiment *noun* prattick NE.

expert *noun* deacon; (*called in a court case*) man *or* woman of skill.

adjective, see also **skilful**; cannie, slee, profite NE.

expire *see* **die.**

expiry (*of a lease etc*) ish.

explain (*a dream, riddle etc*) rede; (*esp Scripture*) expoon(d); (*something in detail to someone*) pit someone throu a maitter.

explanation (*valid*) quittance; (*esp of Scripture*) exposeetion.

expletive *see* **swear-word.**

explode 1 pluff; (*with a sharp hiss*) flist N; (*cause to explode*) set aff. **2** (*with rage*) lowse, flist N, spunk up.

explosion flist N; (*mild*) pluff; (*loud explosive noise*) reboon(d).

exploit *noun* splore.

explore reenge.

exploration explore.

export: exporting (*of fresh fish to waiting factory ships*) klondyking.

exporter (*ship or person, as above*) klondyker.

exposed (*of a place*) fusslebare NE.

expound expoon(d).

express: try to express ettle at.

expression (*on the face: pathetic, to gain sympathy*) sair face.

extend 1 *see also* **stretch, reach**; stent, rax, rack. **2** (*a lease etc*) prorogate.

extension eik; (*of a building*) ootshot.

extent (*amount*) boon, thing; (*limit*) stent.

to some extent some: '*She cam tae hersel some*'.

to the fullest possible extent tae the mast-heid.

to that extent that: '*He wis that scared*'.

extinct wede awa *literary*.

extinguish (*a fire etc*) slock(en), smore NE; (*a candle etc*) whuff oot.

extol heeze, heyze NE, ruise, reese N.

extort: ruin by extortion herrie.

extortionate (*of prices*) menseless.

extra *adjective* extrae, tither, tidder SHETLAND, NE.

extra charge tae-fa(w).

extract *verb* (*a tooth*) pou.

extraction (*family*) kin: '*o gentle kin*'.

extraordinary *see also* **exceptional**; extraordinar, by-or(di)nar, byous, nae or(di)nar, unco, undeemous SHETLAND, N.

extraordinarily by-or(di)nar, forby: '*he wis forby kind*'.

extravagant expensive, spendrif(e) NE, wasterfu, wastrif(e), haveless N, (*lavish*) fallauge NE, lairdlie NE.

extravagance wanthrift SHETLAND; (*extravagant living*) fill an fesh mair; (*extravagant profusion*) dem an lave NE.

live extravagantly live at heck an manger.

extreme *adjective* sevendle.

extremely *see also* **very**; terrible, unco, sair.

extricate howk; **extricate yourself** (*from a difficulty*) redd yer fit.

exuberant cadgie, on the keevee, croose.

eye *noun* ee, blinker, een-peeper *child's* word, yak *mainly gipsy*, S.

eyebrow broo, ee-broo, ee-bree; **eyebrows** breers o the een N.

eyelash ee-breer, (ee-)winker; **eyelashes** breers N.

eyelid eelid, (ee-)winker.

eyelet pie-hole.

F

fabricate feingie.

fabrication *see* invention.

face *noun* (*of a person*) neb, gizz *informal*, gruntle *contemptuous*, snoot *contemptuous*.

facing *preposition* forenent, ower fae.

(flat) on your face on yer groof, breidth an lenth.

in the face atween the een.

not look someone (straight) in the face skook.

make a face *see also* grimace; chowl the chafts.

facetious knackie.

facile owerlie NE.

facility faceelitie.

factory: factory siren bummer.

factory workers mill yins.

faculty (*for doing something*) ingine.

in full possession of your faculties solid.

fad *see also* whim; freit, whigmaleerie, fyke, norie S.

be faddy stan(d) on freits.

faddy eater pike-at-yer-mait, fyke.

fade *see also* wither; wallow, wallae, spire SE, dwine; (*of colours*) thraw, dowe.

faded (*of colours*) casten; (*withered*) dowit; (*of flowers*) wallan(t) NE; (*shabby*) scawt, scaddit.

faeces *see* excrement.

fag *verb, see also* weary; (*work too hard*) pingle; (*make weary*) tash.

faggot (*bundle*) faggald.

fail *verb, see also* go bankrupt (*under* bankrupt); (*to grow, develop; to happen; to do something*) miss: '*they nivver miss tae find oot*', slip; (*go wrong*) misgae NE; fail in (*a job*) stick; (*cause to fail*) misgie.

failed (*in a profession*) stickit: '*stickit minister*'.

failure *see also* bankruptcy, ruin; (*to do something*) failzie; (*poor performance*) blue do; (*in business*) brak.

fail on one small point eat the coo an worry on the tail.

faint *verb* fent, fant N, fa awa SHETLAND, NE, gang awa, gae awa, dwam, soon(d), swarf; (*appear to faint*) dwamle.

noun (*fainting fit*) fent, fant N, dwam, drowe, soon(d) SHETLAND, ORKNEY, swarf SHETLAND.

adjective (*weak*) dwamie, filsh, wauch, waumish.

faint-hearted fushionless, hen-hertit.

faint turn dwamle.

make a faint sound peep.

fair¹ ferr: *adjective* 1 (*just*) jonick, richtlik(e) NE. 2 (*tolerable*) middlin. 3 (*of complexion*) fair-avised; (*extremely, esp of albinos*) blin(d) fair. 4 *see* beautiful. 5 (*of weather*) *see* fine, pleasant.

fairly (*tolerably*) middlin.

head of fair hair tap o lint, tap o towe.

a fair number *or* amount a gey wheen.

fair play fair hornie, jonick.

fair-sized dentie.

fair² *noun, see also* market; ferr; (*at which farmworkers were engaged*) hirin fair, hirin market, feein market, Mucklie, Muckle Friday; (*for men who were not employed at the regular fairs*) †Rascal Fair NE; (*funfair*) the shows.

fairy eemock NE; (*benevolent, household*) broonie, whuppitie-stourie; (*wicked, to frighten children*) murmichan; (*mis-

chievous Scandinavian) trow(ie) SHET-LAND, ORKNEY; **fairies** guid fowk(s), little fowk(s).

fairy-hill sithean HIGHLAND, trowie knowe SHETLAND, ORKNEY.

fairyland Elfin.

fairy-ring elf-ring.

faith: faithful *see also* **loyal;** aefauld, leal-hertit.

break faith with mistryst wi.

have faith in lippen tae *or* on.

lack faith in mislippen.

fake *see* **fraud.**

fall *verb* fa(w): **1** clype NE; (*from a height*) hurl; (*suddenly*) whummle, snapper SHETLAND, NE; (*down flat, esp to hide*) flap; (*heavily*) cloit, play dad, sklyte NE, flype NE, doist NE; (*with a sharp thud*) rap, sclype NE; (*heavily, into water*) plowt, plype NE; (*rapidly in drops*) rap SHETLAND, ORKNEY. **2** (*of rain, heavily: see also* **rain**) plump, ding (on *or* doon); (*with a splash*) clash; (*intermittently*) leck; (*of snow etc*) smore. **3** (*of prices*) be on the doon han(d) NE.

noun fa(w), clink N; (*tumble*) whummle, cowp; (*esp when skating*) lander; (*sudden*) clink N; (*heavy: see also* **thud**) dunt, cloit, plunk, sklyte, sclype NE, pergaddus NE, FIFE; (*violent*) pardoos SHETLAND; (*esp into water or mud*) sclatch NE, plowt; (*with a splash*) clash; (*esp on something soft*) flaip S; (*into soft earth etc*) plert; (*heavy and noisy*) clype NE; (*and stunning*) dird NE; (*and awkward*) soss; (*on the buttocks*) dowp-scoor NE; (*on your back*) keel-up; (*of rain, snow: heavy; see also* **downpour**) plump, onfa(w), dooncome; (*of snow: slight*) skiffin.

fall out *see also* **quarrel;** cast oot, skew NE, cut harrows S.

fall over cowp, cave, whummle.

fall to pieces *see also* **crumble;** fa(w) a(w) tae staps, murl (doon).

fallow *adjective* lea, ley, white.

verb (*break fallow ground*) fauch.

fallow ground lea break, fauch.

lie fallow rest.

false fause, lee-lik(e) SW, S; (*underhand*) sleekit.

falsehood *see also* **lie**[1]; fausehood, falset.

falseness pit-on, swickerie NE.

false step snapper NE.

false teeth wallies CENTRAL.

falter 1 *see also* **stumble;** stammer. **2** (*in speech: see also* **stammer**) stoiter.

famed *see* **famous.**

familiar *see also* **friendly;** fameeliar, (weel-)kent, lang-kent, kenspeckle; (*homely*) hamelt, hameower, couthie.

familiar communication traffeck.

familiar term of address *see* **address.**

familiar with uised wi, yaised wi, eest wi N.

become familiar with (*something new*) get intae.

family faim(i)lie; (*ancestry*) kin; (*your relatives*) yer fowk; (*brood*) cleckin; (*of small children*) sma faimilie; (*of two children*) doo's cleckin.

family prayers (faimilie) worship.

of good family weel come.

last child of a large family poke-shakkins, shakkins o the pok(i)e.

famine faimine.

famish faimish, hunger.

famished howe.

famous fawmous NE, faur kent, namelie.

fan *verb* waff; (*a flame*) flaff.

noun, see **winnowing fan.**

fancy *noun, see* **whim, liking.**

adjective wallie, fantoosh.

verb (*a person of opposite sex*) lik(e).

take a fancy to fa(w) in fancy wi, be taen up wi.

fantastic pawkie.

far faur, ferr S.

farther farder, faurer, ferrer S, fa(u)ther.

farthest *see also* **furthest in;** farrest, fardest, ferrest S.

far away hyne-awa, hyndies awa *child's word*, NE.

far gone (*in illness*) (sair) awa wi't.
far-sighted faur-seen, forehandit, niz-wise NE.
as far as the lenth o.
from far and near faur an aboot.
far too ... useless: '*useless monie*', ees(e)less NE.
farce ferce S.
fare *verb* fa(w): '*foul fa ye*', luck SHETLAND, N, betide NE.
noun **1** *see also* **food**; farin. **2** (*for transport by water*) fraucht.
fared *past participle* forn SHETLAND.
farewell fareweel, fare ye weel.
farewell feast foy.
farewell meeting (*eg of a council*) greetin meetin.
fare badly come huilie tae.
farm *noun, see also* **croft, home farm**; ferm, place, room, grun(d), tack; (*buildings and surrounding area*) toon; (*outlying*) oot-ferm; (*small, outlying, managed by employee*) led ferm; (*tenant*) mailin; (*hill, for sheep-rearing*) storefarm SW, S.
verb ferm.
farmer fermer, guidman, (*female*) guidwife, muck-the-byre *contemptuous*; (*tenant*) tacksman; (*leasing animals and grazing rights*) bower, bowman; (*dairy*) coo-feeder.
farmer's eldest unmarried daughter missie.
farmer's wife dame NE, FIFE, guidwife.
farm animal baist, beast, beas; (*which remains outdoors in winter*) ootlier; (*work-animals*) stryth CAITHNESS.
farm bailiff grieve.
farm buildings (*with or without farmhouse*) *see also* **homestead**; (ferm) steidin, steid, ferm steid, onsteid, onset; (*when forming four sides*) square; (*outbuildings*) mains.
farm cottage cot hoose; (*tied*) †cottar hoose; (*group of*) cot toon; (*row of*) toon end.
live in a farm cottage cottar.

farmhouse *see also* **farm buildings**; ha, ha-hoose SHETLAND.
farmland grun(d); (*near the farm, in continuous cultivation*) †infield, †intoun NE; (*outlying*) †outfield, †out-toun NE; (*adjoining house*) (toon) loan; (*cleared of crops*) redlan(d).
farm-lease of nineteen years nineteen.
farm overseer grieve.
farm sale (*of stock, implements etc*) displenishing sale.
farm servant *see also* **farmworker**; hirer; (*who looks after horses*) horseman; (*kitchenmaid*) (kitchie) deem NE.
farmstead *see* **homestead**.
farmstock *see* **stock** 1.
farmworker *see also* **farm servant, cattleman, ploughman**; jock(ie), joskin, cley davie NE; (*female*) jennie; (*adolescent*) halflin, loon N; (*piece worker*) tasker; (*receiving some wage in kind*) benefit man SW; (*married, with farm cottage*) cottar, hind S, (*left in charge when others are away*) toondie NE, toonkeeper NE; (*doing odd jobs*) orraman, orra loon NE, quarterer, pirler.
farmworkers ferm fowk; (*male*) men fowk; (*on large farm*) hash NE; (*living in farm cottages*) cot fowk.
farmworkers' quarters (*for unmarried men*) bothy, hyne hoose NE, chaumer NE, berrick.
farmyard yaird, close, backside; (*paved or hand-beaten around house*) cassie.
farrier *see also* **blacksmith**; ferrier.
farrow *verb* ferry.
farther *see* **far, further**.
farthing farden, ferthin S, curdie.
fashion fasson.
fashionable tippie.
after a fashion in a kind.
fast[1] *adjective, adverb* **1** *see also* **quick**; fest, fost; (*very*) ding-dust ULSTER. **2** (*of a watch*) forrit.
as fast as possible at the ivver-leevin (gallop) NE.

make fast rance.

play fast and loose play Jock needle Jock preen NE.

fast[2] *noun* fest.

fasten fessen, steek; (*tightly*) hankle; (*esp with a loop*) hank; (*with a catch*) snib, sneck; (*with a hook*) cleek; (*with a hasp*) hesp.

fastener *see* **catch, latch**.

fastening hiddin NE, huidin SHETLAND, ORKNEY, steek NE.

fastidious *see also* **fussy**; perjink, dainshach, primp; (*about dress*) saucy, jeetie NE; (*about food*) skeichen NE, nice-gabbit, pe(r)neurious NE.

fastidiously perjink.

fat *noun* creesh; (*esp of pigs*) (soo-)saim, (swine's) saim.

adjective **1** (*greasy*) creeshie. **2** (*of persons: see also* **stout, plump, corpulent, chubby**) bowsie, bulfie; (*very*) fat as a puggie, lipper-fat S; (*flabby*) fozie, gowstie NE; (*and inactive*) brosie-heidit NE.

fatten mend.

being fattened (*of a sheep etc*) feedin: '*feedin sheep*'.

of the back view of a small fat man aa erse an pootches NE.

the fat's in the fire the deil's gane ower Jock Wabster N, the kiln's on fire, the ba(w)'s (up) on the slates.

short fat person pult, punch(ik)ie NE, pellock ORKNEY, NE.

fat clumsy person fodge SE, hush NE, selch NE.

fat unshapely person trollie-bags.

fat clumsy woman clatch, hotch, flodge, mardle SHETLAND, NE.

big fat woman hoose-en(d), sodie.

fat sluggish person hillock.

fat easy-going person sugg ORKNEY, NE.

short fat girl cuttie.

fat clumsy young man stilch.

fat hen (*plant*) midden-weed, melgs N.

fate weird: '*ye maun dree yer (ain) weird*'.

fatal deedlie.

fated (to die) fey.

fateful weirdfu.

father *noun, see also* **dad**; faither, fader SHETLAND, NE, auld yin.

verb faither, fader SHETLAND, NE.

father-in-law guid-faither.

fatherlasher cumper ORKNEY, NE, gundie NE, hardheid.

show who your father is (*by resemblance*) faither, fader N.

fathom *noun, verb* faddom.

fatigue *noun* tire.

verb, see also **exhaust**; tash, stress, jaup.

fatigued *see also* **exhausted, tired**; ramfoozelt, traikit.

faucet *see also* **spigot**; stroop.

fault *noun* faut: **1** (*geological, esp in a mine*) tribble, back, thraw, step AYRSHIRE. **2** (*in character: see also* **flaw**) shortcome, mote NE. **3** blame: '*it's no ma blame*', wyte.

faultless *see* **perfect**.

fault-finding capernicious NE, nurrin SHETLAND, CAITHNESS.

find fault with hae a faut tae, faut, challenge, quarrel, cabal NE, be at (someone about something).

commit a (moral) fault step aside.

favour *verb* (*someone to the exclusion of others*) no see past (someone), nae see by.

noun (*act of kindness*) obleegement.

favourable *see also* **lucky**; cannie; (*of weather: for crops*) forcie NE, (*for work*) fordersome.

general favourite a(w)bodie's bodie.

in great favour faur ben.

be in favour be i the guidman's buiks NE.

be in favour with hae an infit wi NE.

curry favour *see also* **flatter, fawn**; sook in, sook up (till), haud in, cheek in NE, hing in, smool.

owe someone a favour hae a day in hairst wi someone.

fawn *verb* beenge, feeze, plaister, foonge NE, smool, fleetch.

fawn on phrase NE.

fawning *adjective* lick-lip, inhaudin N, FIFE; (*and deceitful*) sleek(ie).

fear *see also* **dread**: *noun* dree.

fearful 1 *see also* **afraid, timid**; skeer, timorsome, feart for the day ye nivver saw. **2** (*disquieting*) frichtsome, oorie SHETLAND. **3** *see* **awful**.

fearless *see* **bold**.

fearsome-looking person, source of fear fley.

feasible faisible.

feast *noun, see also* **harvest-home**; eat NE, belly-rive(r) NE; (*after a birth*) blithemait; (*funeral, esp of drink*) dredgie; (*farewell*) foy.

verb (*immoderately*) gilravage.

feat (*difficult*) kittle; (*acrobatic, gymnastic*) henner EDINBURGH.

feather *noun, see also* **tuft**; fedder SHETLAND, ORKNEY, N, pen.

featherbrain sodie-heid, glaik, ceepher, monument.

featherbrained *see* **flighty** (*under* **flight**[1]).

get feathers (*of a bird*) feather.

feature *noun* (*trait*) track SHETLAND; (*facial, in a family*) swap SHETLAND; (*distinguishing feature*) kenspeckle, meith; (*feature in common*) swatch.

February †Februar.

feckless haveless N, smeerless, knotless, daeinless, paidlin.

fed-up scunnert, uggit.

become fed-up sta(w).

feeble (*of persons: see also* **weak, tottery, faint**) fushionless, faur awa wi't, waff(lik(e)), waffle, wammilie, mauch(t)less, peelie-wallie, dwaiblie, dowless.

feeble-minded *see* **mentally handicapped**.

feed *verb, see also* **fed-up**; stowe, mait; (*and clothe*) fettle; (*of a nursing mother*) foster SHETLAND, ORKNEY, NE; (*cattle and horses with hay etc*) fother; (*a horse with oats or grain*) corn NE; (*cattle with turnips*) neep.

feel *verb, noun* fin(d).

feeling (*attitude*) souch.

without feeling tebbitless.

feet *see also* **foot**; lyomons NE.

feign *see also* **pretend**; feingie.

feigned feingit, simulate.

feint *see also* **pretend**: *verb, noun* (*threaten*) mint NE.

felicity *see* **happiness**.

fell[1] *verb* (*strike down*) foon(d)er; (*trees*) hag.

fell[2] *adjective, see* **fierce**.

felloe fillie.

fellow *noun, see also* **man, chap**[2]; fella(e), follow, fallie SE, chiel(d), billie, callan(t), loon *mainly* N, carle, wicht.

female *see also* **woman**.

female head (*of something*), **female boss** hersel(f).

femur *see* **thigh-bone**.

fence *noun* **1** pilin SW, S; (*of stakes and twigs*) stake an rice; (*of furze bushes*) whin dyke; (*over stream, to stop animals straying etc*) watter gate; (*eg as windbreak in front of a door*) skathie. **2** (*receiver of stolen goods*) resetter.

verb (*with stakes*) stob.

fencepost (*fence*) stob, pailin stab.

strainer in a wire fence stentin post.

fend fen.

fend for yourself fork.

able to fend for yourself fendie, fendfu.

ferment *verb* barm, berm S.

fermenting (*of grain*) het.

fern *see also* **bracken**; firn, rannoch; (*lady*) leddy bracken, leddy fern.

ferocious *see* **fierce**.

ferret foumart, thoumart, whitrat, futrat NE.

ferrule virl, bee SW, S.

ferry *verb* **ferry across** set ower.

noun bait NE.

ferry-boat coble NE.

fertile *see also* **prolific**; (*of vegetation*) growthie.

fertility growthieness.

fertilize *see* **manure.**
fertilizer *see* **manure.**
fervent *see* **eager.**
fester beal, etter.
festering bealin, atterie.
festering sore *see also* **boil;** bealin.
festive blithe, rantin.
festive gathering rant.
period of festivities at Christmas and New Year the Daft Days.
festivities when a bride comes to her new home hame-come SHETLAND, NE, hame-fare SHETLAND, ORKNEY.
fetch fess, fesh, seek S.
fetched *past tense* fuish, fotch, feess NE. *past participle* fessen N, fuishen.
fetid *see* **putrid.**
fetlock cuit.
fetter *see also* **hobble;** hapshackle.
fettle kilter, tift, kippage.
feud †feid.
fever (*esp scarlet*) fivver; (*scarlet*) rush-fever; (*sudden high, esp puerperal*) weed.
sudden fevered state feem.
feverfew featherfoolie NE.
few fyow N; **a few** a (wee) pickle, a pucklie, a wheen, a curn, nae monie, twa-three, three-fower.
fewer less.
fiasco *see* **disaster.**
fib *see also* **lie;** feeb.
fibre (*esp fibrous roots*) taw, tanners.
fickle *see also* **capricious;** kittle, flichtersome NE, flichterie NE.
fiddle *noun* (*cheating*) pauchle.
verb **1** (*play the fiddle*) diddle. **2 fiddle (about)** *see also* **potter, waste time, dawdle, fidget;** fouter, plowter, palaver, pirl NE; (*nervously with the fingers*) ficher SHETLAND, NE; **fiddle with** nibble. **3** *see also* **cheat;** pauchle.
fiddler (*nickname*) fiddlie NE, gutscraper.
fiddling, fiddly fouterie, pernicketie, skitterie, scutterie NE, tooterie NE, titersome NE; (*of work*) pinglin.
fiddle-peg thoomack NE.

fiddle-player *see* **fiddler.**
fiddle-string thairm.
sound of the fiddle plink.
fidget *verb, see also* **fiddle;** fidge, fyke, hushle NE; (*esp restlessly*) rowe; (*esp impatiently*) hotch, hodge NE.
the fidgets the fykes.
fidgety fykie, ficherie NE.
field *noun, see also* **meadow;** park, perk S, feedle NE, glebe; (*long, rather than broad*) rig; (*of old grass*) lea field, lea park.
fieldfare skitterie feltie, feltie, feltiflier, feltifer.
field labourer ootby worker; (*female*) ootumman NE.
outlying field ootfield.
fiend *see also* **devil;** fient.
fierce 1 bang, fell, bowsterous, turk NE, ramsh. **2** (*of a battle, a struggle*) sair.
fierce person teeger.
look fierce teeger.
fiery (*in temperament*) het-skinnt.
fifteen feifteen.
fifteenth feifteent.
fifth fift.
fifty fuftie.
fig feg.
fight *see also* **struggle:** *verb* fecht, faucht; (*eg in skirmish, in street*) bicker; (*quarrel*) tulyie, sharrie NE, tyarr CAITHNESS; (*noisily*) tirr-wirr.
noun, see also **dogfight;** fecht, faucht; †brattle *literary*; (*eg in street*) bicker; (*battle*) hubble, stour; (*scuffle*) rammie, tulyie, yokin NE, shangie, sharrie NE; (*to settle a grudge*) han(d)-shakin S; (*against odds*) pilget NE, pingle.
fighter fechter, kemper; (*intrepid, esp in a cause*) bonnie fechter.
ready to fight fechtie.
fight with your own shadow fecht wi yer ain taes.
figure *noun* feegur, (*stucco*) stookie.
verb feegur, jalouse.
figurehead †tulchan.
filch *see also* **steal;** skech, pike NE, pauchle.

file[1] (*row*) raw.
file[2] *verb* (*smooth off*) risp, resp s.
 noun (*coarse*) risp.
fill *verb, see also* **cram**; prime, fou; (*a container*) eik up; (*to capacity*) stap; (*of the contents*) sleek; (*esp the stomach: see also* **gorge**) stowe, stech, puist s, (*eg a hole*) colf NE; (*with mud etc*) clatch up; (*crevices in masonry*) sneck NE.
 noun fou, (*esp of food*) sairin.
 filling *adjective* (*of food*) fousome.
film *noun* (*thin layer*) scruif SHETLAND, ORKNEY, N, screef NE, striffin SHETLAND, ORKNEY, CAITHNESS; (*of vapour etc*) (y)oam SHETLAND, ORKNEY, NE, yim NE, gum N.
 become covered with a film (*eg of condensation*) gum NE, yim NE, scam.
 filter *noun, verb, see also* **sieve**; sye, sile, sythe.
filth *see also* **dirt, excrement**; fulyie, cla(i)rt, glit, geing.
 filthy fousome NE, maukit, maukie, unfeel s; (*of persons*) brockit; (*muddy*) cla(i)rtie, (*esp with excrement*) keechie, dirten.
fin (*pectoral, with attachments*) lug.
final hin(der)maist.
 finally hin(d)maist, at the hinneren(d), at (the) lang an (the) lenth, at lang an last.
finance: your finances yer pootch.
 help someone financially turn someone's han(d).
finch *see* **bullfinch, goldfinch, greenfinch.**
find *see also* **found**[1]; fin, (*by looking*) get, git, airt oot s.
fine *adjective* **1** *see also* **first-rate**; braw, brave, gey (lik(e)), gran(d); (*of persons*) pretty. **2** (*of weather*) braw, leesome NE. **3** (*in texture*) sma.
 finery (*in dress*) bravitie, braws.
 become fine (*of weather*) fair (up).
 stay fine (*of weather*) keep up, haud up.
finger *noun* (*little: see also* **little finger**)

pinkie; (*index*) coorag CAITHNESS; (*middle*) mid-finger.
 verb pawt; (*excessively*) thummle SW.
 white speck on a fingernail present.
 finger-stall finger-stuil, finger-steel N, SE.
 fingertip finger neb, finger en(d).
 use fingers deftly nabble; (*in something intricate*) niddle.
finicky (*fussy, intricate*) fykie, (*fussy*) perjink, jinipperous, peremptor SHETLAND.
finish *verb* feenish; (*food, drink*) perish *humorous*, cowe.
 finished 1 gaed duin; (*esp of work*) byhan(d); (*of a meeting etc*) oot. **2** (*done for*) awa wi't.
 finishing time (*at work*) lowsin time.
 finish off (*eg in a fight*) doctor.
fiord *see* **fjord.**
fir: fircone fir yowe NE, yowie NE, (fir) tap, peerie s, burr N, dirken N; (*of the Scots pine*) sheepie NE.
 fir-root *or* (**-**)**knot** knab NE.
 bog-fir moss-fir.
fire *noun* lowe; (*on a hearth*) ingle; (*large, bright*) gleesh(ach) NE; (*glowing*) greeshoch; (*blazing*) tover SHETLAND, N; (*from wood-friction, supposed magic*) †needfire.
 firedamp wildfire.
 fire-engine the butts.
 fireplace chim(b)ley NE, brace; (*whole structure*) lum; (*in a kiln*) sornie CAITHNESS; (*open-air, with sods and iron bar*) lunkart N.
 stone at back of fireplace backstane, hud s, cat-hud.
 firescreen sconce.
 fireside ingle(-neuk), ingle-cheek, chim(b)ley-lug NE, fire-en(d).
 firewood *see also* **fuel, kindling**; browl(s); (*small pieces*) chirls NE.
 firework (*rocket*) racket; (*squib*) squeeb; (*homemade*) peeoy.
 fire off (*shot etc*) set aff.
 catch fire gae on fire, tak lowe, tak lunt.

column of fire and smoke lunt.

draw up to the fire come in tae the fire.

make a fire *see also* kindle; big a fire; (*to keep burning*) hap a fire.

on fire on haud: '*yer lum's on haud*'; (*specif of a chimney*) up.

set on fire (*chimney*) set up: '*set the lum up*'

set fire to *see also* kindle; lunt S.

sit lazily by the fire leep, hoker ower the fire.

firm *adjective* (*stable, secure*) sicker, stench NE, solvendie, stieve.

firmly (*securely*) hard, stieve(lie).

firmly fixed stieve.

make firm sicker, stieve.

first (*foremost*) forehand.

first light (*of day*) mornin blink SHETLAND.

first-rate *see also* excellent; tap, nae din-bonnets NE, principal SHETLAND, NE.

take first place be the heid o the heap, bear the gree *literary*.

fish *noun* fush; (*caught inshore on small lines*) sma fish; (*no longer fresh*) Monday's haddie; (*spent*) spyntie NE, slink; (*putrid*) scag.

verb, see also troll; fush; (*inshore with a small net*) screenge; (*with the hands*) guddle.

fisherman fisher; (*who shares in profits*) half-deal man.

fisherman's hut lodge SHETLAND; (*for salmon-fishers*) bothy.

fishing boat *see also* trawler; (*kind of small*) skiff, yole SHETLAND, ORKNEY, N; (*kind of light*) scaith NE; (*kind of carvel-built*) ba(u)ldie; (*kind of Dutch*) bum NE; (*line-fishing*) liner; (*herring*) drave boat; (*kind of herring-boat*) Fifie E COAST, nabbie; (*flat-bottomed for salmon-fishing*) (saumon) coble.

member of a fishing community (*male or female*) fisher.

fishing hook preen.

fishing line (*inshore*) sma line; (*hand-line*) handlin; (*which bobs up and down*) dandie (line) SHETLAND, NE; (*first shot from boat*) teeset NE; (*last section to be shot*) tide-line NE.

cord *etc* attaching fishing line to hook snuid, tippin N, FIFE, tippet NE, tome SHETLAND, ORKNEY, N, imp.

leave fishing lines to allow fish to take bait tide the lines.

fishing net (*next to boat*) buird N; (*first shot from boat*) trail-en(d) SHETLAND, NE, tail-net SHETLAND, CAITHNESS; (*first after buoy*) powe net; (*seine*) trawl; (*between two boats which sail closer together*) ring-net; (*used in deep-water fishing*) greatlin; (*suspended, into which fish are driven by splashing*) splash net; (*on long handle*) ave N.

place a fishing net in water shuit a net.

fishing rod (fishin) wan(d), spaingie wan(d) NE, gaud.

segment of a fishing rod skair.

fishing village fisher toon NE.

fish-hawker (fish-)cadger.

stuffed fish-heads crappit heids, stappit heidies N.

fish refuse goories NE.

fish-spear (*with several prongs*) leister, waster.

fish-trap (*esp of stakes across a river*) cruive, croy; (*esp of stone etc across a river*) yair SW; (*esp for lobsters*) creel.

fish and chips fish supper.

person who cleans and prepares fish washer SHETLAND, NE.

person who splits fish and removes backbone spleeter SHETLAND, CAITHNESS, NE.

fissure clift, rift, rive SHETLAND.

fist nieve, niv.

clenched fist steekit nieve.

fistful nievefu.

fisticuffs nieves.

fit[1] *verb* 1 (*of clothes*) ser. 2 (*a bootlace, cart wheel, with a metal tip, band etc*) shod; (*one edge of (a plank) to another*) seam.

fit

adjective 1 (*suitable*) settin, confeerin NE; (*law: admissible*) habile. 2 (*physically*) able, kneef N, solvendie, umbersorrow S.

fitted-out boden NE.

fitting *adjective* (*suitable*) wicelik(e).

badly-fitting (*of shoes*) sha(u)chlin.

fittings (*esp of metal on wood*) munts.

fit in with complouter wi.

fit out (*with clothes etc*) pit oot NE.

fit²: fitful (*changeable*) flichtrif(e).

fit of rage *see also* **rage**; tirrivee.

five: group of five fivesome.

fix *verb* (*in position*) stell; (*firmly*) sicker.

fixed (*of wages*) upstannin.

fizz *verb* (*of liquids*) bizz; (*make a fizzing noise*) fiss NE.

fizzy fuzzie NE.

fjord, fiord sea loch, voe SHETLAND, ORKNEY.

flabbergast *see also* **dumbfound**; stammygaster.

flabby fozie, gowstie NE.

flabbiness foziness.

flabby-cheeked guffie.

flag *verb* (*become weary*) fag.

flagon stowp.

flail *noun* frail.

beater of a flail swingle, soople.

handle of a flail han(d)staff.

flail about (*with the limbs*) spra(u)chle, sprawlach NE.

flair flerr.

flake *noun* (*esp of snow: see also* **snowflake**) flichan, fla(u)cht, pirl; (*thin slice*) skelf, skelb, skelp.

verb skelf, skelb.

fall in flakes (*of snow*) fla(u)cht; (*large*) flag NE.

flamboyant (*esp in dress*) prinkie, kickie; (*of colours*) roarie, skyrie ORKNEY, NE.

flame *noun* flam, lowe, glaim; (*bright*) gleesh; (*very small*) peep, peek; (*of a candle etc*) doozie.

burn with a bright flame lowe.

go up in flames tak lowe, gae ableeze.

flange lug.

flank (*of the body*) lisk.

flannel flannen.

flannelette flannenette.

flap *noun* 1 (*of a shoe, cap etc*) lug. 2 (*flapping motion*) waff.

verb, see also **flutter**; flaff, fluffer NE, waff, waffle, wap, wallop; (*esp of bird's wings*) flochter; **flap about** wampish; (*cause to flap*) flaff, wap.

having flaps luggit.

flare up 1 lowe, bleeze. 2 (*in anger*) lowp up (at), flist NE, spunk up, loss the heid.

flash *noun* (*of light: see also* **gleam**) gliff, glisk, skime, glent; (*of lightning*) (fire-)fla(u)cht.

verb **flash past** glint.

flashy *see also* **showy**; fantoosh; (*of colours*) roarie, skyrie ORKNEY, NE.

in a flash in a glint, lik(e) spottie NE.

flask flesk S.

flat *adjective* flet: 1 (*level, even*) plat SHETLAND, plain; (*of feet, and splayed*) shuilie; (*of a dish*) skleff. 2 (*dull*) fushionless. 3 (*of beer*) wersh.

noun (*apartment*) hoose, hoosie; (*one-roomed*) single-en(d); (*two-roomed*) room an kitchen.

adverb (*on your face*) flatlins, belly-flaucht, grooflins.

flatten flet; (*crops*) lay, buff NE.

flat-chested skleff S.

flat foot sclaffer, bap fit NE.

flat-footed plain-soled, sclaff-fittit, spagach N, plat-fittit S.

block of flats (*usually three or four storeys*) tenement.

person with flat shuffling feet shuil-fit.

flatter *see also* **wheedle**; blaw up, blaw in someone's lug, claw someone's back, ruise, reese NE, fleetch, fraik, phrase NE, foonge (on) NE, sleek, cuittle SW, S, sook in wi.

flatterer *see also* **wheedler**; sook, fraik; (*excessive*) plaister, lick-ma-dowp, lick-spit.

flattering *adjective, see also* **obsequious, wheedling**; buttery-lippit, fair-ca(w)in, fair-farran(t).

approach in a flattering way cuddle (up tae), sook up tae.

flattery ruise, reese NE, fraik, phrasin NE, flairdie SW, whillywha.

flatulence pumpin, curmur(rin), rummle-gumption(s) *humorous*.

flatulent heftit.

relieve flatulence brak the win(d) SHETLAND, CAITHNESS, NE, pump.

flaunt *see* **show off** (*under* **show**).

flavour *noun, see also* **taste, savour**; (*disagreeable*) kneggum, touk.

give flavour to kitchen.

having a strong coarse flavour ramp SW, S.

lacking flavour *see also* **tasteless**; wersh, fen(d)less NE.

sharpness of flavour nip.

flaw mote NE, defection, gaw; (*in character*) shortcome; (*esp in cloth*) jesp SE, felter FIFE, (*gap*) gaw; (*in stone*) awte NE.

flax lint.

flax-dresser lint-dresser.

flax-factory lint-mill.

flax-flower lint-bell.

flax-seed linget N.

flax-seedpod lint-bowe.

flax-spinning-wheel lint-wheel.

bundle of flax (*ready for processing*) lint-beet; (*dressed and put in distaff*) †lint tap, †tap (o lint).

pile of flax refuse †pob-towe.

white as flax (*of hair*) lint-white.

flea *see also* **sand-flea**; flech, flae.

fleas cattle.

rid (*a person or animal*) **of fleas** flech.

fleck *noun* spreckle.

verb spreckle, (*esp with snow*) grime.

fledgling *see* **nestling**.

flee flicht, tak the gate, †tak tae the bent; (*at once*) be uptail an awa; (*from justice*) tak leg bail.

flee the country lowp the country NE.

fleece *noun* fleesh; (*matted*) ket.

flesh *noun* (*of poultry or game*) white mait; (*tainted, esp of sheep*) ket SE.

fleshy pluffie, sappie, chuffie.

flexible *see also* **supple**; dwaible, dwamfle NE, swack N, waffle.

flibbertigibbet sodie-heid.

flick *verb* spang.

noun flisk, (*esp of the fingers, to move a marble*) plunk.

flicker *verb* (*of a light*) flichter, blinter NE, chitter *in poetry*; (*of the eyelid etc*) wicker.

noun (*of a light*) flichter; (*of the eyelid etc*) wicker.

flight[1] **1** (*act of flying*) flicht. **2** (*flock of birds*) flocht.

flighty *see also* **frivolous**; flichtie, flauntie, fliskie, licht-farran(t), hawkit, stane pirrie S, sturdie(d) SHETLAND, CAITHNESS, daft as a yett on a windy day; (*esp of a girl*) skeerie.

flight[2] (*act of fleeing*) flicht.

put to flight skail, fley, gie heels tae.

take flight *see also* **flee**; flicht.

flimsy silly; (*esp of clothes*) slim SHETLAND, N, flindrikin NE.

flimsy thing (*esp cloth*) flindrikin NE, reevick S.

flinch flench, jouk, scunner, resile, crulge.

fling wap, hove, shine S, fung.

fling together hush.

flint arrowhead (*thought to be used by fairies*) elf-arrow.

flipper (*of a seal*) meg SHETLAND, ORKNEY, CAITHNESS.

flirt *verb* gallant, glaik, haud a fyke, jink, gawk, mird, tig, tig-towe, daff(er); (*sloppily*) floan NE; **flirt with** rush.

noun (*girl*) jillet.

flirtation pawkie, dafferie.

flirtatious *see* **coquettish**.

float *verb* fleet SHETLAND; (*gently*) cowd(le).

noun (*glass etc, on a fishing line*) pallet; (*cork, to mark sunken lines etc*) stoy NE.

flock *noun* paircel; (*esp of sheep*) hirsel; (*of birds*) flocht.

arrange (*sheep*) (**in flocks**) hirsel.

flog *see also* **whip, beat**; flag, belt, leather, whang, lamp, skeeg NE.

flood *noun* flude, fleed N, soom SHETLAND, N: '*in a soom*', (*esp in a river*) spate.

verb, see also **overflow**; flude, fleed N, (*esp of a river*) spate.

floor *noun, verb* flair, fleer NE, fluir.

ground floor first flair.

floored with wood wuidlaid.

on the ground floor laich.

flop *verb* **flop down** clap doon; (*esp to hide*) flap; (*noisily*) clank doon; (*for a short rest*) flype NE.

florid *see* **showy**.

flotsam (and jetsam) (*floating rubbish*) wrack, god('s)-send, spreath.

flounce[1] *verb* flunce SHETLAND, NE, flird, fling.

flounce[2] *noun* (*on a dress etc*) squirl N, fabala.

verb (*in sewing*) mush.

flounder[1] *verb, also* **flounder about** floonder, spra(u)chle, wallop, walloch N, spralloch NE, plowster S, spalter, swatter, welter; (*in mud*) slutter NE.

flounder[2] *noun* (*fish*) floonder, flunner N, fleuk, grayback NE, FIFE.

flour floor.

flourish *verb* 1 (*of plants*) blaw NE, blume, bleem N. 2 (*thrive*) forder, dae guid, mak oot. 3 *see* **brandish**.

noun (*eg in handwriting*) pirlicue, squirl N.

flourishing 1 (*of plants*) raffie NE. 2 (*of a business etc*) guid-gaun.

flout hoot.

flow *verb* fleet, pirr, trinnle NE; (*esp of rain or sweat*) hail.

noun (*of water*) rin; (*of blood etc*) shot.

flower *noun, see also* **bunch**; flooer; (*artificial*) gum-flooer.

verb, see **flourish**.

flowering currant son-afore-the-faither.

flowery flooerie.

flowerbed knot.

flower vase pig.

flu haingles, hingles NE.

fluctuate swither.

flue (*of a chimney*) vent.

fluent (*in speech*) gabbie, glib, tonguie.

fluency tongue-raik.

fluff (*from cloth etc*) oos(e), oother S, caddis.

fluffy oos(s)ie.

fluid *noun, see* **liquid**.

flurry *noun* 1 (*of snow etc*) skirlie, tirl NE, waff; (*esp of sleet*) snifter. 2 *see also* **bustle, commotion**; flocht, swither, fudder NE, hatter S.

move in a flurry *see also* **bustle**; flocht, swither.

flush *verb* (*with clean water*) reenge, synd.

fluster *noun, see also* **bustle**; swither, pilget NE.

verb fluister, flochter.

flustered hattert S.

flute *verb* (*cloth*) pipe.

flutter *verb* 1 fluther, flichter, flauchter, flaff(er), fluff(er), wavel, flird, whitter, wamfle; (*of a leaf etc*) wag; (*esp of birds in water*) squatter, swatter. 2 (*be excited*) flichter, fidder.

noun (*flapping*) flaff, flichter, flauchter.

fly[1] *verb* flee, flicht, (*lightly*) skiff; (*off at a tangent*) skite; (*of birds, awkwardly*) flichter.

noun 1 (*of a spinning wheel*) flichts SHETLAND, NE. 2 (*in trousers*) shop door, spaiver, spare, ballop.

flying (*of clouds*) rackin.

flywheel (*of a spindle*) whurl.

let fly lat sing, lat fung NE.

send flying skite.

fly[2] *noun* (*insect*) flee; (*angling: dubbed with a hare's ear*) hare('s) lug; (*types of artificial*) heckum-peckum, professor.

foal *see* **colt, horse**.

foam *noun, verb* faem, fro, freith, ream; (*of a strong sea*) kav SHETLAND, NE.

foaming (*of ale etc*) nappie, barmie.

fob (*watch pocket*) spung.

fob off jank aff, set aff.

fodder *noun, verb* fother.

foe *see also* **enemy**; fae *in poetry*.

fog *see also* **mist**; loom, rouk; (*thick*) smoch; (*cold, esp on* E COAST) haar; (*dense, from sea*) thickness.

foggy *see also* **misty**; haarie, roukie.

foist on to pawn on tae.

fold[1] *verb, see also* **wrap**; faul(d); (*cloth*) faik; (*fold back*) flype; (*wrap*) wap, wup; (*work into folds*) ruckle; (*cloth lengthwise after weaving*) crisp; (*arms*) plet.

noun faul(d); (*of a garment*) faik NE, flype; (*layer*) ply; (*crease*) kink, lirk, ruckle, gruggle NE.

fold[2] (*for animals: see also* **enclosure, sheepfold**) faul(d), crue, criv NE, lair.

folk fowk.

follow fallow, follae.

follow (*someone*) **about** traik efter.

folly madderam SHETLAND, ORKNEY.

foment (*a sore in hot water*) plot.

fond: fond of browden on NE, fain o; (*extremely*) daft aboot, daft for, daft on.

be fond of be keen o, browden.

I am very fond of leeze me on.

fondle *see also* **cuddle, grope**; culyie, daut; dossach (wi) NE; (*sloppily*) slaik; (*a child*) daidle.

fontanelle open o the heid.

food fuid, mait, scran, vivers, parritch, pottitch NE, kail, belly-timber, farin, meal('s) corn, chuck, leevin, fend NE, scaff; (*small amount*) pickin; (*insubstantial*) gnap-at-the-win NE; (*liquid: eg gruel*) blearie; (*small amount*) drabble; (*watery*) spleuterie NE; (*soft*) spuin-mait; (*messy*) plowter, soss, kirn, sowce CAITHNESS; (*sloppy*) slaiger, slubber; (*unpalatable*) slaister, slitter; (*unappetizing*) spoot-ma-gruel NE.

food and drink meal an maut NE, gear.

having a plentiful supply of food maitrif(e) S.

provide food for mait.

scrap of food peck, snap; **scraps of food** (*for beggars*) scran NE.

fool *noun, see also* **idiot, blockhead**; fuil, feel N, daftie, geck, gawk(ie), gawkus, gawpus, haiverel, gumph, stupe, docus, bawheid; (*simpleton*) coof, gowk(ie), gumph, guff; (*feeble*) sookin teuchit NE: '*he hisna e wit o a sookin teuchit*', sookin turkey; (*chattery*) blether(um)skite.

verb jamph, pit intae, tak the turn oot o, begowk, begunk.

foolish *see also* **stupid**; fuil, feel N, fuil-lik(e), daft, glaikit, tuim-heidit, eediotical, gypit, gowkit, menseless, unwicelik(e) N, saikless S.

foolishness daftness, gyper(t)ie NE, bladrie.

fool's errand (*esp on 1 April: see also* **April fool**) huntiegowk.

make a fool of *see also* **pull someone's leg** (*under* **pull**); lead (*someone*) by the neb, tak the rag (oot) o, tak the lift o NE, gype.

play the fool kiow-ow, gype, gawk(ie), act the daft lassie *or* laddie.

foot *noun, see also* **feet**; fit, fuit, cloot, spyog CAITHNESS; (*esp large clumsy*) spag CAITHNESS; (*of an animal*) spag CAITHNESS, luif; **front part of foot** forefit.

regain your footing gaither yer feet.

footling fouterie, scutterie NE, skitterie, kirnin NE.

football fitba(w), kick-ba(w); (*esp as* (*formerly*) *played on Shrove Tuesday*) the Ba.

foothold fit: '*miss yer fit*'.

footless stocking *see* **stocking**.

footpath *see also* **path**; fit-road, fit pad sw, pad.

footstep (*heavy*) clamp N.

footstool *see also* **stool**; creepie (stuil).

change your footwear shift yer feet, change yer feet.

on foot Tamson's mear, shanks'(s) naig(ie).

journey *etc* **on foot** traivel.

travel on foot pad, traivel.

foppish *see also* **affected**; fussy, prinkie.

for *preposition* fur, fir, till SHETLAND, N,
tae: '*he worked tae Mr G*', on: '*wait on
me*'.

forever 1 (*for all time*) for aye. **2** (*continually*) aye.

for all that fra'at NE.

forage reenge; (*scrounge food*) sorn N.

foray †raid, †spreath, †creagh, †heir-
ship.

forbearance *see* **tolerance.**

force *noun* bensel, bellum, poust S,
strouth; (*energy*) birr, virr, smeddum,
fushion NE, farrach NE.

verb (*make to do*) gar, dwang.

forceful forcie SHETLAND, NE, fell SE,
feckfu.

forcibly, by force swap SHETLAND.

force your way into mak intae.

force your way through rive throu.

ford *noun* fuird, f(y)oord N, rack.

verb fuird, f(y)oord N, ride.

forearm gardie NE.

forebears *see* **forefathers.**

foreboding *noun* bodement NE, foregang SHETLAND, N, freit N.

forecast spae.

forecastle (*of a herring boat*) den.

forefathers forebeir(er)s, forefolk.

forefinger coorag CAITHNESS.

forefront forebreist NE.

be in the forefront be heid o the
heap.

forehead foreheid, broo, bree, brinkie-
brow, broo-brinkie *used to children*.

foreign furrin, fremmit, fremd, oot-
lan(d), ootlin.

foreigner *see* **stranger.**

foreknowledge *see* **forewarning.**

forelock tap, swirl SHETLAND, dossan
N.

foreman 1 *see also* **overseer;** fores-
man. **2** (*of a jury*) chancellor.

foremost forehan(d), foremaist.

forenoon forenuin, for(a)neen NE.

foresee spae.

foreshore ebb, tide; (*lower part*)
grun(d) ebb SHETLAND, N.

foresight foresicht.

have foresight see far afore yer neb.

having foresight forethochtie.

forestall foresta(w).

forester pun(d)ler NE.

foretell spae *literary*.

foretell the future read (the) cups *or*
cards *etc*.

**something which foretells the arri-
val of a stranger** guest SHETLAND,
ORKNEY.

forethought forethocht.

forewarning moyen NE: '*get a moyen
o*'.

forfeit *noun* (*in a game*) wad.

verb tyne NE.

forfeiture (*law*) †escheat.

**game in which forfeits are de-
manded** wads.

forgave *past tense of* **forgive** forgied.

forge *noun, see* **smithy.**

forgery (*law*) falsehood.

forget foryet SHETLAND, disremember,
misremember, lose min(d) o.

forgetful forgettle.

forgetfulness forget.

be forgotten gae oot o heid; (*esp of a
rumour etc*) dill doon SHETLAND, NE.

forgive forgie.

forgiven forgien.

fork 1 (*for digging*) graip; (*for potatoes*)
tattie-graip. **2** (*of a tree*) breeks, glack
NE, cloff S, boucht(ie).

forkful fork.

fork up graip.

forlorn tint, disjaskit.

form *noun, verb* furm, firm.

formal dress regimentals.

former yae-time S; (*mainly of persons*)
umquhile *now literary*.

fornicate play the loon, lift a leg.

fornication houghmagandie, sculdudderie.

forsake *see also* **abandon;** forsak, forleet, quat.

forswear forsweer.

fort (*prehistoric round tower*) broch,
(*small*) dun.

forth furth, furt SHETLAND.

forthright *see also* **honest;** rael.
forthrightly even oot.
forthwith the noo, eenoo, ivnoo.
fortify fortifee NE.
fortified house tower (house), (*esp in Borders*) peel.
fortitude *see also* **endurance;** saul.
fortnight fortnicht.
fortress *see* **fort.**
fortune *see also* **luck;** fortoun; (*fate*) weird; (*good*) seil, sonse.
fortunate *see also* **lucky;** seilfu, seilie, happy, cannie.
fortune-teller (*female*) spaewife, weird-wife; (*male*) †spaeman.
fortune-telling (*using egg-white*) castin the glass(es).
tell fortunes spae *literary.*
have good fortune luck.
be a bringer of good *or* **bad luck** be a guid *or* ill fit.
stroke of good fortune (*gained without effort*) peeled egg.
forward *adverb* forrit, furrit, for(r)ad SHETLAND, CAITHNESS, forelins NE, en(d)weys.
adjective, see also **impetuous, impudent;** forritsome, ignorant, gumptious, gallus, hard-neckit.
go steadily forward nivver leuk ower yer shouder.
rush forward impetuously breenge.
foster *verb, see* **encourage.**
foster-mother †nourice.
fought *past tense of* **fight** focht.
past participle focht(en).
foul *adjective, see also* **filthy;** fool, laithlie.
verb, see also **soil;** nestie, befyle, bedrite.
foul-mouthed ruch, ill-gabbit; (*esp of a woman*) randie.
found[1] *past tense, past participle of* **find** fun(d).
found[2] *verb* foon(d).
foundation *see also* **site** 1; foond(s), steid SHETLAND, ORKNEY, CAITHNESS,

larach, (*specif of a stack*) stathel, stale.
foundation stone grun(d)-stane.
founder foon(d)er.
fountain funtain; (*public*) pant SE.
four fower.
fourteen fowerteen.
fourth fowert.
four-poster bed stoop bed.
group of four people fowersome.
fowl *see also* **chicken;** fool.
fox *noun* tod, (tod-)lowrie *literary.*
verb quirk NE.
foxglove lady's thummles, thummles, witches' thummles, witches' paps, deid man's bells NE, King's Ellwand S, tod's tails S.
foxhunt tod-hunt.
fracas *see also* **commotion;** fraca.
fraction (*small amount: see also* **particle, fragment**) stime, mention, haet.
fractious *see also* **peevish;** fashious, peengie, pe(r)neurious NE, tiggie; (*esp of a child*) teedie.
fracture (*in a coal seam*) vise.
fragile *see also* **brittle;** bruckle.
fragment *noun, see also* **particle, fraction, crumb, scrap, shred, splinter;** nip, murlin, nimsh N, lab SE, crottle SW, mote; **fragments** *see also* **smithereens;** flinders, scowes ORKNEY, CAITHNESS, shalls SHETLAND.
reduce to fragments murl, mak murlins O, mak mice feet O SHETLAND, NE.
frail *see also* **weak;** silly, far awa wi't, dwaiblie.
frame (*for carrying two pails from shoulders*) gird; (*triangular, spiked for drying fish*) heck; (*for smoking fish, meat etc*) reest SHETLAND; (*on which cornstack is built*) fause hoose, kill, boss; (*on cart, to increase load*) heck NE.
frank fair-spoken, frugal SHETLAND, CAITHNESS, NE, furthie, furth the gate NE, evendoon; (*of speech*) fair oot.
frankly fair (oot).
frantic dancin mad.
fraternize *see* **friendly.**

fraud 1 fausehood, cheatrie, intak, skin, snipe NE. **2** (*person*) *see* **swindler**.

fraudulent *see* **deceitful**.

fray[1] *see* **battle, fight**.

fray[2] (*of cloth etc*) faize, frizz.

frayed (*of cloth etc*) chattert, chattit NE, thrummie NE; (*of rope*) fozie NE.

freak dandrum NE.

freckle fern(i)tickle, spreckle.

freckled fern(i)tickelt.

free *adjective* quat (o); (*free to travel*) lowse-fittit.

verb (*yourself or another*) redd (o).

become free lowse, win free.

freedom (*scope*) scowth.

free-for-all rammie, reerie NE, stramash.

freestone freestane.

break free of conventions get oot yer horns.

freeze *verb, see also* **frozen**; jeel, lapper NE.

freight *see* **load**.

frenzy frainesie, raise, feem.

drive into a frenzy raise.

frequent *verb* howf.

frequently *see* **often**.

fresh (*of air, water, fish, vegetables etc*) caller; (*of milk: new*) green; (*untreated, not sour*) sweet; (*of butter: unsalted*) sweet; (*of fish: newly caught*) lowpin an leevin; (*esp herring: unsalted*) green.

freshen *see also* **stimulate**; caller; (*of wind*) kittle NE.

fresh-complexioned (*and plump*) gawsie.

freshwater fish (*species of, found in Loch Lomond and Loch Eck*) powan.

fret freet, girn, peenge, narr, canker NE, orp, fyke, peefer, chirm.

fretful *see also* **peevish**; girnie, canker(i)t, crankous, peeng(e)in, wurpit.

be fretful girn.

friable *see also* **brittle, crumbly**; frush, murlie, knappie; (*of soil*) mealie.

friar freir.

friend *see also* **companion**; freen(d), billie, fere *literary*; (*female*) cummer.

friendless freen(d)less.

friendly (*intimate*) freen(d)lie, great, chief, cosh, pack W, S, siblik(e), big NE, tosh; (*very*) far ben, thickan-three-faul(d), thrang; (*on good terms*) gracious; (*towards others*) couthie, hamelie, cadgie, oncomin, fair-spoken; inner S; (*in appearance*) sonsie, smirkie.

be very friendly with be gey chief wi, be great guns wi SHETLAND, N, be gran billies wi NE, troke wi.

in a very friendly way cheek for chow(l).

friendly term of address *see* **address**.

friendliness freen(d)liness.

friendship fraca.

fright *see also* **scare**; fricht, fleg, fley, gliff; '*get a gliff*', fear.

frighten *see also* **scare**; fricht(en), fear, fleg, fley, gliff, flocht NE.

frightened *see also* **afraid**; frichtit (for), frichtenit (for), feart (for), fleyt (for), rad, shan.

frightening frichtsome, fleysome.

frightful *see* **awful**.

stop in sudden fright (*of the heart*) be cawed aff the stalk FIFE.

frigid (*in manner: see also* **cold**) freff.

frill *noun* frull.

having a frilled edge (*of lace*) peakit.

fringe freenge.

frippery whigmaleeries, trappins.

frisk (*caper*) flisk, fud, daff.

frisky hippertie-skippertie NE; (*of an animal*) spankie; (*esp of a horse*) fliskie, skeich.

fritter away moot awa.

frivolous *see also* **flighty**; freevolous, daft, hippertie-skippertie NE, licht-far-ran(t).

frivolity *see* **fun**.

frivolous person flee-up-i-the-air; (*silly*) sodie-heid.

frizz: frizzy swirlie.

frizzled setten-on.

frog puddock, paddock, paddie.

frogspawn puddock cruddles, (puddock) redd, crud NE, FIFE, rodd.

frolic *noun, see also* **fun, romp, caper**; cantrip, tear, jink, set, kiow-ow, randie, rigmarie.

verb daff, splore.

frolicsome *see also* **playful**; kim NE.

from fae, frae, thrae SE, furth.

from the time that f(r)ae: *'She's been that wey fae she wis a bairn'*.

away from aff.

out from oot.

front *noun (of something)* foreside, forebreist NE; *(projecting, eg of a cart)* breist N.

front garden front.

front part fore-en(d).

in front afore.

in front of afore, forenent, anent.

frontier *see* **boundary**.

frost *noun, see also* **hoar-frost**; freest NE; *(hard, prolonged)* ringin frost.

frosty rimie.

frostiness jeel.

frost nail shairp, cog.

Jack Frost nip-nebs.

there is frost it's frost.

thin coating of frost garb SW.

froth *noun, verb, see also* **foam**; fro, freith, fraith SW, S; *(esp on ale etc)* ream; *(on plants) see* **cuckoo-spit**.

frothing reamie.

frown *verb* froon, smool.

noun froon, skook NE, gloom.

frowning look loor-brow.

frozen frozent, geelt.

frugal througal, cannie, inhaudin NE.

fruit: fruitcake *(rich, spiced)* black bun, (Scotch) bun.

fruit-machine puggie.

fruit-slice fly cemetry, muck midden NE.

frustrate pall SHETLAND, ORKNEY, NE, langle.

frustrated lummed SW.

fry[1] *verb* †fryth.

small number of fish for frying fry: *'here a fry o haddies tae ye'*.

sound of frying sotter.

fry[2] *noun (of the minnow etc)* peen-heid; *(newly-hatched, esp of herring)* sile.

fuddled *see also* **drunk**; mixit, moidert, ree, reezie.

fudge *noun (of a crisp, friable consistency)* ta(i)blet.

fuel *noun* fire, eldin.

add fuel to *(a fire)* beek.

fuggy smuchtie NE.

fugitive fugie, rinagate.

fulcrum pall.

fulfil: fulfil the conditions of *(law: a contract etc)* purify.

fulfilment *(law: of a contractual obligation)* implement.

full[1] *adjective* fou, ful; *(ample)* luckie; *(quite full, full to the brim)* bung-fou, lippin(-fou) SHETLAND, NE, pang(-fou), rovin-fou; *(of a place)* stowed (oot); *(of frothy liquid)* reamin-fou; *(of a person: of food)* drum-fou, stappit (fou); *(to bursting point)* riftin fou, heftit, fou as a wulk, fou as a bit; *(to vomiting point)* spuin fou, boakin fou, byock fou NE.

fully fou, fullie.

fullness fouth.

full-bodied *(of a liquid)* maumie.

to the full oot ower.

full[2] *verb (cloth)* waulk.

fulling mill waulk mill.

fulmar mallduck SHETLAND, ORKNEY, mallimoke SHETLAND, ORKNEY.

fulsome phrasie NE, phrasin.

fumble fummle, ficher SHETLAND, NE, fouter, plowter, peuther, pirl NE, thrummle NE.

fumbling *noun* fummle.

adjective han(d)less, picherin NE.

fumblingly aside yer thoum NE.

fume *verb* feem; *(with anger)* beal, barm, reek.

fumes smuik, smeek, guff.

fumigate *(with smoke)* smeek, smuik SW, S.

fun dafferie, daffin, gyper NE; *(boisterous)* madderam SHETLAND, ORKNEY; **piece of fun** *see also* **romp**; ploy, tear, pant, set, guise.

function

funny (*of conversation etc*) knackie.
funny bone dirlie-bane.
funny story farce, baur.
funfair the shows.
fond of fun hertie.
have fun rin the rigs.
have (a bit of) fun (with) hae a guise (wi) SHETLAND, NE.
keep the fun going hail the dools.
make fun of *see also* **mock**; tak the nap aff, joke SHETLAND, N, knack, geck.
function (*social*) swaree, suree.
fund *noun* foon(d), fond.
funeral fooneral S, bural, beerial NE.
invitation to a funeral funeral letter, burial letter.
fungus (*esp stalked*) puddock stuil.
funk *verb* (*chicken out*) hen.
funnel *noun* **1** (*of a ship etc*) lum. **2** (*for pouring liquids*) filler.
furious *see also* **angry, fury**; radge, dancin mad, wuid, reid mad, hyte.
furiously angry *see* **furious.**
furnish *see also* **provide**; (*a house*) plenish.
furniture plenishin, haudin.
furrow *noun* **1** (*made by plough*) furr, sheuch, scart; (*eg of turnips*) stitch SW; (*preliminary*) scrat ORKNEY, NE, scrape, croon, rit; (*second*) hause-furr; (*deep*) gore; (*between two rigs*) mid-rig, mids NE, hintin; (*last of rig*) muild furr(ow); (*in which grain is sown*) seed-furr N; (*for drainage*) gaw (furrow), watter furr. **2** (*in skin*) score.
verb (*make furrows in*) furr.
land at the end of a furrow en(d)-rig.
furry oos(s)ie.
further *see also* **farther** (*under* **far**): *adverb, adjective* forder, farder.
verb forder.
furthest in benmaist.
furthermore forby, mairatour *literary*.
furtive thief(t)ie, hidlin, hintbacks SHETLAND, ORKNEY, huggerie(-muggerie), sleekit.

furtively stow(n)lins, hidlins, huggerie(-muggerie).
behave furtively *see also* **skulk**; smool NE, snaik, mowdie, sloonge.
furtive look skook NE.
fury *see also* **rage**; tirrivee, stramash SHETLAND, CAITHNESS.
like fury in a wuiden dream.
furze *see* **gorse.**
fuse *noun* (*mining*: *of an explosive charge*) strum.
fuss *noun, see also* **commotion, bother, bustle, uproar**; carfuffle, stushie, stashie, stooshie, souch, adae, fizz, fraca, sang: '*mak a sang aboot*', souch, din, wark, gae, ongae, fykerie, boorach(ie) N, HIGHLAND; (*ostentatious*) palaverin; (*about nothing*) palaver, a hair tae mak a tether.
verb **1** (*make a fuss*) fizz, mak (a) maitter, gae on, plaister; raise a reek; (*doing very little*) peuther, pyocher SHETLAND; (*about nothing*) (mak a) fyke, stand on freits; (*noisily*) rant. **2** **fuss over** connach, phrase wi NE, kirn wi NE, dossach NE, SOSS NE. **3** **make a fuss about** mak a wark aboot, mak a fraik aboot. **4** **make a fuss of** (*pet*) daut.
fussy fykie, fouterie, perjink, pointit, tooterie NE, phrasie NE, peremptor(ie) SHETLAND, pea-splittin, kiow-owie; (*specif about food*) pe(r)neurious NE, skeich NE, saucy, nice-gabbit, dainshach.
fussy person, fusspot fyke, finick, palaver.
fussy eater pike-at-yer-mait, pickie, fyke.
fussiness *see also* **fuss**; fykerie; (*about food*) skeichen.
fusty *see also* **mouldy**; foostie, mozie, mochie NE, mothie.
fustiness foost.
futile knotless.
do something futile seek for a key that's i the lock.

G

gab *verb, see also* **chat, chatter, gabble;** blether, claver, clishmaclaver NE, gash, yatter.

gabble *verb, see also* **gab;** yabber, yabble, gutter, raible, slaver.

gable ga(i)vel, gale NE, hoose-en(d).

   gable-end ga(i)vel-en(d).

   steps on the sloping edge of a gable crawsteps, corbie-stanes, cat-steps S.

gad about *see also* **roam;** stravaig, traik, gallant, traipse, vaig, raik, haik (aboot).

   gadabout rinaboot, vaiger, flee-aboot, shanker NE, traik, raik, haik: '*he's an awfu haik*'.

gadfly (*horsefly*) cleg, gleg, gled S; (*attacking cattle*) warback.

gadget *see* **contraption.**

Gaelic Gylick NE, Hielan(d) (language), Tartan, †Erse.

   Gaelic music heedrum hodrum *contemptuous.*

gaff *noun* (*salmon-hook*) cleek, clep.

gag *see* **joke.**

gain *verb* (*earn*) win.

gait gang; (*slow, heavy*) stowff NE; (*slow, hobbling*) hoit; (*trailing, heavy-footed*) skleush N; (*shuffling, shambling*) sha(u)chle; (*tottery*) tooter NE; (*swinging, vigorous*) sling; (*swaggering*) swash; (*haughty*) strunt.

gaiters (*leggings*) leggums, gramashes; (*cloth*) cuitikins.

gale *see also* **wind**[1]**, storm;** gell, gurl, driffle, blowster.

gall *noun, verb* (*sore, boil*) ga(w).

   galling chawsome, chawin.

gallant *adjective* pretty, †pauchtie.

gallery (*in a church*) cock-laft, laft, bauks; (*for clock*) knock-laft.

galley gaillie.

gallivant *see* **gad about.**

gallon †quart.

gallop skelp, binner NE, wallop.

   at a gallop lowpie for spang NE.

gallows widdie.

   gallows-bird *see also* **rogue, villain;** widdiefu, minker, †hempie.

   gallows rope widdie, towe.

   gallows tree †dool tree.

galore *see* **plenty.**

gambol whid, flisk.

game *noun, see also* **match**[2]; gemm, play SHETLAND.

   adjective (*plucky*) stuffie.

   gamebird (*young*) pout.

   gamekeeper gamie, gemmie, gamewatcher NE.

gander ganner, steg S.

gangling: **big gangling person** pallion NE.

ganglion luppen sinnon.

gangster *see* **villain.**

gannet gant; (*young*) guga HEBRIDES.

gantry gantree.

gaol *see* **jail.**

gap open NE; (*eg in a wall, hedge etc*) slap; (*between hills*) nick SW, S; (*esp between threads in a loom*) shed.

   bridge a gap kep a slap.

   make a gap in (*a wall etc*) slap.

gape *verb* 1 *see also* **stare;** gaup, gowp. 2 (*of clothes*) girn.

garb *see also* **clothes;** ootrig, onpit.

garbage *see* **refuse**[2]**, rubbish.**

garden *noun, see also* **kitchen garden, market garden;** gairden; (*esp of a cottage*) yaird.

   gardener gaird(e)ner.

   garden-seat (*of turf etc outside cottage*) deas.

garden wall yaird-dyke.

foot of a garden yaird-fit.

garish roarie, skyrie, skyrin.

garlic *see* wild garlic.

garment *see also* clothes; (*loose, outer*) jupe, slug, (*esp as worn by women*) robe-coat SHETLAND, ORKNEY; (*loose, ill-fitting*) polonie NE; (*untidy*) scash; (*untidy, ill-fitting*) laib NE; (*ill-fitting, shabby*) pilsh NE; (*shabby, for rough work*) peltin-pyock NE; (*tattered, trailing*) loorach N.

garret (*esp in a bothy*) gaillie NE.

garrulous *see also* talkative; bletherin, haiverin, gabbie, newsie NE.

garrulous person blether, blether(um)skite, haiverel.

garter *noun, verb* gairter, ga(i)rten.

garter-tab (*of a kilt stocking*) flash.

gas: small jet of gas peep: '*the gas is at a peep*'.

gash *verb* gulliegaw N, raze.

noun screed; (*in the face*) †Lockerbie lick.

gasp *verb* (*for breath*) pech, fesh, whaisk; (*specif from exertion*) stech; (*in coughing*) kink; (*with a cold, surprise etc*) gliff.

noun pech, hauch, stech; (*eg in whooping cough*) backdraucht.

gate yett; (*self-closing*) liggat SW.

gatepost stoop.

gateway gate-slap; (*esp of a walled town*) port; (*arched*) bow.

gather gaither, gether, gadder SHETLAND, NE; (*of people*) forgaither; (*together confusedly*) houster.

gather in (*crops*) ingaither.

gathering *see also* collection, crowd; gaitherin; (*large*) reesle, hirsel; (*noisy*) hurroo, helm NE; (*social*) shine: '*tea shine*', coarum NE, jine NE; (*for making toffee*) taffie jine.

gaudy skyrie, skyrin, glairie, gyre NE; (*specif of colour*) roarie.

gaunt peesweep.

gave *past tense of* give gied, gid, gien.

gawky *see* awkward, clumsy.

gawky man muckle tae hae.

gawp *see* gape 1.

gay *see also* merry, cheerful; croose, lichtsome, vogie, gleg.

gaiety *see also* merry-making; dafferie.

gaze *see also* stare: *verb* (*esp vacantly*) gove, gowk, waul S; (*intently*) glower; (*open-mouthed*) gowp.

noun (*esp vacant*) gove, gowp; (*intent*) glower.

gear *noun, see also* equipment, tackle; graith, orders.

geld *see also* neuter; lib, sort SHETLAND, NE.

gelding staig.

gender gener.

general store (*small*) Jennie a'thing(s), Johnnie a'thing(s), shoppie NE.

generous *see also* hospitable; guidwillie, hertie, lairge, furthie.

genial *see also* pleasant; lithesome, hertie, lithe NE, sanshach NE.

genitals (*male*) doddles N; (*female*) fud.

genteel gentie.

gentian bad money.

gentility genteelitie, gentrie, gentrice; (*in a lady*) ladyness.

gentle lithe(some); (*of a person*) douce, cannie; (*of wind*) lown.

gentlemanly gentlemannie SHETLAND, NE.

gently huilie, cannie; (*esp of wind*) lown.

gentry gentrice, genteelitie, (k)nabberie.

gentry and commoners (alike) gentle an semple.

genuine *see also* honest; jonick, rael, evendoon.

the genuine article the real Mackay.

germinate breir(d), braird, come awa; (*during malting*) acherspyre.

gesture gester; (*feeble*) paw; (*with the hand*) wag; (*of goodwill*) sain.

get *see also* got, obtain; git.

get at (*try to express*) ettle at.

get away *see also* escape; win awa, win aff NE.

get by warsle throu, chaave awa NE.

get off (*be acquitted*) win aff NE.

get off with (*a person of the opposite sex*) click, cleek, lumber.

get on *see* **succeed.**

get out (*escape*) win oot.

get out of (*a friendship*) weir oot o.

get over *see also* **recover;** get abuin, owercast.

get round (*a person*) come (the) paddy ower.

get through get by: '*If we can jist get by the next three days*'.

get the upper hand of get ower.

get up 1 (*stand*) win up, lift. **2** (*in the morning*) rise, shak yer feathers NE.

get-up (*odd clothes*) paraffin.

gewgaw *see also* **trinket, trifle, contraption;** geegaw.

ghastly gashlie, gruesome, alagrugous; (*ill-looking*) gowstie NE.

ghost ghaist, bogle, boodie NE, doolie, bawcan ARGYLL.

ghostly *see also* **supernatural;** eldritch *literary*.

ghost of your former self eemage.

giant †tetin.

giantess (*ogress*) gyre carline.

gibber gabber, roiter W.

gibberish *see* **nonsense.**

gibbet *see* **gallows.**

gibe *see also* **mock, jeer, taunt:** *noun* dunt, sneist, jamph NE, rub.

verb **gibe at** lat at, jamph, lant NE, snite (someone's niz).

giblets harigals, emmlins NE.

giddy *see also* **dizzy;** licht i the heid, sturdie; (*esp from drink*) capernoitie, reezie.

become giddy swander.

gift *noun, see also* **present;** compliment; (*small, eg as a token of goodwill*) mindin: '*it's jist a wee mindin*'; (*for luck for something new or just beginning, eg a coin in a new purse*) han(d)sel; (*esp from a fair*) fairin; (*at New Year, esp of food or drink*) Hogmanay: '*gie them thir Hogmanay*'; (*at Christmas*) Christmas: '*He wants it for his Christmas*'.

give as a gift gift: '*£1 000 was gifted to the society*'.

give a gift to in order to celebrate something new han(d)sel.

give a small gift to mind.

gigantic wappin.

giggle *see also* **snigger:** *verb* geegle, gaggle, keckle, keechle, kicher, sneeter, snitter.

noun geegle, keckle, keechle, kicher.

gild gilt.

gills (*of a fish*) ginnles, chollers SW, S.

gimlet wummle.

gimmick *see* **contraption.**

ginger *noun* ginge.

ginger beer ale NE.

gingerbread ginge(r)breid, gibberie N.

ginger snap snap.

gipsy *see also* **vagrant, tinker;** jockie; **gipsies** waun(n)erin fowk.

girl lass(ie), quine NE; jilt *contemptuous*, dosh *contemptuous*, SHETLAND, NE, teenie-bash *contemptuous*, bird *contemptuous*; (wee) hairy *contemptuous*, GLASGOW; (*small*) lass(ock)ie, quinie NE, wifie, wifockie N, wench; (*older*) deem N, dame NE, cummer NE, chiel(d); (*attractive*) blinker, stoater; (*light-footed*) linkie S; (*awkward*) maukin; (*thin, adolescent*) scargivenet; (*lively, tomboyish*) gilpie; (*giddy*) taupie, hallock, kittie SHETLAND, NE, gillie-gawkie SW, S, lintie; (*mischievous*) hempie, limmer, clip; (*cheeky*) yip S.

girlish lass-lik(e).

girlfriend lass(ie), quine NE, lovie, hing-tee N, tairt, click, cleek, lumber.

girth grist; (*on shafts of cart*) tram girth.

large of girth gurthie.

gist rinnin NE, heids (o something).

get the gist of get the richt threid o.

give *see also* **gave;** gie; (*hand to*) see.

given gien, gied.

give me gimme, gie's, see me, see's: '*see's* (*me*) *ower the teapot*'; (*by stretching*) rax me (ower).

give us gie's, see's.

give and take giff-gaff.

give in see also **yield**; (esp cringingly) snuil.

give up (abandon) quat, gie ower SHETLAND, NE, jeck, pass; (surrender) lat the towe gang wi the bucket, fauchat ARGYLL.

cause (someone) **to give** (something) **up** spean fae.

give way (submit) knuckle; (prudently) jouk an lat the jaw gae by.

gizzard gizzern, queern NE, caibie N.

glad gled, blithe, prood, (to do etc) fond.

  gladly blithe.

  gladness blitheness.

glamour glamourie literary.

glance see also **glimpse, peep**[1]: verb **1** (look quickly) glent, teet, glisk, gliff, keek; (sideways: see also **squint**) sklent, gley, glime. **2** (fly off obliquely) skite.

  noun glent, glisk, gliff, glimp, teet, keek, blink, scance; (sidelong) sklent, gley, glime, skellie, skew NE, (esp angry) skime.

  glancing blow scuff, scud.

gland: swollen glands kirnels.

glare noun (of light) gliff.

  glaring (of a colour: see also **gaudy, garish**) glairie-flairie.

Glasgow Glesca, Glesgie EDINBURGH.

glass gless, glaiss NE.

  glasses see also **spectacles**; glesses.

  glass marble glessie (bool), glesser.

  drinking glass see **goblet**.

  pane of glass peen, lozen.

glazed lozenit NE.

gleam see also **glimmer, shine**: verb glaim, leam literary, skime, glint, lowe, sheen, skinkle literary, scance, skimmer.

  noun glim, leam literary, glint, glisk, scance, skime; (faint) scarrow SW, scad; (small) pink(ie); (of sun) sun blink.

glean (with a rake) rake.

  gleaner (with a rake) raker.

  handful of gleaned corn singlin.

glee see **fun**.

glib gleg-tonguit, gleg-gabbit W, gash-gabbit E CENTRAL.

glide (move easily and quickly) scrieve, link, skimmer; (at an easy pace) snuve; (quietly) sloom; (furtively) sleek.

glimmer see also **gleam**: verb blinter NE, gleet S.

  noun glim, flichter, spunk(ie), stime literary, gleed SE, gleet S.

glimpse see also **glance, peep**[1]: verb get a sicht O, get a swatch O.

  noun glim, glimp, gliff, swatch, twig NE, went NE, waff, vizzy SHETLAND, skime, glisk.

glint verb glent.

  noun glent, gliff, skime.

glisten see also **glitter, gleam, shine**; glister, sheen, gleet S.

  glistening noun gleet S.

glitter see also **glisten, gleam, shine**: verb glent, glister, prinkle, skire, skinkle literary, gleet SE.

  noun glent, glister, gleet SE.

  glittering adjective glaizie.

globe (eg on a fishing net) pallet.

globules (of fat in soup) een.

globe-flower butter-blob, luckengowan S.

gloom mirk(ness).

  gloomy mirk(ie), mirksome, dreich, dowie, grumlie, douth S; (specif of persons) hingin-luggit, drumlie, dowf, heavisome SW; (of weather) drumlie, immis NE, dour.

glory glore literary.

  glorify glorifee.

gloss noun, see **shine**.

  glossy glaizie.

glove see also **mitten**; gluive, gliv SHETLAND, ORKNEY, N, han(d)sho ORKNEY; (with or without fingers) mitten.

glow see also **shine, gleam**: verb glowe, lowe, leam.

  noun glowe, lowe, leam; (bright, of a fire) gloss, gleed SE.

  glowing in a lowe; (of a fire) glossie.

  glowing embers drieshach NE.

glower see **frown**.

glue noun batter.

glum see also **sad, downcast**; dowie, drum, doon o mou, demuirit, glumshie.

be glum glumph.

look glum glumsh, stour SHETLAND.

why are you so glum? wha stole yer scone?

glut *see* plenty.

glutinous claggie, glittie.

glutton guts(er), belly gut NE, midden NE, knacker's midden, gorb, hecker, Rab Ha, slaik, troch, gulch N, slaister kyte.

gluttonous *see also* greedy; guts(ie), guttie, belly gut NE, geenyoch w.

gluttony gutsiness.

eat gluttonously guts, gorble, heck.

gnarled *see also* stunted; gurlie, swirlie SHETLAND, N.

gnash (*teeth*) chirk, chark; (*eg with rage*) girn.

gnat *see* midge.

gnaw *verb* gnyauve N, chittle SW; (*gnaw with the teeth*) scob.

noun gnyauve N.

gneiss (*esp large boulder of*) haithen NE.

go *verb, see also* went, gone; gae, gang, gan CENTRAL, S, gyang NE, ging NE, (*very quickly*) streek, skelp; (*smoothly*) jeck NE; play: '*the door played clink*'.

noun (*energy*) smeddum.

going *present participle* gaun, ga(a)n, gya(u)n SHETLAND, NE, gaein.

going to gaunae.

goings-on ongauns, wark.

keep going knype (on) NE.

go-ahead *adjective* throu-gaun, furthie NE.

go away haud awa, gang yer weys; go away! abree *gipsy*; (*expressing disbelief*) awa wi ye!

go-between (*of lovers*) †blackfoot; (*intriguer*) †trafficker.

go off (*of food*) chynge N, gae wrang.

go out (*energetically*) timmer up NE.

go slow huilie.

go with hae wi.

goad *noun* gaud, brog, brod.

verb brod.

ploughman who goaded horses or oxen gaud(s)man, goad(s)man N.

goal (*in games*) dale, dool w, hail s.

shout when a goal is scored hail.

goat gait; (*castrated he-goat*) haiver.

gob (*of spit*) spittle.

gobbet gabbit.

gobble *verb* snap, lay intae, hanch, glunsh, heck, gorble.

goblet tass(ie) *now literary*.

goblin *see also* hobgoblin, bog(e)yman; blackman, wirricow, boodie NE.

gobstopper ogo-pogo-eye.

God Goad, (the) Guid, (the) Gweed NE, Dyod NE, (the) Almichtie, (the) Michtie; (*specif as mild oath*) dod, od, nyod NE, Goad Almichtie!

godly guidlie NE.

godforsaken dreich (lik(e)).

godmother cummer.

gold gowd, goold.

golden gowden, goolden.

golden plover *see* plover.

goldcrest golden crest(ie), muin s.

goldfinch goldie, gooldie, gowdspink.

golf gowf.

golfer's attendant caddie.

act as a golfer's attendant caddie.

golfball gowfba(w), guttie (ba(w)).

golf club (*stick*) gowf stick; parts of golf club: (*flat bottom*) sole; (*socket on head, for shaft*) hozle.

goloshes galashes N.

gone *past participle of* go gane, geen SHETLAND, N, forn SHETLAND, N.

good *adjective, see also* fine, excellent, first-rate; guid, gweed NE; (*specif of character*) honest; (*fairly good*) nae bad.

goodly guidlie.

goodness! *see* gracious!

goodness knows! Deil kens, guid kens!, gweed kens! NE.

for goodness sake! for onie sake!

goods graith, gear: '*guids an gear*'; (*esp worthless*) troke.

your worldly goods pack NE, gaitherins, githerins N.

good-for-nothing *noun, see also* rogue, rascal; dae-na-guid, hallockit, scum, reebald SHETLAND, ORKNEY, rap, dyvour, (weary) warroch.

adjective little worth, nochtless, waff(lik(e)).

in good condition bien.

good evening guideen.

good gracious! *see* **gracious!**

in good health hardy.

good-humoured *see* **cheerful.**

good-looking *see also* **handsome, beautiful;** weel-faured, braw, sonsie, lik(e)ly, pretty, nae bad leukin.

good-looking woman stoater, brammer.

good-natured *see* **kindly.**

having a good-natured expression smirkie.

good person the hert o corn.

good-sized gey.

good-tempered (*of an animal*) handie NE.

good turn cast.

make good mak weel.

very good *see* **excellent.**

not very good at nae great sticks at SHETLAND, NE.

goosander saw neb.

goose *noun, see also* **gannet;** guse, geese SHETLAND, ORKNEY, N; (*brent*) ware goose; (*brent or greylag*) quink goose ORKNEY.

gooseberry groset, groser, grosart; (*large yellow*) hinnie-blob; (*green*) greenberry.

gooseflesh cauld creep(s), hen's flesh, hen's picks NE, hen's plouks S.

goosefoot *see* **fat hen.**

gore[1] *noun, see* **blood.**

gore[2] *noun, see* **gusset.**

gore[3] *verb* (*with the horns*) stick, pork SW, S, porr SW.

gorge *noun, see also* **ravine;** cleuch, heuch.

verb stap, pang NE, stech, puist S.

gorgeous *see also* **beautiful;** braw.

gorse whin(s), fun(s) NE.

gosh! goshens!, gosh me!, gweeshtens! NE, go!

gosling gaislin.

gossamer slammachs NE.

gossip *verb, see also* **chat;** blether, clash, clatter, claver, clack, cleck, news, clish-maclaver NE, clypach NE, cummer S.

noun **1** (*idle talk: see also* **chitchat**) clavers, clack, cleck, clatter(s), clish-clash, ferlies, speak, souch, clype, news, claiks, causey clash; (*of the district*) countra clash; (*of the town*) toon's speak. **2** (*piece of gossip*) say, raverie NE. **3** (*person: see also* **scandalmonger**) clatter NE, clapperdin NE, claik, clishmaclaver, clash(er), cracker, clypach NE; (*man or woman*) (auld) sweetie-wife.

gossipy glib-gabbit, newsie, clashie.

got *past tense of* **get** gat.

past participle gotten.

Gouda (cheese) goudie.

gouge *verb, noun* gudge SHETLAND, ORKNEY, NE.

govern *see* **control.**

gown goon.

grab *verb, see also* **snatch;** grabble, cla(u)cht, glaum at, glammach at NE, grip till SHETLAND, NE, reeve ORKNEY, pin NE, nam SHETLAND, S, mitten SHETLAND, NE.

noun grabble, claut, cla(u)cht, glammach NE.

grace *noun* (*mealtime prayer*) bethankit.

verb (*adorn*) mense.

graceful jimp, gentie.

gracious couthie.

(good) gracious! fegs!, ma patience!, dear be here!, gweeshtens NE, lovanentie, michtie (me)!, losh.

grace note NB in piping = a short note played over a melody note; series of these are essential to a piping melody; **types of grace note:** (*which simulates the repetition of a note*) doubling; (*with all fingerholes closed, sounding low G*) grip; (*series preceding a higher note*) throw; (*series used in pibroch*) taorluath, (*more complex*) crunluath.

into someone's good graces on someone's saft side.

say grace (*before a meal*) say awa ORKNEY, NE.

graduate: graduation address (*to honorary graduates*) laureation.

person about to graduate graduand.

grain *noun* **1** *see also* **particle**; tick, starn NE; (*of oats, barley, wheat*) pickle; (*of oats*) corn; (*at top of stalk*) tappickle, en(d)-pickle. **2** (*cereal crop*) stuff, meal('s) corn SHETLAND, ORKNEY, N, grits; (*esp before or after harvesting*) vittal; (*mixed, often with pulses*) mashlum. **3** (*in stone*) greet; (*in wood or stone*) awte NE; (*direction of*) reed.

grammar gremmar NE.

grampus herrin hog ULSTER.

granary grainerie, †girnel.

grand gran, graun(d).

grandchild gran(d)-bairn, gran(d)-wean, oe N, ARGYLL; (*esp reared by grandparents and spoilt*) grannie('s) bairn CENTRAL.

grandchildren gran(d)childer ULSTER.

grand-daughter grandochter.

grandfather gran(d)faither, gran(d) fader, grandaddie, granda, aul(d)-faither, bobbie, guidsire, gutcher, deyd(ie) NE, luckie daid(ie) NE, pawpie.

grandmother gran(d)mither, aul(d)-mither, luckie (minnie) NE, deyd(ie) NE, guid dame.

grandson nevoy.

grand-uncle *see* **great-uncle**.

granite (*kind of dark, used for curling stones*) Crawfordjohn; (*with marled granular surface*) peasie whin NE.

grannie *see* **grandmother**.

call (*someone*) **grannie** grannie at: '*Dinna you grannie at me*'.

grant *see* **give**.

granule *see* **grain, particle**.

granular quernie NE.

graphite wad SW.

grapnel creeper ARGYLL; (*small, for searching for fishing lines*) sucken NE.

grapple graipple, dacker NE.

grasp *verb, see also* **seize**; gresp,

cla(u)cht NE, tak a ha(u)d o; (*by fumbling*) thrummle SW.

noun gresp, cla(u)cht; (*often ineffectual*) glaum; (*sudden*) cla(u)tch.

grasping *noun* grabble.

adjective, see also **greedy, miserly**; nabal NE, menseless, glamshach.

grasp at (*money*) grub.

grass *noun* gress, girse; (*wild, luxuriant*) naitur girse NE; (*long, reedy, on marshy ground*) bennel, sprat; (*types with long thin stalks*) windlestrae; (*types growing on marshy ground*) star (grass); (*coarse, esp on waste ground*) reesk NE; (*coarse, on dunged ground*) go(r)sk NE, tathe; (*rank, not eaten in summer*) fowd N; (*withered during winter*) beust SW; (*growing on stubble*) fuslach SW.

grassy girsie, (*of land*) green SHETLAND, ORKNEY, CAITHNESS.

grassy patch on a hill gair SW, S.

grassy (cattle) track (*through arable land*) loan.

grasshopper cricket S.

grassland (*not recently ploughed*) ley (girse); (*marshy, used for hay*) meedow, meedie E CENTRAL; (*boggy, low-lying*) misk W.

covered with (coarse) grass (*rather than heather etc*) white.

second crop of grass (*after hay*) foggage, hey fog.

grate[1] *noun, see also* **fireplace**; chim(b)ley NE.

grating (*on a window or door*) tirless; (*in or over a stream*) heck, watter gate; (*over a street-drain*), syver, stank W, brander NE, cundie ANGUS, pen(d) SW, S.

grate[2] *verb* (*make a grating sound*) risp, chirk, scart, (*also teeth*) jirg.

grating sound risp SHETLAND, NE, jirg ARGYLL, screeve, screed; (*eg by scraping on wood*) scrunt; (*of a sharp point on a hard surface*) rauk.

grateful thankrif(e).

gratify graitifee, glack someone's mitten NE.

gratified prood; (*by some honour*) knichtit NE.

gratitude graititeed NE.

gratuity *see also* **tip**³; maggs; (*from an employer*) pauchle; (*for drink*) drink siller.

grave¹ *noun, see also* **burial plot**; graff, graft, delf CAITHNESS; (*the grave*) mool(s).

gravedigger †beadle.

gravestone lairstane NE; (*horizontal*) table stone, thruch(stane) SW, S.

graveyard *see also* **churchyard, burial ground**; graveyaird.

grave² *adjective, see also* **serious**; (*of a person*) thochtie, drummure.

gravel *see also* **shingle, grit**; graivel, channel, chad NE, chingle(s) NE, grool SW; (*fine*) grush.

gravelly chinglie ORKNEY, NE; (*of soil*) shairp, sherp.

gravy bree.

graze¹ *verb* (*touch lightly*) scuff, skiff, scutch N; (*the skin*) screeve; (*the ground with a golf club*) sclaff.
noun (*light touch*) scuff, skiff, scutch N; (*on skin*) screeve.

graze² *verb* (*of animals*) gae NE; (*nibble*) nip, moup (on).

grazing *see also* **pasture**; girsin ORKNEY, N.

grease *noun, verb* creesh.

greasy *see also* **oily**; creeshie, glittie, tauchie.

great 1 grit, gret, gryte NE; (*in size, amount*) muckle, bonnie, gey, queer; (*remarkable*) unco. **2** (*of relationships*) auld-: '*auld-uncle*'.

the greater part (of) the muckle feck (o), the maist (o).

greatly *see* **very, extremely**; notorious.

great-aunt aul(d)-auntie.

greatcoat *see also* **overcoat**; big coat, bavarie, jockie coat.

great-grandchild ieroe.

great-grandfather grandsher.

great-grandson nevoy.

great tit ox-ee.

great-uncle aul(d)-uncle.

greed *see* **gluttony**.

eat greedily guts, heck (in).

greedy *see also* **gluttonous, avaricious**; hungry, gutsie, grabbie, ill-hertit NE, mislearit NE, menseless, glamshach, pegral.

greedy person *see also* **glutton**; gled, gutser.

be greedy hae a crap(pin) for a(w) corn.

green 1 *adjective* (*pale, dull*) haw NE. **2** (*naïve, gullible*) hielan(d): '*no sae hielan*'.

greenish greenich(t)ie NE.

greenfinch green lintie, greenie.

greengrocer (*female*) kailwife.

greet goam: '*she nivver goamed them*'.

greeting *see* **familiar, friendly term of address** (*under* **address**).

pass on greetings min(d): '*mind me tae yer mither*'.

grey gray; (*dark*) parson gray; (*mixed black and white*) grim.

greyish-white (*esp of mixed wool in cloth*) riach SHETLAND, ORKNEY, N.

greyhound grew, grewhound.

greyhound racing the grews.

grey mullet pelcher CAITHNESS.

griddle girdle.

gridiron brander.

grief *see also* **sorrow**; teen, sair, anger, harm(s) SHETLAND, dool *now literary*; (*constant*) hert-sair; (*source of bitter grief*) hert-scaud.

grief-stricken (hert-)sair, doilt NE.

come to grief misfare SHETLAND.

grieve *see also* **mourn**; fyke; **grieve over** mane (for).

grievance eelist, plaint, grummle, gaw i the back, sta(w); (*source of grievance*) clyre.

deeply grieved hert-sorry, sair vext.

be grieved grudge.

grievous sair.

grill *verb* brander, branner.
noun, see **grating** (*under* **grate**¹).

grim (*of a person*) dour, raucle, (ala)grugous, sture s; (*of a struggle etc*) stieve.

grimace *see also* **scowl**; *noun* girn, showl, shile sw; **grimaces** mudgins.

verb girn, murgeon, sham; (*wryly*) grue; (*in disapproval etc*) mak a mow NE; (*from pain, disdain etc*) thraw yer gab; (*from vexation, bitter taste etc*) showl, shile sw.

grime *see* **dirt**.

grimy brockit, brookit.

grin *noun, verb* girn.

grind 1 (*to smaller fragments: see also* **crush**) mak doon, runch, chap. **2** (*two surfaces together*) scrunt, (*also teeth*) risp NE; (*teeth; see also* **gnash**, **grate²**) jirg.

grindstone grun(d)-stane.

(back to) the daily grind (back tae) auld claes an parritch.

grip *verb, noun* grup.

gripped *past participle* gruppen.

grippers (*of tongs*) palm.

grisly *see* **ghastly**, **gruesome**.

grist girst.

gristle girsle.

grit *noun, see also* **gravel**; grush.

verb (*teeth*) cramsh NE.

gritty (*of soil etc*) shairp.

grizzled (*of hair*) lyart.

groan *verb, noun, see also* **moan**, **sigh**; grain.

grocer *see* **shop, general store**.

groin lisk.

groom *noun* (*for a horse*) strapper.

groove *noun* (*scratch, score*) rit, rauk; (*deep*) rat s; (*cut in stone or wood*) raggle, raglet; (*esp for roof-slate under coping stone*) rag(g)lin; (*esp for a scythe blade*) den NE.

cut a groove in rat; (*stone or wood, eg for the edge of a roof*) raggle; (*a board to fit a 'tongue'*) gruip; (*eg in a horseshoe*) swedge NE.

grope *verb, see also* **fumble**; graip, growp, fin(d), ripe, grabble, grapple, glaum, pirl NE, gump; (*indecently*) graip

s, fin(d), ficher wi SHETLAND, NE; (*in streams for fish*) guddle.

gross *adjective* (*of a person: see also* **coarse**) guttie.

in gross owerheid.

ground *noun, see also* **land, soil**; grun(d); (*poor, infertile*) ill-bit SE, scaup SHETLAND, NE, scarp, hirst; (*sandy, undulating, near seashore*) links E COAST; (*low-lying*) howe; (*on which a building stands*) solum.

groundsel grundsel, grundiswallow NE.

group *noun* boorach, curn, paircel; (*huddled together*) parrock NE; (*of people, to gossip or drink*) cabal NE; **groups** wheens.

group of four, six etc persons or things fowersome, saxsome *etc*.

grouse¹ *verb, see also* **grumble**; girn, natter, yammer, chunner, molligrant, mane, scronach NE.

noun mane.

grouse² *noun* (*bird*) groose, (*red*) muirfowl, (*male*) muircock, gorcock *literary*, (*female*) muirhen, (*young*) muir pout; (*black: male*) black cock, (*female*) gray hen; (*wood-grouse*) capercailzie.

grove plantin, shaw *literary*.

grovel beenge.

grow growe, weir up SHETLAND, NE; (*of plants, rapidly*) come awa.

growing fast (*of vegetation*) growthie.

stop growing (*of plants or animals*) set; (*of plants*) sit.

grown-up *see also* **adult**: *adjective* up, muckle; (*of a man*) man-grown, man-big, man-muckle; (*of a woman*) wumman-grown, wumman-lenth, wumman-muckle.

growth growthe; (*of plants: rank*) rush SHETLAND, ORKNEY, N, raff NE.

grow longer (*of days in spring*) creep oot, rax.

grow shorter (*of days in autumn*) creep in, come in.

grow smaller creep in, crine.

grow up come tae NE.

growl *see also* **snarl:** *verb* grool NE, gurr, gurl, wurr NE, snagger NE, grunch; (*specif of a dog*) yirr SHETLAND, nurr.

noun gurr, gurrie-wurrie, gurl, wurr NE, habber NE, grunch; (*specif of a dog*) yirr SHETLAND, nurr.

grub *verb* (*about in soil*) muddle; (*like a pig*) hurk SW.

noun (*of the cranefly*) torie NE, storie SHETLAND, ORKNEY, CAITHNESS.

grudge *noun* grummle.

grudging ill-willie.

bear (*someone*) **a grudge** hae a pick at, tak a pike at.

gruel blearie, lithocks, stourin NE, stourie (drink); (*with fresh butter and honey*) wangrace.

gruesome growesome, ugsome.

gruff stroonge, sture S.

grumble *verb, see also* **complain, grouse**[1]; grummle, grumph, girn, chunner, yammer, mump, thraw, craik, pewl, glumsh, peek NE, witter NE, croup NE, gronach NE; (*ineffectually*) greet; (*perpetually*) narg.

noun grummle, pewl, mane.

grumbler grumph.

grumbling *adjective* grumlie, cronachin, peesie-weesie.

noun girn; (*continual*) narg.

grumpy grumphie, greetin-faced, torn-faced.

grunt *verb* grumph, grunch, gruntle; (*like a pig*) grumphie.

noun grumph, grunch, gruntle; (*eg from exertion*) stech; (*of a pig*) guff SHETLAND, ORKNEY.

guarantee *verb* uphaud, stan(d) guid for, caution.

noun, see also **security:** warrandice, (*now esp on sale of livestock*) warranty.

guard *verb* gaird, weir S; (*esp at night*) wauk.

noun gaird.

guardian (*law: until 1991*) curator; (*of a pupil* (*boy under 14, girl under 12*)) tutor.

be on your guard watch yersel.

guess *verb* jalouse, ettle.

guffaw *verb, noun* gaff(aw), guff, heffer, bullie (o a lauch) NE.

guide *verb* (*a person to a place*) airt, wice; (*the course of something*) ettle.

guild: head of guild in royal burgh †Dean of Guild.

member of a guild guild brither.

guile sneck-drawin, pawkerie.

guileless saikless, ill-less SHETLAND, NE, aefauld.

guillemot queet NE, marrot, sea hen CAITHNESS, lavie HEBRIDES, scoot; (*black*) cuttie, teistie SHETLAND, ORKNEY, CAITHNESS, Jennie Gray CAITHNESS, sea doo ARGYLL.

guillotine (*for beheading*) †maiden.

guilt: guiltless *see* **innocent.**

guilty-looking doon-leukin.

feel guilty about tak tae yersel.

guinea geenie, (yella) geordie.

gull[1] *noun* goo N, sea goo NE, (sea) ma(w), loch-ma(w); (*young*) plee; (*herring*) gray Willie N, willie goo NE, (*esp young*) pleengie NE; (*black-headed*) pictarnie, pewlie(-Willie) NE, pirr-maw SW, pick(ie)maw S, huidie craw SHETLAND, huidit craw ORKNEY.

gull[2] *verb, see also* **cheat, deceive:** whillie.

gullet thrapple, hause, craig, neck, reid road, reid lane, reid brae, scroban, wizzen.

gullible fond.

gullible person daft Erchie.

gully *see also* **ravine:** gullet, gill, lirk, gowl; (*in the sea*) slock; (*deep, narrow, where tide rumbles in*) rummlin kirn SW.

gulp *verb* gowp, gollop, glog (ower) NE, pootch NE, slooster, glut.

noun gowp, gaup, glock, glog NE, glut; (*noisy*) sloor NE.

gum (*in the mouth*) goom, geem NE.

gumboil gumbile.

gun: gunshot brattle.

gun-wadding colfin NE.

the recoil from a gun putt.

sight on a gun vizzy.

gunwale: board round the gunwale rimwale.

gurgle *verb* gurl, jirg, glock, glog, clunk NE, buck NE, goller; (*in the throat*) souch, glag(ger) NE, glutter, gluther; (*of a baby*) groozle.

noun gurl, glock, glog NE, clunk, groozle SW, goller; (*in the throat*) glag(ger) NE, glutter, gluther.

gurgling *adjective* gurlie.

gurnard crooner, gowdie; (*grey*) goukmey.

gush *verb* **1** (*of liquid*) teem, pish, buck NE, hush, faem ORKNEY, strone; (*in spurts*) skoosh. **2** (*in speech*) phrase NE.

noun **1** (*of liquid*) stour NE, strone, hush SHETLAND, ORKNEY; (*spluttering*) spleut NE. **2** (*in speech*) phrasin.

gushing (*of a person*) phrasie NE.

gusset gushet, eik, (*specif triangular*) gair.

gust *see also* **blast**: *noun* (*of wind etc*) gowst, gliff, flan SHETLAND, ORKNEY, N, wap SHETLAND, NE, sweevil SHETLAND, ORKNEY, blaw NE; (*sudden*) brash, blowder NE, flocht NE, whid SHETLAND, ORKNEY; (*with rain*) flaw, bluffert, blirt NE; (*slight*) skiff; (*howling*) gowl; (*of hot air*) (y)oam SHETLAND, NE.

verb (*of wind*) dad, tear, flaff, flan, hushle, whid SHETLAND, ORKNEY, bleester; (*with rain*) scudder NE, (*strongly*) snifter.

gusty *see also* **blustery**: gowstie, blashie, blastie NE, cankert NE, reezie, reevin; (*with rain*) ragglish NE.

gusty wind hushle, blinter.

gut *noun* thairm; **guts** *see also* **bowels, intestines**; puddins.

gutter *noun* gitter, trink, channel; (*in a cowshed*) gruip, greep NE; (*roof-gutter*) rone (pipe), spoot; (*street-gutter*) syver, stank, brander NE, cundie ANGUS, straun, sheuch, stripe.

guttersnipe gutterbluid.

guttural *adjective* (*of the voice*) howe.

guzzle *see also* **glutton, greedy**; guts, gilravage.

gym: gymnastic feat henner EDINBURGH.

gymshoes sannies, san(d)shuin, san(d)sheen N, gutties W.

gypsy *see* **gipsy**.

H

habit *see also* **routine**; (*custom*) haunt, trade NE: '*mak a trade o*'; (*whim*) kick NE, ginkum NE; **habits** (*manners*) gates NE.

bad habit ill-gate, ill-lair CAITHNESS, gaw-i-the-back.

have a habit of be in the wey o, wont: '*playin the games we wont tae play*'.

habitable biglie.

habitation inn(s), haud: '*hoose an haud*'.

hack *verb* hawk, hag, haggle, hash, gullie-gaw N, chack.

noun hawk, hag, haggle, chack.

hackle heckle.

had *past tense of* **have** hid, haid.
past participle haen, hid, haid.

had not hidna, hidnae, hadna, hadnae.

haddock haddie, hoddock NE; (*after spawning*) cameral NE, harrowster NE; (*small*) poot(ie), snap ORKNEY, N, chat NE; (*unsplit, smoked*) (Arbroath) smokie; (*unsplit, half-dried*) piper NE; (*small, unsplit, smoked in chimney*) pin-the-widdie; (*split, smoked in peat smoke etc*) Finnan haddie; (*split, dried or smoked*) speldin SHETLAND, N, speldrin; (*half-split, for curing*) lucken NE; (*dried or smoked*) Crail capon FIFE.

haft heft.

hag runt, (auld) rudas NE, carline, †luckie.

haggard shilpit, shirpit, pookit, gluntie SE.

haggle haigle, argie-bargie, niffer, prig, tig-tag SHETLAND, hick SW, S.

hail[1] *verb* (*summon*) hoy.

hail fellow well met aw hinnie an jo.

hail[2]: **hailstone** hailstane, bullet (stane) NE.

hailstorm blatter.

hair *noun* herr; (*in long tangled locks*) dabberlacks NE; (*thin wispy*) strag.

hairy †birsie.

hairband (*worn by young unmarried women*) †snuid.

haircut cowe, dock, poll.

hair-splitting *adjective* pea-splittin.

hairstyle (*with hair gathered on top of the head*) †cockernonie, (*using a pad of false hair*) †cock-up.

made of hair hairen.

luxuriant growth of hair rush.

tangled mass of hair sheemach NE.

hake herrin hake.

hale and hearty lowpin an leevin, livin-lik(e), yaul(d).

half *noun, adjective* hauf.
adverb halflins NE.

halves haufs.

be only half alive pewl.

half-blind (*as of an albino*) san(d)-blin.

half-grown (*esp of a boy*) half-lang, halflin.

half-grown boy halflin.

work half-heartedly plowter, plyter NE.

half-holiday halfie.

half light *see also* **twilight**; half licht, gloamin.

half-past four *etc* hauf fower *etc*.

halfpenny bawbee, maik, hey ANGUS.

your last halfpenny the hin(d)maist rook, the hin(d)maist maik.

look half-starved pit yer mait in an ill skin.

halfway hauf-road(s), halflins, half-gates.

halfwit *see also* **idiot**; halflin, daftie.

halfwitted *see also* **mentally handicapped**; hauf-jack(it), no richt, feel N,
far frae a yonner NE.

go halves gae haufers, ging halvers.

halibut turbot, blacksmith NE.

hall ha.

hallow sain.

Halloween bonfire shannack, sownack, †tannel.

halo (*round sun or moon, latter indicating
storm*) broch, gowe; (*round sun*) sun
broch; (*round moon*) cock's ee N,
faul(d), muin broch.

halt *see also* **stop**: *verb* haut: **1** deval,
huilie, stint NE; (*temporarily*) ha(u)d
(aff). **2** (*bring to a halt*) reest NE, stell.
noun haut, deval, stick.

halter *noun* (*for horse etc*) helter, heid-
ban(d), mink, branks.
verb helter, brank.

halter-rope helter-shank.

halve *see also* **half**; hauf, halver.

halyard (*to set peak of mainsail*) tappin
lift SHETLAND.

ham: hams hunkers.

hamstring hoch.

hamlet toon, biggin; (*usually with a
church*) clachan; (*round a farm*) ferm-
toon.

hammer *noun* haimmer, hemmer, hawmer NE: **1** Glesca screwdriver, Paisley
screwdriver W; (*heavy*) mell. **2** (*ship-
yard*) peltie NE, (*heavy*) mundie, (*heavy,
double-faced*), plyin hammer W. **3**
(*stonemason's: peen hammer*) peener,
(*medium-weight*) reel, (*small*) clatchie-
hammer; (*stone-breaker's*) mash (hammer), (*small*) (stane-)knapper. **4**
(*miner's pick-ended*) hack.
verb haimmer, hemmer, hawmer NE; (*as
in a smithy*) chap; (*with a heavy hammer*)
mell; (*pieces of metal together*) stave.

hammer at whinner at.

hammer and tongs (*vigorously*) pick
an mell.

hamper *verb, see also* **hinder**; taigle,
habble S, langle.

hand *noun* haun(d), han, handie (*esp to

a child*), cleuk NE, spyog CAITHNESS;
(*large*) crog CAITHNESS; (*large, clumsy*)
spag CAITHNESS, maig; **hands** (*raised
to fight*) gardies.
verb, see **hand over**.

handful haunfae, nievefu, luiffu, claut,
cla(u)cht NE, glack; (*the fill of two
hands*) gowpen(fu); (*handful of unthreshed grain etc*) rip; (*of gleaned corn*)
singlin, single; (*of hay*) lachter.

handy hantie.

handball (*as played at certain holidays
in the Borders and Orkney*) the Ba; (*as
played in the Borders with a small ball*)
handba.

hand's breadth haun-breed.

handcart hurlie(-barrow).

handcuffs snitchers, shangies.

hand-picked han(d)-waled.

handrail ravel.

handwriting han(d)write, han(d) o
write, write NE; (*piece of*) scrieve.

wholly in one person's handwriting
(*law*) holograph.

at hand aboot haun(s), forrit.

hand over lat see.

lend a hand pit tae yer han(d).

live from hand to mouth cuil an sup
s.

having powerful hands rackle-
handit.

**two hands held together to form a
receptacle** gowpen.

handicap *noun* (*burden*) doon-haud,
haud-doon, doon-drag NE, doon-
draucht.

handkerchief naipkin, snochter-dich-
ter, snifter-dichter NE.

handle haunle, hannle: *noun, see also*
shaft; horn SHETLAND, ORKNEY; (*eg
of a cup*) lug; (*of an implement*) heft.
verb (*esp children, animals*) guide;
(*awkwardly with the fingers*) thrummle
NE; (*too much*) maig s.

handlebars guys NE.

fit with a handle heft, shank.

having a handle heftit, luggit.

handsome *see also* **good-looking**;

hang

braw, bonnie, lik(e)ly, weel-faured, wice-leukin, clivver, eesome; (*and healthy-looking*) gawsie.

hang *verb, see also* **hung**; hing; (*a person*) rax, †strap up; (*of clothes etc, untidily*) trollop, trailep N, wingle.

hanger-on *see also* **parasite**; onhanger, gie's-a-piece.

hanging untidily (*of clothes etc*) huggerin, trollopy, trailepie N.

hangings hingers.

escape hanging cheat the widdie.

hangdog look *see also* **shamefaced**; doonleuk NE.

hangman *see also* **executioner**; †hangie.

hangman's noose towe; †(hempen) gravat, †St Johnston('s) ribbon.

hangnail ragnail.

hang about *see also* **loiter**; haingle, hanker, hulk aboot, sloonge.

hank hesp, waft clew NE, bowt.

hanker ettle N, green, myang NE.

hankering crave.

haphazard antrin.

hapless *see also* **unfortunate**; donsie.

happen: happen to happen, come o: '*whit'll come o them?*'; (*mainly of misfortune*) come ower; (*mainly in curses, blessings*) fa(w): '*foul fa her*'.

happenings (*esp rowdy*) ongauns.

happy *see also* **cheerful, glad**; blithe, blide SHETLAND, ORKNEY, seilfu, seilie, content, vogie.

happily blithe.

happiness seil.

harangue *noun* lay-aff, screed, la(m)gam(m)achie NE, scrieve.

harass hash, tra(u)chle, deave, murther, dwang, hashter, haister, taigle, pook at, pursue, hatter.

harassed *see also* **hard-pressed**; tra(u)chelt, hurried, taskit, fa(u)chelt, focht(en) NE, taigelt, ticht-hauden SW, S, pingelt, hauden doon.

harbour *noun* herbour, hythe NE, hine, (the) shore N, FIFE.

hard *adjective* (*very*) hard as the horn, hard as Henderson's erse NE; (*of a struggle etc*) sair, stieve; (*of a blow etc*) uncannie, sicker SHETLAND, ORKNEY; (*trying*) coorse; (*difficult, troublesome*) ill; (*difficult to understand*) crank; (*of a bargain*) strait; (*of persons, actions: see also* **severe, stern**[1]) dour.

adverb (*laboriously*) sair NE.

harden (*your heart*) steek.

hardly *see also* **scarcely**; harlie, hardlins, harlies, jimp, scantlins.

hardship hard, throucome SHETLAND, NE, skaith.

suffer hardship come throu the hard, fin frost.

hard cash dry siller.

hard-hearted *see also* **inflexible**; whunstane, stieve.

hard-packed (*of earth etc*) saddit.

hard-pressed *see also* **harassed**; wi yer back tae the wa, hurried, ill-pit, sair made, hard pit(ten) tae, sair pit(ten) tae, ticht-hauden.

hard-up ticht, slack, grippit NE, sair aff, plackless.

hard-worked sair wrocht, sair vrocht NE.

hard-working *see also* **diligent**; warslin.

hard-working person hinger-in.

hard to please *see also* **unappreciative**; ill tae please, perskeet SHETLAND, dortie SW.

be hard on (*clothes*) be sair on, be heavy on, be a heavy neibour on.

hardy hard as the horn, derf, umbersorrow S.

hare bawd, maukin, myaakin NE, bawtie S, puss(ie), donie *in poetry*.

harebell bluebell, blawort, blaver NE, gowk's thimmles NE, lady's thummles.

hare-brained *see also* **flighty** (*under* **flight**[1]); cat-wittit, hallach, hallirackit, kae-wittit, stane-pirrie S, cude S, beeheidit.

hare-lip hareshaw, hairshach, hareskart.

the movement of a hare whid.

run like a hare whid.

hark herk.

harm *verb* hairm, herm, skaith, bla(u)d, middle, injure, mischieve SHETLAND, NE, dae ill till; (*specif physically*) mittle, mar *gipsy*, S.

noun hairm, herm, skaith, ill; (*specif physical*) mischief, faut SHETLAND, NE.

harmful sair, ill.

harmless saikless, ill-less SHETLAND, NE, mows NE.

harmony (*concord*) greement.

harmonious (*in accord*) greeable.

harmonize (*in music*) cord.

live in harmony gree.

work in harmony kep kinches SW.

harness *noun* harnish, herness, graith; (*of a plough etc*) yoke N.

verb (*a horse*) graith.

harnessed (*of a horse*) dra(u)chtit NE.

harp *noun, see also* **Jew's harp**; hairp, herp; (*wire-strung Highland*) clarsach.

harp on *see also* **drone on, nag²**; yap, yirp, threap, rane, be on (aboot): '*she's aye on aboot the price o fish*'.

play on a harp hairp, herp.

harridan *see* **hag, shrew**.

harrow *noun* harra; (*large, heavy*) drag; (*iron, esp for weeding in drills*) grubber.

verb (*land*) harra, straik; (*a field along the furrows*) en(d)lang.

harrowing sair.

harrow-marks straik.

harry *see also* **plunder**; herrie.

harsh (*of a person: see also* **severe**) sair, ill, ill-set, fell, stere; (*of the voice*) groff SHETLAND, NE; (*of sound*) sture; (*to the taste*) ramsh, hask, (*and dry*) stroonge; (*of weather etc*) sicker.

harshly sair, snell.

make a harsh noise chirk, jirg.

not speak harshly to no say a wrang word tae.

treat harshly ool.

harum-scarum *see* **flighty** (*under* **flight¹**).

harvest *noun* hairst, hervest, shearin; (*potato*) tattie-howkin, tattie-liftin.

verb hairst, hervest, lift, win; (*growing potatoes, without disturbing the tops*) lib.

harvester (*person*) hairster, cutter NE, shearer SHETLAND; **harvesters** hairst-fowk.

harvest-home (festival) *see also* **sheaf**; kirn, clyack NE, meal an ale, cailleach.

large roll *etc* eaten on harvest field shearer's bannock.

time between harvest and winter hint-hairst.

has his, huz, hes, haes.

has not hisna, hisnae.

hash *verb, see also* **hack**; hag, haggle.

noun (*of chopped meat etc*) hashie.

hasp hesp.

haste *noun* heist, hist NE, chase, whirr NE, kip S.

hasten *see also* **hurry**; heist, hist NE, hastie NE, heeze, lick, hoy.

hasty heestie; (*and sharp-tongued*) whippert.

hat *see also* **cap, cloth cap, beret, bonnet, top hat** (*under* **top¹**); hot SE; (*tweed, worn by farm overseer*) pickie-say (hat) NE.

hatch *verb* (*eggs*) cleck, clock.

hatching cleckin.

about to hatch (*of an egg*) (hard-)sitten, hard-birdit.

hatchet *see* **axe**.

hate *verb, see also* **loathe**; ill-will NE.

noun, see **hatred** *below*, **loathing**.

hateful hatesome CAITHNESS, ill-faured.

hatred ill will.

haughty *see also* **proud, arrogant, disdainful**; heich, heich-heidit, hauchtie, pauchtie, upsettin, high-bendit, heidie, primp, proudfu, stinkin SHETLAND, NE.

haughtily heich.

act haughtily cairry a heich heid.

look haughtily cock (up) yer neb.

haul *verb, see also* **drag**; hale SHETLAND, NE, harl.

noun (*of fish*) drave.

haul someone over the coals *see also* **scold**; claw someone's kaim.

haunches *see also* **hip**[1]; hainches, hurdies; (*of an animal*) rumple.

on your haunches on yer hunkers.

squat on your haunches hunker doon.

haunt *verb* †hant.

noun hant, howf.

haunted boglie NE.

have *see also* **had, has**; hae, ha, hiv *esp emphatic or interrogative*: 'Hiv ye seen im?'

have not hinna, hinnae, haena, haenae, hivna, hivnae.

haven *see also* **harbour**; hine.

havoc dirdum.

hawk[1] *noun* gled.

as sharp as a hawk as gleg as a gled.

hawk[2] *see also* **clear the throat**; clocher, rauk.

hawk[3] (*sell, peddle*) cadge, traivel the roads.

hawker cadger, traiveller, treveller, candyman, gang-aboot, fleein merchant NE; (*who exchanges rags for crockery*) pig-an-ragger NE, mugger.

hawser swing rope.

hawthorn chaw NE; (*tree*) haw-tree, haw-bush.

hay hey; (*meadow hay*) mawin-girse.

haycock *see also* **stack**; cole, quile, kyle, shig; (*compressed by tramping*) tramp-cock, tramp-cole.

hayfork hey-fowe.

hay harvest hey.

hay harvesters hey-fowk.

haystack *see* **stack**.

hay-truck hey-bogie, hey-cairt.

hazardous *see also* **dangerous**; unchancie.

haze *noun, see also* **heat haze**; loom, gum CAITHNESS, NE, scaum; (*esp with sunbeams*) ure; (*frosty*) rime.

hazy *see* **misty**.

cover with haze scam.

hazel hissel; (*used on Palm Sunday*) palm (tree).

hazelnut cracker nut; (*double*) St John's nut.

hazel stick hissel.

covered with hazels hazellie.

he e, ei S.

head *noun* heid, powe, tap; (*implying stupidity*) neep.

verb (*a ball*) heidie, neeger EDINBURGH.

header 1 (*a ball*) heider. **2** (*masonry*) inban(d).

heady (*of liquor*) nappie *mainly literary*.

headache sair heid.

head-butt *verb* pit *or* stick the heid on, gie (someone) a Glasgow kiss.

headland ness *mainly* SHETLAND, ORKNEY *and in place-names*, mull *mainly in place-names*.

person with head-lice scabbie-heid.

headlong ramstam.

rush headlong skelter, breenge.

headmaster *see also* **headteacher**; heidmaister; (*at small country school*) the maister, dominie.

headstall heidsteel.

headstone lairstane NE.

headstrong *see also* **wilful** (*under* **will**[2]); heidie, ramstam, ootheidie, tapthrawn.

headteacher heidie; (*of a secondary school*) rector.

go to your head (*make giddy*) tak yer heid.

head for airt for, draw till.

head off kep.

with head held high heid-heich.

head over heels *see also* **somersault**; heelster heids, heelster gowdie NE, heels ower hurdies.

a fall throwing you head over heels kelter SW, S.

lift the head proudly geck.

put our *etc* **heads together** lay oor *etc* lugs thegither.

heal hail, sort, sain, mend.

skilled in healing skeelie.

woman skilled in (supernatural) healing powers skeelie wife.

health halth SW, ULSTER, (*good*) (guid) heal, weelness; (*normal state of*) usual: '*He's in his usual*'.

healthy *see also* **in good health** *below*, **fit**[1], **well**[2], **hale and hearty**; hail, caller, weel, at yersel, yaul(d), fendie, (hale an) fere.

in bad health *see also* **ill**; badly, traikie, hingin(-lik(e)), nae weel.

health-giving hailsome.

health visitor green lady W.

in full health and vigour hale an fere, a(w) richt.

in good health braw (an weel), hardy, on fit SHETLAND, ORKNEY, NE, kneef, stench NE, stuffie, solvendie; (*esp after illness*) stoot.

be in good health haud the gate NE.

good health! (*as toast*) slainte (mhath)!

in poor health hard up SE, traikie, hingin(-lik(e)).

improve in health *see also* **recover**; haud forrit.

ask about the health of ask for, inquire for, speir for.

heap *noun* haip; (*round*) roon(d)el; (*small*) hot, dossie NE, humple, hump(h)lock; (*confused*) rickle, rauchle, boorach NE, FIFE, hatter, hushoch NE, FIFE, hushle SHETLAND, CAITHNESS, hudder, (*esp of clothes*) dilgit NE; (*of stones, sand etc*) toorie; (*of stones, large*) bunker NE; (*of stones, esp as a marker or memorial*) cairn; (*of stones etc, esp as a marker*) prap; (*of peats etc*) ruck NE; (*of waste from a mine*) bing, redd bing; (*of manure, hay etc, small*) coop.

verb haip, hot, hudge NE, boorach; (*untidily*) hudder.

hear (*with attention, eg someone's lessons*) hearken.

hard of hearing dull (o hearin), deef kin.

hear yourself speak hear yer ears.

hearse pail.

heart hert, hairt; (*as source of emotions*) wame.

hearten hert, upsteer, upheeze.

hearty hertie, hertsome, sonsie, guidwillie; (*vigorous*) gowst(e)rous; (*of a meal*) hertsome SW.

heartily hertilie, gustilie.

heartache hert-scaud.

heartbeat (*strong*) wallop.

heartburn watter brash, hert-scaud.

heart disease hert-kake SHETLAND.

heart-sore hert-sair.

in the heart of inthrow ORKNEY, NE.

pain at the heart hert-stoun(d).

suffering from a weak heart hertie.

hearth hairth, herth, chim(b)ley NE.

hearthstone firestane ORKNEY, NE, ingle-stane.

heat *noun* hait; (*sweltering*) swither; (*sudden state of*) feem NE; (*sudden glow of*) gliff.

verb het, hait; (*partially*) leep; (*a house*) fire: '*keep the place fired*'.

heated *past tense, past participle* het.

become heated (*in anger etc*) spunk up.

heating (*act of*) heat: '*come awa in an get a heat*'.

heat haze (y)oam SHETLAND, NE, simmer cowts.

on heat (*of a cow*) rinnin.

be on heat (*esp of a sow*) breem, brim.

heath *see* **heather, moor**[1].

heathen haithen.

heather hedder SHETLAND, ORKNEY, NE, hather, dog-heather NE; (*with bell-shaped flowerets*) bell-heather, carline heather.

heathery hedderie NE.

heather-twig, broom of heather twigs heather-cowe.

flower of heather heather bell.

stalks and roots of burnt heather heather birn(s).

heave *verb* have NE; **heave (up)** heeze, hoise, hodge; (*something heavy*) hoy; (*with the shoulder*) hunch.

noun hoy; (up)heeze, heezie, hyzie NE: '*gie's a hyzie up*', hoise; (*with shoulder*) hunch.

heaved *past tense* hove, haved NE.

heaven heiven, the land o the leal, the guid place; **the heavens** the lift; **heavens!** *see* **surprise** (*exclamations of*).

heavenly heivenlie.

heavenly body blinker.

heavy hivvie; (*weighty*) wechtie, unfreelie NE, loordie; (*corpulent*) wechtie NE, gurthie, bursten NE; (*sluggish*) loordie; (*oppressive*) grief, gurthie; (*of dough*) sad, saddit.

heavily souse NE.

hector hatter S.

heddles calmes ANGUS.

hedge *noun* dyke SW.

hedgehog hedger, hurcheon, erchin NE, FIFE.

hedge-sparrow hedgie, hedge-spurdie, spurdie, fieldie, whin-sparra, dykie SW, hempie S.

foot of a hedge (*hedge*) ruit.

heed *see also* **attention**: *noun* tent.

verb tent, tak tent o, leet; **not heed** nivver heed, no fash yersel, no goam, no fash yer thoum.

heedful tentie.

heedless *see also* **reckless**; tentless, ramstam, regairdless, throu-the-muir NE.

heedlessly *see also* **recklessly**; blin(d)lins.

give heed to tak tent tae.

heel: heel-piece (*to strengthen boot or shoe*) heel-shod, cauker, cuddie-heel; (*round*) heel-ring.

take to your heels mak yer feet yer freen(d)s NE.

hefty (*of person*) *see* **stout, corpulent**.

heifer *see also* **cow**[1]; heefer.

height heicht, hicht; (*of a person*) lenth; (*of an arch*) spring.

heighten heicht, hicht(en).

heir (*who inherited land*) †heir-at-law, †heir-of-line.

heiress *see* **co-heir**.

declare (*a person*) **heir** †serve heir.

held *past tense of* **hold** heeld NE.

past participle hauden, hadden.

hell the bad place, the ill place, the bad fire, the ill pairt NE, elfin *euphemistic*; (*as curse*) Hecklebirnie NE, Hexham S.

go to hell! gae tae Freuchie (an fry mice)!, gang tae Buckie (an bottle skate)! NE.

depths of hell muckle hell.

helmet (*woollen*) magirkie NE.

help *verb* (*lend a hand*) pit tae yer han(d); **help!** harro!

noun cast; (*attentive*) notice SHETLAND, NE; (*onto a wall, vehicle etc*) dookie-up E CENTRAL, S, punt-up W.

helpful *see also* **obliging**; helplie.

helping (*of food*) raik.

give a helping hand to gie a lift tae.

helpless mauch(t)less, dowless, doless, daeless; (*unable to cope*) silly; (*on your back, eg when drunk*) awald; (*with laughter*) soople.

made helpless owertaen.

help yourself (*to food or drink*) mak a lang airm, pit oot yer han(d).

helter-skelter *see also* **confusion**; ding-dang NE, FIFE.

hem *noun* bord; (*with a drawstring*) slot; (*with upper edge sewn down over lower one*) splay; (*with one part of cloth folded down over the other*) owerlay.

hem in hamphis, humfish, stell.

hemlock humlock, hech-howe W, SW, scab S.

hen *see also* **chicken, broody**; chookie (hen); (*crested*) tappit hen, tappie *mainly pet name*, SHETLAND, ORKNEY; (*breed of short-legged*) golaich.

hen-coop (hen-)ree, (hen-)cavie, hen-crae, crib, cruive NE.

hen-droppings hen-pen, hens' muck.

hen-harrier gled.

henpeck drum-major, hoolet, craw in someone's crap.

hen-roost hen-laft, reest.

hen-run (hen-)ree.

hence (*of places*) hyne.

her hir.

herald: chief herald in Scotland Lord Lyon (King of Arms).

Court of Heralds in Scotland Lyon Court.

herb yerb.

herd *noun* paircel.

verb, see also **tend**; wirk.

herdsman *see also* **shepherd**; herd, hird.

hereabouts hereawa.

hermaphrodite scart; (*male*) Jennie Wullock; (*fowl*) faizart.

hernia rimburst(in); (*strangulated*) knot i the puddin.

heron hern, heronshew S, (h)erle, cran, (lang-)craigit heron NE, lang Sandie NE, Jennie heron SW.

herring herrin, scattan NE, W; (*half-mature*) halflin; (*half-mature female*) mattie SHETLAND, NE; (*sexually mature*) matfull; (*as food*) twa-eyed (beef)steak *humorous*; (*salt*) Dunbar wether, Glesca bailie, Glesca magistrate, magistrate, white herrin.

herring boat drave boat; (*types of*) nabbie W, SW, Fifie E COAST.

herring fishing drave; (*in summer, off Fife coast*) Lammas drave.

herring fry (herrin) sile.

herring net *see* **net**.

herself hersel.

by herself (by) her lane, er leen NE, bird-alane.

hesitate *see also* **dither**; swither, swander SHETLAND, N, waffle, hover, teeter, hum(ph) an hae, dachle NE, huilie, hick SW, S; (*scruple*) stickle; (*eg in speaking*) hanker.

hesitant ergh, sweirt, sweir-drawn.

hesitation swither, dachle NE, fiddletie-fa NE, hank S, hum(ph) an hae: '*wi a hum an a hae*'.

heterogeneous mixter-maxter.

hew howk, hag.

hiccup *noun, verb* hick, yesk.

hid *past tense of* **hide** hed, hod NE, hoddit, hidit N.

hidden *past participle* hid, hod NE, hoddit SHETLAND, NE, hidit NE, dernit.

adjective (*also good for hiding in*) hidie, hoddie ANGUS, dern.

hide[1] *verb, see also* **hid**; hod NE, hoid SHETLAND, howd FIFE, dern, hiddle, heal, scug; (*esp something for later use*) plank, plunk, pose; (*esp your feelings*) smuir; (*duck out of sight*) jouk.

hiding place hidie-hole, hideance, hiddle.

hide-and-seek hidie, hide-an-gae-seek, Hi-Spy, keehoy, hunt-the-tod NE, lurkie, seek-an-haud, cook FIFE.

hide your feelings hae't an haud it NE.

hide[2] *noun* (*skin*) leather.

hiding *see* **beating**.

hideous laithlie.

higgledy-piggledy *see also* **topsy-turvy**; hickertie-pickertie, tapsalteerie, throuither, throwder NE, heels ower gowdie, heelster heid(s), heids an thraws, reel-rall, rach-ma-reeshil.

high *adjective* heich, hie; (*of wind*) teirin; (*esp of prices*) lang NE; (*of taste*) humphie.

higher (*than its surroundings, of a relief pattern etc*) prood.

highest heichmaist, eemost NE.

highest part heid.

highest up heidmaist.

highly *see* **very, extremely**.

high-born gentie.

Highland Hielan(d).

Highlander Hielander, teuchter *contemptuous*; (*male*) Hielan(d)man, (Hielan) Donal(d) N; (*esp Gaelic-speaking*) Gael.

Highlands Hielan(d)s; (*esp Gaelic-speaking*) Gaidhealtachd.

in the Highlands upthrou SHETLAND, ORKNEY, N.

high-minded major-mindit.

high-pitched (*shrill*) snell, squallochie NE.

high-pitched sound skirl, squalloch NE; (*esp of a bird*) wheeple.

high-rise flat multi.

high-water mark rowe N.

hilarious (*from drink*) glorious.

hilarity madderam SHETLAND, ORKNEY.

hill *see also* **hillock, mountain;** hull, heich, hope S; (*esp higher*) ben; (*long, narrow*) rig; (*rounded, often conspicuous*) law; (*steep, rocky*) fell; (*steep, eroded*) scaur; (*of over 2 000 feet (610m), in the Lowlands*) Donald.

hillock knab, knowe, nabb, humple; (*esp fairy hill*) tulloch N; (*in a bog*) hag; (*small*) hiller CAITHNESS, tummock; (*covered with long grass*) dog hillock N.

hilly hill-run N; (*and exposed*) fusslebare NE.

hillcrest *see* **crest.**

hill-dweller heather-lowper NE.

hill-face (*steep*) shin.

hillside brae, sidelin(s); (*stony*) sclenter.

hilltop *see* **summit.**

hills and dales heichs an howes.

himself himsel, hissel.

by himself (by) his lane, bird-alane, him lane, im leen NE.

hind: hind leg (*of an animal*) hint-leg, hoch.

hindmost *see also* **last²;** hin(d)maist, hintmaist, hint-han(d).

hindquarters *see also* **buttocks;** hin(t)en(d); (*of an animal: see also* **haunches**) hinders.

hinder *see also* **hamper;** hinner, block, pit fae, taigle, mar, ersie SHETLAND, ORKNEY; (*delay*) hing (someone) on NE, (*with something unimportant*) scutter.

hindered hinnert, hamperit.

hindering, causing hindrance taiglesome.

hindrance hinner, hinnerance N, hing-on, mar, stick, haud-again NE, affset, taigle.

hinge *noun* hiddin NE, huidin; (*of a door*) harr SHETLAND, ORKNEY, ban(d) NE.

hint *verb* mint (at) NE, moot SHETLAND, NE.

noun moot SHETLAND, NE, mump NE, witterin; **not a hint** nae a cheep.

he never gave a hint he nivver loot myowt NE.

hinterland erse ORKNEY, N.

hip¹ *see also* **haunches: hips** hurdies.

hip-bone hurkle-bane; (*of an animal*) lunyie-bane.

having sticking-out hips happerersit, happer-hippit S.

hip² *see also* **rosehip** (*under* **rose²**); (*fruit*) hap, buckie, buckie faulie CAITHNESS, choop SW, S, dog(gie)'s hip; **hips** hippans NE.

hire *see also* **lease:** *verb* (*as a servant*) fee; (*something in advance*) tryst.

noun (*of a boat*) fraucht.

hiring out (*law*) location.

his heez.

hiss *verb* (*of liquid*) bizz; (*of a cat etc*) fuff; (*make a hissing sound*) fiss NE; (*to drive away an animal etc*) hish.

noun (*eg of a cat*) fuff; (*to drive away animals etc*) hish; (*of an object flying through the air*) swiff SHETLAND, NE.

hissing *adjective* fuzzie NE.

hit *verb, see also* **strike, knock, slap;** gowf, skite, ding, fortak NE, swap, snite S, lift yer han(d) (tae); (*hard*) melt, stookie.

noun, see also **blow², slap;** gowf.

past tense hut, hat SHETLAND, N.

past participle hutten, hitten, hut.

hit out loonder, lat sing; (*in all directions*) lay fae yersel, let flist (at) NE; **hit out at** lat at.

hitch *verb* **hitch up** hotch up, hodge up, hilch up, keytch.

noun **1** (*movement*) hotch, hodge SHETLAND, NE. **2** (*snag*) whaup *or* thraw i the raip.

hither hereawa.

hither and thither hither an yon(t), hereawa thereawa.

hive *noun, see also* **beehive;** byke, bink.

hoar: hoary hair; (*of hair*) lyart.

hoar-frost haar(-frost), cranreuch, rind.

hoard *see also* **store:** *noun* huird, hoord NE, stockin, rake, hogger, fallachan ARGYLL; (*esp for later use*) pit-by, plank, plunk, pose; (*of money*) moggan.

verb huird, hain; (*esp for later use*) plank, plunk, pose N.

hoarder gear-gatherer.

hoarse hairse, roupie, roostie, croupit; (*and deep, rough*) sture.

hoarseness the roup.

speak hoarsely *see also* **croak** 1; croup NE, FIFE.

hoax *noun, see also* **deceit, trick**; rise.
verb, see also **deceive, cheat**; play the rig wi.

hob (*on a fireplace*) bink.

hobble *verb* 1 *see also* **shuffle** 1, **totter**; habble, hirple, hochle, lamp, hilch, hainch, cripple, hodge SHETLAND, ORKNEY, NE, hammle S, pauchle (alang). 2 (*an animal*) langle, lingel NE, hapshackle, hoch-ban(d) SHETLAND.
noun (*for an animal*) lingel, langle, hapshackle, hoch ban(d).

hobby-horse habbie-horse.

hobgoblin *see also* **bog(e)yman**; bockie SHETLAND, ORKNEY, N, wirricow, boodie NE, trowe SHETLAND, ORKNEY, doolie, grapus.

hobnail tacket.

hobnailed tacketie, tacketit.

hobnailed boots tacketie buits.

hobnob *see also* **associate**; †big sandy mills (wi).

hock (*of animal's leg*) hoch.

hockey-like game (*played mainly in the Highlands: see also* **stick**[1]) shinty.

hod hudd.

hoe *noun* howe, hyowe N, paidle, claut; (*horse hoe*) hurkle.
verb howe, hyowe N, paidle; (*slightly*) scutch N; (*turnips*) rin.

hoeing (*slight*) scuffle.

hoe out (*seedlings*) sinder NE.

hog *noun* 1 (*castrated pig*) gaut. 2 *see* **glutton**.

hogshead hogget.

hogweed humlock, kex SHETLAND, ORKNEY, coo-cakes, bunnel.

go the whole hog gae yer dinger, gie it laldie.

hoist *see also* **lift**: *verb* hyste, heeze, hize

NE, heft; (*a sail*) hoise; (*a load*) humph, hulster; (*a person by the buttocks*) dook(ie) (up) SE.
noun (*lifting-up*) hyste, heeze, hoise, hulster; (*on the back*) backie; (*of a person, from below*) dook(ie)-up, punt-up, hochie-up NE.

hold[1] *verb, see also* **held, confine**; haud, had, howld SHETLAND, ORKNEY, N, ARGYLL, ULSTER.
noun 1 (*grasp*) haud, had, howld SHETLAND, ORKNEY, N, ARGYLL, ULSTER, catch, claut. 2 (*over a person*) a hair in someone's neck.

holding haudin, haddin, howldin SHETLAND, ORKNEY, N, ARGYLL, ULSTER; (*esp of property: see also* **lease, smallholding**) hau(l)d, place, placie ORKNEY, N.

hold back dachle NE.

hold forth lay aff, say awa, loonder (at).

hold off haud aff.

hold on *see also* **wait**; behaud.

hold on to grip till SHETLAND, NE.

hold out *see* **last**[2].

hold over refer.

hold your tongue haud yer wheesht, steek yer gab.

hold up 1 uphaud; (*hair, with a comb etc*) kep. 2 **hold things up** hing the cat ANGUS, FIFE. 3 (*work in a factory*) steg W.

catch hold of *see also* **snatch**; grip, cla(u)cht.

hold[2] (*of a ship*) howld.

hole *noun, see also* **hollow**; thirl; (*esp as hiding place*) bore; (*in ground, esp marshy*) powk; (*in river*) pot, (*deep*) pootch; (*made by auger*) wummle-bore; (*in wall for sheep to pass through*) lunkart W, SW; (*in ground, for marbles game*) kypie NE, dump, mug.

full of holes holiepied NE.

holiday *noun* hoaliday; (*esp break from business*) vacance; (*annual summer*) the Trades *esp* EDINBURGH, the Fair: '*the Glasgow Fair*'; (*from school etc*) the play; (*from school for potato harvest*) tattie hoalidays.

on holiday on the daffin NE.

hollow *noun, see also* **hole;** hallow; (*esp in land*) howe; (*esp marshy*) wham SHETLAND; (*wet, marshy*) swail NE, slunk; (*eg where peats have been cut*) hag; (*among hills*) hope S; (*esp between hills*) slack, slock N, lirk; (*esp with a road*) swire; (*on side of a hill*) corrie; (*narrow, steep, on hillside*) slidder; (*in flour when baking*) sprent.

verb **hollow out** *see also* **scoop out;** hallow, howk, gowp.

adjective hallow, howe, boss, hullie SE; (*of sound*) tuim, teem N, dowf, howe; (*in shape*) cappie.

hollow-backed howe-backit.

hollow-trunked (*of a tree*) pumped.

holly hollin NE.

holy halie.

home *noun* hame, heem ORKNEY, hem SHETLAND, heyime S, yer hoose at hame, midden heid *humorous:* '*on yer ain midden heid*'.

homely hamelie, hamel(t), hamit, hameower, hamewart, hodden; (*esp of a person*) hame-made.

homely person hodden gray.

home farm mains.

home-grown *see* **home-made.**

home-loving hame-drachtit NE, ha-mit.

home-made hameart, hamit, hamelt.

homesick hame-drachtit NE.

homespun raploch.

homestead *see also* **farm buildings;** (ferm) steidin, ferm toon.

homeward hamewart, hamewith NE.

homeward bound hame-gaun.

homewards hamewith NE, hameower; (*straight*) hame-throu SHETLAND.

(school) homework tasks.

at home hame.

away from home ootby.

(act of) going home hame-gaun.

make your home sit doon.

make your home with rely till NE.

see (*someone*) **home** set hame, follow SHETLAND, ORKNEY.

seeing someone halfway home Scotch convoy.

staying at home hame-farin, hame-drachtit NE.

hone *see* **whetstone.**

honest jonick, furth-the-gate NE, rael, suithfast; (*sincere*) aefauld, evendoon, leal.

honestly aefauldlie.

honesty furth-the-gate NE, leal.

honey hinnie.

honey bag (*of a bee*) blob.

(earthenware) honey jar hinnie pig NE.

honeysuckle hinniesickle, bin(d)wuid.

honour (*decency*) honesty; (*credit*) mense; (*eg in a contest*) gree: '*win the gree*'.

honourable *see also* **honest, worthy;** honest, guid.

honour with your presence, do honour to mense.

hood huid.

hooded huidit.

hooded crow huidie (craw), hoodie craa NE, grayback, corbie.

hoodwink *see also* **deceive, cheat;** draw straes afore someone's een.

hoof *noun* huif, hiv CAITHNESS, NE, luif, cloot, (*originally a cloven hoof*) cluif.

hook *noun* heuk, cleek, click; (*esp for a pot*) cruik, clep; (*for hanging things on*) knag.

verb (*also a man*) cleek, click.

hooligan *see* **ruffian.**

hoop *noun* gird, girr; (*large, for holding a barrel during construction*) passer, parson hoop NE; (*canvas-covered for winnowing grain*) wecht, blin sieve.

rod for guiding a child's hoop †cleek.

hoot *verb* (*of or like an owl*) hoo.

hop *verb* hap, hip S, hitch, haut.

noun (*act of hopping*) hap, hip S, haut; (*eg in hopscotch*) hitch; (*in a dance*) stot.

hopper (*in a mill*) happer.

hopscotch beds, peever(ie) beds, peever(s), pallal(s) E CENTRAL, skeetchers N, FIFE, hap-the-beds SW, hoppin beddies NE.

stone *etc* **used in hopscotch** peever, pallal E CENTRAL, skeetcher N, FIFE.

hop about lowp.

hop, step and jump hap, step an lowp.

hope *verb* howp, hoop SHETLAND, ORKNEY.

noun howp, hoop SHETLAND, ORKNEY, wan SHETLAND, ORKNEY, CAITHNESS.

hopeful howpfu.

in a hopeless situation up a clos(i)e.

in the hope of doing in howp(s) tae dae.

horde *see also* **crowd**; fleesh NE.

horizon easin(s) NE, wa-heids SW.

look along the horizon sky NE.

horizontally flatlins, skleff S.

horn *noun* (*musical*) tooter; (*small, loose, on hornless cattle*) scur SW.

hornless (*of cattle*) hummel doddie NE.

hornless cow *or* **bull** doddie NE.

horn spoon gebbie SHETLAND, ORKNEY, NE; (*of ramhorn*) ramhorn (spuin).

cow with crooked horns crummie.

having downturned horns scoul-hornit.

having upturned horns kippie S.

having short upright horns stookit.

play on a horn rowt on a horn.

strike with the horns snug.

toss the horns cave.

horrible *see also* **dreadful, terrible**; grue, ugsome, pooshionous, laithfu, fousome NE.

horribly laithfu NE.

horror (*feeling of*) grue.

feel horror grue: '*it gars me grue*'.

horse *noun* **1** horse-baist, cuddie, naig, gry *gipsy*; (*small, sturdy, used in hills*) garron; (*kept for odd jobs*) orra horse;

(*young, male*) frog NE; (*young, not broken to work*) staig; (*young, castrated*) staig; (*one-year-old*) eean NE; (*old*) bassie; (*old, worn-out*) glyde, yaud S, garron, aiver; (*worthless*) jaud. **2** (*gymnasium horse*) cuddie.

horse-collar brecham.

horsefly *see* **gadfly**.

horse-hoe shim NE.

hospitable cadgie, guid-willie, hielan, frugal, furthie.

hospital hoaspital, ospital.

hospitality mense.

host[1] landlord.

hostess landlady.

host[2] *see* **crowd**.

hostile *see also* **malicious**; awkwart, ill-willie, ill, ill-kindit.

hostility hosteelity, ill-will.

hot het; (*uncomfortably*) roastit, sweltrie.

hothouse hothoose.

hot-tempered birsie.

hot-water bottle (*earthenware*) pig.

be(come) very hot *see also* **swelter**; be(come) a-heat.

hotchpotch *see also* **mixture**; hodgepodge, mixter-maxter, pronack.

hotel hottle.

hound *noun*, *see also* **dog**; hun(d).

verb hun(d).

hour *see also* **early, late 1**; oor; (*whole* (*long*) *hour*) stricken oor.

keep irregular hours mistime NE.

respectable hours elders' oors.

house *noun*, *see also* **cottage, hovel, hut, farmworkers' quarters**; hoose, hoosie, ruif-tree, byke, heft; (*dwelling-house, as opposed to other buildings*) hoosin NE, fire hoose NE, lodgin; (*inhabited, ie with smoking chimney*) reekin lum, smoke HIGHLAND; (*large, belonging to a landowner*) big hoose, ha(ll); (*one-apartment*) single-en(d); (*having separate entrance etc*) self-contained hoose, hoose within itsel; (*on ground floor*) maindoor (hoose), maindoor flat; (*badly-built, rambling*) jamb; (*dilapi-*

dated) ra(u)chle; (*of dry stone and turf*)
†black hoose HIGHLAND; (*of stone and lime*) †white hoose CAITHNESS, HIGHLAND; (*with slate roof*) sclate hoose; (*forming angle between two roads*) gushet hoose; (*small, between two taller*) hole i the wa.

verb hoose.

housebound hoosefast, hoose-tied.

household equipment plenishin, hoose gear; (*loaded for removal*) flittin.

householder hooseha(u)dder.

head of the household (*male*) himsel; (*female*) hersel.

housekeeping hooseha(u)ddin, hizzieskep.

houseleek foos NE.

housemaid *see* **maid**.

houseman (*in a hospital*) resident.

house-martin wunda-swalla.

house-owner laird.

house-warming (party) hoose-heat(in).

housewife guidwife, dame NE, FIFE; (*slovenly*) Mrs MacClarty.

change of house shift: '*We want a shift tae a main door*'.

in(to) a house inby.

set up house, become a householder tak up hoose.

move house flit.

hovel *see also* **hut**; puidge, boorach, cruive.

hover (*indecisively*) swither, teeter, hing.

hovering *adjective* (*indecisive*) sweirt.

how *adverb* hoo, foo SHETLAND, ORKNEY, N.

conjunction hoo, foo SHETLAND, ORKNEY, N, hoo that, foo that NE.

however hooivver, howanever, foosomever SHETLAND, ORKNEY, N.

how are you? hoo's a(w) wi ye?, foo's a wi ye? N, fit like? NE.

howl *see also* **roar, yell, bellow**: *verb* gowl, wow SHETLAND, NE, yowt, yammer; (*esp of a dog*) yowl; (*of the wind*) gurl, hoo.

noun gowl, wow, yowt; (*esp of a dog*) yowl.

hoyden hallockit.

hubbub *see* **commotion**.

huddle *verb* hiddle, hunker, coorie in; (*with cold*) nither, hugger.

noun hiddle; (*eg of buildings*) rickle.

hue and cry *see* **outcry**.

huff *see also* **sulk**; dort(s), fung, towt, strum(s), strunt(s): '*tak the strunts*', fuff.

go into a huff fuff, strum, strunt, tak the tig.

huffy snottie, bungie NE, birkie.

hug *see also* **cuddle**: *verb* smoorich.

noun chirt sw, Scotch gravat, lovie *child's word*, smoorich, bosie.

huge *see also* **big, large**; wappin, muckle big, great muckle.

hull *see also* **husk, shell**: *verb, noun* huil.

hullabaloo *see* **commotion, fuss**.

hum *verb* (*esp of a bee*) bum, bummle; (*a tune*) souch, sowff NE, sooth NE; (*to accompany dancers*) diddle.

noun (*humming sound*) bum, dirr S; (*continuous*) bum-bummin NE, FIFE; (*low singing*) sooth, sowff NE.

human: human being bodie, buddie; **human beings** fowk.

human race Jock Tamson's bairns: '*We're aw Jock Tamson's bairns*'.

humane cannie, couthie.

humanity *see* **mankind** (*under* **man**).

humble *adjective* hummle, lown.

verb hummle, tak doon a hack, tak a stap oot o someone's bicker; **humble yourself** below, come doon wi yer spirit, jouk.

humbug *see* **pretence**.

humdrum *see also* **dreary**.

humdrum workaday world *see also* **routine**; auld claes an parritch: '*It's back tae auld claes an parritch the morn*'.

humid *see also* **close**[1] 3; growthie.

humiliate *see also* **humble**; bemean, tak doon a hack, snuil.

humiliation doon-tak, doon-come.

humour *noun, see also* **mood**; eemir NE.

humourless dour.
humorous humoursome, pleasant.
hump humph, hulk.
  humpback humph.
  humpbacked *see* **hunchbacked.**
hunch: hunched humphed.
hunchback hump(h)(ie-back), hunchie.
hunchbacked hump(h)ie(-backit), humph-backit, boo-backit, booliebackit, crootchie, hurkle-backit.
hundred, hundredth hunder, hunner.
hung *past tense of* **hang** hingit, hang SHETLAND, NE.
  past participle hingit.
hunger *noun* (*ravenous*) hert-hunger NE; (*growing*) curnawin NE.
hungry hungert, hungrysome, tuim, teem N, yaup, howe; (*very*) gleg as a gled.
  be hungry yaup; (*ravenously*) fin(d) the grun(d) o yer stamack.
  causing hunger hungrysome.
  pinch of hunger nip o hunger.
  pinched with hunger nippit.
hunk *see also* **chunk, lump**; knoit, gunch, knoll, knoost.
hunt *see also* **search**: *verb* (*prowl*) snoke.
  noun fork.
  hunt for fork for.
  hunt-the-slipper shuffle-the-brogue.
  hunt through ripe.
hurdle *noun* (*used as a gate*) flake; (*to stop a gap in a hedge etc*) let SW.
hurl *verb, see also* **throw**; pick; (*a weapon*) wage.
hurly-burly *see* **commotion.**
hurricane skailwin(d).
hurry *see also* **haste, rush², bustle, hustle**: *verb* lick, streek, hoy, leather, hing in, heeze, chase, breeshle, hill on NE, spur, pey on NE, hastie NE, kip; (*cause to hurry*) heeze, gie heels tae.
  noun chase, kip S.
  hurried hush(l)ochie.
  hurriedly fiercelins.

hurt *verb* hort CAITHNESS: **1** *see also* **injure**; skaith, wrang, mischieve, malagrooze NE, mishanter NE; (*esp on the head*) brain; (*badly*) kill, mairtyr. **2** *see also* **offend**; heelie.
  past tense, past participle hurtit.
  noun **1** *see also* **injury**; skaith, mishanter SHETLAND, ORKNEY, N. **2** (*to feelings*) scaud, scam NE.
  adjective bemang't.
  hurtful hurtsome, sair.
  be hurt tak skaith.
  easily hurt frush; (*of feelings*) henhertit.
hurtle *verb* hurl.
husband *noun* man, guidman, neibour.
  my husband oor ane, oor yin.
hush *verb* (*a child to sleep*) ba(w), hushie-ba(w).
  noun, see **quiet.**
  interjection hish!, wheesht!
  hushed wheesht, lown.
husk *noun, see also* **shell, pod**; huil, sloch, pile, pilk; **husks** (*removed from grain*) (sheelin) seeds.
  verb, see also **shell**; huil.
husky *see also* **hoarse**; roupie.
  huskiness the roup.
hussy besom, limmer, jaud, quine NE.
hustle *verb, see also* **hurry, rush², bustle**; rooshel NE, dreel, fluister.
  hustling *adjective* forcie.
hut *see also* **shed²**; puidge; (*fishermen's, climbers'*) bothy; (*fishermen's*) lodge SHETLAND; (*for shepherds or fishermen*) †shiel(in).
hyacinth: wild hyacinth *see* **bluebell.**
hydrangea hedder-reenge NE, FIFE.
hygienic (*esp in cooking*) parteec(u)lar.
hymn *noun* hime.
hypochondria heepocondrie.
  hypochondriac heepochondreeoch.
hypocrite heepocreet, hypocreet.
  hypocritical heepocreetical.
hysterics: go into hysterics gae hyte.

I

I A(h), aw.

I shall I'se: '*I'se warran*'.

ice frost; (*icy surface*) s(c)lidder NE, slipper NE; (*thin covering*) glaister SW, scum; (*half-melted, eg in a river*) grue; (*large, loose piece, eg in a river*) shud S.

icicle (ice-)tangle, eeshogel, shockle, bobantilter CAITHNESS.

icy *see* **slippery** 1.

ice-cream (*vanilla, with raspberry juice*) macallum.

ice-cream cone pokey hat.

ice-cream shop Tallie shop *humorous*.

ice-cream wafer slider; (*two with marshmallow filling and chocolate edge*) black man CENTRAL.

cold as ice jeel caul(d) NE, fair jeelit NE.

stretch of ice (*for skating etc: see also* **slide**) s(c)ly; (*down the centre of a curling rink*) howe-ice.

idea idaia NE, consait NE.

identical self an same.

idiosyncrasy particularity.

idiot *see also* **mentally-handicapped person, fool, blockhead, simpleton**; eediot, eejit, idiwut, daftie, heidbanger, bawheid, gomerel, stot, neep-heid, snot, docus, guff, oanshach NE, ARGYLL, hinkum sneev(l)ie NE, dingle E CENTRAL; (*clumsy*) muckle sumph: '*ye muckle sumph, ye!*'

idiocy eediocie.

idiotic *see also* **stupid, foolish**; eediotical, feel NE.

idle *adjective* idleset, lither; (*completely*) horn idle, stane-tired S.

verb, see also **potter**[2], **loaf**[2]; sloonge, slope, sotter, gamfle, gawk.

idler waster, sloonger, jotter, †blellum.

move *or* **work idly** pirl NE.

stare idly gawk, gaik NE.

idleness idleset, idletie.

idling *adjective* (*of machinery*) tuim.

with idle hands han(d)-idle.

idle talk *see also* **gossip, chitchat**; clavers, clish(ma)clash, clashmaclaver(s), clishmaclaver NE.

idol eedol NE.

idolize idoleese.

if gin, an, in NE, gif *mainly literary*.

ignite *see* **kindle**.

ignoble *see* **mean**[1].

ignominy tash SHETLAND.

ignorant far back N, unkennin SHETLAND, iggerant *humorous*.

ignore (*a person*) (sling someone a) deefie: '*he deefied me*'.

ill ull: *adjective, see also* **unwell, ailing**; no weel, unweel, badly, sair pit on; (*slightly*) seeckrif(e) *literary*; (*seriously*) far awa wi't; (*dangerously*) far throu.

be ill traik.

become ill tak ill, tak nae weel.

illness ill SHETLAND, N, unweelness NE, dishealth, distress; (*ailment*) tribble, ail, jallisie NE; (*esp of unknown origin*) income, onfa(w) S; (*esp epidemic*) traik; (*in children, with no particular cause*) hives; (*sudden*) owercome, brash, dwam, toit, drowe; (*sharp attack*) oncome S; (*slight: see also* **touch** 2) towt, skiff, twine NE; (*about which a fuss is made*) fraik ORKNEY, N.

be out of action because of illness be laid aside.

ill-assorted mismarrowed.

ill-bred menseless, mislearit, ill-guidit.

ill-disposed *see* **malevolent**.

ill-fated unchancie, mischancie, weird-less, misluckit NE.

ill-favoured ill-faured.

ill-gotten wrangous.

ill-health *see* illness.

ill-humour *see also* bad temper, sulks; canker; (*fit of*) thraw, towt, ill tid, ill teen NE.

ill-looking hingin-lik(e), peelie-wallie, nae weel lik(e).

ill-mannered *see also* ill-bred; ill-faured, ignorant.

ill-natured *see also* bad-tempered, sulky; grumphie, wickit, canker(i)t, natterie, ill-thrawn, neukit NE.

ill-omened unchancie.

ill-spent ill-waured.

ill-tempered *see* bad-tempered, surly.

ill-treat ool, ill-guide, injure, bad-use SHETLAND, NE, mischieve SHETLAND, NE, demain NE.

ill-will *see also* enmity, rancour; un-freen(d)ship SHETLAND, gum.

illegal wrongous.

illegitimate (*of a child*) merry-begot-ten, ill-come N, ill-gotten.

illegitimate child *see also* bastard; misfortune, come-o-will NE, luve-bairn.

have an illegitimate child cowp the creels, cast a shae.

illustrious *see* distinguished.

image eemage.

the (very) image of *see also* likeness; the spitten eemage O, the parrymauk O NE, the marrow O: '*She's the marrow o her mither*'.

imagine jalouse.

imbecile *noun, see also* idiot, men-tally-handicapped person; daftie, haiverel, object, feel NE.

adjective, see mentally handicapped.

imitate eemitate.

immature bairnlik(e).

immediately immedantlie NE, stra(u)cht, richt noo, in a crack, bedeen, belyve, at aince.

immense *see also* huge; undeemous SHETLAND, N, great muckle.

immerse dook; (*in boiling water*) plot.

immersion dookin; (*in boiling water*) plot.

imminent *see* soon.

immobile (*rigid*) stieve.

immoderate surfeit.

eat and drink immoderately *see also* eat; gilravage.

immodest heich-kiltit.

immoral lowse.

immoral person dyke-lowper S.

live immorally gae an ill gate.

living immorally ruch-livin.

imp deevilock NE, limb o the deil.

impact dunt, skelp.

impartial *see* fair[1] 1.

impatient (*short-tempered*) fuffie, on nettles; (*hasty*) whippert; (*restless*) lik a hen on a het girdle.

impatience (*excited*) reeho NE.

be impatient with fash at.

exclamation of impatience ach!, och!, in the name (o a(w))!, michtie (me)!, toots!

impeccable evendoon.

impecunious *see* poor.

impede *see also* hamper, hinder; dachle NE, pester, habble S.

impediment (*in speech: see also* stam-mer) mant.

have a speech impediment mant.

having a speech impediment tongue-tackit.

imperious *see* domineering.

impertinent *see* impudent.

impertinence *see* impudence.

impetus *see also* force; (*sudden*) rummle; (*eg behind a curling stone*) wecht.

impetuous *see also* rash[2], bold; heid-ie, ramstam, rammish, raucle.

impetuous person breenger.

impetuously *see also* rashly (*under* rash[2]); fiercelins, ramstam, breengin.

implacable unbowsome S.

implement *noun, see also* tool; luim,

leem N; (*for slicing turnips*) hasher; (*for scraping dung etc*) claut; (*long-handled, for weeding etc*) paidle.

implicate insnorl N.

impolite *see* **rude.**

import *verb* (*into a place*) inbring.

important: important person nae sheep shank.

think yourself important think yersel nae sma drink, hae a guid consait o yersel.

most important heid.

of what importance is it? whit reck(s)?

importune *see also* **beg, entreat, dun;** prig, fleetch, thrain FIFE, pursue.

impose: imposing (*of things*) vogie, gawsie.

imposition imposeetion, humbug NE.

impossible (*out of the question*) oot the windae.

attempt the impossible (mak a brig tae the Bass an) ding doon Tantallon.

impostor mak-on SHETLAND, NE.

impotent (*powerless*) mauch(t)less.

impound (*stray animals*) pund, poind.

impoverish povereese, herrie, tak doon ORKNEY, N.

impregnate bairn, sneck.

impress pit on.

impression *see* **imprint.**

impress a fact on insense intae SW, ULSTER.

imprint *noun* steid SW.

imprison *see also* **jail;** (*put in prison*) prison SHETLAND, ORKNEY, nick; (*shut away*) steek, †ward.

imprisonment †ward(ing).

impromptu affluif.

improper (*out of place*) misbehadden SHETLAND, ORKNEY, NE; (*unjust*) unricht.

improperly (*illegally*) wrangouslie.

improve impruive; (*character etc*) mend; (*in health*) mak better SHETLAND, kittle NE; (*continue to get better*) haud forrit.

improvement (*in health*) betterness: '*There's nae betterness for him*'.

not improve no mak a better o't; (*in health*) mak naethin o't, nae mak muckle o't SHETLAND, NE.

improvident weirdless, doless, daeless.

imprudent *see also* **foolish;** unwicelik(e) N.

impudent *see also* **cheeky, insolent, rude;** impident, gallus, braisent, forrit(some), dortie, facie, nebbie, clippie, sneistie.

impudence *see also* **cheek, insolence;** impidence, snash, gash, hard neck, ill-chat, tongue, backjaw, cutlack NE, nash(-gab) S.

impudent woman quin(i)e NE.

speak impudently gange; (*in reply*) speak back.

impulsive furthie, raucle, ramstam.

in i; (*inside, forming a part of*) in o, intil: '*there's ingan intil't*'; (*in respect of*) o(f): '*it's a queer thing o me*'.

ins and outs oots an ins.

inability inabeelitie.

inactive thowless, daichie; (*and fat*) brosie-heidit NE.

remain inactive lie by.

inadequate (*not enough*) scrimpie, scrimpit, jimp.

inadmissible (*law*) †inhabile.

inadvertently unwittins *literary*.

inattentive tentless.

inaudibly (*speak*) intae yersel.

inaugurate (*with a ceremony, for good luck*) handsel, sain NE.

inauguration handsellin.

inauspicious unchancie, wanchancie.

incalculable undeemous SHETLAND, N.

incantation *see* **spell**[3].

incapable weirdless, haiveless N; **incapable of** unable for.

incapacitate (*through illness*) lay by.

incessantly even on.

incidentally i the bygaun, i the bygaein.

incise *see also* **notch;** sneck; (*a mark on wood etc*) scrieve.

incision *see also* **notch, earmark;** whack, sneck; (*small*) nitch.

incite *see also* **urge on**; airt, egg (up), eik(el) NE, pouss; (*a mob*) sherrack w; (*a dog to attack*) hish.

inclement *see also* **severe, stormy**; coorse, weatherfu, hashie.

incline *noun, see* **slope**.

inclination inklin SHETLAND, ORKNEY, N, list.

  follow your own inclination hae yer ain road, gang yer ain gate.

  inclined (well-)set.

incoherent (*rambling*) raivelt.

income: constant source of income dreepin roast.

  incomer ootrel; (*to Falkland* (*Fife*) *or Peebles*) stourie-fit; (*to Shetland*) sooth-moother; (*to Orkney*) ferry-lowper.

incomparable marrowless.

incompatible ill-yokit.

  join incompatibles together mismarrow.

incompetent han(d)less.

  incompetence han(d)lessness.

incomprehensible haithen.

inconceivable haithen.

incongruous: two incongruous companions (the) gowk an (the) titlin.

inconvenient disconvenient.

  inconvenience *noun* disconvenience, fash.

  verb disconvenience, fash, pit aboot, jam, fouter.

incorrect *see* **wrong**.

  incorrectly wrangweys SHETLAND, NE.

incorrigible past mendin.

increase *verb* (*in length*) rack; (*make bigger*) eik (tae); (*become bigger*) fill up. *noun* eik.

incrust *see* **encrust**.

  incrustation (*of scab etc*) kell.

indebted *see* **beholden**.

indecent *see also* **obscene, improper**; undecent, heich-kiltit, foutie.

  indecency (*esp in language*) sculdudderie.

suggestion of indecency blue threid.

indecision swither, whittie-whattie; (*fussy*) haiver(s), aff-pit.

indecisive twa-fangelt NE, whuther-or-no, aff an on (aboot).

indeed *adverb* deed, atweel.

interjection d'ye tell me (so)!, fegs!, hech ay!, na! SHETLAND, NE, yea! SHETLAND, ORKNEY, N.

indentation *see also* **dent, notch**; (*ridged*) runkle.

independent(ly) on for yersel, on yer ain coat-tails.

  begin to act independently (*of a young person*) leuk ower the nest.

index finger coorag CAITHNESS.

indicate *see also* **show**; lat see.

  indication tint.

indict indick, (*law*) libel.

  indictment (*law*) libel.

indifferent (*not caring*) jeck-easy; (*apathetic*) cauld-watter, dowf; (*cold in manner*) cauldrif(e); (*of health etc*) sic-lik(e).

  treat with indifference slowth NE.

  be indifferent no jee yer ginger.

indigenous kindly, hamelt.

indigent *see also* **poor**; needfu.

indigestion indisgestion.

indignant *see* **annoyed**.

  indignation *see* **annoyance**.

indirectly (*of speech or look*) sidelins.

indiscreet unwicelik(e) N.

  indiscreetly braid (oot).

indiscriminately han(d) ower heid.

indispensable: indispensable person in a group stang o the trump NE.

indisposed *see also* **ill**; no weel, ees(e)less SHETLAND, ORKNEY, N.

  indisposition *see also* **illness**; (*slight*) towt.

indistinct: make an indistinct sound gummle.

indolent *see also* **lazy**; sweir(t), drochlin NE, thowless; (*naturally*) hert-lazy.

  indolence sweirtie SHETLAND, NE.

indoors inby, therein.

indubitably

indubitably dootless.

induce (*someone to do something*) moyen NE, wice; (*something criminal*) procure.

indulge 1 *see also* **spoil, pamper;** cock up (wi), pettle S. **2** (*in high living*) gil-ravage.

industry (*industriousness*) t(h)rift ORKNEY.

industrious eydent, warklik(e) SHETLAND.

inebriated *see* **drunk.**

ineffective ill, rhymeless, knotless, bauch.

ineffectual *see also* **inefficient;** fushionless, thowless, picherin NE, pinglin.

act ineffectually whustle on yer thoum, pyocher SHETLAND.

work ineffectually pauchle, diddle, pingle, tooter N, picher (aboot) NE.

inefficient *see also* **ineffectual, ineffective;** han(d)less, kirnin NE; (*disorganized*) throuither, throwder NE.

inefficiency throuitherness NE.

he's inefficient he couldnae run a menodge.

inept fouterie, ill, weirdless, nae great sticks SHETLAND, NE.

ineptly aside yer thoum NE.

inert waffle.

inevitable tied.

infamous *see* **wicked.**

infant *see also* **child, baby;** bairn(ie), wean CENTRAL, geet NE, getlin *contemptuous.*

infancy bairnheid.

infant school wee scuil, little skweel(ie) NE.

infatuated fond: '*she must hae been fond*', daft (aboot), browden (on) NE, begottit.

infect infeck, smit.

infected (*of a wound etc*) atterie, bealin.

infection smit: '*gie the smit tae*'; '*get the smit*'.

infectious smittle, smittin.

inferior *see* **low-class** (*under* **low**[1]); (*of coal*) duffie.

infertile *see* **barren.**

infest owergae.

infestation (*of sheep by maggots*) strik.

infested hoatchin, hotchin, lowpin, quick; (*with fleas*) flechie; (*with cranefly grubs*) toriet NE, (*of land*) torie-eaten NE.

be infested with (*vermin*) creep ower wi.

infinite infineet, undeemous SHETLAND, N.

infirm *see also* **weak;** crazed, failed, dwaiblie.

inflame *see also* **infuriate.**

inflamed (*sexually*) gyte, awa wi't.

inflammation (*between toes*) galtags CAITHNESS.

inflate *see* **swell.**

inflexible (*of character: see also* **stubborn**) stench NE, sture S.

inflict inflick.

influence *noun* hank, infit NE: '*hae an infit wi*', moyen NE.
verb wark on.

use influence mak moyen(s) NE.

influenza *see* **flu.**

inform 1 witter; **inform of** lat wit. **2** *see* **tell (tales).**

informant author.

information witterin(s), wittin; (*got by enquiry*) speirins; (*in advance*) moyen NE: '*get moyens o*'.

ask for information from inquire at, speir at.

not inform no lat dab.

pass on information leet.

infrequent *see* **seldom.**

infuriate *see also* **rouse;** raise.

infuriated *see* **furious.**

infuse (*tea: see also* **tea**) mask, mak, scaud SW, S.

become infused (*of tea*) draw.

ingenious knackie, auld-farran(t), crafty, soople.

ingenuity ingine.

ingenuous saikless.

ingoing ingaun.

ingratiate: **ingratiate yourself with** *see also* **curry favour**; sook in wi, mak in wi, smool in wi, cuddle (up tae).

ingratiating *see also* **obsequious, sycophant**; inhaudin, beengin, sookie, (*specif in speech*) phrasin.

ingratitude ingraititeed NE.

inhabit bide in.

inhabitant indwaller; **inhabitants** fowk.

inheritance heirship.

pooling of inheritances (*law: equitably among heirs*) collation.

inhospitable: being inhospitable caul(d) comfort.

inhuman ill-set, ill-kindit.

iniquitous *see* **wicked.**

initiate (*into a trade*) brother.

injection jag, prod NE.

injunction (*law*) interdict.

injure *see also* **hurt, harm, mutilate**; skaith, mischieve SHETLAND, NE, bla(u)d, mittle, gulliegaw N, malagrooze NE.

injured bemang't.

injury *see also* **hurt**; ill, mischief, skaith, mishanter SHETLAND, ORKNEY, N, amshach NE; (*severe*) massacker SHETLAND, NE; (*caused by over-exertion*) burst.

injurious *see* **hurtful, unjust.**

ink: ink-bottle inker, ink-pud.

inland upthrou NE.

-in-law guid-: '*guid-faither*'.

inlet *see also* **creek**; inlat; (*narrow rocky*) gote; (*long, deep between rocks*) slock.

inn change-hoose, howf.

innkeeper †hostler, †change-keeper.

inner *see also* **inwards**: in the inner part ben, inby.

innermost howe, benmaist.

innocent ill-less SHETLAND, NE, saik-less.

play the innocent act the daft laddie *or* lassie.

innocuous *see* **harmless.**

innovation newfangle.

innumerable *see* **numerous.**

inoculation jag.

inoffensive *see* **harmless.**

inquest (*esp into a fatal accident*) inquiry.

inquire speir.

inquire after see aboot, ask for.

inquisition inquiseetion.

inquisitive *see also* **curious**; inqueesitive, queesitive, speirin, nebbie; (*rudely*) lang-nebbit, ill-fashiont SHETLAND, NE.

be inquisitive spy ferlies.

insane *see also* **mad, crazy, off your head**; gyte, daft, awa wi't, no wice, wuid, wrang NE, awa in the heid.

insanity *see* **madness.**

insect baist(ie), beast(ie).

insecure *see also* **unsteady**; crankie, tolter.

insensitive (*of the body*) dowf.

inside *preposition* inower, intil, in o.
adverb ben, inby, inower.

inside out backside foremaist EDINBURGH.

turn inside out flype.

insidious *see* **underhand.**

insignificant *see also* **nondescript**; little-boukit.

insignificant-looking shilpit.

insignificant person ablach, nyaff, yaff, messan, smowt, snite SHETLAND, NE, smool NE, snauchle SW.

insignificant thing *or* **person** *or* **animal** skiddle.

insincere pitten-on, sleekit; (*of speech*) phrasin.

insincerity pit-on, flairdie SW.

insinuate moot, mint; (*yourself into something*) draw a sneck.

insinuation moot.

insipid *see also* **tasteless**; (*esp of food*) wersh, walsh, fushionless, saurless; (*of liquor*) shilpit, slushy; (*esp of persons*) fushionless, palie, peelie-wersh S; (*of things*) smeerless N.

insipid person toohoo.

insist

insist (*strongly*) threap, prig.
  insistence threapin.
  be insistent with threap at *or* wi.
  insist on insist for.
insolent *see also* **impudent**; ill-mou'd, pauchtie.
  insolence, insolent language *see also* **impudence**; clack, ill-jaw, ill-gab, snash(-gab).
  use insolent language to cheek up.
insolvent astarn.
insomniac *adjective* waukrif(e).
inspect leuk, see, sicht, vizzy; (*a newborn animal for its sex*) sicht.
  tour of inspection reenge.
  inspector (*in a mine*) owersman.
instability instabeelitie.
instal (*a minister*) induct, settle.
instant *see also* **moment**; rap, gliff, han(d)clap, short NE.
instead insteid.
instil insense intae SW, ULSTER.
instruct *see* **teach**.
instrument *see also* **tool, implement**; luim, leem N.
insubordinate *see also* **insolent, impudent**; camstairie.
insufficient scrimp, jimp.
insult *see also* **abuse**: *verb* injure, snash, lichtlie, misca(w).
  noun dunt; (*insulting remark*) snash.
  make insulting remarks throw snawba(w)s.
intact intack.
integrity mense.
intellect intelleck.
  weak in intellect *see also* **mentally handicapped**; hazy.
intelligent *see also* **clever, quickwitted**; heidie, mensefu.
  intelligence *see also* **common sense, shrewdness**; mense, wit, uptak, harns.
intemperate *see* **immoderate**.
intend ettle, mint, be a mind (tae).
intense (*deep*) howe; (*excessive*) odious.
  intensely *see* **extremely**.
intent *adjective* eydent; **intent on** browden on NE.

intentionally willintlie.
inter *see* **bury**.
intercept kep, mar.
intercourse 1 *see* **dealings. 2** (*sexual*) †tail-toddle; (*illicit sexual*) houghmagandie, sculdudderie.
  have (sexual) intercourse mow (wi), dance the reel o Bogie, curdoo, †mix yer moggans (wi); (*illicitly*) play the loon, lift (a) leg, ride.
interest: looking after your own interests hame-drachtit NE.
  lose interest in loss taste.
  take an interest in leuk the gate o, leuk near(han) NE.
  take no interest in a person no leuk the road someone is on.
interfere *see also* **meddle**; pit in yer spuin, scaud yer lips wi ither folk's kail, mak or meddle; **interfere with** middle, intromit wi, parry wi, prat wi.
  interference fittininment NE.
intermediate (*in size*) halflin, hauflin.
intermittently aff an on.
internal organs intimmers *humorous*, harigals *humorous*.
interpret (*dreams, signs etc*) read: '*read the cups*'.
interrogate speir, tarragat.
  interrogation speirin.
interrupt interrup.
intertwine warple.
interval: at intervals atweenwhiles, noo(s) an aan(s) NE.
  in the interval atweenhan(d)s.
interview (*private*) collogue.
intestines thairms, trollie-bags, painches, puddins, intimmers *humorous*; (*esp of an animal*) harigals, draucht, inmait.
intimate *adjective, see also* **close**¹ 2, **friendly**; far ben, chief, pack.
  noun, see also **friend**; (*female*) cummer.
  intimated *past tense, past participle* intimat.
  intimation (*of a funeral*) burial letter.
  be intimate with big sandy mills wi, mell wi.

intimidate coonger, dare NE, daunton.
into intae, intil, until NE, in.
intolerable past a(w).
intonation (*of speech, accent*) tune; (*nasal*) sneevil.
intoxicate fill (someone) drunk, fill (someone) fou; (*of alcohol*) tak someone's heid: '*whisky taks his heid*', turn someone's heid.
  intoxicated *see* **drunk**.
  intoxication *see* **drunkenness**.
intractable *see also* **stubborn**; dour, thrawn, kittle, ill-contrivit SHETLAND, N, stieve.
intrepid *see also* **bold**; campie.
intricate kittle, fykie, pernicketie, quirky.
  intricacy wimple N.
intriguer mowdiewort.
introduction innin.
intruder incomer.
intuition: flash of intuition glent.
inundate *see* **flood**.
inure brither NE.
  become inured to use tae.
invade *see* **attack**.
inveigle insnorl N, wice.
invent (*think up*) cleck.
  invention (*something made up*) upmak SHETLAND, NE.
invert whummle.
invest: invested (*law: with legal possession*) infeft.
  investing (*with legal possession*) infeftment.
investigate pit throu han(d)s, howk, speir oot.
  investigation speirin.
invite inveet, seek, speir; (*to a wedding etc*) bid; (*encourage*) tryst.
  invitation inveet; (*to a wedding*) bode SHETLAND; (*to a funeral*) murnin letter, burial letter; (*written*) bodword NE; (*to do something*) biddin; (*last-minute*) fiddler's biddin, piper's biddin.
  invite someone to eat or drink ask if someone has a mou.
  he never even invited me to have something to eat he nivver said collie wull ye lick.
invocation (*of goodwill*) sain.
involve insnorl N.
  involved (*confused*) misred.
  be involved in be rowed intae.
inwards inweys, inwith NE, inwan; (*eg towards a fire*) introw SHETLAND; (*esp in a mine*) ben.
irascible *see also* **angry** (*under* **anger**), **bad-tempered**, **irritable**; crabbit, natterie, het-skinnt, flistie NE, whippert.
ire *see also* **anger**; birse: '*his birse is up*'.
iris (*flower, esp wild yellow*) seg, seggan W.
  with a white circle round the iris (*of the eye*) ringit.
Irish person Irisher.
irksome *see also* **annoying**; fashious.
iron *noun* **1** airn, erne. **2** (*smoothing*) airn, erne; (*with polished surface*) facin iron; (*tailor's*) gusin iron.
  verb (*cloth*) dress.
  ironing airnin.
ironstone (*of inferior quality*) maggie; (*coarse type*) doggar.
irregular (*at irregular intervals*) orra; (*unpunctual*) mistimeous N.
  irregularity gley NE; (*in a coal seam*) foulness, lipe.
  keep irregular hours mistime NE.
irrelevant talk *see also* **nonsense**; buff (an styte), buller.
irreligious regairdless.
irreparable past mendin.
irresolute: be irresolute *see* **hesitate, vacillate**.
irresponsible *see also* **thoughtless, hare-brained, flighty** (*under* **flight**[1]); glaikit, rhymeless NE, rudas NE.
irritate *see also* **annoy**; fash, kaim against the hair, gaw, taisle, taiver.
  irritable *see also* **angry, bad-tempered, irascible**; crabbit, carnaptious, towtie, capernoitit, kittle i the trot NE, toostie.
  irritation 1 *see* **anger, bad temper. 2** (*of the throat*) kittle.

is

is: is not isna, isnae.
island (*small*) inch.
issue *noun, see also* result; (*main*) heid
  ORKNEY, NE.
  verb, see stream out.
it 1 hit, hut, 't, hid ORKNEY, CAITHNESS.
  2 (*children's games*) het, hit, mannie NE.
Italian Tallie *humorous or contemptuous*.
itch *verb* yeuk, youk, yock NE.

noun yeuk, youk, yock NE, fykes.
itching (*to do something*) fidgin (fain)
  NE, FIFE.
itchy yeukie, youkie, yokie NE.
item eetim.
itinerant gaun-aboot.
itself itsel.
  by itself its lane.
ivy bin(d)wuid.

J

jab *see also* **prick**: *verb* job, prog.
noun 1 job, prog. 2 (*injection*) jag, prod
NE.
jabber *see also* **chatter**; gabber, yammer.
Jack 1 Jake, Jeck, Jock. 2 jack (*bowls*)
kittie. 3 jack (*cards*) jock, munsie NE.
jackdaw jaikie, kae.
Jack Frost nip-nebs.
jacket jaicket; (*woollen*) fecket.
jaded *see also* **tired, exhausted, worn
out**; forjeskit, jaskit, jaffelt sw, dowf,
doon kin NE.
jagged pikie.
jail *noun, see also* **prison**; jile; (*of a town*)
†tolbooth; (*of a village*) kittie.
verb jile.
jailer jiler.
be sent to jail get the jile.
jam jeelie.
jamjar jeelie-jaur, jeelie-can, jeelie mug,
jeelie-pig NE.
jam pan jeelie pan.
bread and jam jeelie piece, piece on
jeelie, piece an jeelie.
jamb (door-)cheek.
jangle *see* jingle.
January Januar *mainly literary*.
jar¹ *noun, see also* **jamjar**; jaur; (*esp
earthenware*) pig, crock; (*for whisky*)
whisky pig.
jar² (*shake*) *verb, noun* dirl, rees(h)le.
jaundice jandies, gulsoch, gulsa SHET-
LAND, ORKNEY; (*esp in the newborn*)
(yella) gum.
jaunt *see* outing.
jaunty croose.
jaw *see also* **chin**; (*of a fish*) gip; **jaws**
chowks, chafts, gams, muns *gipsy*.
jawbone chaft-blade.

jay jay pyot.
jealous jeelous, jaelous.
make jealous chaw.
jeer *see also* **mock, taunt**: *verb* lant NE,
jamph, snag.
noun afftak, jamph.
jell jeel.
jelly jeelie, jeel; (*specif table-jelly*)
trimmlin tam(mie).
jellyfish scalder, scowder, loch liver
NE, lubbertie NE, switherel.
jerk *see also* **twitch, jolt, tug**: *verb*
fidge, yerk, yark SHETLAND, ORKNEY,
N, tit SHETLAND, NE, jirt, snig, ferk NE,
kilch S; (*up and down*) hotch.
noun yerk, yark SHETLAND, ORKNEY,
N, jink, fidge, tit SHETLAND, NE, hotch,
rees(h)le, jirt; (*sharp, forward, esp of a
marble with finger and thumb*) plunk.
jerky movement hirtch.
move jerkily *see also* **stagger**; hainch,
hodge.
jersey (*fisherman's etc*) gansey, frock,
surcoat.
jest *see also* **joke**: *verb* jeest NE, daff.
noun baur, jeest NE.
jet¹ (*of liquid: see also* **squirt, gush**)
skoosh, scoot, strone, strintle, skit.
jet² (*mineral*) jeet NE.
jetsam *see also* **flotsam**; spulyie.
jetty *see also* **quay**: (*from a riverbank, eg
to protect it*) putt S.
jewel jowel NE.
excessive jewellery plaister.
Jew's harp trump.
tongue of a Jew's harp tang.
jib *verb* (*of a horse*) reest, set.
jibe *see* gibe.
jiffy short NE, glisk.
jig jeeg.

jiggle

jiggle jeegle.

jilt *verb, see also* **abandon, deceive**; begunk, gie (someone) the gunk, fling, gie (someone) the fling.

be jilted get the fling.

jingle *verb* jing, dingle NE, tingle.

noun jing, tingle.

job *noun* 1 *see also* **situation**; sit-doon.
2 *see also* **task, odd jobs, botch, bungle**; ontak, turn; (*fiddly*) fouter, pickle.

jocular jokie, pleasant, joco.

jog *verb* 1 (*push: see also* **nudge**) shog, jundie. 2 **jog along** dodge, knype NE, shoggle.

noun (*push: see also* **nudge**) dunch, shog, jundie.

joggle *verb, noun* joogle, shoogle, shoggle.

join *verb* jine; (*esp by splicing*) wap, wip SHETLAND, ORKNEY, N; (*roughly, with rough stitches*) ranter.

noun jine.

joiner *see also* **carpenter, cabinetmaker**; jiner, wricht NE.

joint jint; (*of the body*) lirk; (*of the finger or toe*) lith; (*esp in backbone*) link; (*of meat for roasting*) roast.

joint venture pairtisay.

join in hing tae.

joist *see also* **beam** 1; jeest.

joke *noun* baur: '*jist a baur*', mows, bourd; (*piece of fun*) terr, set; (*funny story*) farce; (*practical joke*) pliskie, ploy, rise, heeze NE, prat.

verb mak game, bourd.

no joke nae mows NE.

enjoy a joke at the expense of hae a rag oot o.

jolly *see also* **cheerful, merry**; (*of persons*) sonsie, gawsie.

jollification skite: '*on the skite*', splore, rant NE, rerr terr: '*We'd a rerr terr at the waddin*'.

jolt *see also* **jostle, jog, jerk**: *verb* hotter, rummle, shoogle, shoggle, jag NE, jundie, hodge, junner.

noun shoogle, shoggle, jundie, hodge, hotch, jag.

jolting *noun* rummle, hotter.

jostle *see also* **jog, jolt**: *verb* oxter, cadge NE, jowe; (*football*) rummle up.

jot *noun, see also* **particle**; stime, dottle.

journey *noun* raik, vaige EDINBURGH, veage SHETLAND, gate, gang, traivel.

verb raik.

set out on a journey steer, road NE, tak a stap.

jovial hertie, joco.

jowl *see also* **cheek** 1: **jowls** chollers.

joyful *see also* **cheerful, merry, glad**; blithe, blide SHETLAND.

judge *noun* joodge, jeedge NE; (*of the Court of Session*) law lord.

verb jeedge NE; (*law: decree*) decern.

judgement (*law: final*) decree, †decreet.

Day of Judgement hin(d)maist day, lang day.

jug *noun* joug; (*esp milk- or cream-*) stowp NE; (*esp cream-*) poorie; (*for liquor, with lid like hen's crest*) tappit hen.

verb joug.

juggle joogle.

juice joice SHETLAND, ORKNEY, N, bree, broo, wuss.

juicy (*of meat*) sappie.

July Julie.

jumble *see also* **confuse, muddle**: *verb* jummle, jurmummle, taigle, taisle, sotter NE.

noun jummle, taigle, kirn, mixter-maxter, hatter.

jump *see also* **leap**: *verb* lowp, jimp.

noun lowp.

jumped *past tense* jamp, jaump, lowpit.

jumper *see* **jersey**.

junction (*of two roads*) infa NE; (*where a side road meets a main one*) road-en(d).

June Juin.

juniper jenepere NE, etnach NE.

junk *see* **rubbish**.

junk food snashters, gulshichs NE.

jurisdiction (*over a territory, granted by the sovereign*) †regality, †stewartry.

jury assize.

foreman of a jury chancellor.

just *adjective* jonick, richt-lik(e) NE. *adverb* jist, juist, jeest NE, een, nae bit NE; (*newly*) new.

just as (if) the same as (if), e same's NE.

just now the noo, ivnoo NE.

just so ay ay.

justice jonick.

justify justifee.

juvenile *see* **youthful**.

K

keel over cowp, tirl, whummle.

keen *adjective* **1** *see also* **eager, zealous**; (*excessively*) hyte; **keen on** on for, ill aboot NE; **keen to** wuid for, wuid tae. **2** (*in perception*) gleg; (*specif in hearing*) gleg-luggit. **3** (*of wind etc*) snell, thin, fell, haarie.

keenly snell.

keenness (*sharpness*) glegness.

keen-edged gleg.

keen-eyed gleg-eed.

keep *verb, see also* **kept**: **1** (*guard*) kep. **2** (*continue*) haud.

noun, see **livelihood**.

keepsake mindin.

keep away haud aff; (*keep someone away*) herd fae; **keep away from** haud by NE.

keep your end up keep yer ain pairt.

keep going shog.

keep in order coonger, haud in aboot.

keep in with haud in wi, sook up till.

keep off *see* **keep away**.

keep out haud oot.

keep to a path haud the gate.

keep the pace up keep the puddin het.

keep up haud on.

not be able to keep no fa(w).

keg cag, knag.

kept *past tense, past participle of* **keep** keepit.

kerb crib, crib-stane.

kerchief curch.

kernel kirnel, paip; **kernels of oats** grits.

kestrel keelie (hawk), willie-whip-the-win(d).

kettle snippie.

key (*for a door: see also* **lock**[1]) check.

keystone putt-stane, peat-stane.

fasten with a key key.

kick *verb, see also* **kick about**; dump, winch, sub *school slang*, w; (*esp of a horse*) fling, fung; (*of a horse*) fit; (*a football etc, hard but ineffectually*) blooter. *noun* fung, fleg, pawt; (*restless*) fowe NE; (*from an animal*) fling.

kicker (*animal*) funker.

kick about (*restlessly*) spartle, wallop; (*esp in bed*) fowe NE.

kid (*informal*) *see* **child**.

kidnapping (*law*) plagium.

kidney (*now esp of an animal*) neir.

kill *verb, see also* **murder, slaughter**; en(d), fell, nail, claw someone's mittens.

killer *see* **murderer**.

kiln kill.

kiln fire(place) killogie, ingle, sornie CAITHNESS.

kilt philabeg *literary*.

man wearing a kilt kiltie.

kin *see* **relation**.

kind[1] *noun* (*sort*) keind, kin, thing: '*wull ye hae white breid or the broon thing?*'

all kinds a kin-kin(d) NE.

what kind of . . .? whatna . . .?, whit kinna . . .?, fit kinna . . .? NE.

kind[2] *adjective, see also* **generous, friendly, kindly**; couthie, cannie, furthie.

kindly *adjective* hamelie, guid-willie, lithe.

take kindly to tak wi.

act of kindness obleegement.

kindle kennle, kinnle, set on, pit tae, lunt.

newly-kindled (*of a smouldering fire*) green.

kindling kennlin, kinnlin, kinnlers NE.

kindred *see also* **relation**; kinred, sib SHETLAND, freen(d)s.

king keeng.

 kingdom kinrick *literary*.

 kingfish *see* **opah**.

king's evil cruels.

kink *noun* (*twist, coil*) snorl, jink NE; (*in character: see also* **quirk**) lirk NE.

kipper twa-eyed (beef)steak *humorous*.

kiss *verb* pree the lips O; (*loudly*) smack; (*sloppily*) slaik, slooster; (*exchange kisses*) smoorich.

 noun smoorich, smirk NE; (*light*) (*wee*) cheep(er); (*demanded from someone wearing something new*) beverage.

 kissing game bee-baw-babbitie.

kitchen keitchin, kitchie N; (*of a but-an-ben*) but, but the hoose N.

 kitchen garden kailyaird, yaird, (*plant*) taft CAITHNESS.

 kitchen-boy scodge, †scuddler.

 kitchen-maid scodgie; (*on a farm*) (kitchie) deem NE.

kite 1 (*toy*) (fleein) draigon. **2** (*bird*) gled.

kitten *noun* kittlin.

 verb kittle.

kittiwake kittie, weeg SHETLAND, tarrock.

kitty (*in a game*) puggie; (*for a social gathering etc*) jine.

knack swick: '*the swick o*', gate, catch, slicht.

 having lost the knack aff the fang.

knapweed horse's knot.

knave 1 *see* **rogue, villain. 2** (*cards*) pam.

knead kned, kyauve NE, chaave N, taw, chaff.

knee: knee-breeches knee-breeks, breekums.

 kneecap knee-lid, knap.

 having swollen knee joints knule-kneed.

 bend your knees cruik yer hochs.

kneel cruik yer hochs.

knell *see* **toll**[2].

knew *past tense of* **know** kent.

knick-knack nig-nag, whigmaleerie, boch CAITHNESS.

knife *noun* whittle, futtle N; (*large*) gullie (knife); (*small*) beetyach; (*weapon*) chib *slang*; (*worn in kilt stocking*) sgian dubh; (*clasp-knife*) jockteleg; (*for gutting fish*) guttag; (*for scooping out mussels for bait*) sheel-blade; (*for prising limpets from rocks*) sprod NE.

 verb chib *slang*.

 knife-grinder shantieglan W.

 knife-thowing game knifie.

knight knicht.

knit tak a loop; (*esp stockings*) wyve NE; (*stockings*) shank NE.

 knitter (*of stockings*) shank.

 knitting wyvin NE.

 knitting needle wire, weer NE; **set of knitting needles** wires, weers NE.

 knitting-needle holder (*pad worn at waist*) sheath, wisker NE.

knob (*bump, lump*) knoit, knule SW, S; (*esp an elbow*) noop; (*ornamental, on top of something*) tappietoorie, toopican NE, toopie SHETLAND.

 knobby swirlie SHETLAND, N.

 having knobbly knees knule-kneed.

knock *verb, see also* **strike 1, beat 1, thump**; chap, dunt, ding, ca(w); (*sharply*) knap, rap; (*at a door*) chap; (*loudly*) rees(h)le.

 noun, see also **blow**[2], **thump**; chap, dunt, da(u)d, ding, ca(w); (*sharp*) knap.

 knocker (*on a door*) chapper.

 waken by knocking rap up.

 person whose job is to waken by knocking chapper-up DUNDEE, GLASGOW.

 knock off (*work*) lowse.

 knocking-off time lowsin time.

 knock-kneed in-kneed, weaver-kneed, knule-kneed, sha(u)chlin.

 knock about touse, cadge NE, chaave NE, touther, mishannle.

 knock down ca(w) doon, flocht NE, whummle; (*specif a person*) cowp by the heels; (*violently*) swash.

knoll *see also* **hillock**; knowe.

knot

knot *noun* **1** boucht NE; (*running: see also* **slip-knot**) kinch; (*badly-tied*) soo's tail; (*to join parts of fishing line*) huidin; (*twist in rope etc*) snorl, swirl; (*tangle in hair*) rug; (*of ribbons etc*) doss NE. **2** (*in wood*) knar, knag, swirl.
verb (*of thread etc: run into knots*) snurkle s.
knotted snorlie, swirlie.
knotty (*of wood*) swirlie.
knot-grass midden-weed, feenich NE.
knot-hole (*in wood*) navis-bore NE.
know *see also* **knew**; ken, knaw, wite NE; (*intimately*) ken by heid an horn N; (*intuitively*) ken o yersel SHETLAND, NE.
knowing wice; (*shrewd*) cannie, skeelie.
knowledge ken, knawledge, wittin(s), lair.
person of great knowledge dungeon o learnin.
known kent.
make known lat ken.
not know misknaw.
knuckle *noun* (k)nickle, knockle; (*of beef*) skink.

L

labour *noun* **1** *see also* **work, toil;** lawbor, dwang. **2** (*in childbirth*) cryin NE, shoutin.
verb lawbor, warsle; (*hard*) swink; (*ineffectually*) stra(u)chle.
laborious typin NE, pinglin.
laboriously sair NE.
labourer *see also* **farmworker;** †piner; (*casual*) darger NE, orraster NE; (*on piece-work*) tasker.
labour exchange *see* **employment exchange.**
be in labour shout, cry NE, FIFE.
labour of love love-darg.
laburnum hoburn sauch NE, pea(se cod) tree S.
lace 1 (*ornamental*) stringin; (*lace trimmings*) pearlins. **2** *see* **shoelace.**
edged with lace pearled.
lacerate rive, ratch S.
lack *verb* want, wint NE.
noun inlaik, scant, ingang, haud-in, (*esp of food*) faut.
lackey †leckie.
lad *see also* **boy, youth** 2, **adolescent;** la(u)d(die), chiel(d), callan(t), gillie, loon *mainly* N; (*sturdy*) knap NE, stirrah; (*promising*) lad o pairts.
ladder ledder; (*eg to a loft*) trap.
ladle *noun* divider; (*for skimming*) scummer.
lady leddy.
ladylike qualities leddiness.
ladylike woman leddy bodie ORKNEY, N.
ladybird leddy launners, (reid) sodger, king('s) doctor ellison NE, clock leddy.
lady's bedstraw leddy's beds.
lady's smock spink.
lag (*act idly*) dagglc.

lagging behind lag.
laid out (*of a corpse: see also* **lay out** (*under* **lay**)) underboard.
lain *past participle of* **lie** lien NE.
lair (*of an animal*) bourie, flap.
lake loch; (*small*) lochan, peel NE.
lake-dwelling (*on artificial island*) crannog.
lamb *noun, see also* **sheep, call** *noun* 3 (2); lammie(-meh) *esp as pet name*; (*female*) yowe lamb; (*male*) tuip-lamb, (*castrated*) wedder-lamb; (*premature*) keb SW, S; (*ailing, undersized*) palie; (*reared by hand*) pet (lamb), sick (lamb) NE, sickie NE, caddie (lamb) SHETLAND, ORKNEY.
shelter for young lambs keb-hoose SW, S.
lame *adjective, see also* **limp²;** cripple, palie, hippitie; (*esp of a horse*) cruikit.
lamely (*with a limp*) hippitie.
walk lamely *see also* **limp²;** hirple, cripple.
lameness hainch.
lame person lameter.
lament *noun, see also* **lamentation;** croon; (*funeral: see also* **dirge**) coronach.
verb, see also **mourn;** greet, yammer, croon N, remorse NE.
lamentable awfu, sad.
lamentation greetin, scronach NE, molligrant, yammer, plaint.
lamp leerie; (*esp flickering*) winkie; (*oil*) (eelie) dolly NE, (*boat-shaped with rush wick*) cruisie, collie SHETLAND, ORKNEY; (*miner's*) tallie lamp, (*for testing for gas*) glennie.
lamplighter leerie.
lamprey lamper eel, ramper (eel).
lancet lance.

land

land *noun, see also* **ground, farmland;** lan, glebe; (*rough, uncultivated*) muir; (*low-lying, by river*) carse, haugh, merse SW, inks SW; (*low-lying, behind shore*) machair HEBRIDES.

landing (*on a stair*) plat, plettie DUNDEE; (*at top of common stair*) stairheid.

landing place the shore N, FIFE.

landlady *see also* **landowner;** (*of an inn*) luckie, guidwife; (*of St Andrews student's lodgings*) bunkwife.

landlord *see also* **landowner;** (*to whom feu duty is paid*) superior; (*esp one liable for upkeep of church etc*) †heritor.

landmark (*esp used by sailors*) meith; (*heap of stones, esp on hill top*) cairn.

landowner laird; (*small*) portioner, cock laird NE, sma laird, †bonnet laird; (*of small farm: male*) guidman, (*female*) guidwife.

piece of land (*portion: see also* **croft**) dale; (*esp separate from surroundings*) shed; (*small*) paffle; (*let to sub-tenant*) pendicle.

lane trance, throughgate; (*grassy, leading to pasture*) loan(in); (*between houses*) wynd, vennel.

language langage, leid.

talk in a strange language clytach NE.

languid smerghless N, sauchen NE, lither, fushionless.

languish dwine.

lanky *see* **thin, skinny.**

lanky person *see also* **skinny person;** lingel N, stilpert NE, streeker NE, trallop.

lantern *see also* **turnip lantern;** bouet.

lantern-jawed lang-chaftit NE, chandler-chaftit.

lap *verb* **1** (*drink*) laip, laib, lerb NE. **2** (*of water: see also* **ripple**) lapper.

lapping sound lapper.

lapse *verb* (*law: of an action*) sleep; (*of a right, action etc*) prescribe.
noun (*law*) prescription.

lapwing peesweep, peewee(t), peesie, teuchit, teewheet, wallopie(weet).

larceny *see* **theft, robbery.**

larch larick.

lard *see also* **fat;** (*swine's*) saim.

larder aumrie, spence.

large *see also* **big;** lairge, muckle, wallie SHETLAND, ORKNEY.

largely *see* **mainly.**

something large of its kind wheesher, beezer.

lark[1] *noun* (*bird*) laverock, larick NE.

lark[2] *verb* daff.

larva *see also* **caterpillar;** (*of the cockchafer*) cob-worm FIFE.

larynx thrapple.

lash *noun* **1** *see* **eyelash. 2** (*with a whip etc*) screenge, cracker, whang, sleesh, leash, leerup N.
verb **1** *see also* **whip;** leash, leerup N, cleesh S, whang. **2 lash down** (*of rain: see also* **pour**) plash, leash, ding doon.

lass *see* **girl.**

last[1] *noun* (*shoemaker's*) iron fit, tacketie jock, deil NE, deil's fit, priest an devil.

last[2] *adjective, adverb* laist, lest, hin(d)maist, hinnermaist; (*esp of a curling stone or player*) hint-han(d).
verb (*endure*) lest; **last out** pit ower, get ower NE, dree.

last drops (*from a container*) sypins, sype SHETLAND, ORKNEY, dreepins.

last night yestreen, the streen ORKNEY, N, estreen NE.

last year fernyear.

at last at (the) lang an (the) lenth, at lang an last, at (the) lang lenth.

last part hinderen(d), hinneren(d).

latch *noun, see also* **hasp, catch;** sneck, cleek.
verb sneck; (*so that the door will not open*) rack.

latched (*but not locked*) on the sneck.

late *adjective* **1** (*after the event*) ahin(t) (the) han(d), ahin(t); (*after the expected time*) yon time: '*He didnae get hame till yon time*'. **2** (*deceased*) umquhile *now literary.*
adverb hyne NE, ower SHETLAND, NE.

later (*at a later time*) again: '*Keep it an I'll get it again*'.

late hours (*of the night*) blin oors NE, (wee) sma oors.

grow late weir ower.

lath *noun* spail; (*esp across roof beams for storage*) lat.

lath-and-plaster *verb* (*a wall etc*) stoothe SW, S.

lathe lay, turnin luim.

lather *noun* (*soap suds*) saip(ie)) sapples, (saip(ie)) graith, sowp, freith. *verb* freith.

Latin Laitin; (*as university subject*) humanity.

translation into Latin version.

latrine *see* **privy**.

latter hinner.

latterly at *or* i the hinneren(d).

lattice tirless.

laudanum lodomie.

laugh *see also* **giggle**: *verb* la(u)ch; (*heartily: see also* **guffaw**) bicker NE, heffer; (*noisily, excitedly*) keckle; (*in a suppressed way: see also* **snigger, smirk**) smudge, smue.

noun la(u)ch NE; (*hearty: see also* **guffaw**) heffer; (*loud*) keckle, goller, gullie (o a laach) NE; (*suppressed*) guff.

laughed *past tense* la(u)cht, leuch N, looch N.

past participle la(u)cht, la(u)chen NE.

(no) laughing matter (nae) mows NE.

laughing stock moniment SHETLAND, ORKNEY, N.

laughter la(u)chter; (*irrepressible*) kink: '*gae intae kinks*'; '*He went intae sic a kink*'.

burst with laughter rive.

choke with laughter kink.

shake with laughter hotch, hotter NE, hodge NE.

laugh your head off, die laughing la(u)ch yer hinneren(d) NE, la(u)ch yer kill NE.

get a laugh out of hae a rag oot O.

launch *verb* lench.

laundress *see* **washerwoman**.

laurel larie.

lavatory *see* **W.C., privy**.

lavish *adjective* lairge NE, lairdlie NE, fallauge NE, lovage, furthie, rowthie.

law laa NE.

lawyer *see also* **solicitor**; lawer, lawvyer, writer, man o business.

lawful lawfu, lawfae.

lawless lowse.

law-abiding leal.

lawbreaker brakker.

chief law officer of the Crown in Scotland Lord Advocate.

lawsuit *see also* **action**; law-plea.

state in a court of law propone.

lax (*of character*) lither, sachless S.

lay *verb* (*a table*) set in; (*of a hen, away from the usual place*) lay awa.

layer (*of hay, peats etc*) dass; (*of corn sheaves in a stack etc*) gang; (*thin layer*) skliffer; (*thin surface layer*) scruif, screef NE; (*hard surface layer*) scrump NE.

layabout sloonge, snuil, slotch, sn(u)ivie, haiver.

lay aside pit by, set by.

lay hold of *see* **catch**.

laying on onlayin.

lay out (*a corpse*) streek, stra(u)cht NE, straik.

layout ootset.

well laid out snod.

lazy *see also* **idle**; sweir(t), doxie NE, haingle NE, latchin NE, drochlin NE, mautent NE, daeless, doless, lither; (*rather*) sweirie; (*very*) hert-lazy, stane-tired S; (*apt to be lazy*) easy-osie.

work lazily fa(u)chle, sneet NE.

laziness idleset, sweirtie SHETLAND, NE; (*fit of laziness*) lazy.

lazy person *see also* **layabout**; snuil, brochle, slemmer, sloonge.

be lazy, laze snuil, sloonge.

lea ley.

lead[1] *noun* (*metal*) leid.

black lead, lead pencil wad SW.

lead[2] *verb* **1** (*guide, direct*) wice. **2** (*singing in church*) precent HIGHLAND.

leader 1 *see also* **manager**; (high) heid

yin, heidsman. **2** (*of singing in church*) precentor HIGHLAND.

leaf 1 (*of a cabbage, turnip etc*) blade; (*mature*) ruch blade; (*enclosing corn-stalk and ear*) shot blade; **leaves and stalks** (*of potatoes, turnips etc*) shaws. **2** (*of a door*) lid.

league: in league pack.

be in league collogue, colleague NE.

leak *verb* leck, laik, seep, rin oot, (*esp slowly*) sype; (*mining: of a bucket*) pass watter; (*of a boat*) tak in.

leakage seep(age), sype.

leaky (*of a dried-up wooden container*) gizzen.

become leaky gizzen SHETLAND, ORKNEY, NE, geyze.

leak out skail; (*of news*) spunk oot NE.

lean[1] *verb* (*to one side*) heeld SHETLAND, ORKNEY; (*out of a window to watch*) hing.

noun (*out of a window to watch*) hing.

lean-to tae-fa(w), fa(w)-tae.

lean[2] *adjective, see also* **thin, puny**; tuim, teem NE, nakit, slink; (*esp of a formerly fatter person*) swamp.

leap *see also* **jump, skip**: *verb* lowp, lup SHETLAND, ORKNEY, sten(d), spang.

noun, see also **bound**[1] 2; lowp, lup SHETLAND, ORKNEY, sten(d), spend, wallop; (*sudden*) sowt SW.

leapt *past tense* lowp(i)t, leapit.

past participle lowp(i)t, leapit, lowpen.

leapfrog lowp-the-cuddie, cuddie-lowp(-the-dyke).

learn lairn, leern NE; (*find out*) lear, tak wit O.

learned far i the buik.

very learned person dungeon o learnin.

speak learnedly speak lik a prent buik.

learning lair; (*education*) buik-lair, buik leir.

lease *noun* less, †tack; (*esp from the lessor's point of view*) set.

verb (*take on lease*) tak.

remain at the end of a lease sit on.

leather *noun* ledder SHETLAND, ORKNEY, NE.

strip of leather whang.

leave[1] *noun* (*permission*) freedom.

give leave to leave.

leave[2] *verb, see also* **quit**; lea, lave; (*abandon*) quat; (*depart*) win awa; (*in a hurry*) be uptail an awa.

leavings *see also* **leftovers, scraps**; hinneren(d), ootwales, quinkins.

leave-taking wa-gang NE.

lecher *see* **libertine**.

lecture *noun* lecter; (*see also* **scolding**) hearin, creed, chaw N.

ledge *noun, see also* **shelf**; (*projection*) cantle NE; (*on a hillside etc*) dass; (*on a building*) scarsement; (*in a byre where cattle stand*) sattle.

lee (*lee side*) lithe N.

leech gell(ie).

leek *see* **houseleek**.

lees grun(d)s.

left[1] *see* **leave**[2].

leftovers *see also* **scraps, leavings**; orts, orra(l)s, pan-jotrals, brakkins NE.

left[2] *adjective* (*opposite of right*) car, ker S. *adverb* (*as a direction*) wast.

left-hand ketach, kippie E CENTRAL.

left-handed car(rie), corrie(-fistit), car(rie-)handit, ker(-haundit) S, pallie-handit, kippie, skibbie, katie-handit, soothie, skerrie-handit S.

left-handed person corrie-fister W, clootie, kippie.

call to a horse to turn to the left *see* **call** *noun* 3 (1).

leg *noun, see also* **wooden leg**; sham, lyomon, spyog CAITHNESS; (*long, thin*) spurtle-leg; (*of meat*) shank; (*of lamb or pork*) gigot; (*of a stocking etc, esp while being knitted*) shank; (*of a table etc*) stoop; **legs** trams *humorous*; (*sturdy*) stumparts NE.

leggings *see also* **stocking (footless)**; leggums.

leg-up hainch.

having long thin legs spurtle-leggit, pipe-shankit.

on your last legs on yer hunkers.
legal papers (*in court for an action*) process.
legend leegen(d).
leisure leesure, laiser SHETLAND, easedom SHETLAND, NE.
leisure time by-time.
lemon leemon.
lemonade skoosh, leemonade, sproosh NE, ginger W, ale NE, lang ale NE.
lemon sole *see* sole².
lend len, laen SHETLAND, ORKNEY.
length lenth.
lengthen rax; (*esp of days*) rax oot, creep oot; (*eg clothing*) eik.
lengthwise, at full length en(d)lang, at full streek.
full length streek.
your full length yer lang lenth, breadth an lenth.
at length *see also* **at last** (*under* last²); at lang lenth, at (the) lenth an lang, syne.
go into (*something*) **at length** simmer an winter.
lenient *see* soft.
lest least, (in) case be NE.
let *verb* 1 (*allow*) lat. 2 (*lease*) set.
past tense lat, leit, luit.
past participle latten, luitten, letten, lat, let.
let alone (*leave alone*) lat a-be, lat be; (*much less*) lat be.
let fly lat gird, lat skelp, lat sing, loonder, let flist, let fung.
let (*someone*) **down** misgie.
let-down snipe NE.
let go lowse.
lethargy *see* laziness.
lethargic *see also* lazy; thowless, mautent NE, doxie NE, lither.
letter 1 *see* capital letters. 2 (*postal*) scrieve, scribe SHETLAND; (*short, hasty*) scrape o the pen; (*from abroad*) faurawa screed.
lettuce laituce.
level *adjective* (*smooth, even*) snod, evenlie NE, plain SHETLAND, plat SHETLAND, skleff S.

noun (*in a mine*) mine.
verb (*level off in a measure*) straik, strik SW, sleek.
level-headedness rum(mle)gumption.
bring to the same level even.
lever *noun, see also* **crowbar**; lewer SW, S, gavelock, prise, swey SHETLAND; (*heavy, for lifting a millstone*) lewder NE.
verb pinch, pry.
levy *see* tax.
lewd *see also* obscene; ruch, roch (kin) NE.
liar leear.
greatest of all liars waghorn *literary*.
libel *noun* leebel; (*law*) defamation (= Eng *libel and slander*).
liberal *see also* generous; leeberal, hertie, guid-willie.
liberate leeberate.
liberty *see also* freedom; leebertie.
libertine loon, dyke-lowper.
library leebrarie.
lice *see also* louse; cattle.
licence *see also* permission: *noun, verb* leeshence.
person who has been licenced (*esp as a minister*) licenciate.
licentious *see* dissolute.
lichen fog; (*types used for dyeing*) crottle, stane raw SW.
lick *verb* slaik; **lick up** laib, lerb NE.
noun slaik, lerb NE.
licorice *see* liquorice.
lie¹ *see also* **liar**: *verb* lee, whid.
noun lee, whid; (*mild*) slide NE, flaw; (*deliberate*) made lee.
tell a mild lie slide NE.
lie² (*be horizontal: see also* lain) lig *now literary*; (*lie down*) lean.
lie to one side sklent.
lie-in long lie.
lieutenant lieutenand.
life (*life itself*) wizzen.
lifeless (*absolutely*) as deid as a mauk.
full of life lifie, green.
show no signs of life no play paw.

lift *see also* **hoist**: *verb* heeze, heicht; (*to estimate weight*) heft; **lift up** hoise, heyze NE, upheeze; (*something heavy*) humph.
noun **1** (*heave up*) heeze, hoise. **2** (*in a vehicle*) cairry, hurl.

light[1] *noun* (*brightness*) licht, leam *literary*; (*faint*: *see also* **gleam**) gloam NE, scarrow SW; (*quick flicker*) spunk(ie); (*flash*) glaik; (*of a candle etc*) doozie; (*for a cigarette etc*) lunt; (*light thought to foretell death*) deid licht.
verb licht(en); (*a fire, match*) spark, sperk S; (*a lamp*) blink SHETLAND.
adjective licht.
come to light spunk oot NE.
lightning firefla(u)cht; (*without thunder*) wildfire.
flash of lightning fla(u)cht SHETLAND, NE.
light[2] *adjective* (*not heavy*) licht.
lighten lichten.
lightly licht(lie).
light-fingered tarry-fingered, sticky-fingered, picky-fingered.
light-footed lichtsome.
light-headed (*esp from drink*) reezie.
something light and flimsy flindrikin NE.

like[1] *adjective, preposition* lik, lek SHETLAND, CAITHNESS.
noun maik: '*they nivver saw the maik o't*'.
likely lik(e).
likelihood lik(e)ly.
more like (mair) liker.
likeness limn; (*exact*: *see also* **image**) spitten eemage, model.
likewise siclike, an a(w).
like[2] *verb* lik.
likeable fine, innerlie S.
liking goo (of *or* for), wan SHETLAND, ORKNEY, CAITHNESS; (*affection*) notion (o *or* tae), dint (o) NE, wanness SHETLAND; (*longing*) ee.
have a liking for hae skeel o, be keen o; (*special liking*) hae a saft side tae; **have no liking for** hae nae broo o.
like very much lik(e) fine: '*We lik it fine*', fair lik(e).

lilac lilyoak, laylock.
limb *see* **leg**.
lime *see also* **chalk**.
limekiln limewark.
limestone limestane.
limit *noun, see also* **scope**; leemit; **limits** stent.
verb leemit, punish, stent.
limp[1] *adjective, see also* **weak**; wamfle NE, waffle.
limp[2] *see also* **hobble**: *verb* hirple, lamp, hilch, hainch, haut, clinch, hammle S.
noun hirple, hilch, clinch NE, hainch.
limping *adjective, see also* **lame**; hippitie.
noun (*act of*) haut.
limpet lempit, lempeck.
linchpin lin-pin, lin-nail, spar.
line[1] *noun, see also* **fishing line**; (*boundary line*) ma(i)rch; (*of fishing nets from the end of a boat*) swing.
arrange in a line raw; **be arranged in a line** streek.
line off (*land with a plough*) dra(u)cht N.
out of line aff the straucht.
line[2] (*a roof with wood*) sark.
lineage kin, strin(d).
of the same lineage sib.
trace lineage redd oot kin.
linen (*coarse*) plainen, harn; (*thin, coarse, in strips*) scrim; (*medium fine*) twal-hunner.
linen clothes linens.
linen cupboard naperie press.
linen thread (*washed but not bleached*) whitie-broon.
table linen naperie.
ling[1] *see* **heather**.
ling[2] (*fish: young*) stakie NE.
linger *see also* **dawdle, loiter**; hinder, wait on, taigle, dachle NE, tarrow SHETLAND, ORKNEY; (*expectantly*) hing on.
lingering (*slow*) lag.
liniment leenament.
bottle of liniment rubbin bottle.
link arms (with) cleek (wi).
linnet lintie, lintwhite, heather lintie, whin-lintie.

livid

linoleum waxcloth.

linseed linget N.

lintel (*wooden, for additional support*) safe lintel; (*with initials and marriage date of owners*) mairriage lintel, mairriage stane.

lip *noun* mull; (*drooping underlip*) faiple.

having a thick, protruding lower lip spuin-gabbit.

liquid bree, broo; (*quantity of*) sup; (*in which something is dipped*) dook; (*rising to the top of a container*) shirins; (*strained off, eg potatoes*) poorins; (*stirred up with sediment*) jabble; (*small quantity: see also* **drop, trickle**) skite, jibble, poor(in); (*poured out*) jirble; (*spilt*) jilp.

be covered in liquid sail.

separate a liquid from dregs shire.

liquor 1 *see* **liquid. 2** (*alcohol: see also* **whisky**) wheich, pundie; (*esp weak*) skink, jute ORKNEY; (*small amount of*) skite, skirp NE, tuithfu.

liquorice lickerie, sugarallie, alicreesh, black sugar.

liquorice drink sugarallie watter.

liquorice root (*chewed by children*) lickerie stick.

list (*of candidates for a post*) leet: '*long leet*'; '*short leet*'; (*of cases etc in court*) roll; (*of people at a meeting*) sederunt.

put on a list of candidates leet.

listen (*carefully*) preen back yer lugs; **listen to** hark (tae), hearken, tent, speak tae; (*carefully*) tak tent tae.

listener hearkener.

just listen to him *etc*! hear till him *etc*!

refuse to listen steek yer lugs.

listless *see also* **spiritless**; fushionless, thowless, palie, heepochondreeoch.

listlessly davielie.

be listless sneet NE.

become listless weary.

literary lceterarie.

literary work quair *literary*.

lithe *see also* **supple, agile**; swack, slamp, swank, leish SW, S, wannle S.

litigate pursue.

process of litigation law-plea.

litter *noun* (*of animals*) brod, brodmel NE, cleckin.

verb, see **produce young.**

smallest of a litter *see also* **runt**; rig, cricklet W, ricklin, crowl NE, shargar NE, croot S, the shakkins o the pokie.

little *see also* **small**; wee, peedie SHETLAND, ORKNEY, CAITHNESS, FIFE, peerie SHETLAND, ORKNEY, CAITHNESS.

a little (*a (very) small amount*) a bittock, a wee (bit), a kennin, a (wee) tait, a (wee) thocht, a (wee) pickle; (*somewhat*) a piecie, a (wee) bit, a (wee) tait, a (wee) thocht, a wee thing(ie).

little finger pinkie, crannie(-doodlie) NE, pirlie-winkie, peerie-winkie *in nursery rhymes*.

little girl lassock(ie), wee quine NE.

little lamb lammie.

little man mannie.

every little helps monie a mickle maks a muckle.

live[1] *verb* leeve; (*see also* **dwell**) stey, bide, haud oot, †won.

living *see* **livelihood.**

make a living mak saut tae yer kail, mak oot; (*with difficulty*) witter NE.

live from hand to mouth pewl.

live in (*at a farm*) kitchie NE.

live on leeve aff.

live[2]: **lively** *see also* **active, restless, spirited, cheerful, merry**; (*active*) gleg, leevin-lik(e), forcie SHETLAND, NE, fendie; (*of an animal*) keen; (*spirited*) cantie, hertsome, skeich, heich, lifie, sparkie, brainie, birkie W, kirr SW, sprack; (*in conversation*) knackie; (*bustling*) steerie; (*restless*) steerin.

liveliness smeddum, lifiness.

livelong leelang *literary*.

livestock gear, cattle-baists, ferm stockin, bestial; (*maximum a farm will carry*) cover.

live wire the stang o the trump NE.

livelihood brose, throu-beirin.

livid 1 (*colour*) blae. **2** *see* **furious.**

147

lizard heather-ask, man-keeper SW, S, ULSTER, dirdie-lochrag CAITHNESS.

loach bairdie (lotchie), Katie bairdie, bessie (bairdie) S.

load *noun, see also* **burden;** laid, draucht, lift; (*amount carried at one time*) raik, gang, fraucht; (*small load*) pauchle; (*full load*) fou.
verb laid, prime.

loaded *past tense* laidit, laid.

past participle laidit, laid, laidin.

loaf[1] *noun* laif, breid, half-laif; (*old enough to cut*) cuttin laif; (*white, baked in tin*) pan laif; (*white, baked in batch*) plain laif; (*wheaten*) clod; (*coarse, wheaten*) tammie; (*fat, round, wheaten*) fadge; (*small, crusty*) rumpie; (*long, rye*) anchor stock; (*kind of fancy loaf*) Jenny Lind; (*rich fruit, made in Selkirk*) Selkirk bannock, Selkirk bannie.

end of a loaf heel, sole-shaif.

loaf[2] *verb, see also* **dawdle, loiter, lounge;** sloonge, sotter, hawm, sneet NE, haiver, mump, snuil.

loafer slute, sloonger.

loan *noun* len, laen SHETLAND, ORKNEY; (*brief use*) shot: '*gie's a shot o yer bike*'; (*of a book*) read(in); (*law: given free but recallable*) precarium.

loath *adjective* laith, sweir(t).

loathe laith, ug *literary*.

loathing laith, scunner, ug NE.

object of loathing scunner.

feel loathing (at) scunner (at).

look with loathing leuk lik Wattie tae the worm.

loathsome laithsome, laithlie, scunnersome, uggin NE, fousome.

lobby entry, trance.

lobe (*of the ear, liver*) lap SHETLAND.

lobster lapster, labster.

lobster trap (lapster) creel.

box to keep lobsters alive in water lapster kist.

local *noun* (*pub*) howf.

locality airt, gate-en(d), quarter ORKNEY.

local-authority housing estate (housing) scheme.

lock[1] *verb* key.

fastened by a lock, secure under lock and key lockfast.

lockjaw jaw-lock.

lock, stock and barrel stoup an roup, skin an birn.

lock up sneck up.

lock[2] *noun* (*of hair*) fla(u)cht, tossel, link, swirl.

lodge *noun* ludge; (*small, hunting*) lunkart ANGUS.

verb ludge, wait, howf; (*for the night*) nicht NE.

lodger ludger.

lodging(s) ludgin(s), up-pittin; (*of a St Andrews student*) bunk FIFE.

loft laft.

lofty (*in manner: see also* **arrogant, haughty**) heich(-heidit), heeliefu.

log *noun* (*of wood*) clog, stock NE.

loggerheads: at loggerheads at the knag an the widdie NE, striven NE, oot lik a pat fit NE.

loin (*of beef, various parts*) backsey.

loiter *see also* **dawdle, loaf**[2]**, lounge;** lyter, haingle, dring, haik, dwadle, mollach NE, howk (aboot), lowder, dwingle S.

loiterer jotter.

lonely lanelie, lanerlie, lanesome, hertalane; (*through missing your usual companion*) misslie.

long *adjective* lang; (*and large*) side an wide.

verb **long (for)** green (for), think lang (for), glagger (for) NE, mang (for), myang (for) NE; (*esp for a long time*) weary (for).

longing *adjective* awid.

noun ill-ee NE; (*for affection*) hert-hunger SHETLAND, NE.

long ago lang syne, lang back, far back.

a long time a guid bit.

tall, long-legged person stilpert NE.

person with long ears lang lugs.

long-necked (*of a bird*) lang-craigit.

long-suffering patientfu, thole-moodie.

long-winded (*of a person*) en(d)less; (*of speeches etc*) dreich.

look *see also* **glance, stare, peep**[1], **peer**[2]**, blink**: *verb* leuk, luck, deek *originally gipsy*; (*long and earnestly*) leuk wi clear een NE.

noun leuk, luck, deek *originally gipsy*; (*close*) sicht; (*quick*) scance, swatch.

-looking *in compounds* -lik(e): '*daftlike*'; '*queerlik*'.

look about (yourself) sky NE.

look after *see also* **see to, care for**; leuk ower, guide, tend, tent, cast aboot; (*specif a person*) see efter, see aboot.

look at leuk till SHETLAND, NE, see; (*closely*) vizzy SHETLAND; (*critically*) scance.

look for 1 *see* **search for. 2** (*expect*) lippen, bode NE.

look here! leuk see!

look like (*of weather*) mak for: '*It's makkin for snow*'.

look longingly (*esp at food*) growk.

look out! mind whaur ye're gaun!, mind yersel!

be on the lookout *see also* **watch out**; be on the haik (for), keep shot(tie) (for): '*keep shot for the polis*'.

it's a poor lookout for it's a(w) up a clos(i)e wi.

look out of the window leuk ower the windae.

look sideways *see also* **squint, glance**; sklent, gley.

loom *noun* luim, leem N.

loop *noun* kinch, mink N, latch; (*esp for fastening*) latchet; (*to attach a fishing hook*) snuid.

verb hank.

loose *adjective* lowse, dwamfle NE; (*of soil*) frush.

loosen lowse, lowsen.

loose-fitting (*of clothes*) lowse.

loose woman limmer, radge, randie.

become loose lowse.

loot *see* **plunder.**

lop (off) sned, sneck.

lope lowp, lamp.

lopsided lab-sidit, skellie, a(w) tae the one side lik Gourock.

loquacious *see also* **talkative**; gabbie, glib(-gabbit), gash(-gabbit), tonguie.

loquacity tongue-raik, click-clack NE, bletheration, blethers.

loquacious person blether, gab, say-away S.

lord *exclamation* losh (me)!, laird!, lod!, lorie! SHETLAND, ORKNEY, N.

lordly lairdlie.

lorry larrie; (*refuse collector's*) scaffie('s) cairt, midgie motor.

lose loss, loass, tyne.

lose ground gae back.

lose your way get tint NE, tyne yer fit NE.

loss loass, miss: '*She's a big miss*'; (*by being cheated*) snipe NE; (*damage by loss*) †tinsel; (*law, due to an 'Act of God'*) damnum fatale.

at a loss ill-aff, pichert NE.

cause the loss of tyne.

lost tint, loast; (*having lost your way*) forwandert *literary*.

get lost! gae tae Freuchie (an fry mice)!, gang tae Buckie (an bottle skate)! NE.

horse *or* **dog which has lost a race** binger.

lot[1]**: a lot** *see also* **many**; a lump, an awfie, an awfu: '*There an awfu wasps here the day*'.

the lot *see also* **whole**; the hail jing-bang, the hail tot.

lot[2] (*lot cast*) cavel NE.

lottery lucky pock.

cast lots draw straes.

loud lood, fell.

loudly, in a loud voice lood oot, heich.

speak loudly bairge NE.

loud-mouthed glowsterin.

loud-voiced (*of a(n aggressive) woman*) randie.

lounge *verb, see also* **dawdle, loaf**[2]**,**

loiter; loonge, sloonge, floan NE, hing the cat, hurk SW, S.

lounger haiverel, hurk SW, S.

louse *see also* **lice**; loose, Jerusalem traiveller, poolie, gray horse; (*head-louse*) tra(i)veller *humorous*.

lout *see also* **boor, fool**; scurryvaig, filsh NE, fleep ORKNEY, N, keelie, yaup, cowt NE, coof, lubbard SW, S; (*stupid*) gype SHETLAND, NE.

loutish ill-shakken-up SHETLAND, ORKNEY, NE, miraculous N, orra.

love *verb* luve, loo *literary*; (*esp a person of the opposite sex*) lik(e).

noun luve, hert-likin SHETLAND, NE, fainness SHETLAND.

lovable loosome, douce, leesome.

lover *see also* **mistress** 2; lovie, billie, chap, jo *literary*.

ex-lover auld shuin.

loving *adjective, see also* **affectionate**; fain, hert-warm SHETLAND.

loving look luve-blink.

lovingly condinglie N.

lovely *see also* **beautiful**; bonnie, loosome.

love-child luve-bairn.

lovesick gyte.

fall in love get the smit.

make love curdoo FIFE.

low[1] *adjective* laich, law; (*mean, dishonest*) wheetie NE; (*in spirits*) doon o mou.

lower *adjective* (*esp of a place*) nether; (*of a river*) sma.

verb laich; (*the head*) loot; (*the price of*) lat doon; **lower yourself** *see* **humble**.

lowest nethmost.

low-class *see also* **common**; main, waff, schemie.

low-class person keelie, schem(i)e, gutterbluid, scaff.

lowland lawlan(d), lallan.

low-lying inby.

stretch of low-lying ground by a river haugh, howm.

low-spirited *see* **depressed, morose.**

low tide *see* **ebb-tide.**

low[2] *verb* (*of cattle*) rowt, belloch; (*in a low tone*) drizzen NE.

lowing rowt; (*in a low tone*) drizzen NE.

lower (*of weather*) loor.

lowering cankert NE.

loyal leal, sicker, stench NE, stieve.

loyally leal.

loyalty lealtie.

lozenge (*sweet*) lozenger.

lubricate creesh.

luck: good luck sonse; **piece of luck** *see also* **windfall**; luck SHETLAND, ORKNEY, nibble S; **bad luck** misluck, wanluck SHETLAND, deil's luck; **bringing bad luck** ill-fittit; **have bad luck** be ill-luckit (wi).

luckless *see* **unfortunate.**

lucky cannie, sonsie, happy, seilie, seilfu, chancie.

lucky dip lucky poke.

be lucky luck.

money given by a seller to a buyer for luck luck('s) penny, lucky penny.

lug *verb* humph, haigle S.

lukewarm lew (warm).

lull *verb* (*to sleep*) ba(w), hushie-ba(w).

noun (*in weather*) daak N; (*at sea*) sma.

lullaby hushie-ba(w), lillilu, baloo.

lumbago lumbaigie.

lumber *noun, see also* **rubbish**; troke, rottacks NE.

verb, see **burden.**

lump *noun, see also* **excrement**; (*large piece*) da(u)d, claut, knoit, kneevle, toldie NE, doldie, lab, dodgel; (*very large*) clunkart, kneeplach NE; (*of mud etc*) clag; (*of something soft*) gob; (*esp of food*) dunt, junt NE, kemple NE; (*eg of cheese, butter*) skelp; (*esp of cheese*) kneevlick NE; (*in porridge*) knot; (*bump*) knurl, knap ORKNEY, NE, clunker; (*caused by a blow*) cloor; (*under the skin, eg a swollen gland*) kirnel; (*of dung etc hanging from an animal's coat or tail*) knapdarloch NE.

verb **1** (*form lumps, of porridge etc*) knot. **2 lump together** slump.

lumpy knottie, knappie NE, knurlie CAITHNESS; (*of a person's shape*) bumfie.

lumpfish paidle, cock-paidle NE, hush-paidle NE, runker CAITHNESS.

the lump (*in building industry*) the grip.

lunatic *see* **insane, mad**.

lunch *see* **packed lunch**.

lung: lungs lichts, buffs.

lungwort thunner-an-lichtenin, William an Mary NE.

lunge loonge.

lurch[1] *see also* **stagger, sway**: *verb* rowe, stoiter, swaver SHETLAND, ORKNEY, NE, hyter NE, howd NE.

noun stoit NE, hyter NE, swaver NE; (*esp of a ship*) howd.

lurch[2]: **leave in the lurch** lant NE, mistryst S.

lure *verb, see also* **entice**; wile, wice.

lurid *see* **garish**.

lurk *see also* **skulk**; lirk, skirt.

luscious maumie.

lush (*of vegetation: see also* **luxuriant**) grushie, growthie.

lustful radgie.

luxury: luxuries (*food*) *see* **delicacies**.

luxuriant (*of vegetation*) ruch, grushie, growthie, go(r)skie NE, prood SHETLAND, NE.

M

mace-bearer *see* porter.

machine *see* engine.

machinery graith; (*of a mill*) gaun gear.

piece of machinery furliemajig(ger) NE.

mad *see also* crazy, insane, off your head; gyte, daft, gane, wuid, doitit, begoyt, feel NE, in a creel; (*temporarily*) deleerit; (*esp with excitement, rage*) hyte, radge; (*completely*) re(i)d wuid, horn daft.

madden raise.

maddening *see* annoying.

madness madderam; (*mad state*) wuiddrim.

mad person bampot, bammer, gyte.

go mad gang gyte, gae by yersel, gae hyte, rin wuid.

like mad lik(e) a hatter.

madam (*as form of address*) mem.

made *past tense, past participle of* make makkit.

maggot mauk, maithe SHETLAND, ORKNEY, N.

maggoty meithie, maukie; (*esp of sheep*) maukit.

become infested with maggots maithe NE.

magic *noun* glamour(ie), gramarie *literary*, cantrip.

magician warlock.

magistrate (*until 1975*) bailie, bylie.

magnificent *see also* wonderful; magneeficent.

magpie maggie, pyot, deil's bird.

maid (*servant: see also* kitchen-maid) lass(ie), quine NE, maiden, servin lass, girzie.

maiden *see also* girl; dame NE, deem N.

maid-of-all-work scuddler.

die an old maid die lik(e) Jenkin's hen.

maim *see also* mutilate, injure; mishannle, mank, mittle, mar.

main: mainly fecklie NE, maist SHETLAND, N.

mainlander sooth-moother SHETLAND, ferry-lowper ORKNEY.

main street toon gate S.

maintain (*a person*) fend; (*yourself in a certain state*) haud: '*She never hauds hersel in richt order*'; (*in argument*) uphaud.

maintenance *see also* upkeep; uphaud, throu-bearin; (*law*) aliment.

major: majority feck, plurality, force.

major part (*of something*) ruch.

make mak; pit: '*He pits me mad*'; (*compel*) gar: '*It gars me greet*'; (*a bed*) mak up.

make-believe mak-on.

makeshift *noun* by-pit NE, dae-nae-better; (*esp a meal*) pit-by, pit-ower NE, aff-pit.

make as if to offer tae.

make do pit by, pit ower N; shuit by.

make down (*a garment*) tak doon.

make for haud for, airt for.

make much of daut.

make off *see* clear out.

make or mar mak a kirk or a mill o.

make up to chim NE.

male *noun* he.

desire the male (*of a sow etc*) breem.

malediction †malison.

malefactor ill-daer.

malevolent *see also* malicious, hostile; ill-hertit, ill-willie, ill-intendit NE, ill-gien.

malice ill(-will).

malicious *see also* **hostile, malevolent**; maleecious, ill-hertit, mislushious, warlock, uncannie, pooshionous.
malicious person keek NE.
malignant (*evil: see also* **malevolent**) uncannie.
malinger fraik.
mallard mire-duck, moss-duck, muirduck.
mallet bittle.
mallow (*plant*) maw(s) S.
malt maut.
maltster mautman.
man *see also* **fellow, chap, lad, old man**; carle, he, chiel(d), gadgie LOTHIAN, S, *originally gipsy*, boy *esp* HIGHLAND, tuip *contemptuous*, CAITHNESS; (*as opposed to a woman*) man-bodie; (*the common man*) jock, jack NE; (*as a form of address*) min, mon; (*informal: see also* **address**) mac; (*to an older man*) callan(t) NE.
manhood manheid.
grown to manhood *see also* **adult**; man-big.
mankind fowk, Jock Tamson's bairns.
manly pretty.
mannish-looking woman he, rudas NE.
manhandle (*indecently*) graip S, ficher wi SHETLAND, NE.
manservant (*young*) servan(t) chiel.
manslaughter (*law*) culpable homicide.
any man alive the face o clay NE.
effeminate man (big) jessie; (*who concerns himself with women's affairs*) henwife, sweetie-wife.
manage manish; (*arrange, direct*) guide, cast aboot; (*look after*) tak aboot, owersee; (*cope*) shuit by, mak a fen(d); (*succeed*) win: 'win tae dae it', maun, get: 'he couldna get sleepin'; 'he couldna get sleepit'.
manageable fleet NE.
manager *see also* **overseer**; guider, heid bummer *often sarcastic*; (*of an estate*) factor, gr(o)un(d) officer.

managing fendie.
manger foresta NE; (*rack above manger*) heck NE.
mangle (*damage*) massacker, mishannle; (*cut roughly*) hash, haggle.
mangy scawt.
manifest: make manifest kythe.
manifestation kythin.
manipulate (*dishonestly*) pauchle.
manner *see also* **way**; mainner, gate, shape.
mannerism ginkum NE.
mannerly *see also* **polite, courteous**; mainnerlie, mensefu.
manners *see also* **bad manners**; mainners, (*fair*) fashions, mense, havins.
manoeuvre *verb* wice, airt; (*a small object by poking*) pirl.
mansion(-house) big hoose, ha (hoose).
mantelpiece lintel, chim(b)ley-heid, (chim(b)ley-)brace.
mantle †manteel.
manure *see also* **dung**: *noun* mainner, muck, guidin.
verb mainner, muck; (*with seaweed*) ware; (*of animals dropping dung*) tathe.
liquid from manure addle, aidle, midden bree, green brees NE.
many monie, plenty.
(a good) many *see also* **lot**; a hantle, a guid few, a spreath NE.
many a monie's the.
many a person monie ane, a hullock N: 'a hullock o loons'.
very many monie a monie.
map caird.
mar *see also* **spoil, botch**; spulyie, mank, durk.
maraud spulyie.
marble (*toy*) bool, chippie, commonie, commie GLASGOW; ruckie S; (*thrown rather than rolled*) pick NE, pitcher NE; (*large*) doller NE, dollicker EDINBURGH, dabber S; (*small*) peasie, peever; (*glass*) glessie (bool); (*steel*) steelie; (*clay*) clayey; (*red clay*) reidie W; (*earthenware*) crocker, jaurie, pottie (bool)

NE, pigger; *(large brown earthenware)* ston(e)der NE; *(small earthenware)* peerie NE; *(small coloured earthenware)* stonie.

game of marbles bools, chippie; *(played along a road)* chasie NE; *(with circle on ground as target)* ringie; *(in which marbles are aimed at others in holes)* holie; *(in which winner keeps gains)* winnie; *(in which gains are returned)* funnie; *(in which winner takes all)* rookie; *(played by flicking with the thumb and forefinger)* plunkie.

march[1] *see also* **walk**: *verb* mairch, merch; *(purposefully)* stramp.

noun mairch, merch; *(eg in protest)* parawd.

march[2] *see* **boundary**.

March Mairch, Merch.

last three days of March *(old style)* borrowin days.

period of bleak wintry weather in March teuchit's storm.

mare mear(ie); *(old)* yaud.

marguerite *see also* **daisy**: cairt wheel, white gowan.

marigold *see also* **marsh marigold**; yella gowan.

mark *noun, see also* **scratch, landmark**; merk; *(imprint, track)* steid; *(of a burn)* scam; *(distinguishing mark)* kenspeckle; *(of ownership on an animal: see also* **brand, earmark, sheepmark**) kenmark; *(in a game: see also* **target**) gog, mott, *(starting line)* score.

verb merk; *(a boundary etc with markers)* prap; *(sheep with owner's mark)* buist.

marker *(eg as a boundary, in ploughing, as a target)* prap; *(heap of stones on a boundary etc)* cairn.

off the mark aff the stot.

market *noun, see also* **fair**[2]; mercat, ootgate; *(esp for sale of livestock)* mart, tryst; *(market on 1 November)* Hallowfair.

market cross (mercat) cross.

market garden(er) †mail-gairden(er).

marketplace tron *esp in place-names.*

marriage mairriage.

marriage bond ban(d).

marriage partner *see* **mate**.

marriage settlement sittin-doon, tocher *literary.*

join in marriage yoke, buckle, tether *sarcastic,* N, souder, sowther.

marrow *(in bones)* mergh SHETLAND, mergie SHETLAND, ORKNEY.

marry *see also* **wed**; mairry, merry, tether *sarcastic,* N, buckle, yoke, marrow (wi), tak; *(get for a spouse)* get.

married to merrit on *or* wi.

be married be tied, be yokit.

get married forgaither, get wad, get yokit.

newly-married couple *(of any age)* young fowk.

desire to marry clockin.

plan to marry *verb* mak it up.

marsh *see also* **bog, quagmire**; gullion, quaw, slag, slump; *(marshy ground: see also* **marshland**) moss, flush, plowter, fluther; *(patch among heather)* gair; *(hollow)* sink, swail, slack S; *(esp with a stream)* syke.

marshy mossy, spootie, slumpie, wauchie.

marshland moss; *(very wet)* flow.

marsh marigold wildfire, lapper gowan.

marshal †marischal.

martin *see also* **sand-martin**; *(house-martin)* (hoose-)mairtin, swalla, wundaswalla.

martyr mairtyr.

marvel *noun* ferlie.

verb ferlie, strange SHETLAND.

masculine(-looking) woman he, rudas NE.

mash *verb* *(vegetables)* chap, champ, rummle; *(malt)* mask.

noun, see **mush**.

mashed potatoes chappit tatties, champit tatties, champers.

masher *(for vegetables: see also* **potato masher**) bittle.

mask *noun* (*face-shaped*) fause face.

mason *see* **stonemason, chisel, hammer.**

masonry stane an lime; (*of square-hewn stone*) aislarwark; (*badly-built*) rummle SHETLAND, NE.

masquerade guise.

masquerader (*now esp of children at Halloween*) guiser.

mass[1] *noun, see also* **heap, swarm**; (*big, unwieldy*) hulk; (*of tiny crushed fragments*) smush; (*tangled*) hushoch; (*untidy*) hushle; (*of something soft*) sklone NE.

mass[2] *noun* (*Eucharist*) †mess.

mast (*of a boat*) most NE.

master *noun* maister; (*of a craft*) maister, cork, deacon.
verb get roon(d), maugre NE, maun, owergang.

mastery grip, poustie, owerance.

domineering master master an mair.

master of the house guidman.

mastitis (*in female animals*) weed, simmer weed.

mat *see* **rug.**
verb taut.

matted tautit, tautie; (*of wool*) waulkit.

match[1] (*for lighting*) spunk, lunt.

match[2] *noun* **1** (*curling*) bonspiel, spiel. **2** (*equal*) marrow, neibour, maik: '*There wisna his maik at waddins*'.
verb marrow, neibour, peel, come.

not matching (*eg of gloves*) mar(row)less, neibourless.

matchless (*without equal*) marrowless.

be a match for tak the swatch o.

meet your match meet wi yer merchant.

mate *noun* (*marriage partner*) marrow *literary*, half-marrow, neibour.

matrimony *see also* **marriage**; mink NE.

matron (*older woman*) wife, wifie, guidwife, cummer.

matted *see* **mat.**

matter *verb* maitter.

noun, see also **pus**; maitter; (*waxy, in the eye*) goor SHETLAND, ORKNEY, N.

it doesn't matter there's nae (muckle) maitter, it disna mak N.

in the matter of O.

what does it matter? whit maitter?, whit reck(s)?, whit's adae?, fat's adee? NE, fit dis't mak? N.

mattress mattrass, tike; (*chaff-filled*) caff-bed.

mattress cover tike, tikin.

mature *adjective* (*adult*) muckle; (*of fruit*) maumie; (*of herrings*) full.
verb (*of manure*) mak.

maul *see also* **mutilate, injure**; rive, massacker, mell.

maunder *see also* **babble**; maunner, rander.

may mith NE.

maybe *see also* **perhaps**; mibbie, mebbe.

May Mey.

mayfly (*just after larva stage*) scur.

stormy weather in early May gab o Mey.

high tide in May Mey flude.

mayor provost.

me us, iz.

meadow meedow, meedie E CENTRAL, haugh, lizour, park, leens CAITHNESS, howm.

meadow pipit moss cheeper, muir cheeper, gray cheeper, heather peeper NE, titlin.

meadowsweet queen o (the) meedow, lady o the meedow.

meagre scrimp(it), seldom.

meal[1] male, male o mait, meltith, diet, eat NE; (*main meal*) kail; (*cooked*) made diet SHETLAND, NE; (*frugal*) pickin; (*hasty*) aff-pit, pit-ower NE, shuit-aboot NE; (*light: see also* **snack**) pit-by, pit-past, chat NE, pike; (*heavy*) rive, rimrax(in) NE, rimfu; (*afternoon*) efternuin SHETLAND; (*at 4pm*) †fower-oors.

mealtime diet-oor, brose-time, cornin-time.

meal[2] (*esp oatmeal*) male.
  mealy-mouthed *see also* **prim**; mim(-mou'd), bird-mou'd.
  meal-chest meal-kist, (meal-)ark, girnel.
mean[1] **1** *see also* **avaricious, stingy, miserly, greedy**; grippie, ticht, hungry, meeserable, scrimpit, scruntie, meechie, moolie, ill-hertit NE, ill-willie, scuffie NE, wheetie NE, clem *school slang*. **2** (*contemptible*) foutie, scawt, dirten NE.
  act meanly snuil, pinch.
  meanness grippiness.
  mean person *see also* **miser**; nipscart, scrunt.
  be mean hae a guid grip o the gear, be some grippie NE.
mean[2] *verb* **1** (*to do something*) ettle. **2** (*signify*) bear.
  get someone's meaning pick someone up.
  meaningless haiveless NE, rhymeless NE; (*of speech*) pyot.
  what do you mean? whit are ye at?
meander *see also* **bend**: *noun* (*of a river*) wimple, jouk, wample.
  verb (*of a river*) wimple.
means: by means of wi, inthrow NE.
  by no means nane, at nae rate.
meantime, meanwhile (a)tween han(d)s.
measles maisles, mirls.
measure *noun, for specific measures see table on p 302* mizzer SHETLAND, NE, mett; (*liberal*) Moffat measure.
  verb mizzer SHETLAND, NE; (*by pacing*) space, spang; (*exactly, with a tape measure*) tape.
  measurement mett.
  measuring rod ellwan(d).
  measure out (*food*) mess.
  take the measure of tak the swatch o.
meat *see also* **cut, slice, butcher**; mait, flesh, beef.
  meat market skemmels NE.
mechanism intimmers.
meddle *see also* **interfere**; middle, mak

or meddle, mak or mell, mell, pit in yer spuin, scaud yer lips wi ither fowk's kail, mird NE, pingle, fyle yer fingers: '*Wad ye fyle yer fingers wi crime?*'
  meddlesome inbearin.
  not to be meddled with unchancie.
mediation moyen.
medical certificate (*that you are unfit for work*) (doctor's) line.
medicine (*drug etc*) feesick, graith.
  medicinal hailsome.
mediocre †guidless ill-less.
meditate (*think hard*) lay the brains asteep.
  meditative pensefu.
medium *adjective* (*of medium size, quality etc*) middlin.
meek patientfu.
meet *verb* (*encounter*) meet in wi, kep; (*meet together*) forgaither; (*by arrangement*) tryst.
  meeting forgaitherin, tryst; (*of a council etc*) †sederunt; (*informal gathering*) sederunt.
  meeting place tryst, trystin place, (*esp a pub*) howf.
  arrange a meeting tryst.
  time for a meeting trystin time.
  last meeting (*of a council before an election*) greetin meetin.
melancholy *adjective, see also* **sad, sorrowful**; dowie, oorie, dowf, douth, heepochondreeoch NE, unhertsome, glumsh.
  make a low melancholy sound chirl.
mellow *adjective* (*of fruit etc*) maumie.
melodeon box.
melody souch.
melt mouten.
  melt away (*of snow*) mizzle.
  melt down (*fat*) rind.
membrane *see also* **caul**; striffin.
memento mindin.
memorandum jottin.
memory (*recollection*) mind(in).
  have memory of remember o, min(d) on.

memorial heap of stones cairn, cyaarn NE.

menace *verb, see also* **threaten**; mint, cock.

noun, see **nuisance**.

mend *see also* **repair, patch, cobble**; sort, fettle, beet; (*by sewing*) ranter, (*patch*) cloot; (*heels of shoes or stockings*) heel-cap.

mend your ways mend.

menial *noun* scodgie.

do rough menial work scodgie.

menstruate see her ain.

mental: mental twist lirk.

mentally handicapped wantin, no richt, silly, feel NE, far frae a yonner NE, gytit.

mentally-handicapped person daftie, saftie, gowk(ie), eediot, feel NE.

be mentally handicapped hae a want, want tippence o the shillin, be feel NE.

mention *verb* mint, mou, mooth; (*make mention*) leet.

not mention no say cheese, nae say eechie nor ochie.

merchandise *noun* (*small articles*) troke.

merchant merchan.

travelling merchant packman.

mercurial (*in temperament*) either (i) the muin or the midden.

mercy: at the mercy of in the merciment o, in the reverence o.

merge gae thegither.

merit mense SW, S.

mermaid †marmaid(en).

merry *see also* **cheerful, lively, jocular**; croose, blithesome, joco, hertie, rantin, gleg, mirkie NE.

merrily mirkie NE.

merry-making daffin, dafferie; (*noisy*) rant, gilravage.

make merry splore, rant, gilravage, heeze NE.

mesh (*of a net*) mask SHETLAND, ORKNEY, N.

make the meshwork of (*a herring net*) wyve NE.

mess *noun, see also* **muddle, shambles, bungle**; midden, guddle, gutter, carfuffle, bullox, sclatch, plaister, Paddy's market, Annicker's midden, bucker NE, maschle NE, quigger NE, sotter, throuither, boorach(ie) N, HIGHLAND; (*dirty*) spleuterie; (*wet*) slitter, skiddle, blitter; (*wet and dirty*) slutter, slaister, soss; (*wet or sticky*) cloiter; (*of food*) plowter; (*disgusting*) slaiger, slorach, mairtyr, sludder.

work, eat, drink etc messily slaister, slitter.

messy *see also* **muddy**; (*and wet*) slitterie, slutterie, cloiterie; (*and dirty*) slaisterie; (*and muddy*) gutterie, sotterie.

messy person slitter, slaister; (*slobberer*) slabber; (*worker*) gutter.

messy way of working slaik.

messy work kirn NE, sotter.

it's messy it's a(w) mince.

make a mess of *see also* **spoil**; bullox, moger, soss Shetland, NE, sotter up, scutter SHETLAND, ORKNEY, N.

make a mess of things gae throuither; (*make messy*) slaister, slitter.

mess about plaister, guddle, quigger NE, cloiter; (*with housework*) scuddle.

mess about with poach: '*The baby's poachin his porridge*'.

messenger (*unfaithful*) corbie messenger.

metal: fit with metal rims *or* **tips** *etc* shae, shee NE.

fitted with metal tips (*of a shoelace*) shoddit.

metal tag of a bootlace horl.

put metal toe and heel pieces on (*a shoe*) shod.

meteor *see* **shooting star**.

method *see also* **way**; road, gate.

methodical purposelik(e).

lack of method throuitherness.

methylated spirit, meths *see also* **wine**; (*for drinking*) feek NE.

meticulous *see also* **precise**; pinglin, pludisome NE.

mettle *see also* **drive, spirit**; saul.

mettlesome *see also* **spirited, lively; mettle.**

mew[1] *noun* (*gull*) maw, maa SHETLAND, ORKNEY.

mew[2] *verb, noun* (*of a cat*) maw, miauve NE; (*piteously*) waw.

miaow *see* **mew**[2].

mica (*white, esp in small scales*) sheep siller.

midday twaloors.

midday snack *or* **meal** twaloors SHETLAND, ORKNEY.

midden *see* **dunghill.**

middle mid(s): '*in the mids*'.

middle-aged aul(d)-young.

middle course mids NE: '*there's aye a mids in the sea*'.

a middle-sized man a cut o a man.

midge mudge HIGHLAND, midgie, midgeck NE, mudgeick SHETLAND, ORKNEY.

midnight midnicht, the turn o the nicht, the twal (o nicht), the howe o the nicht.

midst mid.

Midsummer Day Johnsmass SHETLAND, ORKNEY.

midway *see* **halfway.**

midwife howdie, howdie-wife, cummer, cannie-wife, luckie.

midwifery howdyin.

midwinter the howe o (the) winter, the howe o the year.

might[1] *past tense of* **may** micht, mith NE: '*I mith a geen*', †mocht, †mote.

might[2] *noun, see also* **power;** micht, maucht, strouth.

mighty michtie.

with all your might hail hole, wi a(w) yer pith.

mignonette minnonette.

milch cow milk coo.

mild (*of weather*) saft, maumie, lithesome; (*and bright*) leesome NE.

mildew foost, foosht NE.

mile *see table on p 302.*

milk *noun* mulk.
verb mulk, draw.

milking stool milkin steel NE, sunkie S.

milking time kye-time.

milk container *see also* **milk pail;** (*broad, shallow*) (milk) boyne.

milk jug (*small*) poorie.

milk pail (*wooden with stave handle*) milk bowie, hannie, bally (cog) NE, leglin.

milk strainer milk sye, sile, sey dish, search.

add milk to (*tea*) milk, mulk.

first milk from a cow after calving *see also* **cheese;** beest(ie), beestin.

give milk (*of a cow etc*) milk, mulk.

not giving milk (*of a cow etc*) yeld, eil(d), farra.

squeeze the last drops of milk from (*a cow etc*) strip, strib, drib NE, jib, efter.

last drops of milk from a milking strippins, stribbins, jibbins, efterins.

mill *noun* mull, †miln.

miller millart, mullert NE, †milnar.

last milling of a season dusty melder.

mill dam mill caul(d).

millrace (*into wheel*) (mill) lade, (mill) lead.

millrace outlet back-fa(w).

millstone stane, steen NE; (*lower*) understane.

bind (*land or tenants*) **to a particular mill** †thirl.

obligation to use a certain mill, payment for use of this mill †sucken.

duty on grain ground at a mill †multure.

small amounts of corn given to mill servants †sequels.

mill around kirn (aboot).

milt (*of a male fish*) melt, melg NE.

mimic *noun* (*person*) afftak.

mince *verb* minch.

minced meat mince, minch; (*cooked with oatmeal, onions etc*) mince(d) collops.

pie filled with minced meat mince pie.

mincing (*esp in speech*) mim-mou'd.
mind *noun* wame.
bear in mind keep mind o.
call to mind mind.
change your mind tak the rue.
frame of mind pin: '*in a merry pin*', tune, teen NE: '*Fit kinna teen are ye in?*'
never mind nivver heed, nivver leet.
out of your mind *see also* **insane, mad**; by yersel, oot o yer rizzon.
pass out of mind (*of news etc*) dill doon SHETLAND, NE.
set your mind to a problem set yer harns tae steep.
mine¹ *pronoun* mines.
mine² *noun, see also* **pit, coal**; heuch AYRSHIRE; (*graphite*) wad SW.
verb howk.
miner pickman, Jock brit *contemptuous*, coomie.
miner's lamp tallie lamp.
miner's (*usu blue-grey*) **singlet** peeweet, peesweep.
mineshaft sink, shank, heuch.
mineworkings winnins.
method of mining by leaving pillars of coal to support the roof stoop-an-room.
mineral meeneral.
minimum meenimum.
minister meenister, black coat *taboo name,* E COAST; (*who presides over a church court*) moderator: '*Moderator of the General Assembly*'; (*student who has been licensed to preach*) probationer.
be a minister wag yer powe in a poopit.
minister's house manse.
land assigned to a minister glebe.
person who has failed to become a minister stickit minister.
son or daughter of a minister son or daughter o the manse.
minnow *see also* **stickleback**; minnon, mennen(t) S, guttie; (*large*) baggie (minnon), doctor; (*red-breasted*) podlie, sodger.
minstrel bard, †menstral.

mint (*field*) lamb's tongues.
mint imperial pan drop, grannie's sooker, auld wifie's sooker.
minuet †minuwae.
minute¹ *noun* meenit, minent.
minute² *adjective, see also* **small**; peerie-weerie.
miracle meeracle.
mire *see* **mud**.
mirror seein gless, keekin gless.
mirth *see also* **laughter, merry-making**; (*noisy*) hirdum-dirdum.
misapprehension: under a misapprehension in a mistak(e).
misbehave gae ower the score.
miscall misca(w).
miscarriage (*abortion*) slip.
miscarry miscairry: **1** (*suffer a miscarriage*) pairt wi bairn. **2** (*of a plan etc*) gley, misgae.
miscellaneous orra.
mischief 1 ill, deviltrie NE. **2 piece of mischief** cantrip, prattick NE, prat CAITHNESS.
mischievous mischievious, ill-deedie, ill-duin, ill-contrivit SHETLAND, N, mirkie NE; (*unruly*) rummlin, gallus; (*esp of a child*) royet, roit NE, ill-trickit SHETLAND, ORKNEY, N.
mischievous person or animal limb o the deil, deil's bairn; (*esp a child*) tike N; (*esp a girl*) clip.
mischievousness ill-gates.
bring mischief on yourself bring an ill kaim tae yer heid.
misconduct ill-daein.
misdemeanour ill-daein.
miser *see also* **hoarder**; misert, nabal, grab, scrunt, heather-piker NE, niggar, nipscart, peyzart, rake.
miserly *see also* **stingy, mean¹,** avaricious, niggardly; misert, grippie, meeserable, hungry, near-begaun, near the bane, near the bit, nairra-begaun, pegral.
miserable 1 meeserable, ill-aff; (*from cold etc*) oorit. **2 miserable-looking** oorie, oorlich.

miserable-looking person greetin face, soor-lik(e) bodie.

look (cold and) miserable pinge.

be miserable hoolet.

misery meeserie, pine SHETLAND, ORKNEY, NE.

in (a state of) misery in the sheuch.

misfortune see also trouble: 1 mischief, misluck, mishanter SHETLAND, ORKNEY, N, wanluck SHETLAND. 2 (a misfortune) amshach NE, conter, begunk, begeck, traik, dree.

misgiving: have misgivings hae yer doots: 'Ah hae ma doots aboot him'.

misguided left tae yersel, will, gley(e)d.

mishandle misguide.

mishap see also accident; skavie NE, mishanter SHETLAND, ORKNEY, N.

misinform mistell.

misinformed mislearit.

mislay see lose.

mismanage see also bungle; misguide, blunk, fa(w) throu.

mismanaged ill-guidit.

mispronounce misca(w).

miss verb (fail to get) tyne; (fail) misgae NE.

missed (because of absence) misslie.

missing amissin.

miss something good (by not being there) miss yersel: 'Ye fair missed yersel at the pairtie'.

missel-thrush storm-cock, Hielan(d) pyot NE, feltieflier.

misshapen thrawn, camsha(u)chelt; (esp of shoes) ba(u)chelt; (of a person: see also hunchbacked) wrang NE.

mist noun rouk; (esp morning) reek SHETLAND, NE; (haze) gum N; (rising from ground) flim; (driving) rack; (dense) roop SW, S; (dense, on sea) thickness; (cold, from sea on E Coast) haar; (freezing, coastal) barber NE; (damp) ure; (wet) rag SHETLAND, ORKNEY, NE; (cold, wet) drowe SE; (cold, with breeze) gull NE; (thin, light) smuchter NE.

misty reekie, roukie, haarie, daggie NE, drowie, drackie; (oppressively) mochie.

mistake verb, noun mistak.

mistaken mistaen, in a mistak, aff (o) yer eggs, mislearit, gley(e)d, up the sheuch W, SW.

be mistaken hae the wrang soo by the lug.

I'm very much mistaken I'm cheatit, it cheats me: 'It cheats me gin he disna fin oot'.

make a mistake mistak yersel.

by mistake in a mistak(e).

say by mistake lee, skellie.

retrieve a mistake tak up a steek.

mistress 1 (of a house: see also landlady, housewife) guidwife, hersel; (used by servants) she. 2 (sexual partner) hing-tee N, preen-tae, limmer; (cohabitee) bidie-in.

mistrust see distrust.

misunderstood (of a remark etc) mistaen.

misuse disabuse.

mitigate licht, souder, sowther.

mitten pawkie, moggan, doddie-mitten, hummel-mitten NE, hummel-doddie NE.

mix verb 1 (mingle: see also stir) mell; (esp liquids, messily) soss; (flour etc with water) draigle NE. 2 (socially) see associate.

mixture see also hotchpotch; mixtermaxter, menyie N, rummle; (messy) keeroch NE; (messy, of food) soss, perlaig NE, slaister, slitter, powsowdie; (weak, of liquid) jabble; (of grains growing together) mashlum.

mix up see also muddle, jumble; taigle, taisle, jurmummle; (messily) keeger NE.

mix-up see also muddle; snorl N, squeeter NE, farrach, complouter, keeger NE.

mixed-up row-chow.

moan verb, noun, see also complain(t); mane.

moaning adjective greetin-faced.

mob noun, see also rabble, riff-raff; canallie, ferkishin s.

mock *see also* **jeer, insult;** tak the nap aff, jamph, lant NE, geck at, lichtlie; (*with exaggerated gestures*) murgeon.

mockery *see also* **banter;** afftakkin, jamph.

mocking *adjective* mockrif(e), afftakkin.

mocking remark afftak; (*reply*) knack.

moderate *adjective* middlin.
verb (*of wind*) *see* **die down.**

moderately middlins.

moderation mense.

modern modren.

modest *see also* **timid;** blate.

moist *see also* **damp, wet;** sappie; (*of warm atmosphere*) moch(ie).

moisten slock(en).

moisture moister.

molar aisle-tuith sw, S, chaft-tuith.

molasses *see* **treacle.**

mole[1] (*animal*) mowdiewort, mowdiewarp, mowdie.

mole-catcher molie, mowdie, mowdieman.

molehill mowdie(wort)hill.

skin of a mole mowdieskin.

mole[2] (*on skin*) rasp, mowdiewort *humorous.*

molest *see also* **pester;** steer, sturt.

mollycoddle *verb, see also* **pamper;** kirn wi NE, fraik.

moment *see also* **instant;** mament, blink, rap, crack: '*in a crack*', gliff, glisk.

at the moment the noo, eenoo, ivnoo, this weather.

in a moment, a moment ago the noo, eenoo, ivnoo.

momentum virr.

Monday Monanday.

money siller, bawbees, penny: '*a bonnie penny*', plack, brindle *slang,* NE, clinker ANGUS, gcar: '*guids an gear*', jowldie *gipsy;* (*earning interest in a bank*) clock-in hen; (*received for a first sale etc*) handsel.

monied sillert.

moneybox (*earthenware*) pig, pirlie pig, penny pig, misert-pig, thriftie.

moneygrubber scrub, grab, earthworm NE, lick-penny.

make money mak rich, mak siller.

without money boss, sillerless.

mongrel tike *contemptuous,* messan *contemptuous.*

monkey pug(gie).

monkey-flower frog's mou(th).

monotonous dreich.

talk monotonously paiter, boo.

tell (*a story etc*) **monotonously** psalm NE.

monster *see also* **bog(e)yman;** on-beast; (*esp female*) gyre carline.

monstrous *see* **huge.**

month (*lunar*) muin S.

monument moniment.

mood 1 muid, tune, teen NE, key, tid: '*ill tid*', bin(ner) NE, bon, taik SHETLAND, NE, lay SHETLAND, ORKNEY, pin: '*in a merry pin*', tift. **2 bad mood** *see also* **sulks;** bad cut, gee.

moody tiftie, tunie S.

moon muin, meen NE, †Macfarlane's bouet, †Lochiel's lantern.

crescent moon quarter muin.

ring round the moon (*sign of bad weather*) (muin) broch, gowe, faul(d), cock's ee N.

broad bar of light across the moon (*sign of bad weather*) stiffie.

moor[1] muir, meer NE.

moorland muirland.

moor[2]: **mooring post** pall.

mop: mop up swaible S, dicht up.

mope *see also* **grumble, complain;** mump, map ANGUS, tak on, hing the lugs, pinge.

moral: self-righteously moral people the unco guid.

morass *see also* **marsh, swamp;** flow, slag, slump.

more *adjective, adverb* mair, mae.

moreover *see also* **furthermore;** mair, by token, by (th)at.

and more so an some, by's (th)at.

161

no more than nae bit NE.

morning *see also* tomorrow morning; mornin, fuirday; (*very early hours of*) (wee) sma oors.

morose *see also* sullen; still, stroonge N, glump(ie), dowie.

morsel *see also* crumb, fragment; glack, bittock, minschie, snag NE, gnap.

mortal illness deid ill.

mortar lime: '*stane an lime*'; (*poured into crevices and left to set*) run lime.

mortgage *verb* hypothecate, impignorate.

noun standard security, hypothec, impignoration.

mortgagee grantee of security.

mortgagor grantor of security, reverser.

mortuary deid-hoose.

moss fog; (*esp decomposed*) duff (muild) SHETLAND; (*spongy, on boggy ground*) flow moss.

mossy foggie.

become moss-covered fog.

most maist.

mostly, for the most part maistlie, maist, maistlins.

most of *see also* majority; the feck o.

most of all maistlie.

moth moch, witch NE; (*clothes moth*) mowd.

moth-eaten mochie, moch-eaten.

mother *see also* mum; mither, midder SHETLAND, NE, auld wife *contemptuous*, auld yin *contemptuous*, minnie *affectionate name*.

mother-in-law guid-mither.

motion *see also* movement; (*sudden*) stot; (*of an object flying through the air*) swiff; (*of the tide*) draig.

motley mixter-maxter.

motley crew ragabash.

mottled *see also* speckled, skin; marlie, spreckelt.

having mottled legs *see also* skin; mizzle-shinned.

mould[1] (*fungus*) foost, foosht NE; (*on cheese, jam etc*) hair(y)-mool(d).

mouldy foostie, fooshtie NE, moolie,

mozie, hoamt, mochie NE; (*covered with mould*) hair(y)-mooldit.

become *or* smell mouldy foost, foosht NE, mool.

mouldy condition *or* smell foost, foosht NE.

mould[2] (*earth*) mool, moold, meel(d) NE.

mouldboard mool(d)bred, reest, cleathin NE, cleedin.

moulder muilder, mooler, murl, moost NE, moze SHETLAND, ORKNEY, CAITHNESS.

mould[3] (*pattern*) mool, meel NE.

moulding (*round skirting board*) moose mouldin.

moult *verb* moot.

noun the moot, pook: '*in the pook*', pluck.

mound *see also* hillock; moond, humple; (*esp fairy mound*) tulloch.

mount[1] *verb* munt, rise; (*a horse*) lowp on, win on N.

mounting-stone †lowpin-on stane.

mount[2] *noun, see also* mountain; munt.

mountain *see also* hill, mount[2]; muntain; (*one of the higher Scottish mountains*) ben, (*over 3 000 feet, 914m*) Munro, (*2 500–3 000 feet, 762–914m*) Corbett.

mountain ash rowan(-tree), rodden(-tree).

mountain pass bealach.

mourn murn, croon, mane (for).

mourner (*hired, at a funeral*) †saulie.

mournful *see also* sad, sorrowful; dowie, dool.

mournful sound mane.

mournfully dowielie.

mourning murnin.

mourning clothes murnins, blacks.

mouse moose.

mousetrap (moose-)fa(w).

moustache mouser, moutache, matash, fusker NE.

mouth *noun* mou, mooth, gab, gob, geggie, gebbie E CENTRAL, muns *gipsy*, tattie-trap *contemptuous*; (*esp when pouting*) buss CAITHNESS, HIGHLAND: '*he has a buss on*'; (*of an animal*) mull; (*of a river*) watter-mou.

-**mouthed** -gabbit: '*gash-gabbit*' = having a misshapen mouth.

mouthful *see also* **snack, drink**; moufae, moothfae; (*esp of liquid*) laib, lerb NE, howp NE, spairge, sup(pie): '*a sup tea*'.

mouth-organ moothie.

move *verb* muve, meeve NE: **1** mudge; (*budge*) jee, (*recklessly, carelessly*) breenge; **move about** (*unsteadily: see also* **stagger**) wammle; (*awkwardly, jerkily*) walloch, hodge; (*awkwardly, restlessly*) hushle NE; (*awkwardly, quickly*) wallop; (*fidget*) rowe; (*slightly, restlessly*) fitch SHETLAND, ORKNEY, CAITHNESS; (*quickly, lightly*) skiff, link, skilt S; (*nimbly*) jink, bush; (*quickly, energetically*) skelp, spank, leash SHETLAND, ORKNEY, N, pin ORKNEY, N, timmer (up) NE; (*quickly, noisily*) bicker; (*laboriously*) warsle, (*with a heavy burden*) humph. **2** (*a church congregation*) transport; (*a bowl or curling stone by knocking it with another*) rub.

movement mudge; (*slight*) paw, (*unsteady*) wa(u)chle; (*quick, noisy*) bicker NE; (*sudden, erratic*) stot; **movements** (*esp of the face*) mudgins.

move along (*to make way for others*) hirsel yont.

move house flit.

move to and fro wampish.

on the move on the leg.

mow maw, scythe.

mower mawer, scythe NE.

Mrs Mistress.

much *see also* **lot**[1]: *adjective, adverb* muckle, meikle, mickle; (*with comparative*) hantle (sicht): '*a hantle sicht caulder*'.

very much *see also* **very**; fine, a heap: '*a heap better*', richt NE, sair, uncolie *literary*.

much alike eeksie-peeksie, neibours, gey sib.

much less forby NE.

muck *see* **dirt, dung**.

muck-rake cleek, hack (muck), harl.

mucus glit, goor; (*from the throat etc*: *see also* **phlegm**) clocher; (*from the nose*) snotters, snochter, bubble, meldrop; (*piece of hardened mucus in the nose*) black man CENTRAL, boakie NE.

mud cla(i)rt, gutters, glabber, dubs, goor, lagger, drookit stour, lair CENTRAL; (*soft, sticky*) glaur; (*sediment*) grummel.

muddy *adjective* cla(i)rtie, gutterie, glaurie, lairie, dubbie, clattie, clatchie NE; (*full of sediment*) g(r)umlie, jummlie; (*splashy*) jaupie, platchie S; (*of a road*) slabberie, slunkie ULSTER.

verb glaur, grummel, drummle.

muddy place plowter, gorroch.

cover with mud slaiger, dub, platch SHETLAND, NE.

completely covered with mud glaursel S.

make muddy *see* **muddy** *verb*.

walk in mud plowter, platch.

sink in mud lair.

muddle *noun, see also* **mess, confusion, mix-up, bungle, botch**; raivel, fankle, midden, carfuffle, kirn, reel-rall, gutter, guddle, taigle, ming-mang, snorl SHETLAND, CAITHNESS, NE, picher NE, soss, sotter, moger, boorach(ie) N, HIGHLAND.

verb, see also **jumble, mix up**; raivel, taigle, ramfeezle, ming-mang; (*a speech etc*) gae throu N.

muddled 1 *see also* **untidy, messy, disorganized**; raivelt, throuither, throwder NE, guddelt, hither-an-yon(t). **2** (*in mind: see also* **confused**) bumbazed, taivert, wauchelt; (*with drink*) mix(i)t.

muddle-headed *see* **muddled 2**.

muddle-headedness throuitherness.

muddle along puddle, picher NE.

person who gets in a muddle puddle ANGUS, picher NE.

muff (*woollen, for wrists*) wristie SHETLAND.

muffler gravat.

mug (*drinking*) moog N, joug, stowp; (*small, tin*) tinnie.

muggy *see also* **close**[1]; mochie, muithie, roukie.

mugwort muggart (kail), muggins.

mullet: grey mullet pelcher CAITH-NESS.

multicoloured lyart, sprittelt S.

multitude *see* **crowd**.

mum, mummy mam(mie), minnie *affectionate name*, maw CENTRAL.

mumble *verb, see also* **mutter, murmur**; mummle, mump, mum, hummer; (*toothlessly*) nattle.

mummer *see* **masquerader**.

mummy *see* **mum**.

mumps branks, buffets E CENTRAL.

munch *see also* **crunch**; hash, hanch, cramp N, gumsh NE, moup (on), ramsh.

murder *see also* **kill**; murther.

murderer murtherer.

murk mirk.

murky mirkie, drumlie.

murmur *see also* **mutter, mumble**: *verb* croon, hummer, murmell; (*of the wind*) sowff, souch, SOO SHETLAND; (*of a child*) murther.

noun (*of talk*) curmurrin; (*of discontent*) murmuration; (*murmuring sound*) murr, (*low*) hush NE.

make a murmuring sound murr NE.

not a murmur no a mum, no a smiach CAITHNESS, nae a myowt NE.

mush *noun* powsowdie, pronack.

reduce to mush (*eg food in a dish*) poach.

mushroom puddock stuil, puddock steel NE.

music muisic, meesick NE.

musician musicianer, musicker.

mussel (*large*) clabbydhu W; (*large freshwater*) horse-mussel SHETLAND, N.

mussel-bed mussel-scaup.

must *verb* maun, most SHETLAND, boost, buist, beest N.

must not mauna.

mustard 1 mustart. **2 wild mustard** *see* **charlock**.

musty foostie, fooshtie NE, foostit, fooshtit NE; (*specif of food*) auld-tastit, hoamt NE.

become musty moze SHETLAND, ORKNEY, CAITHNESS, dowe SHET-LAND, NE, foost, foosht NE.

mute *see* **dumb**.

mutilate *see also* **maim**; massacker, mittle, mar S, mank.

mutilated mankit.

mutter *verb, see also* **mumble, murmur**; mump, mum.

mutton (*from diseased sheep*) traik, (*from sheep which has died of braxy*) braxy (mutton), goniel S.

leg of mutton gigot.

mutual help giff-gaff.

muzzle *noun* mizzle, (*of an animal*) mull SHETLAND, ORKNEY.

verb mizzle.

my ma, mi SHETLAND, ORKNEY.

my own mine ain SHETLAND, NE.

myself masel, mysel.

mystery meesterie.

mysterious *see* **supernatural**.

N

nag[1] *see* **horse.**

nag[2] *verb, see also* **scold, criticize;** natter, nyatter NE: '*aye nyatterin on*', yatter, yap, yerp, n(y)arg SHETLAND, ORKNEY, CAITHNESS, antle, nip someone's heid; **nag at** haud at, threap at.

nagging *see also* **scolding;** natter, nyatter NE, yatter, yap, n(y)arg SHETLAND.

nail *noun, see also* **hobnail, bradnail;** (*large*) caddle NE, cathel; (*short thick*) stob (nail); (*headless*) blin(d) nail; (*used in flooring*) plensher (nail); (*joining axle to cart*) garron-nail, carron-nail, cannon-pin, cannon-nail S; (*fixing planks of clinker-built boat*) seam SHETLAND: '*seam an ruive*'; (*frostnail on horseshoe*) shairp.

naïve hielan(d): '*no sae hielan*'.

naked nakit, scuddie, in the scud.

state of nakedness (bare) scud(die).

name *noun, see also* **nickname;** nem, neem SHETLAND, ORKNEY, CAITHNESS; (*formal, as opposed to familiar*) Sunday name.

verb, see also **call;** nem, neem SHETLAND, ORKNEY, CAITHNESS.

person after whom you are named name faither, name mither.

nap *see also* **doze, snooze:** *noun* dover, dot, slug w, SW.

verb dwam (ower), dover (ower).

nape of the neck cuff o the neck, howe o the neck NE.

napkin *see also* **table napkin, nappy;** naipkin, neepyin.

nappy hippin, cloot.

narcissus lily.

nark *verb, see also* **nag**[2]**, scold;** yap, yerp.

narrow *adjective* nairra(e); (*of things*) sma.

- *noun* (*narrow stretch of water: see also* **strait**) hause ORKNEY.

narrowly near.

narrow-hipped lingel-tailt.

narrow-minded nippit, nairra-nebbit.

narrow part (*eg of an axle*) hause NE.

nasty nestie, naistie.

nasty-minded ill-thochtit.

nasty person skite.

national naitional.

native *adjective* (*belonging to, grown or made at home*) hamewart, hameart, hamel, (*to a place*) kin(d) SHETLAND.

native district cauf kintra.

natural naitral, kindly; (*plain, simple*) hameower.

natural death strae daith: '*a fair strae daith*'.

nature naitur.

naught nocht.

naughty coorse NE, ill-contriven SHETLAND, N, ill-trickit SHETLAND, ORKNEY, N.

naughty child *see also* **scamp, rascal;** wick.

nausea scunner, sta(w), ug NE, pya(u)vie N.

nauseate *see also* **disgust, sicken;** scunner, scomfish, set NE, ug, gar the hert rise; (*with too much food*) sta(w).

feel nauseated scunner, sta(w), skeichen NE, ug.

easily nauseated skeichen NE.

nauseating *see also* **disgusting;** scunnersome, scunnerfu, stawsome, fousome.

nauseous stawsome, walsh.

navel †ny(v)le SW.
  navelwort maid-in-the-mist SW, S.
navvy cley davy NE.
near *preposition* nar, nearaboot, aside, inby.
  adverb nar, nearaboot(s), aside.
  adjective nar, nearhan(d).
  nearer narrer; (*closer to the speaker*) nar.
  nearest narrest.
  nearby nar(by) NE, narhan(d), near-aboot(s).
  nearly *see also* **almost**; near, nar, near-by, nearhan(d), narhan(d), near-aboot(s), gey near, verra near.
  nearly (as good) as near.
  very nearly at the edge o, gey near, ver-ra near.
  be near neibour wi.
  near enough as near.
neat 1 nate; (*and small*) cantie; (*tidy: see also* **spruce**[1]) ticht, perjink, conceitie, snod, snog, nacketie, jeetie NE, faisible, dockie SW, fettle SW; (*specif of a person*) gentie, jimp; (*esp of women*) dink; (*esp in dress*) trig, gash, feat, spree; (*of places*) couthie. **2** (*of spirits*) nakit.
  neatly ticht, triglie, tosh, dinklie.
  neatly-made pretty SHETLAND, ORK-NEY, N.
  make neat *see also* **tidy**; snod (up), trig, doss NE.
  small neat person bodsie NE.
necessary necessar.
  necessaries necessars, needcessities.
  necessitate necessitat.
  necessity needcessitie, mister; (*un-avoidable*) maun-be.
neck craig, hause; (*of land*) hause ORK-NEY.
  -necked -craigit: '*lang-craigit*'.
  necktie owerlay.
  break the neck of neck.
  crane the neck rax the neck.
need *verb* (*lack*) want.
  noun, see **necessity**.
  needy needfu, scrimp, skybald NE.
  still in need of no oot o (the) need o.
  supply the needs of fettle (for):

'*She'll fettle for ye an mak yer den-ner*', see till.
  what need is there . . .? whit needs . . .?: '*Whit needs ye speak sae lood?*'
needle (*knitting: see also* **knit**) wire.
  needlecase (*small, pocket*) hussie.
  needlewoman shewster NE.
  needlework shewin, seam.
ne'er-do-well *see* **good-for-nothing**.
neglect *verb* negleck; (*overlook*) mislip-pen; (*treat badly*) misguide, mak a stap-bairn o.
  noun negleck.
  neglected disjaskit.
negligent *see also* **careless**; thriveless.
  act of negligence (*law*) quasi-delict.
negotiate: negotiation *see* **transac-tion**.
  difficult to negotiate (*of a bend etc*) kittle.
negro bleck.
neigh *verb, noun* nicher.
neighbour *noun* neibour, neiper NE; (*next-door*) door-neiper NE.
  neighbourhood neibourheid, pairt SHETLAND, ORKNEY, NE, roon(d).
  in the neighbourhood of *see* **near(ly)**.
  in this neighbourhood hereawa.
  neighbouring nearhan(d).
  neighbourly neibourlik(e).
  neighbourly relations neibourheid: '*guid neibourheid*'.
  neighbourliness neipert(r)ie NE.
  have as neighbour be neibours tae.
neither naither, naider SHETLAND, ORKNEY, NE, nane o the twa.
  conjunction naither, naider SHETLAND, ORKNEY, NE, nor.
  neither one nor the other hauf an atween, neither eechie nor ochie, neither buff nor stye.
nephew nevoy, oe; (*son of sister*) sis-ter('s)-son SHETLAND, ORKNEY; (*son of brother*) brither-sin.
nervous nervish, skeer(ie), aff (o) yer eggs, timorsome, skeichen NE; (*of a horse*) startie.

nervousness (*state of*) swither.
be very nervous be sittin on preens, be lik(e) a hen on a het girdle.
nest *noun* est s; (*wasps' etc*) byke, boick NE.
nestling *noun* younker, gorb, gorblin NE, gorbel, scud(d)ie w, get sw, s, goggie *child's word*.
nestle coorie (in), hiddle NE.
net *noun* (*fishing: bag-shaped, of various kinds*) poke(-net); (*seine-net*) trawl; (*scoop-net*) scum(min) net; (*drawn to catch fish*) draucht net; (*suspended between two boats to form a circular sweep*) ring-net; (*suspended in water, into which fish are driven by splashing*) splash-net; (*small seine, used to fish sea bottom*) screenge net; (*closest to the side of a boat*) buird N; (*first cast after the buoy*) powe net; (*furthest from boat*) tail-net SHETLAND, CAITHNESS; (*small circular, used in crab-fishing and salmon-poaching*) rippie NE; (*salmon-net between shore and boat*) toot-net; (*stocking-shaped, to force out fish from riverbanks*) powt net; (*bag-shaped, to catch esp salmon as tide ebbs*) halve-net sw.
verb (*catch with a net*) mask SHETLAND, ORKNEY, CAITHNESS; (*herring*) mast.
set of nets (*from a single boat*) fleet.
nettle jennie nettle, jaggie nettle, jobbie nettle; (*of various kinds*) day nettle.
neuter *verb*, *see also* **castrate**; (*a cat*) dress.
neutrality (*in children's games*) *see* **truce.**
never nivver.
nevertheless *see also* **however**; still an on, hoo an a(w) be, fra'at NE, whitivver.
never a . . . deil a . . ., fient a . . .
never mind never heed, nivver leet.
a time that never comes nevermas(s).
new (*completely: see also* **brand-new**) split-new CENTRAL, spleet-new SHETLAND, ORKNEY, N.
newly new, newlins.

newcomer *see* **incomer.**
newfangled new-farran(t) NE.
New Year's Day Ne'er(s)day.
New Year's Eve Hogmanay, Ne'er('s) Even, †singin een.
New Year gift (*esp of food or drink*) Ne'erday: '*We'll gie ye yer Ne'erday*'.
first Monday in the New Year (*on which gifts were given*) Handsel Monday.
(be) the first visitor in the New Year first fit: 'we're gaun first-fittin'; '*He wis oor first fit*'.
news uncos, speirins, hearin SHETLAND, knittins NE, wittins; (*news in advance*) moyen NE: '*get a moyen o*'; (*piece of surprising news*) ferlie.
local newspaper the squeak *humorous*.
stale news, old news caul(d) kail het again, piper's news, fiddler's news, cadger's news.
tell your news gie yer crack: '*gie's yer crack*'.
newt ask, mankeeper.
next nixt, neist; (*of days of week*) first: '*Monday first*'.
next but one (*of days of week*) next: '*Monday next*'.
nib (*of a pen*) neb.
nibble *verb* moup, chattle, nattle, smacher; (*half-heartedly*) smurl; (*of an animal: graze*) pike, nip; (*gnaw*) chittle sw; (*like a young animal*) mattle; (*like a rabbit or sheep*) map; (*like a rabbit*) mump.
nice clivver; (*sympathetic*) innerlie s.
to a nicety tae a shavin.
nick: in the nick of time at the clippin time NE.
nick-nack *see* **knick-knack.**
nickname tee-name NE, eik-name.
niece (*daughter of a brother*) britherdochter.
niggard *see also* **miser**; niggar, nipscart.
niggardly *see also* **mean**[1], **miserly, stingy, avaricious**; nippit, nippie, scrimp.

become niggardly wratch.

nigger neeger.

night nicht, mirk.

nightcap (*hat: see also* cap) nicht mutch ORKNEY; (*type of*) pirnie-cap S; (*large, worn by old women*) hoomet.

nightfall mirkin, sky-set(tin), day-set.

nightgown goon(ie).

nightingale nichtingale.

nightjar fern owl.

last night yestreen, the streen ORKNEY, N.

the night before last erethestreen.

middle of the night *see also* midnight; riggin o the nicht NE; (*dead of night*) mirk nicht.

pass the night nicht.

nimble *see also* agile, active; nimmle, knackie, gleg, licht-set, swack, snack(ie) NE, swipper, kim NE, leish SW, S, whippie, waul; (*of animals*) spankie.

nimbly soople, swipper NE.

nine: ninth nint.

nineteenth nineteen(t).

ninepins kyles; (*as played at fairs*) rowlie-powlie.

group of nine ninesome.

nip *verb* (*eg a finger in a door*) sneck, chack, check; nip off (*eg leaves*) stoo SHETLAND, NE.

noun nib.

nippy nebbie.

nipple tit.

nit (*louse-egg*) neet.

no *adjective, adverb* nae.

negative reply na(w).

no one *see* nobody.

no fear (of) nae frichts (o).

not take no for an answer tak nae na(e)-say.

say no (to) na-say: '*He'll no can na-say ye*'.

noble †thane.

nobody naebodie.

nod: nodding (*repeatedly, as when dozing*) (nid) nid noddin.

nod off dover (ower).

node (*eg in a plant stem*) knot.

noise *see also* sound[2], clatter, rattle, rumble; (*din*) dirdum, yammer, brain NE, dindee NE, reemis(h) NE, bellum; (*repeated*) ruddie; (*loud, rattling*) blatter; (*sharp cracking or clicking*) knack ORKNEY, NE; (*of children playing*) squalloch NE.

noisy roarie.

move (about) noisily breenge.

talk noisily blatter.

annoy with noise deave.

make a loud noise yammer, mineer NE; (*repeatedly*) ruddie.

make a sharp cracking noise knack.

nominate (*to a list of candidates*) leet.

nondescript orra, peelie-wersh.

none *see also* not any; nane.

nonentity *see also* insignificant; roun(d) O, ceepher, vision, wunner, peek NE, wiffer-waffer NE, shurf S, yaff, nyaff.

nonplus *see also* bewilder, dumbfound, perplex; raivel, fickle, dumfoutter NE.

be nonplussed (*eg after a snub*) whustle on yer thoum.

nonsense blethers, bletheration, haiver(s), clavers, (buff an) styte, raible, troke SHETLAND, N, stoit ORKNEY, CAITHNESS, NE, clytach NE, gyter NE; nonsense! blethers!, haivers!, hoot awa!, hoot(s) toot(s)!, toots!, fine day!

nonsensical haiverin, gyte.

talk nonsense haiver, blether, slaver, rhyme, gyper NE, gutter, roiter W.

non-traveller *see* traveller.

nook neuk.

nooks and crannies creeks an corners NE.

noon *see also* midday; nuin, neen N, twaloors.

noose *noun* kinch, mink N, fank.

nor yet neit NE.

normal kindly, warldlik(e), (*esp of a newborn baby*) weel an warldlik(e), lik(e) the warl(d).

normally for ordinar.

north nor-, heich SW.

northerly norlin S.

most northerly normost.

northern norlan(d).

northern lights merry dancers SHETLAND, ORKNEY, N, pretty dancers N.

northwards northart SHETLAND, ORKNEY, NE, norlins SHETLAND, ORKNEY.

north of benorth.

person from the north norlan(d).

nose *noun* neb, nob, snotterbox, snoot *contemptuous*, grunyie *contemptuous*, niz *humorous*, cooter *humorous*, N, snubbert *humorous*, NE, wulk *humorous*: '*pick yer wulk*'.

verb **nose about** snoke.

-nosed -nebbit: '*lang-nebbit*'; '*reid-nebbit*'.

nosy nebbie, lang-nebbit.

nosy person neb.

nosebag (*horse's*) mou-bag, mou-poke.

lead by the nose lead by the neb.

speak *or* **breathe through the nose** sneevil.

nostril nosethirl SHETLAND, N.

not no, nae.

not any nae, nane, nae neen NE, deil a, fient a.

not at all nane: '*she can sing nane*'.

not a thing *see* nothing at all.

not counting leave aside.

certainly not! *see* certain.

notable namely, markit, weel-kent.

notary †writer, †notar.

notch *noun* natch, nitch SHETLAND, ORKNEY, N, gneck NE, sneck; (*esp on an animal's horn*) nick; (*on blade*) lip, (*slanting, on wood*) skair.

verb natch, sneck; (*a blade*) lip.

note *noun* **1** (*musical: see also* grace-note) (*esp as written*) spatril; (*shrill, intermittent, esp of a bird*) wheeple. **2** (*short letter*) scrape o the pen; (*explaining a child's absence from school; from a doctor, confirming illness*) line.

verb **note down** mark.

noted namelie.

notebook (*school*) jotter.

notepad scroll ORKNEY, NE.

noteworthy parteec(u)lar.

take note tak tent.

nothing naethin, nocht, nowt S.

nothing at all fient a(w), deil a haet, neither hint nor hair NE, naither gear nor guid NE.

notice *verb* tak tent; **not notice** no goam.

noun (*attention*) tent.

take notice of leuk efter NE; (*take an interest in*) leuk the gate o, see till.

notion norie S.

notorious notour.

nought *see* nothing.

nourish *see also* feed; nourice, mait.

nourishment *see also* food; fushion.

badly-nourished ill-thriven, shargart NE.

looking well-nourished lik(e) yer mait.

novel *adjective* new-farran(t) NE.

noun novelle.

novelty newfangle, newin, unco; (*esp in dress*) kick; (*curiosity*) ferlie.

now noo; (*just now*) the noo, eenoo, presently, this weather: '*Hoo are ye this weather?*'

nowadays nooadays, thir days.

now and again ilka sae lang.

now and then noo(s) an than(s), noo an aan NE, whiles, files N, filies N, puckles NE.

nowhere nae place, naewey.

noxious hurtsome, ill, pooshionous.

nude *see* naked.

nudge *verb* nidge, nodge, dunch, putt.

noun nidge, nodge, dunch, shog, putt.

nuisance provoke, scunner, fash, vex, bucker NE, humbug NE, deavance, sta(w); (*specif a person*) sorra; (*esp ingratiating*) plaister.

null: (*law*) **making null and void** irritant: '*irritant clause*' = clause in an agreement which does this (if something is done against its terms).

nullification (*of a deed*) irritancy.

nullify irritate.

numb

numb (*without feeling*) taibetless, fushionless NE, dowf.

number *noun, verb* nummer.

considerable number guid few, hantle, (gey) wheen, sort S.

large number *see also* **crowd**; heap,
vast, feck, whack, thrang, hullock N,
mardle NE, hirst NE, threave, fleesh NE;
(*of fish*) bodie.

numerous lairge NE, thrang.

nurse *noun* (*child's, wet-nurse*) nourice
literary.
verb (*tend*) cuiter, notice, sort NE; (*with
excessive care*) soss NE.

nurture fess up NE.

nut nit; (*without a kernel*) deef nit; (*ripe*)
leamer SW, S.

nuzzle snoozle.

O

oaf *see also* **lout, boor**; sumph: '*ye muckle sumph*', nowt, fleep ORKNEY, N.

oak *see also* **bog oak**; aik.

oak stake speeach.

oar air.

oats aits, yits, corn, haver; (*potato-oat*) tattie-aits; (*kind of black*) shiak(s).

oaten aiten.

oatcake aitcake, bannock, kyaak (o breid) NE, scone SHETLAND; (*usu triangular, fourth part of a round*) farl, fardel, quarter NE; (*small, thick*) fole ORKNEY; (*circular*) roon(d)-aboot, (*notched*) nickie; (*baked for Shrove Tuesday*) †sautie bannock; oatcakes breid N, cakes NE, kyaaks NE; (*thin*) gnap(-at)-the-win NE; (*made with cream*) ream breid NE; (*crumbled in milk*) milk an breid.

oat-grass (*false*) swine('s) arnit.

oatmeal 1 meal, male, white meal, haver-meal SW, S, blaw *tinkers' cant*, NE, (*coarsely-ground*) pinheid (oat)meal, roon(d) meal NE. 2 (*oatmeal dishes: see also* **porridge**) (*with boiling water*) brose: '*kail brose*' = brose made with liquid from boiled kail; (*mixed with hot water, for chickenfeed*) daich; (*with cold water*) crowdie, drammock, cauld steer(ie) N; (*with hot milk or water, forming lumps*) knotty tam(s) N; (*with cream*) cream crowdie, crannachan; (*with cream or buttermilk*) foorach NE; (*with cream and whey*) froh milk NE; (*fine meal steeped with oat husks and then boiled*) sowans, (*eaten raw*) rawsins NE; (*oatmeal fried in fat*) mealie-creeshie, creeshie-mealie ANGUS, (*with onions*) skirlie.

oatmeal container meal kist, girnel.

oatmeal pudding white puddin, mea-

lie puddin, (mealie) jimmie.

oath *see* **swear-word**; aith.

obedient bowsome.

obey (*law: esp a court order*) obtemper.

object *noun, verb* objeck.

objection pleen.

what objection do you have (to)? whit ails ye (at)?

objectionable *see also* **nasty, disagreeable**; scunnersome.

oblige obleege.

obligation obleegement, tie, common; (*law: limiting an owner's use of property*) servitude.

be under an obligation fa(w) SHETLAND, hae a day in hairst, be in the reverence (o).

bind by a moral obligation thirl.

obliged bunsucken NE.

obliging helplie, bowsome.

oblique squint, sklent, skave, sidelins.

obliquely squint, agley, (a)sklent, sidelins.

move obliquely sklent, skew NE.

obliqueness gleytness NE.

obliterate disannul SHETLAND, ORKNEY, N, smore NE.

obnoxious ill-faured.

obscene (*esp of language*) randie, groff, ruch.

obscenity sculdudderie.

obscure *adjective* mirk, dern; (*puzzling*) kittlie.

verb smoor.

obsequious sleekit, sleek(ie), lick-lip, inhaudin, inbearin NE.

be obsequious *see also* **curry favour**; beenge.

observe leuk till SHETLAND, NE, see at NE.

observant tentie.

observation observe.

obsess: be obsessed with (*a person's virtues etc*) no be able tae see past *or* by.

obstacle stick SHETLAND.

obstinate *see also* **stubborn, perverse**; thrawn, dour, positive, (ill-)set, contermacious, maroonjous NE, stickin, unbowsome S.

obstinately rizzon *or* nane NE.

obstreperous *see also* **unruly, wild**; radge, ramstam, maroonjous NE, tousie.

obstruct *see also* **hinder**; mar, stap, pester; (*a water channel etc*) gurge up.

obstruction hinder, mar.

remove obstructions from redd.

obtain *see also* **get**; obteen.

obvious as plain as parritch, kenable SHETLAND, NE.

occasion 1 *see also* **opportunity**; tid. **2** (*need*) use: '*there was nae use for it*'.

occasional *see also* **rare**; antrin, orra, drappit NE, daimen, happenin S.

occasionally *see also* **now and then**; at a time, puckles NE, at the edge o a time, whiles, files NE.

mark a special occasion (*eg with a gift*) handsel.

occupy occupee.

occupied (*busy*) fest NE.

occupied with in han(s) wi, on the heid o.

occur: occur to glance (up)on.

occur to you come up yer humph.

ocean tide, dub *humorous*.

odd *adjective* **1** *see also* **occasional, unmatched**; orra. **2** *see also* **strange**; parteec(u)lar, unco.

oddity (*thing or person*) queerie, magink, ferlie, (*person*) jigger.

odd jobs jots NE, jotterie.

odd-job man orraman, jotter.

odd-looking person *see also* **oddity**; ticket, track NE, munsie NE, shape SW, S; (*esp overdressed woman*) Teenie fae Troon, Teenie fae the neeps E CENTRAL.

odd person queerie.

odds and ends orras, orrals, clattertraps, troke, trantles.

odour *see also* **smell**; (*slight*) waff.

of o; often omitted in Sc in expressions of quantity: '*a drap milk*'; '*a bit breid*'.

off *adverb* aff, oaf.

preposition aff (o).

adjective (*of food etc*) *see* **mouldy** (*under* **mould¹**), **rotten**.

off your head *see also* **insane, mad**; aff at the heid, oot o yer heid, aff (at) the knot.

offal emmledeug, emmlins NE.

offend offen, pet, miscomfit NE, misfit NE, tramp on someone's taes.

take offence *see also* **sulk**; tak the gee, tak the rue; (*quickly*) flee up, fung NE.

offended struntit.

be offended at something tak something ill oot.

offender (*esp against church discipline*) fauter.

seat where offenders against church discipline sat to be rebuked †stuil of repentance, †repentin stuil.

offensive ill-faured.

offer *verb* (*esp insistently*) bode NE.

noun bode.

offhand affluif, jack-easy.

office offish.

officer offisher.

official offeecial.

officious offeecious, inbearin NE.

be very officious (about) ride on the riggin (o).

offset (*building: on a wall*) intak.

offshore (*of wind*) ooterlie SHETLAND.

offspring bairn, wean, geet NE, get *contemptuous*.

often af(t)en, aft *literary*.

ogle †blink.

ogre etin.

ogress gyre carline.

oil ile, uilie, eelie NE.

verb ile, uilie, creesh.

oily 1 *see also* **greasy**; ilie, glittie. **2** (*of* a *person*: *see also* **obsequious**) sleekit, slid.

oilcan (*small, with spout*) poorie.

oilcloth wax cloth.

oil jar uilie pig SHETLAND.

oil lamp eelie dolly NE; (*with rush wick*) cruisie, collie SHETLAND, ORKNEY.

ointment eyntment, saw.

old *see also* **aged, elderly**; auld, aul, owld SHETLAND, ORKNEY, N, ARGYLL, ULSTER; (*very*) tike-aul(d) NE; (*physically*) auld i the horn.

   oldest (*in a family*) aul(d): '*auld brither*'.

   old age eild.

   old-fashioned auld-farran(t), auld warld.

   old-fashioned little girl grannie mutch(ie).

   old-fashioned-looking woman Auntie Beenie.

   old maid maiden NE, wanter.

   die an old maid die lik(e) Jenkin's hen.

   old-maidish primsie.

   old man bodach *often contemptuous,* CAITHNESS, HIGHLAND.

   old woman cailleach HIGHLAND, N, W, ULSTER, grannie mutch(ie), luckie: '*Luckie Broon*', deem NE, carline *contemptuous*, heuk *contemptuous*, NE, kail-runt *contemptuous*.

   grow old turn ower in years, weir doon (the brae), gang doon the hill.

   not make old bones (*not reach old age*) no claw an auld man's heid.

omen *see also* **portent**; warnin, freit; (*esp of death*) forego.

   ominous uncannie.

   of bad omen uncannie.

   of good omen cannie, sonsie.

omentum (*of an animal*) wab.

omit (*not to take into account*) hip.

   omission (*intentional*) pass-ower.

on in, o; (*along*) awa: '*come awa tae yer bed*'.

once aince, yince E CENTRAL, wance W, eence SHETLAND, ORKNEY, NE.

at once *see* **immediately**.

   once or twice a time or twa.

one ane, yin CENTRAL, S, wan W, SW; (*mainly emphatic*) ae SHETLAND, ORKNEY, N, E CENTRAL: '(*the*) ae wey', yae CENTRAL, S; (*in children's rhymes*) eentie, eendie.

   one after another efter ither.

   one another ither, ilk ither.

   the one and only wha but he.

   the one . . . the other . . . *see* **other**.

   all of one kind sic mannie sic horsie NE, eeksie-peeksie.

   oneself yersel.

   by oneself yer lane.

   to oneself (*in a whisper*) intae yersel.

onion *see also* **spring onion**; ingan.

   onion leaves tails.

only (*child*) ae SHETLAND, ORKNEY, N, E CENTRAL, yae CENTRAL, S: '*oor ae bairn*'.

   only child bird-alane.

onset onding, (*esp of an illness*) oncome S.

onslaught onding.

onward *see* **forward**.

ooze *see also* **leak**: *verb* weeze, sip, sype; (*of a wound etc*) teicher.

   noun seep, sype, glaur; (*from a wound etc*) glit.

   oozings sypins.

opah Jerusalem haddie.

open *adjective* apen, wuppen S; (*of a door: partly*) ajee, (*wide*) wide tae the wa; (*of land*) plain; (*of weather*) fresh.

   verb, see also **reopen**; apen, wuppen S; (*a bag etc, to search*) gae intae.

   opening (*gap*) open NE; (*eg in a wall*) slap, (*small*) bole; (*gateway*) gate slap; (*in a wood*) glack; (*esp between threads in a loom*) shed; (*in clouds*) (blue) bore NE, (*foretelling better weather*) Meg's hole.

   openly fair.

   do something openly dae something at the kirk door.

   in(to) the open air furth.

   stare open-mouthed gype.

   be wide open (*of a door*) stan(d) tae

the wa, be wide tae the wa SHETLAND, ORKNEY, NE.

opinion opeenion, braith, consait NE, souch; (*strongly held*) threap: '*stan tae yer threap*'.

have a good opinion of yourself hae a guid consait o yersel, think yersel nae sma drink, think yersel nae sheep shank.

have an unfavourable opinion of hae nae broo o, hae an ill broo o.

my *etc* **own opinion** ma *etc* ain think NE.

opponent unfreen(d).

opportune timeous, i the tid.

opportunity (*chance*) inlat, cast NE, kep, dunt SHETLAND, sklent; (*unexpected*) kinch; (*scope*) scowth; (*favourable time*) tid.

oppose (*contradict*) conter, contrair; ca(w) again; (*thwart*) thorter, thraw (wi); (*withstand*) gainstand.

opposed contrair.

opposite *adjective* opposeet, conter(gates) N.

preposition forenent, foregain, anent.

noun **the opposite** the opposeet, the contrair, the conter N.

opposition opposeetion, haud-again.

in opposition to conter.

oppress haud doon, owergang, ool.

oppressed hauden-doon, doon-hadden, ill-hauden, sair made, pingelt; (*by heat*) muith.

oppressive gurthie, sair.

oppressively hot and humid muith(ie), glorgie AYRSHIRE.

optician opteecian.

opulent *see* **rich, wealthy**.

orange *see also* **segment**; oranger.

orchid (*wild, esp heath spotted*) balderrie; (*spotted*) puddock's spindle.

ordain ordeen.

ordeal throu-the-mill, throu-come SHETLAND, NE, handlin.

order *verb* (*goods etc*) speak; (*in advance*) tryst; (*order drinks*) ca(w).

noun (*orderliness*) ranter N.

orderly *see* **tidy**.

orderliness *see* **noun**.

in order that till.

in good order in gweed reel NE, weel redd.

keep in order haud in aboot, keep in aboot, pit the hems on.

put in order *see also* **tidy**; redd (up), sort, snod, see till.

out of order (*out of control*) oot o theat NE; (*not working*) nae jaikin NE.

ordinary ordinar, ornar; (*of a person*) raploch.

ordinarily ordinar, for ord(i)nar.

ordinary person a scone o the day's bakin.

no ordinary person nae ilka bodie.

organ (*musical*) kist o whustles.

organically sound hert-hale.

organ-gallery (*in church*) organ-loft.

internal organs intimmers *humorous*, harigals.

organize guide.

origin (*descent*) oreeginal NE.

original *adjective* oreeginal.

noun (*of a document*) principal.

resembling the original (*of a picture etc*) vieve.

the true original the real Mackay.

ornament *noun, see also* **decoration, gewgaw**; affset, ootset, whigmaleerie, tirlie-whirlie, variorum; (*esp spiral or fancy*) whirligig.

verb, see also **decorate, trim**; (*fancifully*) fineer; (*with a chequered pattern*) dice; (*with a knitted border*) pearl.

ornamental wallie CENTRAL, S; '*wallie dugs*'.

ornamental flourish (*in handwriting*) pirlicue, squirl.

ornate fantoosh.

orphan orphant.

ostentation bladrie, swash.

ostentatious *see also* **boastful, proud**; palaverin, swashie N, prinkie ORKNEY, N, braggie.

(piece of) ostentatious behaviour palaver.

other ither, idder SHETLAND, NE, aither.

   the other the tither, the tidder SHETLAND, NE.

   the one . . . the other . . . the tane . . . the tither . . ., the teen . . . the tidder . . . NE.

   otherwise itherwise, idderwise SHETLAND, NE, ithergates, ither-roads, else, ense.

   at other times itherwhiles.

ought ocht, boost.

   ought rather to hae mair need tae.

ounce unce.

our oor, (*unstressed*) wir, wur, (*stressed*) weer NE.

   ourselves oorsels, wirsels.

   ourselves (alone) oor lane, wir lane.

out *see also* **outer;** oot.

   out and out ringin, main, polist, sevendle, evendoon.

   out of *see also* **outside;** oot (o), ooten; (*a door etc*) oot at.

   out of doors *see also* **outdoor;** ootby, oot aboot, ootwith NE, oot ower the door, on the street(s), furth.

   out of hand *see* **out of control** (*under* **control**).

   out of place misbehadden.

   out of sorts *see also* **ailing;** oorlich, nae a(w)fu weel.

   out of the way *see also* **outlying;** oot the gate, (faur) oot the road, (faur) oot aboot.

outbuildings (*of a farm*) (*ferm*) stead-in, mains, e hooses NE.

outburst eruction, erumption, gowster; (*esp of noise*) onding; (*eg of oaths*) goller; (*of rage*) rampage, fuff, flist NE; (*of emotion etc*) spate; (*of weeping*) blirt.

outcast *see also* **fugitive;** ootlan(d).

outcome upcome.

outcry *see also* **fuss, commotion, uproar;** sang, yammer, scronach NE, machreach NE, dirdum.

   make a great outcry yammer, scronach NE.

outdo *see* **surpass.**

outdoor *see also* **out of doors** (*under* **out**); oot aboot NE, ootby.

outer ooter; (*esp of the outer room of a cottage*) but N, FIFE.

   outer room (*esp of a two-roomed cottage*) but, but-the-hoose N, but-en(d); (*reached by a separate door*) oot-room.

outfit graithin.

outflow (*steady gush*) stour NE.

outgoing (*of a person*) *see* **friendly.**

outing veage EDINBURGH, vaige SHETLAND, oot aboot NE.

outlandish haithen.

outlaw: outlaws ootlins; (*in the Highlands and Borders*) †broken men.

   proclaim as an outlaw †put to the horn.

outlay ootgang.

outlet ootlat.

outline *noun* (*of a story etc*) rinnin NE.

   in outline only (*sketchy*) stake an rice.

outlive ootleeve.

outlying ootby, oot SHETLAND, ORKNEY: '*oot isles*', ootwith NE.

   outlying land ootlan(d); (*of a farm, before enclosures etc*) †ootfield; (*outlying piece*) ootlie NE.

output throu-pit.

outrageous maroonjous NE, heronious AYRSHIRE.

outright ootricht, richt oot, plat an plain SHETLAND.

outset affset.

   at the outset in the mou o the poke.

outside *adverb* ootside, ootwith NE; (*out-of-doors*) ootby, ootins, furth SHETLAND, NE; (*after an illness*) ower the door: '*He's no been ower the door for a week*'.

   preposition furth; (*beyond*) outwith, furth o(f) *now law, literary and* NE.

   outsiders the fremd, the fremmit.

   go outside (*esp out of the house after illness*) leuk ower the door.

outskirts: on the outskirts of ootby: '*ootby the toon*'.

outsmart win ahin NE, grip NE; (*esp in bargaining*) nip SW.

outspoken *see also* **blunt**; tongue-be-trusht NE.

outstanding sad NE, by-or(di)nar, past or(di)nar.

outstanding thing *or* **person** *or* **animal** bummer, beezer.

outwards ootby, ootwith NE, ootwan.

outwit raivel SHETLAND, ORKNEY, N, begowk, begunk.

ouzel *see* **ring ouzel**.

ovary egg-bed; (*of a fowl*) lay bag, lay p(y)ock SHETLAND, NE.

oven ovven, une.

over *preposition* ower, oot ower, †atour. *adverb* ower; (*past*) by: '*when the holidays are by*'; (*of a meeting etc*) oot.

over and above forby, atour *law*.

over and done with by wi, by-han(d) N.

over the top of, over to the other side of oot ower.

over the way owerby.

overall *noun* carsackie; (*esp household*) wrapper; (*for dirty work*) slug.

over-anxious: be over-anxious rack SW, S.

overawe coonger, daunton.

overbalance cowp.

cause to overbalance ca(w) ower, ca(w) the feet fae.

overbearing ringin.

overburdened *see also* **harassed**; tra(u)chelt.

overcast owercast, loorie, hingin.

overcharge saut.

overcoat muckle coat, big coat, jockie coat.

overcome *verb, see also* **defeat**; owercome, bang, warsle, waur, win abuin SHETLAND, NE, gang ower ORKNEY, NE.

adjective, see also **exhausted**; (*esp with drink*) owertaen.

overcooked (*of meat*) sair duin, gey weel deen N.

overdressed fantoosh.

overdue ahin(t) the han(d).

overeating gutsin; (*bout of*) guzzle.

over-excited raised, dementit, ree, yiv-verin NE.

overflow *verb, see also* **flood, spill**; skail, ream ower, owergae, juitle SW, lipper.

water which overflows ground fleet water.

overgrown (*of ground*) grown-up; (*of crops*) prood SHETLAND, N.

overhang owerhing.

overheads (*mining*) oncost.

overlook *see also* **neglect**; owerleuk; (*neglect*) mislippen.

over-particular jinipperous NE, fykie.

overpower *see also* **defeat, overcome**; ower-pooer, owergae SHETLAND, NE, win N.

over-precise perjink.

overrate owerrate.

overreach ower-rax.

over-refined prick-ma-dentie.

overrun *verb* ower-rin, owergae. *adjective* hoatchin, hotchin: '*the hoose is hoatchin wi mice*'.

oversee owersee.

overseer (*on a farm*) grieve; (*esp at potato harvest*) tattie-swinger; (*in a mine*) owersman.

oversleep sleep in.

overstep owerstap N.

overtake owertak; (*catch up with*) mak up on, tak in NE; (*excel*) mak by.

overtax *see* **overwork**.

overthrow *verb* owerthraw, whummle, ding doon.

overtime by-hours NE.

overturn *verb* cowp, owercowp, whummle, kilt, heeld SHETLAND, ORKNEY, keel.

easily overturned cogglie.

overturning cowp, whummle.

overweening *see* **arrogant**.

overwhelmed *see* **overworked**.

overwork *verb* (*cause to work too much*) hash, stress, tirraneese NE, hatter S.

overworked *see also* **harassed**;

tra(u)chelt, sair hauden doon by the bubbly jock.

owe awe, yaw NE, aucht, ya(u)cht NE, be due: '*He's due me wages*'.

owing owe: '*he's owe me £5*'.

owing to wi: '*Wi the rain we hid tae cancel the barbecue*'.

owl hoolet, ool SHETLAND, NE, oolet; (*barn owl*) white hoolet; (*long-eared owl*) hornie hoolet.

own *verb* awn, awe, yaw NE, aucht, ya(u)cht NE.

adjective ain: '*it's ma ain hoose*'.

owner awner; (*law: of the fee simple of a property*) fiar.

ownership aucht: '*in yer aucht*'.

of my *etc* **own** o ma *etc* ain(s).

own up to haud wi.

who owns . . .? wha's aucht . . .?, wha is awe . . .?, fa echt . . .? NE.

ox *see also* **bullock**; owse, nowt NE; (*castrated incompletely or when fully grown*) shag N.

oxen owsen.

ox-bow, ox-collar brecham, (owsen-)bow.

ox-eye daisy *see* **daisy**.

oyster †oo *only in Edinburgh street cry*: '*Caller oo!*' = fresh oysters.

oyster-catcher sea-pyot, reid-neb NE, skirlie-wheeter NE, shalder SHETLAND, ORKNEY, pleep, mussel-picker.

P

pace *noun* 1 (*step*) pass, spang. 2 (*speed*) raik; (*steady*) jundie; (*quick*) steek AN-GUS: '*at sic a steek*'.
verb, see also **measure**; pass; (*hither and thither*) reenge, snodge SE.
keep pace with haud up wi, keep tack till, keep steeks wi SW, S, keep tee till NE.
keep the pace up keep the puddin het.
at a quick, steady pace lik(e) a mill sheelin.
pacify *see also* **soothe**; pecifee, cowshin NE, dill.
pack *verb, see also* **stuff**; stap; (*full, tightly*) pang; (*herring in ice*) fresh.
noun, see **bundle**.
packed (*of a room etc*) stowed (oot).
group packed together parrock NE.
pack-saddle (*of a pad of straw etc*) shee-mach N, †sunk; (*wooden*) clibber SHET-LAND, ORKNEY.
pack-thread skeenie.
packed lunch piece(-denner), denner-piece, nacket SW, S, chit.
packed-lunch box piece box.
pack of cards pair o cairds.
pad *noun* (*piece of padding*) pluff.
paddle *verb* paidle.
paddock *noun* parroch SE.
paid *past tense of* **pay** peyed.
paid in advance forehandit, fordel N; (*of rent*) forehan(d).
put paid to something gie something its soorldab.
pail *see also* **tub, bucket**; cog, bowie: '*milk bowie*'; (*wooden, esp for water*) stowp.
pain *noun* 1 bide NE; (*sharp: see also* **stitch**) steek, steenge, catch; (*sudden,*

sharp) twang, (*as of a sting*) stang; (*sharp throb*) stoun(d); **sharp pains** (*esp in the bowels*) grups; (*attack of, esp in childbirth*) shour; (*in back etc from stooping*) hurdie-caikle. 2 (*trouble*) fash; (*grief*) hert-sair.
painful sair; (*of a blow, wound*) suckie.
painful injury sair yin.
painfully sair.
causing pain sair (on): '*it's sair on the back*'.
exclamation expressing pain oh-ya!, it-ye! NE.
take pains fash.
paint *noun, verb* pent.
painted pentit.
paintwork pent.
lick of paint slairie; (*rough*) cleeroch NE.
pair *noun* perr, twasome, twaesome.
one of a pair neibour, marrow: '*Thae gloves are nae marrows*'.
an incongruous pair (the) gowk an (the) titlin.
pal *see* **friend**.
palace pailace.
palate: palatable suppable.
delight the palate gust (the gab).
palaver *see* **fuss**.
pale *adjective* whitely; (*wan, tinged with blue or green*) haw N; (*brownish*) fyaachie N; (*of a person*) peelie-wallie, paewae, gowstie, gash *literary*; (*gaunt*) pickit(-lik(e)).
made pale blaikent.
paling pailin.
paling post pailin stob, pailin stucken SE.
palisade †peel.
pall *noun* (*over coffin*) mortclaith.

pallid *see also* **pale**; palie, peelie-wallie, paewae, pickit(-lik(e)).

palm (*of the hand*) luif, liv NE.

palpitate flaff(er), dunt, flichter, gowp.

palpitation dunt.

paltry fouterie, sober NE, waff, nae wirth.

pamper *see also* **spoil**; cuiter (up), daut, browden on, dossach wi NE, fraik, pettle S; (*esp a child*) waste, fortifee NE; cock (someone) up (with something); **pamper yourself** socher.

pampered leepit N, peppint NE, finger-fed; (*of an animal*) fence-fed NE.

pan *noun* (*flat, iron*) tillie-pan NE, (*small, shallow, long-handled*) pingle-pan.

pancake English pancake; NB *in Sc refers to a small round cake of thickish batter baked on a girdle etc, also known as a* dropped scone, screever, bannock NE.

singed *or* **burnt in the pan** sitten-on, sung.

pancreas (*esp of a sheep*) breeds NE.

pane (*of glass*) peen, lozen.

panelling *see* **wainscoting**.

pang stang, stoun(d), twang; (*specif of pain*) thraw, (*esp in childbirth*) shour; (*specif of emotion*) rug.

panic *noun* swither, pirr SHETLAND, ORKNEY, NE, pilget NE, panshit NE.

pannier packet NE; (*esp for manure, earth*) hut SW; (*straw*) cassie SHETLAND, ORKNEY, N.

pant *verb* pech, hechle, stech, fob NE: '*fobbin lik a fat kittlin*', blast NE, fesh, thock S.
noun pech.

pantry aumrie.

paper (*brown, for wrapping*) gray paper SHETLAND, ORKNEY, N.

paper bag poke: '*piece poke*', pyock N.

parade parawd.

paralyse paraleese.

paralysis *see also* **stroke**; paraleesis, the pairls S.

paralysed blastit, palie, pairlt S.

parapet (*of a bridge*) parpen, ravel.

paraphernalia orders, trock N.

parasite *see also* **scrounger**; (*person*) eat-mait NE, gie's-a-piece.

act as a parasite sorn.

parboil leep.

parboiling leep: '*gie it a leep*'.

parcel *noun* paircel; (*clumsy*) dudgit NE.
verb paircel.

parch birsle.

parched drouchtit, gizzen.

pare white, fite NE, skive; (*surface soil from land*) skin, scaup; (*turf from ground*) fla(u)chter, flaw, flae, tirr.

paring *noun* (*eg of cheese*) scruiffin.

parent pawrent.

parish pairish.

parishioner pareeshioner.

parish church †muckle kirk.

park pairk, perk.

park-keeper, (public) park attendant parkie.

parliament: member of parliament parliamenter.

parlour room, chaumer, spence.

paroxysm (*esp of rage*) rapture.

parrot papingo *now literary, or of a representation of a parrot used as an archery target*.

parry kep.

parsimonious *see also* **stingy, avaricious, mean**[1]**, miserly**; ticht, scrimp, nippit, grippie.

part *noun* pairt; (*share*) dale; (*one of two unequal parts*) half.
verb pairt, twin(e), sinder (wi); **part** (*a person*) **from** spean fae; (*hair etc*) shed, split.

parting (*in hair etc*) shed, score, seam.

parting drink deoch-an-dorus.

parting of the ways shed(din).

partly pairtlie, haufweys, halflins NE, kinna.

greater part *see also* **majority**; muckle feck.

for your own part for yer ain han(d).

particle *see also* **crumb, jot, fraction, grain, piece**; rissom: '*no a rissom*', stime, flow NE, starn NE, dottle.

not a particle no a haet, fient a haet, fient a bit.

every particle hair an hoof, ilka hilt an hair SW, ilkie bit NE.

particular *adjective* parteec(u)lar; (*exact*) perjink, pe(r)neurious NE.

particularly *see also* **especially**; particular, parteec(u)lar.

more particularly tae the mair mean taikin NE.

partition *noun, see also* **screen**; parteetion; (*wooden*) pairple; (*between stalls in a stable or cowshed*) travise.

partner *noun* pairtner, neibour; (*marriage*) neibour, half-marrow, marrow *literary*.

partnership partnerie; (*law: limited, for a specific purpose*) joint adventure.

hold in partnership halver N.

partridge pai(r)trick.

party (*social gathering*) pairtie, ploy SHETLAND, han(d)lin, awthegither, soirée *informal*, shine: '*cookie shine*'; '*tea shine*' = tea party; (*convivial*) core, horoyally HIGHLAND; (*with music etc*) ceilidh; (*with drink*) splore; (*esp organized by a church etc*) swaree.

pass *verb* **1** (*of time: towards an event*) weir in; (*spend time*) pit by. **2** (*go past: with a whizzing sound*) whinner; (*overtake*) win by. **3** (*hand to someone*) see: '*see's ower the jeelie*'.

noun (*mountain*) bealach, slack, slap.

passing bell deid bell.

passing through throu-gaun.

in passing in the bygaun.

pass away *see also* **die**; win awa.

pass by haud by NE.

pass over 1 (*cross*) win ower. **2** (*omit: see also* **overlook**) hip; (*omit to do something*) slip.

a pretty pass a fine time o day.

passageway (throu-)gang, throu-gate, throu-gaun, trance; (*in or between houses*) entry, close; (*between houses*) wynd, vennel, (*vaulted*) pend; (*in a cowshed*) walk; (*along a wall, for grading sheep*) race.

passion *see also* **rage, excitement**; patience, feem.

passionate birsie, heidie.

go mad with passion gae hyte.

passive (*of a person*) thowless, fushionless.

past *preposition* by: '*by their best*'; (*beyond*) yont; (*of hours*) efter: '*hauf an oor efter ten*'.

adverb (*of time*) bygane.

things past *or* **in the past** (*eg offences, injuries*) byganes.

get past get by.

paste *noun, verb* (*eg as adhesive*) batter; (*used in weaving*) pap.

pastern paster.

pastime play SHETLAND.

pastries snashters, sweet-breid SHETLAND, ORKNEY, gulshichs NE, fine pieces NE.

pasture *noun* paster, gang, raik; (*old-established*) ley girse; (*accustomed*) heft; (*for sheep*) sheep-gang; (*for a cow*) coogang S; (*open, for cattle*) ootgang SW; (*small enclosed, for cattle*) ootca(w) SW; (*spring*) springin; (*remote summer*) †shielin; (*outlying*) ootrin; (*dry, heathy*) birn.

verb girse, gress.

pasturage lizour, girsin N; (*surface of*) sole; (*amount which will support a certain number of livestock*) soum; (*proportion of a common allocated to each tenant*) stent; (*area allocated to a flock and shepherd*) hirsel.

pasty *noun, see* **pie**.

pasty-faced etten an spued, peelie-wallie, fauchie N.

pat *verb, noun, see also* **stroke**; (*affectionately*) clap: '*gie the dog a clap*'.

patch *verb* cloot, eik, lap, spatch S, clamp SHETLAND, NE, jam SHETLAND, ORKNEY; (*a leak in the clinkers of a boat*) tingle.

noun **1** (*mended*) cloot, eik, spatch S, clamp SHETLAND, ORKNEY. **2** (*part of a surface*) platch: '*an ugly platch on his cheek*'.

patch up (*a quarrel*) souder, sowther.

patella see **kneecap**.
paternity: determining the paternity (of a child) (law) filiation.
path pad, road(ie), gang, gate; (esp in a forest) rack; (narrow, esp sheep-track) roddin; (in a ravine) peth; (garden) bauk.
pathetic expression (to arouse sympathy) sair face.
patience thole.
patient tholemoodie; (very) patientfu, tholin.
be patient thole.
patient waiting onhing.
have patience with forbear.
patronage cheenge NE.
patter verb whitter; (of feet) fitter; (of rain etc) rap.
pattern noun, see also **mould³**; pattren; (checked, in tartan) sett; (veined) marl; (dressmaking) shape; (sample of cloth) swatch.
paunch painch, bag, wame.
pause verb (hesitate) hover, huilie.
noun (of the tide, between ebb and flow) still.
pave causey.
pavement causey, plainstanes, plettiestanes E CENTRAL.
pavilion paveelion.
paw noun luif, spag, spyog CAITHNESS; (large clumsy) maig.
verb (the ground, of a horse) pawt.
pawn verb pawnd; (law) impignorate.
noun pawnd: 'Ma waddin ring's in the pawnd'.
pawned impignorat.
pawnshop pawn(d); (unlicensed) †wee pawn(d).
pay verb pey; (for others' drinks etc) pey aff; (esp as a bribe, tip) creesh (someone's) luif.
noun pey; (wages) penny-fee in poetry.
avoid paying slope.
payment peyment, quittance; (law: by tenant at renewal of lease) grassum.
pay attention see **attention**.
make (someone) pay dearly cauk NE: 'He'll cauk ye for that'.

pay down (money) doss(ie) doon NE.
pay for pey: 'it'll pey the coal'.
pay its way (of a business) wash its face.
pea see also **pease**; pey NE, S, pizzer NE.
peas pizz, pizzers NE.
peanut puggie nut.
pea-pod (pea-)cod, (pea-)shaup, (pea-)huil, whaup, cob, swab S.
peashooter scooter, scoot(-gun), pluffer, pluff(-gun), skiter SHETLAND, NE; (made of a bird's quill) pen-gun.
pea soup pea bree.
peas and beans (grown together) black victual, †black crap.
leaves etc of the pea plant (used as fodder etc) pease strae.
peace pace, lown, saucht.
peaceable greeable.
peaceful(ly) lown.
peaceful place lown.
be at peace still.
hold your peace keep a quiet souch.
peacock paycock.
peahen paysie.
peak (apex) peen; (something which rises to a peak) tappietoorie; (of a hill) kip SE; (of a cap) skip, snoot, stem SW.
peaked (of a cap: see also **cloth cap**) skippit, snootit, stemmit SW.
peal noun (of a bell) jowe, jowl; (of thunder) brattle.
verb (of a bell) jowe, jowl; (of thunder) dinnle.
pear peer.
pearl pairl.
string of pearls pearlins.
pease see also **pea**; pizz, pizzers NE.
pease flour peasemeal; (mixed with boiling water) pease brose.
cake made with pease flour pease bannock.
made of pease flour peasie: 'peasie bannock'.
peat pate; (spongy) foggie peat, duff (muild) SHETLAND; (spongy and tough) ket SW; (spongy or wet) fum SW; (piece of) (peat) clod, divot; (surface) turf,

turr, sod; (*esp with grass attached*) ruch-heid.

peaty water peat bree.

peat-bank moss-bank, skemmel, hatch NE.

peat basket (*deep, for carrying on the back*) (peat) creel, (peat) cassie.

peat bog (*where peat is cut*) (peat) moss, (peat) hill SHETLAND, ORKNEY, N, mire SHETLAND; (*very wet*) flow.

peat-cutter 1 (*person*) peat-caster, mosser. **2** (*tool: see also* **turf-cutter**) peat-spade, tusker N.

peat-cutting peat-castin.

peat dust peat coom, peat muild, drush NE, (peat) smoorach N, HIGHLAND.

peat embers (peat) greeshoch.

peat fire (*or its glow*) peat lowe.

peat-stack stack, ruck NE, hill N; (*of a specific size*) leet NE; (*esp against a house, for winter supply*) peat bing; (*small heap*) (peat) rickle.

base of a peat-stack steid.

end of a peat-stack (stack) mou NE.

peat working *noun* (*old*) peat(-hag), moss-hag, skemmel; (*esp water-filled*) peat-hole.

area of ground where peats are cut *see* **peat bog**.

area of ground where peats are laid to dry (peat) lair, peat larrach, spread-field.

face where peats are cut (peat) bank.

corner where peat is stored (*enclosed recess*) peat-ree; (*eg in kitchen, for immediate use*) peat neuk.

setting peats on end to dry (*in small stacks*) fittin; (*turning the peats, and rebuilding the small stacks*) turn-fittin.

track leading to a peat moss moss road.

tuft of peat used as a seat hassock.

pebble peeble, chuckie (stane).

pebbly rocklie.

peck *verb* pick NE, paek SHETLAND, dab, dorb NE.
noun dorb NE.

peckish *see* **hungry**.

peculiar *see also* **strange**; parteec(u)lar, unco, clem.

peculiarity unconess.

pedantic lang-nebbit.

peddle *see also* **pedlar**; cadge, traivel (the roads).

pedestrian ganger; **pedestrians** fitfowk(s).

pedlar *see also* **hawker**; cadger, packman, packie, troker, Scotch cuddie, pedder, dusty-fit.

pedlar's wares troke, troggin.

peel *verb* pilk.

peep[1] *verb* (*glance*) keek, glent, glisk, teet, deek *originally gipsy*.
noun keek, glent, glisk, deek *originally gipsy*.

peeping Tom keeker, skiver.

peep-bo keek(ie) bo, teet(ie) bo.

peephole keekhole.

peep[2] *verb* (*esp of birds: make a shrill noise*) pleep, queeple, wheep(le).

peer[1] *noun* (*equal*) maik.

peer[2] (*look closely*) stime, pie.

peering *adjective* (*of the eyes*) glimmer-in.

peevish *see also* **bad-tempered, short-tempered, fretful**; girnie, fashious, peeng(e)in, pe(r)neurious NE, natterie.

peewit *see* **lapwing**.

peg *noun* (*for hanging things on*) (k)nag, nab; (*wooden, on plaster wall, for holding a nail*) dook; (*to fasten a tether*) baikie NE.

insert pegs into (*a wall*) dook.

take someone down a peg tak someone doon a hack, tak a stap oot o someone's bicker, snite someone's niz, pit someone's gas at a peep.

pellet skirp NE; **pellets** (*small shot*) hail, (leid) draps; (*of sheep dung*) trottles, trintlets.

pelt[1] *noun* (*skin*) pellet, sloch.

pelt[2] *verb* **1** (*with missiles*) clod, da(u)d; (*with stones*) stane, pin. **2** (*of rain*) bicker, blatter, stot.

pen[1]: **pen-case** penner.
  penmanship *see also* **handwriting**; han(d)write.
  pen-nib pen-point, neb.
  pen-nibful of ink stolum N.
  stroke of the pen straik.
pen[2] *noun, see also* **enclosure, sheepfold**; cruive, crue, ree(ve); (*square*) pumphal NE.
  verb (*an animal*) pumphal NE.
penance mends.
pencil *noun, see also* **slate pencil**; pincil, keelivine; (*coloured*) keel.
  pencil-point nib.
pendulum *see also* **cord**; pendle.
penetrate thirl, prog; (*like a needle*) needle; **penetrate into** (*investigate*) howk.
penis pintle, pill(ie), tossel, whang, toby *humorous*, taw *child's word*, Robin *child's word*, tot *child's word*, N; (*of an animal*) wan(d).
penitent: place in a church where penitents stood †place of repentance.
penny stuir SHETLAND.
  penniless plackless.
  penny-farthing speeder ORKNEY, NE.
pensioner (*army*) foggie.
pensive pensefu, tholemoodie, thochtish S.
pent up inhauden.
penury *see* **poverty**.
  penurious scuddie NE.
peony speengie rose.
people *see also* **person**; fowk, shither CAITHNESS, cattle *contemptuous*.
pepper spice.
  peppery spicy.
  peppermint sweet (*mint imperial*) pan drop; (*bull's eye*) black-strippit ba(w).
  pepper and salt dab-at-the-stuil.
perceive fin(d); (*by smell or taste*) feel.
  perceptive nizwise NE.
perch *noun* (*bird's: see also* **spar**) spaik.
percolate *see also* **trickle**; seek, seep, sype.

peremptory cuttit.
perfect(ly) perfit.
perfidious *see also* **treacherous**; sliderie.
perforate thirl, puil.
perhaps aiblins *literary*, maybe, mebbe, mibbie.
pericardium huil.
peril wanchance *literary*, S.
period (*of time*) track (o) time, stoun(d) SHETLAND; (*short*) sketch S, whilie, filie NE.
perish (*die*) tyne, torfle S.
periwinkle (*winkle*) wulk, buckie.
perjure: perjured †mansworn.
  perjure yourself †manswear.
perk[1]: **perk up** spunk up.
  perky birkie.
perk[2] *see* **perquisite**.
permit *verb, see also* **allow**; lat, leave.
  permission permeeshion, freedom.
perpendicular (*esp of rain*) evendoon, fair doon.
perpetually *see* **eternally**.
perplex *see also* **confuse, bewilder**; fickle, kittle, tickle, raivel, waun(n)er, pall SHETLAND, ORKNEY, N, denumb NE, habble S, haister SW.
  perplexed bumbazed, wa(u)chelt, pichert NE, will NE.
  be perplexed swither.
  perplexity maze, swither.
  in perplexity in a creel, held again NE.
perquisite(s), perk(s) chance(s); (*for drink*) drink siller; (*small quantity taken by employee*) pauchle.
persecute *see also* **harass**; murther, pursue, pook at.
persevere hing in, stick in; (*esp at work*) plowd NE; **persevere in** haud at.
  person who perseveres hinger-in, stick-in.
persist: persist in haud at.
  persistent (*dreary*) dreich; (*of a cold*) sitten-doon.
  persistently even on.
person *see also* **people**; bodie: '*could ye no leave a bodie in peace?*', golach

contemptuous, N, wicht *contemptuous or pitying*; (*anyone*) leevin: '*He nivver telt a leevin*', sowl.

perspire *see* **sweat.**

persuade *see also* **coax**; perswad, wice, gow (ower) NE; (*law: to something criminal*) procure.

pert *see also* **impudent**; forritsome, nebsie.

  chatter pertly chant.

  pert child nacket.

  pert person yaff, nyaff.

pertain perteen.

perturb *see* **disturb.**

perverse thrawn(-heidit), tap-thrawn, dour, rigwiddie, camstairie, ill-duin, ill-gatit, contermacious, camsheuch NE, contermint NE, essart, ersit SW, frawart *literary*.

  perversity thraw, ill-gatitness.

  pervert *verb* (*a meaning*) thraw.

  perverse streak (*in character*) thrum.

pest (*nuisance*) provoke, sorra, staw, scunner.

pester *see also* **disturb, annoy**; pest, steer, soss NE, haud at, tarragat, roast, fash, threap at.

pestle *see* **potato-masher.**

pet *see* **term of endearment** (*under* **endearment**).

  verb, see also **fondle**; daut, browden, fortifee NE, dossach NE.

  pet name (*for a ewe*) maillie SW.

  petted deltit NE.

  petted child sookie.

petition *noun* peteetion; (*law*) crave.

petrify *see* **terrify.**

petticoat coat(s), quite(s) NE.

petty pea-splittin.

petulant *see also* **sulky, touchy**; tiftie, bungie NE, carnaptious.

pew dask, deas; (*square*) pumphal NE.

pewit *see* **lapwing.**

pewter pewther.

phantom *see* **ghost.**

pharmacist poticary SW.

pheasant phaesan(t), feesan(t), ephesian.

phlegm fleem, glit, defluxion.

phosphorescence (*on the sea*) fireburn, watter-burn N.

photograph *noun* photie, limn.

phrase *noun* (*repeated*) rame, owerword, rane.

physic (*medicine*) feesick.

physician physeecian.

physics natural philosophy.

pick *verb* pike; (*fruit, flowers*) pou; (*dust, fluff etc from*) mote NE.

  noun pike.

  pickaback *see* **piggyback.**

  pick at (*food: see also* **nibble**) pewl at, pewl amang; **pick at food** smurl.

  pick and choose lift an lay.

  pick out *see also* **choose**; chaps, wale.

  pick up 1 (*stitches in knitting*) lift. **2** (*after illness: see also* **improve**) cock.

pickle *see also* **muddle, confusion**; picher, steer.

picnic (*riverside, esp by the Tweed, of newly-caught salmon*) kettle SE.

picture *noun* picter.

piddle *see also* **urinate**; strone.

pie NB in Sc often refers to a round individual 'mutton pie', also known as a 'Scotch pie'; (*circle of pastry folded over, with meat filling*) (Forfar) bridie.

  pie dish ashet W.

piebald (horse) pyot.

piece *noun, see also* **bit**[1]; (*small, esp of food*) dorle NE; (*very small: see also* **fragment, crumb**) nip, crumch(ickie) NE, jinsh NE, (n)imsh N, (*esp of food*) snap; (*large: see also* **lump, chunk**) da(u)d, knoit, doll NE, dolder NE, lob, kneep(lach) NE, dorlach NE, thump, (*esp of food*) knoll, (*clumsy*) divot; (*long piece of string etc*) leash.

  piecemeal in smas.

  piece of work handlin, turn.

  pieceworker tasker.

  all to pieces tae pigs an whustles, a(w) tae sticks an stanes, a(w) tae crockaneetion(s).

  (in)to pieces oot o ither.

pied wagtail *see* **wagtail.**

pier *see* **quay.**

pierce *see also* **prick, stab**; jag, prog, deg NE, stob NE, brog, thirl, stug; (*slightly*) dab; (*with emotion*) dirl, thirl.

piercing (*of wind, see also* **keen**) snell.

pig *noun, see also* **sow**[1]**, boar**; swine, grumph(ie), chattie NE, gruntie *humorous*, Sandie (Campbell) *taboo*, harkie *taboo*, SHETLAND; (*esp hog or boar*) gaut; (*esp young*) gussie; (*esp young suckling*) grice; (*young, after weaning*) shott; (*smallest of a litter: see also* **runt**) poke-shakkins, shakkins o the pok(i)e, titlin, doorie W, SW, ULSTER.

piggyback backie, coalie-back; (*on the shoulders*) shouderie, high shouder.

piggy-bank *see* **moneybox.**

pig-headed *see also* **stubborn**; thrawn, positive.

pignut (*lousy*) arnit, knotty-meal N.

pigsty cruive, crue, craw, pig-hoose, ree(ve), puidge.

pigswill swine-mait.

pigtail pleat.

pig in a poke blin bargain.

pigeon doo, pud(die) doo; (*tame*) rook-ettie doo; (*stray*) strag; (*wood pigeon*) cushat, cushie (doo), croodlin doo NE.

pigeonhole *noun* doocot(-hole).

pigeon-toed hen-taed, in-taed, pirn(ie)-taed, tickie-taed.

having a pigeon-toed gait partan-taed SHETLAND, ORKNEY, NE.

walk in a pigeon-toed way plet.

pike[1] (*fish*) ged.

pike[2]: **pikestaff** †pickstaff.

pile *see also* **heap**: *noun* bing; (*esp loose*) rickle; (*eg of peats*) ruck NE; (*eg of unthreshed grain*) mou.
verb **pile up** bing; (*loosely*) rickle; (*peats, turnips*) clod SW.

pilfer *see also* **steal**; pauchle, sneck, pike NE, pilk SHETLAND, NE, FIFE, cab NE, skech.

pilgrim pilgrimer.

pill peel.

pillage *see also* **plunder**; reive, herrie.

pillar stoop, pall.

from pillar to post fae wig tae wa, hither an yont: '*Ah went hither an yont tae pick up the bairns*'.

pillow *noun* pillae, cod.

pillowcase pillowbere.

pilot *noun* (*steersman*) lodesman SHETLAND.
verb airt.

pimple plouk, blob, shilcorn; (*inflamed*) esscock NE; (*on face, supposedly from too much whisky-drinking*) whisky-tacket.

pimply ploukie, ploukit.

pin *noun* preen, peen; (*large, for fastening a shawl*) grannie preen, Wullie Cossar; (*on a cart axle*) *see* **nail.**
verb preen, peen.

pincushion preen-cod.

pinhead preen-heid.

pinpoint *noun* neb.

game played with pins heidicks an pinticks NE.

have pins and needles prinkle.

pinafore peenie, daidlie, carsackie.

pincers pinchers, (*esp blacksmith's*) turkas.

pinch *verb* **1** (*squeeze*) nevel. **2** (*with cold*) nirl, nither. **3** *see also* **steal, pilfer**; skech, wheech, wheek.
noun (*of meal, salt etc*) nip, hummie; (*of snuff*) sneesh(in), snuff.

pinched 1 (*lacking*) scrimp: '*scrimp o claes*'. **2** (*with cold, ill-health etc*) peeng(e)in, shilpit, shirpit, huggert.

take a pinch of (*snuff*) lick.

pine[1] (*Scots pine*) bonnet fir.

pine-cone *see* **fircone.**

pine-needle preenack NE.

pine[2] *verb* (*waste away*) dwine, peenge; (*pine away*) traik, torfle S; (*of an animal*) pewl.

pining *see* **sickly** (*under* **sick**).

pink (*flower: maiden pink*) spink.

pinnacle peenacle.

pint *see table of measures on p 301.*

pious gracie, guidlie NE.

pip *noun* (*of a fruit*) paip.

pipe *noun* **1** (*tobacco*) gun; (*short, stumpy, clay*) cuttie (pipe), cuttie clay.

2 (*musical: toy, made of oat-stems*) corn-pipe; (*made of a reed*) doodle; (*of the bagpipes: on which melody is played, or separate pipe for practising*) chanter; (*bass pipe*) drone. **3** (*pipe from a roof gutter*) rone-pipe.

pipeclay cam(stane), stookie; (*piece of, for whitening doorsteps*) rubbin stane.

pipe-cleaner pipe-riper.

leader of a (regimental) pipe band pipe major, pipie *informal*.

pipit *see* **meadow pipit, rock pipit**.

piquant *see* **sharp**.

pique *see also* **huff**: *noun* heelie.

piqued thin, struntit.

pirate *noun* †caper.

pirouette *verb* wheel.

piss *verb, noun* pish.

pit 1 (*coal mine*) heuch, winnin, sink. **2** (*hollow: see also* **sandpit**; *place dug out*) delf. **3** (*of the stomach*) grun(d): '*Ye'll hae gotten the grun o yer stomach*' = you've been very sick.

pitted (*roughened*) pickit.

pithead hill.

pithead shelter ludge.

pitch[1] *noun* (*resinous*) pick.

pitch-dark(ness) pick-black, pick-dark, pit-mirk.

pitch[2] *verb* **1** *see also* **throw**: pick, keytch, lab. **2** (*of a boat*) howd.

pitchfork *noun* fowe.

pitcher (watter) pig, graybeard.

pith (*essence*) sense; (*energy*) smeddum, smergh, bone, fushion.

without pith fushionless.

pity *noun* peety, sin SHETLAND.

verb peety, mane, rue on, be vext for.

pitiable peetifu.

to be pitied tae mane: '*they're muckle tae mane*'.

expression of pity the (wee) sowl!, the craitur!

it's a pity it's a sin.

pivot peevot.

pizzle wan(d).

placate dill.

place *noun* **1** (*spot*) bit, spat; (*site*) steid, locus *law*. **2** (*area*) pairt, airt.

verb, see also **put**; (*in position*) stell, steid, plank; (*down flat*) plat.

placed (*in a certain spot*) stanced NE.

all over the place *see also* **everywhere**; a(w) roads, a(w) wye(s).

in place of in room o.

in that place yonner-aboots, onner NE.

out of that place thereoot, oot o onner NE.

put someone in his *or* **her place** pit someone's gas at a peep, sort.

placenta *see* **afterbirth**.

placid *see* **contented**.

plagiarize thig.

plague *noun* (*esp bubonic*) †pest.

verb, see also **pester, annoy**; pest, deave.

plaice plash N, plashack (fleuk) N, splash(ack) N.

plaid plaidie, plad, hap, rauchan, †brechan; (*checked, worn by shepherds*) maud; (*of fine quality and intricate pattern*) †harnish plaid; (*long, fastened with belt*) †belted plaid(ie).

wrap *or* **dress in a plaid** plaid, plad.

corner of a plaid (*in which shepherds carried lambs*) plaid neuk, maud neuk S.

plain *adjective, see also* **ordinary**; hamelt, hameart, (*also of food*) hameower.

noun (*along a river; see also* **meadow**) carse.

plaintiff pursuer; (*victim of a crime*) complainer.

plait *noun* plet, pleat.

verb plet, warp.

plan *noun, see also* **scheme**; (*esp light-hearted*) ploy.

verb ettle: '*whit are ye ettlin?*', mak it up (that), mint.

plane *noun* han(d)-plane; (*large*) hauflin.

verb (*roughly*) scrunt.

plank *noun, see also* **board, lath**; clift; (*thin, esp for barrel staves*) scowe SHETLAND, N, knappel.

verb **plank down** plat, plowt.

plant *noun* (*young*) settin.

verb **1** (*a hedge*) lay; (*esp potatoes*) pit doon; (*temporarily, for later transplant*) sheuch (in). **2** *see also* **place, plank**; stell; (*your feet against something to steady yourself*) stell.

plant out set aff.

plantation plantin; (*esp to shelter sheep*) stell.

plantain (*greater or ribwort*) curl-doddie, carl-doddie; (*greater*) healin blade, waverin leaf SHETLAND; (*stems and flowerheads, used in a game*) sodgers; (*hoary*) lamb's lugs, lamb's ears.

plaster *noun* plaister; (*eg for a broken limb*) stookie.

verb **1** plaister; (*a wall*) stoothe SW, S; (*smear*) cleester, skaik NE. **2** (*a broken limb*) stookie.

plate *noun, see also* **trencher**; (*large oval, for serving*) ashet; (*soup-plate, or other hollow plate*) deep plate; (*flat, under a gravy boat etc*) sole NE.

plate-rack (*eg on a wall*) bink, bench, binch.

platter *see* **plate**.

plausible sleekit, fair-farran(t), fairfaced.

play *verb* **1** (*roughly, boisterously*) rampage. **2** (*a bowl, curling stone*) rowe. **3** (*a wind instrument*) doodle. **4** (*with your food*) *see* **pick**. **5** (*a curling stone: so that it fails to cross the score*) hog; (*with such force that it moves an opponent's stone in its way*) ride (oot); (*one stone off against another*) wick; (*striking the inside of another stone*) inwick; (*striking the outside of another stone*) ootwick.

noun (*entertainment by boys at New Year's Eve or Halloween*) Galatians, Galoshins.

player (*curling: first on each side*) leader.

playful *see also* **skittish**; geckin, kim NE.

act playfully daff.

playing (*of a curling stone: towards the tee*) shot; (*with handle inwards*) inturn, (*with handle outwards*) oot-turn.

playing cards *see also* **card**[1]; cairts, cairds, deil's picter buiks NE.

plaything *see also* **toy**; playock, playfare.

fair play fair hornie, jonick.

play fair play fair hornie.

play truant *see* **truant**.

play a lively tune †rant.

plead (*with someone for something*) prig, fleetch.

pleaded pled.

please *verb, see also* **satisfy, gratify**; pleesure, kittle (up).

pleasant *see also* **agreeable**; cantie, cannie, couthie, lichtsome, shortsome, seilfu, dentie; (*esp of a person*) douce, fine, leesome, sanshach NE; (*esp in appearance*) sonsie, eesome; (*jovial*) gawsie; (*esp of weather*) braw, nae (that) ull.

pleasantly mirkie NE.

pleased *see also* **satisfied**; prood, pridefu, suitit, set NE, upmade S, cantie, vauntie *literary*; (*very*) fair awa (wi): '*She's fair awa wi her new computer*'; **pleased with yourself** croose, joco.

not be pleased no please: '*he wadna please*'.

pleasure pleesure, pleesur.

do what you please play yer ain spring, gang yer ain gate.

pleat plet.

pledge *verb* wad, hecht, impignorate *law, rare*.

noun wad.

Pleiades Seven Sisters.

plenty *noun* fouth, galore, rowth, raff, feck.

plentiful rife, rowth, lairge NE, raffie NE; (*plentifully supplied*) ruch: '*a guid ruch hoose*'.

plentifully rife.

having plenty of rife o, rife wi.

pliable *see also* **supple**; dwaible, swack N, dwamfle NE, waffle N.

pliant

make pliable swacken SHETLAND, ORKNEY, N.

pliant *see* **pliable.**

pliers pinchers, (*esp blacksmith's or shoemaker's*) turkas NE.

plight pliskie, snorl SHETLAND, N, pilget NE.

plimsolls sannies, gutties W.

plod *see also* **trudge**; stodge, stowff NE, plowd(er) NE, lowder NE, FIFE, fauchle N, stug, bap, snodge SE.

plodder stodger.

plop *verb* plowp, plowt, plunk; (*of small drops*) pink.

noun plowp, plowt.

make a plopping noise plump.

plot *noun* **1** (*of land*) dale NE, glebe; (*small*) paffle, bit. **2** (*conspiracy*) pack.

verb collogue, colleague.

plough *noun, see also* **horse-hoe**; pleuch, ploo; (*light American type*) Rabbie Burns.

verb pleuch, ploo, furr; (*crosswise*) thorter; (*throwing soil onto a ridge*) gaither; (*in rigs*) rig; (*esp replough in spring*) steer; (*start ploughing*) streek NE; (*every alternate furrow*) rib.

division of a ploughed field (*ploughed in a single operation*) rig.

ploughing (*act of*) furr; (*of grassland*) ley-fur(row); (*ploughing along the side of a slope*) side-castin.

plough-handle (pleuch-)stilt, hilt, stoop NE, stiel S.

ploughman pleuchie, hind, Jock hack NE, Jock muck CAITHNESS.

ploughshare (pleuch) sock.

plough-spade pattle.

plough-traces (pleuch) soam, (pleuch) theats.

break with the plough rive oot.

movement of plough across a field (and back) bout, landin.

parts of a plough *see also above and* **coulter, mouldboard** (*under* **mould**^{2}), **swingletree: metal parts** ploo airns; **left-hand side** lan(d)-side; **right-hand side** fur-side.

plover pliver.

golden plover yella plover, gray plover.

green plover *see* **lapwing.**

ringed plover sandy lairick N.

pluck *verb* pook, (*esp fruit or a bird*) pou; (*wool from a sheep, feathers from a bird*) plot.

noun, see also **courage**; gumption.

plucking movement pook.

plucky *see also* **spirited**; stuffie.

plug *noun, see also* **stopper**; (*of tobacco in a pipe*) (pipe-)dottle.

verb (*stuff, block up*) stap.

plum ploom.

plume *noun* pen.

plump *adjective* pluffie, fodgel, (*and healthy(-looking)*) sonsie, gawsie, sappie, tidy ORKNEY, weel at yersel; (*well-nourished*) lik(e) yer mait.

plump person fodgel; (*small*) pud; (*sturdy child*) stoussie.

plunder *verb* spulyie, reive, rook, ripe, roop, rump, scoff, (*also a nest*) herrie.

noun spulyie, fang, (*from Highland raid*) †creagh.

plunderer (*esp in Border raids*) †reiver; (*esp of a nest*) herrie-hawk.

plunge *verb* plype NE, slunge, plowt, dook; (*carelessly, into something*) breenge.

noun plype NE, slunge; (*noisy*) plowt, dook.

plunger (*of a churn*) plumper NE, kirnin rung, kirn staff, kirn stick.

pneumoconiosis stourie lungs, stifle.

pneumonia pneumonie *humorous*.

poach spoach S; (*salmon with weighted hooks*) snigger.

poacher spoacher S.

poacher's hook geg S.

pocket *noun* pootch, poacket; (*breast-pocket*) gushet; (*watch-pocket in trousers*) spung.

verb pootch.

pocket money Saturday('s) penny, Friday's penny NE.

provide with pocket money keep (someone's) pootch.

188

pock-marked pock(y)arred.

pod *noun, see also* **pea-pod** (*under* **pea**); huil, cod, sloch, shaup, swab; (*esp immature*) whaup, swap.

verb, see **shell**.

podgy *see also* **fat, plump**; pudgie, pudgetie s.

poem pome *humorous*.

poet makar *literary*, (*esp in Gaelic contexts*) bard.

pogge poach.

point *noun, see also* **peak**; pint, peen SHETLAND, N; (*eg of a pen, pin, knife*) neb.

verb pint; (*inside joints of slates*) shouder.

pointsman (*mining*) sneck-shifter.

bring to a point peen.

put a point on (*a pencil etc: see also* **sharpen**) neb.

poison *noun, verb* pooshion, pushion, puzzen s.

poisonous pooshionous, pooshionable.

poke *see also* **prod**: *verb* powk, prog, pork SW, S, powt, proke; (*with a stick*) poach, proadge; (*with the elbow etc*) punce; (*with the nose*) snoozle; (*a fire*) pirl SHETLAND, NE, kittle.

noun powk, prog, pork SW, S, powt, ripe; (*with the elbow etc*) punce.

poker proker.

poke about ruit, kirn, reemage NE, pirl NE, spoach (in) s.

poke ashes from (*a fire*) reenge.

poke your nose into howk, snoke.

pole *noun* powl, pall, stang; (*eg to push off a boat*) sting; (*long, heavy, as thrown in Highland games*) caber; (*projecting from window etc, for drying clothes*) perk; (*on wheels for transporting logs*) janker; (*for hanging fishing lines to dry*) spile-tree NE; (*butcher's, for hanging carcasses*) hangrell.

polecat foumart, thoumart.

police polis.

policeman polis(man), hornic *slang*, bulkie *slang*, NE, snoot *slang*, peg *slang*.

police station nick.

polish: polished (*of manners*) †Falkland bred.

polish off (*food*) perish, connach.

polite *see also* **courteous, mannerly**; mensefu, discreet; (*superficially*) fair-faced.

politician politeecian.

poll cowe.

polled (*of cattle*) hummel(t), cowit.

pollack lythe, skeet N.

pollute smit, fyle.

polysyllabic lang-nebbit.

pompom (tappie)toorie.

pompous fou, pensie, poochle NE, massie.

pond *see also* **pool**; pound, dub, stank, coble NE; (*for steeping flax*) lint-hole, lint-pot.

ponder *see* **reflect**.

pony pownie; (*esp* SHETLAND) sheltie.

pooh! *see also* **nonsense!**; hoot (toot)!

pooh-pooh hoot.

pool *noun, see also* **pond, puddle**; puil, peel NE, pound, stank, waterhole; (*shallow*) hole; (*esp marshy*) powe SHETLAND, N; (*deep, in a river*) pot(tie), plumb, weel; (*below a waterfall*) linn; (*from a natural spring*) wall; (*of stagnant water*) stank, (*from a dunghill*) strang hole, green brees NE; (*esp of muddy water*) dub; (*of mud*) gullion.

poor puir, peer NE; (*see also* **needy, hard-up**) ill-aff, sober NE.

poorly *see also* **ailing**; badly, tender, ill-aff, no weel, hard-up SE.

poor fellow puir sowl, peer breet NE.

list of poor people in a parish †puir's roll.

pop *verb* **pop out** lowp.

popping sound (*of a cork*) plunk.

popgun spoot-gun.

pope pape.

popery paperie.

popish paipish.

poppy puppie.

popular *see* **in great favour** (*under* **favour**).

porcelain *see also* **tile**; (*dish, ornament etc*) wallie.

porch entry, rochel NE.

pork purk SHETLAND, NE, Sandie *humorous*.

porpoise pellock, puffie (dunter), dunter.

porridge *see also* **oatmeal**; parritch, pottitch NE, gruel SHETLAND, ORKNEY, poshie *child's word*.

porridge bowl (parritch) cap; (*esp of staves*) bicker.

stick for stirring porridge spurtle, spurkle, theevil, theedle N, FIFE.

port *see* **harbour**.

portend bod.

portent *see also* **sign foretelling death** (*under* **death**); wa(i)rnin, freit N.

porter: chief porter (*and macebearer, in some Scottish universities*) bedellus.

portfolio bla(u)d.

portion *see also* **share, quantity**; dale, lab.

portrait-painter (*esp royal in Scotland*) limner.

position *noun* poseetion, locus *law*.

put in position *see also* **place**; (*specif a millstone*) lair.

take up your position sconce NE.

positive positeeve.

positively positeevely, exacklie, fairly: '*he'll fairly dae it*'.

possess *see also* **own**; aucht, aicht ORKNEY, NE, belang.

possessed jointly (*esp of farmland*) mean.

possession 1 (*joint*) commonty. **2** (*property*) haddin; **possessions** gear: '*guids an gear*', graith.

act of giving possession (*law: of feudal property*) sasine.

possible: possibly maybe, mebbe, mibbie.

possibility maybe: '*a maybe is not always a honey bee*'.

post *noun, see also* **pole, stake** 1; stoop, pall, stob: '*fence-stob*', stab; (*upright*) stan(d)art.

posterior *noun, see* **buttocks**.

postman post(ie).

postpone (*law: a case etc*) continue, supersede.

postponement continuation, affpit(tin).

posture *noun* shape.

posy *see* **bouquet**.

pot *noun, see also* **cauldron**; pat; (*large cooking*) kettle; (*small, iron, with straight handle*) goglet; (*three-legged cast-iron*) yetlin; (*earthenware jar*) pig.

potful pottle.

potted meat plowt *humorous*; (*from the head of a cow or pig*) pottit heid, (*from the shin*) pottit hoch.

pot-bellied guttie, muckle-kytit, kettle-bellied.

pot-belly cog wame.

pot-handle pat-bool.

pot-hanger (*above fire*) swey, swee, cran.

pot-hole (*in the street*) powe SHETLAND, N.

pot-leg pat-fit NE.

pot-lid (*wooden*) pat-brod.

pot-scourer scrub; (*of heather twigs*) (heather) range, (heather) reenge NE.

go to pot gae gyte, gae worth NE.

keep the pot boiling keep the puddin het.

potato tattie, tawtie, pitawtie, (*potato-seller's street-cry*) †peerieorie EDINBURGH; (*small*) chat; **small potatoes** brock; **potato dishes** (*cooked in skins*) peel-an-eat, peelock SW, skinny tatties; (*with salt*) dab-at-the-steel NE, pick an dab; (*dipped in gravy etc*) tatties an dab; (*mashed*) champit tatties, chappit tatties; (*mashed with fried fish*) hairy tatties NE; (*mashed with mashed turnip*) clapshot; (*mashed with milk, butter etc and sometimes other vegetables*) rummle(de)thump; (*stewed with onions and sometimes meat etc*) stovies, stovit tatties; (*fried in slices*) sleeshacks N.

potato bag tattie poke, tattie pyock NE.

potato basket tattie creel; (*of wire*) scull.

potato cake (*thin, baked on girdle*) tattie scone, potato scone, fadge ULSTER, tattie bannock SHETLAND, ORKNEY, CAITHNESS.

potato clamp *see* **potato pit.**

potato-digger (*person*) tattie howker; (*machine*) tattie deevil NE, FIFE; (*harrow*) tattie grubber.

potato field tattie park.

potato harvest tattie howkin, tattie liftin.

school holiday when children helped with potato harvest tattie holidays.

potato leaves and stalks (tattie) shaws.

potato-masher tattie-champer, (tattie-)chapper, tattie-beetle.

potato-peeler tattie-parer.

potato pit tattie bing, tattie pit.

potato seedbox tattie ploom.

potato skin tattie peel(in).

potato soup tattie soup, tattie claw SE, tattie broth.

potato water (*poured from pot*) tattie poorins.

meal of potatoes only tatties an pint.

thinning of potato crop tattie-roguin NE, ANGUS, PERTHSHIRE.

potent *see also* **strong**; (*eg of drink*) stieve.

potential (*scope*) scowth.

potter, potter about *see also* **idle, waste time**; fouter, plowter, gutter, diddle, daidle, dauble NE, fite the (idle) pin NE.

pottering *noun* kirn NE.

pottery *see* **earthenware.**

pouch pootch, poke; (*for money*) hogger, spung, (*also for tobacco*) spleuchan.

poultry pootrie.

poultry enclosure *see* **hen-coop.**

poultry woman henwife.

pound[1] *noun* (*weight or money*) pun(d).

pound note note, single (note), flaffer.

pound[2] *verb* (*impound*) pun(d).

pound[3] *verb* (*mash*) champ, chap, bittle, knock; (*hit hard*) ding, nevel.

pour poor: **1 pour out** (1) (*from a container*) tuim, teem, tim; (*carelessly*) jaw, sklyter NE; (*unsteadily*) jirble; (*liquor*) birl; (*from one container to another*) skink. (2) *see also* **gush**; spue, buck NE; (*of smoke*) (y)oam SHETLAND, NE. **2** (*of rain*) tuim, tim, hale, dish (on), rash.

pouring out *see* **gush.**

pour the liquid from poor: '*poor the tatties*', bree NE.

pour off (*top liquid*) shire.

pour out *see also above* 1; (*tea*) poor: '*poor the tea*'.

pout[1] (*fish*) *see* **bib** 2.

pout[2] *verb, see also* **sulk, grimace**; poot, lat doon the lip, have a bus(s) on CAITHNESS, HIGHLAND.

poverty puirtith, scant.

poverty-stricken *see also* **poor**; ill-aff, in the grubber SE.

be poverty-stricken drink oot a toom cappie NE.

complain of poverty (*eg as an excuse for meanness*) mak a puir mou.

powder *noun* poother, pooder; (*fine*) smeddum, (*eg from peat*) smoorach N, HIGHLAND.

verb poother, pooder.

powdery pootherie.

power pooer, poustie, poust S, micht, virr, (*esp physical*) ma(u)cht; (*to harm*) danger.

powerful pooerfae; (*strong*) pithy, maisterfu, stootrif(e) SW, S; (*forceful*) feckfu; **most powerful** (*of a person*) maist.

powerless mauch(t)less.

in the power of in the reverence o HIGHLAND.

at the height of your powers in yer potestator SHETLAND, NE.

practice *noun* (*habit*) haunt.

practise *verb* practeese.

practicable prestable.

practical joke *see* **joke.**

praise

praise *verb, noun* (*esp flatteringly*) ruise, reeze NE.

prance *verb, see also* **strut**: brank, link, stairge S; (*of an animal*) winch.

prank *see also* **practical joke** (*under joke*); pliskie: '*play a pliskie on*', cantrip, pant, skavie NE, prattick NE, prat N.

play pranks prank.

prattle *see also* **chatter**: *verb* gash, trattle, paiter, gibble-gabble.

noun gash, gibble-gabble.

prawn praan N.

pray (*begin to pray*) engage NE.

prayers (*esp children's*) guid words.

family prayers (faimily) worship, (faimily) exerceese.

say a prayer mak a prayer, pit up a word.

preach: preacher (*itinerant, evangelical*) missionar NE, ULSTER; (*lay, in the Free Churches*) missionary HIGHLAND.

listen to the preaching of sit below.

precarious (*tricky*) kittlie; (*unsteady*) tolter ORKNEY.

precious praicious.

precious stone *see* **jewel**.

precipice heuch, scaur, clint SW, S.

precipitous *see also* **steep**[1]; brent.

precise preceese; (*exact*) nate; (*of a person*) perjink, pintit; (*over-precise*) sanshach NE, perskeet, peremptor, dink.

precisely preceese, juist that.

precocious (*of a child*) auld-farran(t), ancient.

precocious child nacket SHETLAND, ORKNEY, NE.

predicament *see also* **plight**: snorl, kinch, firris NE, plet S, pirkas CAITHNESS.

predict spae *literary*, †weird.

prediction †spae, †weird.

pre-eminence gree *literary*: '*bear the gree*'.

pregnant on the road, (muckle-)boukit; (*at halfway stage*) hauf gone; (*heavily*) heavy(-fittit), heavy o fit; (*of an animal: see also* **ewe**) baggit; (*of a cow*) tidy.

be pregnant biggen; (*of an unmarried woman*) miscairry SHETLAND.

she's pregnant her coats are kiltit, there's a trootie i the well NE.

become pregnant fa(w) wi bairn.

make pregnant bairn.

prejudiced nairra-nebbit.

premature: act prematurely cut afore the point.

give birth to a premature baby pairt wi bairn.

(give birth to a) premature lamb keb SW, S.

premonition forego, warnin.

preoccupied jammed, taen up (wi).

be completely preoccupied with ride on the riggin o, be fair taen up wi.

prepare graith, busk, redd (up), boon NE, mak way NE, rank NE, rig SHETLAND, NE; (*a meal*) ready; (*ground for sowing*) mak.

prepared boon NE, clair SHETLAND, boden *literary*, yare *literary*.

prepare for mak for.

preposterous *see* **ridiculous**.

preposterous idea megrim.

prescience *see* **forewarning**.

prescription (doctor's) line, receipt.

present *noun, see also* **gift**; praisent, compliment NE; (*esp of food, eg from a fair*) fairin.

verb gift.

adjective (*at hand*) forrit.

presentable weel tae be seen, gate farrin NE, faisible.

at present presently, the noo, ivnoo, meantime.

preserve *verb, see also* **keep**: preser, hain; (*cattle, for stock*) haud.

(God) preserve us! sers!, sirs!

preside (*over a church court*) moderate.

president preses, convener; (*of a trade in a town*) deacon; (*of all the trades*) (deacon) convener.

press *verb, see also* **hard-pressed**: preese, brizz, birze; (*squeeze*) chirt, thrummle; (*esp with the feet*) paidle; (*esp with the knee*) knidge SHETLAND, N; (*press close to*) bore.

noun preese; (*squeeze*) chirt, brizz, birze.

press down clap, knuse, pram SHETLAND, NE, trist SHETLAND, ORKNEY; (*esp clothes in washing*) poss, post NE.

press (*something*) **on** (*someone*) bode NE.

pressure 1 brizz, birze; (*esp with the knee*) knidge. **2** (*of work*) thrang(itie); (*excessive*) hash.

presume *see* **suppose**.

I presume I'm thinkin.

presumption *see* **effrontery**.

presumptuous *see also* **forward**; ignorant.

pretend mak on, lat on, pit on; **pretend to do** mak a fashion o NE.

pretended simulate.

pretence pit-on, mak-on SHETLAND, NE, phrase NE; (*excuse*) scug.

get by false pretences sconce.

pretentious *see also* **affected**; half-hung-tee NE, fantoosh.

pretentious person knab.

pretend to be busy haiver, smatter.

pretext *see also* **excuse**; scug.

pretty *adjective* bonnie.

adverb, see also **very**; gey (an), lucky SHETLAND, NE.

a pretty pass a fine time o day.

pretty well geylies, weel eneuch, no bad.

prevail upon *see also* **persuade**; weir roon(d).

be prevalent (*of an illness*) gae aboot.

prevaricate hunker-slide, hum(ph) an hae, whittie-whattie.

prevarication whittie-whattie, weeshie-washie.

prevent pit fae, kep; (*law: forcibly from carrying out a duty*) deforce.

to prevent for: '*he canna wait for missin the bus*'.

previous umquhile *literary*.

previously, previous to afore.

price *noun* (*very low*) wanworth; (*very high*) dearth NE; (*exorbitant*) ransom; (*price fetched at auction*) roup price SHETLAND, NE; (*of grain, used to fix ministers' pay*) †fiars.

at an average price per item owerheid.

high price bonnie penny.

prick *verb* jag, prog, job, jabbie NE, dob SHETLAND, ORKNEY, NE, brog, stug.

noun jag, prog, job, dob NE, prod SW, stug.

pricker (*for marking etc*) progger.

prickle *noun* jag, job, prog, stab, prod SW, pike.

verb prinkle.

prickly prickie, jaggie, jobbie, sticklie, stobbie NE, prinklie S.

prickly sensation prickle.

pride: full of pride pridefu.

prig primp.

priggish pensie, perjink.

prim *see also* **priggish**; perjink, mim (as a Mey puddock), primsie, dink; (*in speech*) mim-mou'd, mim-spoken, tattie-peelin.

primly perjink, mim.

behave primly mim, primp.

prime *verb* (*a pump etc*) fang.

in your prime in yer potestator SHETLAND, NE.

primrose pinkie, spink, meysie, buckie-faulie CAITHNESS.

primula (*auricula*) dusty miller; (*flower-cluster of denticulata*) kirrie dumplin ANGUS, PERTHSHIRE.

principal *adjective* heid, maist.

noun (*of a secondary school*) rector.

print *noun, verb* prent.

printed book prent buik.

printer prenter.

prior to in front o, afore.

prison *see also* **jail**; jile, nick, kittie S, ULSTER.

prisoner (*at the bar*) panel.

be sent to prison get the jile, be nickit.

private *adjective* quate.

private conversation, private interview collogue.

privet (hedge) privy hedge.

privy *noun, see also* **W.C.**; wee hoose, little hoose, mickey, offic, John Gunn NE, duffie SE.

privy

193

prize *noun* **1** gree *literary*: *'bear the gree'*. **2** *see also* **plunder**; tak.

probable lik(e).

probation: student minister on probation probationer.

probe *verb* (*investigate*) speir; (*poke around*) prog.
noun **1** (*investigation*) speirin. **2** (*instrument*) prog.

problem *noun* (*puzzle*) tickler; (*baffling*) fessener; (*difficult problem*) kinch, (*confused*) raivelt hesp, raivelt pirn.

proceed ca(w) awa, ca(w) the girr; (*esp against difficulty*) win.

proceed against pit at.

proceed with (*a legal action*) insist in.

open the proceedings of (*a court, with a formula forbidding interruption*) fence.

procession (*ceremonial*) walk, parawd.

proclaim lat wit NE.

proclamation (*public*) scry NE; (*written*) paper SHETLAND.

procrastinate latch NE, parry.

procrastinating *adjective* snifflin NE, aff-pittin.

procrastination weeshie-washie, mafflin SW, aff-pit(tin).

procrastinator aff-pit, by-pit NE.

prod *verb* prog, poach, pork SW, S, porr SW, powt, putt; (*with a long instrument*) proadge.
noun prog, nib, pork SW, S, porr SW, dorb NE, powt.

prodigal *adjective, see also* **extravagant, spendthrift**; wastrif(e); (*with money*) fallauge NE.

produce *noun* ootcome; (*of the land*) profit.

production ootcome; (*output*) throupit.

produce young (*of animals*) ferry; (*of small animals*) kittle, kindle SW.

profane *adjective* ill.

proficient *see also* **skilful**; profite NE.

profit *noun* ootcome, fore; (*unreasonably high*) rug.

profound (*of a person*) lang-heidit.

profuse *see also* **lavish**; rowth(ie), fallauge NE.

profusion rowth, lick an skail, lashangallaivie S; (*extravagant*) dem an laive NE.

progeny *see also* **offspring, brood**; get, geet NE.

progress *noun* oncome SHETLAND, NE, forder, ongae, en(d)wey.
verb (*well*) spin NE.

make progress (*eg in business*) forder, mak redd; (*esp in growth*) mak forrit.

we're not making any progress we canna(e) get oot (o) the bit.

prohibit (*law: by an injunction*) interdict.

project *noun* projeck; (*undertaking*) prattick NE.
verb projeck.

projecting piece of land hip; (*on a hill*) kip; (*downward spur*) shank.

projection neb, cantle NE.

prolific (*apt to breed*) breedie.

prominent (*conspicuous*) kenspeckle.

become prominent heave.

promise *verb, noun* hecht.

promising young man lad o pairts.

promising young woman lass o pairts.

show promise few, shape (tae).

I give you my promise! there's ma thoum!

promontory *see* **headland**.

promote *see also* **encourage**; forder.

prompt (*quick, ready*) gleg, olite, yare, timeous *formal*.

prone (*flat on your face*) grooflins, on yer groof, agroof.

prong (*of a fork etc*) tae, prang, grain, stang NE, (*esp of a digging- or pitchfork*) tang.

pronounce pronoonce.

pronouncement speak NE.

proof *noun* pruif, prief, clearance NE; (*law: corroborating*) adminicle.

produce (*a person*) **in proof** (*law*) adduce.

prop *noun* prap, haud, rance, pall; (*in a mine*) gib, stell, tree; (*eg for a beached boat*) steet N.

verb prap, stuit, steet N, stell; (*eg a building*) rance; (*a mine roof*) tree.

propel (*eg a swing with the body*) pile, beam SE.

proper *see also* **respectable**; wicelik(e).

properly richt, the richt gate NE; (*very*) fine an . . .

property (*possessions*) gear: '*guids an gear*', pack NE; (*property held*) haud, haudin; (*wealth*) hullion.

piece of property (*law*) subject.

act of giving possession of feudal property (*law*) sasine.

strip of land dividing properties ma(i)rch bauk.

taking possession of another's property (*law: with or without permission*) intromission.

the person first named in a title to property (*law*) institute.

prophecy *see* **prediction**.

prophesy spae *literary*.

prophetess weird wife.

propitious *see also* **favourable**; seilfu.

proportion: a large proportion of plenty o: '*plenty o them play fitba*'.

the greater proportion *see also* **majority**; plurality.

propose 1 (*for discussion*) propone. **2 propose to** (*a woman*) seek, speak tae, speir (for), speir someone's price.

proposal (*of marriage*) speirin.

proposition proposeetion.

proprietor *see also* **owner**; (*of an estate*) laird; (*one formerly liable for upkeep of church property etc*) †heritor.

propriety *see* **decency**.

prose: long piece of prose screed, scrift NE.

prosecute pit at.

prosecutor (*law: in a criminal action*) complainer.

public prosecutor procurator fiscal.

prosper luck SHETLAND, N, come (guid) speed, thram NE.

prosperity seil, sonse, speed, thrive SW.

prosperous bien, weel-daein, fouthie, pithy.

prostitute *noun, see also* **whore**; hairy, tail, cookie.

prostrate *adjective* **1** *see also* **prone**; (*lying on your back*) awald. **2** (*with illness*) felled.

verb foon(d)er.

protect proteck, perteck; hain, scug; (*with a thick covering*) theek; (*eg with earth or straw, against cold*) hap; (*from attack*) weir; (*from harm with a ritual sign*) sain.

protection bield *literary*, hap; (*of a rock etc*) scug.

give protection to (*a criminal etc*) reset.

protest *noun* (*complaint*) plaint; (*loud outburst*) reird.

verb, see also **grumble, complain**; murmell.

Protestant Prod(die), Prodistan, Billy *slang*, blue nose *contemptuous*.

protrude (*of the eyes*) boggle.

protuberance knap.

proud *see also* **conceited, haughty, arrogant**; prood, poochle NE; (*conceited*) full, great, croose, bigsie ORKNEY, NE, vogie, conceitie, voostie; (*haughty*) proodfu, heich(-heidit); (*self-confident*) poochle NE; (*very proud*) as big's bull beef NE.

proudly heich, heid-heich, voostie.

prove pruive, prieve; (*law: by evidence*) qualify, instruct.

proved *past participle* proven.

proverb wice-sayin SHETLAND, say SHETLAND, ORKNEY, N, speak NE; (*old and worn*) auld sang.

provide (*with sustenance*) fend; **provide for** sort.

provided boden NE.

provided that gin, sae bein('s), perconnon that NE.

provident forehandit, forethochtie.

provision 1 proveesion. **2 provisions**

proveesions, scran, vivers, stuff, scaff, tammie, yer mait, fend NE, †belly-timber; (*esp titbits*) sunkets.

provoke *see also* **annoy;** chaw, teen.

provoking angersome.

provocation provokshin SHETLAND.

prow horn SHETLAND.

prowl *verb* **prowl about** scunge, screenge NE; (*like a dog*) skive, scoorie NE, snoke, ratch S; (*furtively*) mowdie; (*restlessly*) rink NE.

prowler scunger NE, skiver.

on the prowl on the skech.

prudent cannie, auld-farran(t), forehandit, forethochtie, sicker, wicelik(e), tentie NE; (*esp in business*) stieve.

prudish mim, perskeet SHETLAND.

prune *noun* ploom damas.

verb sned, sneck, snod; (*esp a hedge*) scutch, switch, (*severely*) roop.

pry spy (ferlies), neb, snoke, spoach SE.

prying lang-nebbit.

psalm saum; (*first in a service*) gaitherin psalm.

pub *see also* **inn;** howf.

puberty *see* **youth.**

pubes (*female*) fud.

public: publican (*female*) †browster wife, †brewster wife.

public house *see* pub.

publication (*of banns of marriage*) proclamation, cries: '*pit in the cries*'.

in all the public affairs kirk an market.

make public cry at the cross.

public well *see* well[1].

publish (*banns of marriage*) proclaim, cry.

pucker *noun* bumfle, lirk.

pudding *see also* **black pudding;** (*boiled in a cloth*) clootie dumplin; (*steamed in a cloth bag*) poke puddin; (*rich fruit, steamed*) dumplin; (*of sheep's offal, oatmeal etc*) haggis, jaudie FIFE; (*of oatmeal, suet etc*) white puddin, fite puddin NE, (*mealie*) jimmie, (*mealie*) jerker, (*round*) mealie dumplin, (*sausage-shaped*) mealie puddin.

water in which a pudding has been boiled puddin bree.

puddle *noun, see also* **pool;** dub, hole, poach NE; (*small*) loch, lappie; **muddy puddles** gutters.

puerile bairnlie.

puerperal fever weed.

puff *verb* (*blow gently*) pluff, fuff; (*breathe heavily*) pech, stech; (*give out puffs*) lunt; (*at a pipe: see also* **smoke**) feuch NE.

noun (*of air, wind etc: see also* **gust**) pluff, fuff, gliff, guff, waff, peuch, pew SW; (*of smoke, steam*) lunt; (*of a tobacco pipe*) draw, blaw, blast, reek, feuch NE.

puffy (*of the face*) chuffie.

puffball blin man's buff, deil's snuffbox.

puff candy pluffie.

puff out pluff, pew SW.

puffed out 1 bumfelt; (*of the body*) flozent NE. **2** *see also* **breathless;** pecht, puggelt.

with a puff pluff.

puffin Tammie norrie, norie SHETLAND, Tammie cheekie NE, reid-nebbit pussy NE, patie W.

pugging (*of a building*) deefenin.

pugnacious fechtin, randie.

pugnacity fecht.

pull *verb, see also* **drag, tug, jerk;** pou, pul; (*haul*) harl; (*vigorously*) rug, (*rug an*) rive; (*suddenly, sharply*) pook, yank, yerk, yark SHETLAND, ORKNEY, N, snig CAITHNESS; (*stretch*) rax, rack.

noun, see also **tug, jerk;** pou, pul; (*vigorous*) rug, rive; (*sudden, sharp*) pook, yank, yerk, yark SHETLAND, ORKNEY, N, snig CAITHNESS.

pull about touse; (*roughly*) tuggle.

pull apart *see also* **pull to pieces;** spelder.

pull someone's leg draw a bodie's leg, tak a bodie on.

pullover *see* **jersey.**

pull to pieces rive, knip.

pull through (*an illness*) ca(w) throu, thole throu.

pull yourself together gaither, tak yersel up.

pull up (*nautical*) hale.

pullet poullie, earock.

pulley block; (*small, eg in a winding gear*) horl; (*esp for drying clothes from a window*) pulleyshee; **pulley(-wheel)** shave, cheeve N.

pulp *noun* (*esp of food spoilt in cooking*) potterlowe NE.

  reduce to pulp pran NE.

pulpit poopit.

  canopy over a pulpit soondin box.

pulsate *see also* **throb**; putt, skelp, stoon(d).

pulverize *see also* **crumble**; murl (doon), meel NE.

pummel *verb* knuse, nevel.

pump *see* **suction**.

punch *verb, see also* **strike** 1; nevel. *noun, see also* **blow** 2; nevel.

Punch-and-Judy show puppie show.

punctilious(ly) pintit(ly).

punctual(ly) pintit(ly).

puncture *see* **prick**.

pungent snell.

  pungency nip.

  pungent taste kneggum, took.

punish *see also* **beat**; pey, sort, paik, saut, pran NE, norter NE, gie (someone) his fairins; (*fully*) pey hame; (*severely*) soosh; (*eg by caning the soles of the feet*) ram.

  be severely punished get yer heid in yer han(d)s.

  punishment *see also* **beating**; peys, paikin, fairin(s), unction NE, droddum(s): '*dree the droddum*', laldie: '*gie him laldie*'.

  instrument of punishment (*iron bridle*) †branks; (*iron collar*) †jougs.

  punishment before trial Jeddart justice, †Cupar justice.

punt-pole sting, kent.

puny shilpit, shilpie, shirpit, peeng(e)in, drochlin NE, smallie, weanlie, shargart NE, singit, wirlie, wandocht *literary*.

  puny person drochle, shargar NE.

pup *see* **whelp**.

pupil 1 scholar; (*top of a class or school*) dux; (*of a class*) heids S; (*bottom of a class*) fits, fittie, dult w; (*kept in as a punishment*) keepie-in. **2** (*of the eye*) sicht, star o the ee, starn o the ee S.

puppet show puppie show.

puppy *see* **whelp**.

purchase coff.

  purchases (*shopping*) messages: '*pit the messages doon here*', eeran(t)s.

purge *verb* (*bowels*) scoor; (*of a medicine*) wark.

  purgative (*of bitter aloes*) †hickery-pickery.

purify (*a liquid of dregs*) shire.

purl[1] (*knitting*) pearl.

purl[2] (*of water*) gurl.

  purling gurl.

purlin rib, pan.

purple purpie.

purpose *noun* mint, ettle; (*of something*) heid ORKNEY, NE.

  verb ettle, mint.

  for the express purpose aince-erran(d).

  to little purpose tae little maitter.

  without purpose, purposeless lik(e) a knotless threid, fushionless.

purr *verb* curmur, thrum NE, sing (gray) thrums, hurr SHETLAND, ORKNEY, CAITHNESS, nurr S, murr. *noun* murr, three threids an a thrum.

purse *noun* (*esp with a spring clasp*) spung; (*esp leather*) spleuchan; (*esp ornamental, worn with kilt*) sporran. *verb* (*the lips*) thraw.

  pursing (*of the lips*) thraw.

pursuit: set off in pursuit of set efter.

purulent att(e)rie.

pus *see also* **matter**; humour, etter, wursum SHETLAND, ORKNEY, CAITHNESS.

  discharge pus *see also* **fester**; rander, etter.

push *verb, see also* **shove, butt**[1], **nudge**; pouss; (*a person*) gie (someone) the heave; (*urge on*) puist; (*knock*) cave; (*gently*) putt; (*shove*) bray NE, dab N,

ram, kilch SW, S; (*roughly*) burrie NE,
shuit SHETLAND, ORKNEY; (*forcibly*)
ding, dush ORKNEY, N, dird NE; (*eg
with the elbow*) jundie; (*of cattle, with
the horns*) snug SHETLAND.

noun 1 *see also* **shove, nudge**; pouss;
(*gentle*) putt; (*shove*) kilch SW, S; (*heavy*)
doose SHETLAND, ORKNEY, NE, doosht
NE; (*sharp*) ding, dush NE; (*upwards*)
hulster; (*esp with the elbow*) jundie. 2
(*energy*) *see* **drive**.

push along (*on wheels*) hurl.

pustule *see also* **pimple**; plouk, girran
CAITHNESS, ARGYLL.

put *see also* **place**; pit.

past tense pit, put, pat.

past participle pit, pitten, putten.

put aside (*for future use*) pit by, set by.

put(ting) away wa-pit SHETLAND.

put down (*with a thump*) plank, plunk,
plype NE.

put (*someone*) **off** (*something*) pit
f(r)ae.

put in order redd.

put out 1 (*forcibly*) set oot. 2 (*a fire,
light*) smore NE.

put yourself out (*trouble yourself*)
mismak.

put together (*prepare hastily*) rattle
up.

put up with thole (wi), bide: '*He cannae bide his mither-in-law*'.

putrefy *see* **moulder** (*under* **mould**^{2}).

putrid *see also* **smelly**; humphed.

putty pottie.

puzzle *verb, see also* **perplex**; fickle,
tickle, kittle, bleck NE, pall SHETLAND,
ORKNEY, N.

noun (*problem*) tickler; (*see also* **riddle**^{1})
fickle.

puzzling (*difficult*) kittle, kittlie, ficklie,
ticklie.

Q

quack *verb* quaik NE, whaak SHET-
LAND, ORKNEY; (*like a duckling*) queeple.

quaff *verb* cowp, wa(u)cht.

quagmire bobbin-quaw, quakin bog,
quakin moss, shog(gie) bog, hobble bog
NE, hobble quo s, quaw sw, gullion.

quail *verb* jouk, scunner.

quaint *see also* **odd** 2; (*of a child*) aul(d)-
farran(t) (as a nickit bake).

quake *verb* quak, grue.

quaking grass (siller) shaker(s), shak-
ie-tremlies NE.

qualify qualifee.

insufficiently qualified stickit:
'*stickit minister*'.

qualm: I have qualms about it Ah
hae ma doots (aboot it).

quandary *see also* **predicament;**
swither, plet s, hobble quo s.

put in a quandary lant, jam.

quantity *see also* **amount, number;**
(*considerable*) hantle, kit s; (*vague*)
da(u)d; (*large*) feck, lump, muckle,
whack, vast, slap, wecht, hudge ORK-
NEY, N, mask NE, mense; (*of spirits*)
blybe; (*untidy*) ferkishin s; (*small*)
pickle, (wee) tait, lick, fingerfu; (*of food*)
peck; (*esp of drink*) smell.

quarrel *see also* **dispute, wrangle, ar-**
gue, argument: *noun* thraw, threap,
ootcast, split, tulyie, argie-bargie,
grummle, cabbie-labbie, pilget NE, sharrie NE, skew NE, deil-speed-the-liars NE,
jirr NE, snifter s; (*noisy*) catterbatter,
brulzie(ment), tirr-wirr, collieshangie;
(*on the landing of a tenement*) stairheid
rammie.

verb thraw, threap, cast oot, differ,
tulyie, strive SHETLAND, NE, eggle

ORKNEY, N, jirr NE, scash NE, sharrie
NE, skew NE, fratch SW, S; (*violently*)
flyte; (*noisily*) catterbatter s, tirr-wirr.

quarrelling tift(er); (*abusive*) flytin.

quarrelsome carnaptious, camstairie,
argle-barglous, din-raisin, tiftie, ill-
greein, ettersome SHETLAND, ORKNEY,
N, wranglesome SHETLAND, ORKNEY,
NE.

quarrelsome woman randie.

quarry *noun* (*stone-quarry*) quarrel,
heuch.

verb (*stone*) howk.

stone from a quarry quarrel.

quarter 1 (*of a round of oatcakes*) farl,
fardel. **2** (*direction*) airt. **3 quarters** *see*
lodging(s).

quarter day (*for payments, leases etc*)
term day.

Scottish quarter days Candlemas (2
Feb), Whitsunday (15 May), Lammas
(1 Aug), Martinmas (11 Nov).

quarter pound quarter.

quartz (*type of*) cow-lady-stane s,
colladie-stane s.

quaver *see* **tremble.**

quay shore N, FIFE.

land beside a quay shore-heid FIFE.

queasy: rumble queasily (*of the
stomach*) wammle.

queer *see also* **strange, odd** 2; clem.

queer-looking thing *or* **person** magink.

quench (*thirst or a fire*) slock(en);
(*emotions*) smuir.

quench your thirst weet yer thrapple,
slocken yer drouth.

querulous *see also* **peevish, fretful;**
girnie, peeng(e)in, fashious, carnaptious, orpit, yatterie SHETLAND.

be querulous yatter, yabble.

query *noun, verb* speir.

quest *see* search.

question *noun* speir.
verb speir (at); (*closely*) tarragat, streek SE, backspeir.
questioning speir, speirin(s).
person who is always asking questions speir.

queue: stand in a queue stan(d) yer ben.

quibble *noun* fittiefie NE.

quick *adjective* gleg, clivver, swith; (*active*) swipper(t) NE, shuttle.
quickest suinest.
quickly swith, swipper(t) NE, snell; (*without delay*) tite, belyve.
walk more quickly pit in a fit, hoy on.
quick-tempered snappous NE.
quick-witted gleg (i the uptak), snack(ie), sparkie, edgie, sharp as a Kilmaurs whittle AYRSHIRE.

quiet *see also* calm, silent: *adjective* quate, quietlik(e), lown.

noun quate, lown, saucht.
quietly quate, quietlik(e), (*esp of wind*) lown; (*in speaking*) sma: '*speak sma*'.
be quiet haud yer gab, steek yer gab.
be quiet! *see also* hold your tongue (*under* tongue); (haud yer) wheesht!, quate wi ye!, hish!
keep quiet about steek yer nieve on NE.
quieten qua(i)ten, lowden.

quill (*feather*) pen; (*of an animal*) pike.

quilt *noun* twilt, (*specif for a bed*) hap.
verb twilt.

quirk fittiefie NE, norie S.

quit *verb* quate, quite ORKNEY, N.
past tense quat, quate.
quits equal-aqual.

quite 1 *see also* completely; hail, perfit. 2 *see* rather.

quiver *verb, see also* shake, tremble; queever, dirl, twitter, thirl, bever S.
noun hotter.

quoin inban(d), ootban(d).

quota *see* share.

R

rabbit kinnen, kyunnen SHETLAND, bawtie S; (*pet name*) mappie, map-map, moppie, mup-mup; (*young*) leprone.
rabbit's burrow rabbit's hole, clap SW, S, †cuningar.
rabbit's tail bun, fud.
rabble *see also* **riff-raff**; clamjamfrie, trevallie, canallie.
rabid *see also* **furious**; (*of animals*) wuid.
race[1] ilk, etion NE, *often contemptuous*.
the human race Jock Tamson's bairns.
race[2] *see also* **rush**[2]; (*of the heart*) lowp.
rack *noun* heck; (*for drying, eg cheese, indoors*) tirless NE; (*on a grate to hold a pot etc*) winter.
racket *see also* **uproar**; ricket.
racquet (*wooden*) clackan.
radiance *see also* **gleam**; lowe.
radish reefort.
horse-radish redcoll.
wild radish wild kail SW.
raffle lucky-poke.
rafter raft, raghter, bauk, bougar, caber NE, couplin.
pair of rafters (*forming a V-shaped roof support*) couple.
rag 1 cloot, trail; (*fluttering*) wallop; (*long, trailing*) trollop, trailep NE, loorach SHETLAND, NE. **2** (*poor garment*) brat; **rags** cloots, duds, dewgs, pallions, tatterwallops.
ragged raggit, raggetie, raggie, duddie, haggertie-taggertie NE.
ragman ragger N, candyman.
made of rags clootie: '*clootie rug*'.
ragwort ragweed, bunweed, tansy, stinkin Willie, weebies, bowlocks SW.
ragamuffin skybald, tattie-bogle,

tatterwallop ORKNEY, NE, caddie, minker, ticket.
rage *noun* tirrivee, tirr, tit, feem NE, rapture, madderam SHETLAND, ORKNEY, tak S, taum; (*great*) fizz, desperation, feuch; (*sudden*) pirr, flist NE.
verb fizz; (*of a storm*) tear.
fly into a rage gang gyte, fuff, flist NE, fung NE, ree ORKNEY, gae hyte.
be full of rage beal.
rage and curse jeedge NE.
in a (towering) rage dancin mad, lowpin mad, wuid, reid mad.
raid (*Highland*) †creach; (*for cattle*) †spreath.
raider †reiver.
Border cattle raider †moss-trooper.
rail[1] *noun* ravel; (*in a fence etc*) spar NE.
railing ravel.
railway points (*mining*) snecks.
rail[2] *verb* flyte.
rain *noun, see also* **drizzle, downpour, shower**; weet, sowp, saft, black weet ORKNEY, NE, bleeter NE, pani S, *originally gipsy*; **spot of rain** skirp NE, scuff(in).
verb (*heavily*) teem, plump, pish doon, spate, plash, ding on *or* doon; (*violently*) blatter; (*with a crash or splash*) clash; (*gently*) smirr, dew NE; (*slightly*) skiff, spitter, skirp NE, spark.
rainy saft, blashie, plowterie, weetie, spleuterie, feechie, some weetie kin NE, (*very wet*) trashie.
rainy day (*emergency*) sair fit: '*lay aside for a sair fit*'.
(lower) part of a rainbow, regarded as a sign of bad weather weathergaw, wattergaw, tuith NE, stob.
raindrop spark.

be likely to rain draw tae rain, be on for rain: '*We're on fur rain the nicht*'.

threatening *or* **beginning to rain** scowderie.

raise 1 *see also* **hoist;** heeze, heyze NE, hoise, uphaud; (*the head or eyes, to look, listen*) rax (up); (*a hand or foot in attack*) draw; (*the fist threateningly*) cock. **2** (*a legal action*) pursue. **3** (*a price while bargaining*) lowp up.

rake[1] *noun* scartle; (*wide-toothed shoulder-rake*) smiler N; (*for scraping*) harl.
verb (*hay into small heaps*) quile, cole; (*loose hay or straw from a stack*) kaim.

rake together harl.

rake[2] (*dissolute man*) rap.

at a rakish angle skew-whiff.

ram *noun* tuip, teep NE.

young ram tuip lamb.

ramble *verb* **1** *see also* **wander;** rammle, dander, stravaig. **2** (*in speech: see also* **maunder**) raivel, rander, rove. **3** (*of plants*) ramp.

ramshackle ricklie, sha(u)chlie.

ramshackle article rauchle, rickle.

ramsons ramps.

ran *past tense of* **run** run, rin.

rancour gum, ill bree NE.

random: at random beguess.

randy radg(i)e.

range *verb* (*wander over*) reenge.
noun (*distance, limit*) reenge NE.

range over raik.

rank[1]**: of high rank** muckle.

rank[2] *adjective* **1** (*of plant growth*) go(r)skie NE, ruch. **2** (*of taste*) wild, ramsh, ramp SW, ULSTER.

rank growth raff NE.

ransack ransackle, ripe NE.

rant *verb* rane, whudder NE.

rap *see also* **knock:** *verb* knap, knoit NE, pap; (*at a door*) chap, rees(h)le S; (*your knuckles*) clyte.
noun knap, knoit; (*smart, sharp*) stot.

rapacious person gled.

rape (*plant*) rap(s) SW.

rapid *see also* **fast**[1]: *adjective* (*of running water*) strick.

rapidly *see* **quickly** (*under* **quick**).

move rapidly (*rush about*) fleg SW; (*of things*) dreel.

rare seendil, antrin, daimen; (*very good*) rerr.

rarities uncos SHETLAND, NE, ferlies.

find something rare fin(d) a fiddle.

rascal *see also* **rogue, scamp;** laidron, widdiefu, rinagate, moniment, radical SHETLAND, NE, hallion, fang NE, trusdar N, HIGHLAND, ARGYLL; (*mischievous child*) limmer, hurb NE, smatche(r)t SHETLAND, ORKNEY, N, sorra, tike, (*boy*) loon.

rascally *see* **disreputable.**

rash[1] *noun* rush, nirls, hatter, ootstrikin.

have a rash be in a hatter.

rash[2] *adjective, see also* **impetuous, reckless;** ramstam, raucle, ootheidie, lik(e) fire an towe, frush, reevin.

rashly ramstam, lik(e) fire an towe.

rasp *verb* (*make a grating sound*) risp.
noun (*a file*) risp.

raspberry rasp, hindberry; (*wild*) siven; **raspberries** thummles NE.

raspberry-picking berry-pickin, the berries.

rat ratton.

rat-trap stamp, ratton fa.

water-rat watter dog NE.

rate *noun* **1** (*speed*) raik. **2** *see* **tax.**

at any rate oniewey(s).

at a great rate at an awfie skelp, at an aafu surrender NE.

rates and taxes public burdens, cesses.

rather 1 (*sooner*) raither, as lief, liefer. **2** (*somewhat*) raither, ratherlie CAITHNESS, freelins NE, geylies, gey an . . .

rather than or.

ratify (*esp a defective contract etc*) homologate *archaic*; (*a bargain*) chap.

ration raition.

rational *see* **sane.**

rattle *verb* dirl, brattle, shatter; (*of rain, hail*) blatter, bleeter NE; (*of doors, crock-*

ery etc) rees(h)le, rickle.

noun 1 (*sound*) dirl, blatter, bleeter NE, brattle, splatter, clitter-clatter, rees(h)le, rickle, rink NE. 2 (*child's*) corn-craik, craw mill; (*wooden, as used eg by football supporters*) ricketie.

rattle on *verb* (*a door*) tirl.

raucous roupit.

ravage *see* **harry**.

rave *verb* rame, raivel, rove, taiver, raible.

raving *adjective, see* **mad**.

noun raverie NE.

ravel (*become tangled*) fankle.

raven corbie.

ravenous geenyoch.

ravine cleuch, heuch, gill, glack, gullet, lirk.

raw 1 (*of liquor*) hard. 2 (*of weather*) wersh, oorie, oorlich N.

raw-boned runchie.

ray (*of light*) leam, straik; (*small*) peek.

razor razzor; (*as weapon*) malky *slang*.

razorbill scoot, marrot, lavie HEBRIDES.

razor-fish spootfish, spoot.

slash with a razor malky *slang*.

reach *verb* reak, win at, win tae; (*extend*) rack.

noun 1 reak. 2 (*of a river*) rack.

reached *past tense, past participle* raucht.

reach out (*the hand or arm*) **to grasp** rax (oot).

reach over *see also* **stretch out**; rax ower, ower-rax.

reach up to (*of water, on a person*) tak up tae.

read: reading book (*child's first*) †readiemadeasy, †penny book(ie), †penny buff; (*second*) †tippeny (book).

indistinct reading bummle.

read aloud read up; (*fluently*) screed aff.

read with difficulty hamp.

ready olite, weel-wallie, guid-willie, frank, clair, yare *now literary*; (*to do something*) boun, free.

in readiness for again, gin NE.

ready cash lyin siller.

get ready rank NE.

make ready graith, busk.

make ready for mak for.

ready for rife for.

real *adjective* rael.

really! (*expressing surprise*) fegs!, niver a bit!, (ou) yea! NE; (*expressing wild remonstrance*) noona!

realm kinrick *literary*.

reap raep, share.

reaper cutter NE, sharer.

rigs reaped by a band of reapers set.

band of three to eight reapers bandwin.

first strip to be cut in hand-reaping forewin.

rear[1] *noun* 1 hin(t), hin(t)side, hin(t)-en(d), hinneren(d). 2 *see also* **buttocks**; hin(t)-en(d), hinneren(d), hinder(s) SHETLAND, behoochie, bahookie.

adjective hin(t), hinder, hin(d)maist.

towards the rear of something eft.

rear[2] 1 (*children*) fess up NE; (*animals in a field or enclosure*) park. 2 (*of a horse*) kaim.

rearing (*of children*) upfeshin NE.

reason *noun* rizzon NE, raison; (*sanity*) judgement, wit; (*for something*) use.

reasonable (*of a person*) wicelik(e).

beyond the bounds of reason ower the score.

for what reason? whit wey?, fit wey? NE.

the reason why the wey at, foo NE: '*Foo e's deein't, 's . . .*'.

without reason rhymeless NE; (*of a person*) unsensible, no wice.

rebellious *see* **headstrong**.

rebound *verb* skite, stot, stoit.

rebuff *see also* **snub**: *verb* snuil.

noun turn, sloan S, snotter.

rebuild rebig SHETLAND, ORKNEY, N.

rebuke *see also* **scold**: *verb* rebook, check, quarrel, challenge, dreel, gie

someone his fit, snot, speak a word tae.
noun rebook, snotter S, come-again NE, redd-up.
recalcitrant reestie.
recall *see* **remember**.
receipt quittance.
receive (*stolen goods*) reset.
  receiver (*of stolen goods*) resetter.
  receiving of stolen goods reset (of theft).
recent raicent.
  recently (in the) new, newlins NE, shortlins, shortly, short (sin)syne.
  as recently as nae farrer gane than.
reception: good reception *see also* **welcome**; innin.
  reception room public room.
recess (*in a wall*) crannie NE, neuk, (*especially used as a cupboard*) bole.
recipe receipt.
recite rame, scrift.
  recitation scrift.
reckless rackless, ramstam, rhymeless NE, raucle, gallus.
  recklessly racklessly, ramstam.
  move recklessly breenge: '*he breenged in*'.
  reckless person neeger, ramstam, rummlegarie.
reckon rackon.
  reckoning rackonin; (*in an inn*) lawin.
  beyond reckoning untellin.
reclaim (*land*) rive (oot); (*waste or rough ground*) tear in N.
  reclaimed land intak, ootset.
recline lean, lig *now literary*; (*lazily*) floan NE.
recluse mowdiewort.
recognize ken; (*as a relation etc*) own.
  not recognize misken, no goam, nae ken.
  easily recognizable kenspeckle, kenable SHETLAND, NE.
  hardly recognizable unco NE.
  recognition kennin SHETLAND, ORKNEY, N.
recoil *verb* resile.
  noun (*from a gun*) putt.

recollect recolleck, mind, mine.
  recollection mindin, mind NE, mine NE.
recommend (*a person*) moyen NE.
recompense *see* **reward**.
reconcile (*people*) gree.
  to be reconciled gree, come tae.
reconsider forethink NE; (*law*) advise.
record *noun* (*law, written*) writ.
recount *verb, see* **relate**.
recover (*from illness*) win ower, sturken S, betak yersel NE; (*your health or spirits*) cantle up; (*your faculties*) gaither.
  recover from (*illness*) get throu, get abuin NE, come throu, mend O, owercast.
  recovered (*from illness*) till yer fit, tae the road NE; (*completely*) better; (*and going about*) aboot: '*Tam's aboot again*'.
  recovery betterness.
recrimination back-come, castin up.
recruit *verb* (*into the army*) list.
rectify richtify, stra(u)cht.
recuperate *see* **recover**.
red reid, rid.
  redden reid, rid.
  redcurrant rizzar.
  lesser redpoll rose lintie.
  redshank pellile NE, pleep.
redemption: right of redemption (*of mortgaged lands*) reversion.
redress *noun* remeid; (*of a civil wrong*) reparation.
  calling for redress clamant.
reduce (*the intensity of*) lowden.
  reduce to silence *see* **silence**.
  reduction inlaik; (*in rent*) lat-aff.
reed sprot.
  reed bunting ring fowl(ie) NE.
reef skellie NE, skerrie SHETLAND, ORKNEY.
reel *noun* 1 (*of thread, for fishing-rod*) pirn; (*for winding yarn onto reels*) yairn winnles, yarlins NE. 2 (*lively dance*) spring.
  verb 1 *see also* **stagger**; slinger SHETLAND, NE, skavle ORKNEY, N, welter N.

2 (*a fishing line*) pirn in *or* oot.

reel off yerk, scrift, screed aff.

refer: referring (*of something to another authority*) remit.

referee (*in a dispute*) thirdsman.

with reference to anent.

refined *see also* **prim**; perjink.

reflect refleck.

reform (*a person*) mend; (*yourself*) mend, tak up.

refrain *noun* (*of a song, repeated remark*) owercome, owerword.

refresh brisken up, caller NE.

refreshing caller.

refuge (*place of refuge*) bield, hau(l)d, howf.

take refuge howf, scug.

refund *verb* repeat.

refurbish replenish.

refurnish replenish.

refuse[1] *verb* refuise, refeese NE, na-say, grunch, ort; (*to do something*) deny NE; (*to do work*) renaig.

refusal refuise, refeese NE, na-say.

refuse to move reest, (*esp of a horse*) tak the reest.

refuse[2] *noun, see also* **rubbish, scraps;** hinneren(d), hinderen(d), redd, ootwales, ootwalins, drabble; (*of threshed corn*) oot-dichtins, gray meal, pluffins S; (*of oats, barley etc*) shag; (*of corn after riddling*) riddlin heids; (*of fish*) goories NE; (*of melted lard or tallow*) rittocks SW; (*picked up by beggars*) scran.

refuse collection (*of bulky articles*) special uplift.

refuse-collector scaffie.

refuse collector's cart *or* **lorry** scaffie('s) cairt, midgie motor.

regalia (*Scottish Crown, Sceptre, Sword of State*) the Honours of Scotland.

regale treat.

regard *verb, noun* regaird.

with regard to anent, o.

region kintra, country.

register *noun* catalogue.

regret *verb* forthink NE, rue, tak the rue; (*a promise*) rue.

regular reglar, raiglar; (*of wages*) upstannin.

reign ring.

reimburse *see* **repay.**

reiterate threap.

reject *verb* rejeck, ort.

relapse back-gang(in), cast-back.

have a relapse (*in illness*) be thrown back.

relate 1 (*tell volubly and at length*) screed aff. **2** (*pertain*) effeir *law*: '*the land effeiring to the hotel*'.

related (*by blood*) sib.

relating to anent.

relation (*blood*) sib, kin, freen(d), blood freen(d) SHETLAND.

relations sib SHETLAND: '*sib an fremd*'.

relationship sibness.

claim relationship with coont kin wi.

relative *noun, see* **relation.**

relax lint; (*after a good meal*) swage ORKNEY, N.

release lowse.

reliable sicker, moleskin; (*of a person*) cannie.

relief (*from physical discomfort*) easement; (*law: from an obligation etc*) exoneration.

relieve 1 (*law: from an obligation etc*) exoner. **2** (*a person at work*) speel. **3** (*sorrow, pain etc*) souder, sowther.

religion releegion.

religious releegious, guidlie; (*churchgoing*) kirkie.

relinquish *see* **quit.**

relish: without relish kitchenless.

reluctance sweirtie.

reluctant thrawn, sweir(t), sweirdrawn, dour, laithfu, ergh.

rely (on) lippen (till).

remain bide, stey; (*in a place or house*) sit on.

remainder lave, ootwales.

remains (*of a meal*) orrals, brakkins NE.

remark *noun* observe, say, word.
  remarkable unco, parteec(u)lar, sad; (*of its kind*) fell.
remedy *noun, verb* remede.
remember mind (o *or* on), keep mind o.
  I remember (*doing something*) I've seen masel: '*Ah've seen masel gaun on a Sunday*'.
  remember (someone) to (someone) mind tae: '*Mind me tae yer mither*'.
  remind mind, remember: '*Remember me tae pey the milkman*'.
reminiscence mindin, mind NE.
remnant (*of cloth*) remainder.
  remnants aff-fa(w)ins, orrals.
remorse: express remorse remorse NE.
  feel remorse tak the rue.
remote farawa, ootlan(d), faur oot aboot, hiddlie, hyne awa NE.
remove remuve, remeeve NE; (*clear away*) redd; (*from one place to another, to another house*) flit.
  removal (*esp by theft*) wa-takkin; (*to another house*) flit(tin), shift; (*from a tenancy*) ootgang.
remunerate *see also* **pay, wage**; mak up.
rend rive, rent, screed.
render (*fat*) rind.
rendezvous *noun, verb* randyvous, tryst.
rennet yirnin, thickenin w.
renounce renunce.
renovate replenish: '*Ah've replenished that auld hoose*'.
rent[1] (*tear*) *noun* rive, screed.
rent[2] *noun* (*payment: for a farm*) mailing.
  renting (*act of*) location.
reopen (*of a school etc, after a holiday*) tak up.
repair *verb, see also* **mend**; sort, replenish, beet.
  keep in good repair uphaud.
  reparation *see also* **compensation**; mends, upmak.

repartee giff-gaff.
repay repey, repeat.
  repayment repetition.
repeat 1 (*monotonously*) rhyme; (*again and again*) rane; (*from memory*) say ower. **2** (*of food*) come back on a person: '*Ingans come back on me*'.
  repeated saying owerword, auld sang.
  have (*food*) **repeating** hae the rift o.
repel: be repelled by be scunnert at, scunner at.
repent tak the rue, mak a rue, remorse NE.
  repent of forthink NE.
repetition repeteetion, (*monotonous*) rame.
replete *see also* **full**[1]; fou, ful.
replica limn, model, marrow.
reply *verb* (*in argument*) speak back.
  give a curt reply rebat NE.
report *noun* (*account*) din, hearin. *verb* clype.
repose *see* **rest**[2].
representative *see* **sovereign**.
repress haud in aboot.
  repressed doon-hauden, haudendoon.
reprimand *see* **scold**.
reproach *verb* rag, scance at, upcast. *noun* wyte, upcast.
  reproach someone with something cast something up tae someone.
reprobate *see* **rascal**.
reproof *see also* **scolding**; (*severe*) waukenin; (*slight*) rub.
  reprove *see also* **scold**; repree.
repudiate *see* **reject**.
repugnance scunner.
repulse (*someone*) gar (someone) grue.
  repulsion hert-scaud.
  feeling of repulsion set.
  cause a feeling of repulsion in scunner.
  repulsive ugsome, ill-faured.
repute: of good repute namely.
  reputation word.
  bad reputation ill-name.

act up to your reputation be lik(e) yersel.

request *verb* seek, speir.

make a formal request protest.

require requare NE.

research *see* **investigate**.

resemble favour; (*a person*) tak aff, kin(d) tae S; (*closely*) stare i the face; (*esp facially*) swap.

resemblance compare.

resent: resented ill-taen.

show resentment murn.

reserve *verb* hain, pit by, pose up, set by.

noun fordel NE.

reserved (*in manner*) ootward S, stench NE, still, unco.

reserve team wee team.

reservoir pound; (*mining, underground*) lodgement.

reside stey, bide, haud oot.

resident residenter, indweller, indwaller, hamebider (*esp a native of Bo'ness (West Lothian) or Anstruther (Fife)*).

residue lave.

resign: resign membership of a particular congregation lift yer lines.

resign yourself to something tak o it NE, hunker.

resin *noun* roset.

resinous roset(tie).

covered with resin rosettie.

rub with resin roset.

resist gainstan(d).

resistance fend.

resolute stieve.

resolve (*a problem*) redd up.

resort *noun* (*haunt*) howf.

resort to seek tae.

resound dingle NE, stoun(d).

resource: resourceful quirkie, fendie SW, fendfu.

at the end of your resources puggelt, fair deen NE.

reach the limit of your resources win tae the end o yer tether SHETLAND, ORKNEY, N.

relying on your own resources on yer ain poke.

respect *verb* respeck, leuk efter NE.

noun respeck.

respectable douce, honest(-lik(e)), weel-faured, wicelik(e); (*of dress*) honest, gash, pensie NE, gate farrin NE.

not quite respectable wafflik(e), waffish.

respectability honesty.

have little respect for haud licht by NE.

in every respect a(w) weys.

in that respect that wey.

respite lissance.

responsible (*of character*) pensie NE.

responsibility responsibeelity.

(the taking of a) responsibility ontak SHETLAND, NE.

have some responsibility (*on a farm*) hae a pickie (o) say.

rest[1] (*remainder*) lave.

rest[2] *verb* rist NE, faul(d) yer fit NE, faul(d) yer hoch, lean, lint.

noun rist NE, saucht; (*short*) floan NE; (*time of rest from work*) speel.

rested sleepit oot.

restive skeer(ie); (*of a horse*) startie, fliskie NE.

restless fykie, fliskie, wanrestfu; (*esp of a child*) steerin, stourie; (*with eagerness*) fidgin fain.

restlessness fyke.

fit of restlessness the fykes.

in a state of restlessness lik(e) a hen on a het girdle.

move restlessly (*of the feet*) fitter.

be at rest still.

cause to rest lay by.

re-steel (*a plough-iron etc*) lay.

restitution (*repayment*) repetition.

make restitution of repeat.

restore kep, keep in aboot; (*to strength*) sturken S.

restrain pit the branks on, tether, haud in aboot, pit the haims on; **restrain yourself** (*from striking*) keep in yer han(d).

restrained mim, lown.

restraint rander.

beyond restraint neither tae haud nor tae bind.

restrict restrick; (*unduly*) jimp; (*supplies*) scrimp.

restricted scrimpit.

restrict the freedom of tether.

result *noun* affcome, eftercast, eftercome, ootcome, upcome.

end results efterins.

retailer merchant.

retain kep.

retch *verb* reach, boak, byock NE, byochy-byochy ANGUS, cowk.

noun boak, byock NE, spue, cowk NE.

retching with nothing to bring up dry boak.

retinue trevallie, †menyie; (*of a Highland chief*) †tail.

retirement retiral.

retort *verb* speak back, cheek back, cheek up, rebat NE.

noun back-chap; (*sharp*) knack.

retract resile, hen.

retreat *verb* tak leg bail.

noun place o haud SHETLAND.

retribution dirdum, lawin.

return *noun* (*home*) hame-comin.

be returned to a lender with addition (*of something borrowed*) gae lauchin hame.

reveal kythe.

revelation clearance.

revel *verb* rant.

noun splore, carrant; (*riotous*) merry-courant SW.

revelry (*uproarious*) rippet, gilravage; (*disorderly*) †deray.

revenge: revenge yourself on get yer penny(s)worths (oot) o.

be revenged on be upsides wi, be upsides doon wi N.

take revenge on saut.

reverberate dirl, dunner, stoun(d).

reverberation dunner NE, stoun(d), reboon(d), ruddie.

reverie dwam, sloom.

reverse *noun* conter, snifter, thraw NE, whummle.

review *verb* scance.

noun (*quick*) scance.

under review throu han(d)s.

revile *see* abuse.

revive 1 (*in health or spirits*) spunk up. 2 (*law: a legal process*) waken.

revolting *see* disgusting.

revolve *verb* birl, wammle, whummle; (*cause to revolve*) feeze.

revolving *adjective* row-chow.

revulsion scunner, sta(w), forlaithie NE.

reward *see also* deserts; rewaird, hire.

rheumatism rheumatise, the pains.

rheumatic disease spavie *humorous*.

rheumatic joint shot joint.

rheumatic pains rheums.

rhododendron rosidandrum.

rhubarb rewburd, roobrub.

rhyme (*counting-out*) pye NE.

rhythm lilt, stot.

out of rhythm aff the stot.

ribald *see also* indecent; reebald.

ribald talk hash.

ribbed rigged an furred.

ribbon trappin, tial SHETLAND, ORKNEY; (*tying the hair of an unmarried woman*) †snuid.

ribbon grass gairdner's gartens, tailor's gartens.

ribwort plantain ripple-grass, sodger, carl-doddie.

rich *see also* well-off (*under* well²); bien, fouthie, (weel-)gaithert; (*too rich*) ower fou hauden S; (*of food*) fousome.

make someone rich mak someone up.

rich in rife O, lairge O NE.

rick *see* stack.

rickety ricklie, shooglie.

rickety thing rees(h)le, braiggle SW.

ricochet skite.

rid redd.

get rid of redd O, tyne, sha(u)chle aff NE, gie the heavy dunt tae.

be rid of be shot o.

difficult to get rid of (*of a cold etc*) sitten-doon.

good riddance to you merry hyne tae ye NE.

riddle[1] (*puzzle*) guess, quirk.

ask riddles speir guesses.

riddle[2] *noun* (*large sieve*) ree, harp, search; (*wide-meshed*) slogie-riddle s; (*esp for coal*) scree.

verb ree; (*esp coal*) scree; (*ashes*) rees(h)le.

ride *verb, see also* **rode**; (*in a wheeled vehicle*) hurl; (*round boundaries*) ride *or* redd the ma(i)rches.

noun (*in a wheeled vehicle*) hurl; (*in a cart or barrow*) showd N; (*in a wheeled vehicle or on horseback*) sail.

riding equipment ridin graith.

riding horse pownie.

ridge *noun* 1 (*of land*) soo('s) back, hirst, drum, shin; (*high*) rig(gin); (*long, narrow*) kaim. 2 (*in a cultivated field*) rig; (*with the hollow next to it*) rig an fur(row). 3 (*of a roof*) riggin, riggin heid, heid.

ridicule *verb* mak a bauchle o, (mak a) gype (o), tak yer watter aff.

ridiculous *see also* **nonsense**; rideeculas.

riff-raff scruff, scuff, scaff (an raff), clamjamfrie, trag, troke.

rifle *verb, see* **plunder**.

rifle-shooting competition wapinschaw.

rift *noun* rive, clift; (*between friends*) split.

rig (*an election*) pauchle.

rig out reik, pink.

right *adjective* richt.

adverb (*as a direction*) east.

rightly richtlie, richtlins SHETLAND, NE.

right hand thoum han(d) NE.

all right (then) weel a weel.

call to a horse to turn to the right *see* **call** *noun* 1 (3).

put to rights sort, richtify, stra(u)cht.

righteous: self-righteous people the unco guid.

rigid 1 stieve; (*taut*) strait. 2 (*in manner*) stench NE.

rigmarole lay-aff, laberlethin, raible, sclore, say-awa, leetanie SHETLAND, NE, la(m)gam(m)achie NE, lingie; (*nonsensical*) rat-rhyme.

rigorous snell, stere, (*of laws, weather*) sicker.

rim (*on a wheel*) fillie, tread.

rime cranreuch, rind.

rind huil; (*of a cheese*) heel.

ring[1] *noun* raing NE; (*of people*) raw.

ringed plover *see* **plover**.

ring-dove *see* **wood-pigeon**.

ring-ouzel heather blackie, chack.

ring[2] *verb* 1 (*of a bell*) tingle, jowe, (*ring when struck*) dirl. 2 (*a bell*) tingle, jowe.

noun (*ringing of a bell*) ringle, tingle, jowe; (*ringing sound*) chang *in poetry*.

rinse *verb, noun* reenge, syne, synd, sweel.

riot *noun* hurry, gilravage.

verb gilravage.

run riot rin the rig.

riotous dinsome, randie, bellihooin FIFE, camsteerie.

riotousness bellihooin FIFE.

riotous living rampage.

rip *verb* raip NE, rive, screed.

noun raip NE, rive.

make a ripping sound risk.

rip up slite.

ripe (*of fruit etc*) maumie; (*very ripe*) drap-ripe.

ripple *verb* swaw, switter, lipper, lapper, pirl, souch.

noun swaw, lipper, lapper, pirl.

rise *verb, see also* **rose**[1]; (*above the surface*) heave, hove; (*stand on end*) prickle; (*of dust in a cloud*) stour; (*of wind*) tak up.

noun 1 (*of water in a river: sudden*) spate; (*slight*) fluther. 2 (*of an arch*) spring. 3 (*in a coal-seam*) upgae.

well risen (*of bread*) hovie.

late riser capper NE.

rise hastily bang up.

take a rise out of tak the nap aff.

risky mischancie, unchancie.

riven *see* **torn**.

river *see also* **stream, brook**; wat(t)er: '*Water of Leith*'; (*most rapid part*) strick; (*shallow part used as ford*) garth NE, rack SW.

    riverbank (*steep*) brae; (*overhanging*) broo; (*with steps down, where clothes etc are dipped*) dippin.

    riverbed (*gravelly*) claddach.

    river meadow *see* **riverside**.

    rivermouth wat(t)er mou(th), wat(t)er-fit *now in place-names*, inver *now in place-names*.

    riverside (land) (*low-lying*) inks SW, inch *now in place-names*; (*low, alluvial*) haugh, carse, merse SW.

    river valley *see also* **valley**; rin, wat(t)er (gate) S.

rivet *verb* ruive, clink.

    noun ruive, clink.

    riveter's assistant hauder-on.

rivulet *see* **stream**.

roach braze.

road rod, gate; (*for driving cattle*) †drove-road.

    road-fork sindrins, sheddin.

    roadside recess (*for storing road-metal*) lie-by.

    roadstead (*for ships*) raid.

    roadway 1 causey; (*short stretch of*) step. **2** (*inclined, in mining*) dook.

    on the road roadit NE.

    middle of the road croon o the causey.

roam *see also* **gad about**; stravaig, traik, reenge; (*aimlessly*) vaig, scurryvaig, taiver, scuddle, raik; (*from place to place, like a dog on the hunt*) scurry NE, squeerie NE.

    roaming *noun* stravaig: '*on the stravaig*'.

roan *adjective* grim.

roar *verb* rair, goller, gollie, buller NE, rowst, yowt; (*of cattle*) rowt; (*of other animals*) rowt, roup; (*of wind etc*) root, gurl.

    noun rair, reird, goller, gollie, buller NE, rowst, gallyie, yowt, snore; (*of cattle*) rowt.

roaring *adjective* roarie.

roast *verb* sneyster, plot; (*on embers*) harn.

rob *see also* **plunder**; reive, rook, spulzie, roop; (*bird's nest*) herrie.

    robber briganner, †reiver; (*Highland*) †cateran; (*of nests*) herrie-hawk.

    robbery †rapt, †stouth.

    robbery with violence stouthreif.

robin reid Rab, mason's ghost S.

robust *see also* **sturdy, stalwart**; hail, stoot, hardy, rambust, stuffie, umbersorrow S.

rock[1] *noun* **1** (*crag*) craig, clint SW, S; (*sheer*) scaur; (*projection of rock*) snab. **2** (*in the sea*) *see also* **reef**; (*flat*) leck; (*tall column rising out of the sea*) stack ORKNEY, N; (*exposed at low tide*) buss NE. **3** (*crushed*) breese AYRSHIRE; (*broken pieces*) clinkers; (*broken up and used in roadmaking*) metal.

    rocky *see* **stony**.

    rock-pipit rock lintie.

rock[2] *verb* **1** *see also* **stagger, totter**; shoogle, shog, coggle, hobble, howd NE, hyke, showd, shue S; (*gently on waves*) cowd; (*of a boat*) jowe. **2** (*cause to rock*) coggle NE, shoogle, shog, (*also rock to sleep*) showd N.

    rocking (motion) shue, shog, showd; (*esp of a ship*) howd.

    with a rocking motion rocketierowe.

rocket racket.

rod stang, wand, swabble S.

rode *past tense of* **ride** rade, red.

roe[1] (*deer*) rae.

roe[2] (*of fish*) rawn.

rogue *see also* **rascal, scamp**; dyvour, widdiefu, skellum, cheat-the-widdie, bleck, loon, radical SHETLAND, NE.

    roguery joukerie-pawk(e)rie.

    roguish pawkie, ill-trickit SHETLAND, ORKNEY, N.

roisterous rantin.

roll *verb* rowe, pirl, trinnle, trowe, slinger; (*roll about*) wammle; (*at play*) row-chow; (*of a ball*) hurl; (*the eyes*) waul S; (*of waves etc*) sweel.

noun 1 rowe. 2 (*register*) catalogue. 3 (*of bread*) rowe, bap, skinnie; (*floury*) fite bap NE; (*large thick*) foustie; (*crisp-surfaced*) hardie ANGUS; (*flat*) luiffie ANGUS; (*of coarse flour*) sod; (*circular, of coarse flour*) roon(d)aboot NE; (*flaky, made with a lot of butter*) buttery, rowie NE, buttery rowie NE. 4 (*of cloth*) bowt. 5 *see* drum roll.

rolling pin (*esp grooved for oatcakes*) rower.

suitable for rolling trinnlie.

roll along trinnle.

roll over trowe.

roll to and fro walter.

roll towards the jack (*of a bowl*) rowe.

roll up untidily bumfle.

rollicking tousie.

Roman Catholic *see* **Catholic**.

Romany: speak Romany mang the can.

romp *verb* rant, rample, heeze NE; (*boisterously*) ramp; (*amorously*) tig SHETLAND, NE, tig-tow.

noun rant, ramp, heeze NE, randie.

romping hempie.

roof *noun* ruif, reef NE, riggin, hooseheid; (*sloping*) camceil.

roof-boarding sarkin.

roof-gutter rone(-pipe), spoot.

roof-ridge riggin, riggin-heid.

take the roof off tirl, tirr.

rook *noun* craw, corbie.

rookery craw widdie.

room 1 (*of a house*) en(d); (*best room*) chaumer, ben, the room, (*of a but-and-ben*) room-en(d); (*small middle room*) mid hoose NE. 2 (*scope*) scowp N, scowthe.

roomy sonsie, scowthie NE, gawsie, gutsie, great.

in *or* **to the inner room, in** *or* **to the best room** ben: '*they're aw ben the noo*'.

in *or* **to another room** ben (the hoose).

in *or* **to the outer room** but (the hoose).

make room (in) redd.

roost *noun* reest NE, (*hen-roost*) bauk, hen-laft.

roosting bar spaik, reest NE.

root *noun* 1 ruit, reet N; (*small fibrous*) tanner; (*main branch of a root*) taupin. 2 (*of a matter*) grund.

verb (*of a pig*) howk.

gather root-crops lift.

root and branch reet an rise NE.

strike root (*of a plant*) haud NE.

rope *noun, see also* **cord, hawser:** 1 raip; (*length of rope*) towe, girdin, lingel; (*of twisted willow wands*) widdie; (*for lowering coffin into grave*) cord. 2 (*fishing: esp head rope*) bauk N; (*float-rope with corks*) heid-bauk SHETLAND, NE; (*head rope in herring net*) heid towe NE; (*for nets of a drift*) bush-rope; (*bottom rope of a net*) sole raip, skunk W; (*weighted*) grun(d) bauk SHETLAND, ORKNEY; (*side-rope*) gavel ORKNEY, NE, FIFE. 3 (*farming: attaching draught horse to plough*) soam; (*tying cattle in stall*) thrammel NE; (*hobbling an animal*) lingel; (*of twisted straw*) strae raip, thraw raip, thrawcruik S, whippie; (*of straw or hay twisted round the thumb*) thoum raip. 4 (*thatching: to secure thatch*) thack-raip; **ropes securing thatch** raip, (*with stone weights*) simmens SHETLAND, ORKNEY, N; (*cross-rope on stack or thatch*) edderin NE.

verb raip.

rope-twister thrawcruik, thrawheuk, thraw-raip, strae heuk, splicer S, tweezle NE, glaiks SW, ULSTER, wyle.

ropeworks raperee.

rose[1] *past tense of* **rise** raise.

rose[2]: **rosebush** (*wild*) breer, buckie-breer SW, ULSTER.

rosehip dog-hip, doggies' hip NE, hap, buckie, choop SW, S; **rosehips** hippans NE.

rot

rot *verb* daise; (*become musty*) moze SHETLAND, ORKNEY, CAITHNESS.

rotten daised, mozie; (*of wood, fruit etc*) dosinnit; (*of wood, cloth etc*) dozed, frush.

become rotten (*of meat, meal etc*) moch(t) NE.

rotate birl; (*rapidly*) tirl; (*cause to rotate*) pirl, tirl, trowe.

rotation of crops (*each crop*) shift.

rough ruch, roch, haskie, buirdlie NE, unfeel S; (*somewhat rough*) ruchsome, roch kin NE; (*of persons*) raucle, heatherie, teuch, groff, randie, yeukie, tousie; (*in manner*) coorse, ramstougerous, sture; (*in work*) hashie; (*of speech*) raucle; (*of the voice or throat*) roostit; (*of weather*) ill, teuch, gurlie.

roughen (*metal, wood*) faize NE; (*tools*) fluise SW; (*of the skin*) hack.

treat roughly chaave NE, touther.

push roughly burrie NE.

handle roughly *see also* **rumple**; rummle, misguggle, touther; (*esp a woman*) touse.

be roughly handled gae ower the heckle-pins.

rough handling touther, throu-pittin, yokin NE.

roughcast *noun, verb* harl.

rough projection (*on something, after sawing*) rag.

rough and ready hamit, hielan, ramstampish, reuch an richt; (*of a worker*) ramstoorie.

rough treatment norter NE.

round roon(d).

rounders hoose-ba.

round face (*usu stupid*) ba(w)face.

round-faced (*and usu stupid*) ba(w)-faced.

round-shouldered rowe-shoudert NE, howe-backit, tanker-backit, booliebackit, loot-shouthert, loor-shouthert S.

round up (*sheep*) haud S; (*and confine animals as surety for damage done by them*) poind.

roundel roon(d)el.

rouse roose; (*to action etc*) upsteer, rowst.

rout *noun* scatterment NE.
verb skail.

rout out rowst.

route road, gate; (*over a natural obstacle*) pad.

routine job-trot, or(di)nar.

old *or* **usual routine** auld claes an parritch, (the) auld hech how.

depart from your routine mistime NE.

out of your routine aff the stot.

rove raik, haik; (*esp with evil intent*) scamp NE; (*esp for plunder*) gilravage.

rover land-lowper, traik, rinaboot, rinthereoot NE.

roving rinaboot.

row[1] *noun* **1** raw; (*of objects tied together*) stringle NE; (*of people skating or sledging together*) tuckle S. **2** (*in knitting etc*) gang.

row of houses raw; (*mining*) (miners') raw.

set out in a row raw.

row[2] *noun, see also* **quarrel, argument**; stramash, stooshie, stushie, stashie, rammle, reerie NE, ricket.

row[3] *verb* (*a boat*) rowe, oar.

rower (*in stern, in front of helmsman*) hank(-oar)sman NE.

Gaelic rowing song iorram.

rowlock thow(l) (pin).

rowan (*tree*) rodden(-tree).

rowan berry rodden N.

rowdy *adjective* bowsterous, tousie.
noun, see also **ruffian**.

be rowdy stramash.

rowdy behaviour ongaeins.

royalty (*on minerals, books etc*) lordship.

rub *verb* (*in order to dry*) dicht; (*between the fingers*) thrummle SW; (*vigorously*) screenge, fauch NE, ferge up NE; (*wear*) chaff; (*graze*) scuffle NE.
noun dicht; (*polish*) kittle NE; (*act of rubbing*) screenge NE.

rubbed (*chafed*) chattit NE.

rub against skliff.
rub the skin off peel.
rub up the wrong way rub again(st) the hair.
rubber cahootchie, guttie.
made of rubber guttie, guttie-perkie: *'guttie-perkie ba'*.
rubbish *see also* **refuse**[2]; rubbage, muck, brock, clamjamfrie, houstrie, trashtrie, troke, trumpherie, rooster NE, brolach N; ((*to be*) *cleared away*) redd; (*domestic*) midgie; (*piece of rubbish*) rottack NE; (*brought down by a river*) watter-wrack.
rubbish! *see also* **nonsense!** blethers!, hoot(s)!
rubbish dump cowp, tuim.
rubble grummel; ((*to be*) *cleared away*) redd.
ructions *see* **disturbance**.
rudder rither, steerer.
ruddle keel.
mark with ruddle keel.
rude *see also* **impudent, ill-mannered**; indiscreet, ill-mou'd, misbehadden SHETLAND, ORKNEY, NE, mislearit, unmainnerfu, ramgunshoch.
rudely ramstam.
rue *see* **regret**.
ruffian *see also* **rogue**; rochian, randie; (*from Glasgow*) (Glesca) keelie.
ruffle *noun* bord.
verb, see also **rumple**; runkle, snorl, fuffle, touse; (*irritate*) kaim against the hair.
ruffled touslie.
be ruffled (*of water*) lipper ORKNEY, CAITHNESS, NE.
rug (*for wrapping*) hap; (*floor rug: made of rags*) clootie rug.
rugged *see also* **rough**; (*in character*) umbersorrow S.
ruin *noun* **1** (*building etc*) rummle SHETLAND, NE. **2** (*state of ruin*) brolach N, crockaneetion NE, massacker SHETLAND, NE, potterneetion NE, wrack, stramash.
verb cowp, durk, malafooster, wrack; (*a piece of work*) pox; (*a person*) bring tae

the roup, pit tae the door NE, (*by extortion etc*) herrie.
ruination ruinage.
ruined awa wi't, by wi't, throu wi't, shent, in the sheuch, awa for ile, gane tae potterlowe NE; (*bankrupt*) broken.
go to ruin gae tae pigs an whustles, gae tae staps, gae worth NE.
ruin the health *etc* **of** ool.
in ruins a(w) tae sticks (an staves), hyter NE.
road to ruin black gate NE.
rule *see* **reign**.
as a rule for ordinar.
rumble *verb* rummle, dunner, bluiter; (*of thunder etc*) root, hurl; (*of the stomach*) wammle.
noun rummle, dunner NE; (*resounding*) reemis(h) NE.
ruminant *see* **stomach**.
rummage howk, ruit, reenge, kirn, rink NE, ripe NE, hurk SW, spoach SE, tow(in) SW.
rummaging kirn NE.
rummage about in tousle.
rummage through rees(h)le throu.
rumour *noun* clatter, souch, whimper, soon(d), mudge.
verb, see **gossip**.
rump curpin; (*specif of an animal*) rumple, runt SW.
rump-bone rumple-bane.
rump-steak heuk-bone, Pope's eye, round steak.
rumple *see also* **crease**: *noun* lirk, bumfle.
verb lirk, gruggle NE, misguggle, touse, taffle, tuffle SW, S.
rumpled bumfelt.
rumpus splore, sherrack GLASGOW, Kelton Hill Fair SW.
run *verb, see also* **rush**[2]; rin, leg, lift a leg, scoor; (*quickly*) whid, stour, chase, binner NE; (*with clattering footsteps*) splatter; (*with outstretched arms, of children*) flichter.
noun rin, race; (*for a specific purpose*) raik.

runner (*for unloading barrels*) slipe.
runny (*of nose*) snotterie, snochlie.
in the long run at the hinneren(d).
run about (*wildly, of cattle*) startle, tig SW, S.
runabout rinaboot.
run away tak leg, tak leg bail, tak yer heels, mak yer heels yer freen(d)s, tak the gate, skirt; (*in fear*) scar.
runaway *noun* fugie.
run close behind rin ahin.
run over (*a person*) ower-rin.
rung spar, spaik.
runnel *see also* ditch; trink.
runt (*of a litter*) *see also* weakling; dorneedie NE, rag SW, S, titlin, poke-shakkins, shakkins o e pyockie NE.
rupture ripture, ripter; (*hernia*) rimburst.
  ruptured rimburs(t)in.
rural landward.
ruse wimple N.
rush[1] *noun* (*plant*) rash, sprot; (*coarse*) sprat.
  clump of rushes rash bush.
  made of rushes rashen.
  of *or* like *or* overgrown with rushes rashie, sprottie, sprattie.
rush[2] *verb* stour, breeshle, skirr, whidder; (*recklessly*) breenge; (*violently, headlong*) brainyell, ramstam, slash, skelter; (*with a roaring sound*) snore; (*through the air*) wheech; (*from place to place*) fleg SW; (*of liquid*) jaw, pish.

noun scoor N, whirr; (*violent*) breenge, rummle; (*violent forward or downward*) hurl; (*impetuous*) whidder NE; (*headlong*) ram-race, spoot; (*of work*) hurry, hash; (*of water*) jaw, (*noisy*) hurlie-come-gush.
rushing sound whush; (*of water*) hush.
  make a rushing sound whush, souch.
  with *or* in a rush lik(e) stour.
rush about whidder NE; (*excitedly*) flichter, skavie NE; (*frantically*) rammish, rin the hills.
rush downwards hurl.
rush through (*a job*) slim ower.
Russian Rooshian.
rust *noun* roost, iron-eer N.
  verb roost.
  rusty roostie; (*of water*) iron-eerie NE.
  rust mark (*on cloth*) mail.
rustic *adjective* hame-made, landward.
  noun geordie, jock, coof, Michael, teuchter.
rustle *verb* rees(h)le, souch, fissle; (*of ripe grain*) buzzle NE; (*cause to rustle*) rees(h)le, fissle.
  noun (*rustling sound*) rees(h)le N, souch, fissle, stichle NE, hushle NE, hirslin NE.
  with a rustling noise rees(h)le.
rut *noun* rat S, trink NE; (*cut by plough for drainage*) furr.
  rutted trinket NE.
ruthless fell.

S

sack[1] *noun* **1** seck; (*small*) sacket, poke, pyock NE; (*of coal: of a certain measure*) †met. **2** (*dismissal*) **the sack** the heave: '*they gied him the heave*', yer leave, the shift, the road: '*she got the road*', yer jotters.
verb (*dismiss: see also noun 2*) seck, pit awa, set aff.
sackcloth harden, harn.
sack[2] *verb, see* **plunder**.
sacrament (*of the Lord's Supper*) *see* **communion**.
sacrifice secrifeese.
sad *see also* **sorrowful, woeful, melancholy**; sod N, dowie, drearifu, demuired, dowf, dool(some), sairie; (*sad-looking*) drummure.
sadly dowie(lie).
sadness *see* **sorrow**.
saddle *noun* **1** *see also* **pack-saddle**; saidle; (*with hooks for panniers*) cruik saidle; (*pad of straw etc*) sheemach N, †sunk. **2** (*in hills*) sneck.
verb saidle.
saddler saidler.
saddle-girth gird(in).
safe *adjective* sauf, sicker; (*of things*) solvendie N.
safety †sauftie.
place of safety (*in games*) den.
safe-conduct conduck.
sag *verb* swag.
sagging *adjective* dwamfle NE.
sagacious *see also* **wise**; aul(d)-farran(t), wicelik(e), gash.
sagacity *see* **wisdom** (*under* **wise**), **shrewdness**.
said *past tense of* **say** sayed, quo, co N.
past participle sayed, sain.
sail: sailor tarry-breeks.

sailyard rae SHETLAND.
rope attaching sailyard to sail raeband SHETLAND, CAITHNESS.
saint sant, saunt, †sanct.
saintly sauntlie.
saithe *see* **coalfish**.
sake: for goodness sake for onie sake.
salary sellarie; (*minister's*) steepend, stipend.
sale *see* **auction**.
travelling salesman fleein merchant NE.
saliva slavers, slivver(s) NE.
salivate slerp, gush NE.
wet with saliva *verb* slabber, slubber.
sallow *adjective, see also* **pale**; din.
salmon saumon, fish; (*young, at early stage, with dark stripes*) parr; (*at next stage*) smowt; (*on first return to fresh water*) grilse; (*beginning first journey up-river in August*) Lammasman; (*male, at spawning time*) reid-fish; (*newly-spawned*) ligger SW, black fish; (*on autumn run*) grayback SW, S; (*on its way back to the sea after spawning*) kelt.
salmon fishers' hut bothy.
salmon fishing boat (saumon) coble.
salmon leap saumon lowp.
salmon spear leister.
salmon trap (*esp across a river*) cruive, yair SW.
salt *noun* saut.
verb saut; (*specif to preserve*) poother; (*fish*) roose.
salty sautie; (*very*) saut as lick, saut's sel.
salt container (*salt-cellar*) saut dish, saut fat; (*salt jar*) saut willie; (*box on wall*) saut(ie) backet.

salt-maker sauter.

salt water saut bree.

lacking salt wersh.

salute *see also* greet; (*by raising the hat*) hat.

salve saw.

salver server.

same samen, efter ane NE: '*he's aye efter ane*'.

the very same *see* image.

all of the same kind a(w) ae oo.

all the same still an on, whit reck(s).

much the same muckle aboot it, siclik(e).

of the same name of that ilk: '*Moncrieffe of that Ilk*'.

in the same way siclik(e).

in the same way as the same as.

sample *noun* preein N; (*of cloth*) swatch; (*test-piece*) †sey-piece.

verb pruive, pree N.

sanctimonious: sanctimonious person Holy Willie.

sanctimonious people the unco guid.

sanction *see* ratify.

sanctuary bield *literary*, haud SHETLAND.

seek sanctuary (*of a debtor, esp in Holyrood Abbey*) †retire.

sand san, saun.

sandy sannie.

sand-eel san(d)le, san(d)lin NE.

sand-flea sand(y) lowper, sand jumper, sea flech SHETLAND, NE.

sandman Willie Winkie.

sand-martin sandy swallow.

sandpiper sand laverock NE, sand dorbie NE, fiddler, heather peeper, Tibbie thiefie.

sandpit (*on a golf course*) bunker.

sandstone brie-stone; (*easily worked*) freestane; (*very hard*) kingle; (*laminated*) gray slate.

sandwich sangwitch, piece: '*egg-piece*'; '*piece on cheese*'.

sane wice(lik(e)), at yersel, thorow, solid.

sanity wit, judgement: '*lose yer judgement*'.

not quite sane no wice.

sapwood sap-spail.

sarcasm *see* mockery.

sarcastic snell, setterel NE, afftakkin, tuithie.

make a sarcastic thrust at lat at.

sardonic *see* scornful.

sash (*of a window*) (windae-)chess.

sat *past tense of* sit sut, set.

past participle sutten.

Satan *see also* devil; Sawtan.

sate *see* satiate.

sated *see also* full[1]; sairt, gizzent, stappit, stankit NE, no boss; (*thoroughly*) sick-sairt ORKNEY, NE.

satiate ser, sta(w), stowe, stench NE.

satiety *see also* surfeit; ser, sairin.

satin saitin.

satisfy saitisfee, pleasure; (*esp with food or drink: see also* satiate) ser, stench; (*thirst*) slock(en): '*slocken yer drouth*'.

satisfaction saitisfaction.

satisfied fittit, suitit; (*with food: see also* sated) (weel-)sairt, fine; (*of thirst*) slockit.

satisfying (*of a meal*) hertsome.

get satisfaction get (the) mends o.

satisfactory no bad.

satisfactorily bonnilie, richt.

saturate *see* soak.

Saturday Saturday; (*on which no pay is given to fortnightly-paid workers*) blin Seturday.

sauce gravy.

saucy *see also* impudent; pauchtie, skeich.

saucepan *see* pan.

saucer flat, flattie NE, shell NE.

drink (*tea etc*) from a saucer flet.

saunter *see also* stroll, wander: *verb* dander, daun(d)er, daidle, daiker.

noun dander, daun(d)er, stot NE.

sausage sassenger; (*with haggis stuffing*) saster; sausages links, slingers, hingin mince *humorous*; (*sliced*) Lorne sausage, square sausage.

savage *adjective, see also* **fierce**; catwittit, gurlie.

save *verb* sauf; (*money*) gaither.

savings hainins.

savings club menadge, menodge.

save money fog: '*We'll hae tae fog a wee*'.

save up hain (in), pose (up) N.

savour *see also* **taste**; saur, gust, guff.

savoury (*tasty*) gustie, smervie NE.

saw[1] *noun* Rob Sorby N.

verb (*roughly*) risp.

sawing (*wood*) **along the grain** rip.

sawdust *see also* **shavings**; sawins; (*of oak, used for smoking kippers*) mush SHETLAND, NE.

saw[2] *past tense of* **see** seen, seed.

say *verb* (*utter*) moot; (*by heart*) tell: '*tell me yer tables*'.

saying say SHETLAND, ORKNEY, N, word; (*popular*) speak; (*old*) auld sang, threap; (*repeated*) owercome.

say no more about it lat that flee stick tae the wa.

say on say awa.

you don't say! d'ye tell me (sae)?, weel a wyte na.

scab *noun* scur(l), scruif; (*on the head or face*) kell.

verb (**form a) scab** scur NE.

scabbed scabbit, scabbert.

scabby scawt.

scabious curl-doddie.

scaffolding gaberts, brander.

supports for scaffolding branderin.

scald *verb* sca(u)d; (*in hot water to clean etc*) plot, leep.

scalding *noun* scadd(in), scaud(in), plot, leep.

adjective **scalding (hot)** plot(tin) het.

scale[1] (*of a balance*) shall NE.

scales wechts, wey-bauks, wey-wechts; (*public*) weys, †tron.

scale[2] *see* **flake**.

scallop *noun* (*shellfish*) clam(shell).

verb (*sewing*) mush.

scallywag *see* **scamp** *noun*.

scalp *noun* scaup, powe.

scalpel lance.

scamp *verb* (*work*) slim (ower), skiff (by).

noun, see also **rascal, rogue**; nickum, loon, skellum, sacket ANGUS, smatchet.

scamper *verb* skelter, whitter; (*esp of a hare*) whid.

scamper along skelp (on), stour.

scan *verb* scance.

scandal clatter(s), souch, ill-win(d) NE; (*piece of*) din.

scandalize scandaleese.

scandalous michtie.

scandalmonger *see also* **telltale**; clashpyot, clatterer, sclave NE.

scandalmongering speak.

spread scandal clash, clish, clatter, sclave(r) NE.

scant scrimp.

scanty scrimpit, jimp, skintie, seldom NE.

scanty measure scrimpie (measure).

scantily jimp.

scantiness scrimpness.

scapegoat (*public, in a fishing village*) burry man.

scar *noun* scaur, arr, score, blain NE, waum.

verb scaur.

scarred arr(e)d, pock(ie)-arr(e)d.

scarce *see also* **scanty**; scrimp, jimp; (*of money*) slack.

scarcely *see also* **hardly**; scarcelins, scantlins, jimp.

scarcity scant.

scarcity or plenty a hunger or a burst.

scare *verb, see also* **frighten, terrify**; scar, skeer, fleg, fley, fear, gliff.

noun scar, fleg, fley, fear, gliff.

scared *see* **frightened**.

be scared (get a) fleg.

easily scared skeichen NE, easy fleggit.

scarecrow (tattie-)bogle, (tattie-)boodie NE, scaurcraw, craw-bogle, crawnancy.

217

scarf

scare away (*birds etc with a* (*hissing*) *noise*) hish, hush.

scarf (*esp woollen*) gravat, cosie; (*bulky*) brecham.

scarifier scarifeer, grubber.

scarlet fever fivver, rush-fever.

scatter *verb, see also* **sprinkle, spatter**; skail, splatter, sperfle; (*seed, dung*) spark in; (*coins to children at a wedding*) logan NE, strive S.

noun (*of coins to children at a wedding*) poor-oot E CENTRAL, scoor-oot E CENTRAL, scramble W, logan NE, strive.

scattering skail, strinkle.

scatterbrain scatterwit, sodie-heid; (*esp a girl*) taupie.

scatterbrained *see also* **flighty**; scatterwittit, sodie-heidit, stane pirrie S.

scatter about squatter, straw, strowe, strinkle, sheel oot NE.

scavenge *see* **scrounge**.

scent *verb* (*as a dog*) snoke.

scheme *noun* ploy, schame.
verb schame.

scheming *adjective* lang-drauchtit.

schist (*type of*) sclate-ban(d).

scholarship (*endowment to a student*) bursary.

holder of a scholarship bursar.

school scuil, skweel NE, skeel N (*north of Moray Firth*); (*infant school*) wee school; (*subsidiary school in an outlying area*) †side-school.

school attendance officer †whipper-in.

schoolbook *see* **reading book**.

schoolchild *see* **school pupil**.

school dinner hall dinner scuil.

school-leaving party (*at primary school*) quallie (dance) EDINBURGH.

schoolmaster dominie, domsie NE, maister, dick NE.

school pupil scuil bairn, scuil wean, scholar.

be a pupil at school learn the scuil.

scissors chizors, shears.

pair of scissors shears, scissor: '*Gie me the scissor*'.

scoff *verb, see also* **mock**; geck at, scorn at.

noun afftak, bob SHETLAND, N.

scold *verb* scaul(d), tongue, rage at, dreel, sort, redd up, be intae, flyte at, challenge, yaff, coonger, rally on, boast SHETLAND, ORKNEY, N, driffle NE, cyaard NE, siege NE; (*severely*) heckle, targe, gie someone his coffee, kaim someone's hair, gie someone his dixies, gie someone his heid in his han(d)s, gie someone his kail throu the reek, gie someone it het an reekin, gie someone hey-ma-nannie NE.

noun scaul(d), cyaard N, flyter; (*woman*) targe, bard.

scolding scaul(d), redd(in) up, upreddin, ragin, dirdum, dreel, clearin, setawa, targin, waukenin, come-again NE, driffle NE, sederunt NE, cyaardin NE.

scolding match flytin.

get a (severe) scolding get yer heid in yer han(d)s, get yer kail throu the reek, get it het an reekin, get hey-ma-nannie NE.

scone (*triangular*) farl; (*of barley- or wheat-meal and hot milk*) scaddit scone; (*of oatmeal, flour, egg and milk*) skair scone, (*of oatmeal and potato*) drogget scone.

round of six scones cat's face.

scoop *verb* **scoop out** scuip, scob, howk, gowp; **scoop up** (*water*) gowp.

noun scuip; (*used by shopkeepers, seedsmen etc*) scuif; (*for taking samples, eg of cheese*) pale; (*for lifting fish from a net*) spootcher.

scope scowp N, scowthe, tether, heidroom.

scorch *verb, see also* **singe, scald**; birsle, scowder, scam, plot, haister S, sneyster.

become scorched scowder.

score *noun, verb* (*groove*) rit.

have equal scores (*in a game etc*) stan(d) peels, peel.

have a score to settle with hae a day in hairst wi.

what's the score? whit's the Hampden (roar)?

scorn *verb, see also* **mock**: lichtlie, geck. *noun* laith.

scornful mockrif(e), lichtlifu NE.

be scornful sneist.

act scornfully mollop S.

scot-free hailscart.

Scots (language) Scoats, Scoatch, Doric *literary* (*often referring to* NE *Scots*), Lallans *literary* (*usually referring to the language of the 20th-century Scottish Renaissance*).

scoundrel *see also* **rogue, rascal**; scoon(d)rel, skellum, skybal(d).

scour *verb* scoor, reenge; (*energetically*) screenge.

scouring scoor.

scourer *see* **pot-scourer**.

scourge *verb, see also* **whip**; screenge.

scowl *verb, noun* scool, glunsh, gowl, smool SW, gloom.

scowling gowlie.

scrabble scraible.

scraggy (*of a person: see also* **thin**) ill-thriven; (*of an animal*) mean.

scramble *verb* scrammle; (*struggle*) hirsel, sprattle, wa(u)chle; (*about with the hands*) scra(u)chle, scraffle; (*climb clumsily: see also* **clamber**) spra(u)chle, scra(u)chle; (*eggs*) rummle, cotter.

noun scrammle; (*struggle*) spra(u)chle, sprawl NE, sprattle; (*for goods, esp noisy*) rushie, rooshie-doo.

scrap *noun* perlicket N, nick; (*of food*) pick, peck, snap; **scraps** orrals, smatters, smush; (*of food: see also* **leftovers** (*under* **left**[1])) brock, scran NE.

scrape *see also* **scratch**: *verb* scrap, scart, scrab, scrunt; (*eg to clean*) claut; (*scrape skin off*) peel.

noun scrap.

scraper scartle, claut.

scraping noise screeve, screed, scrunt.

scrape an existence, scrape along fend.

scrape through warsle throu.

scrape together scart, harl S; (*in little bits*) scartle, scran.

scratch *see also* **scrape**: *verb* scart, scrat, screeve, rauk SHETLAND, NE, fauch NE; (*make a groove*) rit, rat, ratch S; (*claw*) cleuk NE; (*gently, eg to relieve itch*) claw.

noun scart, scrat, rive, screed; (*large*) screeve; (*deep*) rit, rat, ratch SW, S; (*of the head, eg in astonishment*) claw.

scratched scorie.

make little scratching movements scartle.

scratch around (*as a hen for food*) spur S.

scrawl *see also* **scribble**: *noun* (*hasty letter*) scrape o the pen; **scrawls** hen's taes.

scream *see also* **screech, shriek, yell**: *verb* skirl, skelloch, screel, skraich, spraich, scronach NE, squalloch NE, walloch NE.

noun skirl, skelloch, skraich, spraich, scronach NE, walloch NE.

screaming and shouting yellyhooin W, SW.

scree sclenters, sclithers, glidders S.

screech *see also* **scream, shriek**: *verb* skreek, skraich, screel; (*esp of a bird or animal*) squaik; (*make a screeching noise, eg with a fiddle bow*) screeve.

noun skreek, skraik; (*esp of a bird or animal*) squaik.

screen *see also* **shelter**: *noun, see also* **covering**; (*shelter of wood, stone etc*) sconce; (*between door and fireplace in an old cottage*) †hallan.

verb scug.

screw *noun* feeze; (*wooden, on spinning wheel*) temper-pin.

verb **1** *see also* **twist**; feeze. **2 screw (up)** (*the face*) shevel, showl N, shile SW, thraw.

scribble *see also* **scrawl**: *verb* scart.

noun scart; (*hasty note*) scrape o the pen.

scribbler scriever.

scrimp *verb* jimp, pinch, haud in aboot.

script *noun* write, scrieve.

scripture scripter.

scrofula the cruels.

scrounge *verb, see also* **sponge;** scroonge, scunge, skech, scran, sloonge, scoff, sorn.

scrounger scunge, skech, sloonge, gadger NE, sorner, scranner; (*in dustbins etc*) bucket-scranner, midgie-raker.

scrounging skech: '*on the skech*', scran.

scrub[1] *verb* screenge; (*eg a pot*) reenge.

scrubbing brush rubber.

scrub[2] (*brushwood*) scrogs.

scruff[1] (*of the neck*) cuff (o the neck).

scruff[2] *see* **scruffy person.**

scruffy *see also* **shabby;** waff(lik(e)), scawt, scoorie, scuddie, loon-lik(e), schemie, scaffie.

scruffy person tattie bogle, ticket, (*very*) scaff, scheme, schemie.

scruple *verb* stickle.

scrupulous pe(r)neurious NE.

scrutiny sicht, vizzy; (*brief*) scance.

scrutinize sicht, vizzy, scance, tak (a) swatch o.

scud whid.

scuff *verb, noun* skliff, sha(u)chle, scutch.

scuffle *noun, see also* **disturbance;** rammie, yokin, tulyie.
verb, see also **fight;** tulyie.

scullery-maid *see also* **kitchen-maid;** assiepet, scodgie.

scullion scodgie.

scum *noun* **1** *see also* **froth;** quinkins, (*esp on broth etc*) float. **2 scum of the earth** scuff.

scurf *noun* scruif, screef NE, luce; (*esp on head or face*) kell.

covered with scurf kellt.

scurry *verb* skelter, whidder, fudder NE, scuddle, skirr, squeerie NE.
noun fudder NE.

scutch knock, †strik, †switch.

scutcher lint-dresser, cogster S.

scutter *see* **scurry.**

scuttle *see* **scamper.**

scythe *noun* hey-sned, whittle, Rob Sorby N.

verb maw; (*edges of a field to make space for a reaping machine*) redd roads NE.

scytheman scythe NE.

scythe-sharpener (scythe-)straik, scythe-brod NE.

scythe-shaft (scythe-)sned.

sea *see also* **tide, choppy;** sey MORAY COAST, S, tide; (*full, in May*) sab E COAST.

sea anemone (sea-)pap.

sea beach *see also* **beach;** (*gravelly*) mowrie.

sea bottom, sea floor grun(d); (*rough, out to sea beyond seaweed*) hettle E COAST.

sea-eagle earn.

sea fog (sea-)haar E COAST.

seagull *see also* **gull;** (sea-)maw.

seaman: leading seaman killick W.

sea mist *see* **sea fog.**

sea-pink sea-daisy.

seaport (town) sea toon.

sea scorpion *see* **fatherlasher.**

seashore *see* **beach, foreshore.**

seaside (*as holiday area, on the Clyde coast*) doon-the-watter.

sea-thrift sea-daisy.

sea trout (*kind of*) bill SW; (*young: see also* **salmon**) whitlin, yella fin, finnock, herlin SW, S.

sea urchin hairy hu(r)tcheon.

seaweed (*coarse*) tang(le), currack NE, bellware NE; (*green, slimy*) green gaw NE; (*types of edible*) badderlocks, dabberlacks NE, keys ORKNEY, N, hen's ware NE; (*often made into a jelly*) slake, sloke; (*laminaria digitata*) reid-ware SHETLAND, ORKNEY, N, FIFE, slattyvarrie ARGYLL; (*in slimy strips*) blibbans; (*stems, esp of oarweed*) rowps NE; (*massed on (sunken) rock*) buss NE; (*coarse, washed up by tide*) (sea)ware; (*deep layer, cast ashore in storm*) brook (o ware) SHETLAND, ORKNEY, N; (*roll, along highwater mark*) rowe N.

arm of the sea sea loch.

seal[1] *noun* (*of Court of Session*) signet; (*used to authenticate a royal grant*) privy seal; (*specif for appointment of a QC or of a lord lieutenant*) great seal.

seethe

seal[2] (*animal*) selch, selkie SHETLAND, ORKNEY, silkie SHETLAND, ORKNEY.
seal people (*imaginary race of seal-like sea creatures*) selkie folk, silkies.
seam *noun* saim: **1** (*sewing*) *see* **hem**. **2** (*mining*) *see* **coal-seam** (*under coal*).
search *verb* fork (for), kirn SHETLAND, N; (*a place, thoroughly*) reenge, range, ripe, seek; (*a bag, drawer etc*) gae intae; (*with official warrant*) dacker NE; (*noisily*) reemage; (*eagerly*) screenge; (*a person*) rake; **search for** seek.
noun reenge, fork.
season *noun* saison, sizzon NE; (*favourable*) tid.
verb saison; (*food*) kitchen, hire NE.
seasoning kitchen.
between seasons in the deid thraw NE, on the turn: '*the year is on the turn*'.
seat *noun* **1** sate; (*esp wooden, also used as bed or table*) deas; (*long, wooden*) bink; (*chest used as a seat*) bunker; (*of turf, eg against a cottage gable*) sunk; (*formed by two people crossing hands*) queen's chair, cat's carriage. **2** (*spell of being seated*) sit-doon. **3** *see* **buttocks**; (*of trousers*) dowp.
verb set.
be seated set.
you may be seated set yersel(s) doon.
take a seat lean, plunk yersel doon, plank yersel doon.
secluded oot-the-wey, oot-the-road.
second saicant.
second cousin half-cousin.
second hand (*of a timepiece*) moment han(d).
second-hand *adjective* second-handit.
secret *adjective* saicret, hidlin(s), dern.
noun saicret.
secrecy hidin(s), hudge-mudge.
secretly, in secret (in) hidlins, hidlinwise.
keep (*something*) **secret** steek yer nieve on.
tell a secret lat oot the poother NE.

secretary secretar.
sect profession.
section *see* **segment**.
secure *adjective* sicker; (*strongly made*) sevendle.
verb sicker; (*make secure*) ticht; (*with a loop*) hank.
securely sicker.
security (*law*) caution; (*something deposited as security*) wad.
give security (*law*) set caution.
give *or* **take as security** (*law*) hypothecate.
sedate douce.
walk sedately spyog ORKNEY, N.
sedge seg.
sedgy seggie.
sedge-warbler Scotch nightingale.
sediment grummel, grun(d)s.
full of sediment g(r)umlie.
seduce mistryst.
be seduced (by) (*of a woman*) fa(w) wrang (till) SW.
see *see also* **saw**[2]; sei S.
be unable to see (*in the dark*) no be able tae see yer thoum.
you see? seestu?
seeing that sae bein('s) that.
see to *see also* **look after**; notice SHETLAND, ORKNEY, NE, own.
seed: seedy (*ill, weak*) bauch.
seed-basket ruskie.
seed-potato set.
seed-time sawin time NE.
go to seed shuit, sheet N.
gone to seed shot.
sheet from which seed was scattered †sawin sheet, †sawin happer.
seek *see also* **sought, search for**; sik; (*in marriage*) sik, come aifter NE.
seemly mensefu, wicelik(e).
seep sype, sook.
seer *see* **soothsayer**.
seesaw *noun* shoggie-shoo.
play seesaw cowp the ladle.
seethe (*boil hard*) hotter.
seething hoatchin, hotchin.

221

seething mass hotter.

segment noun (eg of an orange) leaf, lith, skliff, pap NE, gussie ANGUS.

seize see also catch, grab, capture, snatch; saize, cleek, cla(u)cht, grip, nick, nip, mitten SHETLAND, NE; (esp greedily) sneck; (quickly) snap, nam; (law: goods for debt) poind, reest S.

seized past tense, past participle cla(u)cht.

seizure 1 (law: of goods for debt) poinding. 2 see stroke.

seldom seendil, sinnle.

select verb, see also choose; seleck, wale, wyle.

selection walin, wylin.

self sel; (emphatic) ainsel, nainsel NE: 'her nainsel', the sel O: 'the sel o't'.

by yourself see also alone; yer lane: 'he wis aw his lane', im leen, er leen NE, on yer ain.

selfish sellie, hame-dra(u)chtit NE; (excessively) mislearit NE.

selfishness sellie.

self-assured poochle NE.

self-confident poochle NE, croose (i the craw).

self-conscious (esp of children) strange.

self-heal puir man's clover, crochle-girse NE, hert o the yearth S.

self-important see also bumptious, cocky (under cock); pensie, muckle, massie, pauchtie.

self-important person wha but he.

self-indulgent free-livin.

self-reliant person man o his mind.

be self-reliant hing by yer ain heid.

having self-respect pensie, pridefu, sodger-clad but major-mindit.

self-righteous people the unco guid.

selfsame self an same.

self-satisfied croose, kirr SW.

self-willed see also stubborn; thrawn, set, contermacious, pet-willed NE.

sell verb, see also sold; (by auction) roup.

sell up (esp a bankrupt's possessions) roup (oot).

selvage ruind.

semi-detached house hauf-hoose NE.

send sen, set, hae: 'He wis had tae bed', pit: 'It pits me tae sleep'.

send flying skite; (in panic) ramscooter.

send off set (aff); (eg on an errand) road; (on foot) shank.

send out ootpit, (specif smoke, flames etc) tove.

senile dottelt, donnert, doitrified, doitert, superannuate, veed S, veeand S.

sensation (physical) fushion; (momentary) gliff; (pleasurable) kittlin.

cause a sensation set the heather on fire.

sense sinse NE; (good sense: see also common sense) mense, wit; senses intellecks: 'hae yer intellecks', judgement: 'oot o yer judgement'.

senseless see also mad, crazy, insane; glaikit, eediotical, smerghless N; (meaningless) haiveless.

sensible mensefu, wice(lik(e)), pensie NE.

sensibly wice(lik(e)).

sensitive kittlie.

sentence noun (law: now only for capital punishment) doom.

pronounce sentence against doom.

sentiment souch.

separate verb, see also part; saip(a)rit, sinder, twin(e) SHETLAND, (esp sheep from lambs) shed; (disperse) skail; separate from spean fae.

adjective saip(a)rit, sindry.

separately sindry.

separate grain from straw caave the corn NE.

septic see also festering; atterie, etterie.

serene see calm.

sergeant sairgint.

serious see also severe; sairious; (no laughing matter) nae mows NE.

sermon (*esp at Communion service*) †preachin; (*much-used, esp by a candidate for a church*) gallopin Tam; (*eg to a presbytery, by a divinity student*) †exercise.

the manuscript of a sermon the paper.

servant *see also* **farm servant, kitchen-maid, scullery-maid**; (*girl*) (servan(t)) lass, quine NE, (*junior*) teenie; (*young man*) servan(t) chiel; (*servant who does rough work*) scodge, scodgie; **servants** fowk.

servants' quarters (*on a farm*) *see* **farmworkers' quarters**.

serve *verb* ser, sair; (*food at table*) lift; (*wine etc*) birl.

serving (*eg of refreshments at a funeral, of elements at Communion*) service.

serving spoon divider.

serve someone right be chape o(n) someone: '*I think ye're chape o't*', be the price o someone.

serve a (useful) purpose dae the turn, dae a turn.

service 1 (*attendance*) onwaitin. **2** (*church*) diet o worship; (*esp at Communion*) preachin.

serviette *see also* **table napkin**; servit.

servile *see also* **flattering, smooth-tongued**.

act in a servile way tim the foreman's po.

set *verb* (*of jam etc*) mak, jeel.

past participle setten.

noun pair (*not necessarily two*): '*pair o bagpipes*'; (*eg of knitting needles: see also* **knit**) stan(d).

set aside set by, pit past, pit by.

setback *see also* **reverse, snag**; thraw, set NE.

set down (*esp with a thump*) plank, plunk, plowt.

set off set awa, tak the road, tak the gate, steer.

set (up) on (*attack*) set tae.

set out *see* **set off**.

set to yoke tae, lay in.

set-to *see also* **quarrel** fa(w)-tae.

set up (*place in position*) stell.

settle *verb* sattle; (*affairs*) redd (up); (*a quarrel*) souder, sowther; (*make your home*) sit doon.

become settled (*in a place*) heft; (*of weather, after rain*) harden up.

settlement (*esp in marriage*) doon-set(tin), doon-sit(tin), sittin-doon.

settling down 1 (*in a place*) doon-sittin. **2** (*of the surface of the ground etc*) sit.

settle for (*a price*) steek yer nieve on NE.

seven seeven, saiven NE, syven N; (*in children's rhymes*) seater, teven; (*sheep-counting*) lecturi.

seventeenth seeventeen.

seventh seevent.

seventy seeventie, sintie W.

group of seven seevensome.

sever *see* **part, separate**.

several (*several people*) severals, sinnerie(s): '*sinneries o fowk*', pucklies NE.

severe *see also* **harsh, stern**[1]; snell, dour, fell, ill, side (on) NE, (*strict*) snar; (*specif of laws, weather*) sicker; (*specif of weather*) snell, soor, thin, veecious, thrawn NE; (*of pain*) commandin; (*of a blow*) uncannie.

severely *see also* **harshly**; snell.

sew shew, steek; (*hastily*) ranter.

sewing shewin; (*act of*) shew.

sewing kit hussie.

sewer jaw-hole; (*sewage pit*) scuttle(-hole).

sex *noun* (*sexual intercourse (see also* **intercourse 2**): *illicit*) houghmagandie.

verb (*newborn animal*) sicht.

have sex(ual intercourse) *see also* **intercourse**; dance the reel o Bogie, (*of males*) mow (wi), (*illicitly*) lift a leg (on).

sexually excited radg(i)e, yeukie.

illicit sexual intercourse (*by a woman, resulting in an illegitimate child*) misfortune, mistak.

sexton beadle, kirk officer, church officer.

shabby *see also* **scruffy**; scuffie, ill-faured, yeukie, orra, shan, loon-lik(e); (*uncared-for*) drumshorlin, ill-towdent NE; (*of clothing*: *threadbare*) pookit, (*faded*) ill-faured.

shabby person ticket: '*he looks an awfu ticket*'.

shackle *verb, noun* sheckle, hapshackle.

shade *noun* **1** (*shelter*) scug. **2** *see also* **particle**; mention.

verb (*fishing*: *a patch of water, to see the bottom*) sky NE.

shadow *noun, verb* shedda, sha(i)ddae SE, scaddow S, scarrow SW.

shaft 1 *see also* **barrow-shaft**; (*of a cart etc*) tram, stang; (*of a scythe*) sned; (*of a brush etc*) shank. **2** (*in a mine*) shank.

fit (*an implement*) **with a shaft** shank.

shag scarf, scart, scrath NE.

shaggy tautit, tautie, hudderie; (*dishevelled*) tousie.

(person with a) shaggy head of hair heatherie heid, hudderie heid NE.

shake *see also* **shiver, quake, joggle, totter**: *verb, see also* **shook**; shak, shog, shug, shoogle, bevver S; (*violently*) jag, (*up and down*) jirg; (*wave*) wag, wap; (*vibrate*) dirl, dinnle; (*totter*) coggle, jossle, roddle; (*with laughter*) hodge NE, hobble NE, (*also with cold, fear*) hotter NE; (*something, eg to make it rattle*) rees(h)le; (*contents of a sack etc, by knocking on the ground*) dunt.

noun shak, shog, shug, shoogle; (*violent*) jag, cadge NE; (*vibration*) dirl.

shaken *past participle* shakken, shooken, shucken.

shaking *noun* hotter.

shaky *see also* **unsteady, tottery**: shooglie, cogglie, jeeglie; (*esp of a person*) sha(u)chlie, (*weak*) dwaiblie.

no great shakes (at) nae great sticks (at).

shake hands chap han(d)s, crack luifs.

shake off sha(u)chle aff.

shake up cadge NE.

shall *see also* **should**; will, sall; (*after*

personal pronouns) s(e): '*ye'se hae yer supper*'.

shall not *see also* **will not** (*under* **will**[1]); shanna, sanna.

shallow *adjective* shalla, shaul(d); (*esp of the ground in ploughing, or of the mind*) ebb; (*of a dish*) skleff.

noun shalla, shaul(d).

sham *noun, see* **pretence** (*under* **pretend**).

adjective, see also **false**; leesome.

verb, see also **pretend**; feingie; (*illness*) fraik.

shamble *verb, see also* **totter**; sha(u)chle.

shambles *see also* **confusion, chaos, muddle**; knacker's midden, Paddy's market, Annicker's midden, poach, soss, plaister.

shame *noun* (*intense*) black burnin shame.

shamefaced hangit-lik(e), hingin-luggit, doon-leukin.

shameful *see* **disgraceful**.

shameless braisant.

feel shame get a rid face.

it's a shame it's a sin: '*it's a sin, so it is*'.

be overcome with shame gae throu the flair.

put to shame *verb* shent.

shanks's pony shanks('s) naig(ie), shanker's naigie, Tamson's mear.

shape *noun* (*arrangement*) set.

verb coll.

shapeless *see* **out of shape**.

out of shape (*of shoes*) sha(u)chlin; (*knocked out of shape*) bogshaivelt NE; (*twisted*) squeegee.

share *verb* pairt, skair, bunce EDINBURGH.

noun dale, bunce EDINBURGH; (*half*) halfer(s), halvers; (*contribution*) inpit; (*esp of a quality*) rug; (*in some affair*) han(d)lin.

go shares rin snips.

in equal shares hackum-plackum S, eeksie-peeksie.

share equally gae halfers, ging halfers NE.

greatest share, lion's share muckle feck.

not do your full share of work sit in the britchin.

shark *see also* **basking shark;** sherk.

sharp *adjective* shairp, sherp; (*sharp-edged*) gleg; (*mentally: see also* **quick-witted, alert**) gleg, snack(ie), flinty, sparkie; (*astute*) lang-nebbit; (*in manner: see also* **curt**) nebbie, nippit, snell; (*of or to the senses*) snell.

sharpen *see also* **whittle;** shairp(en), sherp(en); (*a scythe*) straik, sha(i)rp, sherp; (*whet*) cuttle.

sharpening *noun* shairp, sherp.

sharply (*of the mind*) shairplie, sherplie.

sharpness (*keenness*) glegness.

sharp-eared gleg-luggit.

sharp-eyed gleg-eed.

sharp-featured peesie-weesie.

sharp-nosed nairra-nebbit.

sharp-pointed *see also* **prickly;** (*of a tool*) gleg.

sharp tongue tongue that wad clip cloots.

sharp-tongued snippie, nebbie, birkie.

shatter chatter NE, smatter.

shattered state smash; '*in smash*', stramash.

shave (*pare*) skive.

(wood) shavings *see also* **sawdust;** spail(in)s, flaesocks NE.

shawl hap, faik NE; (*small*) shawlie; (*worn on the shoulders*) shouderie; (*long rectangular tartan*) plaid; (*of fine quality and intricate pattern, made in Paisley*) Paisley shawl, harness shawl.

she shae, sheu SHETLAND, ORKNEY, †scho.

sheaf shaif, shave; (*small*) tait; (*set up in a field to dry*) gait, gyte NE; (*last on top of a rick etc*) heidin shaif.

band round a sheaf strap SW.

group of sheaves stood to dry stook.

last sheaf on harvest field (*often in the shape of a doll: see also* **corn**[2]) cailleach, carline, (maiden) clyack NE, clyack shaif NE, hare SW, ULSTER, grannie ULSTER.

shear share.

shebeen cheepin shoppie, (*in Lewis or Glasgow*) bothan.

shed[1] *verb* cast.

shed[2] *noun, see also* **hut;** (*for straw*) strae-hoose; (*for salmon-curing etc*) corfhouse; (*rough shelter, for shepherds or sheep*) shiel; (*for cattle*) byre, (*with open court attached*) hemmel; (*of stone, in an exposed place, to preserve food*) skeo SHETLAND, ORKNEY.

sheep *see also* **lamb, ewe, ram;** sheepie(-meh) *child's word;* (*in second year*) towmond S; (*young, until first shearing*) hog(g): '*yowe hog*'; '*tuip hog*', hogget; (*breeds of sheep: white-faced*) Cheviot; (*small, native to Shetland*) Shetland sheep; (*crossbred: blackface and Leicester*) gray face, brockle SW; (*sheep lying on back, unable to get up*) cowpie SW, S; (*which has died a natural death*) morkin SW, S.

sheepish bauch.

sheep-clippers *see* **sheep-shears.**

sheep disease (*types of: usually fatal intestinal*) braxy; (*causing leaping*) lowpin ill; (*brain disease causing staggering etc*) sturdy; (*causing paralysis etc*) thorter ill; (*causing paralysis and trembling*) tremmlin; (*causing itch*) scrapie; (*caused by mineral deficiency*) pine, pinin, vanquish SW; (*dropsy*) watter; (*sheep-rot*) pluck NE, pock.

sheepdog collie.

sheep dung (sheep) purls, (sheep) troddles.

sheep enclosure (*for dipping, shearing etc*) (sheep) fank, (sheep) stell.

sheep-flock hirsel.

sheepfold sheep (bucht), faul(d), ree; (*circular*) roon(d)el, roon(d) SW, S.

sheepmark kenmark, buist; (*on ear*) lugmark, nip, rit, stoo, (*V-shaped*) eel-stab, (*flap*) lap ORKNEY; (*made with ruddle*) keel; (*small, round*) pop SW, S; (*brand on lower part of face*) hingin burn.

sheep pasture sheep gang, (sheep) raik.

sheep-rot *see* **sheep disease.**

sheep-shearing (sheep) clippin.

sheep-shears shears, gangs CAITHNESS.

sheepskin (*separate from wool*) fell S; (*of a sheep that has died a natural death*) mort.

sheep-tick (sheep) taid, keb, ked.

sheep-track (sheep) roddin.

sheer *see also* **complete(ly)**; evendoon.

sheldrake burrow duck, stock annet.

shelf *see also* **ledge, shelving**; skelf, dale; (*eg on a wall, for plates etc*) bink; (*by an old fireplace, for pots etc*) bink, hud.

shell *noun, see also* **shellfish**; shall SHETLAND, ORKNEY, N, sheel.

verb shall SHETLAND, ORKNEY, N, sheel, (*peas etc*) huil, shaup.

shellfish *see also* **whelk, mussel**; (*pyramid shell*) siller-willie; (*cowrie*) John o Gro(a)t's buckie; (*kind of cowrie*) groatie buckie SHETLAND, ORKNEY, N; (*small, delicately coloured*) motherie; (*found on rocks between high and low tide*) scaup.

shelter *verb* **1** (*give shelter to: see also* **protect**) scug, bield *literary*; (*from weather*) lown, lithe N; (*animals*) tak in, hoose; (*a criminal*) reset. **2** (*take shelter*) hiddle, scug, howf.

noun shalter SHETLAND, N: **1** (*sheltered place*) lown, lithe N, jouk; (*refuge*) bield, haud; (*rough: see also* **hut**) howf. **2** (*eg of a rock*) scug; (*against weather etc, eg of wood, stones*) sconce; (*eg windbreak in front of a door*) skathie NE.

sheltered hiddlie, lown, lithe N, bieldie S, innerlie S, lee-laik SW.

shelving *adjective* (*of a riverbank*) shelvie.

shepherd *noun* herd, hird.

shepherd's crook nibbie, crummock; (*for catching ewes at lambing time*) lambin stick.

shepherd's purse leddy's purse.

shepherd's wrap maud, rauchan.

sheriff (*Scots law officer*) shirrif, shirra.

shield *noun* shiel.

shift *verb* mudge; (*awkwardly*) hirsel; (*cause to move*) mudge, jee, fotch; (*along, to make room for others*) hotch yersel.

noun (*at work*) yokin.

shiftless *see also* **feckless**; haiveless, fen(d)less, knotless.

shifty loopie, wheetie NE, hielan NE.

act shiftily hunker-slide.

shilling shullin.

shilly-shally *see also* **hesitate**; waffle, whittie-whattie, ditter.

shimmer *verb, see also* **shine**; skimmer.

noun (*of air on a hot day*) *see* **heat haze.**

shin *verb, see* **climb.**

shine *see also* **gleam, glitter, sparkle**: *verb* sheen, scance, glent, blink, blent, gleet S, leam *in poetry*; (*brightly*) skire, gloze; (*dimly*) blear; (*with reflected light*) skime; (*of the sun: brightly*) beek.

noun glent, gleet S; (*brief*) blink, blent.

shiny glancie; (*esp from wear or friction*) glaizie.

shingle (*gravel*) chingle NE, jingle SW, ULSTER, channer, channel, stanners, mowrie NE.

ship *noun, see* **boat, yacht, barge.**

shipwreck *see* **wreck.**

factory ship (*esp for herring or mackerel*) klondyker.

shirk renaig, slope, hing, jouk.

shirker sloper, slootch, slunk.

shirt *see also* **tunic**; sark, serk.

shirt-collar band sark-neck.

provide with a shirt sark.

wearing only a shirt sark alane, jist in yer bare sark.

shit *see* **excrement.**

shiver *see also* **tremble, shake, shudder**: *verb* chitter, grue, nither, oor, hotter NE, hugger NE, rissle SHETLAND, shither S.

noun grue, hotter NE.

shivery oorit, oorie, greeshach N, groosie, agrue.

shoal[1] *noun* (*of fish*) drave, scuil, skreed SHETLAND, ORKNEY, CAITHNESS.

shoal[2] (*shallow water*) shaul(d).

shock[1] *noun* gliff: 'get a gliff', conflummix NE, stammygaster; (*sudden*) scunner; (*disappointment*) dunt, snifter S, (*stunning*) flamagaster NE.

verb conflummix NE, stammygaster; (*the feelings of*) scandaleese.

shocking awfu.

shock[2] (*of bushy hair*) hassock NE, wizzie SHETLAND.

shock[3] (*group of sheaves*) stook.

setting up blown-down shocks stook parade.

shod *past tense, past participle of* **shoe** shaed, sheed NE.

shoddy *see* **shabby**.

shoe *noun* shae, shee NE, *plural also* shuin, sheen NE, shoon *literary*; (*light, loose-fitting*) sclaff; (*old, worn*) ba(u)chle, sha(u)chle, skliff, scushle NE.

verb, see also **shod**; (*a horse*) shae, shee NE, shod.

shoelace (shae) pint, steeker; (*esp leather*) whang.

shoemaker souter, cordiner; (*apprentice*) snab.

shoemaking souterin, snabbin.

shoemaker's (waxed) thread en, lingel(-en), rosettie-en, rosettie-eyn NE, souter('s) ens, sutter's lingels.

change your shoes change yer feet.

make *or* **mend shoes** souter.

wearing shoes but no stockings slipshod.

shook *past tense of* **shake** shuk(e), shakit.

shoot *verb, see also* **shot**[1]; shuit, sheet N; (*a missile*) pap.

noun (*of a plant: young*) imp, hempe; (*small, slender*) spirl; (*green, on haw-* *thorn*) cheese-an-breid, breid-an-cheese.

shooting competition *see* **rifle**.

shooting star fire-fla(u)cht, †shot star(n).

send out shoots stock N; (*of corn etc, from side or base of stem*) tiller.

(make something) shoot off at an angle skite.

shoot up (*of a plant*) rapple.

shop *noun* chop, shap, tchop NE; (*small, general*) Jennie a'thing(s), Johnnie a'thing(s); (*selling small cheap goods*) penny-rattler NE.

shopping messages, eeran(t)s.

shopping list line.

do the shopping gang the messages, dae the eeran(t)s.

shop assistant coonter-lowper *contemptuous*; (*female*) shop lassie.

shopkeeper (general) merchant; (*of a small, general store*) Jennie a'thing(s), Johnnie a'thing(s).

basement shop laich shop.

shore[1] *noun* strand CAITHNESS, stron ORKNEY.

shore[2]: **shore up** stoot NE.

short *adjective* **1** jimpit; (*stunted*) stumpit, struntie; (*short and thickset*) gudgie, cuttie; (*short and stumpy: of people or things*) fuddie; (*of clothes*) scrimp. **2** (*of pastry etc*) free, frush.

shortage shortcome, inlaik.

shorten (*clothes*) dock; (*of daylight hours*) creep in.

shortly *see also* **soon**; shortlins, in a wee, eenoo, ivnoo.

shortbread shortie.

short (clay) pipe cuttie (pipe).

short cut near cut.

short-tailed fuddie.

short-tempered on short trot, short i the trot, short i the pile, cat-wittit, fuffie, snottie, setterel NE, capernicious NE.

a short time a short NE, a wee, a whilie, a fylie NE.

a short time ago short (sin)syne, short ago, nae lang syne.

in a short time shortlins, in a wee.

short-winded pechie, pechin.

short, stocky person *or* **animal** dottle, laichie-braid, stump(ie) NE.

in short supply scrimp.

shot[1] *past tense of* **shoot** shuit, sheetit NE.

past participle shotten NE, sheetit NE.

shot[2] **1** *see also* **pellets**; (*sound of a shot*) tooch SE, knell NE. **2** (*in curling: played carefully so that it comes to rest at a particular spot*) draw; (*forceful, which knocks a lying stone out of the 'house'*) chap; (*which glances off the inside of another stone*) inwick; (*which strikes the outside of another stone*) ootwick.

should shid, sood, suid, sid NE: '*ye sid dee't*'.

shoulder shouder, shouther, spaul(d); (*of beef, mutton etc*) spaul(d) NE.

shoulder-bone spaul(d).

shoulder joint shouder heid.

shout *see also* **scream**: *verb* cry, goller, gollie, skrauch, rowst, rowt; (*loudly*) blast, toot; (*esp with glee, often in a dance*) hooch.

noun goller, gollie, rowst; (*of joy, esp in a dance*) hooch.

shove *see also* **push**: *verb* shuve, shiv, oxter, ram, bray NE, jundie; (*smartly*) dab N.

noun jundie; (*rough*) hodge SHETLAND, NE.

shovel *noun, verb* shuil, sheel NE, shuffle, shiffle SHETLAND, N.

show *verb* shaw, kythe, lat see; (*point out*) wiss.

noun shaw.

showy fantoosh, dashie NE, swashie NE, glairie-flairie, flarie SW; (*esp in dress*) kickie; (*of things*) gawsie; (*of colours*) roarie, skyrie ORKNEY, NE.

show off pross, splore, kick N, pavie.

show-off primp S.

showing-off bladrie.

show promise of being *etc* shape tae.

make a show of mak a fashion o.

shower *noun* shour; (*specif of rain: esp*

gusty) scoor; (*slight*) skiffle, spitter; (*slight, flying*) scowder, scuff, skarrach; (*short, sharp*) skite, raff NE; (*wind-driven*) spleiter NE: '*it cam on a spleiter o rain*'; (*heavy*) blash, oncome; (*sudden, heavy: see also* **downpour**) sc(r)ow, plype NE; (*often with thunder*) (thunner-)plump; (*heavy but localized*) planet; (*very heavy*) plash, poor, onding, dingon, pelsh NE.

showery plowterie, plooterie, drappie NE, scoorie; (*with cold wind*) scuddrie NE.

shred *noun* shreed, screed, target NE; **shreds** flitters, taivers: '*bile tae taivers*'; (*of cloth etc*) caddis NE.

shrew 1 (*animal*) screw, shirrow, shearmoose, strae-moose, thraa-moose NE. **2** (*woman*) shirrow, targe, sauter, tearer.

shrewd cannie, pawkie, gash, langheidit, fell, far north; (*in business*) stieve; (*because of long experience*) auld i the horn.

shrewdness lang heid, rumgumption.

shriek *verb, noun* skirl, skreich, skraich, skrauch, skelloch NE, squalloch NE, scronach NE.

shrill snell, skraichie.

cry shrilly skelloch NE, squalloch NE, weeack NE.

shrill cry skelloch, squalloch NE.

(make a) shrill sound (*on the bagpipes*) skirl.

shrimp (*freshwater*) screw.

shrink 1 creep in, crine (in), gae in, skrunkle, nirl, screenge SW, S; (*with cold or age*) creep thegither; (*with heat or drought*) scrocken SHETLAND, NE; (*of wood etc, in drying*) gizzen, cling; (*of cloth after wetting*) waulk; (*from a swollen state: of floods, of the stomach*) swage SHETLAND, ORKNEY, N. **2** (*in disgust, fear etc*) grue, gruse, coordie, resile.

shrink back scunner.

shrivel crine, nirl, gizzen SHETLAND, ORKNEY, NE; (*with cold etc*) nither.

shrivelled wizzent, skrunkit, shrunkelt; (*with cold etc*) nither, scruntit,

scruntie, gizzen, clung; (*of grass*) piskie
SW; (*of food*) tewed S; (*in cooking*) setten-on.

shroud shrood, weed, deid claes, linens.

Shrove Tuesday fastern's een, Bannock Day, Bannock NICHT.

football game on Shrove Tuesday
the Ba.

shrub *see* **bush**.

shrug *verb* hirsel, hotch, hussle S.
noun fidge, hotch, hunch.

shrunken (*of a person or animal: see
also* **shrivelled**) picket, wainisht, shilpit, clappit, scruntit, struntie; (*of a person, with age*) cruppen doon.

shudder *see also* **shiver**: *verb* (*with fear,
disgust*) shidder, shither, grue, hotter
NE, girl S.
noun shidder, shither, scunner, grue.

shuddery greeshach.

shuffle *see also* **scuffle**: *verb* **1** shiffle,
sha(u)chle, scush(le) NE, sclatch,
pauchle (alang *etc*), fuffle. **2** (*cards*)
pauchle.
noun scush NE.

shuffling *noun* scush NE, skliff.

shuffling walk sha(u)chle.

shun evite, skulk ORKNEY, NE; (*by not
visiting*) gae by someone's door.

shut *verb* **1** steek; (*a door: see also* **slam**)
pit tae, pul tae, faul(d), lay till; (*property*) shut tae; (*the eyes*) steek, faul(d); (*a
book*) steek. **2** (*of a door*) sneck, gae tae.

shutters shuts, windae-brods.

shut up 1 (*animals in a pen*) parrock,
cruive. **2** (*not speak*) (haud yer)
w(h)eesh(t), save yer breath tae cool yer
parritch, haud *or* steek yer gab, dit NE.

keep shut haud (a door) tae.

shut with a bang dirl (a door) tae.

shut the door as you leave dra(w) the
door tae, tak the door wi ye, pul the
door tae.

shuttle spule.

shy *adjective* ergh, freff, laithfu, blate,
willyart; (*esp of animals*) scar; (*of children*) strange.
verb skeich, (*of a horse*) funk.

shy away from scar.

shy away from a responsibility
renaig.

sick *see also* **ill**; seeck, bad(ly); (*slightly*)
seeckrif(e), nae weel.

sicken *verb* seecken, scunner, scomfish
SHETLAND, NE.

be sickened (by) scunner (at), ug
(at).

sickly unweel, nae (a(w) that) weel,
wersh, peelie-wallie, peelie-wersh S,
peel-an-eat, palie, hingie, hingin, peengie, pyaavin N, dwamie, paewae, dwinie.

sickly-looking etten an spued, fauchie
N.

sickly-looking person graveyaird deserter, kirkyaird deserter NE.

sickness *see* **illness**.

sickbed carebed.

become sick dwam.

sickle Rob Sorby N.

reap with a sickle shear.

side *noun* (*esp of a door, fireplace etc*)
cheek; (*of the face*) haffet.

sidelock haffet.

sidelong sidelins, (*of a glance*) sklent.

give a sidelong glance *see also*
peep[1]; gledge.

sidesaddle side legs.

sideways sidieweys, sidelins.

move sideways skew NE, sklent, jee.

at your side at yer lug.

choose sides chap.

side by side fit for fit, han(d) for
nieve.

to one side ajee, skellie.

on this side of adist.

on that side of ayont, beyont.

on the other side of (*a wall*) throu.

sidle siddle, hirtch.

sieve *noun* seeve, search NE, harp; (*esp
for milk*) sile, sythe, sey; (*esp for coal,
sand etc*) scree.
verb seeve, sye, search NE.

sift (*flour etc*) bout, search NE; (*grain,
meal*) dicht.

sigh *verb* sich, sech, souch; (*of the wind*)
souch, soo.

sight

noun sich, sech; (*deep*) souch; (*of the wind*) souch.

sight 1 sicht. **2** (*odd figure: see also* **spectacle**) ticket, trag NE, baigle, tattie-bogle.

sightless sichtless.

a welcome sight a sicht for sair een.

sign *see* **signal**.

show signs of (*of weather*) mak for.

signal seegnal; (*made by waving*) waff; (*with the hand*) wag: '*gie a wag*'.

signify beir.

silence noun seelence, lown; (*absolute*) neither hishie nor w(h)ishie.

verb w(h)eesh(t).

interjection w(h)eesht!: '*wheesht wi ye!*'

silent *see also* **quiet**; seelent SHETLAND, ORKNEY, NE, w(h)eesh(t); (*completely*) stane-dumb SHETLAND.

be *or* **keep silent** (haud yer) w(h)eesh(t), sing dumb, be quairt NE.

keep silent about clap yer thoum on.

silicosis stourie lungs.

sill sole.

silly sully, daft, tuim-heidit, taibetless, fuil, feel NE, gaupit, gypit, saikless S, sappie-heidit; (*completely*) as daft (CENTRAL) *or* feel (NE) as a maik watch.

silly person sodie-heid, bawheid, gomerel, sumph, gype NE.

silly talk *see also* **nonsense**; jibber, gyper(t)ie NE.

silt noun sleek.

silver noun siller.

adjective siller; (*of coins*) white.

verb siller.

silvery (*of the hair*) lyart.

silver coins white siller.

similar *adjective* siclik(e), saelik(e).

point of similarity swatch.

similarly siclik(e).

having similar qualities sib, lik(e) ither NE.

simmer sotter, tottle, hotter; (*of a pot*) prinkle.

simper smudge.

simple semple; (*plain*) hamelt, hameart; (*naïve*) blate.

simply (*with verbs*) een.

simple-minded no richt, wantin, waffish, sappie-heidit, feel NE.

simpleton *see also* **fool, silly person**; daftie, saftie, coof, sot, gowk(ie), guff, mowdiewort, sumph, feel NE.

simulate feingie, mak on.

simulated simulate, feingit, made on.

sin: bring sin on yourself (*esp by lying*) sin yer soul.

since *conjunction* **1** (*from that time*) sin, syne, fae: '*She's been away fae this mornin'*. **2** (*because*) sin.

adverb sin, syne.

since then sinsyne, fae aan NE.

sincere aefauld, evendoon, leal-hertit.

Yours sincerely (*in letter*) Yours aye, Aefauldlie.

sinew sinnon, leader.

sing tweetle; (*in a low voice*) croon; (*in a low clear voice*) lilt; (*softly*) souch, sowff NE; (*badly*) bummle NE; (*shrilly*) skirl; (*a tune, without words*) diddle, teedle; (*for dancing*) doodle, diddle; (*of a bird*) tweedle.

bad singer bummle NE.

singsong horoyally HIGHLAND.

singe *see also* **scorch**; *verb, noun* sing, scowder, scam.

singed *past tense, past participle* sung, singit.

become singed scowder, get sung.

single 1 aesome. **2** (*unmarried*) free, marrowless, his *or* her lane, im leen NE, er leen NE.

singular *see* **peculiar**.

single-minded aefauld.

sinister weirdlie.

sinister-looking person huidie craw.

sink *verb* (*in mud etc*) lair, lagger, (*gradually*) slump.

noun (*kitchen-sink*) jawbox.

sip (*esp continuously*) sirple.

siren (*factory*) bummer, whustle ANGUS.

sissy *see also* **effeminate**; (big) jessie.

sister tittie.

sister-in-law guid-sister.

sit *verb, see also* **sat**: **1** *see also* **sit down**; (*in a crouching position*) hunker, hurkle; (*lazily*) clatch, clock N; (*as if ill*) clorach NE. **2** (*make to sit*) set.

sitting (*for a meal*) doon-sittin: '*at ae doon-sittin*'.

sitting room (public) room, spence.

sit close cuddle.

sitting close together curcuddoch.

sit in the dark sit lik(e) craws i the mist.

sit down 1 cruik yer hochs, dowp doon; (*suddenly*) clyte, plunk doon; (*heavily*) dyst (doon) NE, souse; (*to a meal, at table*) sit in. **2** (*make to sit down*) set doon.

sit-down (*of a meal*) set-doon.

sit on (*eggs*) clock.

sit still! (*eg to a child*) sit at peace!

site *noun* **1** (*of a building*) stance, steid(in), lan(d); (*with the buildings on it*) onset; (*esp of an old building*) larach. **2** (*place, position*) pairt, locus *law*.

situate: **situated** situate *law and* NE.

be situated near neibour wi.

situation seetiation; (*position*) pouster; (*job*) bit, sit-doon; (*of a servant*) up-pittin, hoose place.

six sax; (*in children's rhymes*) heeturi; (*in sheep-counting*) hecturi.

sixteen saxteen.

sixteenth saxteent.

sixth saxt, sixt.

sixty saxtie.

sixpence saxpence, sick(ie).

group of six saxsome.

period of six months sax-month, †halyer.

six and half a dozen eeksie-peeksie, sixes an saxes.

size *noun* bouk, grist.

sizeable roon(d).

sizzle *verb* seezle; (*esp in cooking*) papple, skirl.

skate[1] *verb* skeet, sketch, skeetch N, skytch, s(c)ly; (*slide*) scurr NE, scutch NE.

noun **1** (*blade*) skeet ANGUS, sketch,

ske(e)tcher. **2** (*act of skating*) sketch, s(c)ly.

skater skeetcher, skytcher.

skate[2] *noun* (*fish*) gray skate.

skate soup (*supposed to have aphrodisiac qualities*) skate bree.

ovarium of a skate skate purse.

skein hank, heap.

skeleton skelet; (*very thin person*) rickle o banes, frame, gaishon SW, S.

sketchy stake an rice, stab an rice.

skewer (*esp for hanging fish to dry*) speet.

skid *noun, verb, see also* **slide**; skite, scurr NE.

skill *see also* **knack**; skeel, slicht, airt, can NE.

skilful *see also* **deft, smart**; skeelie, knackie, profite NE, gleg; (*highly*) far seen; (*dexterous*) cannie, handy; (*ingenious*) crafty, kittle.

skim *verb* **1** (*remove scum from*) scum; (*remove cream from*) ream. **2** (*move lightly*) skiff(le). **3** (*a stone over water*) *see* **ducks and drakes**.

skimmed milk scum milk.

dish for skimming milk scummer, reamer, scale.

skin *noun* **1** (*of a person or animal: see also* **bare skin**) huil, leather, ledder SHETLAND, ORKNEY, NE; (*of a person*) bark, hide *humorous*. **2** (*of a plant*) huil.

verb (*remove skin from*) scruif, screef N; (*in strips*) flype; (*esp accidentally, eg from a leg*) peel.

skinny *see also* **thin, slender**; skrank, shilpit, shirpit.

skinny person skinnymalink(ie).

skin disease (*scaly*) scaw.

having a skin disease in a sotterel NE.

skin eruption *see* **eruption, rash**[1].

skinflint *see also* **miser**; nipscart, peyzart, sneck.

loose piece of skin flype.

mottled skin on the legs (*from sitting too near the fire*) grannie's tartan, tinker's tartan, fireside tartan.

having an unblemished skin hail-skinnt.

skip *verb* **1** (*move lightly*) skiff, skilt S; (*dance*) lilt, link; (*hop*) hip. **2** (*pass over*) hip.
noun link.

skipping game (*jumping over waving rope*) pavey-waveys; (*with fast turns of the rope*) bumps EDINBURGH, firies ANGUS; (*with two ropes turned in opposite directions*) londies SHETLAND, NE.

skipping rope jumpin raip, skip(pin) raip, tow raip.

skipping stones *see* **ducks and drakes.**

skip along skelp.

skipper (*of a curling team etc*) skip; (*of a fishing boat*) mannie.

skirmish *noun, verb, see also* **fight;** skrimmish, bicker, tulyie.

skirt *noun* coat, quite NE.

skirting board skiftin (board).

having a long trailing skirt tingel-tailt.

skittish *see also* **flighty** (*under* **flight**[1]); skeich, fliskie, skeer(ie).

skittles kyles.

skua dirten allan ORKNEY, N; (*great*) bonxie SHETLAND; (*Arctic*) allan (hawk) SHETLAND, ORKNEY.

skulk skook, skowk, jouk, slootch, smook, snoke, smool NE, scug NE, mowdie, scunge aboot; (*idly*) hulk aboot.

skulking person skook, sloonge SW.

skull (harn)pan, powe; (*as* (*heraldic*) *symbol*) mort-head.

sky *noun, see also* **opening;** lift, pen(d), cairry NE; (*clear sky above the horizon at twilight*) weather-gleam SE.

skylark laverock, liv(e)rock NE, laveroo ORKNEY.

slab *noun* (*large slice*) skelp; (*flat stone*) leck NE, SW; (*in baker's oven*) henshel-stane.

slack *adjective* **1** (*of shoes*) sha(u)chlin. **2** *see also* **lazy;** haingle, lither.
verb (*work idly*) jauk, jamph (at) NE, pirl NE, jotter, pingle S.

slacker fouter, cuil-the-loom S.

slackening *noun* slack.

slacken off slack.

slag *noun* (*clinkers*) danders.

slag-heap bing.

slake (*lime or thirst: see also* **quench**) slock(en); (*lime*) soor.

become slaked (*of thirst*) slocken.

slam *verb* (*a door*) clash, dad.

slander *noun* ill-tongue, ill win(d) NE; (*slanderous talk*) ill-speakin; (*law*) defamation (NB also covers Eng 'libel').
verb misca(w), lee on, splairge, sclave(r) NE, say (someone) wrang.

slandered ill-spoken.

slandering *adjective* ill-tonguit.

slanderous (*of a person*) ill-speakin; (*of the tongue*) ill-scrapit.

slant *see also* **slope:** *verb* (*slope*) sklent; (*move slantwise*) s(k)lent, skew.
noun sklent.

at a slant, slanting *see also* **askew;** squint, skellie, sklent, skew.

slap *verb, see also* **smack, hit;** skelp, sclaff, scud, scult, slop N, gowf, cloot; (*esp to crush*) scone; (*a person's face etc*) tak yer han(d) aff.
noun, see also **smack, blow** 2; skelp, sclaff, scud, scult, slop N, scone, cloot, sclatch NE, bluffert NE; (*hard*) sclap NE, sclype NE, fornacket NE; (*used as a threat*) back o ma han(d)!: 'Ye'll get the back o ma han!'

slapdash *adjective* (*of a person*) rummlin, hashie, ramstourie; (*of work*) haisert, yeukie, hairy.
adverb (*rashly*) ramstam.

slash *see also* **cut:** *verb* hash, screed, gulliegaw N; (*sharply*) knack.
noun screed, sned.

slat (*of wood*) rin(d), reen N.

slatted sparred.

slate *noun* sclate, scailie, scallie NE, skylie NE; (*soft, shaly*) blaes.
verb sclate.

slate pencil scailie, scallie NE, skylie NE, screevie.

have a slate loose want a sclate.

slattern *see also* **slovenly person, slut**; laidron, clatch, daw.

slatternly *see also* **sluttish, slovenly**; slutterie.

slaughter *verb* sla(u)chter, fell; (*specif an animal for meat*) butch.
noun sla(u)chter.

slaughterhouse butch-hoose, skemmels NE, killin hoose.

slave sclave.

slaver *verb, see also* **slobber**; slivver NE, slabber.
noun slavers, slever(s), slivver(s) NE.

slay *see also* **kill, slaughter**; en(d), nail.

sledge sled; (*for moving heavy loads*) slipe; (*esp for peat or hay*) car SW; (*for hay etc*) puddock.

sleek *adjective* sleekit, snug SHETLAND, ORKNEY, slaip S; (*specif of a person*) sappie.

sleep *see also* **doze, snooze**: *verb* (*lightly*) dover, gloss NE, snoozle; (*very soundly*) sleep as soon(d) as a peerie, sleep as soon(d) as a horn; (*fall asleep: see also* **get to sleep** *below*) fa(w) ower, fa(w) aff.
noun sowff, slug W, SW; (*child's words*) baw-baw(s), beddie-ba(s), Willie Winkie; (*light*) dover, gloss NE, snoozle; (*light, unsettled*) sloom; (*short, disturbed*) growf.

sleepless, unable to sleep waukrif(e).
be sleepless wauk.

sleepy *see also* **drowsy**; sleeperie.

get to sleep win asleep, get sleepit NE.
lull to sleep hishie.

having slept your fill sleepit oot, sleepit.

suffering from loss of sleep misrestit.

wink of sleep blink.
sleight slicht.

slender *see also* **slim, skinny**; sclinner NE, sma, jimp(ie), spirlie; (*slightly-built*) sober NE.
slender person spirlic.
sleuth-hound sluan, slowan.

slice *noun* sclice, sleesh; (*large*) skelp, whang, fang N, wadge, fardel NE; (*thin*) slive S; (*long, thin*) tag; (*thin, flat: see also* **flake**) sclaff NE; (*of bread, cheese etc*) shave, sheave, shaif, shive, sheed ANGUS; (*of bread with butter, jam etc*) piece; (*end of loaf*) heel, (*with one crusty side*) slab; (*of meat*) collop, (*large*) tailyie.
verb sclice, shave, skelf, slive S; (*thinly*) skive; (*thickly*) whang; (*eg turnips for fodder*) hash.

slice open (*eg fish*) speld SHETLAND, ORKNEY, N.

slick *see also* **skilful**; gleg, snack, soople.

slid *past tense of* **slide** slade, sled.
past participle slidden.

slide *verb, see also* **slid, slither**; ((*as*) *on ice*) s(c)ly, scurr NE, scutch NE; (*suddenly on a smooth surface*) skite; (*on ice, in a crouched position*) hunker-slide.
noun ((*as*) *on ice*) s(c)ly; (*children's*) rone NE; (*skid*) skite.

slight *adjective* slicht; (*of a person, slightly-built: see also* **slender**) sma, smallie, sober NE.
noun heelie.
verb lichtlie, wallipend NE.

slightly some, a piecie, a wee.

slim *adjective, see also* **slender, thin, slight**; sma, slamp.

slime glaur, goor; (*eg on fish*) glit, glet, slam NE.

slimy glittie, slaisterie, slochie, glutherie, goorie N; (*esp from a runny nose*) snotterie.
make slimy glaur.
slimy mass blash NE.

sling *verb, see* **throw, hurl**.
noun (*for hurling stones*) slung.

slink *see also* **prowl, skulk**; sleek, smook aboot, smool NE, snuve S.

slip *verb, see also* **slide, slither**; sklyte, (*cause to slip*) s(c)lidder; (*jerkily*) skitter; (*on a slippery surface*) skite.
noun (*sliding*) s(c)lidder, (*sudden*) skite.
slippery 1 slippie, skitie, skitterie, sli-

slipper

die, s(c)lidderie, sleekie, glib, slibberie ANGUS. **2** (*of a person*) sleek(it), joukie.

slipperiness, slippery condition slipper, glaur.

slippery customer jouk.

slip-knot (*pulled tight*) rin-knot.

slipshod *see* **careless.**

give the slip to jouk, jink.

slip away skice NE.

slip past glent.

slipper baff(ie), carpet NE; (*soft*) saftie; pantin SHETLAND; (*loose, worn*) ba(u)chle, sclaff, sha(u)chle; (*made of strips of cloth*) ruind shuin.

slit *verb* slite; (*a sheep in the ear*) rit. *noun* (*in a skirt etc*) spare, fent; (*in a sheep's ear*) *see* **sheepmark.**

slither *see also* **slide, slip:** *verb* s(c)lidder, sclither, scurr NE, sklyte, hirsel. *noun* s(c)lidder, sclither, hirsel.

sliver *see also* **splinter:** slive S; (*of wood*) spail, splice SE.

slobber *verb* (*in eating or drinking*) slubber, slabber, slaiger, slorach, slairg S; (*messily*) slitter, slaister; (*in drinking*) lerb NE; (*eat in a slobbering way*) sloch, slerp, slorp, slork, logger, slooster. *noun* slubber, slabber; (*slobbering sound*) slerp, slorp, slorach, slork.

slobberer slabber.

slobbering blibberin NE.

sloe slae.

slop *verb, see also* **splash, slobber;** skiddle, sklyte(r) NE. *noun* **1** slutter. **2 slops** slaps, slaister, soss.

slop basin slap bowl.

sloppy 1 (*of food etc*) slidderie, slitterie. **2** (*sentimental*) sapsie.

sloppy food *see also* **slops;** slubber.

mouthful of sloppy food sloor NE.

sloppy mess kirn; (*of food*) plowter.

slope *noun* **1** sklent, deval, swaip S; (*of an arch etc*) spring. **2** brae; (*on hill(side)*) sidelins; (*steep*) shin; (*steep, short*) snab; (*grassy*) gair. *verb* sklent.

sloping sidelins; (*of a ceiling: see also* **ceiling**) coomed.

slosh *see* **slop, splash.**

sloth *see also* **laziness;** sweirtie.

slothful sweir(t), lither.

slouch *verb* sloonge, lootch, s(c)lutter, s(c)lidder, sloit(er), loonge, slotch. *noun* lootch.

slouching person slotch.

slough *noun, verb* (*outer skin*) sloch.

slovenly *adjective, see also* **sluttish;** throuither, throwder NE, slaigerin, huddderie(-dudderie), hashie, mistimeous N, trooshlach NE, haingle NE, strushie NE, gotherlisch NE, owerheid SHETLAND, ORKNEY, oozlie SW, hush(l)ochie; (*in appearance*) untowtherlie NE, tashie.

slovenly person *see also* **slut;** guddle, habble, trollop, trailep NE, slooter N, schamlich NE, hugmahush NE, foongil ANGUS, harl SW, S, mowdiewort, hudderon, scurryvaig; (*big*) sklyte(r) NE; (*very messy*) midden, slitter, slaister.

do something *or* **work in a slovenly way** guddle, clart, gutter, plaister, scuddle, scutter, slitter, slaister, soss, clorach NE, keeger NE.

slow *adjective* slaw; (*of a person: see also* **lazy**) (*tardy*) lag, langsome, latchin NE; (*dilatory*) latchie NE; (*reluctant*) dour, dreich; (*lazy*) doxie NE; (*sluggish*) snifflin NE; (*mentally or physically*) dawlie.

slowly huilie, heelie NE.

move slowly widdle.

slow-witted *see also* **sluggish, stupid;** timmer, donnert, fozie, dauk, donsie S.

slow-witted person mowdiewort.

slow-worm slae.

be slow sniffle NE; (*delay*) latch NE, dringle; (*hesitate*) dackle.

slow down (*go more slowly*) ca(w) cannie.

sludge slutch.

slug snail; (*esp large grey or black*) snake.

sluggard *see also* **lazy person;** s(c)lidder, drool, stump SHETLAND, N.

sluggish *see also* **slow(-witted), lazy;** smerghless, dauk, dour, thowless, waffle, lither, mautent NE, snifflin NE.
fat, sluggish person hullock.
sluice *noun* sloosh, cloose.
slumber *see* **sleep.**
slum-dweller (*woman*) hairy; (*man*) keelie.
slump *see* **fall.**
slur *noun* (*on character*) tash, smitch.
slush slash, (*esp in running water*) snawbree, grue, goor SHETLAND, NE.
slushy slashie, glushie.
slut *noun, see also* **slovenly person;** clatch, heap, hotch, trail(ach), wallydraigle, mardle SHETLAND, NE, strushie NE, dollop NE, toosht NE, harl, soss, slerp, flag; (*esp a housewife*) Mrs MacClarty.
sluttish *see also* **slovenly;** slaigerin, slutterie, ropach HIGHLAND.
sly *see also* **cunning, crafty;** slee, s(c)lidderie, sleek(it), slim, joukie, datchie.
slyly slee.
having a sly sense of humour pawkie.
smack *verb, see also* **beat, slap, spank**[1]; skelp, skeeg NE, scuff; (*esp with the tawse*) scud, scult.
noun skelp, skeeg NE, souflet, sclatch NE, leerup N, slype NE; (*esp with the tawse*) scud, scult, palmie, luiffie.
smacking skelpin, skelpit leatherin.
smack someone's bottom skelp someone's dock, scone someone's dock, pey someone's dowp.
small *adjective, see also* **little, slight;** sma, wee, peedie SHETLAND, ORKNEY, CAITHNESS, FIFE, peerie SHETLAND, ORKNEY, CAITHNESS; (*very*) wee wee, little wee, wee sma, tot(t)ie (wee); (*compact*) sma-boukit; (*slight*) smallie; (*worthless*) nochtie.
small amount sma, (wee) tait, (wee) pickle, smatterin SHETLAND, ORKNEY, N, toosht(ie) NE.
small piece bittie, flichan.

small person *or* **thing** *see also* **insignificant;** smowt, dottle; (*thing*) pink; (*person*) dance-in-ma-luif.
describing a small but capable person guid gear gangs in sma buik.
small change smas.
smallholder crofter, crafter NE, pendicler.
smallholding croft, craft(ie) NE, placie, pendicle, mailin, toft.
smallshot *see* **pellets.**
smallwares smas.
smart *adjective* smairt, smert: **1** (*in appearance: see also* **neat**) snod, perjink, ticht, spree, tosh, gash, knackie. **2** (*see also* **lively**) gleg, edgie, kirr SW.
verb, see also **tingle;** nip, gell SHETLAND, CAITHNESS.
smash *verb* smush, smatter, trounce SW; (*to pieces*) ding tae scowes.
noun stramash.
smear *verb* sclatch, cleester, straik, slair(ie), slairg, skaik NE; (*very messily*) slaister, slaiger; (*esp with the tongue*) slaik; (*with mud*) cla(i)rt, clort; (*a sheep with tar etc*) lay, smairg, smoor.
noun sclatch, slaik, slairie, slairg, skaik NE.
smell *see also* **stink, stench:** *noun* **1** (*slight*) waff; (*bad*) guff, fum, kneggum, feff N; (*very bad*) goo, stew, steuch, (*of decay*) humph; (*esp stifling*) smeek; (*sulphurous*) smush; (*of fumes from burning*) yowder. **2** (*act of sniffing*) snoke.
verb **1** (*have a certain smell*) saur. **2** *see also* **sniff;** snoke.
smelly smeekie, mingin, bowfin.
cause a bad smell guff, stech, stew, steuch.
fill with a bad smell stink.
smelt *noun* spirlin, doobrack NE.
smile *see also* **smirk:** *verb* (*pleasantly*) smirk; (*ingratiatingly*) smue; (*affectedly*) smicker.
noun (*pleasant*) smirk; (*wry*) shevel.
smirk *verb, noun* smudge, smirtle.
smith *see* **blacksmith.**

smithy smiddy.

smithereens shivereens, crockaneetion, lames, spails, potterlowe NE, shaups NE, smatters, scowl(s) ORKNEY, N.

smock wrapper, slop(e), slug, carsackie, curseckie ANGUS; (*child's*) jupe.

smoke *noun* 1 reek, rick NE, smeek, smuik; (*thick, eg from damp fuel*) smuchter; (*thick, choking*) smoch; (*stifling*) smoor, smore; (*column of smoke*) lunt; (*jet of thick, billowing*) (y)oam SHETLAND, NE; (*thick cloud of smoke*) smush ORKNEY, NE. 2 (*at a pipe*) blast, draw, reek, rick NE, feuch NE, (y)oam NE.

verb 1 smeek, smuik, reek, rick NE; (*give out smoke*) smeek, smuist, vent, guff; (*thickly*) tove, smuchter NE; (*of a chimney*) reek. 2 (*a pipe*) reek, blast, blaw, lunt, fuff NE. 3 (*dry food in smoke*) smeek, smuik, reest.

smoky smeekie, reekie, rickie NE, smochie.

make smoky smeek.

smoke-covered reekit, rickit NE.

smoke(-cure)d reekit, rickit NE, reestit.

smoke-filled reekie, rickie NE.

smoke-stained smeekit.

puff of smoke spue (o reek), pewl; (*from a pipe*) lunt.

there's no smoke without fire there's aye some watter whaur the stirk(ie) droons.

smolt smowt.

smooth smuith, smeeth N, sleekit, snod, feel, slid; (*esp of the brow*) brent; (*smooth and slippery*) sleekie; (*smooth and glossy*) sleekit; (*even*) evenlie.

smoothly smuithlie, smeethlie N.

move smoothly jeck NE.

smooth-tongued sleekit, slid(derie), fair-ca(w)in, gleg-gabbit, glib-gabbit.

smooth-working (*of an engine etc*) gleg, jeckin fine NE.

smooth down (*hair*) daik NE.

smooth out stra(u)cht.

smooth over glaze SHETLAND, NE.

smother smither, smudder, smuir, smoor, smore; (*a fire, for the night*) smoor, reest.

be smothered smore.

smoulder smooder, smuik, smuist, smoost, smuchter NE.

smudge *noun* smit, slair, slaurie, tash, smird SHETLAND, NE; (*large*) sclatch, sklatter.

verb slair, tash.

smug croose, kirr SW.

smuggling †free trade.

smuggling boat †bucker.

smut smit, bleck, smad SHETLAND, NE; (*on plants*) bleck.

smutty brookie NE, mottie SHETLAND, NE; (*of language*) groff.

snack piece, chack, snap, chat NE, pit-by, pit-past, snag NE, by-bite; (*eaten during school break*) play-piece, schoolpiece, leave-piece E CENTRAL; (*eaten after a swim*) chitterin bit(e), shivery bite; (*break for a snack*) piece-time.

midday snack twaloors.

mid-morning snack mornin, forenuin bite.

snag thraw *or* whaup i the raip.

snail-shell buckie.

snap *noun* knack; (*esp of a dog*) snack.

verb knack, knip, knick, snash; (*with the teeth*) snack, hanch; (*specif of a dog*) gansh.

snapdragon grannie('s) mutch(es), mappie('s)-mou(s).

snap your fingers crack yer thoums.

snare *noun* girn, crank SW, S; mink.

verb (*catch in a snare*) girn, fankle, snarl.

snarl *noun* girn, gurl, habber N, wurr NE, nurr.

verb snag, snagger NE, yirr SHETLAND, gansh, wurr NE, nurr.

snatch *noun* glamp, glaum.

verb sneck, hanch, snap NE, glaum.

snatch at glaum at, (let) glammach at NE; (*forcibly*) reeve at; (*of a dog*) gansh.

snatch away wheech awa, wheek awa NE.

snatch up clink up.

sneak *noun* hinkum sneev(l)ie, tod, snaik, pick-thank NE, sloonge SW, snuive S.
verb snaik, sleek, smook, smool NE, snuive S.

sneer *noun* sneist.
verb girn, snash (at).
sneering sneistie.

sneeze *noun* neeze SHETLAND, ORKNEY, NE.
verb sneesh, neeze SHETLAND, ORKNEY, NE.

sniff *noun* snift(er), snoke.
verb snifter, snoke, snook, snowk.

snigger *noun* snicher, sneeger, nicher, snifter, sneeter, snirt, snirk.
verb snicher, sneeger, nicher, snirt, snoke, sneeter, snirt.

snip *verb* nick, sneck, sneg, whang.

snipe heather-bleat(er), earn-bleater NE, blitter SW, moss-bluiter SW, mire-snipe.

snivel *noun* sneevil, snifter.
verb sneevil, snifter, bubble, snotter.
snivelling *adjective* sneevlin, bubblie.

snob flee-up, cockapentie, knab.

snobbish pridefu, stinkin SHETLAND, NE, wallie-close-gless-door W, fur coat an nae knickers EDINBURGH.

snooze *noun* dover, gloss NE, souch SW.
verb dover, snotter, gloss NE, snoozle.

snore *noun* snocher.
verb snifter, snoit(er), snork; (*esp loudly*) snagger NE.

snort *noun* snirt, snifter, snirk, snocher, guff, sneer.
verb snirt, snirtle, snift(er), snirk, snork, guff, snotter.

snot snotter, bubbles, snochter, snochles NE.
snotty snotterie, bubblie(-nosed), snochlie NE.

snout snoot, (*of a pig*) grunyie, gruntle S.

snow *noun* snaw, snyauve NE; (*drifting*) blin-drift; (*slushy*) lapper; (*powdery*) dry drift; (*driven by the wind*) speendrift NE, yowdendrift *literary*.
verb snaw, snyauve NE.

snowy snawie, snyauvie NE.

snow-bunting snawflake.

snow-covered snawsel.

snowdrift (snaw-)wreath, snaw(-wride), blin smoor.

snowfall (*heavy*) oncome, onfa(w), ding-on (o snaw); (*esp when lying on the ground*) storm.

snowflake pile, flichan, fla(u)cht; (*large*) flag N.

snowstorm stour, yowdendrift *literary*.

bank of snow *see* snowdrift.

snub *noun* chaw, sneck, snotter.
verb saut, snot, snool, snib, chap in the taes NE.

snuff *noun* sneesh(in); (*home-made*) graddan.
verb 1 (*poke with the nose*) snoke. 2 (*a candle*) snite.

snuffbox mill, mull, sneeshin-mill, sneeshin-horn, †sneeshin-box.

snuff-spoon sneeshin-pen.

pinch of snuff snuff, sneesh.

take snuff snuff, sneesh.

snuffle *noun* sneevil, snifter, snocher, snochle NE.
verb snifter, snocher, snork, snotter, sneer, guff, snochle NE.

snug *see also* cosy; snog, snoog, snod, cosh, couthie, ticht, tosie, lithe N, curmud S.

snuggle (down) coorie (doon).

snuggle up coorie in.

so sae, sic NE; (*to such a degree*) that: '*that big*', this; (*in that case*) syne: '*an syne ye're no gaun*'.

so-and-so sic a bodie, sic-an-sic.

it is so! it is sot!, it is sut!

soak *verb* drook, drookle, dook, draik, logger, steep, sap, sowp, slock NE, sotter; (*esp clothes in soapy water*) sapple.
noun, see soaking.

soaked *see also* sodden; drookit, drookelt, seepit, sypit, draigelt, soggit NE, sypin.

soaking *adjective* (*very wet*) plashin,

soap

platchin S, seepin, in a soom SHET-
LAND, ORKNEY, NE.
noun dookin, drook.
soak through seek throu.
soap *noun, verb* saip.
soapy saipie.
soapsuds (saipie) sapples; (*dirty, used*)
graith.
soar tove NE.
sob *noun* sab, greet, bubble, bibble NE.
verb sab, bubble, bibble NE, toot(er), isk
CAITHNESS, byke SW; (*noisily*) hick S.
sober 1 (*not drunk*) richt, fresh; (*completely*) due sober. **2** (*sedate*) douce, richt.
sociable couthie, oncomin, sonsie;
(*convivial*) hertie, joco, innerlie.
social: social gathering soirée, swaree, suree, ba(ll), ploy SHETLAND, ceilidh
HIGHLAND, jine.
social upstarts fite-iron gentry NE.
sock (*old, worn as slipper etc*) hogger E
CENTRAL, fittock ORKNEY, CAITH-
NESS, NE.
pull up your socks pou up yer
breeks.
socket (*for a tool-handle*) hose, ho(o)zle.
sod[1] clod, flag, fail N; (*thinner*) divot;
(*esp surface peat*) turr.
sod[2] *see* **contemptuous term.**
soda sodie.
sodden *see also* **soaked;** steepit, sappie
NE, saddit, sypit, platchin.
soft saft; (*spongy*) fozie, duffie; (*to
touch*) feel; (*of soil*) nesh; (*esp in character*) sapsie.
soften saften.
softly saftlie, muithlie; (*quietly*) lown.
soft drink *see* **lemonade.**
soggy sotterie SE; (*of food*) sappie, sapsie.
soil[1] *noun* **1** *see also* **earth;** sile, muild,
mool; (*thin, shallow*) scaup SHETLAND,
NE; (*red, gravelly*) ure SHETLAND. **2** (*the
land*) glebe.
soil[2] *verb* sile, (be)fyle, suddle, smad
SHETLAND, NE, glaur; (*clothes*) scuddle;
(*with food*) laiber S; (*with excrement*)
bedrite, fyle, dirt, skite.

soiled foul, brookit, daidelt NE; (*with
excrement*) dirten.
soirée swaree, suree.
sojourn *noun* stey.
verb stey, bide, pit-by.
solan goose *see* **gannet.**
sold *past tense, past participle of* **sell**
sellt, sauld.
solder *verb* souder, sowther.
soldier sodger; (*veteran*) foggie; (*in a
Highland regiment*) kiltie.
sole[1] howe o the fit.
sole[2]: **Dover sole** rock sole NE.
lemon sole tobacco fleuk NE.
sole[3] *adjective* ae, yae W, S.
solely *see also* **just;** allenarly *now law.*
solicit peuther, fleetch.
solicitor soleecitor, (law) agent, writer,
advocate ABERDEEN.
solicitous *see* **helpful.**
solid (*of things*) sufficient, sonsie; (*of
bread*) sad; (*of a meal*) hertsome SW;
(*strong, robust*) pithy.
solitary *see also* **alone;** aesome, lane,
waff.
be solitary hoolet.
solve (*a problem*) redd (up).
sombre mirkie.
some *see* **few.**
somehow somewey, somegate.
something sumhin.
some time ago a while back, a file back
NE, a while syne, a file seen NE.
sometimes whiles, whilom, files NE,
filies NE.
somewhat some, a bittie, kin(d) o, kinna.
somewhere someplace, somegate,
somebit, somewey, somepairt.
somewhere else someplace else,
somewey else.
somersault simmerset, henner EDIN-
BURGH, fleepie, kilhailie CAITHNESS.
turn a somersault tummle the cat
SHETLAND, NE, tummle (ower) yer
wullcats *or* wilkies, turn the (wull)cat,
cowp the creels.
somnolent sleeperie.

son sin, lad(die), loon N.

son-in-law guidson.

song sang, sonnet, souch; (*mournful*) croon; (*silly*) strowd NE; (*lively, rhythmical*) lilt; (*sung by farmworkers*) cornkister NE; (*snatch of a song*) sprig.

song-book sang-buik.

song festival sangschaw.

song thrush mavis, mavie, throstle *literary*.

soon suin, sin, shin CENTRAL, seen NE, in a wee, bedeen, belyve, the noo, eenoo, ivnoo, or lang.

sooner or later suin or syne.

sooner than or.

as soon as whenivver, finivver NE.

soot suit, shuit, seet NE, sit NE, bleck, coom; (*on pots etc*) brook.

soothe soother, dill.

soothsayer (*female*) spaewife, weirdwife; (*male*) †spaeman, †weirdman.

sop *see* **soak**.

soppy sappie.

sops saps, steepies, slingers NE.

sorcerer *see* **wizard**.

sorceress *see* **witch**.

sore *noun* sair, gaw, blain NE; (*festering*) bealin; (*big, festering*) lipper CAITHNESS; (*caused by chafing*) scaud; (*on the foot*) guttergaw.

adjective sair.

person who is stiff and sore sarkfu o sair banes.

sorely sair(lie).

soreness sairness.

sorrel soorock(s), soor dock(en), soor leek.

sorrel seeds rabbit's sugar NE.

sheep sorrel lammie soorocks S.

wood sorrel gowk's mait, sookiesoorocks.

sorrow *noun* sorra, sair, dool, teen, harm(s), wae; (*source of sorrow*) hertscaud, vex; (*exclamation of*) hech!, ochone!

sorrowful sorrafu, sair(ie), dool(some), wae(fu), waesome, greathertit, wearifu.

sorrow over mane.

sorry 1 sairie; (*extremely*) sick sorry, illpeyed NE. **2** (*feeble*) bauch.

sorry for yourself wi yer heid under yer oxter.

be sorry for (*a person*) be vext for.

reduce to a sorry plight mak a munsie o NE.

sort *noun, see* **kind**[1].

verb **sort (out)** redd (up), wale.

nothing of the sort no the like, deil e like NE.

so-so siclik(e).

sought *past tense, past participle of* **seek** socht.

soul saul, sowl.

sound[1] *adjective* soon(d); (*unimpaired*) hail(some); (*in health*) fere, ticht.

sound[2] *noun, see also* **noise**: soon(d); (*dull, thudding*) flaip S; (*faint*) peep; (*low, rumbling*) curmur; (*low, melancholy*) drowe; (*short, sharp*) plink; (*ringing*) ringle, chang *literary*; (*grating*) chirk, jirg; (*hoarse, croaking*) craighle; (*of a blow with something soft*) buff; (*of a heavy fall*) plunk; (*popping, of a cork being drawn*) plunk, clunk.

not the slightest sound nae a teet SHETLAND, ORKNEY, N, no a smiach CAITHNESS, neither hishie nor whishie, nae a myowt NE.

with a dull heavy sound plunk, skliff.

sound[3] *see* **strait**.

soup *see also* **broth**: bree, kail; (*thick, vegetable broth*) Scotch broth; (*watery*) blibs NE; (*made with a shin of beef*) skink SHETLAND, NE; (*made with milk*) milk bree; (*made with smoked fish, potatoes, onions, milk*) Cullen skink; (*made with haggis ingredients*) wammle-brees NE.

soup-ladle divider.

soup plate deep plate.

sour *adjective* soor, shilpit SHETLAND, ORKNEY, CAITHNESS, wersh; (*very*) soor as roddens; (*slightly, of milk*) blansht NE; (*of temperament*) *see* **sour-looking**.

sour grapes soor plooms.

sour look glumsh.

sour-looking greetin-faced, soor-faced, torn-faced, glumsh.

sour milk with oatmeal cauld steer.

become sour (*of food*) wynt, change N.

look sour glumsh, glumph.

turned sour (*of milk*) blased.

souse sloonge, sweel.

south *noun* sooth.

southern soothlan(d).

southwards suddart SHETLAND.

south side sunny side.

southernwood sitherwood, suddrenwood, aippleringie NE.

souvenir mindin, memorandum.

sovereign's representative (*at the General Assembly of the Church of Scotland*) Lord High Commissioner.

sow[1] *noun* (*female pig*) soo; (*young*) gilt.

sow[2] *verb* saw, shaave NE; (*for a grass crop*) saw doon, saw oot; (*land, with turnip seed*) neep.

hand-sower (*mechanical, held on shoulders*) fiddle; (*for turnip seed*) (neep) shaaver NE, (*old type*) bobbin John NE.

space *noun* (*room*) waygate S; (*of time*) piece SHETLAND, NE.

spacious spawcious.

widely-spaced (*of writing*) sparse.

spade 1 spaad NE; (*for draining*) rittinspade; (*for turf-cutting*) flauchter (spade). **2** (*in cards: see also* **Jack** 3) pick NE.

span *noun, verb* spang.

spank[1] (*strike: see also* **smack, hit, slap, beat**) skelp, scud, leather, scone, scult, pey (someone's) dock.

spanking *noun* skelpin, skelpit leatherin, scondies NE, buttock mail NE.

spank[2] (*move quickly*) skelp, stour, wallop.

spar *noun* (*eg in a birdcage*) strunt.

fit with spars rung.

spare *adjective* orra, fordel N.

sparing jimp.

don't be sparing with dinna be feart o, dinna be cannie wi.

sparingly jimp.

use sparingly tape.

at spare moments amang (yer) han(d)s, at orra times NE.

spare time by-time.

spark sperk S, aizle, spunk, flaesock NE, gleed, jaup; **sparks** (*eg on the edge of burning paper*) sodgers.

sparkle *verb* glent, prinkle, sheen, skinkle.

noun glent, glisk.

sparrow sparra(e), sp(e)ug, sprug, spurdie.

sparse: sparse crop of grain feuach NE.

spasm (*of anxiety etc*) drowe; (*of coughing etc*) kink.

spat *past tense of* **spit** sput.

past participle spitten.

spatter splatter, splairge, scutter, squeeter NE, spleiter NE; (*with liquid or dirt*) spark.

spavin spavie.

spawn *noun* redd, rodd CAITHNESS.

verb redd.

spawned shotten; (*in poor condition, especially a herring*) spent, spyntie NE.

recently-spawned fish (*esp a salmon*) black fish.

spawning ground redd.

speak *see also* **talk**; spek, spike NE, spick NE; (*a great deal: see also* **chat**) blether; (*softly*) cheep; (*in a whining, fawning way*) crose NE; (*unrestrainedly or exaggeratedly*) rin awa wi the harrows.

not on speaking terms oot lik(e) a pot fit NE.

stop being on speaking terms cut harrows S.

speak of mint at.

speak your mind say awa.

speak out (*boldly, cheekily*) set up yer gab.

speak vehemently *or* **earnestly about** loonder at *or* on SHETLAND, NE.

so to speak like: '*jist fur the day like*'.

spear *noun* (*pronged, for salmon-poaching*) leister.

verb (*fish, with a leister*) leister.

spearmint spearimint.
special speeshal, by-or(di)nar, byous.
specially (*for a specific purpose*) ainceeeran(t).
species speshie.
specify condescend on.
specimen (*of work*) see **test piece** (*under* test).
average specimen scone o the day's bakin.
bigger *or* **better specimen of its kind** beezer, wheesher, clinker SHETLAND, ORKNEY, N.
specious fair-farran(t).
speck pink, smitch, jesp, grott.
specks formed in the eyes during sleep sleepie men.
speckle see also **spot**: *noun, verb* spreckle.
speckled spreckelt, sprittelt S.
spectacle (*person: see also* **sight**) eemage, ticket; (*oddly-dressed woman*) Teenie f(r)ae Troon, Teenie f(r)ae the neeps.
spectacles see also **glasses**; spentacles, windaes; (*weak, to preserve the sight*) preserves.
wearing spectacles speckie: '*that speckie boy in first year*'.
spectre see also **ghost**: doolie.
speculate jalouse, ettle.
speech see also **affected**; (*speaking*) say, gab; (*language*) leid *literary*; (*a talk*) speak NE; (*long, boring*) screed; (*elaborate, flowery*) phrase NE.
speechless dumfoonert.
make a speech tak speech in han(d).
make fine speeches (to) phrase (wi) NE.
speed *noun* raik; (*burst of speed*) lick. *verb* smack.
speedily swith, at a fair lick.
do (something) speedily claa aff *or* awa NE.
speedy see **quick**.
speedwell cat's een.
heath speedwell Jennie's blue een.
at full speed full pin, full slap, hailtear, at an awfu surrender NE.

go at full speed streek, skelp (along).
spell[1]: **spelling, spelling lesson** spell.
spelling book †spell(-book); (*in capital letters*) †big spell(-book); (*in lower-case letters*) †wee spell(-book).
spell[2] (*stretch of time*) speel; (*short*) sketch, swatch; (*of weather*) tack; (*turn*) swatch; (*of work*) turn.
spell[3] (*magic*) cantrip.
spellbind daumer NE.
spellbound taen(-lik(e)).
spend ware.
spending wastefully, extravagantly barkin an fleein.
spent (*exhausted*) matit.
spent before earned forenailt NE.
spendthrift spendrif(e) NE, waster.
sperm (*of a fish*) melt.
spew see **vomit**.
spice *verb* (*food*) kitchen.
spider speeder, wabster, weaver, attercap, nettercap, Meggie(-lickie)-spinnie N.
spider's web moose wab, moose wob.
spignel bad-money, micken.
spigot spicket, spile, spriggit.
spigot and faucet cock an pail.
spike *noun* stug; (*large*) garron nail; (*of a railing etc*) pike; (*fixed to shoe for curling*) †cramp.
verb (*provide with spikes*) pike.
spiked see also **barbed**; pikie.
spiky stobbie NE.
spill *verb* skail, jaw, jibble, jowe, skiddle, drabble; (*with a splash*) jaup; (*dribble*) driddle.
spin *verb* **1** (*yarn*) snuve. **2** (*turn round*) birl, pirl, snuve, sweel; (*like a top*) doze. **3** (*cause to spin*) birl, pirl; (*a top, so fast that it appears motionless*) doze.
spinning jenny jeanie AYRSHIRE.
spinning wheel (*large, horizontal*) muckle wheel; (*small, upright*) spinnie SHETLAND.
spindle spinnle; (*specif on a spinning wheel*) broach.
spindly spirlie.

spindrift speendrift NE, spunedrift SHETLAND, NE.

spine 1 *see also* **backbone**; rig. **2** *see also* **quill, prickle**; prog, pike.

spinster *see also* **old maid**; maiden NE, wanter.

spirit *noun* speerit, spreit: **1** (*supernatural being*) wicht; (*female, thought to foretell death*) banshee; (*in shape of horse*) kelpie, water horse. **2** (*courage*) saul; (*energy*) smeddum, gurr NE. **3 spirits** *see also* **whisky**; aquavita, het watters.

spirited *see also* **lively**; speeritie, mettle, stuffie, birkie W, croose, lifie, kim NE; (*of animals*) spankie.

spiritless *see also* **dispirited, dejected**; fushionless, taibetless, paewae, thowless, smerghless N, saurless NE, dowfart.

drink of spirits *see also* **whisky**; dram, bucket: '*he can tak a guid bucket*'; (*before breakfast*) mornin.

in high spirits heich, skeich, cadgie, on the keevee.

in low spirits *see also* **dejected**; doon o mou, doon at the mou, hingin-mou'd, hingin-luggit.

out of spirits aff the fang.

raise your spirits heeze (up) yer hert.

recover your spirits cantle (up) NE, birk up.

spit[1] *noun* (*for roasting etc*) speet.

spit[2] *verb, see also* **spat**: **1** slerp. **2** (*with rain*) pewl S. **3** (*of a cat*) fuff.
noun **1** *see* **spittle**. **2** (*of a cat*) fuff.

spite *verb* maugre NE.

spiteful cat-wittit, ill-willie, litigious NE, pooshiont, atterie N.

spiteful person ettercap.

in spite of (in) maugre o N.

in spite of someone's efforts, wishes *etc* in spite o someone's teeth *or* neck.

spittle spits, spittin(s), slaver(s).

splash *see also* **squelch, spill, sprinkle**:
verb **1** jilp, jabble, splairge, plash, skite, slutter, sloosh; (*messily*) plowt, skiddle, splitter, splerrie; (*esp with mud*) platch; (*violently*) slash; (*noisily*) splatter; (*wash over*) slunge, soosh NE; (*eg of rain*) skelp; (*spill*) jaw, jilp, jaup, jirble; (*messily*) spleiter NE, splatch; (*in small drops*) skirp NE. **2 splash about** (*messily*) plowt(er), plyte(r) NE, platch, plype NE, sloonge.
noun plash, splitter, jaw, jilp, jibble, sloosh, slutter, spleiter NE, blash; (*esp of mud*) jaup, splairge, platch, splatter; (*violent*) slash; (*noisy*) plowt(er), plyter NE, plype NE; (*made by a heavy object*) slunge; (*small spurt*) skirp NE.

splashy jaupie.

(with a) splash! jaup!, plash!, plype! NE, platch!

splay skew.

splay foot splash fit NE.

splay-footed skew-fittit, deuk-fittit SW, splash-fittit NE.

splay-footed person kep-a-gush S.

spleen 1 melt. **2** *see* **bad temper** (*under* **temper**).

splendid *see also* **fine**; braw.

splendour brawness.

splice *verb* (*pieces of wood*) skair; (*rope etc*) wap.

splint *noun, verb* ((*for*) *a broken bone etc*) spelk, scob NE.

splinter *noun* splinder SHETLAND, ORKNEY, N, spelk, skirp NE, splice SE; (*esp in the skin*) skelf, skelp, skelb, spail, skiver, stob; **splinters** scowes, flinders.
verb spelk, sklinter.

split *verb* spleet, rent; (*burst*) rive; (*esp clothing*) sklent; (*fish*) speld, spalder.
noun spleet; (*crack*) rive.
adjective (*of unseasoned wood*) gelled; (*of fish*) *see* **haddock**.

split peas spilkins.

person who splits fish spleeter.

splodge, splotch *see also* **stain**; splatch.

splutter *verb* splitter, spleuter NE, splooter NE, souch; (*messily*) slerp.
noun splitter, spleuter NE, splooter NE, splurt.

spluttering gush spleut NE.

spoil *verb* spile, spul(y)ie, hash, pooshion, mank, connach, bullox, mak a munsie o NE, malagrooze NE, tash; (*by rough handling*) bla(u)d, tra(u)chle, massacker; (*by over-handling*) maggle SW, maig S; (*a game*) hoax NE; (*with kindness*) waste, delt NE: '*a deltit bairn*', peppin NE, browden.

noun spul(y)ie, †spreath, †reif.

spoilt (*by age, damp etc*) daised.

completely spoilt gane tae potterlowe NE.

spoilt child mither's bairn, sookie, mammie-keekie.

spoke[1] *past tense of* **speak** spak.

spokesman preses.

spoke[2] *noun* spaik.

spoked spaikit.

a spoke in someone's wheel a whaup *or* thraw i the raip.

sponge *verb* 1 *see also* **scrounge**: cadge, scoff, scunge, sorn, spoach SE; (*esp food*) scaff. 2 (*wipe*) spoonge.

noun spoonge.

sponger skech, sorner, spoacher SE, skemler.

spongy fozie, duffie, pory SHETLAND.

spook *see* **ghost**.

spool spule; (*for holding weft yarn in shuttle; also small, for sewing thread*) pirn.

spoon spuin, speen NE; (*wooden*) gabstick.

spoonful spuinfu, spuinfae, speenfae NE, speenifu NE.

sport *noun* play.

verb ramp(le), daff, mird (wi) NE.

sportsman (*who shoots game*) gunner.

sportsman's attendant gillie.

spot *noun* 1 spat, spreckle. 2 (*on the skin: see also* **pimple**) plouk.

spotted spreckelt, mottie SHETLAND, NE, sprittelt S; (*of animals, with white*) hawkit.

spouse marrow *now literary*, half-marrow.

spout *see also* **gush**: *noun* spoot; (*of a kettle, jug etc*) stroop.

verb spoot, scoot, sploit.

sprain *verb, noun, see also* **wrench, strain**; rax, rack, thraw, stave.

sprat garvie.

sprawl *verb* spra(u)chle, spravle CAITHNESS, sprawlach NE, spelder, sprattle.

spray *verb* spairge; (*with dust etc*) stour. *noun* (*cloud of*) stour; (*whipped up from waves*) speendrift NE.

device for spraying skoosher.

throw out a fine spray spark.

spread *verb* 1 spreed; (*spread open*) spelder. 2 (*with something soft*) skaik NE; (*butter with the thumb*) thoum; (*manure etc on the ground*) skail. 3 (*news, gossip*) troke NE; (*gossip*) sclave(r) NE; (*of news, gossip*) clink.

noun spreed; (*of food*) set-doon, doonset(tin).

spreadeagle spelder.

spread about skail.

spread gossip *see also* **tell tales**; clish, ca clashes NE.

spread (something) out speld.

spree splore, skite, bash, screed, rammle, ba(ll) SHETLAND, N.

sprig rice.

sprightly *see* **spry**.

spring *noun* 1 (*of water*) wall(ie), spoot. 2 (*leap*) lowp, sten(d). 3 (*season*) voar SHETLAND, ORKNEY, ware.

verb (*leap*) lowp, sten(d), spoot.

spring onion sybie, syboe.

first day of spring voar day SHETLAND, ORKNEY, ware day.

spring up *or* **forward** breist, brent.

with a sudden spring brent.

sprinkle *verb* splatter, sp(l)airge, straw, strinkle, roose NE; (*with something oily*) straik; (*with dust*) stour; (*esp with snow*) grime.

sprinkler skoosher, rooser NE.

sprinkling splatter, sp(l)airge, strinkle; (*light, of snow etc*) skimmer(in).

sprint *verb* sprunt.

sprite (*benevolent household*) broonie, brownie.

sprout *verb* sproot, brear(d), stock N;

spruce

(*of grain during malting*) acherspyre; (*of potatoes*) chun SW.

noun sproot; (*of grain etc*) brear(d); (*esp of a potato*) chun SW.

spruce[1] *adjective* sproosh, sprush, doss, snod, knackie.

verb, also **spruce up** sproosh, sprush, snod, doss.

spruce[2] (*tree*) sprush.

spry spree, sproosh, sprush, fendie.

spume (*driven from sea onto land*) seagust SHETLAND, ORKNEY.

spur (*for riding*) brod.

spurious fause.

spurn cast at, pit (someone) by the door SHETLAND.

spurrey: corn-spurrey yarr.

spurt *verb* jaw, jilp, scoot, skoosh, strintle, strone.

noun scoot, skoosh, jaw, jilp, splurt, strintle, strone.

sputter *verb* sotter; (*of fat in cooling*) papple, skirl.

spyglass †prospect.

squabble *see also* **quarrel**: *verb* scash NE, tulyie, bargle.

noun stushie, stashie, strush, tulyie; (*noisy*) rooshie-doo, sherrack W.

squabbling *noun* nip-lug.

squalid fousome NE, nestie.

in a state of squalor in a sheuch.

squall *noun* skelp, gurl, bluffert, bowder, brattle SHETLAND, NE, gandiegow; (*from high land over the sea*) flan.

verb (*scream*) squaik.

squally scoorie, blirtie NE, flannie.

squander squatter, misguide; (*heedlessly*) splairge, (*specif money*) sperfle, gae throu, perish.

squandered doon the stank.

squander your fortune ca(w) yer pack tae the pins.

square *adjective* squerr W, fower-neukit.

main square of a town plainstanes.

make square quader.

squash *see* **crush**.

squat *verb* hunker (doon), coorie hunker, cuddle.

adjective setterel, gudgie, laich-set, durkie.

in a squatting position on yer hunkers.

squawk *noun, verb* squaik, chirawk NE.

squeak *verb* squaik, squeck, wheek, wheep NE, weeack NE; (*of things*) cheep, queek NE.

noun squaik, squeck, weeack NE, wheep.

squeal *noun, verb* squile NE, squaik.

squeamish sweamish, waumish, wersh.

squeeze *see also* **crush**: *verb* knuse, chirt, nevel, thrummle, pran NE, knidge SHETLAND, N, trist SHETLAND, ORKNEY.

noun chirt SW, groze; (*forceful*) knidge SHETLAND, N; (*sharp*) jirt SHETLAND; (*crush*) pack SHETLAND, NE.

squeeze down poss.

squelch *see also* **splash**: *verb* chork, plush; (*through mud etc*) plodge, plype NE; (*eg of water on shoes*) slorp S.

squelching plashin.

make a squelching sound jorg; (*in walking*) slork SW, S.

squib squeeb; (*schoolboy's home-made*) peeoy.

squid ink-fish.

squint *noun* **1** (*cast in the eye*) skellie, gley, staul NE. **2** *see also* **glance**; skellie, gley, gledge, skew NE.

verb **1** (*have a squint*) skellie, skew, staul NE. **2** *see also* **glance**; sklent, gledge, gley, skew.

squint-eyed skellie(-e(y)ed), gley(-e(y)ed), jee-eed, pie-eyed.

squirm *verb* wimple.

squirrel skwurrel.

squirt *see also* **spurt**: *verb* scoot, skite, skiddle, skoosh, chirt.

noun scoot, skite N, spoot, sploit; (*syringe*) scoot.

stab *verb* stug, stick, durk, porr, prog, dab.

noun stug, porr, prod, prog.

stabber sticker.

stable[1] *adjective* sicker, stieve.

stably stieve.
stability stabeelitie.
stable[2] *noun*: **stable-stall** *see also*
stall; †travise.
stack *noun* steck S; (*of hay, corn*) ruck,
scroo SHETLAND, ORKNEY, N; (*of hay*)
cole; (*large, oblong*) soo; (*small*) hut,
hooick NE; (*small, temporary*) hutch,
rickle, shig; (*of peats*) ruck, (*small,
loosely stacked*) rickle.
verb steck S; (*corn etc*) big, ruck, scroo
SHETLAND, ORKNEY; (*hay*) cole; (*peats,
loosely, for drying*) rickle, set NE.
stack foundation ruck foon(d), stale,
stathel.
stackyard cornyaird, stack hill, haggard
SW, ULSTER.
stack up ruck.
staff *see* **stick**[1].
stagger *see also* **totter**: *verb* stoit(er),
styte(r) NE, stot(ter), stammer, stacher,
stave, swaver SHETLAND, ORKNEY, NE,
dotter, wammle.
noun stoit(er), styte(r) NE, stot(ter),
stammer, stacher, swaver NE.
stagnant staignant.
stagnant green water goor SHET-
LAND, ORKNEY, N, green brees NE.
stagnant pool stank, sink SHETLAND.
staid douce, as mim as a Mey puddock.
stain *verb* tash, smad SHETLAND, NE,
coom, brook; (*with ink*) blotch.
noun tash, smad SHETLAND, NE,
smitch, jesp; (*on clothes*) gair; (*from
rust*) mail.
stairs stair; (*outside, to an upper flat*)
forestair, oot-stair; (*narrow, enclosed*)
box-ladder.
staircase stair.
spiral staircase turnpike.
foot of the stairs stairfit.
top of the stairs stairheid.
stake *noun* 1 stob, stuckin SE, stower
SW. 2 (*in a game*) stunk.
stale haskie, wauch NE; (*very: see also
mouldy* (*under* **mould**[1])) foostit; (*of
bread*) aul(d).

stale news fiddler's news, piper's news.
stale story *etc* caul(d) kail het again.
stalk[1] *noun* (*of a plant*) pen, shank;
(*hard*) runt, castock, stock; (*withered, of
grass*) windlestrae.
stalks and leaves (*of potatoes, turnips
etc*) shaws.
stalk[2] *verb* (*walk stiffly: see also* **strut**)
steg, stilp NE, dilp, stairge S.
stall 1 sta(w); (*for an animal*) boose,
stance N. 2 (*for selling*) stan(d), crame.
stallion staig.
man who goes round with a stallion
staiger.
stalwart *see also* **robust, sturdy**;
buirdlie, hail-hertit; **stalwarts** †wale
wicht men.
stamina *see* **strength**.
stammer *verb* stut, stot, stoiter, habber
SHETLAND, N, mant, gant CAITHNESS,
gansh.
noun stut, stot, habber SHETLAND, N,
mant, gansh.
stammerer manter.
stamp *verb* 1 (*with the feet*) tramp,
stramp, ramp; (*in anger*) pawt; (*in
water*) japple SHETLAND, N. 2 (*with a
die*) teep.
noun tramp, stramp.
stamp along stam SE.
stamp around palmer (aboot) NE.
stampede *verb* (*of cattle*) prick NE,
startle.
stanch *verb* stench, stainch.
stanchion staincheon ORKNEY, N, pall.
stand *verb, see also* **stood**: 1 stan,
staun(d). 2 (*endure*) bide, thole.
noun stan, staun(d); (*wooden, for barrels*) gantree.
at a standstill hoggit.
bring to a standstill stell.
come to a standstill stell.
stand on end prickle; (*of hair*) be in a
birr.
stand up win up.
stand up and move off lift.
stand up for yourself haud the gullie
ower the dyke.

standard

stand up to stick up tae, teethe NE.
take (up) your stand tak (up) yer stance.
standard standart, stannert.
standard-bearer (*in some 'Riding of the Marches' ceremonies*) cornet.
staple *noun* (*for fastening*) stapple, steeple, haud-fast.
star starn, stern S, blinker.
  starry starnie.
  starfish scoskie N, cross-fit NE.
  starlight starnlicht.
  evening star cowslem S.
starboard faran NE.
starch *noun* stairch, sterch, stiff(en)in.
  verb stiffen.
stare *verb* glower, gowk; (*esp vacantly*) gove; (*open-mouthed*) gowp; (*foolishly*) gype; (*rudely*) geck; (*fixedly*) leuk fae yersel.
  noun gowp; (*wide-eyed*) glower.
  with a wild, staring look fraized S.
stark sterk.
starling stirlin, stuckie, stushie, stirrie NE.
start *verb* stert: 1 yoke tae, get yokit, tak on, set on; (*work*) jine. 2 (*with fright*) glocken SW.
  noun stert: 1 affgo, affset. 2 (*fright*) gliff.
  starting point (*in a race*) butt.
  starting-up (*of machinery, esp a mill*) ongang NE.
startle stertle, start, stert, gliff, flocht NE, flichter, fleg.
starve sterve, hunger.
  starved hungert, nippit.
  starved-looking shilpit.
state *noun* (*condition*) tift, track; (*of affairs*) set.
  statement speak NE, mou; (*formal, legal*) libel; (*in a lawsuit or financial transaction*) state.
  in a state (*of distress or anxiety*) in a wey: '*She's in an awfu wey aboot Rab*'.
station *noun* (*stopping place*) stance.
  verb stance.
  station-master station-agent.
statue (*of plaster*) stookie (eemage).

stature lenth.
  of equal stature heidie-peer.
staunch stench, stainch, sicker, stieve.
  staunchly stieve.
stave *noun* stap.
  verb brak, knick.
stay[1] *verb* 1 (*remain*) stey, bide. 2 (*a legal proceeding*) sist.
  noun 1 (*time in a place*) stey, bide: '*a lang bide*'. 2 (*of a legal proceeding*) sist.
  stay on sit on.
stay[2] *noun* (*support*) haud, uphaud, prap, rance; (*mainly mining*) stell, stoop.
  verb (*a building*) rance.
  stays (*corset*) steys.
steadfast set, sicker, stieve.
steady sicker, stieve; (*in character*) cannie.
steak collop.
steal *see also* **stole, stolen**; nip, scoff, pootch, pauchle, chore *slang*, sneck, thief, reive, spulzie *law*.
stealth: stealthy sneck-drawin, thief-tie.
  stealthily quate, slee, stow(n)lins, hidlins, huggerie-muggerie.
steam *noun* stame, (y)oam SHETLAND, ORKNEY, NE, guff.
  verb stove.
  puff of steam lunt.
steel (*piece for striking sparks from a flintstone*) fleerish.
  steelyard steel, weys.
steep[1] *adjective* stey, brent, stieve, strait.
steep[2] *verb* drook, sap; (*clothes in soapy water*) sapple; (*clothes in lye before bleaching*) bouk.
steer[1] *verb* airt, guy NE.
  steersman lodesman SHETLAND.
steer[2] *noun* stirk, stot.
stem *noun* 1 (*of a plant: see also* **stalk**[1]) pen, shank; (*hollow, used as peashooter*) pluffer, bluchtan SW. 2 (*of an instrument*) shank; (*of a pipe*) (pipe) stapple, pipe shank.
stench guff, humph, stew, wheech; (*from burning*) yowder, yowther, ewder.

step *noun* **1** (*pace*) stap, staup S, stramp, pass; (*long, striding*) sling, sten(d), spang; (*long, heavy*) plowd NE; (*heavy, stamping*) powt; (*hesitant*) dachle NE; (*uneven, of a person with one leg shorter than the other*) lift; (*tottering*) stoit NE, stot. **2** (*of a stair*) stap. **3 steps** (*moveable, to a loft etc*) trap (stair(s)).
verb stap, staup S.
stepping-stones stappin-stanes, steps.
step by step fit for fit.
with weak tottering steps hyter NE: 'hyterin on'.
walk with long vigorous steps spang.
step-: stap-.
step-child stap-bairn.
step-father stap-faither, stappie.
step-mother stap-mither.
sterile (*of soil*) deef.
stern[1] *adjective* dour, raucle, sair, stere, sture.
sternly fell.
stern[2] *noun* starn.
steersman's seat at stern starn-stuil.
towards the stern eft.
stew *verb, noun* stove.
stewed (*of tea*) sitten NE.
steward stewart, factor, doer.
stick[1] *noun, see also* **walking stick, shepherd's crook**; steek; (*long, pliant*) swabble S; (*strong*) rung; (*crooked*) cammock NE; (*gnarled*) rammock NE; (*for stirring*) spurtle, spurkle, theevil; (*used by teething children*) gumstick; (*lit and waved about by children*) dingle-doosie, Robin-a-ree; (*Y-shaped, used in thatching*) stob NE; (*shinty*) caman.
stick[2] *verb* steek; (*in mud*) lair.
sticky claggie, cla(i)rtie; (*of ice in curling*) drug, dour, bauch, dauchie.
stick close to grip till SHETLAND, NE.
stick up (*of hair*) stert.
stickleback banstickle, bandie NE, reid-gibbie, spriklybag; (*three-spined*) bairdie.

stiff 1 stieve, stent(it); (*in movement, in the joints*) stechie, unbowsome S. **2** (*formal*) stickin, stryngie, primpit.
stiffly stieve.
become stiff with cold stock.
stifle *see* **suffocate**.
stifling stifin, smochie.
stigma tash.
stiletto heel peerie heel.
still[1] *adjective* quate, lown.
adverb yet, aye.
stand still stan(d) lik a stookie.
stillness lithe N.
still[2] *noun* (*for distilling*) stell.
stilt stult, stilpert NE, powl.
cross a river on stilts stult the watter.
stimulate steemulate, upsteer, kittle (up), brisken up.
stimulation upsteerin.
stimulus kittle.
sting *noun, verb, see also* **stung**; stang; (*of acid taste etc*) nip.
stinging (*of a wound*) nippie, suckie; (*of nettles: see also* **nettle**) jaggie.
stingy ticht, meeserable, nippit, hungry, neetie, moolie, hard, nairra-begaun, meechie.
be stingy keep in yer han(d).
stink *see also* **smell, stench**: *verb* stew. *noun* stew, wheech.
stinking *see* **smelly**.
stint *verb* stent, scrimp, tape. *noun* (*spell of work*) yokin.
stipend steepend.
stir *verb* **1** steer, cair, pirl SHETLAND, NE; (*eg with a stick*) poach; (*with a churning motion*) kirn; (*vigorously*) rummle; (*something soft or messy*) gorroch; (*mining*) rimle. **2** (*move*) mudge, jee.
noun, see also **commotion**; (*stirring movement*) steer; (*vigorous*) rummle.
stir round whummle.
stir up taisle; (*incite*) set up, egg (up), eggle ORKNEY, N, eickel NE.
stirrup strip.
stirrup cup deoch-an-dorus.

247

stitch

stitch *noun* **1** (*sewing, knitting*) steek, stick; (*in knitting*) loop. **2** (*of clothing*) steek, tack ULSTER. **3** (*pain in the side*) steek, catch, income, spurtle grup, caik SE.
verb steek, stick; (*roughly and hastily*) ranter.

stoat whitrat, futrat N, whitterick, stoat-weasel.

stock *noun* **1** (*breed*) etion NE; (*of a farm*) stockin, haudin. **2** (*from boiling*) bree.
verb, see **store**.
of good stock weel-comed.

stockade peel.

stocking (*woollen*) moggan ORKNEY, N; (*footless*) moggan N, hairy moggan N, hoshen, hogger; (*footless, used as gaiter in wet weather*) fot S, hogger; (*in the process of being knitted*) shank.
stocking leg (*being knitted*) shank.

stocky short-set, laich-set, stowfie NE.

stole *past tense of* **steal** stealt, staw.

stolen *past participle* stealt, stow(e)n.

stomach stamack, gebbie, crap(pin), puddin market *child's word*; (*belly*) kyte, wame, wyme N, painch, peenie *child's word*; (*stomach and bowels*) intimmers *jocular*; (*of a sheep*) haggis-bag; (*of a sheep or pig*) jaudie.
stomachache belly-thraw, mollie-grubs, sair wame.
stomach-rumble curmurrin.
third stomach of a ruminant moniefaul(d).
fourth stomach of a ruminant reed, roddikins.
flat on the stomach belly-fla(u)cht.
upset the stomach fyle the stamack.

stone *noun* **1** stane, steen N, ruckie S, yuck; (*small*) chuckie(-stane), yuckie; (*small, rounded*) knibloch; (*flat*) leck. **2** (*used in building: roughly dressed*) shoddie; (*small, strengthening in a dyke*) pin; (*passing through a whole wall*) parpen, throu-band. **3** (*used in games*) chuckie(-stane); (*in ducks and drakes*) skiffer. **4** (*of fruit*) paip.
verb stane.

stony stanie, steenie N.

stone-breaker stane-knapper, steen-knapper NE.

stonemason dorbie.

stone's throw stane-cast.

stone trough troch stane.

loose stones on a steep hillside scree, slidder S.

heap of stones cairn, stane-bing, rickle (o stanes).

stonechat stane chack(er), chack.

stood *past tense of* **stand** stuid, steed NE.
past participle stuiden.

stool *see also* **footstool**; stuil, steel NE, crockie; (*small*) currie; (*low, three-legged*) creepie.

stoop *verb* coorie, lootch, loot.
noun lootch, loot SHETLAND.

stop *verb* stap, stoap, lay by, deval, quat, gie ower SHETLAND, NE, stint, jeho NE; (*of rain or snow*) upple N; (*bring to a stop*) stell, reest NE; (*obstruct*) mar; (*a mill*) set; (*a person*) kep; (*a legal procedure*) sist.
noun stap.
stop! haud sae!; (*call to a horse: see also* **call** *noun* 3 (1)) stan(d)!
stoppage stick.
stopper prop.
without stopping even on, nivver devallin.
put a firm stop to pit the peter on.
stop growing (*of plants*) stint.
stop in the middle of stick.
stop for a moment haud a wee.
stop short reest.
stop up clag, colf NE.

store *verb, see also* **stow**; kist; (*for future use*) hain, fordel (up) NE.
noun fordel NE, pose N, fallachan ARGYLL; (*secret*) posie, hochie FIFE; (*of barrels ready for use*) stowe.
storekeeper (*of general store*) Johnnie a'thing(s), Jennie a'thing(s).

storey (*of a house*) flat.

storm *noun* weather, snifter, stour, roil ARGYLL; (*heavy*) bowder; (*of wind and* rain) scowe, blatter, bleeter NE; (*sudden*) blowt; (*from the sea*) doister; (*adding more snow*) feedin storm; (*short, spring-time*) gowk's storm.

verb **storm at** *see* **scold.**

stormy weatherfu, coorse, sair, at-terie, gowstie, roit NE, gurlie, rumbal-liach S.

storm about rammish.

story crack, clash, say; (*exaggerated*) sonnet NE; (*funny*) farce; (*long*) *see* **rig-marole.**

storyteller upmakker SHETLAND, NE, talesman SHETLAND; (*of traditional Celtic/Gaelic tales*) shenachie.

magnify a story in the telling gie a story hose an shuin.

old story aul(d) sang.

the same old story the aul(d) hech how(e).

stories of long ago aul(d) fernyears NE.

an unlikely story a fine ham-a-haddie.

stout *adjective* stoot, sture; (*big and stout*) lik(e) a hoose-en(d), buirdlie; (*fat and soft*) brosie, mardle.

stout-hearted stoot-hertit.

stow stowe.

straddle striddle.

straggle straigle, traik, vaig.

straight *adjective, noun* stra(u)cht, strecht SE.

adverb stra(u)cht, strecht SE; (*directly*) brent NE.

straighten stra(u)cht, strechten SE; (*the limbs of a corpse*) *see* **lay out.**

straightforward stra(u)cht-forrit, even-forrit.

straight ahead en(d)weys.

straight away stra(u)cht, richt noo, at the meenit.

straight down evendoon.

straight on en(d) lang, even on.

strain *noun* **1** streen, streend SE; (*sprain*) rax. **2** (*melody*) souch NE.

verb **1** streen, streend SE, rax, shammle. **2** (*sieve*) sye, sile, search NE.

strainer *see* **sieve.**

piece of cloth for straining liquid sye-cloot SHETLAND, ORKNEY, N.

stand up to strain haud haul CAITH-NESS.

strait kyle W COAST.

in straitened circumstances sair aff, ill-aff, nae weel aff.

strait-laced perjink, primsie SHET-LAND, ORKNEY, primp SHETLAND.

strand (*of rope etc*) ply, faul(d), faik N.

strange strynge, unco(-lik(e)), fremmit, ferlie, forby, ootlin; (*unknown*) un(be)kent; (*uncommon*) orra; (*rather strange*) queerie.

stranger *see also* **incomer**; ootrel, ootlin.

strangers unco fowk, the fremmit, nae hereaboot fowk NE.

strangeness fremmitness, unconess.

strange-looking unco-leukin.

strange sight ferlie.

strangle thrapple, guzzle, tak some-one's breath *or* win(d).

strap *noun* **1** (*school punishment strap*) tawse, tards, tag NE, the belt, Lochgelly. **2 straps worn below the knees by farmworkers** nickie-tams, waltams, booyangs, yorks. **3** (*tying an animal's hough-sinew*) hoch-ban(d).

stroke with a strap *see* **stroke.**

stratum (*of clay in limestone*) sclit; (*of intrusive rock*) float; **strata** (*in which minerals occur*) metals; (*of sandstone or limestone*) faiks.

straw strae; (*esp for thatching*) gloy SHETLAND, ORKNEY, CAITHNESS.

straw-band (*to tie up a sheaf*) raip, strap SW.

straw-rope *see also* **rope-twister**; strae-raip, raip, shimee N, whip.

straw-shed strae hoose.

bundle *or* **sheaf of straw** wap, winnlin SHETLAND, ORKNEY, N; (*esp for thatch-ing*) kemple CAITHNESS, stapple, tippet NE, wase NE.

ball of straw used in stack-thatch-ing cloo; (*rugby-ball-shaped*) edderin NE.

cover with straw (*eg a stack*) thack.

the last straw the hinneren(d) o a(w).

loose piece of straw strab NE.

straw in shoes to keep feet warm wisp.

put straw in (*shoes etc*) strae: 'strae yer buits'.

unthreshed straw tremmlin strae(s) NE.

stray *see also* **wander**; gae will ORKNEY, NE.

adjective (*of animals*) waff.

streak *noun* (*of colour etc*) straik, spraing, rand; (*dirty*) gair; (*of light*) flick.

verb straik, skaik NE; (*with dirt*) slaik.

streaked (*with dirt*) brookit NE; (*with different colours*) randit; (*of a fleece*) cairie CAITHNESS; (*of the hair, with white*) lyart.

stream *noun* **1** (*of liquid*) strin(d), strule; (*small*) strintle CAITHNESS; (*of milk from a cow's teat*) strone, strin(d) NE. **2** (*small river*) burn, strand; (*mountain*) scriddan; (*moorland*) caochan N; (*slow*) lane SW; (*slow, in flat ground*) powe; (*small*) rinner, stripe SHETLAND, ORKNEY, NE; (*boggy, that dries in summer*) syke.

verb, see **gush, trickle**.

stream out (*eg of smoke*) tove SE.

street causey, gate *now mainly in street-names*; (*narrow*) vennel; (*narrow, winding*) wynd *now mainly in street-names*.

street drain, street gutter *see* **gutter**.

street-sweeper scaffie.

strength *see also* **energy**; strenth, poustie; (*physical*) ma(u)cht, farrach NE, fushion; (*of things*) docher.

strengthen (*friendship*) souder NE; (*courage etc*) cantle NE.

drained of strength poustit SHETLAND, ORKNEY.

lacking strength mauch(t)less, fendless.

strenuous sair.

stress (*exertion*) sweet; (*excitement*) flocht NE.

stretch *verb* streetch, streek, rax, stra(u)cht; (*by pulling*) rax; (*a part of the body*) rax; (*make taut*) stent; (*expand*) rax; (*extend between two points*) reak.

noun **1** streetch, streek, rax. **2** (*of a river*) rack.

stretch your legs streek yer hochs *or* shanks *etc*, rax yer legs.

stretch out 1 (*a thing*) streek; (*the hand etc*) rax oot, rax ower. **2** (*of time*) rax oot.

stretched out streekit out, ootstreekit.

stretch over rax ower, ower-rax.

strew straw, strinkle, strintle N.

stricken strucken.

strict strick, snar, stret NE, ticht, nairra.

strictly stricklie, stench NE.

stride *verb, see also* **strode**; striddle, steg, strod(ge) S, sten(d); (*with long steps*) lamp, stilp NE; (*vigorously*) spang.

noun striddle, sten(d); (*long, firm*) lamp; (*long, vigorous*) spang.

off your stride aff yer stot(ter).

strident (*esp of the voice*) groff SHETLAND, N, sture.

strife (*battle*) stour *mainly literary*; (*discord*) plea NE, sturt.

strike *verb, see also* **struck, beat, tap**[1], **slap, stab: 1** strik, chap, doose, lamp, paik; (*heavily*) ding, dunt, dush; (*a person*) skite, lift yer han(d) tae; (*the head*) crunt; (*slap*) skelp, gowf, clash, cloot, sclaff; (*sharply*) knap, knack, crack NE, knype; (*roughly*) buckie NE; (*with the hands or feet*) fung NE; (*with a hammer*) chap; (*with something soft*) dowf NE; (*with a sharp thud*) rap; (*with a dull thud*) plunk; (*with a glancing blow*) skliff, scuff; (*with a resounding blow*) knell; (*making a small sharp sound*) pink; (*mainly curling*) chip. **2** (*of a clock*) chap. **3** (*a match*) scart.

strike at lay at.

strike down foon(d)er, nail.

strike off skite.

strike out *see* **hit out**.

strike up (*a tune etc*) yerk aff, yerk up, (*esp on the bagpipes*) dirl up.

string *noun* skainie N, skeenie.

piece of string (bit o) towe; (*for tying*) tial SHETLAND, ORKNEY, N.

string together strap.

string of beads pair o beads.

strip *noun* ran(d); (*small, of wood*) spelk; (*long, narrow*) striffin; (*of cloth, paper etc*) screed; (*eg of flesh from a wound*) target; (*of land*) screed, skelp; (*of ploughed land raised in the middle*) †rig; (*uncultivated, usu marking a boundary*) mearin; (*of green grass*) gair.

verb (*undress*) tirr NE; (*a room etc*) tirr.

strip off tirl; (*turf before digging*) rip, tirr.

stripe *noun, see also* **streak**; strip NE, straik, ran(d); (*bright*) spraing.

verb straik, spraing.

striped strippit, gairit, randit S.

stripling *see* **youth** 2.

strive *see also* **strove, struggle**; kemp, pauchle, warsle, chaave NE, pingle.

strive for seek tae.

strode *past tense of* **stride** strade.

stroke *noun* 1 *see also* **blow²**; straik, skelp, chap; (*sweeping*) swipe; (*with a whip*) screenge; (*on the palm, with a strap*) palmie, pandie, luiffie. 2 (*of work*) chap NE; (*in curling*) shot. 3 (*of a clock or bell*) chap; (*of a clock*) ring. 4 (*paralytic*) shock, blast NE.

verb straik; (*an animal etc, affectionately*) clap.

stroll *verb* dander, daun(d)er, stravaig, raik, tak a step, taik N, stoy NE.

noun dander, daun(d)er, stravaig, raik, range, taik SHETLAND, N: '*tak a taik*'.

strong 1 strang, stench NE, pithy, raucle; (*of people: see also* **sturdy**) bang, kibble NE, stalwart, able, yibble S, sture, stark, stieve, wallie; (*of things*) sevendle. 2 (*of liquor*) hard, nappie; (*of tea*) sitten.

strongly strang(lie), stievelie, fell.

strongly-made stark.

strong taste *see also* **taste, taint**; goo.

strong-tasting wild.

strove *past tense of* **strive** strave, streeve NE.

struck *past tense of* **strike** straik, strak, strook.

past participle strucken, stricken.

struggle *verb, see also* **strive**; fecht, chaave NE, kyauve SHETLAND, NE, warsle; (*esp physically*) stra(u)chle; (*under a heavy burden*) hulster; (*like a drowning person*) switter; (*eg to get through something*) spra(u)chle; (*tussle*) rug an rive, tissle; (*against odds*) wa(u)chle, pingle; (*esp to earn your living*) witter NE.

noun fecht: '*it's a sair fecht*', chaave NE, kyauve NE, struissle, wa(u)chle, warsle, haggle S, widdle, tuggle SHETLAND, N, hechle, tulyie; (*scramble*) spra(u)chle; (*tussle*) tissle; (*against odds*) pilget NE, pingle.

struggling warslin.

struggle on warsle on, pauchle, haggle S, widdle.

struggle through mak throu, warple.

having a (great) struggle with wrocht tae daith wi.

strut *noun* (*support bar*) dwang, warpin, rack; (*wooden post used as a strut: see also* **prop**) rance.

verb bairge, pavie, strunt, prink, brank, gester, strod(ge) S.

stubble stibble; (*unevenly cut*) stugs.

stubbly stibblie, sticklie, stobbie NE.

stubborn thrawn, thrae, dour, rigwiddie, stickin, contermacious, stockit NE, thrawart SHETLAND, ORKNEY, ersit SW.

fit of stubbornness thraw.

become stubborn thra(w) (wi).

stucco stookie.

stuck *past tense of* **stick** stack.

past participle stickit, stucken.

stuck-up *see* **conceited**.

he's stuck he canna(e) get oot (o) the bit.

stud (*small-headed for shoe-heels*) mud.

student collegianer.

study *verb* (*examine closely*) vizzy SHETLAND, bore at, bore in.

stuff

stuff *noun* graith, gear.

verb stap (*also in cookery*), prime, colf NE, puist S; (*with food: see also* **eat**) pang NE, stech, stowe, ram.

stuffed (*also in cookery*) stappit: '*stappit haddie*'; '*stappit heidies*'; (*full of food*) *see* **full**[1].

stuffing (*esp for fish-heads*) stappin.

stuffy *see also* **close**[1]; smochie.

stumble *verb* stummle, stammer, stoit(er), stotter, stacher, miss a fit, doiter, hyter NE, stavel.

noun stummle, stammer, stoit(er), stotter, stacher, hyter NE, stavel.

stumbling-block bumlack NE.

apt to stumble fitless.

a person who often stumbles hamrel NE.

stump *noun* (*of a tree*) stug, scrunt, stock, stole; (*old, decayed*) runt.

verb stodge, stilp NE, dilp; **stump along** stramp, sclunsh, stowff NE.

stumpy stumpit, cuttie.

stun *see also* **stupefy, daze**; doze, daver, daumer NE; (*with a blow*) devel, stoun(d).

stunned donnert, dammisht.

stunned state stoun(d).

stung *past tense of* **sting** stang.

stunt *verb* jimp, nirl.

stunted scruntit, scruntie, stumpit, palie, sutten-on, shargart NE; (*of plants, animals*) nirlie; (*of a tree*) scroggie.

stunted-looking person *or* **animal** shargar NE.

stupefy *see also* **stun, daze**; daver, denumb NE, doze, swarf; (*with a blow*) stoun(d); (*with noise*) mineer NE; (*with much talk*) domineer NE.

stupefied donnert, dammisht, doitrified, dosinnit, moidert, taivert.

in a stupefied state in a creel.

stupid stupit, stippit, daft, donnert, blate, gawkit, glaikit, idiotical, sumphish, feel NE, sumphie NE, (hauf-)chackit, guffie S; (*very*) thick as mince; (*from old age*) dottered; (*from old age, drink etc*) dozent.

stupid person *see* **fool**.

be stupid sumph, daver, hae naethin but whit the spuin pits in the heid.

pretend to be stupid act the daft laddie *or* lassie.

do you think I'm stupid? I didnae come up the Clyde in a banana boat *or* on a bike, d'ye think I'm feel? NE.

you're stupid yer heid's fou o mince, yer heid's wastit.

stupor dwam, stoun(d), swarf.

sturdy *see also* **robust, stalwart**; stieve, stuffie, fell, kibble NE, sture, stark, stowfie NE, raucle; (*specif of animals*) pretty SHETLAND, NE; (*of young children*) sonsie.

sturdy young man stirk.

stutter *see also* **stammer**; stitter.

sty *see* **pigsty**.

stye (*on the eyelid*) styan ORKNEY, NE.

style *noun* souch.

stylish tippie; (*and bold*) gemmie.

suave fair-faced.

subdue lowden, daunton, snuil.

subdued (*of persons*) lown.

subject *noun* (*of conversation, esp gossip*) speak.

kept in subjection hauden-doon, doon-hadden.

leave that subject alone lat that flee stick tae the wa.

subjugate *see* **conquer, defeat**.

sub-lease, sublet *verb* †subset.

noun †subset, †substack.

submit *see also* **yield**; knuckle, hunker; (*tamely, weakly*) snuil.

submissive patientfu.

act submissively sing sma.

subscription: collect subscriptions gaither.

subside seg; (*of floods etc*) swage SHETLAND, ORKNEY, N; (*of news etc*) dill doon SHETLAND, NE.

subsistence leevin.

subsoil sole; (*hard, impervious, stony*) moorband.

substantial sonsie; (*of things*) sufficient; (*of a meal*) hertsome.

substitute *noun* (*temporary*) by-pit; (*poor*) dae-nae-better; (*legal*) surrogatum.
verb (*for someone at work*) speel.
subterfuge *see also* **trick**; scug SHETLAND, NE.
subtle *see* **crafty**.
subtract subtrack, substract.
succeed *verb* (*be successful*) luck, spin NE, mak weel, come speed, maun, throu SW.
 succeeding (*in a post etc*) incomin.
 success *see* **prosperity**.
 successful *see* **succeed**.
 successfully en(d)weys.
 succession: in succession efter ither, efter idder NE.
 in rapid succession hilter-skilter, ding dang.
 succeed in doing win tae dae.
 succeed in reaching win till, manage: '*He'll manage hame*'.
 succeed or fail in a big way mak a spuin or spile a horn.
succinct (*curt*) cuttit NE.
succour *verb, see also* **help**; fend N, gie a lift tae.
succulent (*of meat etc*) sappie.
such sic, sich, siccan, siclik(e), sic a lik(e).
 such a sicna, sic a.
 such-and-such sic-an-sic.
 such a person sic a bodie.
 suchlike siclik(e).
 in such a way siclik(e).
suck sook; (*of a suckling, greedily*) taw S.
 sucker sooker.
 make a sucking noise when eating sorple S.
 suck up noisily slab up NE, slork.
 suck up to sook in wi, smool in wi.
suckle sook, sickle.
 suckling sookie, sookin bairn; (*farm animal*) suckler.
suction (*of a pump*) fang.
 suction pipe (*mining*) rattlehead.
 having lost its capacity for suction (*of a pipe*) aff the fang.

sudden suddent.
 suddenly suddentlie, in a hurry, plunk, at a(e) whip; (*and heavily*) cloit.
 suddenness suddenty N.
 all of a sudden on a suddenty N.
suds sapples, sowp, freith.
sue law.
suet shuet.
suffer *verb, see also* **endure**; dree, thole.
 suffering pine, dool *in poetry*.
sufficient *see also* **enough**; suffeecient.
 sufficiency suffeeciency, sairin.
suffocate *see also* **choke**; (*with smoke etc*) smeek, smoor, whirken S.
 state of suffocation, suffocating atmosphere scomfish ORKNEY.
sugar succar, shuggar.
 slice of bread and butter sprinkled with sugar sugar piece.
 sugar-candy candibrod.
suggest propone, mint.
suicide: commit suicide pit yersel awa, pit han(d) tae yersel.
suit *noun* shoot, shuit.
 suit of clothes cleedin; (*complete*) stan(d).
 verb shoot, shuit, fit, (*of clothes*) serve.
 blue suits you ye suit blue.
suitable sitable, settin, confeerin NE, fettle SW.
 more suitable to liker.
sulk *verb, see also* **huff**; fung, hing the pettit lip, munge, strunt, dort, glumph.
 sulks dods, dorts, humdudgeons, strunts: '*tak the strunts*'.
 sulky glumsh, snuffie, hingin-mou'd NE, glunsh(ie), glumpie, dortie, gowlie, stunkard.
 sulky-looking glumsh, soor-mou'd.
 sulky expression torn face, pettit lip: '*hing the pettit lip*', lang lip, boose CAITHNESS, HIGHLAND: '*have a boose on*', black dug on yer back SE: '*Why is the black dug on yer back?*'
sullen derf, doon-leukin, dour, glumpie, hum-drum, mump, stroonge N.

sullenly dourlie.

look sullen sumph, glum.

sully fyle, suddle.

sulphurous smell smush.

sultry *see also* **close** 3; glorgie AYR-SHIRE, lunk(ie), smochie; (*and humid*) mochie, muithie.

sum *noun* soum; **sums** (*in arithmetic*) coonts.

sum total (the hail) tot.

considerable sum sweetie NE.

small sum triffle.

summarily short an lang.

summer simmer.

spend the summer simmer.

summit heicht, heid, tap, hillheid, knowe heid.

summon cry, hoy, warn; (*before a court*) summons, sist.

summons cry; (*by death*) challenge NE; (*legal*) brief.

sun sin.

sunny side sun side.

sunbeam *see* **beam**.

sun bonnet crasie, huid, stitchie S; (*on high frame*) ugly SE.

sunrise keek o day.

sunset sundoon, day-set.

gleam of sunshine (sun)blink; (*momentary*) simmer-blink.

Sunday Sawbath, Sabbath.

Sunday clothes Sunday claes, Sunday braws, kirk claes.

sunder sinder.

sundry sindry.

sunken *adjective* howe; (*of the face*) clappit (in).

sup sowp; (*noisily, greedily*) slab NE, cuttie.

superb *see* **wonderful**.

supercilious stinkin, dortie, pauchtie, sneistie.

superimpose onlay.

superior: be superior to be a king tae.

supernatural *adjective* no cannie, eldritch *literary*.

having supernatural powers uncannie.

superstition (*superstitious idea, observance etc*) freit, threap.

superstitious freitie.

supervise owersee.

supervision owerance S.

supper sipper.

have supper sowp, get suppert NE.

supplant pit oot (someone's) ee.

supple soople, leish SW, S, swack, slamp, waffle, waul.

supplement *noun* eik.

verb eik tae.

supply *verb, see also* **provide**; plenish.

lavishly supplied fou-handit, solid.

well supplied with rife o.

ample supply fouth.

short supply scant.

in short supply scrimp, scuddie NE.

supply of food for a function purvey: '*Who supplied the purvey for the waddin?*'

support *noun* haud; (*person*) uphaud; (*prop*) prap, stoop, pall.

verb (*prop*) stuit, steet N; (*a person, by the arm*) oxter; (*look after*) tend; **support yourself** fend.

supporter stoop.

means of support haudin.

suppose *see* **surmise**.

suppress (*feelings etc*) smore, smuir.

suppurate *see* **fester**.

supremacy gree *now literary*.

sure shuir, shair, sheer NE, sicker, certaint, solvendie NE.

surely shuir(lie), fairly NE.

surety caution.

person who stands surety cautioner.

be surety for (be)come guid for, stan(d) guid for, stan(d) in for.

to be sure! hoot aye!

make sure mak siccar.

surf lan(d)brist, jaup.

surface (*of water*) scruif NE.

remove the surface layer from (*ground*) tirr.

surfeit *noun* stap, sta(w), lay-on, gulshoch NE, laithie, forlaithie NE.

verb scunner, sta(w).

surfeited *see* **sated.**

surge noun (*violent move forward*) hurl; (*of waves*) jowe.
verb (*of water*) jaw, gurge, walter.

surgical instruments irons.

surly grugous, gurlie, grumlie, calshie NE, maroonjous NE, stroonge N, sanshach NE, snotterie.

surmise *verb* jalouse, soum.

surmount win ower.

surmount a difficulty lowp a gutter NE.

surpass *see also* **beat** 6; bang, cowe, ootding NE, slap.

surpass everything cowe a(w), cowe the cuddie.

surplice †sark.

surplus owerplus; (*small surplus in addition to that specified*) odds.

surprise *verb* surpreese, pall; (*unpleasantly*) stammygaster; (*dumbfound*) mesmerise.
noun surpreese; (*unwelcome*) conflummix NE, stammygaster NE.

surprised taen(-lik(e)).

be surprised (at) ferlie (at).

I wouldn't be surprised if I've seen as muckle as, I wadna muckle say but, I widna wunner but whit.

exclamation of surprise dod!, losh!, husta! NE, gor!, lovanentie!, govie dick!, govanentie!, michtie!, crivvens!

surrender *see also* **submit;** (*property etc*) renounce.

surreptitious hidlins.

surreptitiously hidlins, stow(n)lins.

surround *verb* (*hem in*) humfish NE.

survey *verb* leuk, scance, sicht, vizzy.
noun leuk, vizzy; (*quick*) scance.

survive pit ower.

surviving tae the fore: '*Is he still tae the fore?*'

not survive nae be tae the fore, nae store the kin NE.

you'll survive ye nivver died o winter yit.

suspect *verb* suspeck, doot, jalouse,

dreid, mislippen, misdoot, jubish.
noun suspeck.

suspense tig-tire.

in suspense on nettles, on heckle-pins.

suspicion suspeecion, alagust NE, misdoot; (*grave*) ill dreid.

suspicious suspeecious, ill-thochtit, jubish.

be suspicious jalouse.

clear (*a person*) **of suspicion** free (a person).

sustain (*a person*) pit ower; (*a conversation*) keep NE.

sustenance *see also* **food;** mait, meal('s) corn, fend NE.

suture (*of skull bones*) *see* **fontanelle.**

swab swaible S.

swagger *verb* strunt, sprose, gester, swash, strush CAITHNESS.
noun swash, strush CAITHNESS.

swaggerer gowster.

swallow[1] (*bird*) swalla.

swallow[2] *verb, see also* **gulp, gobble;** swalla(e), pit ower, pit ower yer craig, lat doon, lat ower NE; (*gulp down*) glog (ower) NE, glut; (*noisily*) glutter, slubber, slork; (*noisily, messily*) sloch, slorp; (*greedily*) glutter, gaup; (*quickly*) scoff.
noun. see also **gulp;** swallae.

swamp *see also* **marsh;** latch, flow, moss flow, gullion, slump.

swampy mossie, slumpie, lairie.

swampy place stank.

sward swaird, sole.

swarm noun (*of bees*) swairm, cast; (*of children*) smarrach NE, swarrach NE; (*of small creatures*) swatter NE, squatter; (*crowd*) swairm, hotterel, vermin; (*in motion*) howdle FIFE.
verb **1** (*of bees*) swairm, cast, byke; (*of people*) swairm, tove, hotter, howder. **2** (*be infested*) heeze, hobble NE, creep ower.

swarming with hoatchin wi, hotchin wi, quick wi.

swarthy black-avised.

swathe *noun* sway.
verb sweel.

sway

act of swathing sweel.

sway *see also* **swing:** *verb* **1** swey, hyke, swag, swig, shog, hobble, showd N, swaver SHETLAND, ORKNEY, NE, shue S; (*unsteadily*) shoogle, wammle. **2** (*cause to sway*) swey, hyke, shog, hobble, showd NE.

noun (*act of swaying*) swey, shog, showd NE.

swear 1 (*an oath*) sweer. **2** (*use bad language: see also* **curse**) sweer, spell, ban, jeedge NE, VOO ORKNEY, NE.

swearing plaister.

swear-word sweer, sweerie word, ill word NE.

swear-words ill-tongue, ill win(d) NE.

sweat *verb* sweet, feem NE; (*profusely*) broth.

noun sweet, feem NE; (*heavy*) broth.

sweated *past tense* swat.

past participle swatten.

sweaty sweetin, feemin NE.

Swede 1 Swade NE. **2** swede (*turnip*) swad(e), neep, turneep, turmit.

sweep *verb* soop, swype NE; (*perfunctorily*) scutch N.

noun (*act of sweeping*) soop, swype NE; (*perfunctory*) scutch N.

sweeping movement wap SHETLAND, NE.

sweet *adjective* hinnie; (*pleasant, lovable*) douce.

noun **1** *see* **dessert**. **2** sweetie, sweetenin ORKNEY, NE, snag NE, smag NE; **sweets** snashters, snysters, gulshichs NE, smacherie NE.

sweet-bag sweetie poke.

sweetbreads breids NE.

sweetheart *see also* **girlfriend, lover;** sweetie, jo, hinnie NE, quine NE.

be named as the sweetheart of name tae.

sweet-jar sweetie bottle.

sweet-seller (*female*) sweetie-wife.

sweetshop sweetie-shop.

sweet-stall sweetie-stan(d).

swell *verb, see also* **swollen: 1** swall, hove; (*puff out*) pluff, huff; (*of arthritic joints*) knot; (*of water*) gurge. **2** (*cause to swell*) swall, hove, bag.

noun (*of the sea*) lift, jowe, chap.

swelled out baggit.

swelling *see also* **swollen;** plouk.

swelter *verb* (*of persons or animals*) plot; (*of weather*) swither.

noun plot, swither.

sweltering sweltrie.

swept *past tense of* **sweep** soopit, swypit NE.

swerve *verb* jee, sklent; (*nimbly*) jink, jouk.

noun swey, jee, sklent, jouk.

swift[1] *adjective* clivver, swith, swipper(t) NE; (*of water*) strick.

swiftly swith, swipper(t) NE.

swift[2] *noun* (*bird*) cran(e).

swig *verb* tak awa, scaff.

noun wa(u)cht, willie-wa(u)cht, slorp, slock, swack.

swill *verb* sweel, synd, rin, soosh NE; (*clothes quickly through soapsuds*) freith SW.

noun (*act of swilling*) sweel, synd.

swim *verb* soom, sweem.

swimming-bladder (*of a fish*) soom, soon(d).

snack eaten after a swim chitterin bit(e), shivery bite.

swindle *see also* **cheat, deceive:** *verb* swick, pauchle.

noun swick, pauchle, intak, sook NE; (*petty*) skin.

swindler swick, intak.

swindling swickerie NE.

swine *see* **pig.**

swing *see also* **sway:** *verb* **1** sweeng NE, shog, shoogle, showd N, shue S. **2** (*cause to swing*) sweeng NE, shog, shoogle, showd N, shue S.

noun (*act of swinging, or a child's swing*) sweeng NE, shog, shoggie-shoo, shue; (*act*) showd NE; (*on a rope etc*) shoogle; (*child's*) swey.

swingboat (*at a fair*) sho(o)gie boat, shoggin boat, swey boat.

swingle (*for flax*) scutcher.

swingle-tree swing tree, swivel tree, horse-tree, threap SW.

swipe *noun, see also* blow²; wheech, skliff, slype NE, sweech ANGUS.

verb, see also strike; wheech, flisk.

swipple (*of a flail*) soople.

swirl *verb* swurl, sweel, pirl, tirr, swither.

noun swurl, sweel, pirl, swither; (*of dust*) stour, stew NE.

swish *verb* sweesh, swoof.

noun sweesh, whush.

switch *noun* (*stick*) wan(d).

switch off (*an electrical appliance*) sneck aff.

swivel *noun* sweel, sweevil.

swollen *see also* swell; swallen, swallt, hoven, hovie, boukit; (*of a river*) heavy, great, prood NE; (*of the body*) flozent NE; (*of persons or animals, from over-eating*) bowdent NE; (*of cattle, from eating too much green fodder*) hoven, hoved, tinged.

swollen gland kirnel.

swollen-headed *see* conceited.

swoon *see also* faint: *verb* swelt, dwam, soon(d) (awa), gae awa, gang awa NE. *noun* dwam, soon(d).

sword swurd, spurtle (*humorous*).

Highlander's large double-edged sword *or* basket-hilted broadsword claymore.

thrust a sword through rit.

sycamore plane (tree).

sycophant kiss-ma-luif, sook, plaister, phraser NE, lick-ma-dowp.

syllable syllab.

symbol (*intricate*) whirligig.

sympathy: sympathetic couthie, innerlie s.

show sympathy for mane, mak mane for.

symposium collogue.

syphilis seephilis, †grandgore.

syringe syreenge, scooter, scoot, skite N, skiter SHETLAND, NE.

syrup seerup, traicle, trykle, trekkle.

system seestem.

T

tabby (*cat*) roant cat.

table (*esp spread for a meal*) buird, brod.

  table leg standart.

  table mat bass mat.

  table napkin servit, daidlie w.

  table support tress.

  table surface table heid.

tablet *see also* **pill**; taiblet.

taciturn dour, derf, still NE, stench NE.

tack *noun* (*sailing*) taik; (*direction*) airt, road.

  verb (*sailing*) taik.

tackle *noun* taickle; (*gear*) graith.

  verb taickle.

tact mense.

  tactful cannie.

tadpole taddie, ladle N, kail-ladle, paddie-ladle S, pollywag, powheid, puddock-pownie, podl(i)e.

tag[1] (*of a bootlace*) shod.

tag[2] (*game*) tig, takkie NE, chasie: '*Let's play chasie*'.

tail rumple, bunt S, runt SW; (*of a hare or rabbit*) fud, bun.

  tail-board (*of a cart*) cairt-door, steeker.

  tail-race (*of a mill*) tail-dam, tail-lead, wa(e)-fleed NE, wa-gang.

  turn tail uptail.

tailor tylor; (*humorously contemptuous*) †prick-the-loose, †seam biter; (*itinerant*) fleein tailor, †cardower, †whip the cat.

  tailor's iron guse.

taint *noun* humph, smit; (*bad taste*) took.

  verb smit.

  tainted *see also* **mouldy** (*under* **mould**[1]), **rotten**; humphie, mochie, wyntit.

  become tainted wynt.

take *verb, see also* **took**; tak, hae, pit: '*he wiz jist pittin aff his claes*'.

  taken *past participle* taen, takken, tooken.

  take after kin(d) tae S: '*That laddie kinds till his mither*'.

  takeaway cairry-oot.

  take in intak.

tale *see also* **story**; sonnet NE, spell, spin NE.

  tell tales *see also* **tell**; clype (on).

  tale-bearer *see* **telltale**.

talent ingine.

  talented young man lad o pairts.

  talented young woman lass o pairts.

talk *noun* **1** (*chat*) blether, clash, cleck, crack, gab, gash, speak, say, word, news SHETLAND, N, laig NE; (*confidential*) hudge-mudge; (*empty*) buller; (*gushing, fulsome*) phrasin, phrase NE; (*idle, repetitious*) rane; (*light, entertaining*) gab; (*incessant*) yap(-yappin); (*loud, incessant*) yammer; (*noisy, angry*) yatter; (*noisy, unintelligible*) goller, lig NE. **2** (*of a place*) speak: '*speak o the toon*'.

  verb crack, blether, say, ca(w) the crack; (*incessantly*) jangle, yab SHETLAND, NE; (*cheerfully, familiarly and at length*) tove; (*fluently and at length*) lay aff, laig NE, scrieve; (*in a lively way*) crack, croose; (*in a rambling, incoherent way*) maunner; (*idly, foolishly*) jaunner; (*ingratiatingly*) crose NE; (*loudly and confidently*) craw croose; (*noisily*) clitter-clatter; (*noisily and quickly*) blatter; (*quickly*) whitter; (*snappishly*) nyaff, yap.

  endless talker toner, deave NE.

talking together corrieneuchin.

talkative bletherie, bletherin, gabbie, crackie, glib(-gabbit), glib-mou'd, gabbit, newsie NE, (*annoyingly*) tongue-deavin, nash-gab S.

tall heich, lang; (*large*) sture.

tall thin person lang drink (o watter), lingel N, spirl, skinnymalink(ie).

tallow tallie, tallon, tauch; (*melted*) rind.

tally nickstick.

talon *see* **claw**.

tame *adjective* (*of wild birds*) caif S.
verb cuddom.

tamper with prat wi, parry wi, mell wi.

tan *see* **tanned**.

tangle[1] *noun* fankle, raivel, snorl, burble, rothos NE, taigle; (*inextricable*) pease wisp; (*of hair*) rug.
verb fankle, taut, taigle, taisle; (*get into a tangle*) fankle, raivel, snurkle S.

tangled fankelt, raivelt, snorlie, burbelt, row-chow, misred; (*of hair*) tousie, ruggie, tautie, feesket SHETLAND.

tangle[2] (*seaweed*) currack NE.

tangy *see* **pungent**.

tankard tanker, stowp.

tanned (*of leather*) barkenit.

tansy stinkin Tam(mie) SE.

tantrum *see also* **rage**; fung, tirr, tirri-vee.

tap[1] *verb* (*strike lightly*) chap, tip, tit, tig, pap.
noun tig, pap.

tap[2] (*water tap*) cran; (*cold-water*) well; (*outdoor, esp one supplying a locality*) spicket, spriggit, stroop.

tap-root taupin.

tap-wrench dwang.

tape trappin; (*ornamental*) stringin.

taper *noun* (*waxed spill*) spail.

tapioca birdie's een(ies) NE.

tar taur, ter.

tarred with the same brush buckelt wi ae hesp.

tarry taurie.

tar-boiler tarry biler.

tar box (*for sheep-marking*) tar-buist.

tardy dreich, aff-pittin, hint-han(d).

tare *see* **vetch**.

target (*object set up as a target*) prap NE; (*in curling*) tee, witter.

set up as a target prap.

tarnish ternish, scuff, scuffle NE, tash.

tarnished scuffie.

tarry hover, dwadle, taigle, tarrow SHETLAND, ORKNEY.

tart[1] *noun* tairt, tert.

tart[2] *adjective* **1** *see also* **bitter** 1; wersh, pickant NE, sharrow CAITHNESS. **2** (*brusque*) snar, cuttit NE, nebbie, snell, snippit, birkie.

tartan *noun* plaidin.
adjective chackit.

task handlin, troke, turn; (*dirty, disagreeable*) plowter, plyter NE; (*hard*) handlin, chaave NE, struissle; (*set*) darg, stent; (*small*) jot NE; (*carelessly done*) slip-by.

take severely to task *see also* **scold**; tak ower the rack stock NE.

be taken severely to task get yer lug in yer luif.

tassel toorie, tossel, tappietoorie, knop.

taste *noun* **1** gust, saur; (*bad*) goo, guff, humph; (*disagreeable: see also* **taint**) kneggum. **2** (*tasting*) preein, pruive SHETLAND, ORKNEY, NE; (*esp of drink*) smell.
verb lip, gust, air N; (*have a certain taste*) saur; (*try by tasting*) pruive SHETLAND, ORKNEY, NE, pree *literary*.

tasteless (*in bad taste*) gustless; (*of food*) wersh, walsh, fushionless, fen(d)less NE, keest S, wauch NE.

tasteless food *or* **drink** wabble NE.

tasty goolie, gustie.

a taste for a goo O, a goo for.

tatter: tatters *see also* **rags**; flitters, pallions, taivers SHETLAND, ORKNEY, targets NE, tartles W, tatterwallops, traileps SHETLAND, ORKNEY, N.

tattered duddie, skybald, tatterwal-lopie.

taught *past tense, past participle of* **teach** taucht, teacht.

taunt

taunt *verb* cry (someone) names, upcast, snite someone's niz, towt SE; (*loudly*) bairge NE.

noun upcast, cast-up, towt SE, doon-tak, sneist.

taunting *adjective* sneistie.

taut *see also* **tight**; tacht SHETLAND, ORKNEY, N, strait, stent(it).

tauten, make taut stent, strait NE.

tavern *see* **inn**.

tawdry huddrie, shan SE.

tax *noun, verb* stent, cess.

Norse tax on land skatt SHETLAND, ORKNEY.

tea tae SHETLAND, N, scaud *humorous*; (*weak*) skiddle, blibs NE, jute ORKNEY; (*afternoon meal*) antrum, efternuin SHETLAND; (*high tea*) tea an till't, tousie tea, mait tea.

tea-break piece-time, piece-break, minute NE.

tea-drinker (*who drinks a lot of tea*) tea-jennie, tea-han(d).

tea-leaf (*tea*) blade; (*in a cup, indicating the arrival of a stranger*) stranger.

tea party cookie shine, tea shine, tea skiddle.

teapot snippie, maskin pot, stroopie SHETLAND, NE, track(ie)-pot.

potful of tea mask(in).

cup of tea, drink of tea stroopach N, HIGHLAND; (*last cup, with whisky instead of milk*) birse tea.

make (a cup of) tea wat (a cup o) tea.

teach *see also* **taught**; learn, leern NE.

teacher *see* **schoolmaster**.

team (*in curling, carpet-bowling, quoits*) rink; (*of weavers etc*) pass; (*of plough horses or oxen*) pleuch.

tear[1] *verb, see also* **tore, torn**; teir, terr W, rent; (*rip*) rive, reeve, screed; (*esp clothing*) sklent SHETLAND, NE; (*at a seam*) skail N; (*by rough usage*) ratch S; (*come apart*) screed.

noun teir, terr W; (*eg in clothing*) sklent SHETLAND, NE.

tear apart rive.

tear at rive, rug an rive (at).

tear off (*a covering*) screeve, tirr, tirl; (*skin in strips*) flype.

tear[2]: **tearful** bubblie, bibblie NE, greetin, greetie, snotterie.

tear-stained begrutten.

burst into tears blirt.

full of tears (*of the eyes*) watshod W, SW.

tease *verb* 1 *see also* **irritate**; kittle (up), be at, joke, taisle, tirraneese NE, towt SE, collie-fox ULSTER. 2 **tease (out)** touse, tait.

teasing rub, heeze NE, towt SE, taisle.

teat tit.

tedder (*for turning hay*) kicker.

tedious *see also* **dreary**; dreich, tedisome, langsome, taiglesome.

tedium hing-on.

teeming with hotchin wi, hoatchin wi, heezin wi NE.

teeth *see also* **tooth**; (*large*) gams NE.

teething stick gumstick.

set of false teeth wallies.

provide with teeth teethe.

teetotal total.

teetotum totum.

television televeesion.

tell *see also* **told**: 1 (*mention, esp confidentially*) mou(th); (*incorrectly*) skellie SW. 2 **tell (tales) (about)** clype (on), tell (on), clash, ca the clash NE.

telltale clype, clash-bag, clash-pyot, clasher, tellie-speirie, tale-pyot, clatterer, clatter-bag(s) NE.

let me tell you seestu.

not tell no lat dab, no lat on, nivver let myowt NE, nivver leet NE.

temper *noun* 1 **bad temper** *see also* **rage**; ill nature, cut: '*she's in bad cut the day*', birse: '*his birse is up*', corruption, dirdum, ill-teen NE; (*fit of temper*) fung, pirr, taum, fuff; (*esp violent*) flist NE, ramp NE. 2 *see* **mood**.

verb (*moderate*) licht.

fly into a temper fuff.

lose your temper loss yer rag, loss yer puggie, loss the heid.

lose your temper with fa oot on NE.

in a bad temper *see also* **bad-tempered, short-tempered, hot-tempered;** crabbit, on short trot, short i the trot, short i the pile, in a bung NE.

get up in a bad temper rise aff yer wrang side.

put in a bad temper canker NE.

temperate *see* **calm.**

temperature: slight rise in temperature lew.

tempest *see* **storm.**

tempestuous 1 (*of weather: see also* **stormy**) gowstie, hashie, rumballiach s. **2** (*of temperament*) rumballiach s.

temple (*side of face*) haffet.

tempt temp.

temptation provokshin.

ten (*children's rhymes*) tenaby SHETLAND, ORKNEY, N, †dick NE; (*sheep-counting*) dek sw.

tenth tent.

tenant tacksman NE; (*farmer*) †mailer; (*on entering a tenancy*) ingaun tenant; (*on leaving*) ootgaun tenant.

entry to a tenancy ingaun.

leaving a tenancy ootgaun.

tend keep, see efter, notice SHETLAND, ORKNEY, N; (*animals, children*) tent; (*animals*) herd, guide, oversee, wirk.

tender *adjective* (*easily hurt*) frush; (*of a kiss*) sappie.

tendon tenon NE, leader.

tenon tenor.

tenon saw tenor-saw.

tense (*taut*) strait.

tenterhooks: be on tenterhooks be sittin on preens, be on heckle-pins, be on nettles.

tepid teepid, lew (warm).

term *see also* **limit;** tairm; (*school*) quarter.

on bad terms faur oot, striven NE.

on good terms in good habits, gracious.

on intimate terms faur ben (wi), pack, hyne in (wi) NE.

come to terms gree.

keep on good terms with keep in (guid) wi, haud in wi.

termagant *see* **shrew** 2.

terminate *see* **end.**

termination *see also* **end;** hinderen(d), hinneren(d); (*of a lease, term of office etc*) ish; (*of a contract etc*) expiry.

defer the termination of (*law*) prorogate.

tern pirr, pictarnie SHETLAND, ORKNEY, FIFE, tirrock SHETLAND.

terrible terrel.

terrier tarrie (dug), terrie (dug).

terrify terrifee, fricht, dare NE, gliff.

terrifying fearsome, frichtsome.

terrified fair fleggit.

terror terrification, the shakers; (*feeling of*) grue.

terse (*curt*) nippit, cuttit NE.

test *verb* (*by tasting*) pree, pruive.

test piece †sey (piece).

testament settlement.

testamentary testamentar.

testicle stane, steen NE, cull s.

male with one testicle undescended riglin.

testify testifee, qualify, †depone.

testy *see also* **bad-tempered;** carnaptious, crabbit, crankie, atterie CAITHNESS, bungie NE, cuttit NE.

tetchy *see* **testy.**

tether *noun* tedder SHETLAND, ORKNEY, N, langle, binnen; (*for a cow*) mink NE, FIFE.

verb tedder SHETLAND, ORKNEY, N, bin(d).

tethering peg, tethering post baikie NE.

be at the end of your tether be at ane mae wi't s.

text (*of a sermon*) grun(d).

than nor, as.

thank thenk.

express thanks to someone cun someone thanks.

God be thanked! †bethankit!

thankful thankfu, thankfae.

that *see also* **those;** at, (*unstressed*) it

NE; (*usually of something further away than 'that'*) yon, thon, on NE.

thatch *verb, noun* thack, theek.

thatched cottage thack(it) biggin, thackit hoos(i)e.

thatched with straw strae-thackit ORKNEY, NE.

thatcher theeker, thacker.

thatching pin thack-pin.

thatching ropes raip, simmins.

Y-shaped stick used in thatching stob NE, sting.

(repair) thatch with a 'sting' sting, stob-thatch NE.

thaw *noun* thowe, come, fresh, ice-lowsin, saft; (*after a high wind*) dry thowe; (*without wind or rain*) weet thowe; (*brought on by rain*) dirty thowe. *verb* thowe, fresh NE, lowp N, lowse, saften NE; (*partially*) glotten.

the beginning of a thaw upbrak.

the e(e) N, de SHETLAND, E COAST, da SHETLAND.

theatrical: travelling theatrical show geggie.

theft stootherie, lift, skin, pickerie, spulzie *law*.

taking by theft or violence wa-takkin.

them thaim, dem SHETLAND.

themselves thaimsels, theirsels, thirsels.

by themselves (alone) their lane, thir lane, them lane SHETLAND, NE.

theme (*constant or repeated*) leid NE, owercome *in poetry*; (*esp a complaint*) rone.

then than, an NE, well: '*We're awa, well*', syne.

thence syne.

there: thereabouts thereawa; **there or thereabouts** yonderaboots, eraboot NE.

thereafter syne.

therefore syne.

thereto theretill.

thereupon syne.

there is there: '*there yer tea*', at's N.

there now! noona!

over there yonder, thonder, onner NE.

these thae, thir, is eens NE, this ones HIGHLAND.

thick (*of persons, things*) guttie, great; (*and smooth, of a liquid*) maumie; (*full of body*) stieve.

thicken (*soup etc*) mak, lithe; (*with meal*) meal N; (*of jam, porridge etc*) mak.

thickening (*for soup etc*) lithin NE.

thickness (*a layer*) ply.

thick-headed *see also* **stupid**; mappit.

thickset thick, stumpie, durkie; (*small*) setterel, short-set.

thickset person (*stout*) stab; (*large, coarse*) pilsh NE.

thicket buss, shaw *literary*; (*of brushwood etc*) rone.

thief *see also* **robber**; brigan(n)er NE.

thievery *see also* **robbery**.

thievish *see* **light-fingered** (*under* light^2).

thigh thee, hoch.

thighs fillets N.

back of the thigh hoch.

thigh-bone hunker-bane.

thimble thummle.

thin *adjective* **1** (*of persons; see also* **skinny**) slink, nairra-boukit, skleff S, spirlie, tuim, skrank; (*emaciated*) shilpit, shirpit, nakit, clinkit; (*thin and miserable or ill-looking*) peesweep, peeng(e)in, peengie, peelie-wallie, pikit(-lik(e)), pookie, pookit, slunken; (*of animals*) mean, sma. **2** (*of things: thin and flat*) skleff S. **3** (*of liquid food*) shire, spleuterie, wabblie; (*of liquor*) shilpit. *verb* **thin (out)** (*seedlings: see also* **potato**) single, sinder NE, slap NE.

thin person skelf.

make thin pike.

thing: the very thing the verra dunt.

thingummy thingmy, thingwy, hingmy.

not a thing deil a haet, no an article, nae a bluid, nae a docken.

think: think deeply lay the brains asteep.

think of *or* **about** think on.

third trid SHETLAND.

thirst *noun* thrist SHETLAND, ORKNEY, NE, drouth.

verb thrist SHETLAND, ORKNEY, NE.

thirsty drouthie.

thirst-quencher slockener.

quench the thirst of slocken.

thirteen therteen, thretten, deil's dizzen.

thirteenth therteen, therteent.

thirty threttie, thertie, trettie SHETLAND, ORKNEY.

this is.

this time this: '*There's plenty tae dae atween this an Sunday*'.

thistle thrissel, thrustle, porr CAITHNESS.

sow thistle swine thrissel.

spear thistle burr-thrissel.

inside of a thistle head breid-an-cheese.

receptacle of a thistle cheese.

ribbon of the Order of the Thistle †green ribbon.

thither theretill, till ere NE.

thong whang, thwang, fang N.

thorax kist.

thorn jag, job, pirk, porr CAITHNESS, prod SW, prog.

thorny jaggie, jobbie, jabbie.

thornback ray thornie(-back) SHETLAND.

thorough thorow.

thoroughly evendoon, perfeck, freely, richt, as clean as a leek.

thoroughfare waygate, gang, througang.

those thae S, that, at NE, that ones HIGHLAND; (*of something more remote*) yon, thon, on NE.

though *adverb* (*at end of phrase*) but: '*It isna me but*'.

thought *noun* thocht.

past tense, past participle of **think** thocht.

thoughtful pensefu; (*considerate*) considerin.

thoughtless daft, glaikit.

line of thought braith, lease.

having nasty thoughts ill-thochtit.

thousand thoosan(d).

thraldom †thirlage.

thrash *see* **beat**.

thrashed *past tense* throosh, threesh NE, treush SHETLAND, ORKNEY.

past participle thrushen, thrashen, treshen SHETLAND, ORKNEY.

thrashing *see* **beating**.

thrash about spelder, wallop.

thread threid: **1** (*broken or frayed*) raivel; (*shoemaker's*) lingel, en(d), souteren(d), roset-en(d), rosettie eyn NE; (*strong, unbleached*) whitie-broon threid. **2** (*of a speech etc*) stot.

threadbare pookit.

thread your way in and out (of) needle.

threat *noun* threit, thrait.

threaten threit, thraiten, threiten, boast, shore, offer (tae); (*a person*) mint NE; (*rain, snow*) mak.

threatening (*dangerous*) unchancie; (*of weather*) canker(i)t; (*rain*) heavy-hertit; (*of the sky*) loorie, hingin.

three chree, threy S, tree SHETLAND, ORKNEY, hree W; (*children's rhymes*) tethery.

three-pronged three-taed.

three or four three-fower.

thresh thrash, berry SW, S; (*roughly*) gloy.

threshed *past tense* throosh, threesh NE, treush SHETLAND, ORKNEY.

past participle thrushen, thrashen, treshen SHETLAND, ORKNEY.

thresher barnman; (*pieceworker*) tasker.

threshing floor chap NE.

threshing mill thrashin machine, (thrashin) mull; (*steam-driven*) †steam mill.

threshold threshwart, thrashel, lintel, door-stane, door-sole ORKNEY, CAITHNESS.

thrift

thrift 1 trift SHETLAND, ORKNEY. **2** (*sea-pink*) sea-daisy.

thriftless doless, thrieveless.

thriftlessness wanthrift SHETLAND.

thrifty fendie SW.

be thrifty hain (in).

thrill *noun* dirl, stoun(d); (*of emotion*) dinnle.

verb thirl; (*with emotion*) dirl.

thrive *see also* **throve**; trive SHET-LAND, ORKNEY, thram N; (*succeed*) luck, dae guid, forder, mak oot.

thriven triven SHETLAND, ORKNEY.

thriving growthie, wallie SHETLAND, ORKNEY; (*of a child*) grushie; (*of animals*) fresh, raff NE.

not thriving ill-daein, wanthriven SHETLAND.

throat craig, craig's close, thrapple, swallae, throttle, hause, hause-pipe, gizze(r)n.

clear the throat ha(u)ch(le); (*noisily*) clorach, hask, rauk, slorach.

throb *noun* thrab, stoun(d), gowp, skelp, dirl; (*of the head etc*) lowp, dunt.

verb thrab, stoun(d), stang, gowp, gell SHETLAND, CAITHNESS, putt S, flaffer, soo, dirl, rash; (*of the heart etc*) lowp, dunt, wallop.

throe shower, thraw.

death throe deid thraw, thratch.

throng *noun* thrang, steer, menyie.

verb thrang.

throttle *verb* thrapple, guzzle.

through throu, throw, throuch; (*to an inner room*) ben.

through and through throch-an-throu.

throve *past tense of* **thrive** thrave.

throw *noun* thraw, jass NE; (*violently*) fung; (*underhand, made by striking against the thigh*) hainch; (*with a swing*) lab.

verb thraw, clod, pick, hove, wap, heave (*without notion of effort as in Eng*), have NE, pin: '*pin that tattie at the cat*'; (*esp a line to a boat*) shyve NE; (*a fishing line from a boat*) saw NE; (*esp a stone*) em;

(*by springing from a board, plank etc*) spanghew; (*suddenly and forcefully*) skite; (*violently*) bung, clash, fung, jass NE, shine S, wap; (*with a jerk*) spang.

throw away (*reject*) ort; (*carelessly*) bum.

throw down (*forcefully*) doosht NE; sclype NE, sklyter NE.

throw off (*clothing*) cast.

throw on (*clothing*) hudder on.

throw up 1 *see* **give up. 2** *see* **vomit. 3** (*buildings, carelessly*) clatch up.

thrush *see* **missel thrush, song thrush.**

thrust *noun* thrist, punce, prog, pork SW, S, porr SW.

verb thrist, dird NE, pork SW, S, porr SW, wap ORKNEY; (*suddenly*) shuit.

thrust into stap in.

thud *see also* **thump**: *noun* dunt, dad, doist, sclaff, doosht SHETLAND, N, flaip S, haiches N, sklyte NE, slype NE.

verb dunt, dad.

with a thud clash: '*it fell clash*'.

fall with a thud soss, sklyte NE.

thug *see also* **ruffian**; rochian NE.

thumb thoum.

thumbscrew *see* **torture.**

angle between thumb and forefinger glack CAITHNESS.

handle with the thumb thoum.

thumb your nose spang the nose.

hold under your thumb keep *or* haad in his *or* her ain neuk SHETLAND, NE.

under your thumb sair hauden doon.

thump *noun, see also* **blow**[2], **thud**; belt, dad, dunt, rattle, dird, ding, dump NE, filbow NE, plowt SHETLAND, NE, racket SHETLAND, rung, slatch, souse, thud, yowff NE; **thumps** (*on the back, to mark a child's birthday*) dumps, bumps EDINBURGH, dunts.

verb, see also **hit**; dunch, dunt, cloor, doosht NE, dump, plunk, souse; (*of the heart*) flichter, gowp, tirr.

go thump gae wallop.

put something down with a thump plunk, plank.

thunder *noun* thunner, brattle, hurl, yird din NE.

thunder shower thunner(-plump).

thwart *noun* (*of a boat*) thaft, taft SHETLAND.

verb conter, pit the haims on, thorter, thraw, pall SHETLAND, ORKNEY, N.

thwarted lummed SW.

tick[1] *verb* (*of a clock*) skelp.

make a ticking sound knick.

tick[2] (*sheep-tick*) fag, (sheep) taid, keb, ked.

tick[3]: **buy on tick** forenail NE.

ticking (*mattress cover*) tike.

tickle *noun, verb* kittle; (*anything causing a tickling sensation*) itchy-coo.

ticklish kittle; (*easily tickled*) ticklie, kittle, kittlie.

tiddly *see also* **tipsy**; corant NE.

tide *noun* (*of the sea*) rug.

verb (*pause between ebb and flow*) still.

ebb tide (*low water*) grun(d) ebb SHETLAND, ORKNEY, N.

high tide the tap o the watter.

high tide in May Mey flude.

high, strong tide at the beginning of August Lammas stream N.

irregular tide in the Firth of Forth leaky tide E CENTRAL.

motion of the tide drag.

strong tide rug.

tidings *see also* **news**; speerins, uncos.

tidy *adjective, see also* **neat, spruce**[1]; trig, tosh, weel-redd-up, purposelik(e), nacketie NE, in gweed reel NE, snog CAITHNESS, ORKNEY, faisible.

verb, also **tidy up** redd (up), sort, tosh, sproosh (up), dicht, snod, trig up NE, doss up NE, bush up, upredd SHETLAND.

tidied redd up.

tidily ticht, tosh.

tidily made faisible.

tidiness purpose.

tidying-up redd(in)-up, rid-up, sort, tosh, snod-up, trig-up NE.

tidy yourself sort yersel.

tie *noun* (*fastening*) tial SHETLAND, ORKNEY.

verb, see also **bind**; tether, wap, wup.

tie together leash.

tie up (*tightly*) hankle.

tiff *see also* **quarrel, dispute**; haud.

tig *see* **tag**[2].

tiger teeger.

tight ticht, tacht N, stret, strait; (*of clothes*) jimp.

tighten tichten, strait NE, straiten SHETLAND, NE; (*a loop in a rope, with a stick*) kinch.

tightly ticht, hard.

tight-fitting nippit, strait, scrimp, jimp.

in a tight spot in the wrang close.

tile (*porcelain*) wallie tile.

tiled (*eg of a wall*) wallie: 'wallie close'.

till *verb* (*the soil*) teel SHETLAND, manner, labour.

tillage labourin SHETLAND.

tiller tillie.

tilt *noun* thraw.

verb cowp, heeld SHETLAND, ORKNEY, jig CAITHNESS.

tilt up (*as of the nose*) kip.

full tilt hail wheel.

timber *noun* timmer, †tree *literary*.

timbre souch.

time (*season*) tid.

time-consuming taiglesome.

time-wasting fouterie, scutterie NE.

time-wasting occupation scutter.

beat time with the foot treeple NE.

favourable time tid.

old times lang syne, lang seen NE.

period of time while's time, filie NE.

the end of time the morn-come-never.

this time this.

time when work finishes lowsin time; (*also*) **when a congregation, school** *etc* **breaks up** skailin time.

fix a time for tryst.

take your time tak yer hurry (in yer han(d)).

at all times *see also* **always; at a(w) time.**

a long time (*from the present*) yon time.

a very long time a muin.

a long time ago lang syne, a guid bit.

for a long time this monie a lang day *or* year NE.

a short time a bittie, a wee (bit), a (wee) whilie, a (wee) filie NE, a catlowp, a short NE.

a short time ago short syne, nae lang syne.

in a short time the noo, eenoo, ivnoo, or lang.

at the present time eenoo, the noo, ivnoo.

at times *see also* **now and then** (*under* **now); at a time.**

at an unspecified time yon time: '*He'll no be hame till yon time*'; '*She's been here since yon time*'.

by the time that gin.

for some time past this while back, is filie back NE.

for the time being in the meantime.

from the time that f(r)ae, syne.

from that time sin, (sin)syne.

from time to time noo(s) an than(s) NE, at oos an ans NE.

in good time timeous *law*.

in (the course of) time throu time.

at that time thae days, thanadays NE.

since that time (sin)syne.

some time ago while-syne.

timid timorsome, blate, bauch, coorie, cooardie, ergh, hen-hertit, hennie, shan; (*of animals*) scar.

timidity ergh(ness).

timorous *see* **timid.**

tin: small tin mug *etc* tinnie.

tin box mull(ie) NE.

tin plate fite-iron NE.

tinsmith tinnie; (*itinerant*) tinkler.

tinder tindle, †spunk.

tine tae, stang NE.

tinge *noun* teenge.

verb teenge, lit.

tingle *verb* thirl, dingle, dirl, gell, prinkle, soo; (*esp of the fingers*) dinnle.

tingling sensation (*eg from a blow*) dinnle, dirl.

cause to tingle nip, dingle, pringle S.

tinker tink(ie), caird, ranegill.

tinker's child tinker-bairn.

tinker's wife, tinker-woman tink wife, tinkie bodie.

tinkle: cause to tinkle tingle.

tinkling (*of water etc*) plinkin.

tint *noun, verb* spraing, lit.

tiny (little) wee, tot(t)ie (wee), peedie SHETLAND, ORKNEY, CAITHNESS, peerie SHETLAND, ORKNEY, CAITHNESS, FIFE, pinkie, pirlie (wee).

tiny piece of something *see also* **piece;** (n)imsh.

tip[1] (*end part*) tap; (*iron*) shod; (*pointed projection*) neb.

fit with a metal tip shod.

tip[2] (*upset*) (ower)cowp, cowp up.

tip[3] (*gratuity*) *noun* drink siller, magg, pauchle.

verb creesh the luif o, glack someone's mitten NE.

tipple *verb* cock yer wee finger, dribble, taste, juitle, sirple S, beb S, toot, turn up the wee finger.

tippler *see also* **drunkard;** drouth, troch, toot.

tipsy hauf-cock(ie), tosie, capernoitit, chippit NE, cornt NE, weel upon't NE, hertie.

tiptoe tipper.

tiptoes taptaes, tippertaes: '*on tippertaes*'.

tire fornyaw, kned, staw SE.

tired forfochen, lowsed, fornyawed, fauchelt, jaffelt SW, taigelt.

very tired *see also* **exhausted;** tiketired, stane-tired S, fair forfochen.

tired-looking disjaskit, oorit.

tiredness tire.

tiresome *see also* **annoying;** stawsome, seeckrif(e).

tiring taiglesome.

tissue tishie.

tit: blue tit blue bonnet, ox ee.
　great tit ox ee.
titbit hire, snag NE, smag NE, sweetnin NE.
　titbits gulshichs NE, snysters.
tithe teind.
　exempt from tithe-paying †teind-free.
titillate kittle.
titivate prink.
title teetle.
　title deed title.
titter *see also* **giggle**: *noun* snicher, whicker, kicher.
　verb snicher, flicher, keckle, keechle, kicher.
tittle-tattle *noun, see also* **gossip**; clavers, clash, clash-ma-claver, gab, gibble-gabble.
to *preposition* tae, till, until; (*after verbs of calling, shouting, knocking etc*) on: '*He's shoutin on ye*'; (*before infinitive: in order to*) for tae; (*in telling time*) o(f): '*a quarter o fower*'.
　to and fro *see* **backwards and forwards**.
　move to and fro wampish.
　wag to and fro swag.
toad puddock, taid.
　toadstool puddock-stuil, puddock steel NE.
　toady *noun, see* **sycophant**.
toast *noun* tost; (*drink in honour*) toss, †skole.
　verb (*bread etc*) birsle, harn; (*too much*) scowder.
　toasted (*of cheese*) roastit.
tobacco tabaccae, tabacca SHETLAND, NE.
　tobacco ash dirrie NE.
　tobacco pouch sp(l)euchan.
　as much tobacco as will fill a pipe smoke o tobacco.
　plug of half-burnt tobacco dottle, fuggle NE, strummel.
　roll of tobacco rowe.
today the day, e day NE.
toddle tottle, hotter S, paidle.

toddler tot(t)ie, totum, wean, bairnie, gangrel, eeshan N, pin NE, smool.
to-do *see* **fuss.**
toe tae; (*of a shoe*) nob EDINBURGH.
　toe-cap (*of boot*) freuchan HIGHLAND.
　toe-plate (*front of boot sole*) tae bit.
　little toe peerie-winkie *in nursery rhyme.*
toffee taffie, gundie, black man.
　treacle toffee clack, claggum NE.
together thegither, egither N, (th)egidder NE.
　get on together draw.
　sitting close together curcuddoch.
toil *noun* tra(u)chle, chaave NE, dwang ANGUS, struissle, tulyie, darg.
　verb tra(u)chle, swink, dwang, kyauve SHETLAND, NE, pingle, chaave NE, taw, warsle, darg.
　toilsome pinglin, typin NE.
toilet *see* **W.C., privy.**
token taiken.
told *past tense, past participle of* **tell** telt, telled, tauld.
tolerate bide, thole (wi).
　tolerable tholeable, middlin, geylies.
　tolerably middlin(s).
　tolerance thole.
toll[1] towl.
　toll-keeper tollie.
toll[2] *noun, verb* (*of a bell*) towl, jowe, jowl.
tomboy gilpie, hallockit.
　tomboyish hallockit, hallirackit.
tombstone lairstane NE; (*flat*) thruch-stane SW, S.
tomcat gib(bie)(-cat).
tomfoolery flumgummerie NE.
tomorrow the morn, the morra.
　tomorrow morning the morn's morn, the morra's morn.
　tomorrow night the morn's nicht.
tone (*of voice etc*) souch.
　tone deaf timmer-tuned, timmer-teened NE.
tongs tangs, tyangs NE.
tongue 1 melt. **2** (*of a shoe*) bur SHET-LAND, ORKNEY, NE. **3** (*speech*) gab;

(*malevolent* or *abusive*) ill-tongue. **4** (*language of a country*) leid.

tongue-tied tongue-tackit.

hold your tongue haud yer w(h)eesh(t), save yer breath tae cool yer parritch, haud yer gab, steek yer gab, sing dumb; (*and stay calm*) keep a calm souch.

on the tip of your tongue at the root o yer tongue.

tonight the nicht.

too tae, tee NE; (*also*) an a(w); (*excessively*) overly, ower.

too many ower monie.

too much overly, ower muckle.

took *past tense of* **take** taen, teuk.

tool *see also* **implement**; tuil, luim, leem N, wark-luim, gibble, gibblet; (*inefficient*) futtle CAITHNESS; (*for making a groove jointing two window sashes*) countercheck; (*for smoothing hollow or circular wood*) shavelin NE; (*with ratchet for tensing fencing wire*) monkey.

tools graith.

tool-basket bass.

tooth tuith, teeth; (*large*) gam NE.

toothache teethache, sair teeth.

back tooth aisle tuith SW, S.

top¹ (*highest point*) tap; (*higher part, upper end*) heid: 'braeheid'; 'desk-heid'; (*of a wall etc*) riggin; (*of a class, school*) dux, heids S.

top hat lum (hat), tile (hat).

topknot toorie.

topmost heidmaist.

from top to toe f(r)ae lug tae laggin SW.

on top of oot ower.

top up eik up.

top² (*spinning top*) peerie; (*humming*) bummer.

toper *see* **drunkard**.

topic speak.

favourite topic leid N.

topple cowp, whummle.

topple over tottle.

topsy-turvy tapsalteerie, heels-ower-gowdie, heeliegoleerie, hirdie-girdie, hirdum-dirdum, tersie-versie S.

torch *noun* (*esp for salmon-fishing at night*) †ruffie.

tore *past tense of* **tear**¹ tuir, rave.

torn *past participle* tore, riven.

torment (*with a question*) deave, tarragat.

tornado skailwin(d).

torrent (*mountain*) scriddan; (*of rain*) spate, teem.

fall in torrents leash, plash.

torsk tusk (fish) SHETLAND, ORKNEY, CAITHNESS.

tortoise tortie.

tortoiseshell cat muscovy cat SW.

tortuous: a quick tortuous movement jink.

torture *verb, noun* torter.

instrument of torture (*iron bridle and gag*) †branks; (*thumbscrew*) †thumbikins; (*iron collar*) †jougs; (*of the legs*) †buits, †cashielaws; (*of the fingers*) †pilliewinks.

toss *noun* fung.

verb, see also **throw**; fung, pick, spang, wap; (*the head*) cast, cave; (*of a ship*) howd, jowe.

toss about towin SW, taisle, toosht NE; (*disorder*) roochle ARGYLL; (*restlessly*) rowe, kyauve SHETLAND, NE, chaave NE.

toss down (*money*) doss doon NE.

toss restlessly in bed rummle, whummle, fowe NE.

toss to and fro jowe, keytch, whummle.

tossed about jachelt.

tot 1 (*small child*) *see* **toddler**. **2** (*small drink*) (wee) dram.

total: the total tot, the hail, the hail rickmatick, box an dice, the hail jing-bang.

in total at a slump.

totter *see also* **stagger**: *noun* stotter, stoiter, styter, stacher, stoit NE, swaver NE, toiter NE, staver, hochle.

verb stacher, stoiter, styter, stotter, swaver SHETLAND, ORKNEY, NE, tooter NE, toit NE, toiter, hotter S, tot, jooter, jossle, wabble.

tranquil

tottery fitless, shooglie, wiggletie-waggletie, wammilie, staucherie, stammerie, stotterie.

touch *verb* tig; (*lightly*) scuff, skiff, scutch N, pap.
noun **1** (*slight, in passing*) scuff, skiff; (*light, playful*) tig. **2** (*of illness etc*) whiff, gliff, skiff.
touchy pernicketie, croose, kittle, snuffie, tiftie, towtie.

tough *adjective* teuch; (*from overcooking*) tewed S; (*of persons*) raucle.
noun, see **ruffian**.

tour *see* **trip**.

tourist towerist *humorous*.

tournament †rink.
tournament enclosure †barrace, †rink roume.

tow *verb* towe.
noun towe; (*by a trace-horse*) theat.
towed boat †track boat.

towel too(e)l, han(d) cloot.

tower toor; (*small*) toorack(ie) SHETLAND, NE; (*prehistoric circular*) broch; (*fortified rectangular*) tower house, peel.
towered building tappietoorie.

town toon.
town hall toon('s) hoose, †tolbooth.
townspeople toonsers.
bottom of a town toon fit.
to the centre of a town up the toon.
top of a town toon heid.
native of a town †toon's bairn.

toy *see also* **plaything**; bonnie-die, wheerum, wheeriorum N, playock, boch CAITHNESS.

trace *noun* **1** (*rope or chain for drawing*) tress, theat, soam. **2** (*small amount: see also* **amount**) smitch, pick, inklin, perlicket N, scart.
verb, see **track down**.
trace-horse tracer, theater.
man in charge of trace-horse tracer.

trachea wizzen.

track *noun* **1** (*mark left*) steid SW: '*the steids o his feet i the snow*'. **2** (*narrow path*) pad; (*esp sheep track*) roadie:

'*sheep's roadie*', roddin; (*for cattle*) loanin, raik; (*steep path down a ravine and up the other side*) peth.
track down speir oot.

tract[1] (*of land*) track, straik NE.

tract[2] (*pamphlet*) track.

trade *noun* tre(a)d, traffeck, mercat.
verb dale, niffer, traffeck, troke, cowp NE.
master tradesman cork.

tradition tradeetion, threap.

traffic *noun* (*commerce*) *see* **trade**.
verb traffeck, dacker, troke.

trail *noun* (*track*) steid SW.
verb, see also **trudge**; tra(u)chle; (*in mud etc*) draigle, traipse; (*something behind*) tra(u)chle; (*untidily*) trollop, trailep NE.
trailing (*hanging low*) sloggerin.
trailing piece of cloth *etc* trail, trailep SHETLAND, N, traleel NE, laib NE, loorach N.

train *verb* cuddum; (*specif an animal*) track NE.
training upbring.

trait (*characteristic*) track; (*unusual*) lirk.

traitor †traditor, †tratour.

tramcar ca(u)r, skoosh-car W.

tramp *noun* **1** *see also* **vagrant**; caird, gaberlunzie (man), scurryvaig, minker, gangrel, gaun(-aboot) bodie, hallanshaker *literary*; **tramps** waun(n)erin fowk. **2** (*long tiring walk*) traik, trail, traipse.
verb traik, trail, traipse, stramp.
tramp around traik, stramp, traipse.
tramp down *see* **tread down**.
tramp over hoch.

trample *verb* paidle, patter, pran NE; (*clothes in washing*) poss, post NE; (*crops*) tramp, traissle S.
trample on tramp on, stramp.
trampled down padd(er)it.
trampling *noun* stramp.

trance dwam.

tranquil *see also* **calm**; (*of weather*) lown; (*of places*) lithe.
tranquillity lown, saucht.

transact

transact transack.

  transaction transack, troke, han(d)lin.

  transactions traffeck; (*of an agent with his employer's money*) intromissions.

transfer (*a minister*) translate, transpose.

  transferable (*of money etc*) prestable.

transfix skiver.

transform *see* change.

transgress lowp ower, mistak.

transition: in a transitional state in the deid thraw.

transitory: something transitory glisk.

translate owerset; (*interpret*) rede.

  translation owersettin; (*of English to Latin prose*) version.

transport *verb* convoy, flit; (*in a wheeled vehicle*) hurl.

transverse thort, ower.

  transversely thort.

trap *noun* **1** (*snare*) girn, mink NE, stamp; (*for mice or rats*) fa(w). **2** (*vehicle*) machine.

  verb (*ensnare*) fankle, girn.

  trappings graithin.

trash trashtrie, troke, trooshter NE, perlaig, trudder NE, trag SHETLAND, NE.

  trashy peltrie NE.

  trashy food snashters.

travel *noun, verb* traivel.

  traveller (*usually referring to tinkers etc*) treveller, traiveller.

  travelling bag †pockmantie.

  travelling salesman fleein merchant NE.

  travel along the road at speed tak in the road NE.

  travel fast spank, heeze, skirr, skelp on.

  travel on foot traivel, shank.

  travel through reenge.

  non-traveller scaldie.

  person who travels fast dub-skelper.

traverse *verb* reenge, stravaig.

trawler (*fishing close to 3-mile limit*) scratcher NE.

tray server; (*for bottle or decanter*) wineslide.

treachery traison.

  treacherous traicherous, traisonable; (*dangerous, unreliable*) uncannie, unchancie.

treacle NB in Sc always refers to molasses; traicle, trykle, trekkle, strap, black strap NE.

  treacle ale traicle wheich, traicle peerie.

tread *noun* stramp; (*heavy, noisy*) clamp N.

  verb, see also **trodden**; stramp; (*heavily*) sklute S.

  tread down paidle, tramp, traissle S.

  tread on stramp; (*heavily*) tramp.

treadle (*of a spinning wheel etc*) fit brod NE.

treason traison.

treasure traisure.

  treasurer thesaurer; (*esp of a corporation etc*) gowdie, box-master NE; (*of the Kingdom of Scotland*) †Lord (High) Thesaurer.

treat *noun* trait, cheery pike NE.

  verb trait; (*handle*) guide; (*in a certain way*) ser; (*badly*) demain NE; (*roughly*) haik NE; (*with contempt*) hoot; (*unkindly*) mak a stap-bairn o.

  treatment (*of one person by another*) guideship.

treatise libel.

treble *adjective* threeple.

  verb threeple, treeple NE.

tree: tree-creeper woodpecker, treespeeler.

  tree-pipit wuid-lark.

  tree-stump stog, scrunt, stole; (*old or decayed*) runt; (*gnarled*) scrog.

  new shoot on a tree-stump stole.

  tree-trunk (*long slender*) caber, shank.

  tree at which lovers meet by agreement trystin-tree.

  tree from whose twig a whistle is made whustle-wuid.

  tree in front of a Scottish mansion house where the laird met and said

farewell to his guests †covin tree.
(young) growing trees green wuid.
young trees plantin.
trefoil †triffle.
  bird's-foot trefoil craw-taes.
trellis tirless.
tremble *verb, see also* **shiver, quake:** tremmle, trummle, dinnle, twitter; (*with cold*) chitter; (*of the lips, eyelids*) wicker.
  trembling *adjective* (*with fear etc*) grue.
  fit of trembling (fit o) the shakers.
  cause to tremble dinnle.
tremendous unco, by-or(di)nar.
tremor dinnle, grue.
tremulous: tremulous motion dirl.
  make a tremulous sound reemle NE.
trench *see also* **ditch:** *noun* sheuch, track, trink.
  verb howk, sheuch, heuch, cast N.
trencher truncher.
trend *see* **fashion.**
  trendy fantoosh.
trepidation feerich NE.
tress (*of hair*) fla(u)cht, link.
trestle tress, stuil; (*joiner's*) cuddie, pownie; (*for scaffolding*) horse, mear NE.
trial: stand trial thole an assize.
triangle: triangular piece of land gushet (neuk).
tribulation *see* **trouble.**
tributary (*of a stream*) leader.
trick *noun* (*piece of mischief: see also* **joke**) cantrip, pliskie, swick, begunk, begeck N, gink NE, jouk, kick, prottick NE; (*wild, irresponsible*) reek; (*knack*) slicht; **tricks** (*playful*) jinks.
  verb, see also **cheat, deceive:** jink, jouk, swick, begeck, begunk, quirk NE.
  trickery joukerie-pawk(e)rie, swickerie.
tricky 1 (*of a task etc: see also* **awkward**) fykie, fickle, fashious, kittle, ticklie. **2** (*mischievous*) ill-trickit SHETLAND, ORKNEY, N, ill-contrivit SHETLAND, N, quirkie.

play tricks prat.
play a trick on someone play someone a pliskie.
trickle *noun* dribble, trinkle, dreeple SHETLAND, N, strin(d) NE, strintle.
  verb seep, sype, dreeple N, strin(d) NE, treetle SHETLAND, ORKNEY, NE, trinkle, trinnle.
  cause to trickle trinnle.
trifle *noun* (*thing of little value*) triffle, nig-nay, niffnaff, snuff, wanworth; (*small amount*) kennin, mention; **trifles** trantles, trantlums, kiow-ows N.
  verb fouter, niffnaff, nig-nay, partle, jamph NE, pingle S.
  trifling aff-pittin, skitterie.
  trifle with glaik wi.
trigger tricker.
trill (*before a note in pipe music*) doubling.
trim *adjective* tosh, trig, doss, knackie, perjink, sproosh, dinkie, dink, feat CENTRAL; (*of persons*) nate, snod, ticht.
  verb **1** sned, snod, doss; (*hair*) coll; (*a hedge*) switch, scutch. **2** (*a garment etc*) munt; (*with a lace border*) surfle.
  trimmed (*of hair*) snibbit NE.
  trimly dinklie.
  trimming 1 (*on clothing*) squirl N; (*lace*) pearlin; **trimmings** (*on clothes etc*) trappin. **2** (*of a hedge*) scutch.
  make trim dice up.
trinket bonnie-die, variorum; **trinkets** trokes.
trip *noun* **1** (*journey: see also* **outing**) gate, vaige SHETLAND, veage EDINBURGH, NE. **2** (*stumble*) stammer.
  verb **1** (*see also* **stumble**) stammer, snapper SHETLAND, NE, hyter NE; (*cause to trip*) tirl. **2** (*with light steps*) lilt, link.
  be tripped by tak.
tripe wame, painches, roddikin.
triple *adjective, verb* threeple.
  triplet threeplet.
trivet winter, cran.
trivial fouterie, treeval.
trodden *past participle of* **tread** treddin.

troll

troll *verb (for fish, with a fly etc)* harl.

trolley: supermarket trolley barra(e).

trollop *see* **prostitute**.

trot *noun* jundie.

verb troddle, treetle NE.

trot along *(purposefully)* pad, skelp on.

trouble *noun* tribble, adae(s), fash(erie), sturt, hert-scaud, mischief, sussie, wark, tra(u)chle, tulyie *literary*.

verb fash, tra(u)chle, wark, mismay, pest; **trouble yourself** mismak yersel.

troubled tra(u)chelt, drumlie, thochtit.

troublesome tribblesome, fashious, ill, fykie, hindersome, hinnersome, kittlie, sorrafu; *(of things)* pernicketie.

troublemaker *see* **ruffian**.

have plenty of trouble no hae yer sorras tae seek.

source of trouble tra(u)chle.

trough troch, crub SHETLAND, NE, waterin(s).

trounce *see* **beat**.

trouncing *see* **beating**.

trousers troosers, breeks, strides; *(esp tartan, as worn by some Scottish regiments)* trews; *(wide, baggy)* bushlebreeks; *(short)* breekums.

trouser braces galluses.

trouser flap shop-door, spaiver, ballop, cushie-dreel.

trouser-flies *see* **fly**[1] 2.

trouser-seat trooser-erse, erse o yer breeks.

trouser-straps *(worn below the knees by farmworkers)* nickie-tams, booyangs, waltams, yanks N, yerks.

trousseau *see also* **bottom drawer**; waddin-braws, providin, muntin.

trout *see also* **sea trout**; troot; *(small)* trootie, beeran N.

trout-fly *(dressed without wings)* speeder.

trowel truan, truel ORKNEY, N.

truant troon, trone, fugie, plunker.

play truant troon, trone, fugie (the

scuil), jouk (the scuil), jink (the scuil), plunk (the scuil), plug (the scuil), (play the) kip.

truce *(in games, also* **cry for a truce)** barley, baurlie, keys, parlies NE.

truck[1] *verb (barter)* troke, niffer, hooie, cowp NE, FIFE.

noun troke, niffer.

truck[2] *(mining: for carrying rubbish to the pit-head)* redd box FIFE.

truckle-bed hurlie(-bed), whirlie (bed).

truculent turk NE.

trudge *verb* trodge, traipse, traik, trail, tra(u)chle, hochle, sodger, pauchle, snodge SE.

noun traik, trail; *(heavy)* tra(u)chle.

trudge on dodge awa.

true *see also* **loyal, reliable**; suithfast.

truly truelins, tweel.

truth trowth, truith, trith E CENTRAL, trath SHETLAND, ORKNEY, suith.

the absolute truth the God's truith.

truthful truithfae.

the true story the richt wey o't.

trump-card trumph.

trumpery trumpherie.

trumpet *noun* tooter, tooteroo NE.

sound of a trumpet †tutti-taiti(e).

trumpet (abroad) toot.

truncate sned.

truncheon *see* **cudgel**.

trundle trinnle, trunnle, hurl, whurl.

trunk 1 *(chest)* kist, mail. **2** *(of a tree: long, slender)* caber, shank.

truss *noun, verb* turse, knitch.

trust *noun* truist.

verb lippen, truist.

not to be trusted sleekit.

trusty *see also* **loyal**; stieve.

trustworthy suithfast, *(of things)* sicker.

breach of trust *(law)* malversation.

truth *see* **true**.

try 1 *(attempt)* ettle, shape. **2** *(try out, esp by tasting)* pruive, pree.

try hard warsle.

tub *(for washing clothes)* boyne, (washin) bine, cweed NE, stan(d); *(long-*

handled) skeel; *(for milk)* cweed NE; *(for washing feet)* cuittie-boyne; *(for brewing)* cummen; *(wooden, for carrying water)* sae.

tuck *noun (pleat or fold)* touk.
verb, also **tuck up** touk, kilt.
tuck around faik.
tuck up *(clothes)* kilt, *(esp for farmwork)* breek.

Tuesday Tyseday.

tuft *noun, see also* **crest**; toosht NE; *(of hair, wool etc)* fla(u)cht, tap, tait, pook; *(of hair)* tossel, swirl, taut; *(matted, on animal's tail)* tartle; *(of grass)* tait, tummock; *(of feathers on a bird's head)* tappin.
tufted tappit: *'tappit hen'.*

tug *verb* chug, teug, rug, yerk, pook, rive, tit SHETLAND, NE; *(vigorously)* rug an rive.
noun chug, teug, rug, yerk, pook, rive, tit SHETLAND, NE.

tumble *noun* tummle, whummle.
verb tummle, whummle, cowp, fa(w) aff yer feet.
tumble about *(of children at play)* row-chow.
tumble down *see verb.*
tumble head over heels *see* **somersault**.
tumble over play wallop.

tummy *see* **stomach**.

tumult *see also* **fuss, uproar, commotion**; stushie, stashie, stramash, dirdum, hurry-burry.
tumultuous camstairie.

tumulus †law.

tune tuin, tin CENTRAL, teen NE, lilt, souch; *(lively)* diddle, spring, sprig, rant; *(esp on the bagpipes)* †port; *(main theme in pibroch)* ground, urlar.
verb, see **tune up**.
tuneless timmer.
beat of a tune stot.
out of tune aff the stot.
strike up a tune †lilt up.
tune without words diddle.
tune up kittle.

tunic *(loose-fitting)* slop; *(worn by men)* jupe, curseckie ANGUS.

tunnel cundie.

turbid drumlie, grumlie, jummlie.
make turbid grummel.

turbot rodd(en) fluke, rawn (fleuk) NE.

turbulence *see* **tumult**.

turd tuird, taird CENTRAL, toalie, doldie, jobbie, loit.

turf *noun* turr; *(surface)* turvin SHETLAND; *(used for building or roofing)* fail N; *(sod)* fail, flag, shirrel; *(thinner)* divot, scraw; *(surface)* turr; *(with grass still attached)* rough-head.
turf-cutter *see also* **peat-cutter** 2; *(two-handed, broad-bladed)* flauchter-spade.
turf seat sunk.
turf wall truff dyke, swear-dyke NE.
pare off turf from scaup SHETLAND.
slice of turf *(esp used for thatching)* scaddin.

turkey pullie; **turkey cock** bubbly jock, pownie-cock, habble jock ANGUS.
red membranous part of a turkey cock's beak snotter, snubbert NE.

turmeric †tarmanick.

turmoil *see* **uproar**.

turn *noun* 1 *(turning)* birl, skew, thraw SHETLAND, N. 2 *(spell)* shot(tie), swatch; *(in a game)* crack.
verb birl, thraw; *(quickly)* jink; *(a key, doorknob)* thraw.
cause to turn (round) birl, feeze on.
turning lathe lay.
turning point *(change)* wynd.
in turn turn aboot, tour aboot, tour an turn, shots each.
turn aside *(deflect)* skewl.
turn back *(cause to go back)* kep again, haad again NE.
turn out *(eject)* oot.
turn outside in flype.
turnover 1 *(in trade)* owerturn. 2 *see* **pie**.
turn over a new leaf tak up a bore NE.
turn over and over wammle, wummle.

turn round birl; (*a boat*) lay aboot.

turn up (*a hem*) lay in.

turn-up (*on a garment*) flype.

turned up (*of a nose etc*) kippit.

turn up on end oweren(d).

turn to the left *or* **the right** (*as a direction to an animal*) *see* **call**.

serve a turn kep kinches, dae the turn.

turn to one side swey, swee.

turnip neep, turneep, turmit, tumshie *humorous or informal*; (*swede*) swade, baggie SE.

turnip disease raan.

turnip lantern neep lantern, neepie lantren NE, neepie candle NE, tattie-bogle.

turnip slicer neep-cutter.

turnip-tailer tailer.

turnip top neep shaw.

turnip-topper tapner.

implement for pulling up turnips neep-cleek, neep-hack.

turnpike toll.

turnpike-keeper tollie.

turnstile tirless, tirlie, whurlie-gate, furlin-yett NE.

turret tappietoorie; (*round*) roon(d), roon(d)el.

tush! teh!, chach! NE.

tussle *noun* tissle, tousle, taisle, stan(d)-tae, struissle, warsle.

verb tissle, rug an rive, struissle.

tussock boss.

tut! toot(s)!, tits!

tut tut! uts!, tchick!, bizz! NE, foy! NE.

tutelage tutory.

tutorship tutory.

twaddle *see* **talk**.

twang (*nasal*) sneevil; (*of a dialect*) tune, teen NE, souch.

tweak someone's nose snite someone's niz.

tweed mill oo-mill.

tweezers pinchers.

twelve twal, qual.

twelfth twalt.

twelvemonth towmond.

twelve hours a roon(d) o the clock.

twelve o'clock twaloors.

twenty twintie, toontie.

twice twicet CENTRAL, twise SHETLAND, ORKNEY, N.

twiddle tweedle.

twig boucht(ie), cowe, rice; (*of willow or hazel, esp for thatching*) scob; **twigs** (*collectively*) rice; (*dry, for burning*) browls.

twilight gloamin, gloamin fa(w), gloamin oor, atween the (twa) lichts, darkenin, dayligaun, mirk(in), gray dark, gray (o the evenin); (*morning*) gray (o the mornin).

twill *noun, verb* tweel.

twin-bedded twa-beddit.

twine *noun* skaenie.

verb whip, pirl, rowe, wimple NE.

long piece of twine lonnach NE.

twinge rug, stoun(d); (*sharp pain*) twang.

twinkle *verb* glent, prinkle, skinkle.

noun glent.

twirl *noun* swirl, tirl, birl.

verb pirl, snuve, tirl.

full of twirls tirlie.

twist *noun* skew, cast, swirl, pirl, thraw; (*in thread, rope etc*) snorl; (*in wood*) set, swirl; (*mental*) lirk.

verb **1** thraw, feeze, fank, wammle, snorl, skew, rowe, tirl, pirl, plet; (*straw into rope*) thraw, twine; (*esp the body*) twine; (*esp the feet*) scash NE. **2** (*distort*) runkle, showl; (*a joint etc*) rax, rack, thraw.

twist the face sham.

twisted thrawn, snorlie, shauch, squeegee, fankelt, gleyed, swirlie, pirlie S.

twister *see* **rogue**.

twisting movement jink.

twit *verb* (*mock, criticize*) geck, bairge NE, scance at, towt.

twitch *noun* fidge, pook, tit, fyke, twig SHETLAND, ORKNEY; (*of the lips or eyelids*) wicker.

verb fidge, yank, fyke, pook, tit SHETLAND, NE, hodge NE, twig SHETLAND, ORKNEY; (*of the lips*) moup, mump; (*of the lips or eyelids*) wicker.

twitch the nose sneer.

twite heather lintie, hill lintie, rock-lintie, yella-neb lintie.

twitter *verb* tweeter, cheetle, chitter, twit, whitter, chirl.

two twa, twae; (*in counting rhymes*) teentie.

  two-faced sleekit, twa-faul(d) NE.

  two-faced person sneck-drawer, skook N, swick, twa-faul(d) NE.

  two-fold *see also* **double**; twa-faul(d).

  twopence tippence.

  twopenny tippenie.

  two-thirds twa-part.

  in two atwae.

  just the two of them themsels twa, baith the twa o them.

  two or three twa-three.

type *noun* (*kind, letters*) teep.

  large type groff print N.

typhus †purpie-fever.

typical teepical.

  typical person a scone o the day's bakin.

tyrant tirran, bangster.

tyre (*metal, of a cartwheel*) shod, ring.

U

udder ether, edder NE, vessel, lure, ure SW, S.

let a cow's udder become dry by not milking heft.

ugly *see also* **repulsive**; ooglie, ill-faured, ill-farran(t), ill tae see, grue, grugous.

ulcer bealin, lipper.

ultimate *see also* **last**²; hin(d)maist.

ultimately at the hinneren(d).

umbrage umrage NE.

umbrella umberella, umberellae.

umpire (*in a dispute*) owersman.

un- wan-, on-.

unabashed braisant, furthie NE.

unable (*because of exhaustion etc*) useless, yissless, ees(e)less NE.

unable to awa fae: '*he wiz awa fae speakin*'.

unaccustomed to oot o the road o, no yaised wi, nae eest wi NE.

unaffected hameower.

unaired mothie.

unambitious: be unambitious flee laich.

unappetizing wersh, wauch NE.

unappreciative pick-thank NE, perskeet, dortie SW.

unassuming cannie.

unattractive ill-faured, unbraw, unbonnie, hackit, no bonnie.

unawares unawaurs.

unbalanced (*of a person*) *see also* **mad**; cat-wittit.

unbending stieve, unbowsome S.

unbleached (*of cloth, linen yarn*) green.

uncanny no cannie, nae mows NE, eeriesome NE, oorie, eldritch *literary*.

uncaring regairdless.

uncertain slidderie; (*having doubts*) dootsome; (*of your footing*) stammerie;

(*of weather: see also* **unsettled**) ragglish NE, immis NE.

be in a state of uncertainty swither.

unchanged (*in appearance, esp after death or illness*) like yersel.

uncivil indiscreet, sneistie, unmainnerfu.

uncomfortable unoorament CAITHNESS.

uncommon orra.

uncompromising stench.

unconditionally (*law*) simpliciter.

unconscious: become unconscious *see* **faint**.

unconventional owerlie, heronious AYRSHIRE.

uncouth *see also* **rough**; raucle, lan(d)ward, ruchsome, raploch, hamit.

unctuous sappie.

uncultured coorse, hull-run N.

undaunted *see also* **hesitant**; undauntit, hail-hertit.

undecided dootsome, aff-an-on, in the deid thraw.

be undecided swither.

undemonstrative lown.

under *preposition* (in) alow, (in) ablow, (in) aneath.

adjective nether.

underclothing inside claes, linens.

undercut *verb* (*mining*) boss.

undergo dree.

undergraduate's red gown (*esp Aberdeen University*) toga.

undergrowth scrogs.

covered with undergrowth scroggie.

underhand sleekit, hidlins, foutie, wheetie NE.

underhand person mowdiewort.

do something in an underhand way snaik.

underneath neath, (in) aneath, (in) alow, (in) ablow.

undernourished misthriven, ill-thriven, shargart.

underrate lichtlie.

undershirt *see* **vest**.

undersized scrimpit, palie, shargart, shilpit.

understand un(d)erstaun(d), onerstan(d), uptak; *(a person, what a person says)* tak up, pick up, lift.

understanding *noun* uptak, rum(mle-)gumption, kennin.

have an understanding with collogue wi.

quick in understanding gleg i the uptak.

on the understanding that perconnon that NE.

undertake (to) tak on han(d) (tae).

undertaking ploy, han(d)lin, prottick NE, ontakkin.

undervalue lichtlie.

undiluted *(of alcoholic drinks)* hard, nakit.

undisciplined *see* **unruly**.

undistinguished raploch, hedder-an-dub NE.

undo lowse(n).

undress *(yourself, a person)* tirr NE; *(a person)* tirl.

undulate wammle, kelter *literary*.

unearth howk.

unearthly *see also* **uncanny**; eldritch *literary*.

unease *see* **distress**.

uneasy *see also* **anxious**; on ncttles.

uneasiness wanrest.

unemployed orra.

unemployment idleset.

unemployment benefit b(u)roo money.

unequalled mar(row)less.

unexpectedly in a hurry, at the braidside NE.

unfair no fair.

unfaithful no tae lippen tae.

unfamiliar unkent, fremd, fremmit, unco NE.

unfashionable *see* **odd-looking person**.

unfasten unfessen.

unfastened: become unfastened lowse(n).

unfinished *(of a task etc)* stickit.

unfit for unable for, no able for.

unfledged stob-feathert NE.

unfledged bird *see* **nestling**.

unfortunate *see also* **unlucky**; misfortunate, no chancie, mischancie, black, misluckit NE; *(mainly of people)* weirdless.

unfriendly thin, ill(-willie).

ungainly *see also* **clumsy**; ill-shakken(-thegither) NE.

ungainly movement of the body hochle.

ungovernable neither tae haud nor tae bind.

ungrateful pick-thank NE.

unhappy *see* **sad**.

unharmed hail-heidit N, scart-free, scart-hail, hail an fere *literary*.

unhealthy: unhealthy-looking etten an spued, peel-an-eat, pookie; *(ill-looking)* peelie-wallie.

unhurt *see* **unharmed**.

uninspired fushionless.

unintelligible talk lig-lag NE.

uninteresting dreich, smeerless N.

unite knit; *(in marriage)* souder, sowther, yoke.

university: a *or* **the university** the college: 'she's at the college noo'.

university student collegianer; *(first-year at St Andrews)* bejan(t), *(female)* bejantine; *(first-year at Aberdeen)* bejan, *(female)* bejanella; *(second-year at St Andrews)* semi bejan; *(third-year at St Andrews)* tertian.

academic head of a university principal.

elected representative of students on a university court rector.

body which governs teaching and discipline in a university Senatus (Academicus), (*less formally*) Senate.

unjust wrangous, unricht.

unkempt tashie, tautie, hudderie, ramshackle, untowtherlie NE, ill-farran(t); (*of hair*) lik(e) strae hingin fae a midden, lik(e) strae hingin aff a dyke, tousie.

unkind ill, saut.

unknown un(be)kent, nae kent, unco NE, anonst (tae).

unlatch unsneck.

unlatched aff the sneck.

unless onless N, less NE, athoot, withoot (that), binna.

unlike unalik(e).

unload disloaden CAITHNESS; (*a ship*) liver N, HEBRIDES.

unlucky *see also* **unfortunate**; unchancie, ill, uncannie, ill-luckit SHETLAND, N.

unmanageable (*of people*) *see* **unruly**; (*of animals*) willyart.

unmannerly unmainnerfu, unfarran(t), menseless, ill-mou'd, mislearit.

unmarried his *or* her lane, free, marrowless.

    unmarried man (*of any age, living with parents*) boy.

unmatched (*odd*) orra, marrowless, neibourless, wantin a neibour, wintin a neeper NE.

unmethodical throuither, throwder NE, picherin NE.

unmusical timmer, timmer-tuned, timmer-teened NE.

unnatural *see also* **uncanny**; no cannie.

unobserved (by) unkent (till) N.

unoccupied tuim, teem N.

unpaid: remain unpaid lie ower.

unpalatable *see* **tasteless**.

unpleasant *see also* **disagreeable**, **unattractive**; pooshionous, pooshionable, unoornament CAITHNESS; (*to the taste*) ramsh.

    make unpleasant pooshion.

unploughed white, fite N.

unpolished (*of manners etc*) unfarran(t), hedder-an-dub NE, hameart, reuch-spun; (*of speech*) raucle.

unpopular ill-likit, nae weel likit, ill-lookit-upon.

unpredictable kittle.

unpunctual mistimeous N.

unravel (*thread etc*) redd, unraivel, unfankle, faize, tousle oot.

unreasonable oot o a rizzon SHETLAND, N.

unrefined *see* **unpolished**.

unrelated (*by blood*) fremd, fremmit.

unreliable (*of a person*) slidderie, kittle, here the day an awa the morn, no tae ride the watter wi.

unrest wanrest.

unrestrained *see* **unruly**.

unruly ill-deedie, camstairie, ramstam, neither tae haud nor tae bind, gallus, bowsterous, royet, roit NE, maroonjous NE.

unsafe uncannie.

unsalted (*of fish*) green.

unsatisfactory ill, nae great.

unscathed hailscart, scart-hail, scart free, unscaumit.

unscrew feeze aff.

unsettled (*of a person: see also* **flighty** (*under* **flight**[1])) wanrestfu; (*of the weather*) lowse, grumlie NE, brucklie SHETLAND, NE, bladdie N.

unsheathed bare.

unshorn (*of sheep*) ruch.

unskilful kweerichin NE.

unskilled hielan(d), ill; **unskilled in** unkent tae; (*of a job*) orra.

unsociable stickin.

unsophisticated *see* **unpolished**.

unspeakable past a(w), by aathing NE.

unstable (*of things*) *see* **unsteady**; (*of people*) skeer(ie).

unsteady (*of things*) cogglie, shooglie, showdie N, crankie, cockerie, jeeglie; (*of people*) *see* **tottery**.

unsubstantial silly, (*esp of clothing*) flindrikin NE.

untidy *see also* **slovenly, unkempt**;

throuither, throwder NE, strushlach NE, tousie, huddderie, oozlie SW, owerheid, hither an yon(t); (*esp of work*) hairy; (*of a place*) disjaskit; (*of clothes: hanging loose*) trollopie; (*of hair*) *see* **unkempt.**

untidy person ticket.

untidy place Paddy's market, Annicker's midden, guddle: '*Why's this hoose aye sic a guddle?*'

untie lowse(n).

until *preposition* or.

conjunction gin, or, ere SHETLAND, NE, tae, while *literary.*

untrustworthy *see also* **treacherous;** sleekit, sliddderie, no tae lippen tae, no tae ride the ford wi.

unusual *see also* **exceptional;** by-or(di)nar, unco.

unusual(ly) nae or(di)nar.

unwashed unwashen.

unwelcome: not be unwelcome (for) no come wrang (tae).

unwell *see also* **ill;** no weel, bad, compleenin, shabby, hard up; (*slightly*) poch NE.

unwholesome unhailsome, ill.

unwieldy untowtherlie NE, unfierdie, unfreelie NE.

unwilling *see* **reluctant;** sweir(t); **unwilling to join in** stickin.

be unwilling to think ill tae.

unworthy wanwordie *literary.*

unwrinkled (*of the brow*) brent.

unyielding dour, stieve, unbowsome S.

up oop; (*out of bed*) oot ower.

upsadaisy (*eg encouraging a child to its feet*) oopsie doopsie.

up there upby.

it's all up with it's (a(w)) up a clos(i)e wi.

upbraid *see* **scold.**

upbringing upfeshin NE, fessin up NE.

uphold uphaud.

upkeep keep-up.

upland *noun* brae, heich.

adjective hull-run N, upthrou NE.

upper iver *esp in place-names.*

uppermost umost, eemost N, buin-

most, beenmest NE.

upper hand owerhan(d), owerance S.

get the upper hand of get ower.

upper part of a town toon heid.

uppish *see* **arrogant.**

upright (*of a person*) *see also* **worthy;** upricht.

upright people *see* **self-righteous people.**

standing upright oweren(d).

uproar stushie, stashie, stramash, collieshangie, dirdum, reird, cabbie-labbie, strush(ie).

uproarious rantin.

uproot (*by digging*) howk.

upset *verb* **1** (*overturn*) cowp, owercowp, whummle. **2** (*a person*) pit aboot, pet, mismay, ug.

noun (*overturning*) cowp, whummle.

adjective uggit, up, in a (dreedfu) wey (aboot).

easily upset (*by food etc: see also* **nauseate**) skeichen NE.

upset the stomach fyle the stamack.

upshot upcome.

upside down tapsalteerie, heels ower gowdie, heelster-heid(s).

turn upside down whummle.

upstairs upby.

upstart: social upstarts fite-iron gentry NE.

upward upwart.

upwards upwith, tae the hill, aye haddin up NE.

urchin gorlin.

urge threap at.

urge on ca(w), egg (up), haud at, eggle; (*with shouts*) hurroo, hoy.

urgent clamant.

urgently sair: '*Ye're sair needin a pair o shuin*'.

urine peeins, pish, graith; (*used for dyeing, washing etc*) strang SHETLAND, ORKNEY, N, wash, graith.

urinate pish, strone, mak yer burn, dae a wizzie *child's word,* EDINBURGH; (*in small quantities*) driddle.

act of urinating pish, strone, streel.

us uz, wiz, oo s, (*stressed*) hiz; (*those of our group etc*) us yins, hiz eens NE.

use *noun* eese N, yiss.

verb eese N, yaise, yuise.

used to (*accustomed to*) used wi, yaised wi, eest wi N.

he used to be able to he used tae could.

be used up gae duin, gang deen NE.

useful yuisfae, eesefae NE.

useless uisless, yissless, ees(e)less N; (*of a person*) daeless, no worth cawin oot a kailyard.

usual uswal, eeswal NE.

usually for ord(i)nar.

as usual for ord(i)nar.

utensil *see* **tool**.

uterus (*of a ewe*) lamb-bed.

utmost utmaist.

do your utmost dae yer endaivours.

utter[1] *adjective, adverb* fair: '*ye're a fair disgrace*'.

utter[2] mint, moot SHETLAND, NE, mou, mooth.

uvula pap o the hause, pap o the throat N, clap o the hass.

V

vacant tuim, teem N.
vacate (*a property*) redd.
vacillate swither, swey.
  vacillating *see* **indecisive.**
vacuum vawcum.
vagabond *see also* **vagrant;** vagabon, scurryvaig, rinthereoot NE, waffie.
vagrant *noun, see also* **vagabond, tramp** 1, **fugitive;** vaig, gangrel, gaunaboot bodie, jockie, hallanshaker *literary*, waffinger; (*female*) tramp wife NE; **vagrants** waun(n)erin fowk.
  adjective waffie, vaigin *literary*.
vague *see* **doubtful.**
vain 1 *see also* **conceited;** pridefu, vaudie, vauntie, saucy, set-up, vogie. **2** (*of words*) tuim.
  vanity vainitie.
valance pan(d).
valerian valairie.
valet †wally, †chaumer chiel(d).
valiant *see* **courageous.**
valid: lose validity (*law: through lapse of time*) prescribe.
valley *see also* **ravine;** vailcy, howe; (*esp steep-sided with a river*) glen; (*broad, flat, at lower end of a river*) strath; (*small, among hills*) hope S, wham; (*narrow, esp wooded*) den.
  upper end of a valley watter heid.
valour saul.
value *noun, verb* vailye NE, vaillie.
  valueless *see also* **worthless;** nochtie, wanworth.
  lose value tyne.
  something valueless wanworth, sheemach N.
valve (*in a water- or gas-main*) toby.
  flap of a valve (*mining*) lid.
vanilla vaneela, vaneelie.

vanish vainish, wainish, mizzle; (*mysteriously, suddenly*) saunt; (*gradually*) ely awa S.
  cause to vanish saunt.
vanity *see* **vain.**
vanquish *see* **defeat.**
vapid *see also* **insipid;** smerghless N.
vapour reek, (y)oam SHETLAND, ORKNEY, NE, stew; (*choking*) stife.
  send out vapour reek, stove.
variance: at variance striven NE.
variegated *see also* **speckled;** spreckelt, pyot, lyart; (*esp of birds and animals*) marlie.
variety (*kind*) (aa) kin-kin(d) NE.
various sindry.
varnish *noun* vernish, feenish.
  verb vernish.
vary *see* **change.**
  varied sindry.
vase vawse, pig.
vast *see* **huge;** (*of places*) gowstie.
vat fat SHETLAND.
vault *noun* vowt, pen(d).
  verb vowt.
  vaulted vowtit, coomed.
  vaulted passageway pen(d).
vaunt *see* **boast.**
vegetable: vegetable rubbish wrack.
  vegetation growthe.
  rank vegetation growthe.
  withered vegetation fowd N.
vehemently sair, stark.
vehicle: horse-drawn passenger vehicle machine.
  place for vehicles to stop for passengers stance.
velvety feel.
veneer *verb* fineer.
venereal disease †Canongate breeks.

vengeance *see* **revenge.**

venom *see* **poison.**

venture *noun* ventur, ploy, prattick. *verb* ettle.

verge *see also* **limit.**
 on the verge of at the edge O.
 be on the verge of ettle tae.

verily verilies ORKNEY, NE.

verity suith, troth.
 veritable jonick, evendoon.

vermin (*lice etc*) baists, beasts, cattle.

vernacular *adjective* (*esp of speech*) hameower, hamit.

verruca werrock.

verse (*doggerel*) crambo clink; **piece of verse** screed *often disparaging*.

version: the right version the richt wey o't.

vertebra link.

vertigo mirligoes.

very verra, gey (an), terrible: '*whit a terrible bad cauld ye've got*', braw (an), fine an, awfie, aafa NE, richt, rael, fell, wild, unco, byous, some, muckle, mortal(ly), dooms, by-or(di)nar.
 the very thing the like, the verra tattie.
 very well brawlie.
 not very . . . no that . . ., no a(w)fie, nae aafa NE.

vessel veshel.

vest (*of wool etc, usu men's*) simmit, seemit NE, sarket NE; (*men's long*) wyliecoat; (*child's*) baiklet.

vestibule rochel NE.

vestige stime, glint, toosht NE; (*esp of a moral quality*) spunk.
 not a vestige neither hilt nor hair, neither hunt nor hair.

vet *noun* ferrier.

vetch fitch, moose pea(se), horse pea(se).

veteran (*army*) foggie.

veterinary surgeon *see* **vet.**

veto *verb, noun* na-say.

vex *see* **annoy.**
 vexation *see* **annoyance.**

vibrate 1 dirl, thirl, dinnle, dingle. **2** (*cause to vibrate*) dirl, dinnle.
 vibration dirl(in), dinnle.

 make a continuous vibrating sound murr N.

vice (*tool*) *see* **clamp**[1].

vicious veecious, ill, ill-gien.
 viciously angry wickit.

victor: be victorious bear the gree.
 victory owerhan(d).

victuals vittals, scran.

vie *see* **contend.**

view *noun* vizzy; (*partial*) swatch. *verb* leuk.

vigil (*over a corpse*) *see* **wake.**
 vigilant waukrif(e).
 being vigilant on the keevee.

vigour birr, smeddum, virr, lifieness, fushion NE, poust.
 vigorous caller, hail, raucle, forcie SHETLAND, NE, stuffie, yaul(d), bensin NE; (*for your age*) kneef.
 vigorously *see also* **work;** fell, lik(e) hey-ma-nannie, lik(e) a hatter, lik(e) a day's wark.
 set to with vigour lay in, lowse on.
 do something vigorously gae yer dinger, gie something laldie, skelp, gie something big licks.

vile wile, vild SHETLAND.
 vilify splairge, ill-tongue N.

village veelage, toon, clachan, gaave gipsy, SW, S; (*of farm cottages*) cotto(o)n.
 villain limmer, thief.
 villainous hangit-faced, loon-leukin, gallus.

vindictive *see* **spiteful.**

vinegar veenegar.

violate (*treat cruelly*) abuise, mischieve SHETLAND, NE.

violent (*of persons*) bang, wuid; (*of wind, storm*) snell, stark.
 violence strouth; (*to persons or property*) bangstrie; (*of a storm*) bensell.
 with violence slash.
 violently fiercelins, lik(e) fung, souse, gey roch.

violin fiddle.
 violin peg thoumack NE.
 violin string thairm.

viper veeper.
virago *see* **shrew** 2.
virile pretty.
virtuous gracie.
virulent strang, fell, deidlie.
viscera *see* **entrails**.
viscous substance slaurie, slairg.
visible veesible, weel seen, perqueer ORKNEY.
vision sicht, veesion.
visit *verb* veesit ORKNEY, N, ca(w) for, leuk the gate o, ceilidh HIGHLAND; (*in passing*) cry in (by), roar (in), speak in; (*regularly*) come back an fore, come aboot the hoose.
noun veesit ORKNEY, N; (*in passing*) race, cry (in), roar; (*sociable, evening*) ceilidh HIGHLAND.
visitor veesitor.
not visit when nearby gae by someone's door.
vitality smergh.
lacking vitality fushionless.
vivacious speeritie, lifie.
vivacity lifieness.
vivid (*of colours, impressions etc: see also* **gaudy**) vieve; (*of personality*) gleg.
vividly vievelie.
voice *noun, verb* vice.

having an unmusical voice timmer-tuned, timmer-teened NE.
in a low voice laich doon.
raise the voice bairge NE.
void boss, tuim, teem NE.
volatile wafflie ORKNEY, NE.
vole lan(d)-moose.
volley: volley of oaths plaister SHETLAND.
voluble glib, gleg-tonguit, gleg-gabbit, tonguie; (*irritatingly*) tongue-deavin; (*in an ignorant way*) raw-gabbit.
volume 1 (*quantity, bulk*) vol(l)um, bouk. **2** (*book*) buik.
voluntary voluntar NE.
vomit *verb* boak, byock NE, bowk, loit, pit up, yesk, throw, rowp NE, cowk.
noun boak, byock NE, bowk.
voracious gutsie, hungrysome, geen-yoch.
vote: canvass for votes by flattery peuther.
vouch for haud yer face till NE; (*a fact*) uphaud, instruct.
vow *verb* voo, hecht.
voyage veage EDINBURGH, vaige SHETLAND.
vulgar coorse; (*of language etc*) groff.
vulva fud.

W

wadding (*for a gun*) colfin NE.

waddle *verb* widdle, rowe, hoddle, plowd(er) NE, trinnle, showd N.

noun, also **waddling gait** hoddle, plowd NE.

wade *verb* wad, wyde, paidle; (*messily*) plowter, plyter NE, clatch.

wading (*act of*) wad, wyde, paidle.

waders wyders.

wafer (*ice-cream*) slider; (*with chocolate and marshmallow*) black man.

wag[1] *noun* (*wit*) tear, linkie S.

wag[2] *verb* wingle, wavel.

wagtail seed-bird; (*pied*) willie-wagtail, waggie, waggitie, watterie NE, watterie wagtail, seed-lady; (*yellow*) watterie wagtail; (*grey*) yella wagtail.

wage *noun* wadge, wauge; (*to a harvest-worker*) hairst-fee NE; (*daily*) day tale; (*regular basic*) upstannin wage.

servant's wages fees.

wages given only in food dog's wages.

spend wages in advance forenail NE.

wager *verb* wauger, wad, wage, haud, beat N.

noun wauger, wad.

waggle *see also* **wiggle**: *verb, noun* waigle.

waggon wain.

waif waff.

wail *verb, noun* walloch NE, yowl, croon, pewl, yammer.

wainscoting boxin.

waist: waistband (*esp of trousers*) heidban(d); (*of trousers*) breekban(d), towe-ban(d) NE.

waistcoat weskit, wyskit NE, †surcoat; (*long*) wyliecoat.

wait *verb* wyte NE, bide, hing on.

noun wyte NE; (*long*) onwait NE.

wait a little bide a wee, haud a wee, hover a blink.

wait for wait on, wyte on NE.

wake *verb* wauk.

noun (*vigil over corpse*) wauk, lyke(wake) N.

wakeful waukrif(e).

waken wauken, awauk, raise.

walk *verb* **1** traivel, shank (it), raik; (*go for a walk*) streetch, dander, daun(d)er: '*He daundered doon the toon*'. **2** (*clumsily*: *see also* **stagger, stumble, shuffle, limp**[2]**, totter**) sha(u)chle, hochle, palmer NE, skleush N; (*in a slovenly way*) slutter, sclatch; (*unsteadily*) dover; (*in a flat-footed way*) sclaff, sclap NE, slype NE; (*with a short step*) doit NE; (*with long stiff strides*) steg, stilp NE; (*noisily*) clamp; (*with a clatter*) splatter; (*heavily*) skliff, clunk NE, stumper NE; (*as if laden*) hulster NE; (*heavily and slowly*) sclunsh, stowff NE; (*through mud*) plowter, plyter NE, plodge; (*laboriously*: *see also* **trudge**) wa(u)chle, stra(u)chle; (*eg when climbing a hill*) hechle; (*and wearily*) traik, tra(u)chle, doddle. **3** (*slowly*: *in a leisurely way*; *see also* **saunter**) dander, daun(d)er, stoit NE, shog; (*aimlessly*) traik, paidle; (*idly*) slowt; (*and stupidly*) sneet NE; (*cautiously*) tyce NE. **4** (*quickly*) hoy, leash SHETLAND, N, leather, link; (*more quickly*) pit in a fit; (*with a springy step*) lowp, lunt SW, S; (*with a short, quick step*) fud; (*with a light, scuffling step*) scutch; (*with a quick, heavy tread*) stam; (*hurriedly and clumsily*) wheeber NE. **5** (*purposefully*) stend, stell, snodge SE;

(*with long, vigorous strides*) spang, sling; (*with a springy step*) stunt, lamp; (*with a springy or stately step*) stot; (*energetically*) spad on NE, spang on.

noun, see also **gait**; traivel SHETLAND, N, range; (*long*) straik; (*leisurely: see also* **stroll**) dander, daun(d)er, raik; (*long, weary*) traik, trail, raik.

walking *noun, see also* **gait**; shanks'(s) naig(ie), shanker's naigie, Tamson's mear.

adjective (*of a child*) gaun.

walking stick nibbie staff SW, S, staff, powl; (*with hooked handle*) crummock, nibbie; (*with curved handle*) cloopie SW.

walk before you run creep afore ye gang.

wall *noun, see also* **drystone wall, boundary, turf wall, partition**; wa, dyke; (*badly built*) rummle SHETLAND, NE; (*used as windbreak in front of a door*) skathie NE.

wall-clock (*with unencased pendulum*) wag-at-the-wa, waggitie-wa.

wall-eye ringle ee.

wall-eyed ringle-eed, ringit.

foundation of a wall wa-stade SHETLAND.

front wall forewa.

hole in a wall to let sheep pass through lonker W, SW, lunkie-hole SW, cundie.

opening in a wall bole; (*to let in light and air*) windae-bole.

top of a wall (*esp space as used for storage*) wa-heid.

wallet walgan NE.

wallop *verb, see also* **beat, slap**; loonder.

noun, see also **blow**[2], **slap**; loonder, sing, pergaddus, whustle.

wallow *verb, noun* walloch N, wallae, wammle, plowter, plyter NE.

wan peelie-wallie, haw, wabbit.

wand wan.

wander *verb* **1** *see also* **stroll, roam**; waun(n)er, stravaig, scaff NE, traipse, reenge; (*idly*) squeerie NE, mollach (aboot) NE, vaig, trail; (*aimlessly*) traik, haik, rammle, screenge NE, taiver, ganner; (*in search of food*) skech. **2** (*in thoughts*) rove.

wanderer traik, vaiger, raik.

wandering (*in mind*) waun(n)ert, raivelt, cairried, brainish.

wander over reenge.

wangle (*dishonestly*) pauchle.

noun scraible; (*dishonest*) pauchle.

waning *noun* dwine.

want *verb, see also* **wish**; wint NE, seek; (*very much*) ettle (for); (*eg something to eat*) be for: '*are ye for puddin?*'; (*omitting verb of motion*) want: '*the dug wants in*'.

noun, see also **lack, poverty**; wint NE; (*lack*) faut.

in want of wantin, wintin NE.

suffer want want.

war *noun* weir.

war-cry slogan.

warlike weirlik(e).

warble *verb* chirl, chirm, cheetle, tweetle, whitter.

noun chirm.

ward: ward off weir (aff); (*a blow*) kep.

-wards -wan: '*Aiberdeen-wan*'; '*eastwan*'.

ware: warehouse warehoose.

wares weirs, gibbles.

warm *adjective, see also* **cordial**; het; (*cosy*) cosh, tosie; (*of a garment*) mawsie NE; (*of weather: warm and damp*) mochie, muithie, (*promoting growth*) growthie.

verb (*yourself*) beek; (*warm thoroughly*) birsle; (*become warm*) (get a) heat, lew; (*make warm*) (gie a) heat.

noun (*at the fire*) glaise; (*with legs apart*) meffin N.

warmed up leepit.

fond of warmth leepit N.

warn wairn, warnish, vertise SHETLAND.

warning warnisin NE, tellin: '*lat that be a tellin tae ye*'.

warning call (*of approach of police etc*) shot(tie)!

no warning at all (*of a sudden disaster*) Skairsburn warning SW.

warp *verb* worp, thraw, cap, geyze; (*of wood*) gizzen, kink.

noun worp; (*in a piece of wood*) set.

warp thread (*of yarn or silk*) en(d).

warrant *verb* warran NE, uphaud.

noun warran NE; (*law: to enforce attendance of witnesses etc*) diligence.

warren †cuningar.

warrior †kemp.

wart wrat, mowdiewort *humorous*.

wary ware, sicker.

proceed warily ca(w) cannie.

was wis, wus, wur, wes.

wash *verb* wesh; (*quickly*) syne, synd; (*swill*) sweel; (*mop up*) swaible S; (*bedclothes etc by tramping in a tub*) tramp.

noun wesh; (*swill*) sweel; (*hasty, superficial*) cat's lick, dicht, syne, synd, slaik, laip; (*pre-wash, rinse, of clothes*) ca(w)-throu.

washed *past tense* washt, woosh, weesh NE.

past participle washt, weeshen, washen NE.

washer (*round a drill or bolt to prevent leakage*) shangie.

washerwoman washerwife.

washing-tub washin bine, boyne, wash bine W; (*deep*) possin tub SW, S.

wash-house washin hoose; (*public*) steamie.

wash down (*food*) sweel, syne, synd, rinse doon.

wash out syne (oot), synd (oot).

wash up wash the dishes.

wasp waasp, waps.

waspish *see also* **bad-tempered**; witterous NE, witterie NE.

wasp's nest byke.

waste *verb* **1** connach, misguide SHETLAND, NE, weir throu NE; (*esp food*) ort; (*time; see also* **waste time** *below*) pit aff, hinder SHETLAND, NE; (*time, efforts etc*) tyne, ware. **2** *see* **waste away** *below*.

noun **1** (*esp from a mine or quarry*) redd. **2** (*of time*) aff-pit.

wasted ill-wared; (*by illness etc*) gowstie NE.

wasteful wasterfu, wastrif(e), wastrie, haiveless N.

use wastefully (*food*) ort.

waster prod.

wastepaper basket bucket.

waste away dwine, fa(w) awa, traik, pine, wallow.

waste your breath waste yer win(d).

waste time pit aff (time), partle, daidle, palaver, set aff, dauble NE, driddle, play yersel; (*in footling jobs*) skitter.

watch *verb* **watch over** *see also* **guard**; tak tent o; (*keep guard over*) wauk, weir; (*a sick person, corpse*) wauk; (*protect*) hae a care o, leuk ower.

noun **1** *see* **guard**; (*over a corpse*) *see* **wake**. **2** (*timepiece: large, pocket*) neep.

watchful waukrif(e), tentie.

watchmaker watchie.

watch out watch yersel.

water *noun*, *see also* **well**[1]; watter, waitter SE, pani *gipsy*, S; (*as drink*) Adam's wine; (*small amount*) skite; (*dripping from caves*) wa drap; (*natural flow, eg to drive a millwheel*) rin-watter NE; (*overflowing ground*) fleet watter.

verb watter, waitter SE.

watering can rooser.

watery (*of food etc*) shire, wabblie, spleuterie NE, blear(i)t.

watery-eyed blearie.

watery food *or* **drink** blubber-totum NE.

water-beetle skater, skeeter CAITHNESS, watter clearer.

water-bucket stan(d).

water-bug watter bailie NE.

water-channel syver; (*small*) rinner; (*to a millwheel*) lade, trows.

water-closet *see* **W.C.**

watercress wa girse NE.

waterfall linn, spoot, ess NE.

water-hen stankie (hen), stank hen.

water ousel *see* **dipper**.

water pistol scoot, skiter SHETLAND, NE.

water rat watter dog NE.

water shrew lavellan CAITHNESS.

water-spider wall-wesher SW, S, washer-wife, watter bailie NE.

water sprite water horse, (water) kelpie.

water-tap stroop.

watertight thight SHETLAND, ORKNEY.

water wagtail *see* **wagtail** (*under* **wag**^{2}).

dirty water slaister.

dabble *or* **mess about in water** slitter, plowter (aboot), plyter (aboot) NE.

put too much water in whisky, tea *etc* droon the miller.

splash *or* **cover with water** sloonge.

running water quick watter SW, S.

be over your ankles in water weet (the sma end o) yer moggans NE.

wattles (*of a cock*) chollers SW, S.

wave *noun* **1** (*of the sea etc*) swaw, jaw NE; (*rising to a crest*) shouder; (*breaking on shore*) land brist. **2** (*of the hand: as signal*) waff, wag.
verb waff, wampish; (*wave about*) waffle; (*a weapon etc: see also* **brandish**) swap.

wave-tossed wallie *in poetry*.

form waves swaw.

lapping of waves sweel.

motion of waves ca SHETLAND, N.

noise of waves breaking on the shore sang.

waver waffle, wavel, swither, swey.

wavering weegletie-waggletie.

way *noun* wey, wye SHETLAND, N, gate, road, airt; (*direction*) airt; (*in which something goes or works*) set.

all the way a(w) the road.

force *or* **make your way into** mak intae.

give someone his (own) way gie someone his (ain) gate.

go your own way gang yer ain gate, gang yer ain road.

in any way ochtlins.

in every way a(w)weys, ilkie wye NE.

in your way in yer road.

in no (possible) way nae road, nae gate.

in a sort of a way in a kin(d).

on the way in the gate NE.

a long way (from) a far cry (fae), hyne fae NE.

lose your way gae will ORKNEY, NE, gang wull NE.

way in(to) ingaun, ingate, the road in.

wayward *see also* **stubborn**; waywart, lowp-the-dyke, will, willyart.

W.C. cludgie, shunkie, watterie, duffie; (*esp on a stair*) yuffie.

we OO S.

weak waik, wyke NE; (*physically*) wabbit, wauch, fushionless, weanlie, traikie, waff, dowie, silly, fauchinless NE, bauch, dwaiblie; (*mainly of the legs*) dwaible; (*delicate*) brashie; (*thin*) windlestrae; (*mentally*) saft, silly, waff; (*in character*) facile, fushionless, pinglin; (*of food or drink*) wersh, spleuterie NE, blashie NE, weeshie-washie; (*of drink*) slushie SHETLAND, ORKNEY, CAITHNESS.

weaken (*in health*) tak doon.

weakling wallydrag NE, sha(u)chle, shargar NE, cruit S; (*specif of a litter: see also* **runt**) ooterlin, rig, ricklin.

weakly tender, sober NE, dorbie NE, wanthriven.

weak-minded *see* **backward, stupid**.

weak-willed sapsie.

weak-willed man sapsie Wullie.

weal *see also* **scar**; score, mittle, knur, blain.

wealth walth, gear, graith, hullion.

wealthy walthie.

great wealth gowd in gowpens.

accumulate wealth gaither.

wean spean, spen N.

be weaned spean, spen N.

newly weaned new speaned, new spent.

weapon

weapon wappen.
wear verb, see also wore, worn: 1 weir.
2 (damage: clothes with hard usage)
scuff; (clothes, shoes out of shape)
sha(u)chle; (rub) chaff; (into holes) hole.
wear out (a shoe) bauchle.
wear and tear (rough usage) docher.
giving hard wear to (clothes etc) sair
on: 'She's awfie sair on shoes'.
weary adjective, see also tired, exhausted; wabbit, forjeskit, forfochen,
jaupit, traikit.
verb, see also bore², harass, annoy;
deave, jabb NE; (with hard work etc)
tra(u)chle, staw, tash.
weariness tire.
wearisome see tiresome.
weary effort sair pech.
weary-looking disjaskit.
grow weary of fash o.
very weary of sick-tired o.
weasel wheasel, whitrat, futrat NE,
whitterick, foumart, thoumart.
weather wather, wedder, wither NE,
widder NE.
spell of weather track.
spell of cold stormy weather at the
beginning of May caul(d) gab.
spell of severe weather about
lambing time in March lambin storm
N.
spell of bright weather in the middle of bad weather-gaw NE.
weave verb, see also wove; wyve NE,
warp; (do the work of a weaver) shuttle.
weaver wabster, webster, shuttler.
weaver's assistant tenter.
defect in weaving felter.
web wab, wob; (spider's) moose wab;
spiders' webs slammachs NE.
wed see also marry; wad.
wedding waddin, mairriage.
wedding cake bride(s)cake.
wedding clothes waddin braws, mairriage braws.
wedding party (people) waddin
fowk.
scattering of coins to children by a

wedding party poor-oot, scatter,
scoor-oot, strive, scramble w.
wedding at which guests contribute to the entertainment pey waddin, penny waddin.
wedge noun wadge; (as support) cog; (to
prevent cartwheel from skidding) scutch.
verb wadge; (support) cog.
Wednesday Wadensday, Wodensday.
weed: weeds growthe; field weeds
wrack.
weed-infested dirty, growthie.
week ook SHETLAND, NE, wick NE,
aucht days.
weekly ooklie, ilkie wick NE.
weekday everyday, ilkaday NE; (day
for business) lawful day.
a week on Monday a week come
Monday.
weep see also sob; greet, rair, blirt NE,
bum, byke SW, cown CAITHNESS;
(loudly) gowl, snotter, gullie NE, (and
childishly) bubble, bibble NE.
fit of weeping greet: 'hae a guid greet
tae yersel', bubble, bibble NE.
relieve your feelings by weeping get
yer greet oot.
sound of weeping spraich.
weepy see also tearful; greetie.
weepy person greetin Teenie.
weft waft.
weigh wecht, wacht NE, wey, wye SHET-
LAND, ORKNEY, N, wee SE.
public weighing machine †tron.
weight wecht, wacht NE; (heavy) cairry.
weighty wechtie, wa(u)chtie.
weir caul(d) SW, S, damheid CAITH-
NESS.
weird unco NE, eldritch literary.
welcome walcome.
weld wall, well.
well¹ wall.
first water from a well on New
Year's morning cream or flooer o the
well.
(mouth of a) public well pant(-well)
SE.

288

well up wall NE.

well[2] *adverb, adjective* weel; **very well** fine, brawlie, browlie NE; **fairly well** no bad, nae bad, geylies.

interjection weel; **well then** noona; **very well** weel-a-weel.

well-baked weel-fired.

well-behaved discreet, gracie, mensefu.

person who is well-behaved away from home causey saint.

well-bred *see* **well-mannered.**

well-built buird, kibble NE, clivver; (*of women*) pretty NE.

well-deserved weel-wared.

be well-disposed towards hae a saft side tae.

well-dressed *see also* **well-fed;** weel-pit(ten)-on, braw, gash, spatchell N.

well-earned weel-wared.

well-endowed weel-tochert, weel-plenisht.

well-fed and dressed mait-lik(e) an claith-lik(e).

well-fed-looking lik(e) yer mait.

well-grown growthie, weel-thriven.

well in (*with someone*) fa(u)r ben.

well-informed wice.

well-knit fettle sw.

well-known (weel-)kent, kenspeckle.

well-made (*of things*) slee, pretty SHETLAND, ORKNEY, N; (*of persons*) trig, ticht, fettle sw.

well-mannered mensefu, gentie.

well-meaning weel-willie.

well-nourished *see* **well-fed-looking.**

well-off weel-daein, bien, fou, fouthie, pithie, puist, richt eneuch, (weel-)gaithert.

be well-off hae a guid grip o (the) gear.

well on (*of time*) ower SHETLAND, NE.

well-preserved weel-hained.

well-protected weel-happit.

well-read far i the buik.

well-risen (*of bread*) hovie.

well-spent weel-wared.

well-stocked weel-plenisht.

well-to-do *see* **well-off.**

well-trodden padd(er)it.

as well *see also* **too;** an a(w).

as well (as) forby.

it's all very well it's weel an weel eneuch NE.

well and good guid an weel.

welt *noun* walt.

welter walter.

went *past tense of* **go** gaed.

wept *past tense of* **weep** grat.

past participle grutten.

were *past tense of* **be** wur, war NE.

were not warna(e), wurna(e), wirna(e).

it were twar NE.

as it were lik(e): '*jist for the day lik*'.

west wast, bewast SHETLAND.

western waster, wester, wastlin, westlan(d), wasten.

westernmost wastmost.

westwards wastle, wastert NE, wastlins, wast awa, wast by, wast ower (bye).

in *or* **to the west** wastle.

to the west of wast: '*wast the toon*'.

wet *adjective* weet, wat, weetie, sappie; (*soaking wet*) drookit, sypit, wat as muck; (*rainy*) saft, blashie, plowterie; (*very wet: of weather*) trashie; **wet and windy** blashie, brashie, gowsterie.

verb, see also **soak: 1** weet, wat, plash. **2 wet yourself** †tyne yer dam.

past tense weetit, wat.

past participle weetit, wat, watten, wutten NE.

noun, see also **wet state;** weet, wat.

having wet feet watshod.

wet state; weet, wat.

wet-nurse †mam(m)ie SHETLAND, †nourice *literary.*

wet, dirty scraps (*of cloth etc*) daberlacks NE.

wet state *see also* **splash;** soss SHETLAND, NE, soom, sotter NE.

make wet and dirty soss SHETLAND, NE.

wet with tears (*of the eyes*) watshod.

take off wet clothes cast aff the wat.

wether wedder; (*between first and second shearing, esp Cheviot*) dinmont; (*in second year*) towmond S; (*young*) wedder hogg.

whack *see also* **strike, blow**[2]: *verb, noun* whauk, loonder, rummle, rees(h)le.

whale whaul, whaal SHETLAND, NE, FIFE, faal NE.

wharf shore.

what whit CENTRAL, wha' CENTRAL, fat N, fit N, whatten.

what(so)ever whatsomever, fitivver NE.

what a . . . sic-a-lik(e) . . ., fit a . . . NE.

what a thing to say! whit a like thing tae say!

what else? whit ither?, fit idder? NE.

what is more forby.

what kind of whit lik(e), whatten, whitna, fitna NE.

what the devil whit the hule S.

wheat white NE.

wheatear stane chack(art) SHETLAND, NE, stane chipper, chackie ORKNEY, joctibeet CAITHNESS.

wheedle wheetle, whillywha, teal, tice, fleetch, tryst wi N, gowe ower NE, smool, cuiter.

wheedler whillywha, fraik, flairdie SW; (*esp a child*) smool NE.

wheedling *noun* whillywha.
adjective licklip, slid, fraikie.

wheel *noun* (*in machinery*) whurl; (*on wheelbarrow*) trinnle.
verb hurl, rowe, whurl.

wheelbarrow hurl(ie)-barrow.

wheeze *verb* wheezle, whauze NE, foze NE, hirsel, hurl SHETLAND, ORKNEY, NE, pech, souch.
noun wheezle SHETLAND, NE, whauze NE, foze NE, hirsel, hurl SHETLAND, ORKNEY, NE, pech.

wheezing *noun* sowff.
adjective purfelt.

wheezy pechie.

wheezy chest kist o whustles.

wheezy cough clocher.

whelk wulk, wilk, buckie; (*large*) horse-buckie.

whelp *noun, verb* whalp, folp N, fulp(ie) N.

when whan, whun, fan N, fit time NE.

whence wha(u)r f(r)ae, far fae NE.

where whar, whaur, far N.

wherever whaurivver, farivver NE.

where on earth whar awa.

whet what, cuttle, shairp.

whetstone set(-stane), shairpin stane, rag; (*for scythes*) whittle, futtle NE.

whether whuther, whither, fither NE, fidder NE, gin, gif *mainly literary*.

whey fey N, fy NE.

brose made with whey whey brose, fy brose NE.

which whilk, filk N, that, fit(na) NE.

whiff *noun* whuff, wheef, gliff, pluff; (*unpleasant*) guff.

while *conjunction* whill, file N, the time at.
noun stoun(d).

little while (wee) whilie, (wee) filie NE, handlawhile S.

a while ago a while syne, a while back, a file seen NE.

while away (*time*) pit by.

whim wheem, whigmaleerie, maggot, megrim, flagarie, tantrum, tig, fyke, norie S.

whimbrel Mey bird.

whimper *verb* fumper N, girn, peenge, yammer, wheenge; (*specif of a child*) whicker, murther.
noun fumper N, girn, snifter, yammer, wheenge.

whimsical maggotie, maggotive NE, capernoitit.

whin[1] (*bush*) whun (bush), fun (buss) NE; (*clump*) whins, funs NE.

whinchat whin-chacker(t), whin-lintie, chack.

whin[2] (*rock*) whun, fun NE.

whine *verb* girn, draunt, yammer, yowl,

peenge, peefer, peek NE, pewl, glumsh, wheenge.

noun girn(in), draunt, yammer, wheenge; (*of an animal*) yowl.

whining *noun* girn, yowlin.

adjective girnie, pe(r)neurious NE, peesie-weesie.

whinge *verb* wheenge.

whinny nicher.

whip *verb* **1** *see also* **beat**; whup, fup NE, wheep NE, whang. **2** (*rope etc*) wup, wap.

noun whup, fup NE, wheep NE.

whipping *see* **beating**.

person with the whip hand master *or* mistress an mair.

whiplash whang.

whip-round *noun* lift.

whirl *verb* whurl, furl NE, birl, pirl, tirl, sweel; (*in dancing*) wheel.

noun whurl, furl NE, tirl, sweel.

whirligig *see also* **knick-knack, ornament**; turlie.

whirlpool swelch, swirl, weel; (*in the sea*) swelchie ORKNEY, CAITHNESS.

whirlwind whidder.

whirr *verb* whurr, birr, souch, snore, hurr.

noun whurr, birr, souch.

whish *verb* whush, wheesh, souch.

noun whush, souch.

whisk *verb* wisk, whusk, wheech, whid, flisk.

noun (*movement*) wheech NE.

whisker fusker NE.

whisky 1 whuskie, fuskie NE, bree, barley bree, John Barleycorn, the hard (stuff), the stuffie NE, the craitur, the mercies, wheich, usquebae, †aquavita, †mountain dew; (*cheap, inferior*) speel-the-wa; (*cheap, strong, raw*) kill-the-cairter. **2** (*measure, drink of*) dram, hauf; (*small*) wee hauf.

whisky jar whisky pig, kirstie.

glass of whisky dram, hooker, cauker, roostie nail, wee goldie.

neat whisky raw.

a whisky and half a pint of beer a hauf an a hauf (pint).

whisper *verb* **1** whusper, fusper NE, cheep, tittle, hark. **2** (*something to someone*) hearken (in) tae, roon.

noun **1** whusper, fusper NE, hark SHETLAND, N, whimper, mudge, moot. **2 not a whisper** no a cheep, no a w(h)eesh(t), neither hishie (n)or whishie.

whispering (*behind someone's back*) hudgemudgin NE.

whispering together toot-moot.

in a whisper aneath the breath, intae yersel.

whistle *verb* whustle, fussle NE, wheeber, tweetle; (*softly*) sooth; (*esp to call a dog*) wheep; (*of the wind*) skirl, rees(h)le; (*of a bird or the wind*) wheeple; (*of persons, tunelessly*) wheeple NE; (*a tune*) wheeple NE.

noun whustle, fussle NE, wheeber; (*unmusical*) wheeple; (*low, soft*) sooth; (*policeman's etc, sound of a whistle*) birl; (*of the wind*) skirl; (*shrill, esp of a bird*) wheeple, whaup.

whistle through the air whinner.

whit wheet, haet: 'no a haet', hair.

white fite NE; (*of hair: streaked with white*) lyart.

whiting fitin NE, whitie; (*young*) darg NE.

whiting pout gildee ARGYLL.

whitish whitelie, fiteichtie NE.

whitebeam mulberry.

white currant white rizzer.

white-faced (*of animals*) hawkit NE.

white fish (great) fish, fush.

whitethroat wheetie-whitebaird, bletherin Tam.

whither whaur till *literary*.

whitlow whittle (bcalin), milk-bealin.

Whitsunday Whussunday.

whittle futtle N, white, fite NE, twit SHETLAND, ORKNEY, whitter.

whizz *verb* wheech, souch, fung, whinner, swither, whidder, fudder NE.

noun swiff; (*movement*) swither; (*sound*) wheech, souch, fung.

whizzing blow souch.

with a whizzing noise scuff.

who *interrogative, also relative in angli-cized usage* wha, whae, fa NE.
relative also that, at, it NE.
whoever whasomever.
whom wham, that, at N.
whose whase, that's, at + *possessive adjective*: '*the crew at thir boat wis vrackit*'.
whole hail.
wholly *see also* **completely;** hail, hail-lie.
wholesome hail(some).
the whole lot the hail jing-bang, the hail rickmatick, the hail hypothec, the hail closhach NE.
as a whole at a slump.
deal with as a whole slump.
whoop *verb* (*with mirth*) hooch.
whooping cough kink-hoast, kinkers, kink-cough, chincough.
whopper *see also* **large;** whult(er).
whopping wappin.
whore *see also* **prostitute;** hure, lim-mer.
whorl whurl, thorl, forl NE.
why hoo?, foo?, whit wey?, fit wye? NE, whit for?, fit for? NE: '*Fit did ye dee at for?*'
why not? whit for no?, why for no?, foo nae? NE.
wick week.
burnt wick of a candle snot(t)er.
wicked wickit, ill, ill-deedie, ill-gien, ill-hertit, coorse NE.
wickedly ill.
wicker(work)- wan(d)-.
wickerwork wickers.
wide *see* **broad.**
widely abreid.
widely-known faur-kent, weel-kent.
wide awake wide waukin.
wide of the mark aff the gley.
wide open (*of a door*) wide tae the wa.
widow weeda(e), weedow, weeda(e)-bodie, weeda(e)-wumman, wanter, relict *formal*.
widower weeda(e), weedow, weeda(e)-man, wanter.

width *see also* **breadth;** boon.
wield (*an implement*) wage; (*a weapon*: *see also* **brandish**) wald, weel NE.
wife wifie, wifockie N, wumman, guid-wife, neibour, †luckie; (*of a person of standing in a community*) mistress; (*farmer's wife*) dame NE, FIFE; (*used by a husband of his wife*) she, the auld wife, oor ane.
wig weeg.
wiggle *see also* **waggle;** weegle.
wild (*esp of people*: *see also* **unruly**) wull, will, wile ARGYLL, SW; gall(o)us, randie, ragglish NE, maroonjous NE; (*of children*) royet; (*of animals*) willyart; (*timid*) scar; (*of weather*) gowstie, gurlie, roit NE.
wild cat wullcat.
wild garlic ramps.
wild radish wild kail SW.
wile wimple N.
wily pawkie(-wittit), quirkie, sanshach NE, slim.
wilful *see* **will**[2].
will[1] *verb, see also* **would;** wull.
will not winna, wunna, willnae, wull-nae.
will you? wiltu?
will[2] *noun* wull.
wilful willsome *literary*, heidie, ram-stam, tap-thrawn, breengin, conterma-cious, pet-willed NE, willyart.
willing wullint, well-willie, guidwillie, boun, olite, free.
make a will test.
remember in a will mind.
of your own free will at yer ain will.
will-o'-the-wisp (*often regarded as a death omen*) spunkie, lichtie NE, corp-cannle, daith cannle.
willow willie, sauch, sauch-willie, wid-die; (*low-growing*) sauch buss; (*used to represent the palm on Palm Sunday*) palm.
willow twig widdie, sauch wan(d); (*esp for thatching*) scob.
willow warbler willie-muff, wheelie-oe.
made of willow sauchen.

of *or* **like willow** sauchen; (*like willow*; *full of willow trees*) sauchie.

wilt wult.

win wun; (*a prize, victory etc*) bear *or* win the gree *now literary*.

win staked money from sheel.

win over weir roon(d).

wince resile, jouk.

winch (*for hauling nets on fishing boat*) iron man.

wind[1] *noun* 1 win, wun(d), ween NE, the muckle forester NE; (*light: see also* **breeze**) gray; (*strong: see also* **gale**) skirl; (*strong, with squalls*) blouster; (*with rain*) hash; (*driving storm wind*) skail; (*gusty: see also* **gust**) reevin win; (*boisterous, gusty*) blinter; (*drying, gusty*) hushle; (*east wind*) easter NE; (*cold, easterly*) haar E COAST; (*strong, northerly*) (sea) piner NE; (*bringing thaw*) thowe win; (*whipping round corner*) eddy fup NE. 2 (*sound of wind*) souch, swoof; (*gusty*) sab.

windless quate, lown.

windy wundie, reezie, gowlie S, rowstie; (*very windy*) tatterie.

windbag blether, yap, rummlieguts, rave.

windbreak sconce.

windfall peeled egg, caption NE.

windmill win-mull.

windpipe thrapple, throttle, wizzen, hause-pipe.

blast of wind skelp, howder NE, bleester, bla(u)d, blooter, blouster; (*of wind and rain*) brattle.

break wind *see also* **belch**; lat aff, pump, rowt; (*in a suppressed way*) foost NE.

breaking of wind pump; (*suppressed*) foost NE; (*noisy*) reird NE.

breath of wind saur, gliff, fuff, peuch; (*gentle*) pirr, pew SW.

short-winded pechie.

wind[2] *verb, see also* **wound**[1]: 1 rowe; (*into coils*) hank; (*a cord etc tightly round something*) wup; (*yarn onto a reel*) reel. 2 (*of a river*) wimple, wample.

winding *noun* (*of a river etc*) loop.

winding sheet *see* **shroud**.

wind up rowe (up); (*a piece of machinery*) kirn SW.

windlass windass.

window *see also* **dormer (window)**; winda(e), wundae, winnock.

window bar (*glazing bar*) astragal.

window bolt slot.

window catch windae-sneck.

window frame *see* **window sash**.

window jamb windae-cheek NE.

window sash chess.

top of lower window sash ledgit NE.

window shutter shut, brod, windae-brod.

window-sill windae-sole.

iron bar in a window grating stainchel, staincher.

lean(ing) out of a window for amusement hing: '*time for a guid lang hing oot the windae*'; **person who does this** hingie.

wine (*cheap red, mixed with meths*) red biddy.

(large) wine bottle gardevine.

wing 1 weeng NE, FIFE. 2 (*of a building*) jamb NE; (*on a wing-chair*) lug.

wing-chair lug-chair.

wink *verb* glimmer.

noun **wink of sleep** blink, gliff.

winnow win(d), dicht; (*for first time*) cuff NE.

winnowing machine winnister NE, fanners, dichter SE, windass.

winter wunter.

midwinter howe o (the) winter, howe o the year; (*when days start lengthening*) turn o the year.

winter pasture winterin.

animal kept for winter meat †mart.

wipe *verb* dicht; (*mucus from the nose*) snite.

noun dicht; (*hasty*) scuff, slaik.

wire weer NE.

wise *see also* **shrewd**; wice, slee, wylie,

auld-farran(t), lang-heidit; (*from experience*) auld i the horn.

wisdom wit.

wish *verb* wiss, wuss, wush, want, wint NE, seek.

noun wiss, wush, wull.

wishbone thochtbane NE.

as much as you could wish for at a(w) will.

wish someone were out of the way see someone far eneuch.

without consulting someone's wishes ower someone's heid.

wishy-washy fushionless, wersh; (*of liquor*) shilpit.

wishy-washy food *or* **drink** wabble NE.

wisp wusp, tait.

wistful pensefu.

wit wut; **wits** judgement: '*oot o yer judgement*', intellecks.

witless gypit, doitert, tuim, feel NE.

witty auld-farran(t), knackie, pleesant, humoursome; (*cynically or critically*) pawkie.

witch 1 wutch, carline, gyre carline, wice wumman; (*specif a fortune-teller*) spaewife. **2** (*ugly old woman*) rudas NE.

witchcraft glamour(ie), gramarie.

with wi; in: '*providit in*'; (*of food*) tae, till, to: '*an egg tae his tea*'.

withdraw (*from an agreement etc*) resile, rue; (*from something through cowardice*) hen.

wither wuther, wizen, dowe, wallow, gizzen, dwine, spire SE.

withered *see also* **wither;** fushionless; (*of flowers*) wallan(t) NE.

withered grass winnlestraes.

within *adverb* wi'in, ithin SHETLAND, N, athin, ben, inower, inby.

preposition intae, ben.

without wi'oot, athoot, ithoot, thoot, wantin.

do without want, wint NE, dae wantin.

withstand gainstan(d).

withy widdie.

witness wutness.

wizard warlock.

wizened wuzzent, crined, scruntie; (*of a face*) snirket.

wobble *verb, see also* **shake, totter, sway;** wabble, waible, wa(u)chle.

noun wa(u)chle.

wobbly shooglie, shoggie.

woe *see also* **sorrow, grief;** wae.

woebegone waebegane.

woeful waefu, wae, wearifu NE, waesome.

woeful state pliskie.

wolf oof, wowf NE.

wolf-fish sea-cat.

woman *see also* **lady, girl, old;** wumman(-bodie), umman(-bodie) NE, wife, wifie, manishee *gipsy*, S; (*affectionate or familiar term of address*) hen.

women weemin, weemin-fowk.

grown to womanhood wumman-muckle, wumman-lenth, wumman-grown.

womb wame, wyme NE, bosie, creel NE.

won *past tense of* **win** wan.

wonder *verb* wunner, winner NE, ferlie.

noun wunner, winner NE; (*something to be marvelled at*) ferlie.

wonderful wunnerfae, winnerfae NE, ferlie, byous.

wonderfully ferlie, wunnerfae, winnerfae NE, wunnersome.

wont *see also* **habit;** gate NE, hant.

won't winna, winnae, wunna, wunnae.

woo *see also* **court;** oo, rush, come aifter NE.

wood wuid, widd, wud; (*material*) timmer; (*piece of woodland*) wooding, buss; (*small: see also* **copse**) plantin, shaw *now mainly literary*.

wooden wudden, widden, timmer.

wooden bar *or* **rod** spaik.

wooden leg pin leg.

woody widdie, wuddie.

wood-chips *see* **shavings**.

wood grouse capercailzie.

woodland *see noun above*.

woodlark Scotch nightingale.

woodlouse slater.

wood-pigeon cushat, cushie(-doo), croodlin doo NE.

wood-shavings *see* **shavings.**

infested with woodworm moch-etten NE.

wool oo, woo.

woollen oo(en): 'oo ba'.

natural undyed woollen cloth hodden gray.

woolly ooie, oo.

all one wool a(w) ae oo.

made of natural undyed wool growe-gray.

new wool on sheep at shearing time rise.

word wird.

beyond words untellin, ontellin NE.

keep your word haud (yer) tryst.

not a word no a mum, no a cheep.

torrent of words blash, blatter NE.

upon my word! losh!, by ma sang!, (by) ma saul!

wore *past tense of* **wear** weirit, weir SHETLAND, NE, wure SHETLAND.

work *see also* **energetic, aimless, ineffectual, careless, clumsy, messy, work hard** *below*: *verb* wirk, darg; (*dough etc*) chaave N.

noun **1** wark, thrift. **2 piece of work** seam, turn; (*to be done in a certain time*) stent; (*elaborate, fiddling*) pickle; (*day's work*) darg. **3 works** (*of a mechanism*) intimmers.

worked wrocht, vrocht NE.

worked up vrocht up NE, dementit, on the keevee.

worker (*keen, vigorous*) kemper; (*speedy but careless*) hasher; (*slow, inept*) fa(u)chle; (*feckless*) tooter NE; (*who scamps work*) slemmer; (*dirty, untidy*) scutter, slaister, slitter, huther; (*inefficient, slovenly*) tra(u)chle.

working clothes ilkaday claes, scodgie claes.

workings (*mechanism*) intimmers.

workhouse †puirshoose.

workman *see also* **worker** *above*; warkman.

piece of poor workmanship sair han(d).

workshy sweir(t), haingle NE.

be behind with work be in a pauchle.

begin work yoke (tae), streek NE; (*esp harvest*) enter.

time to begin work yokin time.

time to finish work lowsin time.

domestic *or* **indoor work** inwark.

hard work (*tiring*) tra(u)chle.

have too much hard work be sair hauden doon by the bubbly jock, be in the tag NE.

do light work jot NE.

do rough menial work scodge.

set to work pit tae yer han(d), set on; (*vigorously*) tackle tae.

stop work lowse.

work hard dwang, swink, stick in, chaave NE, fyke, rive; (*with little result*) pingle; (*towards a goal*) plowd NE; (*until you are exhausted*) knock yer pan in.

work hard at teir awa at, yerk at SHETLAND, NE.

work in a harassed way steer.

work for little or nothing work for sweeties.

piece of work done without payment love-darg.

work to rule hing the cat, hing the cleek.

world warld, wardle, warle NE.

worldling warldlin.

worldly wardlie.

for all the world by a(w) the earth.

in this world this side o time.

up in the world up by cairts NE.

worm wirm; (*striped, used as angling bait*) brammel (worm), stripey; (*marine, used as bait*) rigger worm.

worn *adjective, past participle of* **wear** wurn, dashelt; (*into holes*) holed; (*of shoes*) sha(u)chlin.

worn out (*of a person; see also* **exhausted**) (sair) forfoch(t)en, forfauchelt, disjaskit, forjeskit; (*of a person or thing*) sair awa wi't.

worry

worry *verb* wirry, fash, backset, dwang; (*needlessly*) rack SW, S.

noun wirry, fyke, thocht, fash, fry, kauch SW.

worried *see* **anxious.**

worse warse, waur, iller.

worse-looking waur-faured.

(the) worse for (the) waur O.

ten times worse ten waurs NE.

worst *adjective, adverb* warst.

verb warst, waur, maugre NE.

come off worst come by the waur.

if the worst comes to the worst if hard comes tae hard.

worsted *see also* **yarn**; worset, wirset.

wort (*brewing*) wirt, geel.

worth *noun* wirth.

worthless wanworth, nae wirth NE, little worth SHETLAND, ORKNEY, wauch, scabbit, nochtie, nochtless, orra, scootie, skybal(d).

worthless person *see also* **good-for-nothing**; scum; (*small*) (*wee*) nyaff.

worthless person *or* **thing** scaddin NE.

worthless people *see* **riff-raff.**

worthless people *or* **things** dirtrie.

worthy wordie, honest, braw.

be worthy of you be guid yer pairt.

not worth anything no worth a bodle, no worth a flee, no worth a docken.

would *past tense of* **will**[1] wad, wid, wud.

would not wadna(e), widna(e), wudna(e).

wound[1] *past tense of* **wind**[2] wan NE.

past participle wundit.

wound[2] *verb, see also* **injure**; brain, gulliegaw N; (*severely*) mairtyr.

noun, see also **injury**; (*slight*) scrat; (*from heavy blow*) dunt; (*from a sting or sharp object*) stang.

wove *past tense of* **weave** weyvt NE, wuive S.

woven *past participle* wuven, wivven NE, weyvt.

wraith *see* **ghost.**

wrangle *see also* **argue, argument**: *verb, noun* raggle, cangle, carb(le) NE, FIFE.

wrap *verb* wap, lap, hap.

noun hap (warm), faik NE.

wrap up rowe up, buckle, wimple NE; (*a person*) hap, sweel; (*a parcel*) pit aboot.

wrasse runker NE; (*ballan*) soo NE; (*small-mouthed*) sea-soo NE.

wrath *see also* **rage, anger**; wreth SHETLAND.

wreck *verb, see also* **destroy**; wrack, wreak, vrack NE, malafooster; (*esp a ship*) perish; (*a person's health or spirits*) ool.

noun wrack, wreak, vrack NE, (*ship, if profitable*) god('s)-send.

wreckage stramash; (*from ships*) spreath.

wren wran(nie), katie wren, cuttie wran SW, thoumie NE.

wrench *verb, see also* **sprain**; runch, yerk.

noun (*sprain, tool*) *see also* **sprain**; wranch, runch.

wrench yourself by falling with legs apart spelder yersel.

wrench out rive oot.

wrestle warsle, wrastle, warple, chaave NE, fecht, be in grips.

have a wrestling bout shak a fa NE.

wrestling match warsle.

wrestle with warsle (wi), joogle wi.

wretch wratch, vratch NE.

wretched *see also* **miserable, unfortunate**; donsie.

wriggle *see also* **wiggle**; wammle, wample SW, spartle, twine; (*the body*) feeze.

wring thraw, trist SHETLAND, ORKNEY.

wring the neck of (*esp a fowl*) thraw the neck O, lith NE.

wrinkle *verb* runkle, ruckle, lirk, snorl, gruggle NE.

noun runkle, ruckle, lirk, gruggle NE.

wrinkled runklie.

wrinkly wirlie, wizened.

wrinkle the nose snirk.

wrist shackle, sheckle.

  wrist-band han(d)-ban(d).

  wrist-bone shackle-bane.

writ (*to appear in* (*a civil*) *court*) summons; (*from High Court or Court of Session*) letters.

write wreat, vreet NE, scribe; (*compose*) clark NE; (*especially with ease*) scrieve; (*rapidly*) screed.

  writer (*especially contemptuous*) scriever.

  writing *noun* write, writ; (*piece of writing*) writ, scrieve, leebel, scribe.

  writing pad (*for rough notes*) scroll ORKNEY, NE.

  style of writing han(d) o writ(e).

  write down hurriedly scart.

writhe *see also* **wriggle, twist**; warsle, twine, thraw, wample SW; (*esp in the death agony*) thratch.

written *past participle of* **write** writ, vrutten NE.

wrong *adjective* wrang, vrang NE; (*unjust*) unricht; (*acting wrongly*) ill-duin, ill-deein NE.

  noun ill.

wrongful wrangous.

wrongfully wrangouslie.

wrongdoing ill-daein.

be wrong be aff the gley.

go down the wrong way (*of food*) gae doon the wrang hause.

go wrong misgae, gang agley.

have the wrong end of the stick hae the wrang soo by the lug.

something wrong a whaup i the raip.

what's wrong with her? whit ails her?, whit's adae wi her?, fit's adee wi her? NE.

wrote *past tense of* **write** wrait, writ, wrat.

wry thrawn.

  make a wry face showl, grue.

  wry smile shile SW.

Y, Z

yacht yatt W.

yap *see* **yelp.**

yard[1] (*measure*) yaird.

  yardstick ellwan(d).

yard[2] (*enclosed ground*) yaird; (*eg for storing timber, coal*) howf; (*eg for storing coal, wintering cattle*) ree.

yarn *noun* **1** yairn; (*coarse, worsted*) wheelin; (*heavy, woollen*) swarra SHETLAND. **2** (*tall story*) spin NE, sonnet NE.

  size *or* **thickness of yarn** grist.

yawn *verb, noun* gant.

year 'ear, towmond.

  yearling yearaul(d).

  for many years this monie a lang year.

  last year fernyear.

  a year of your life a nick in yer horn.

yearn *see also* **long (for);** green (for), myang (for) NE.

yell *noun, verb, see also* **cry, howl, scream;** yowl, yall SHETLAND, N, yowt, gowl, goller, scronach NE.

yellow yella, yellae, yalla, yallae.

  yellowish yalloch(t)ie NE, faughie.

  yellowhammer yella yite, yella lintie, yorlin, yaldie (yite) NE.

yelp *see also* **bark, yell, howl:** *verb, noun* yowl, (*bark*) nyaff, yaff, yaup, yatter.

yes ay, yea SHETLAND, ORKNEY, N, ya SHETLAND, ORKNEY.

  yes indeed och aye, hoot ay.

yesterday yestreen, e streen NE.

yesterday evening yestreen.

  the day before yesterday ere yesterday.

yet 1 (*still*) yit. **2** (*nevertheless*) still an on.

yield *verb, see also* **submit;** loot, ring in, spit an gie (it) ower, snuil.

  noun (*of a cow etc*) profit.

yielded *past participle* yowden.

yoghurt soor dook.

yoke *noun* yock; (*for carrying pails*) frame.

yokel yochel, geordie, joskin, pleuchie, yaup, teuchter.

yolk yowk.

yonder yonner, onner NE, thonder, thonner, yont.

you ye; (*singular, familiar*) doo SHETLAND, thoo ORKNEY, ROSS-SHIRE, (*objective*) dee SHETLAND, ORKNEY, thee ROSS-SHIRE; (*singular, informal*) youse; (*plural*) yeez, yiz; (*plural, informal*) youse CENTRAL.

young *adjective, see* **youthful** (*under* **youth**).

  noun (*of an animal*) follower.

  youngster younker; (*mischievous, esp girl*) hempie.

  produce young (*of animals*) ferrie; (*of small animals*) kittle.

  young children wee yins, geets NE.

your eer S, (*unstressed*) yer.

yourself yersel; (*emphatic*) the sel o ye.

youth 1 youthheid. **2** (*young man*) lad(die), loon, callan(t), strip o a lad(die); (*adolescent*) halflin; (*big, rawboned*) kelp NE; (*mischievous*) kelpie S, (*smart, active*) birkie, swankie.

  youthful green, youthie.

  promising youth lad o pairts.

  the time of your youth the daft days.

Yule *see also* **Christmas;** Yeel N, Eel N.

yum-yum nimm SHETLAND.

zealous guid-willed SHETLAND.

zigzag jink.

Scottish Currency, Weights and Measure

SCOTTISH CURRENCY, WEIGHTS AND MEASURES

Money

SCOTS	STERLING	DECIMAL
1 penny	1/12 penny	—
2 pennies = 1 bodle	1/6 penny	—
2 bodles = 1 plack	1/3 penny	—
3 bodles = 1 bawbee	1 halfpenny	—
2 bawbees = 1 shilling	1 penny	.42 penny
13 shillings 4 pence = 1 merk	1s 1½d.	5½ pence
20 shillings = 1 pound	1s 8d	8 pence

Weights and Measures

There was much confusion and diversity in early Scottish weights and measures and a succession of enactments from the 15th century failed to improve matters till in 1661 a commission was set up by Parliament which recommended the setting up of national standards, the exemplars of which were to be kept in the custody of certain burghs, the *ell* for lineal measure to be kept by Edinburgh, the *jug* for liquid capacity by Stirling, the *firlot* for dry measure by Linlithgow, and the *troy stone* for weight by Lanark. These recommendations in the main prevailed throughout Scotland, though there was some irregularity between commodities in dry measure; a further recommendation that *tron* weight should be entirely abolished was ignored and this measure fluctuated within fairly wide limits as between 22 and 28 ounces per pound. By Act of Parliament in 1824 uniformity of weights and measures was statutorily established and gradually this was conformed to although the names of the older measures like **firlot, forpet, lippie** were transferred to fractions of the Imperial hundred-weight and are still sometimes heard.

Weights

1. According to the standard of Lanark, for troy weight:

SCOTS	AVOIRDUPOIS	METRIC
1 drop	1.093 drams	1.921 grammes
16 drops = 1 ounce	1 oz. 1.5 drams	31 grammes
16 ounces = 1 pound	1 lb. 1 oz. 8 dr.	496 grammes
16 pounds = 1 stone	17 lbs. 8 oz.	7.936 kilogrammes

2. According to the standard of Edinburgh for **tron** weight:

SCOTS	AVOIRDUPOIS	METRIC
1 drop	1.378 drams	2.4404 grammes
16 drops = 1 ounce	·1 oz. 6 drams	39.04 grammes
16 ounces = 1 pound	1 lb. 6 oz. 1 dram	624.74 grammes
16 pounds = 1 stone	1 stone 8 lbs. 1 oz.	9.996 kilogrammes

Capacity

Liquid measure according to the standard of Stirling.

SCOTS	IMPERIAL	METRIC
1 gill	.749 gill	.053 litres
4 gills = 1 mutchkin	2.996 gills	.212 litres
2 mutchkins = 1 chopin	1 pint 1.992 gills	.848 litres
2 chopins = 1 pint	2 pints 3.984 gills	1.696 litres
8 pints = 1 gallon	3 gallons .25 gills	13.638 litres
1 pint = 104.2034 Imp. cub. ins.	1 pint = 34.659 Imp. cub. ins.	1 litre = 61.027 cub. ins.

Dry measure according to the standard of Linlithgow.

1. For wheat, peas, beans, meal, etc.

1 lippie (or forpet)	.499 gallons	2.268 litres
4 lippies = 1 peck	1.996 gallons	9.072 litres
4 pecks = 1 firlot	3 pecks 1.986 gallons	36.286 litres
4 firlots = 1 boll	3 bushels 3 pecks 1.944 galls.	145.145 litres
16 bolls = 1 chalder	7 quarters 7 bushels 3 pecks 1.07 galls	2322.324 litres
1 firlot = 2214.322 cub. ins.	1 gallon = 277.274 cub. ins.	1 litre = 61.027 cub. ins.

2. For barley, oats, malt.

1 lippie (or forpet)	.728 gallons	3.037 litres
4 lippies = 1 peck	1 peck .912 gallons	13.229 litres
4 pecks = 1 firlot	1 bushel 1 peck 1.650 gallons	52.916 litres
4 firlots = 1 boll	5 bushels 3 pecks .600 gallons	211.664 gallons
16 bolls = 1 chalder	11 quarters 5 bushels 1.615 gallons	3386.624 litres
1 firlot = 3230.305 cub. ins.		

Linear and Square Measures

According to the standard **ell** of Edinburgh.

Linear

1 inch	1.0016 inches	2.54 centimetres
8.88 inches = 1 Scots link	8.8942 inches	22.55 centimetres
12 inches = 1 foot	12.0192 inches	30.5287 centimetres
3½ feet = 1 ell	37.0598 inches	94.1318 centimetres
	(1 1/37 yards)	
6 ells = 1 fall	6.1766 yards	5.6479 metres
	(1.123 poles)	
4 falls = 1 chain	24.7064 yards	22.5916 metres
	(1.123 chains)	
10 chains = 1 furlong	247.064 yards	225.916 metres
	(1.123 furlongs)	
8 furlongs = 1 mile	1976.522 yards	1.8073 kilometres
	(1.123 miles)	

Square

1 sq. inch	1.0256 sq. inch	6.4516 sq. centimetre
1 sq. ell	1.059 sq. yards	.8853 sq. metre
36 sq. ells = 1 sq. fall	38.125 sq. yards	31.87 sq. metres
	(1 pole 7.9 sq. yards)	
40 falls = 1 sq. rood	1525 sq. yards	12.7483 acres
	(1 rood 10 poles 13 sq. yards)	
4 roods = 1 sq. acre	6100 sq. yards	.5099 hectare
	(1.26 acres)	

Yarn measure

1 cut = 300 yards
1 heere = 2 cuts or 600 yards
1 heid = 2 heeres or 1200 yards
1 hank or hesp = 3 heids or 3600 yards
1 spinle = 4 hanks or 14400 yards

The above applies to linen and handspun woollen yarn in the early 19th century. Earlier the measure was considerably shorter, and varied considerably with the kind of yarn spun.